# EVIDENCE-BASED INTERVENTIONS
# FOR STUDENTS WITH LEARNING AND
# BEHAVIORAL CHALLENGES

This book assembles into one volume summaries of school-based intervention research that relates to those who deal on a regular basis with the growing body of students having high-incidence learning disabilities and/or behavior disorders: special educators, school psychologists, and clinical child psychologists. Chapter authors begin with an overview of their topic followed by a brief section on historical perspectives before moving on to the main section—a critical discussion of empirically-based intervention procedures. In those instances where evidence-based prescriptions can legitimately be made, authors discuss best practices and the conditions (e.g., classroom environment, teacher expertise) under which these practices are most effective. A final section deals with policy issues.

# EVIDENCE-BASED INTERVENTIONS FOR STUDENTS WITH LEARNING AND BEHAVIORAL CHALLENGES

Edited by

Richard J. Morris and Nancy Mather

Routledge
Taylor & Francis Group

NEW YORK AND LONDON

First published 2008
by Routledge
711 Third Avenue, New York, NY 10017

Simultaneously published in the UK
by Routledge
2 Park Square, Milton Park, Abingdon, Oxon OX14 4RN

*Routledge is an imprint of the Taylor & Francis Group, an informa business*

Transferred to digital printing 2011

Typeset in Times and Helvetica by EvS Communication Networx, Inc.

**Library of Congress Cataloging-in-Publication Data**
Evidence-based interventions for students with learning and behavioral challenges / edited by Richard J. Morris and Nancy Mather.
p. cm.
Includes bibliographical references and indexes.
ISBN 978-0-415-96454-8 (hardback: alk. paper) -- ISBN 978-0-415-96455-5 (pbk. : alk. paper)
-- ISBN 978-0-203-93854-6 (e-book)
1. Learning disabled children--Education--United States. 2. Problem children--Education--United States. 3. Special education--United States. I. Morris, Richard J. II. Mather, Nancy.
LC4705.E85 2007
371.90973--dc22
2007027715

ISBN10: 0-415-96454-7 (hbk)
ISBN10: 0-415-96455-5 (pbk)
ISBN10: 0-203-93854-2 (ebk)

ISBN13: 978-0-415-96454-8 (hbk)
ISBN13: 978-0-415-96455-5 (pbk)
ISBN13: 978-0-203-93854-6 (ebk)

*To*

*Stephanie and Michael Hoffman and Michael and Lindsay Morris,*
*and in loving memory of Jacqueline Anne Morris*

*And To*

*George and Laura Mather for their love and support*

# Contents

## IV.  ISSUES RELATED TO TEACHING STUDENTS HAVING LEARNING AND BEHAVIORAL CHALLENGES

## V.  COMMENTARY ON TEACHING STUDENTS HAVING LEARNING AND BEHAVIORAL CHALLENGES

# Preface

*Education is helping a child realize his potentialities.*
Erich Fromm

The focus of this book is on evidence-based interventions for students with learning and behavioral challenges. You may wonder why we didn't just narrow the focus to learning or behavioral problems. The reason is that so many students with behavioral problems also have issues with learning, with the converse being true as well. Thus, educators and psychologists must be prepared to deal with a variety of overlapping conditions, such as the student with attention deficit hyperactivity disorder (ADHD) and a reading disability, or the student being disruptive in class and having a language disorder. You may also wonder why we used the word "challenges" instead of words such as "disorders," "problems," "impairments," or "disabilities." The reason is that most of the procedures that are described in this book can be used with many students who are struggling with aspects of learning or behavior.

For example, a number of school-age children and adolescents have certain fears or related anxieties, such as test anxiety, separation anxiety, or public speaking anxiety (e.g., oral recitation, answering or asking questions in class, reading out-loud, etc.) that diminish their everyday enthusiasm for learning and may even prevent them from attending school on particular days. Although these students might not be identified as having emotional disturbances and may not be failing in school, they are challenged on certain days to perform at a level consistent with their academic potential. On the other hand, some students have certain fears and related anxieties that do, in fact, prevent them from attending school and in such cases the emotional difficulties do constitute a bona fide emotional disturbance. The intervention research literature on reducing fears and related anxieties does not necessarily differentiate between the types of intervention that should be conducted with each type of student. In both cases, the behaviors pose a "challenge" to the individuals, as well as to school professionals. Fortunately, the research literature suggests the type of intervention(s) that should be implemented to help such students reduce the frequency and intensity of their fearful and anxious behaviors.

The same is true for children and/or adolescents with learning challenges. For example, a fourth-grade student may be reading two years below grade level, but performing acceptably in other subjects that require minimal reading. Without further investigation, the reason for the poor reading is unclear. The student may have a reading disability, but regardless, his reading difficulties are certainly a "challenge" for himself, the teacher, and even his parents or care providers. Here again, the intervention research literature suggests that certain evidence-based procedures may be used to enhance reading performance, and that these procedures may be the same or quite similar to those suggested for students who have documented reading disabilities. School professionals in practice or training, including administrators, general and special education teachers, psychologists, speech-language pathologists, and counselors, need to understand the challenges and also know about the numerous evidence-based educational or psychoeducational procedures that may be implemented to assist students.

The reader may also ask why, in most of the chapters in the book, the discussion centers solely on evidence-based interventions? The reason is that society is increasingly demanding that educators, physicians, psychologists, counselors, and other educational and child health professionals be accountable for the services that they provide and that they use the "best practice" in the delivery of such services. In many cases, this means being able to independently verify or support the use of the "best practice" that one provides. In the fields of education and school psychology, verification of a practice is often demonstrated by using interventions that have objective evidence of effectiveness derived from the research literature. Thus, in the case of the chapters in this book, the "evidence" for the use of the various interventions is based on empirical research in education, special education, school psychology, school counseling, and clinical child and adolescent psychology. In the case of many of the learning and behavioral challenges discussed, the interventions described have achieved a level of treatment confidence that is often referred to as either "efficacious" or "probably efficacious." These terms signify that experimental control conditions have been used in evaluating the effectiveness of a particular intervention, the intervention includes an implementation manual, and that the intervention was found to be significantly (or appreciably) more effective than the control condition. What separates "efficacious" from "probably efficacious" is the number of controlled intervention studies by different researchers that have been published on students having a particular learning or behavioral challenge. In some cases, less well-controlled research may be cited in chapters—including those studies published by only one investigator team—but the results of the intervention(s) that were used were still found to be effective. These latter studies are often referred to as "experimental."

Important changes have occurred over the past 10 to 15 years in general education, special education, school psychology, school counseling, and clinical child and adolescent psychology—with the common focus being on evidence-based practices. Recognition and implementation of these best practices have resulted in positive benefits for school professionals and the children and adolescents they serve. In this regard, many teachers, school psychologists, and counselors are using interventions that have evidence to support their effectiveness, and the majority of university preparation and training programs include methods courses that provide instruction and practice in the implementation of evidence-based practices. School administrators, as well as the federal government, state education agencies and local education agencies, are demanding accountability and the use of evidence-based interventions where the relative effectiveness of the interventions is assessed through the use of evidence-based assessment practices.

In spite of this increasing emphasis on evidence-based practices, only a few books have addressed this topic in depth, and few attempt to address interventions in both the learning and behavior areas. The chapters in this book cover a broad range of the most common learning and behavioral challenges that school professionals are likely to encounter. All chapters are written by individuals who are leading experts in the field and on the topics being addressed. Although the chapter authors were provided with a general outline for writing their respective chapters, they were encouraged to adapt the outline to fit their particular topic area. Case examples are also presented, in some instances, to further illustrate the implementation of a particular intervention. Some chapters also include a discussion of historical and theoretical issues, but the primary emphasis throughout is on the use of evidence-based intervention techniques and strategies for addressing various behavioral and learning challenges in students.

The central intent of this book is to provide a comprehensive view of the best practices for helping these students overcome their difficulties so that they can accomplish realistic scholastic goals and become healthy, productive citizens. The volume covers an introduction and overview of the field; a discussion of why we need evidence-based practices; ADHD; childhood depression and related difficulties; fears and related anxieties; disruptive behavior problems; oral language;

strategies for younger and older readers; written language; mathematics; strategy instruction; and cognitive processing difficulties. Other chapters address such relevant issues as implementation and selection of appropriate accommodations, effective instruction for English language learners, provision of effective service delivery models, and a discussion of gifted students with learning and behavioral challenges. The final chapter serves as a commentary and reflection to remind us never to forget the importance of the human relationships and special bonds that form between students and practitioners, *a necessary component* of all evidence-based interventions.

This book is, therefore, intended to be an intervention-oriented reference volume for special education teachers, general education teachers, school psychologists, speech-language pathologists, and school counselors who work directly with students having learning and/or behavioral challenges. It will be especially useful for graduate training courses in special education, general education and school psychology, as well as courses in classroom management, and school consultation.

One caveat, however, is in order. Research across the century has also clarified that one instructional method or one psychological or psychoeducational intervention will not work with all individuals. Thus, a method, strategy, program, or intervention may meet the requirements of being "evidence-based," but still not be the most efficacious treatment for a certain student. Many factors affect the choice of a methodology, intervention, or program, including the age of the student, past approaches used and how successful they were, the personal characteristics of the person, the demands of the setting and environment, and the resources that are available. "Evidence-based" indicates that many individuals have made progress using the procedure and that the method is more effective than others, but it does not guarantee that a certain student will respond adequately to the "effective" treatment. For example, much of the research on early reading indicates that when evidence-based interventions are employed with intensity and fidelity, a certain percentage of children can be described as "treatment resistors." Even evidence-based procedures need, at times, to be adjusted, adapted, and refined to meet the needs and unique characteristics of a specific individual.

A number of individuals made major contributions to the completion of this book. First, we wish to thank Lane Akers at Lawrence Erlbaum and Associates for his support and encouragement in every phase of this project. In addition, we express our appreciation to Jackie Collins for her assistance during various phases of this project. We also wish to express our special thanks to Vinnie Morris and Michael Gerner for their support during the preparation of this book.

**Richard J. Morris**
**Nancy Mather**

# Contributors

## EDITORS

*Richard J. Morris, PhD,* is the David and Minnie Meyerson Distinguished Professor of Disability and Rehabilitation and Professor of School Psychology in the Department of Special Education, Rehabilitation, and School Psychology at the University of Arizona. He is a Fellow of the American Psychological Association (APA), Charter Fellow of the American Psychological Society, and Fellow of the American Association on Mental Retardation. He has authored or edited 13 books and more than 120 journal articles and book chapters in the areas of child behavior disorders, child psychotherapy, and ethical and professional practice issues in psychology. Some of his authored or edited books are: *Disability Research and Policy: Current Perspectives*; *The Practice of Child Therapy, fourth edition* (with Thomas R. Kratochwill), *Handbook of Psychotherapy with Children and Adolescents* (with Thomas R. Kratochwill), *Treating Children's Fears and Phobias: A Behavioral Approach* (with Thomas R. Kratochwill), and *Behavior Modification with Children: A Systematic Guide.* His current research interests include: managing childhood aggressive and disruptive behaviors in the classroom, disability and juvenile delinquency, and legal and ethical issues in the delivery of children's mental health services. Dr. Morris is a licensed psychologist, and is a past Chair and Board Member of the state of Arizona Board of Psychologist Examiners and a former member of the Ethics Committee of the American Psychological Association. He currently serves as a member of the Board of Trustees of the American Psychological Association Insurance Trust.

*Nancy Mather, PhD,* is Professor of Special Education in the Department of Special Education, Rehabilitation, and School Psychology at the University of Arizona. She specializes in the areas of reading, writing, and learning disabilities. She has conducted numerous workshops nationally and internationally on assessment, instruction, and issues that affect service delivery for individuals with learning disabilities. She has written numerous books, book chapters, and articles on topical issues in the field of learning disabilities. In addition, Dr. Mather is a co-author of the *Woodcock-Johnson III* with Richard W. Woodcock and Kevin S. McGrew (Woodcock, McGrew, & Mather, 2001) and has co-authored two books on interpretation and application of the WJ III: *Woodcock-Johnson III: Reports, recommendations, and strategies* (Mather & Jaffe, 2002) and *Essentials of WJ III Tests of Achievement Assessment* (Mather, Wendling, & Woodcock, 2001). In addition, she has co-authored: *Essentials of Assessment Report Writing* (Lichtenberger, Mather, Kaufman, & Kaufman, 2004) and has just completed the second edition of *Learning Disabilities and Challenging Behaviors* (Mather & Goldstein, 2008).

# CONTRIBUTORS

*Virginia W. Berninger, PhD*
Professor
University of Washington
Department of Educational Psychology
Seattle, Washington

*Samara Blei*
Doctoral Student
Program in Counseling/School Psychology
The Florida State University
College of Education
Tallahassee, Florida

*Jeffery P. Braden, PhD*
Professor of Psychology
Associate Dean for Research and Graduate
    Programs
College of Humanities and Social Sciences
North Carolina State University
Raleigh, North Carolina

*Robert B. Brooks, PhD*
Assistant Clinical Professor of Psychology
Harvard Medical School
Department of Psychiatry
Boston, Massachusetts

*Milton J. Dehn, EdD, NCSP*
Program Director
Schoolhouse Educational Services
Onalaska, Wisconsin

*Donald D. Deshler, PhD*
Professor & Director
Center for Research on Learning
University of Kansas
Department of Special Education
Lawrence, Kansas

*George J. DuPaul, PhD*
Professor of School Psychology
Chairperson, Department of Education and
    Human Services
Lehigh University
College of Education
Bethlehem, Pennsylvania

*Agnieszka M. Dynda, MS*
Doctoral Candidate
St. John's University
Department of Psychology
Jamaica, New York

*Meaghan Edmonds*
University of Texas at Austin
Vaughn Gross Center for Reading and
    Language Arts
Austin, Texas

*Kathleen R. Fahey, PhD*
Professor of Speech-Language Pathology
University of Northern Colorado
School of Human Sciences
Audiology and Speech Language Sciences
    Programs
Greeley, Colorado

*Patricia G. Gildroy, PhD*
Educational Consultant
Strategic Learning Center
Seattle, Washington

*Sam Goldstein PhD*
Research Professor of Psychology
George Mason University
Fairfax, Virginia
Clinical Assistant Professor of Psychiatry
University of Utah School of Medicine
Salt Lake City, Utah

*Noel Gregg, PhD*
Distinguished Research Professor
University of Georgia
Department of Communication Sciences &
    Special Education
Athens, Georgia

*Shelley J. Hosterman, MEd*
Doctoral Student
Lehigh University
College of Education
Bethlehem, Pennsylvania

**James M. Kauffman, EdD**
Professor Emeritus of Education
University of Virginia
Department of Curriculum, Instruction, and
    Special Education
Charlottesville, Virginia

**Timothy J. Landrum, PhD**
Associate Professor, General Faculty, and
    Senior Scientist
University of Virginia
Department of Curriculum, Instruction, and
    Special Education
Charlottesville, Virginia

**Carl J. Liaupsin, PhD**
Associate Professor of Special Education
University of Arizona
Department of Special Education, Rehabilita-
    tion, and School Psychology
Tucson, Arizona

**Jennifer Lindstrom, PhD**
Assistant Professor
University of Virginia
Department of Curriculum, Instruction, and
    Special Education
University of Virginia
Charlottesville, Virginia

**Nancy Mather, PhD**
Professor of Learning Disabilities
University of Arizona
Department of Special Education,
    Rehabilitation, and School Psychology
Tucson, Arizona

**Devery R. Mock, PhD**
Assistant Professor of Reading Education
Appalachian State University
Department of Language, Reading, & Excep-
    tionalities
Boone, North Carolina

**Marjorie Montague, PhD**
Professor of Special Education
University of Miami
Department of Teaching and Learning
Coral Gables, Florida

**Richard J. Morris, PhD**
David and Minnie Meyerson Distinguished
    Professor of Disability and Rehabilitation
Professor of School Psychology
University of Arizona
Department of Special Education,
    Rehabilitation, and School Psychology
Tucson, Arizona

**Samuel, O. Ortiz, PhD**
Associate Professor of Psychology
St. John's University
Department of Psychology
Jamaica, New York

**Steven I. Pfeiffer, PhD, ABPP**
Professor and Director of Clinical Training,
    PhD Program in Counseling/School
    Psychology
The Florida State University
College of Education
Tallahassee, Florida

**Dawn H. S. Reinemann, PhD**
Assistant Professor
Cardinal Stritch University
Graduate Program in Clinical Psychology
Milwaukee, Wisconsin

**Laura E. Rutherford, MEd**
Doctoral Student
Lehigh University
College of Education
Bethlehem, Pennsylvania

**Sarah Schnoebelen, PhD**
Children's Medical Center of Dallas
Department of Psychiatry
Dallas, Texas

**Gretchen Schoenfield**
Doctoral Candidate, School Psychology
    Program
University of Arizona
Department of Special Education,
    Rehabilitation, and School Psychology
Tucson, Arizona

*Terrance M. Scott, PhD*
Professor and Director of Special Education
    Department
College of Education and Human
    Development
University of Louisville
Louisville, Kentucky

*Melody Tankersley, PhD*
Professor of Education
Kent State University
Department of Special Education
Kent, Ohio

*Annmarie Urso, MSEd*
PhD Candidate
Department of Special Education, Rehabilita-
    tion & School Psychology
College of Education, Room 409
University of Arizona
Tucson, Arizona 85721

*Delinda van Garderen, PhD*
Assistant Professor of Special Education
University of Missouri – Columbia
Department of Special Education
Columbia, Missouri

*Sharon Vaughn, PhD*
H.E. Hartfelder/Southland Corps Regents
    Chair
Professor of Special Education
University of Texas
Department of Special Education
Austin, Texas

*Jade Wexler, MS*
University of Texas at Austin
Vaughn Gross Center for Reading and
    Language Arts
Austin, Texas

# I
# INTRODUCTION

# 1

# Introduction and Historical Perspectives

## Richard J. Morris and Nancy Mather

The research and related scholarly literature on learning disabilities and behavioral and emotional disturbances in children and adolescents have grown at an exponential rate over the past 25 years. In addition, during this time period, the U.S. Congress passed two major revisions of the *Individuals With Disabilities Education Act* (IDEA; 1997, 2004)—legislation that guarantees all children who have a disability a free and appropriate education until they reach 22 years of age. The *Americans with Disabilities Act* (1990) also guarantees individuals with disabilities equal access and protection from discrimination in the work place and all public settings. Another federal act, *No Child Left Behind* (NCLB; 2001 had a pronounced influence on the 2004 reauthorization of IDEA. In this regard, the NCLB Act indicates that states and local school districts need to demonstrate that federal funds are spent on programs that have a "scientifically based research" record (Feuer, Towne, & Shavelson, 2002). Thus, the overarching implication of IDEA 2004 is that special educators must attempt to improve services for students with disabilities by providing meaningful educational programs that are grounded in research-based practices (Yell, Shriner, & Katsiyannis, 2006).

Members of society and political leaders have also sent a clear message that they wish to promote and financially support research and scholarship in the areas of learning and behavioral problems, as well as all other areas of special education. This support is not only because of federal legislation, but is also a result of legal mandates at state government levels and various court decisions that have repeatedly concluded that students with disabilities are entitled to equal access to the same educational opportunities, services, and settings as their peers who do not have a disability. The field of special education, as well as related fields such as school psychology, school counseling, school health, and school administration and policy, have responded to this level of societal support by not only centering major research and policy initiatives on advancing (and understanding) the needs of children with disabilities, but also in expanding the number of professional journals and journal pages that publish research in these areas. In addition, the number of research presentations on students with learning and/or behavioral challenges has also increased at the annual meetings of various professional associations.

Over the past 25 years, new concepts have been introduced into special education and school psychology. For example, terms such as "Curriculum-Based Measurement" (CBM), "Curriculum-Based Intervention," "Functional Assessment," and "Evidence-Based Intervention" (EBI) have all emerged from empirical studies conducted by researchers in special education and psychology. The focus of the present book is on evidence-based interventions. Since the mid-1980s, millions of dollars have been spent on EBI research that centers upon assessing, treating, and even attempting to prevent various learning and behavioral challenges in students.

What has society and the fields of special education and psychology learned from this research and the hundreds of thousands of hours that researchers have spent studying these areas and analyzing the results of their work? Most of the scholars in the field would quickly respond "a great deal." Even the most extreme skeptic would have to agree that considerable progress has indeed been made in gathering evidence regarding what works with students who have learning and/or behavioral challenges—as well as what does not seem to work. For example, substantial progress has been made in our understanding of how to teach reading to students who struggle. Similarly, results from EBI research have demonstrated how to successfully identify and intervene with students having attention-deficit hyperactivity disorder. In addition, a great deal has been learned about how to identify students who have depression or fears and related anxieties and to use data-based methods to successfully reduce the frequency and intensity of these behavioral challenges. The EBI literature is even clarifying now the most successful classroom methods for working with students who are disruptive in the classroom.

Why does it seem that so much progress has been made in the past 25 years when, in fact, students with learning and behavioral challenges have been enrolled in public school settings for at least the past 100 years? In truth, progress has been made by the many dedicated, creative, and competent researchers throughout the last century. The gains that we have seen over the past 25 years have resulted from building upon the work of earlier researchers and advancing their initial findings even farther. One can easily think of many of the early pioneers and spokespeople in the field of learning disabilities, including: Samuel Orton, Grace Fernald, Newell Kephart, Samuel Kirk, Marianne Frostig, William Cruickshank, Janet Lerner, Helmer Myklebust, and Doris Johnson, to name a few.

One can reflect upon the insights and dedication of Lightner Witmer who established the first psychological clinic in the United States in 1896 at the University of Pennsylvania. His first case involved a 14-year-old boy who had difficulty learning and was a "chronic bad speller" (Witmer, 1907/1996, p. 249). Similarly, James Hinshelwood (1902), a Scottish ophthalmologist, made many pertinent observations regarding children with severe reading disabilities. From his intensive, systematic case study observations, he concluded that: (a) particular areas of the brain appear to be involved; (b) the children often have average or above intelligence and good memory in other respects; (c) the problem with reading is localized, not generalized to all areas of academic performance; (d) the children do not learn to read with the same rapidity as other children; (e) the earlier the problem is identified, the better so as not to waste valuable instructional time; (f) the children must be taught by special methods adapted to help them overcome their difficulties; and, (g) persistent and persevering attempts will often help these children improve their reading.

Others attempted to establish successful remedial reading programs within the public schools. For example, in 1937, at the request of the U.S. Congress, Monroe and Backus established remedial reading programs in the Washington, D.C. Public Schools at the elementary, middle school, and high school levels. They summarized their results in a monograph entitled *Remedial Reading: A Monograph in Character Education*, noting the connection between the ability to read and the development of character. They observed that many teachers were familiar with the general techniques of teaching reading, but were inadequately prepared to diagnose and deal with the difficulties of individual students. They recommended that programs would be most successful if they adhered to the following general principles: (a) the remedial work was most effective when given individually, but small group instruction was possible if attention was paid to each child; (b) the teaching needed to be systematic with instruction provided daily; (c) interesting reading materials were needed that matched the level of the child's reading ability; and, (d) teachers must receive specific training regarding the most effective ways to help these children. All of these tenets are still applicable today.

Several decades later Samuel Kirk coined the term "learning disability" and helped us understand the various origins of this disability. In an interview, Kirk explained: "I like to define a learning disability as a psychological or neurological impediment to the development of adequate perceptual or communicative behavior which first, is manifested in discrepancies among specific behaviors…" (Arena, 1978, p. 617). He further indicated on several occasions that many people have unfortunately confused learning disabilities with nearly every type of learning problem (Kirk, 1978; 1984). Through years of study by hundreds and hundreds of researchers, our understanding has increased regarding the prevalence and nature of learning disabilities, the most efficacious methods for assessment and diagnosis, and the most robust procedures for addressing and treating these problems.

Similarly, in the area of behavioral and emotional disturbances, many early psychoanalytically- and psychodynamically-oriented individuals come readily to mind—examples include Sigmund Freud and his daughter Anna Freud, Melanie Klein, Harry Stack Sullivan, Karen Horney, and Bruno Bettleheim. These mental health professionals emphasized the critical importance of early childhood experiences on the development of later emotional disorders. They also contributed directly or indirectly in assisting professionals in schools and clinical settings to formulate treatment plans to reduce emotional and behavioral problems. Others to acknowledge include Alfred Adler, Frederick Allen, and Carl Rogers whose theoretical writings and therapeutic approaches had a large impact on our understanding of the etiology of children's emotional and behavioral disorders, as well as on the types of classroom interventions that were effective for altering behavior. (See Morris, Li, Lizardi-Sanchez, and Morris, 2002, for a more complete discussion of these early theorists.)

One must also acknowledge the creativity and genius of B.F. Skinner (1938) and his work with laboratory rats and pigeons. Skinner demonstrated that behavior was predictable under certain environmental conditions and that animals could learn based on various contingencies of reinforcement. Skinner (1953) and his students and colleagues such as Joel Greenspoon, Frederick Kanfer, Fred Keller, Charles Ferster, and Nathan Azrin, also showed how his work with laboratory animals could be applied directly to human behavior. Others, such as Bijou and Baer (1965), applied Skinner's concepts to understanding child development, while Lovaas and his colleagues (e.g., Lovaas, 1977; Lovaas, Berberich, Perloff, & Schaeffer, 1966) applied Skinner's methods to teaching speech to children having autism and reducing severe self-injurious behaviors in children with serious developmental disorders. Other early researchers whose work with children and youth was influenced by Skinner included Ogden Lindsley, Lee Meyerson, Wesley Becker, Montrose Wolf, and Todd Risley.

The work of Lovaas and his colleagues was also built in part upon the earlier writings of Leo Kanner who, in 1943, described the symptoms of 11 cases of "autistic disturbances of affective contact." These descriptions began to direct the attention of scholars like Lovaas to studying children who may have previously been erroneously labeled as having schizophrenia or mental retardation.

One also can appreciate the creativity and insights of Albert Bandura (1969). Bandura formulated a theory of modeling and explained how such imitation learning contributed to the development (and successful remediation) of a variety of behavioral challenges in children. Time and years of laboratory research were also needed in the areas of children's cognitive learning and memory processes before researchers, such as Don Deshler and his colleagues, could begin to develop intervention strategies for successfully addressing a variety of children's learning and behavioral challenges. These are just a few examples of the foundational research that has helped establish the framework for the multitude of findings over the past 25 years regarding EBIs for children with learning and behavioral problems.

Progress in the area of EBIs could not, however, have taken place if students with disabilities were not enrolled in public schools. That is, without the early public policy research and advocacy work by such giants in special education as Samuel Kirk (e.g., Kirk, 1984), Burton Blatt (e.g., Blatt, 1968, 1970; Blatt & Kaplan, 1966), and Wolf Wolfensberger (1972), as well as the thoughtful writings of the anthropologist Robert Edgerton (1964), the political lobbying of several key U.S. senators and representatives, and the advocacy work of many professional associations and parent organizations, the U.S. Congress may have never passed the *Education for All Handicapped Children Act* (PL 94-142, 1975)—the first such federal law that guaranteed all children with disabilities an equal and free education regardless of the nature and severity of their disability. Given this legislation, as well as the brilliant work of earlier scholars and researchers in both special education and psychology, much progress has been made in the educational services available to children having learning and behavioral challenges.

Some critics, however, might say that such progress is limited only to the confines of academic research journals and scholarly textbooks; that real progress has not yet been demonstrated in classroom settings; that teachers do not use these methods because they have no supervised training in how to implement them or do not have the time. Although this may be true in some special education classrooms in some school districts, it is our firm belief that as more and more teachers are educated about EBIs—and receive supervised training in the application of EBIs—the chances of improved services for all children will increase.

The chapter authors of this book, experts all, many of whom were mentored by the leaders of the past, have been encouraged to sample widely from the empirical research literature and to discuss only those methods that are data-based and have been shown on a repeated basis to be effective in successfully addressing a particular behavioral or learning challenge. For some areas, however, the empirical literature is still not well established. When this is the case, the authors describe the current state of empirical knowledge and suggest additional areas for future research and scientific inquiry.

This book contains descriptions of many research-based strategies and teaching methods that can be used to work successfully with children having learning and/or behavioral challenges. Although the evidence-based practices described can help all teachers meet the challenges of improving educational outcomes for all children, simple solutions do not exist; all classrooms are complex interactive environments that also are affected by the diverse characteristics, temperaments, and personalities of both the students and the teachers. People in schools are embedded in complex and changing networks of social interaction (Berliner, 2002; Odom et al., 2005). Although scientific knowledge is certainly important, we cannot forget Berliner's (2002) point that "We should never lose sight of the fact that children and teachers in classrooms are conscious, sentient, and purposive human beings, so no scientific explanation of human behavior could ever be complete" (p. 20). Because of its complexity, special education "...may be the hardest of the hardest-to-do science" (Odom et al., 2005, p. 139).

Despite the fact that special education research is hard to do because of the complexity and variability of the participants and settings, the chapter authors have all done an admirable job of presenting the current status of evidence-based knowledge within their areas of expertise. Each and every EBI discussed in this book must be implemented by competent, caring professionals. As Kauffman (2005) states, "Effective and humane education of students with disabilities has always depended on the individual actions of competent, caring teachers and other individuals, and this will be the case in the future regardless of legal mandates and prohibitions" (p. 446). Similarly, the child psychotherapy literature has repeatedly indicated that the therapeutic relationship is an important contributing factor to the successful implementation of child therapy procedures (see for example, Kendall & Morris, 1991; Morris & Nicholson, 1993). Although this uniquely human element cannot be easily measured, it is an essential component of effective instruction and therapy.

Although much progress has been made in the past 25 years, we look forward to the next 25 years of educational research. This new research will further clarify and enhance our knowledge about the most effective ways to intervene successfully with students. Because of the changes in IDEA 2004, the focus has shifted to measuring and ensuring children's Response to Intervention (RTI). Perhaps, the acronym of RTI should have an additional meaning: All children have the Right To Intervention (RTI). Currently, we know a lot about evidence-based instruction for students who struggle with aspects of learning or behavior but the challenge remains for special educators, school psychologists, and administrators to ensure that all children receive the best of what we know.

## REFERENCES

Arena, J. (1978). An interview with Samuel Kirk. *Academic Therapy, 13,* 617–620.

Bandura, A. (1969). *Principles of behavior modification.* New York: Holt, Rinehart and Winston.

Berliner, D. C. (2002). Educational research: The hardest science of all. *Educational Researcher, 31*(8), 18–20.

Bijou, S. W., & Baer, D. M (1965). *Child development II: Universal stage of infancy.* New York: Appelton-Century-Crofts.

Blatt, B. (1968). The dark side of the mirror. *Mental Retardation, 1,* 42–44.

Blatt, B. (1970). *Exodus from pandemonium: Human abuse and a reformation of public policy.* Boston: Allyn and Bacon.

Blatt, B., & Kaplan, F. (1966). *Christmas in purgatory: A photographic essay on mental retardation.* Boston: Allyn and Bacon.

Edgerton, R. B. (1967). *The cloak of competence: Stigma in the lives of the mentally retarded.* Berkeley: University of California Press.

Feuer, M. J., Towne, L., & Shavelson, R. J. (2002). Scientific culture and educational research. *Educational Researcher, 31*(8), 4–14.

Hinshelwood, J. (1902). *Congenital word-blindness with reports of two cases.* London: John Bale, Sons & Danielsson, Ltd.

Kanner, L. (1943). Autistic disturbances of affective contact. *Nervous Child, 2,* 217–250.

Kendall, P., & Morris, R. J. (1991). Child therapy: Issues and recommendations. *Journal of Consulting and Clinical Psychology, 59,* 777–784.

Kirk, S. A. (1984). Introspection and prophecy. In B. Blatt & R.J. Morris (Eds.), *Perspectives in special education: Personal orientations* (pp. 25–55). Glenview, IL: Scott Foresman.

Lovaas, I. O. (1977). *The autistic child: Language development through behavior modification.* Baltimore, MD: University Park Press.

Lovaas, I. O., Berberich, J. P., Perloff, B. F., & Schaeffer, B. (1966). Acquisition of imitative speech by schizophrenic children. *Science, 151,* 705-707.

Monroe, M., & Backus, B. (1937). *Remedial reading: A monograph in character education.* Boston: Houghton Mifflin.

Morris, R. J., & Nicholson, J. (1993). The therapeutic relationship in child psychotherapy. In T. R. Kratochwill & R. J. Morris (Eds.), *Handbook of psychotherapy with children and adolescents* (pp. 405–426). Boston: Allyn & Bacon.

Morris, R .J., Li, Huijun, Lizardi-Sanchez, P., & Morris, Y. P. (2002). Psychotherapy with children and adolescents. In I. Weiner (Ed.), *Comprehensive handbook of psychology: Clinical psychology* (pp. 389–405). New York: Wiley.

Odom, S. L., Brantlinger, E., Gersten, R., Horner, R. H., Thompson, B., & Harris, K. R. (2005). Research in special education: Scientific methods and evidence-based practices. *Exceptional Children, 71*, 137–148.

Skinner, B. F. (1938). *The behavior of organisms*. New York: Appleton-Century-Crofts.

Skinner, B. F. (1953). *Science and human behavior*. New York: MacMillan.

Witmer, L. (1907/1996). Clinical psychology. *American Psychologist, 51*, 248–251.

Wolfensberger, W. (1972). *The principle of normalization in human services*. Toronto, Canada: National Institute on Mental Retardation.

Yell, M. L., Shriner, J. G., & Katsiyannis, A. (2006). Individuals with Disabilities Education Improvement Act of 2004 and IDEA Regulations of 2006: Implications for educators, administrators, and teacher trainers. *Focus on Exceptional Children, 39*(1), 1–24.

# 2

# Why the Need for Evidence-Based Interventions?

Jeffery P. Braden and Elisa Steele Shernoff

Given the title and content of this book, it may seem a bit odd to raise the question why evidence-based interventions (EBIs) are needed. After all, if you are reading this book, it implies that you at least have answered the question posed in the title in the affirmative. Professional associations, scholarly articles, and even laws and regulations are encouraging or requiring professionals to use EBIs in their efforts to serve children. Given the current demand and the content of the other chapters in this book, what is the value of considering EBIs? The answer is that, by understanding the historical and current context for EBIs, you will be better able to evaluate the promises and the pitfalls of the EBI movement, and in so doing, be a better EBI consumer and practitioner. Or, as Santayana put it, "Those who do not remember history are condemned to repeat it."

EBIs are an outgrowth of three broad factors: (1) the desire to align professional practices with the current knowledge base, (2) efforts to enhance students' welfare while holding steady or even decreasing costs, and (3) legal and regulatory mandates intended to improve educational outcomes. Each of these factors is considered in the following sections.

## ALIGNMENT OF RESEARCH AND PRACTICE

Although dismay at the lack of alignment between research and practice has been raised many times within education (e.g., Coalition for Evidence-Based Policy, 2002, 2003; Cook, 2001; Shavelson & Towne, 2002), the current push toward evidence-based practice (EBP) was first advanced within the medical profession. Surveys of medical resources found that medical procedures varied substantially by region in ways unrelated to patient needs, and frequently included treatments whose effectiveness was not clearly demonstrated (see Ginzberg, 1991/1994). This led to calls from medical associations and elected officials for physicians to use evidence rather than customary practice, word-of-mouth, or untested treatments in treating patients.

In part in response to this movement, Congress established the Association for Health Care Policy Research (AHCPR), which is now known as the Agency for Healthcare Research and Quality (AHRQ). The goal of this entity was to create panels of knowledgeable physicians and researchers to review medical research regarding treatments for given diagnoses, called Patient Outcome Research Teams, or PORT, studies. The goal of these studies was to identify, based on scientific research, what treatments worked for the diagnosis—and by implication, identify treatments that either did not work or for which there was insufficient evidence to make a decision regarding their efficacy. The panels typically produced a report for physicians to guide practice, and a report for patients to help them become better consumers of medial services. The outcomes of these panel reviews are posted on the AHCRQ Web site, which is included in Table 2.2.

The EBP movement quickly spread to psychology, in part because many psychologists practice in medical settings, and in part because psychology has long embraced the "scientist-practitioner" model of training and practice (Drabick & Goldfried, 2002). Divisions within the American Psychological Association (APA) convened panels of scientists and practitioners to set standards to identify forms of evidence to be used to evaluate the quality of the evidence supporting a particular intervention. Most relevant to this book are the standards that were developed by a joint task force of the Society for the Study of School Psychology and APA's Division 16 (School Psychology), which are reviewed in greater detail later in this chapter. Additionally, APA altered its program accreditation guidelines in 2005 to specify that all psychology training programs include training in EBIs (Committee on Accreditation, 2005). In short, the late 1990s and early years of the 21st century saw a flurry of activity to identify, and then apply, standards of evidence to the extant research. This was in an effort to inform both professionals and consumers of the interventions that did (and did not) work and to improve outcomes for medical and psychological problems. Similar efforts were made in education, including special education, as described in an issue of *Exceptional Children* (2005, Vol. 71–2) and reviewed later in this chapter.

## ENHANCING STUDENT WELFARE AND EFFICIENCY

Social pressures from outside professional associations also contributed to the growth of the EBP movement. Specifically, two forces coincided to support EBP. The first was the drive to ensure that people were informed consumers of health and psychological services. The argument was that informed consumers would be better than uniformed consumers when considering treatment options in ways that balanced research, their own circumstances, and their preferences and values (Ginzberg, 1991/1993). Advocates for consumers of health and psychological services therefore embraced and supported the EBP movement as a step toward empowering consumers by giving them knowledge to make choices that maximized personal goals and values.

The second force encouraging the EBP movement came from third-party payers for services. Because most individuals do not pay their entire health care costs out of pocket, state and federal government programs and insurance companies subsidize the bulk of funds spent each year on health and psychological services. These entities have a strong fiscal incentive to reduce expenditures, particularly when funds are expended on services with unknown or demonstrably ineffective outcomes. By having an independent means to decide which services to fund, and not to fund, third-party payers could hold down costs while enhancing outcomes. In the fields of education and school psychology, evidence-based practices also have the potential to propel research forward and eventually improve the quality of services provided by teachers, school psychologists, school counselors, and other educational professionals.

## LEGAL AND REGULATORY MANDATES

Congress has expanded the EBP movement through legislation and regulation, first in health care (which includes psychology), and then in education. As previously noted, Congress boosted EBP by creating the Association for Health Care Policy Research. The results produced by the AHCPR, and its successor agency, the Agency for Healthcare Research and Quality, are used by government health programs (e.g., MEDICARE, MEDICAID) and many insurers to determine which procedures will (and will not) be funded by third party payers.

Congress also embraced principles of EBP in passing education legislation. The No Child Left Behind Act (NCLB) of 2001 and the Individuals with Disabilities Education Improvement Act of 2004 (IDEIA 2004) dramatically increased accountability demands for general and special education, outlining elaborate and extensive expectations for student performance, and including significant sanctions for failure to meet the ambitious targets in the legislation. Along with setting demands, NCLB and IDEIA 2004 explicitly direct schools to adopt EBPs so that they can improve student performance and meet their goals. For example, the IDEIA 2004 directs schools to use "scientifically based" methods of instruction, and allows local education agencies to diagnose learning disabilities in part on the basis of the student's response to "scientific, research based interventions."

Additionally, legislation and regulations directed resources to develop, identify, and disseminate EBPs to educators. The Coalition for Evidenced Based Policy (2002, 2003) was funded to provide guidelines for evaluating evidence from educational research. The What Works Clearinghouse (WWC) was also created to serve a role similar to the AHRQ; that is, to develop standards for evidence, and then review, identify, and publicly disseminate information about educational interventions that meet those standards. These efforts, along with legal mandates for schools to use scientifically based practices, clearly signaled the belief of the federal government that EBP would improve educational outcomes, and largely provide the mechanism whereby schools could meet ambitious goals for student outcomes each year.

Consequently, pressures internal to professions coupled with the interests of consumer advocacy groups, third-party payers, and legislation encouraged the development of EBP, first in medicine, then in education. The burgeoning of interest in and response to EBP has increased dramatically over the past decade, and has even been incorporated as a training requirement in professional psychology programs. Therefore, EBP is a compelling framework for conceptualizing training and practice in psychology and education.

## DEFINING EVIDENCE-BASED PRACTICE

Although the EBP movement has grown in the past several decades, the terminology related to EBP has not always been well understood or agreed upon. The lack of consensus regarding key terminology is due to complexities related to formalizing criteria, and the broader issues and controversies related to dictating a scientific approach to practice (Chorpita, 2003; Elliott, 1998).

One of the first terms proposed for the EBP movement in psychology was "empirically validated interventions," first used by the American Psychological Association Division 12 Task Force (1995) to describe interventions that were evaluated using acceptable methods of science and proven to be effective (Kendall, 1998). The term "empirically validated" created a firestorm of debate and criticism within psychology, because the term suggested that an intervention could be fully validated, with no further evaluation needed. However, in principle, an intervention can never be fully validated because it cannot produce success under all circumstances. Moreover, the term "validated" also suggested that the mechanisms of effectiveness and change were known, a condition that rarely exists for child or adult interventions (Garfield, 1996; Lonigan, Elbert, & Bennett-Johnson, 1998; Stoiber & Kratochwill, 2000).

The term "empirically validated" was quickly replaced by "empirically supported," which implies that practices are never fully validated, but instead have support along a continuum of scientific credibility (Shernoff & Kratochwill, 2005). Empirically supported interventions were identified based on methodological features of the studies evaluating the intervention, and statistical support for intervention outcomes. The term "empirically supported" also connoted that reviewing evidence is an ongoing process that is subject to change, based on future empirical analysis of interventions (Kendall, 2002; Kratochwill & Stoiber, 2002).

Moving beyond specific interventions or procedures, the term evidence-based practice has been described as a "movement" within the fields of education, psychology, and mental health in which there has been an organized effort to identify, disseminate, and promote the use of practices with demonstrated efficacy and effectiveness (Hoagwood, 2005). Evidence-based practice is a shorthand term denoting the quality, robustness, or validity of scientific evidence as it is brought to bear on decisions regarding the adoption, implementation, and evaluation of services (Cournoyer & Powers, 2002; Kratochwill & Shernoff, 2003). Although evidence is an elusive concept, it is clear that the EBP movement embraces evidence that is empirical.

Evidence-based practices are distinct from empirically validated and empirically supported interventions in several domains. First and foremost, evidence-based practices rest on a coherent body of scientific knowledge relevant to a range of educational and clinical practices. These practices are based on prior empirical findings showing that certain actions performed by practitioners with a particular individual or system are "likely to produce predictable, beneficial, and effective results" (Cournoyer & Powers, 2002, p. 800). Second, evidence-based practice, in contrast to empirically validated and empirically supported interventions, integrate practitioner expertise and values with the best research evidence available (Sackett, Straus, Richardson, Rosenberg, & Haynes, 2000). This distinction is important because it places responsibility on the educator/practitioner to provide high quality intervention practices as it emphasizes integrating, rather than replacing, professional expertise and judgment with best available evidence (Frederickson, 2002). Evidence-based practices are also systematically evaluated to assess the degree to which the predicted results were attained as a direct consequence of the educator's or practitioner's behaviors (Cournoyer & Powers, 2002). This emphasis on evaluating practice is crucial, given that many educational and mental health interventions used in schools are limited in terms of their research base, particularly with respect to the contextual factors that influence their application in educational settings.

## KEY CONCEPTS IN EVIDENCE-BASED PRACTICE:
## METHODS OF INQUIRY AND HIERARCHIES OF EVIDENCE

A critical conceptual issue within the evidence-based practice movement focuses on the methods of inquiry and legitimate sources of knowledge used to evaluate educational interventions, prevention programs, and school-based mental health services. The evidence in support of an intervention is often dictated by the specific conceptual questions of interest. These include questions related to: (a) Efficacy (i.e., Is Intervention A superior to Intervention B?); (b) Effectiveness (i.e., Will the intervention work across different settings?); (c) Implementation (i.e., What training and supervision is required to implement this intervention with integrity?); (d) Acceptability (i.e., Is this practice more or less acceptable than established practices?); and (e) Cost-effectiveness (i.e., What is the relative cost for producing outcomes using this intervention compared to existing practice?).

## Efficacy

Most of the early evidence amassed for evidence-based practices emerged in the context of efficacy trials, defined as systematic evaluations directed at (1) comparing one or more interventions with one or more control or comparison conditions, and (2) establishing whether a particular intervention is beneficial (e.g., improves functioning, reduces symptoms). Above all, efficacy studies are concerned with replication so that researchers can conduct similar studies to test the impact of an intervention (Kazdin, 2004). To maximize the likelihood of detecting treatment effects, efficacy trials are usually conducted under carefully controlled conditions. Factors that may obscure treatment effects are eliminated or controlled, including the setting in which the intervention takes place, sample selection, and how the intervention is delivered (Nathan, Stuart, & Dolan, 2000; Weisz & Jensen, 1999). Efficacy studies are usually conducted in university settings or clinical research facilities using well-designed and precise methodology, usually meaning randomized controlled trials (RCTs) in which participants are randomly assigned to conditions (Fonagy, Target, Cottrell, Phillips, & Kurtz, 2002). Efficacy studies often include research participants who are carefully screened and selected to maximize the homogeneity of the sample, and to increase the link between specific interventions and diagnostic classifications or disabilities. Interventions are manualized, brief, and have a fixed duration to minimize within-group variability (Westen, Novotny, & Thompson-Brenner, 2004). Manualized interventions, which are discussed in greater detail later in the chapter, specify the theory and techniques of a treatment in written form with the goal of standardizing intervention implementation and training. Practitioners are also rigorously trained, supervision is intensive, and there is a strong emphasis on ensuring that the intended intervention (no more, no less) is provided in efficacy studies (Nathan et al., 2000).

These features of efficacy research help maximize the internal validity of the studies or the extent to which the independent variable (in the context of efficacy studies, the intervention) causes any observed differences in the dependent variable (i.e., measures of student outcomes). The conceptual relationship between efficacy, effectiveness, and transportability research is represented in Figure 2.1. The poles represent the degree to which internal or external validity is the focus of the study. Although most studies are not purely constructed along these dimensions, efficacy and effectiveness research have often been regarded as being at opposite ends of the internal-external validity continuum. Typically, efficacy studies are designed to maximize internal validity but usually sacrifice external validity (i.e., generalization of results beyond the observed study) (see Figure 2.1).

Results from broad-based meta-analyses of efficacy trials paint an optimistic picture of the number of interventions shown to be effective. Casey and Berman (1985) conducted one of the first broad-based meta-analyses, in which 75 outcome studies from 1952 to 1983 were examined with children ages 12 and younger. They found that the average treated child scored better on outcome measures than 76% of the control group children. Meta-analytic studies specific to school-based interventions have also established a large body of behavioral and educational interventions as efficacious. Stage and Quiroz (1997), for example, conducted a meta-analysis of interventions for decreasing disruptive classroom behavior in public schools and found that on average, 78% of the students exposed to the interventions reviewed had reductions in disruptive behavior when compared to learners in control groups.

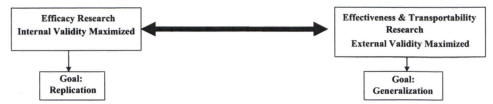

FIGURE 2.1    Conceptual model of the relationship between efficacy and effectiveness research.

Despite compelling evidence for the efficacy of various interventions to address common problems that emerge in school-aged children, controversies exist regarding the hierarchy of evidence needed to establish an intervention as effective. For example, there has been an implicit assumption within the EBP enterprise that efficacy studies and RCTs provide the only valid source of evidence to support an intervention (Roth & Fonagy, 1996). Although RCTs and their logical counterparts are considered the standard for drawing causal inferences about the impact of an intervention, RCTs have also been criticized for their limited generalizability, higher costs associated with training and intervention delivery, and failure to attend to the real world exigencies related to implementing interventions (Carroll & Rounsaville, 2003; Lonigan et al., 1998). Given that there is compelling evidence to suggest that intervention effects previously supported in efficacy trials do not consistently hold under conditions of actual practice, efficacy trials are not the design of choice for all intervention outcome studies.

## Effectiveness

Effectiveness studies, in contrast to efficacy studies, are conducted under conditions that reflect typical practice settings, such as homes, schools, and community mental health agencies (Drake, Latimer, Leff, McHugo, & Burns, 2004). Effectiveness research aims to determine whether interventions are feasible and have measurable benefits across broad populations (Nathan et al., 2000). Effectiveness studies help answer the question "Do intervention effects generalize to the real world?" with a premium placed on external validity (see Figure 2.1). In effectiveness research, participants are in need of immediate intervention regardless of the problem, families do not always seek out services voluntarily, and referral problems are usually more severe and complex (Weisz, Donenberg, Han, & Weiss, 1995). Variables such as differential attrition and lack of random assignment to intervention conditions are common in effectiveness research (Hoagwood, Hibbs, Brent, & Jensen, 1995; Merrill, Tolbert, & Wade, 2003), and practitioners or educators are not always specifically trained in a research protocol or target intervention. In effectiveness research, outcome measures are often broadly defined and often focus on socially valid outcomes, including improvements in quality of life, functioning, or changes in disability status, rather than the scientifically precise (but sometimes less meaningful) measures employed in efficacy research. Effectiveness research embraces extraneous variables, or error variance, that efficacy studies attempt to control. Such messy, "real world" factors are essential to understanding if implementation of an intervention is feasible, effective, and sustainable.

Some promising early stage effectiveness studies include cognitive-behavioral therapy (CBT) implemented in a school for adolescents struggling with depression (Lewinsohn, Clark, Hops, & Andrews, 1990), cognitive therapy to treat depression in community mental health centers (Merrill et al., 2003), and cognitive-behavioral treatment of outpatient children with ADHD (Fehlings, Roberts, Humphries, & Dawe, 1991). An ambitious project was also recently undertaken by the State of Hawaii with the goal of moving from identifying promising interventions in efficacy trials to evaluating the likelihood that such interventions could be successfully applied in educational settings. The Hawaii Project was groundbreaking in its approach to balancing feasibility with high quality research and including key stakeholders (e.g., clinicians, parents) in the process of evaluating evidence-based practices (Chorpita et al., 2002). Despite the significant contributions that the Hawaii Project made to understanding effectiveness, the project also underscored that in contrast to the evidence supporting the efficacy of child and adolescent psychosocial and academic interventions, evidence of effectiveness is quite limited (Chorpita et al., 2002; Hogan, 2002; Weisz & Jensen, 1999).

## Transportability

In addition to longstanding concerns regarding the degree to which intervention effects are replicated in applied settings, researchers across many disciplines have long struggled with the complexities involved in wide-scale dissemination of prevention and intervention programs and the broader organizational and training issues that mitigate the movement of EBIs into practice settings (Blakely et al., 1987; Davidson & Redner, 1988; Hoagwood, Burns, Kiser, Ringeisen, & Schoenwald, 2001; Schoenwald & Hoagwood, 2001). Transportability research is a type of effectiveness research (see Figure 2.1) that focuses on understanding how the intervention works in the real world and who can (or will) conduct the intervention, under what conditions, and to what effect (Schoenwald & Hoagwood, 2001). Transportability research takes into account the contextual variables (e.g., time, training and supervision requirements, and institutional support for EBIs, sustainability of an intervention after investigator support is withdrawn) that mitigate the movement of EBIs into practice settings (Shernoff & Kratochwill, in press). These contextual variables are linked to practitioners' inability to implement EBI protocols in mental health settings (Miller, 2001; Schmidt & Taylor, 2002; Simpson, 2002); unfortunately, well-controlled studies examining the transportability of EBIs to schools have been more limited to date (Storch & Crisp, 2004).

Despite limited research regarding the transportability of EBIs to practice settings, there has been some pioneering work with Multisystemic Treatment (MST) for adolescents with conduct disorders (Henggeler, Melton, Brondino, Scherer, & Hanley, 1997; Henggeler, Schoenwald, Liao, Letourneau, & Edwards, 2002; Schoenwald, Henggeler, Brondino, & Rowland, 2000). The successful transportability of MST to community settings has been attributed to several characteristics that differentiate the model from other EBIs. These include focussing on the multiple determiants of antisocial behavior adherance to principles for implementing the intervention rather than using highly specified treatment manual, and using supervision as a mechanism for enhancing fidelity and corresponding treatment outcomes.

## Additional Methods of Inquiry and Hierarchies of Evidence

Even when strong evidence is available from efficacy, effectiveness, and transportability research, other designs and strategies make important contributions to the knowledge base regarding evidence-based practices. For example, if the goal of the study is to understand research participants' subjective experience with a particular intervention, or the acceptability of specific practices, or how an intervention can be changed to maximize its usefulness, qualitative methods, including semi-structured interviews, may be the best research approach (APA Presidential Task Force on Evidence-Based Practice, 2006; Fredrickson, 2002). Systematic case studies, often involving intensive, longitudinal analyses of an individual, can also be useful for generating hypotheses for future well-controlled studies (Levin, O'Donnell, & Kratochwill, 2003). Single case design strategies have only recently been seriously considered to establish the scientific rigor of educational practices. These strategies offer a high degree of scientific rigor, and also allow for causal interferences to be made regarding behavior changes within individuals. Clearly, different approaches provide complementary evidence regarding effectiveness, and an integral part of the EBP movement requires educators to recognize the strengths and limitations of evidence obtained from different types of research.

## EXAMPLES OF EVIDENCE-BASED PRACTICE STANDARDS

In this section, we will review the key criteria that distinguish evidence-based practices (or interventions) from practices or interventions that lack evidence. We begin by reviewing criteria common to most definitions, and then share some selected criteria to illustrate commonalities and differences among various definitions of EBP and EBIs.

### Elements for Evaluating Evidence

Six key elements are typically applied to decide whether an intervention can be identified as evidence-based. These are listed in Table 2.1 along with the questions each element addresses. An expanded discussion is provided in the following sections. Although these elements are, in some shape or form, common to most definitions of EBIs, they are not used the same way by different entities defining EBP and EBIs. For example, although all definitions attempt to define a particular practice or intervention as responding to a particular problem or set of problems, different definitions do so in different ways. Therefore, the following elements attempt to define common dimensions used across EBI definitions, but do not imply unanimity of agreement regarding how to apply these elements in defining EBP and EBIs.

    Specificity of problem and population. Standards for identifying EBIs are conditional, in that they are usually limited to particular problems and populations. That is, interventions are not in and of themselves judged to be "evidence based;" rather, they are judged to be "evidence based"

**TABLE 2.1**
**Key Criteria for Establishing Evidence-Based Interventions**

| Criterion | Key questions to be addressed |
| --- | --- |
| Specificity of the intervention target population | What problem does the intervention target? In whom does the problem occur? |
| Specificity of the intervention | What is the nature of the intervention? What are the steps and required resources, and are these clearly explained in writing (e.g., a treatment manual)? |
| Research design | Does the research employ random assignment of participants to conditions (or conditions to a single participant)? Is the intervention compared to a previously established treatment? |
| Ability to detect effects or outcomes | Does the study have sufficient power to detect an effect? Does the study use reliable and valid outcome measures? |
| Number and independence of studies needed to support the intervention | Are the intervention effects replicated? Are the replications truly independent investigations? |
| The quality of evidence | What classification does the reviewed evidence merit with respect to its overall strength and quality? |

for a particular problem and within a particular population of children and youth. The most common approach used in medicine, psychology, and education is to define problems via diagnostic classifications, and define populations primarily by the age (or grade level) of the student (although ethnicity and gender are also often used). Just as drug efficacy studies limit claims of efficacy by problem and child's age (e.g., a particular drug is good for a particular problem within adults, but has not been tested in children), so too do EBP/EBI standards delimit the claims of efficacy to the nature of the problem and the age (or grade) of the student.

Specificity of intervention. For an intervention to be considered evidence-based, it must be defined with sufficient precision so that it can be reliably replicated. One common method for meeting this standard is for there to be a treatment manual that clearly specifies the steps in the intervention process, and what to do at each step. This requirement is sometimes expressed as requiring an intervention to be "manualized." Typical requirements for explicitness include exact statements and directions, as well as principles of responding to unanticipated outcomes and circumstances. The criteria should be sufficiently objective and precise to allow different people to produce the same set of behaviors by following the directions in the manual.

Research design. Most criteria specify that the intervention must be found effective in studies using "true" experimental designs. Experimental designs are distinguished from quasi-experimental or pseudo-experimental designs primarily on the basis of random assignment to treatment and control groups (Cook, 2001). Standards typically demand at least two studies using experimental group designs, or a series of single case studies using randomized application of at least two interventions (i.e., the intervention under study and a comparison condition). Most criteria also demand that the experimental design include an alternate intervention in the control condition. Two types of alternatives are identified: first, an intervention that is already established as an EBI (so that the intervention under study can be demonstrated to be equal to or better than the EBI alternative), and second, the equivalent of a psychological or educational placebo intervention condition. Because education is offered to all children, it is inappropriate to test whether a particular intervention is better than no intervention at all (e.g., finding that a particular reading intervention works better than no intervention is hardly illuminating). These features (i.e., random assignment and alternate treatment control condition) apply to group designs, in which individuals are assigned to an intervention or alternate group, and to single-case (or $N = 1$) designs, in which the intervention and the alternate conditions are repeated within an individual to demonstrate the superiority of the intervention to the alternate condition.

Ability to detect effects or outcomes. Most statistical and experimental procedures were developed to reduce the chances of accidentally or erroneously finding a difference between the intervention and alternate treatment conditions. However, there is a complementary problem: failing to find a difference when one exists. The ability of a research design to detect an effect is known as "power." Increasing the sample size of a study is the most direct way to increase power, although using measures with little error also increases the sensitivity of the research to detect actual differences between conditions. Most studies with small samples (e.g., five or ten participants), or with weak outcome measures would fail to find a difference between a new intervention and an established EBI, simply because it lacked the power to detect existing differences. Therefore, most standards for evidence require that the study have sufficient sample size (or more precisely, power) and use reliable, objective measures of outcomes, to detect a difference between the conditions.

Number and independence of research studies needed to support the intervention. Evidential standards require independent replication of findings before accepting an intervention as evidence based. The number of replications varies for single case and group designs. Standards require a large number of $N = 1$ designs to establish an intervention as evidence-based, whereas the minimum number of group designs is typically two. A second feature of replication is that at least two of the sources of evidence be independent from each other. That is, different investigators or teams who are autonomous must report the same finding (e.g., an experimental group study or a series of $N = 1$ studies) for the intervention to be accepted as evidence-based. Replications by individuals in the same lab, or replications by graduate students or employees of an individual do not count toward the independent replication requirement.

Quality of evidence. Finally, when all of the evidence is reviewed, most standards rate the quality of evidence into three categories. These categories typically include a designation for evidence meeting or exceeding the standards, such as "Established," "Empirically Validated," or "Evidence-Based." Likewise, there is typically a designation for interventions that lack most or all of the evidence required by the standards, such as "Experimental" or "Not Established." Finally, most standards provide a designation for interventions where the evidence base meets some, but not all, of the established criteria, such as "Promising" or "Partially Validated." Examples of these categories might include interventions in which an independent replication is lacking, or those interventions tested only against no treatment (rather than alternative intervention or placebo treatment) conditions. Therefore, to declare an intervention as "Evidence-based" implies that the evidence supporting the effectiveness of the intervention meets all of the standards for evidence, whereas those interventions with a less complete body of evidence would be declared as "promising" or "experimental." We use the term "EBI" to designate interventions meeting the standards described in this section, although we recognize that different bodies may define somewhat different criteria to such designations. Therefore, we turn our attention to various standards for evidence relevant to educators, school psychologists, school counselors and other professionals providing services to school-aged populations.

## Examples of Evidential Standards

A number of groups have promulgated standards for defining "what counts" as evidence that an intervention works. These include professional entities (e.g., various practice divisions within the American Psychological Association, The Council for Exceptional Children), governmental agencies (e.g., the US Department of Education, the National Institutes of Health), and nongovernmental organizations (e.g., the Coalition for Evidence-based Policy). These initiatives establish objective, precise criteria for reviewing and coding the empirical status of a range of interventions and practices. There are some similarities across those organizations developing practice standards (e.g., the need for operational criteria and transparency of the process). However, these organizations and initiatives differ along many important conceptual domains, including the criteria invoked for designating interventions as evidence-based, the literature reviewed, and the methodologies embraced (Drake et al., 2004). The various standards for EBP reflect differences in the traditions, values, roles, settings, individuals, and nature of interventions delivered by particular organizations in psychology and education. There is an inherent appeal in developing guidelines that reflect the ideals and values of particular professions. However, divergence across various practice guidelines has created challenges to understanding the "state" of the evidence for evidence-based practices, and complicates conclusions that can be drawn regarding how to integrate this knowledge base into daily practice. For example, one organization's "effective program" can be deemed as "ineffective" by another group. Representative samples of standards from some of the most relevant entities are reviewed in the following sections.

*American Psychological Association.* The Task Force of the American Psychological Association's (APA) Division 12 (Clinical Psychology) Committee on Science and Practice, Division 53 (Society of Clinical Child and Adolescent Psychology) Committee for Empirically Supported Practice, and Interdisciplinary Committee on Evidence-Based Youth Mental Health Care (1998) was one of the first entities charged with establishing criteria for and designating effective interventions to treat specific problems. The Task Force disseminated lists of evidence-based interventions to doctoral and internship programs to influence training, and incorporated EBP guidelines for accrediting doctoral and internship training programs (Task Force on Promotion and Dissemination of Psychological Procedures, 1995). *The Diagnostic and Statistical Manual of Mental Disorders – Fourth Edition (DSM-IV;* American Psychiatric Association, 1994) was the overriding conceptual framework used to link interventions to particular problems (i.e., *DSM-IV* diagnoses), and a high premium was placed on the use of efficacy research and RCTs to establish interventions as evidence-based. Based on Division 12's review of the literature, a list of empirically validated interventions was published for fellow psychologists and doctoral programs. Division 12 of the APA reviewed the literature further and recommended that clinicians and students only be trained in empirically validated interventions, rather than other forms of intervention that lacked "empirical validation" (and were therefore considered outdated and less essential) (Calhoun, Moras, Pilkonis, & Rehm, 1998). The idea of creating lists of empirically validated interventions was compelling at the time, spurred in part by widely disseminated practice guidelines giving priority to pharmacotherapy over other forms of interventions with respect to addressing children's emotional and behavioral problems. Such lists would function in a fashion similar to lists created by the Federal Drug Administration to identify which drugs are effective for which conditions. Also, a strong ethical and professional commitment existed to improve outcomes for children and families through the use of interventions known to be superior to ineffective or inferior interventions, or those treatments that have not been evaluated.

The Division 12 Task Force also developed one of the first manuals to guide the process of reviewing the literature and coding intervention outcome studies for children and adolescents. The coding scheme that was developed was categorical in nature, with the highest level of classification being well-established interventions, which were considered efficacious if they were shown to be more effective than no treatment, psychological placebo treatment conditions, or equivalent to established treatments. Well-established interventions must include between-group design studies replicated by different investigators, or a large series of single-case designs, comparing the intervention to other interventions. In addition, the interventions needed to be described in manuals, and the sample characteristics in supporting studies had to be clearly specified (Lonigan et al., 1998). Probably efficacious interventions met some, but not all, of the criteria for well-established interventions, and were therefore considered promising but in need of additional evidence.

Although the Division 12 practice standards had a monumental impact on training standards and practice guidelines developed by other professional organizations in psychology, operationalizing criteria and publishing lists of empirically validated practices was highly controversial (Elliott, 1998; Garfield, 1996; Norcross, 2001). Aside from the concerns regarding the term "empirically validated," major criticisms were also raised regarding the systematic discounting of certain classes of research (i.e., research other than RCTs); types of interventions (e.g., non-behavioral strategies); and clients (e.g., ethnic minorities) (see Elliott, 1998). The dichotomous coding scheme was seen as a crude estimate of complex interventions, and the rigid reliance on manuals while ignoring non-specific treatment effects (e.g., therapist skill) was condemned (Wampold, Lichtenberg, & Waehler, 2002). Because Division 12 standards relied heavily on efficacy (rather than effectiveness) studies, the practice standards and lists of interventions that evolved were viewed as poorly generalizing from research to practice settings (Kratochwill & Stoiber, 2002; Wampold, 2001).

The field of school psychology, having a vested interest in developing the knowledge base regarding evidence-based practices in schools, created the Task Force on Evidence-Based Interventions in School Psychology in 1999. This Task Force, sponsored by APA's Division 16 (School Psychology), the Society for the Study of School Psychology (SSSP), and the National Association of School Psychologists (NASP), was charged with reviewing and coding prevention and intervention studies for children, youth, and families, and identifying interventions that have sound research support (Kratochwill & Stoiber, 2002; Stoiber & Kratochwill, 2000). The goal of the School Psychology Task Force was twofold: first, to synthesize research on the effectiveness of various educational and mental health programs, and second, to help educators make informed decisions regarding interventions that can be feasibly integrated into school settings. This agenda meant disseminating information to key stakeholders regarding the methodological rigor of intervention outcome studies along with the specific contextual barriers and constraints that make the intervention challenging to implement in schools (Kratochwill & Shernoff, 2003).

The Division 16 Task Force differs from the Division 12 (clinical psychology) Task Force in several fundamental ways. First, the Task Force on Evidence-Based Interventions in School Psychology has invoked a dimensional approach to evaluating intervention research. Methodological criteria were used to evaluate the type and quality of empirical evidence for intervention and prevention programs, rather than simply declaring whether the evidence meets minimum criteria for empirical support. In other words, empirical support was viewed as a matter of degree rather than an absolute value, placing responsibility on the consumer of the information to weigh the evidence in support of a particular practice (Kratochwill & Stoiber, 2000b; Levin et al., 2003). This "consumer reports" approach, linked to a Likert-scale, was intended to help particular audiences understand and apply dimensions of evidence to fit their needs. Key features of an intervention study are rated on a 4-point scale to specify level of evidence (i.e., strong evidence/support, promising evidence/support, marginal or weak evidence/support, and no evidence/support), focus on internal and external validity criteria, and other features considered important for school and field-based implementation. Because a major objective of the Division 16 Task Force is to narrow the research-practice gap, the coding schema describes the overall methodological quality of the outcome evaluation in addition to the degree to which evaluation methods correspond to features of the school environment (Kratochwill & Shernoff, 2003). Studies are also rated descriptively, which may be of value to practitioners who are interested in evaluating how well an intervention matches their specific program needs and settings.

A second feature that distinguishes the School Psychology Task Force from previous evidence-based efforts is the focus on a broader range of methodological strategies to establish evidence for an intervention. A premium is placed on quantitative methodologies as the primary basis for credible evidence (Kratochwill & Stoiber, 2000b). However, qualitative research methods are embraced as a way to understand the community and cultural contexts that contribute to an intervention's success (Hohmann & Shear, 2002). Mixed methods of measurement, such as the use of rating scales along with direct observation, can identify insights into the engagement and retention of research participants. Confirmatory program evaluation strategies, in which researchers use theory-driven evaluations to determine the effectiveness of interventions, are also embraced (Reynolds, 1998). Finally, the School Psychology Task Force has also expanded the focus of its literature review beyond *DSM-IV* clinical disorders, incorporating intervention and prevention programs that focus on a wide range of problems relevant to practice in schools. For example, the Task Force reviewed academic interventions, school healthcare, school-wide interventions, and classroom-based interventions (Kratochwill & Stoiber, 2002).

APA's Division 17 (Counseling Psychology) has taken a unique approach to the evidence-based practice enterprise. Rather than developing a set of criteria that would lead to a list of evidence-based practices, the Special Task Group (STG) on Empirically Supported Interventions in Counseling Psychology decided to articulate a set of principles for identifying interventions and practices as evidence-based (Wampold et al., 2002). These principles are intended to offset some of the significant limitations to ordaining interventions as "evidence based," and recognize the complex relationship that exists between science and practice. In addition, APA's Division 29 (Psychotherapy) Task Force was developed in 1999 to identify, classify, and disseminate information on empirically supported therapy relationships, rather than interventions. This included identifying elements of effective therapy relationships and determining methods for customizing interventions to the unique characteristics that individuals present (Norcross, 2001).

*The Council for Exceptional Children (CEC).* The Council for Exceptional Children (CEC) is an international professional organization focused on enhancing educational outcomes for individuals with exceptionalities and disabilities. The CEC has had a strong role in advocating for policies, standards, and training to assist teachers, administrators, paraprofessionals, and related support service providers to engage in effective professional practice. In 2003, the CEC Division of Research established a Task Force to articulate quality indicators for defining "acceptable" and "high" quality research designs and studies in special education. The CEC identified four types of research methodologies for review: group, single case, correlational, and qualitative designs. The CEC task force places a strong emphasis on how EBPs intersect with effective instruction, including how teachers can access information on EBPs and implement practices with fidelity. See the Special Issue of *Exceptional Children* (Winter 2005) for an overview of the quality indicators for the CEC as they apply to special education research.

*US Department of Education.* The US Department of Education (USDOE) has published a document entitled "Identifying and Implementing Educational Practices Supported by Rigorous Evidence: A User Friendly Guide" (USDOE, 2003). The document contains criteria to classify interventions into one of three categories, from highest to lowest: "Strong Evidence of Effectiveness," "Possible Evidence of Effectiveness," or "Not Supported by Meaningful Evidence of Effectiveness." The aforementioned criteria common to most standards drive the distinctions between these categories, but add a few additional features regarding research design and context. Design features include ensuring random assignment was not violated, ascertaining that the treatment and control groups were equivalent prior to intervention, evaluating subject mortality (i.e., ensuring group differences are not a function of who drops out during the study), reporting both effect size and probability statistics, and reporting all study outcomes, not just those that were significant. Context features include multi-site replications in schools or communities similar to the consumer's site. Distinctions between "Strong" and "Possible" evidence again parallel other criteria, but allow for nonrandom designs in the "Possible" category, provided there is evidence of prospective assignment to groups and evidence that the groups are matched prior to intervention.

*Agency for Healthcare Research and Quality.* The AHRQ commissioned Evidence Practice Centers (EPCs) to generate guidelines for health care quality. The AHRQ did not adopt a single set of standards, in part because different aspects of health must be studied in different ways (e.g., some conditions and treatments lend themselves to experimental studies, and others do not). A report summarizing the key approaches to EBP guidelines (Research Triangle Institute-University of North Carolina Evidence Based Practice Center, 2002) identified standards to rate two types of evidence: the outcomes of randomized controlled trials (RCTs), and the outcomes of systematic reviews. Guidelines for RCTs are similar to those identified by other groups reviewed in this chapter, whereas guidelines for reviews essentially identify the mechanisms by which evidence should be collected, coded, and accepted with respect to the strength of conclusions drawn. Three elements of all criteria stand out as definitive: the quality, quantity, and consistency of outcomes within a review indicate the degree to which evidence meets, partially meets, or does not meet standards for EBP. The AHRQ Web site (see Table 2.2) includes practice guidelines (i.e., approaches meeting standards for EBP in medicine) for a variety of medical problems, with a number of additional studies underway to expand the identification of EBP in medical treatments.

*What Works Clearinghouse (WWC)*. As stated on their Web site, "The What Works Clearinghouse was established in 2002 by the U.S. Department of Education's Institute of Education Sciences to provide educators, policymakers, researchers, and the public with a central and trusted source of scientific evidence of what works in education" (What Works Clearinghouse, nd). The WWC has adopted between-group randomized trials for reviewing evidence and follows procedures highly similar to other entities, in that it empanels groups of scientists to review studies, and rates the studies according to criteria that define the study as "Meets evidence standard," "Meets standard with reservation," or "Does not meet evidence screens" (WWC, 2006). The criteria used to categorize the evidence in each study are similar to standards used by other groups, and to the criteria developed by the USDOE (2003). However, the WWC rates and reports all of the studies that it reviews, leaving it up to the consumer to decide what mix of studies provides sufficient evidence for a particular intervention.

Although intended in large part to provide the definitive resource for educators seeking to enhance EBP, the WWC has suffered from delays, and currently offers limited resources in some critical areas. For example, only one intervention (DaisyQuest; see Foster, Erickson, Foster, Brinkman, & Torgesen, 1994) for early reading was listed as of February 26, 2007, as meeting standards by the WWC. Given the importance of early reading to meeting state and federal expectations for student outcomes, the limited availability of established alternatives listed at the WWC undermines its ability to be "a central and trusted source" for EBP in education.

Non-governmental education agencies. The Campbell Collaboration (named for Donald Campbell, the social scientist who pioneered the experimenting society) is an international, interdisciplinary organization aimed at advancing the integration of research on interventions and enhancing the accessibility of knowledge on evidence-based practices (Schuerman et al., 2002). The primary goal of the Campbell Collaboration is to prepare, maintain, and make accessible systematic reviews of the effectiveness of interventions in social welfare, education, criminal justice, and public policy. Its major product includes a database of over 1,000 systematic reviews of controlled experiments across social, educational, and criminological interventions. Systematic reviews are defined as the use of unambiguous, transparent, exhaustive methods of tracking down controlled experiments that test the efficacy of programs, policies, and practices. The only criteria imposed on systematic reviews are methodological, including studies that used random (i.e., prospective allocation of individuals, schools, or communities to one or two alternative interventions) or quasi-random assignment procedures (e.g., other assignment methods, such alternating assignment). Reviews follow a protocol describing the topics covered and the methods used for including studies in the Campbell Database of Systematic Reviews (see Campbell Collaboration Steering Committee, 2000).

## RESOURCES FOR IDENTIFYING EVIDENCE-BASED PRACTICE IN EDUCATION

Clearly, the intent of this book is to provide resources for EBP relevant to educational contexts. In addition to the resources within this volume, a number of entities are working to provide reviews of evidence to enhance EBP in education. Some of these entities, and their Universal Resource Locators (URLs) are listed in Table 2.2. Although some URLs change without warning, online resources have the advantage of reflecting advances in the field, additional evidence, and other changes over time. Additionally, some illustrative resources (e.g., URLs for evidence standards, resources describing the EBP movement) are included in Table2.2.

## EVIDENCE-BASED PRACTICE: PROMISES AND PROBLEMS

The EBP movement promises enhanced outcomes for individuals and increased efficiency and cost effectiveness for service delivery. However, in addition to these promises, EBP also engenders some problems for educational practitioners. These problems include issues related to ethics, training, implementation, politics, adapting practice to unique contexts, and research. We address each of these in the following sections.

### Ethical Issues

Although EBP seeks to promote ethical practice by encouraging practitioners to select what works for the individual (rather than what the practitioner might find interesting or familiar), the goal of using EBP in contexts where evidence is inconsistent or incomplete creates ethical problems. In the absence of clearly defined EBIs for a particular problem, what should practitioners do? On the one hand, following the Hippocratic dictum (First do no harm) might lead practitioners to avoid intervention altogether until EBIs are available and identified. On the other hand, practitioners who see children struggling to learn or acquire appropriate behaviors are obligated to do what they can to alleviate the problem. In most cases, educators will intervene even in the absence of a definitive evidence base, as "doing something" is better than "doing nothing."

Or is it? Critical reviews of educational interventions have often shown that specialized treatments, even those with appealing theoretical justifications, are worse than customary educational treatments. Examples include perceptual motor training to correct learning disabilities and the Feingold K-P diet for treatment of attention deficit disorder (see Kavale, 2001, for an extensive review). Ethical mandates from professional societies, and legal mandates for identifying and serving student needs, may push practitioners towards providing an intervention, even if it is untested. Practitioners should consider carefully the lost opportunity costs (e.g., what is the student missing, and what resources are being expended that might be expended otherwise, in providing specialized interventions?) when deciding whether to intervene in the absence of a clearly defined evidence base to support a practice.

### Research Issues

There are unique elements of educational research that may limit the application of traditional standards for evidence to educational interventions. First, it is rarely possible to randomly assign individuals to educational treatments, as students tend to receive interventions in groups. Thus, in many cases, the classroom (rather than the student) should be the unit of analysis—although this distinction is rarely honored in research (Levin, 2004). Second, the paradigm of single or double

## TABLE 2.2
### Professional Organizations and Resources Featuring Evidence-Based Practices

| Organizations/Resources | Web site |
| --- | --- |
| Agency for Healthcare Research and Quality (AHRQ) | http://www.ahrq.gov/ |
| American Academy of Child and Adolescent Psychiatry | http://www.aacap.org |
| American Psychological Association | |
| Statement & expanded report on evidence-based practice in psychological health services (American Psychological Association) | http://www.apa.org/practice/ebpreport.pdf |
| Division 12 (Clinical Psychology) | http://www.apa.org/divisions/div12/div12.html |
| Division 16 (School Psychology) and the National Association of School Psychologists and Society for the Study of School Psychology | http://www.sp-ebi.org |
| Division 53 (Society for Clinical Child and Adolescent Psychology) | http://www.wjh.harvard.edu/%7Enock/Div53/EST/index.htm |
| Australian Broadcasting Corp. Health Guide for consumers | http://www.abc.net.au/health/cguides/evidencebased.htm |
| Blueprints for Violence Prevention | http://www.colorado.edu/cspv/blueprints/index.html |
| Campbell Collaboration | http://www.campbellcollaboration.org/index.asp |
| Centers for Disease Control and Prevention | http://wonder.cdc.gov/ |
| Center for Effective Collaboration and Practice | http://cecp.air.org/ |
| Center for Evidence-Based Medicine | http://www.cebm.net/ |
| Center for Evidence-Based Practice: Young Children with Challenging Behavior | http://challengingbehavior.fmhi.usf.edu/ |
| Center for Mental Health Services of the Substance Abuse and Mental Health Services Administration (SAMHSA) | http://mentalhealth.samhsa.gov/ |
| Center for Promoting Research to Practice | http://www.lehigh.edu/projectreach/ |
| Center for the Study and Prevention of Violence | http://www.colorado.edu/cspv/blueprints/contacts/list.html |
| Council for Exceptional Children Evidence-based practice resources | http://www.cec.sped.org/AM/Template.cfm?Section=Evidence_based_Practice&Template=/TaggedPage/TaggedPageDisplay.cfm&TPLID=24&ContentID=4710 |
| Evidence-Based Medicine | http://www.herts.ac.uk/lis/subjects/health/ebm.htm |
| Institute for Education Sciences | http://www.ed.gov/about/offices/list/ies/ncer/ index.html |
| Interagency Education Research Initiative | http://drdc.uchicago.edu/about/drdc_ieri.html |
| Interdisciplinary Council on Developmental and Learning Disorders | http://icdl.com/ICDLguidelines/toc.htm |
| MacArthur Foundation Youth Mental Health Research Network | http://www.macfound.org/site/c.lkLXJ8MQKrH/b.1010061/k.FDFC/Research_Networks__Network_on_Youth_Mental_Health_Care.htm |
| National Association of State Mental Health Directors Research Institute Center of Evidence-Based Practices, Performance Measurement, and Quality Improvement | http://nri.rdmc.org/RationaleEBPCenterReview.pdf |
| National Center for Special Education Research | http://www.ed.gov/about/offices/list/ies/ncser/index.html |

| Organizations/Resources | Web site |
| --- | --- |
| National Child Traumatic Stress Network | http://www.ntcsnet.org |
| National Institute of Mental Health (NIMH) | http://www.nimh.nih.gov/ |
| National Electronic Library for Mental Health (Effective Interventions) | http://www.nelmh.org/page_view.asp?c=22&did=2372&fc=004007 |
| National Information Center on Health Services Research and Health Care Technology (NICHSR) | http://www.nlm.nih.gov/nichsr/healthservicesvideo.ram |
| New York Academy of Medicine Evidence-Based Medicine Resource Center | http://www.ebmny.org/ |
| New York State Office of Mental Health: Evidence-based Practices for Children and Families | http://www.omh.state.ny.us/omhweb/ebp/children.htm |
| Promising Practices Network (Rand Corp.) | http://www.promisingpractices.net/ |
| PsychDirect (McMaster University Department of Psychiatry & Behavioural Neuroscience listing of evidence-based mental health education & information) | http://www.psychdirect.com/ |
| Research and Training center on Early Childhood Development (CED) | http://www.puckett.org |
| Safe Schools/Healthy Students Initiative | http://mentalhealth.samhsa.gov/safeschools/ |
| Social Programs That Work | http://www.evidencebasedprograms.org/ |
| Society for Prevention Research | www.oslc.org/spr/apa/summaries.html |
| UCLA School Mental Health Project | http://www.smhp.psych.ucla.edu/ |
| US Dept. of Education: Coalition for Evidence-Based Policy | http://coexgov.securesites.net/index.php?keyword=a432fbc34d71c7 |
| What Works Clearinghouse | http://www.w-w-c.org/ |

blind treatment delivery is compromised (e.g., it is not possible for either the student or the teacher to be unaware of whether or which intervention is being delivered). This means expectancy effects (on the part of the person delivering the intervention, and on the recipient) may substantially influence outcomes independent of the intervention quality. Third, comparative educational research finds any intervention delivered with fidelity tends to improve outcomes, raising the question of whether controlled studies can truly distinguish effective from ineffective treatments. Comparing students receiving a particular intervention to students getting "general educational supports," which is often referred to in the psychological literature as "usual outpatient therapy" or "customary clinical care" (e.g., Weiz, McCarty, & Valeri, 2006), is more intuitively appealing, but it lacks precision (i.e., it begs the question of what constitutes "usual care"). Despite these limitations, it is still clear that standards for evidence in education still adhere closely to the major elements of research design insofar as they embrace randomized assignment to conditions and comparison to alternative treatments; whereas there is little work to define what would constitute an appropriate "educational placebo" as a control condition in educational experiments. These limitations do not mean that good educational research cannot help to identify which interventions have an evidence base (and which ones do not); rather, it opens the question of the degree to which traditional scientific standards of evidence generalize to educational contexts.

Another major problem is the identification of the "active ingredients" within a particular intervention. Typically, interventions are complex and multi-faceted, engaging a variety of psychological dimensions. The factors to which researchers attribute outcomes (i.e., the actions of the interventionist) may be only partly or not at all responsible for outcomes. Instead, factors such as the strength of the clinical alliance developed between the interventionist and the person receiving the intervention, may largely explain intervention effects. Indeed, there is little if any evidence to suggest that the features to which research attribute effects are in fact responsible for those effects (Wampold, 2005). It is both conceptually and financially challenging to design research capable of identifying which portions of an intervention influence outcomes, yet it is essential if interventions are to be adapted to specific individuals and contexts.

## Intervention Integrity and Differentiation

The study of intervention integrity has received increased attention in recent years and plays a prominent role in the evidence-based practice movement. Integrity refers to the degree to which an intervention is delivered as intended (Yeaton & Sechrest, 1981), with significant evidence supporting intervention failures to be the result of poor integrity versus ineffective interventions (Rossi, Freeman, & Lipsey, 1999; Schoenwald et al., 2000). Differentiation, on the other hand, refers to the degree to which one intervention can be distinguished from another (Schoenwald et al., 2000). For behavioral and cognitive-behavioral interventions, integrity and differentiation are often ensured through the use of treatment manuals that operationally define the treatment strategies used, coupled with intensive training and ongoing supervision of intervention agents. Several key factors are related to the integrity of interventions implemented in school settings. For example, studies have documented the difficulties inherent in adhering to interventions that are complex (Yeaton & Sechrest, 1981), time consuming (Gresham & Kendall, 1987), involve multiple participants (Gresham, 1989), and require extra materials and resources (Yeaton & Sechrest, 1981; Wolf, 1978). Treatment integrity has been found to increase when problems are perceived as severe and when interventions are perceived as effective (Elliott, 1998). Although integrity is associated with stronger treatment outcomes, the exigencies of real world practice make it challenging to implement interventions without making adaptations to meet the unique needs and problems of individuals.

Adapting evidence-based interventions to specific individuals and contexts. Most policies regarding the use of EBIs encourage their application to practice, but also caution professionals to apply them carefully. For example, the American Psychological Association (2005; see also Levant, 2005) encourages psychologists to consider three things as they engage in evidence-based practice: (1) "best research," (2) "patient characteristics, values, and contexts," and (3) "clinical implications." Although the first consideration has been discussed extensively in this chapter, the latter two are given scant attention in the scholarly literature. This is due in part to the lack of systematic research on which characteristics, values, or features of context merit consideration, and how they should be considered. Likewise, "clinical implications" include considerations such as cost, available resources, and other factors that might constrain or alter the selection of an intervention or treatment beyond consideration of the evidence base supporting that treatment. Unfortunately, there is little evidence to guide how educators, school psychologists, or other school-based professionals do (and should) make decisions with respect to these standards, particularly because "adapted" interventions may be less efficacious than those that are consistently, or even rigidly, applied. In many respects, the gap between research and practice can be framed as a division between the nature of evidence traditionally generated in research and the type of evidence educators, school psychologists and other school-based professionals need to make decisions regarding practice (Kratochwill & Shernoff, 2003).

## CONCLUSIONS

In this chapter, we have sought to outline the EBP movement, and describe how EBIs fit within this movement. Although EBIs are currently quite popular, they are but one aspect of the broader EBP movements in medicine, psychology, and education. In so doing, we have attempted to identify the major criteria by which professionals identify particular interventions as being evidence-based. It is essential to note that the criteria used to discriminate evidence-based interventions from other interventions are controversial. Furthermore, the decision to adopt certain criteria over others in and of itself leads to diverse conclusions regarding support for particular interventions, and even for classes of interventions. Therefore, this chapter is intended in part to alert practitioners to the history and issues that lie behind current frameworks for declaring interventions as evidence-based. As Winston Churchill said, "he [sic] who frames the terms of the debate wins."

Therefore, consumers should be acutely aware that any decisions regarding what is and is not an evidence-based intervention are always provisional. Such decisions are based in part on the types of evidence that is valued, and also on the evidence that is available. Although there has been a surge of interest in EBP in the past few years, it is important to note that the knowledge base regarding effective interventions—especially, in the schools—is still in its infancy stage (Jensen, Weersing, Hoagwood, & Goldman, 2005). As evidence becomes increasingly available and the quality of that evidence corresponds to the criteria set forth for evaluating interventions, it is likely that additional interventions will qualify as "evidence-based." Although we concur with professional societies that encourage school- and nonschool-based practitioners to select interventions from a pool so identified, we also appreciate that there are many complexities and vagaries in the application of interventions to real-life settings that may constrain, alter, or shift the selection of interventions. We recognize that the adoption of evidence-based practices is not a straightforward, inexpensive, or a clear endeavor and will require shifts in how scientific knowledge is translated into practice. Nevertheless, it is difficult to argue with the assumption that students, teachers, parents, and administrators will be better served through the adoption and use of interventions that have strong evidence to support their use. Virtually every institution and organization bearing an influence on the profession concur that the practices of education and psychology should be based, in part, on knowledge derived from empirical research. This chapter, then, should serve as a backdrop to the rest of the book, and encourage continued development of interventions, evidence-based evaluations of interventions, and the enhancement of evidence-based practice.

## REFERENCES

American Psychological Association (2005). *Policy statement on evidence-based practice in psychology.* Washington, DC: Author.

Blakely, C. H., Mayer, J. P., Gottschalk, R. G., Schmitt, N., Davidson, W. S., Roitman, D. B., et al. (1987). The fidelity-adaptation debate: Implications for the implementation of public sector social programs. *American Journal of Community Psychology, 15,* 253–268.

Calhoun, K. S., Moras, K., Pilkonis, P. A., & Rehm, L. P. (1998). Empirically supported treatments: Implications for training. *Journal of Consulting and Clinical Psychology, 66*(1), 151–162.

Carroll, K. M., & Rounsaville, B. J. (2003). Bridging the gap: A hybrid model to link efficacy and effectiveness research in substance abuse treatment. *Psychiatric Services, 54,* 333–339.

Chorpita, B. F. (2003). The frontier of evidence-based practice. In A. E. Kazdin & J. R. Weisz (Eds.), *Evidence-based psychotherapies for children and adolescents* (pp. 42–59). New York: Guilford.

Chorpita, B. F., Yim, L. M., Donkervoet, J. C., Arensdorf, A., Amundsen, M. J., McGee, C., et al. (2002). Toward large-scale implementation of empirically supported treatments for children: A review and observations by the Hawaii Empirical Basis to Services Task Force. *Clinical Psychology: Science and Practice, 9*(2), 165–190.

Cournoyer, B. R., & Powers, G. T. (2002). Evidence-based social work: The quiet revolution continues. In A. R. Roberts & G. J. Greene (Eds.), *Social workers' desk reference* (pp. 798–806). New York: Oxford University Press.

Davidson, W. S., & Redner, R. (1988). The prevention of juvenile delinquency: Diversion from the juvenile justice system. In R. H. Price, E. L. Cowen, R. P. Lorion & J. Ramos-McKay (Eds.), *14 ounces of prevention* (pp. 123–137). Washington, DC: APA.

Drake, R. E., Latimer, E. A., Leff, H. S., McHugo, G. J., & Burns, B. J. (2004). What is evidence? *Child and Adolescent Psychiatric Clinics of North America, 13,* 717–728.

Elliott, R. (1998). Editor's Introduction: A guide to the empirically supported treatments controversy. *Psychotherapy Research, 8*(2), 115–125.

Fehlings, D. L., Roberts, W., Humphries, T., & Dawe, G. (1991). Attention deficit hyperactivity disorder: Does cognitive behavior therapy improve home behavior. *Developmental and Behavioral Pediatrics, 12,* 223–228.

Fonagy, P., Target, M., Cottrell, D., Phillips, J., & Kurtz, Z. (2002). *What works for whom: A critical review of treatments for children and adolescents.* New York: Guilford.

Foster, K. C., Erickson, G. C., Foster, D. F., Brinkman, D., &Torgesen, J. K. (1994). Computer administered instruction in phonological awareness: Evaluation of the DaisyQuest program. *Journal of Research and Development in Education, 27*(2), 126–137.

Frederickson, N. (2002). Evidence-based practice and educational psychology. *Educational and Child Psychology, 19,* 96–111.

Garfield, S. L. (1996). Some problems associated with "validated" forms of psychotherapy. *Clinical Psychology: Science and Practice, 3,* 218–229.

Henggeler, S. W., Melton, G. B., Brondino, M. J., Scherer, D. G., & Hanley, J. H. (1997). Multisystemic therapy with violent and chronic juvenile offenders and their families: The role of treatment fidelity in successful dissemination. *Journal of Consulting and Clinical Psychology, 65,* 821–833.

Henggeler, S. W., Schoenwald, S. K., Liao, J. G., Letourneau, E. J., & Edwards, D. L. (2002). Transporting efficacious treatments to field settings: The link between supervisory practices and therapist fidelity in MST programs. *Journal of Clinical Child Psychology, 31,* 155–167.

Hoagwood, K. (2005). The research, policy, and practice context for delivery of evidence-based mental health treatments for adolescents: A systems perspective. In D. L. Evans & et al. (Eds.), *Treating and preventing adolescent mental health disorders: What we know and what we don't know.* New York: Oxford University Press.

Hoagwood, K., Burns, B. J., Kiser, L., Ringeisen, H., & Schoenwald, S. K. (2001). Evidence-based practice in child and adolescent mental health services. P*sychiatric Services, 52,* 1197–1189.

Hoagwood, K., Hibbs, E., Brent, E., & Jensen, P. (1995). Introduction to the special section: Efficacy and effectiveness in studies of child and adolescent psychotherapy. *Journal of Consulting and Clinical Psychology, 63,* 683–687.

Hogan, M. F. (2002). A partly built bridge between science and services: Commentary on the Hawaii empirical basis to services task force. *Clinical Psychology: Science and Practice, 9,* 200–203.

Hohmann, A. A., & Shear, M. K. (2002). Community-based intervention research: Coping with the "Noise" of real life in a study. *American Journal of Psychiatry, 159,* 201–207.

Jensen, P. S., Weersing, R., Hoagwood, K. E., & Goldman, E. (2005). What is the evidence for evidence-based treatments? A hard look at our soft underbelly. *Mental Health Services Research, 7,* 53–74.

Kazdin, A. E. (2004). Evidence-based treatments: Challenges and priorities for practice and research. *Child and Adolescent Psychiatric Clinics of North America, 13,* 923–940.

Kendall, P. C. (1998). Empirically supported psychological therapies. Journal of *Consulting and Clinical Psychology, 66,* 3–6.

Kendall, P. C. (2002). Toward a research-practice-community partnership: Goin' fishing and showing slides. *Clinical Psychology: Science and Practice, 9,* 214–216.

Kratochwill, T. R., & Shernoff, E. S. (2003). Evidence-based practice: Promoting evidence-based interventions in school psychology. *School Psychology Quarterly, 18,* 389–408.

Kratochwill, T. R., & Stoiber, K. C. (2000b). Uncovering critical research agendas for school psychology: Conceptual dimensions and future directions. *School Psychology Review, 29,* 591–603.

Kratochwill, T. R., & Stoiber, K. C. (2002). Evidence-based interventions in school psychology: Conceptual foundations of the procedural and coding manual of Division 16 and the Society for the Study of School Psychology Task Force. *School Psychology Quarterly, 17,* 341–389.

Levin, J. R., O'Donnell, A. M., & Kratochwill, T. R. (2003). Educational/psychological intervention research. In W. M. Reynolds & G. E. Miller (Eds.), *Handbook of psychology* (Vol. 7, pp. 557–581). New York: Wiley.

Lewinsohn, P. M., Clark, G. N., Hops, H., & Andrews, J. (1990). Cognitive-behavioral treatment for depressed adolescents. *Behavior Therapy, 21,* 385–401.

Lonigan, C. J., Elbert, J. C., & Bennett-Johnson, S. (1998). Empirically supported psychosocial interventions for children: An overview. *Journal of Clinical Child Psychology, 27,* 138–145.

Merrill, K. A., Tolbert, V. E., & Wade, W. A. (2003). Effectiveness of cognitive therapy for depression in a community mental health center: A benchmarking study. *Journal of Consulting and Clinical Psychology, 71,* 404–409.

Miller, R. L. (2001). Innovation in HIV prevention: Organizational and intervention characteristics affecting program adoption. *American Journal of Community Psychology, 29,* 621–647.

Nathan, P. E., Stuart, S. P., & Dolan, S. L. (2000). Research on psychotherapy efficacy and effectiveness: Between scylla and charybdis. *Psychological Bulletin, 126,* 964–981.

Norcross, J. C. (2001). Purposes, processes, and products of the Task Force on Empirically Supported Therapy Relationships. *Psychotherapy, 38,* 345–356.

Reynolds, A. J. (1998). Confirmatory program evaluation: A method for strengthening causal inference. *American Journal of Evaluation, 19,* 203–221.

Rossi, P. H., Freeman, H. E., & Lipsey, M. W. (1999). *Evaluation: A systematic approach* (6th ed.). Thousand Oaks, CA: Sage.

Roth, A., & Fonagy, P. (1996). *What works for whom: A critical review of psychotherapy research.* London: Guilford.

Sackett, D. L., Straus, S. E., Richardson, W. S., Rosenberg, W. C., & Haynes, R. B. (2000). *Evidence-based medicine: How to practice and teach EBM* (2nd ed.). New York: Churchill Livingstone.

Schmidt, F., & Taylor, T. K. (2002). Putting empirically supported treatments into practice: Lessons learned in a children's mental health center. *Professional Psychology: Research and Practice, 33,* 483–489.

Schoenwald, S. K., Henggeler, S. W., Brondino, M. J., & Rowland, M. D. (2000). Multisystemic therapy: Monitoring treatment fidelity. *Family Process, 39,* 83–103.

Schoenwald, S. K., & Hoagwood, K. (2001). Effectiveness, transportability, and dissemination of interventions: What matters when? *Psychiatric Services, 52,* 1190–1197.

Schuerman, J., Soydan, H., Macdonald, G., Forslund, M., deMoya, D., & Boruch, R. (2002). The Campbell collaboration. *Research on Social Work Practice, 12,* 309–317.

Shernoff, E. S., & Kratochwill, T. R. (2005). Evidence-based practice. In M. Hersen, G. Sugai & R. Horner (Eds.), *Encyclopedia of behavior modification and cognitive behavior therapy* (pp. 1306–1311). Thousand Oaks, CA: Sage.

Shernoff, E. S., & Kratochwill, T. R. (in press). Transporting an evidence-based classroom management program for preschoolers with disruptive behavior problems to a school: An analysis of implementation, outcomes, and contextual variables. *School Psychology Quarterly.*

Simpson, D. D. (2002). A conceptual framework for transferring research to practice. *Journal of Substance Abuse Treatment, 22,* 171–182.

Stoiber, K. C., & Kratochwill, T. R. (2000). Empirically supported interventions and school psychology: Rationale and methodological issues-Part I. *School Psychology Quarterly, 15,* 75–105.

Storch, E. A., & Crisp, H. L. (2004). Taking it to the schools-Transporting empirically supported treatments for childhood psychopathology in the school setting. *Clinical Child and Family Psychology Review, 7,* 191–193.

Wampold, B. E. (2001). The great psychotherapy debate: Models, methods, and findings. Mahwah, NJ: Erlbaum.

Wampold, B. E., Lichtenberg, J. W., & Waehler, C. A. (2002). Principles of empirically supported interventions in counseling psychology. *The Counseling Psychologist, 30,* 197–217.

Weisz, J. R., Donenberg, G. R., Han, S. S., & Weiss, B. (1995). Bridging the gap between laboratory and clinic in child and adolescent psychotherapy. *Journal of Consulting and Clinical Psychology, 63,* 688–701.

Weisz, J. R., & Jensen, P. S. (1999). Efficacy and effectiveness of child and adolescent psychotherapy and pharmacotherapy. *Mental Health Services Research, 1,* 125–157.

Westen, D., Novotny, C. M., & Thompson-Brenner, H. (2004). The empirical status of empirically supported psychotherapies: Assumptions, findings, and reporting in controlled clinical trials. *Psychological Bulletin, 130,* 631–663.

Yeaton, W. H., & Sechrest, L. (1981). Critical dimensions in the choice and maintenance of successful treatments: Strength, integrity, and effectiveness. *Journal of Consulting and Clinical Psychology, 49,* 156–167.

# II

# STUDENTS HAVING
# BEHAVIORAL CHALLENGES

# 3

# Attention-Deficit/Hyperactivity Disorder

## George J. DuPaul, Laura E. Rutherford, and Shelley J. Hosterman

Attention-deficit/hyperactivity disorder (ADHD) is one of the most common disruptive behavior disorders affecting between 3% to 10% of children and adolescents in the United States (Barkley, 2006). Individuals with ADHD exhibit developmentally deviant levels of inattention and/or hyperactivity-impulsivity (American Psychiatric Association, 2000). Boys are two to six times more likely to be diagnosed with the disorder (Barkley, 2006). ADHD is a chronic, life-long disorder in the majority of cases and is associated with significant impairment in academic, social, and occupational functioning (American Psychiatric Association, 2006; Barkley, 2006).

The purpose of this chapter is to review evidence-based interventions for ADHD that can be used in school settings to reduce symptoms of the disorder as well as enhance academic and social functioning. First, a brief historical perspective on ADHD is provided. Next, the core symptoms are described as well as short- and long-term difficulties that students with ADHD are likely to experience in school. Third, we discuss the major intervention approaches that have been empirically investigated for treatment of ADHD including stimulant medication, behavioral strategies (both antecedent-based and consequent-based), social relationship interventions, and strategies to enhance academic performance. The chapter concludes with a summary and recommendations for future research.

## HISTORICAL PERSPECTIVES

Descriptions of children with ADHD have been evident in the medical and educational literatures since the early 20th century (for review, see Barkley, 2006). Since the beginning of formal schooling in the United States, behaviors such as inattention, impulsivity, and high activity levels have been associated with classroom disruption and problematic school functioning. Thus, the core characteristics of this disorder are the same as they have always been; however, the diagnostic nomenclature and treatment methods to address these challenging behaviors have evolved over time. For example, prior diagnostic terms have included minimal brain dysfunction, hyperkinetic impulse disorder, and attention deficit disorder with or without hyperactivity (Barkley, 2006). It is possible that future iterations of diagnostic manuals will include different terms for the disorder; however, these labels are essentially referring to the same set of behaviors. Further, until the latter half of the 20th century, children exhibiting ADHD-like behaviors were removed from classrooms and/or were subject to high levels of punishment. Vast improvements in treatment have been obtained, including the use of psychotropic medications and positive reinforcement procedures. Thus, school and mental health personnel are better able to identify students with ADHD and effectively manage their symptoms as well as academic and social impairments associated with this disorder.

## CHARACTERISTICS AND SCHOOL-RELATED DIFFICULTIES

The 18 behavioral symptoms of ADHD include 9 inattention and 9 hyperactivity-impulsivity symptoms (American Psychiatric Association, 2000). Specific examples of inattention symptoms include: failing to give close attention to details, difficulty sustaining attention to task or play activities, and not following through on instructions and failing to complete work. Hyperactivity-impulsivity symptoms include: fidgeting with hands or feet, difficulty playing quietly, and blurting out answers before questions have been completed. In order for the diagnosis of ADHD to be made, at least 6 inattention and/or hyperactivity-impulsivity symptoms need to be present at a significantly higher frequency than in others of the same age and sex. Further, symptoms should be chronic (i.e., occur for at least 6 months), begin before the age of 7 years old, and be associated with social and/or academic impairment across at least two settings (American Psychiatric Association, 2000). Thus, this diagnosis is specific to those students who are extremely inattentive and/or hyperactive-impulsive and, as a result, are experiencing significant difficulties in one or more major life activity.

Not surprisingly, students with ADHD frequently experience difficulties with behavior control in classroom settings. For example, children with this disorder often are inattentive and exhibit significantly higher rates of off-task behavior relative to their non-ADHD classmates (e.g., Abikoff et al., 2002; Vile Junod, DuPaul, Jitendra, Volpe, & Cleary, 2006). Rates of on-task behavior are particularly low when passive classroom activities (e.g., listening to teacher instruction and reading silently) are required (Vile Junod et al., 2006). In addition, hyperactive-impulsive behaviors that may comprise ADHD often lead to disruptive behaviors in the classroom and other school environments including talking without permission, leaving the assigned area, bothering other students, and interrupting teacher instruction. Further, from 45% to 84% of children with ADHD are diagnosed with oppositional defiant disorder (ODD) wherein students may frequently disobey teacher commands and overtly defy school rules (Barkley, 2006). The combination of ADHD and disruptive behavior can interfere with learning and classroom activities for students with ADHD and their classmates.

ADHD frequently is associated with deficits in academic skills and/or performance. On average, children with ADHD score between 10 to 30 points lower than non-ADHD control children on norm-referenced, standardized achievement tests (e.g., Barkley, DuPaul, & McMurray; Brock & Knapp, 1996; Fischer, Barkley, Fletcher, & Smallish, 1990). Further, approximately 20% to 30% of students with ADHD also have a specific learning disability in reading, math, or writing (DuPaul & Stoner, 2003; Semrud-Clikeman et al., 1992). Core ADHD symptoms have been found to be significant predictors of concurrent and future academic difficulties (e.g., performance on achievement tests, report card grades, and teacher ratings of educational functioning). The relationship between ADHD symptoms and achievement outcomes is evident for both referred (DuPaul et al., 2004) and non-referred (Fergusson & Horwood, 1995) samples. As a result, students with ADHD are at higher risk for grade retention, placement in special education classrooms, and dropping out from high school (e.g., Fischer et al., 1990). Fewer students with

ADHD go on to post-secondary education relative to similar achieving non-ADHD classmates (Mannuzza, Gittelman-Klein, Bessler, Malloy, & LaPadula, 1993). Thus, poor educational functioning throughout the school years is a frequent outcome for students with ADHD.

Students with ADHD typically have difficulty developing and maintaining positive relationships with peers, teachers, and other school personnel (Barkley, 2006; DuPaul, & Stoner, 2003). Difficulties with inattention and impulsivity inhibit the development of appropriate social relationships in several ways. First, children with ADHD often don't follow the implicit rules of reciprocal conversation (Stroes, Alberts, & Van der Meere, 2003). Thus, a child with ADHD is likely to interrupt during conversation, not listen closely to what others are saying, and respond in an irrelevant fashion (i.e., talk about something that is not germane to the conversation topic). Second, students with ADHD may enter ongoing peer activities (e.g., games and conversations) in an abrupt, impulsive manner, thereby disrupting the activity to a significant degree (DuPaul & Stoner, 2003). Peers may choose to exclude the child with ADHD from activities as a result. Third, children with this disorder are more likely than their non-ADHD classmates to behave in a verbally or physically aggressive manner, presumably due to their problems with impulse control (Barkley, 2006). Finally, given this combination of social relationship difficulties, several studies have indicated that children with ADHD are less popular, more often rejected, and have fewer friends than their non-ADHD peers (e.g., Hoza et al., 2005).

Although most students with ADHD are placed in general education classrooms, they are at higher than average risk to be identified for special education services (Barkley, 2006). Of those children with ADHD receiving special education services, the largest numbers are identified with specific learning disabilities (41%) and speech/language impairments (15%) (U.S. Department of Education, 2005). It is important to note, however, that students with ADHD make up a significant percentage of children identified with a variety of educational disabilities including other health impairment (65.8%), emotional disturbance (57.9%), mental retardation (20.6%), learning disabilities (20.2%), and speech/language impairment (4.5%) (Schnoes, Reid, Wagner, & Marder, 2006). Thus, ADHD may be associated with one or more educational difficulties that further compromise school functioning and may require specialized intervention services.

## EMPIRICALLY-BASED INTERVENTION PROCEDURES

The most widely studied and effective treatments for ADHD in children and adolescents include psychotropic medication (chiefly stimulant compounds, such as methylphenidate) and behavioral strategies implemented in home and school settings (for review, see Barkley, 2006). The combination of these treatments may be necessary for many individuals with this disorder in order to fully address their symptoms as well as areas of functioning that may be impaired. In fact, the combination of stimulant medication and behavioral treatment may lead to greater rates of normalization than either treatment in isolation (cf. Conners et al., 2001).

### Monitoring of Medication Treatment

The single most effective treatment for the reduction of ADHD symptoms is carefully titrated, stimulant medication (MTA Cooperative Group, 1999; 2004). This class of medication includes methylphenidate (i.e., Ritalin™, Concerta™, and Metadate™), dextroamphetamine (Dexedrine™), and mixed amphetamine compounds (Addreal™). These medications lead to reduction in attention difficulties and impulsive behavior as well as enhanced task engagement and rule compliance in the majority of children and adolescents with ADHD receiving this treatment (for review, see Connor, 2006a). Other medications, such as atomoxetine (Strattera™) or clonidine (Catapres™) may be used for those children who do not respond to stimulants or experience significant adverse side-effects (e.g., insomnia and appetite reduction) (Connor, 2006b).

Although school practitioners do not prescribe medication, they can provide critical data to physicians seeking to monitor the initial efficacy and ongoing use of a particular drug. Specifically, information about a student's social, academic, and behavioral functioning may be used to determine the need for medication as well as what compound and dosage are optimal for both reducing symptoms and enhancing functioning (DuPaul & Carlson, 2005; Power, DuPaul, Shapiro, & Kazak, 2003). For example, teacher ratings of behavioral functioning, curriculum-based measurement probes, and parent report of possible adverse side-effects can be gathered during both baseline and several medication dosage conditions. These data can then be communicated to a student's physician who can evaluate (a) whether the medication is effective relative to no-medication conditions and (b) what dosage leads to the most clinically significant change with the fewest adverse side-effects. Given that stimulants typically affect behavior only during the school day, objective classroom data are critical in making accurate treatment decisions.

## Overview of School-based Interventions

A variety of school-based interventions to address the needs of students with ADHD have been studied over the past several decades (for review, see DuPaul & Eckert, 1997; Purdie, Hattie, & Carroll, 2002). Four major treatment strategies are reviewed in this chapter, including behavioral interventions that involve manipulating antecedent events (see Table 3.1), behavioral interventions that involve manipulating consequent events (see Table 3.2), social relationship interventions (see Table 3.3), and academic remediation strategies (see Table 3.4). All of these approaches have received empirical support in reducing disruptive behavior and/or enhancing functioning of students with ADHD.

In considering the use of school-based interventions for this disorder, several core principles are important when designing treatment plans for specific students (DuPaul & Stoner, 2003). First, multiple mediators for intervention should be considered. Obviously, teachers are the primary treatment agent for any classroom intervention plan; however, other mediators (e.g., peers, computers, and parents) should be used whenever possible, given that teachers have many responsibilities that may render effective strategies untenable and impractical. Second, a balanced treatment plan that includes manipulation of antecedent events and academic strategies in addition to the more typical consequence-based approach should be used. All too often, school professionals rely solely on aversive consequences (e.g., negative reprimands, detention, and suspension) to address student disruptive behavior. We advocate a more comprehensive approach using positive consequences, antecedent-based strategies, academic interventions, and social relationship treatments. This combination of interventions may obviate the need for or reduce the frequency of more punitive procedures. Finally, intervention strategies should be individualized in order to account for the unique characteristics of each child with ADHD. Functional behavioral assessment and curriculum-based assessment data can be used to specifically determine exactly which treatment components may be most effective for each student (DuPaul & Ervin, 1996; DuPaul & Stoner, 2003).

## Antecedent Interventions

Antecedents are environmental events that precede behavior. Whereas consequence-based interventions are reactive to problem behaviors, antecedent approaches are both proactive and pre-

**TABLE 3.1**
**Antecedent Interventions for Students with ADHD**

| Intervention type | Key features | Outcomes | Benefits |
|---|---|---|---|
| Task-related choices | Selecting academic tasks<br>Sequencing of tasks<br>Stimulus materials<br>Pace of instruction | Increased level of task engagement<br>Decreases in disruptive behavior | Easily incorporated into curriculum/<br>routine<br>Student empowerment<br>Task compliance |
| Presentation of classroom rules and task instructions | Stated in a positive manner (e.g. raise<br>your hand before speaking)<br>Limited in number (fewer than 5)<br>Publicly and prominently posted<br>Clear and brief<br>May include pictures<br>Actively taught through instruction<br>"Catch" students being good<br>Reminders immediately prior to new<br>activity<br>Attract attention of student(s) before<br>stating rules (e.g. eye contact,<br>proximity, physical prompt)<br>Post schedules with activity specific<br>rules<br>Asking students to repeat rules aloud | Significant improvement in behavior for<br>all students (classwide)<br>Students understand rules and<br>consequences<br>Provides continuous and positive<br>examples<br>Improves overall classroom<br>management<br>Cost effective | Preventative approach<br>Decreased need for negative<br>consequences |

ventative. Antecedent-based interventions focus on reducing the probability of problem behavior. These approaches may also result in increased levels of appropriate behaviors, such as increased attention to task and work completion. Therefore, antecedent strategies may reduce the possibility that punitive consequences will be used (Kern, Choutka, & Sokol, 2002). Antecedent interventions typically involve making prearranged environmental changes to prevent conditions that provoke the problem behavior. Research has shown several of these strategies, including providing task-related choices and presentation of rules, are effective for children with ADHD.

## Providing Task-Related Choices

Choice-making is a simple antecedent-based intervention that embeds self-determination in instruction. Applications of this strategy include offering students choice of stimulus materials, academic tasks, pace of instruction, and order of task presentation. Choice making can be easily incorporated into instructional and inclusive lessons and activities (Moes, 1998). In a comprehensive literature review, Kern et al. (1998) found that choice was an effective procedure for both increasing the quality and quantity of desired behaviors as well as decreasing undesirable behaviors in students with a variety of disabilities. Several studies have investigated the use of choice for students with ADHD. Evidence specific to this population has focused on applying choice the areas of selecting and sequencing academic tasks.

Dunlap and colleagues (1994) provided students with an individualized menu of possible academic tasks and allowed students to select the next classroom activity. This study involved three students with emotional and behavioral disorders, one of whom had ADHD. During the non-choice condition, the teacher wrote two designated assignments on the board and all students were expected to complete those items. During the choice condition, students were first asked if they wanted to choose their assignment and were then provided with a list of 6 to 10 task options. Results showed that students always preferred to choose assignments themselves. They also exhibited increased levels of task engagement and decreases in disruptive classroom behaviors during the choice condition. In a similar study, Powell and Nelson (1997) examined effects of choice on the behavior of one student with ADHD. Results showed the student's levels of undesirable classroom behaviors decreased in the choice condition when he was permitted to select from among three academic assignments.

In the above studies, students were not expected to complete all academic tasks listed. Kern, Mantegna, Vorndran, Bailin, and Hilt (2001) investigated the use of choice when students were asked to complete three required tasks. Three students, two of whom were identified with ADHD, were asked to complete three tasks they found highly undesirable. These academic and classroom routine tasks typically provoked noncompliance and other problem behaviors. Results showed that simply providing students with the opportunity to choose the sequence of tasks led to increases in engagement and decreased problem behavior to near-zero frequencies for both students with ADHD.

## Presentation of Rules

Poor rule-governed behavior, or difficulties adhering to rules and instruction, is a common deficit associated with ADHD (Barkley, 2006). Many behaviors associated with ADHD may interfere with a student's ability to attend appropriately during teacher presentation of rules or instructions. For example, off-task behaviors such as conversations with peers, staring out the window, and fidgeting with items in their desks may prevent students with ADHD from devoting necessary levels of attention to rules and instructions. Clearly a student who is unaware of or not attending to expectations will have extreme difficulty following them. Teachers can use several strategies to actively teach and reinforce rules and expectations.

Establishing general classroom rules benefits all students in the classroom, particularly those with ADHD. General classroom rules should be stated in a positive manner (e.g., "raise your hand before speaking"), rather than as prohibitions (e.g., "don't call out"). Thus, rules tell students what is appropriate or expected. Instead of simply eliminating problematic behaviors, such rules prompt use of positive alternatives. In addition, classroom rules should be limited in number, typically fewer than five (Rhode, Jenson, & Reavis, 1993). Classroom rules should be publicly and prominently posted. Public posting functions as a continuous reminder of expectations and encourages students to make the connection between behaviors and consequences (Kehle, Bray, Theodore, Jenson, & Clark, 2000). Barkley (2006) suggests students with ADHD will benefit from rules that are clear, brief, and delivered through visible and external modes of presentation. Rule prompts with pictures (e.g., and ear for listening) can be placed throughout the classroom as reminders.

Several proactive teacher strategies are valuable during teaching of general rules, expectations, and task-specific instructions and directions. Rules should be actively taught through discussion and always stated clearly. Johnson, Stoner, and Green (1996) found actively teaching classroom rules led to significant improvements in behavior for all students. Asking students to repeat rules aloud is also helpful. Teachers should "catch students being good," and point out natural examples of appropriate behavior by referring to rules. Teachers should also remind students of rules immediately before starting a new activity. Because students with ADHD often have difficulty attending, teachers should ensure these students are paying attention before giving instructions. For example, strategies like making eye contact, standing near the student's desk, or using a discrete physical prompt offer effective and unobtrusive means to obtain student attention. Another option for communicating classroom expectations was described by Sprick, Borgmeier, and Nolet (2002) who suggest posting classroom schedules that feature activity-specific rules for each time block. Teachers can then refer to the appropriate rules at the start of each activity. Following these simple strategies may increase the likelihood that students with ADHD will follow the rules and complete steps of assigned activities.

## Consequent-Based Interventions

The most common type of behavioral strategy used for treating ADHD symptoms in children is the manipulation of consequent events (either positive or aversive) to increase appropriate behavior or decrease disruptive, off-task activities. Included in this category are interventions that involve token reinforcement, response cost, contingency contracting, and self-management. Functional assessment data can optimize treatment effects by ensuring that interventions are directly focused on replacing inappropriate behavior with appropriate behavior that achieves the same behavioral function.

## Token Reinforcement

Token reinforcement strategies involve providing students with an immediate reinforcer (e.g., poker chip, sticker, or points) contingent on a desired behavior in order to increase the probability that the behavior will increase in frequency. The token reinforcer is exchanged at a later time point for a back-up reinforcer (e.g., privileges at home or at school) that presumably has a high degree of salience for the student. Token reinforcement programs have extensive empirical support for the reduction of disruptive, off-task behavior and/or increased task engagement in

**TABLE 3.2**
**Consequent-based Interventions for Students with ADHD**

| Intervention type | Key features | Outcomes | Benefits |
|---|---|---|---|
| Token Reinforcement | Identify several specific target behaviors, including both social and academic<br>Identify reinforcers (tokens) that will be provided by the teacher following display of target behavior<br>Provide back-up reinforcement at school or home on a daily or weekly basis based on number of tokens earned | Increased on-task behavior<br>Decreased disruptive behavior in classroom<br>Higher rate of task completion and accuracy | Improved classroom management<br>Decreased need for aversive procedures |
| Response Cost | Identify several target behaviors that will be reinforced<br>Identify several target behaviors to be reduced in frequency<br>Provide immediate reinforcement (tokens) following display of appropriate behavior and remove tokens following display of inappropriate behavior<br>Provide back-up reinforcement at school or home daily or weekly based on number of tokens earned | Improved on-task behavior<br>Decreased frequency of disruptive behavior<br>Higher rate of task completion and accuracy | Improved classroom management<br>Enhanced maintenance of treatment effects |
| Contingency Contracting | Identify several academic and behavioral goals<br>Identify school and/or home privileges that can be earned on a daily or weekly basis<br>Contract signed by student, parent(s), and teacher(s)<br>Privileges earned on basis of goal attainment<br>Contract reviewed and renegotiated on a regular basis | Increased frequency of appropriate behavior and decreased frequency of inappropriate behavior | Highly feasible to implement<br>Enhanced collaboration among school personnel and student |
| Self-Management | Identify several target behaviors<br>Teacher ratings of behaviors for specified intervals (e.g., by class period)<br>Students trained to rate own behavior using same rating criteria as teacher<br>Points earned for goal attainment and matching teacher ratings<br>Backup reinforcers provided at school or home based on points earned<br>Teacher ratings faded gradually so that eventually reinforcement is based solely on student self-ratings | Increased frequency of on-task behavior<br>Decreased frequency of disruptive behavior<br>Higher rate of task completion and accuracy | Highly feasible to implement<br>Enhanced maintenance and generalization of treatment effects |

students displaying ADHD symptoms (for review, see DuPaul & Eckert, 1997; Pelham, Wheeler, & Chronis, 1998). In order to maximize the potential success of a token reinforcement program, several strategies should be followed including: (a) selection of a few relevant goals that clearly identify expected behaviors, (b) initial use of the program during most problematic times of the school day, (c) immediate and consistent follow-through in providing token reinforcement, (d) exchange of tokens for back-up reinforcement on at least a daily basis, and (e) modifying the expectations and reinforcers over time to address additional difficulties and to maintain student interest in the program (DuPaul & Stoner, 2003).

Classroom-based token reinforcement programs can be supplemented by the use of home-based reinforcement for school behavior (i.e., daily school report card). Daily report cards identify several behavioral goals (e.g., complete assigned seatwork) that students must achieve in school in order to earn reinforcement at home (Chafouleas, Riley-Tillman, & McDougal, 2002; Kelley, 1990). Teachers provide written quantitative ratings for each goal (e.g., 1 ["did not meet goal"] to 5 ["met goal completely"]) that serve as the immediate contingencies. These ratings are converted to points at home and exchanged for home-based reinforcers (e.g., access to television and/or video games). A daily report card system is one of the cornerstones of the classroom component within the Summer Treatment program developed by Pelham and colleagues (2002). As such, there is substantial empirical support for the use of this system, especially in combination with classroom-based behavioral interventions. Further, the potential effects of a daily report card system are enhanced when (a) goals are few in number and stated in a positive manner; (b) both academic and behavioral goals are included; (c) feedback is provided by subject or class period; and (d) parents are included in the planning process (Chafouleas et al., 2002; DuPaul & Stoner, 2003; Pfiffner, Barkley, & DuPaul, 2006).

## Response Cost

Response cost is a form of token reinforcement strategy that involves removal of tokens contingent on inappropriate behavior in order to reduce the probability that the behavior will happen in the future. This treatment strategy has been found to increase on-task behavior and work productivity in classroom settings (e.g., DuPaul, Guevremont, & Barkley, 1992; Rapport, Murphy, & Bailey, 1982). Response cost is particularly effective when it is combined with an ongoing positive reinforcement system (DuPaul & Stoner, 2003). In fact, some studies have shown that behavioral changes induced by response cost are better maintained over time than are the behavioral effects of an all-positive approach (Pfiffner & O'Leary, 1987). Further, in some cases, the effects of response plus token reinforcement interventions are equivalent to those found for psychostimulant medication (e.g., Pelham, Carlson, Sams, Vallano, Dixon, & Hoza, 1993; Rapport, Murphy, & Bailey, 1982). Of course, care should be taken to ensure that students don't lose more tokens than they earn in order to maintain motivation and emphasize positive changes made by students. For example, teachers should only take one token away for a specific behavior even if the latter continues after token removal. In such instances, additional contingencies (e.g., time out from positive reinforcement) may be necessary to curtail the inappropriate behavior.

## Contingency Contract

Typically, formal token reinforcement and response cost systems are not feasible or developmentally appropriate for middle and high school students with ADHD. One treatment alternative to secondary school students with ADHD is contingency contracting wherein a contractual agreement is negotiated between a student and teacher (DeRisi & Butz, 1975). The contract simply identifies the desired classroom behaviors and consequences available contingent upon their performance. As with a token reinforcement program, specific academic and behavioral goals are identified that the student must meet in order to gain access to preferred activities or other rewards. Contracting usually involves a direct connection between target behaviors and primary contingencies, rather than the use of secondary reinforcers such as tokens. As such, there may be a longer time delay between behavior completion and reinforcement than with a token economy program.

The choice of target behaviors, and the manner of incorporating them into an intervention program are important determinants of a behavioral contract's success. For example, during the initial stages of a contracting procedure care should be exercised to avoid large numbers of goals, extremely high standards of quality, and completion of complex (e.g., multi-step) tasks (DuPaul & Stoner, 2003). More difficult or complex goals could be incorporated gradually into later iterations of the contract such that terminal objectives are reached with minimal failure along the way.

Another important consideration in designing a contingency contract is the identification of appropriate reinforcers. All too often, identified reinforcers take the form of activities or items that are assumed by school personnel to be motivating for students. Because reinforcer preferences can be very idiosyncratic, individual reward menus should be derived for each student. This can be accomplished most directly by including the student in negotiations regarding potential privileges. Direct negotiation not only assures identification of salient reinforcers, but also enlists the student's cooperation and investment in the contractual process.

## Self-Management

Several studies have indicated that self-management, particularly the combination of self-monitoring and self-reinforcement, is effective in improving a variety of behaviors including task-related attention, academic accuracy, and peer interactions (e.g., Barkley, Copeland, & Sivage, 1980; Hinshaw & Simmel, 1994). In fact, Reid et al. (2005) obtained a combined effect size of greater than 1.0 for these interventions in relation to changes in on-task behavior, disruptive activity, and task completion.

Self-monitoring plus self-reinforcement strategies may be particularly helpful for addressing ADHD-related problems in two situations. First, students can be taught to monitor and reinforce their own behavior while fading the use of a teacher-managed, contingency management intervention (Barkley, 1989). In such cases, it is assumed that positive behavior change will be maintained despite the reduction in teacher feedback or other forms of reinforcement. Of course, backup reinforcers (e.g., classroom or home privileges) should continue to be used as teacher monitoring and feedback are faded. A second situation where self-monitoring plus self-reinforcement is an appropriate treatment for ADHD is at the secondary level where teachers and students may be reluctant to use token reinforcement, contingency contracting, or response cost. Thus, self-management may be a more acceptable intervention at the secondary level, and, therefore, presumably more likely to be implemented on a consistent basis.

An example of self-monitoring and self-reinforcement procedures useful for ameliorating ADHD symptoms is based on the work of Rhode, Morgan, and Young (1983). These researchers used these strategies to facilitate the mainstreaming of six elementary students with "behavioral handicaps." Initially, a token reinforcement program is used wherein teachers rate student behavior during specific intervals (e.g., every 5 minutes) in the classroom. Ratings of targeted behaviors are provided using a 6-point criterion hierarchy ranging from 0 (unacceptable) to 5 (excellent). Teacher-provided points are exchanged for backup reinforcers in school or at home as in a standard token reinforcement system.

Once target behaviors improve, students are trained to evaluate their own behavior using the same criteria. At this stage, the teacher's ratings continue to be used to determine how many points students have earned. In addition, students can earn a bonus point for matching teacher ratings exactly. If the student ratings deviate by more than one point from the teacher ratings, then no points are earned for that interval. Thus, contingencies are associated with both behavioral improvement and rating one's performance in a manner similar to the teacher.

Over the course of time, the teacher ratings are gradually faded such that the student ratings are the primary arbiter for earning backup reinforcement. This is facilitated by (a) the use of random "matching challenges" that occur on a periodic basis, and (b) the gradual reduction in frequency of these matching challenges. For example, the initial cutback in teacher ratings may involve a matching challenge that occurs every other day, on the average. Then, the teacher matches are faded to every third day, once weekly, and once biweekly, on the average. If, at any point in time, the student's performance deteriorates and/or the teacher suspects inflation of student ratings, then matching challenges are conducted more frequently.

In the program described by Rhode, Morgan, and Young (1983), the students eventually employed self-ratings only with no backup reinforcers. This led to maintenance of significant behavioral improvements across resource and regular classroom settings. This self-reinforcement system has been extended to children with ADHD and related disruptive disorders in elementary (Hoff & DuPaul, 1998), middle (Shapiro, DuPaul, & Bradley-Klug, 1998), and high (Smith, Young, Nelson, & West, 1992) school settings. A critical variable influencing the success of these procedures is the continued use of external reinforcers contingent on student ratings.

## Assessment of Behavioral Function

When possible, consequent-based interventions should be designed using functional assessment data (O'Neill, Horner, Albin, Sprague, Storey, & Newton, 1997). Initially, a small number of clearly defined behavioral targets likely to have an impact on academic functioning should be selected. Next, functional assessment data should be used to determine the contingencies maintaining the target behaviors. In most cases, the intervention should include frequent and immediate positive reinforcement and/or response cost. Ideally, the specific consequences used in an intervention should be matched to the presumed function of the target behavior. For example, if a student with ADHD appears to be talking out of turn and disrupting the activity of classmates to gain peer attention, then the intervention should include the provision of peer attention contingent on appropriate behavior (e.g., through the use of peer tutoring). Presumably, an intervention that includes consequences matched to the function of behavior will be more effective than one designed through a trial-and-error approach (i.e., that does not consider behavioral function). Although, in general, research findings in support of this critical assumption have been equivocal (for review see Ervin, Ehrhardt, & Poling, 2001), several single subject design studies that included students exhibiting ADHD symptoms (e.g., Eckert, Martens, & DiGennaro, 2005; Ervin, DuPaul, Kern, & Friman, 1998; Northup & Gulley, 2001) have highlighted the value of an assessment-based approach to intervention design. Finally, data (e.g., systematic direct observations of behavior) should be collected on a regular basis to assess the effects of interventions and to determine modifications that might be necessary.

## SOCIAL RELATIONSHIP INTERVENTIONS

According to Barkley (2006), approximately 50% of children diagnosed with ADHD have considerable problems in their social relationships with other children. In fact, social difficulties are so prevalent that some investigators have argued that disturbed peer relations should be a defining feature of the disorder (Gentschel & McLaughlin, 2000; Landau, Milich, & Diener, 1998). Certain characteristics of ADHD, such as having difficulty taking turns; often interrupting and intruding on others in games, in conversations, and classroom discussions; and the frequent tendency to appear not to be listening when spoken to (American Psychological Association, 2000) contribute to social skills problems. As a result of these problems, children with ADHD often are rejected by their peers (Hinshaw, 1992), have fewer friends (Hoza et al., 2005), show low levels of social competence (Campbell, 1994), and often exhibit aggressive behaviors (Campbell & Ewing, 1990).

## Social Skills Training

Although social skills trainings (SST) seem a logical solution to these difficulties, many common training strategies do not produce successful outcomes for children with ADHD. This may be due to the fact that many SST address social skills deficits, when many children with ADHD primarily have performance deficits (Barkley, 2006). That is, the student may know the appropriate rule for interaction, but fail to follow that rule in natural settings. Therefore, interventions designed for children with ADHD should focus on reinforcing their use of appropriate social skills and teaching them to use existing skills in various contexts (Stormont, 2001). Although traditional programs produce gains during SST sessions, research shows these changes rarely translate into natural settings (Gresham, 2002). Thus, particular attention must be paid to programming for generalization of skills.

It is also important to target and prioritize behaviors based on individualized assessment. For example, observations and rating scales (e.g. Social Skills Rating System (SSRS); Gresham & Elliott, 1990) from multiple informants are valuable tools for determining key areas of need for a particular student (Colton & Sheridan, 1998; Stormont, 2001). Students with ADHD often require assistance with the following target social skills: cooperation, problem solving, recognizing and controlling anger, assertiveness, conversations, and accepting consequences (Antshel & Remer, 2003).

Multicomponent SST programs are most successful for students with ADHD. Key features of such programs include modeling, behavioral rehearsal, self-monitoring, reinforcement, and parent/teacher training. During modeling, adults demonstrate use of inappropriate behavior and ask students to identify mistakes and positive alternatives. Next, adults perform the skill appropriately, incorporating suggestions from students. Behavioral rehearsal involves role-playing, in which students attempt the desired skill while receiving positive reinforcement and constructive feedback from peers and adults. Practice continues until students achieve a certain level of proficiency with the new skill. Ang and Hughes (2002) showed outcomes are influenced by SST group membership, with greater improvements associated with diverse peer groups (e.g., including children with and without problem behaviors).

Inattention and impulsivity often prevent children with ADHD from considering different behavioral options or associated consequences before they act (DuPaul & Weyandt, 2006). Self-monitoring offers a practical method for addressing this performance deficit. After practicing the target skill during SST sessions, students are asked to observe and track their use of this skill in natural environments. For example, students may rate performance of the skill (whether the skill was used, whom? the skill was used with, when it was used, and how it went). In addition, students may assign a number rank (e.g., on a scale from 1 to 5) describing how they felt they performed in a particular setting (recess, lunch) (Sheridan, Dee, Morgan, McCormick, & Walker, 1996).

Self-monitoring systems should be accompanied by a reinforcement system. Many students

**TABLE 3.3**

**Social Relationship Interventions for Students with ADHD**

| Intervention type | Key features | Outcomes | Benefits |
|---|---|---|---|
| Social Skills Training | Reinforce appropriate use of social skills | Improvements in assertion skills | Positive peer interactions |
| | Practice existing social skills in context (e.g. lunch, recess, free time) | Gains in social entry/initiation behavior | Decreased conflict |
| | Program for generalization (e.g. discuss upcoming situations) | Positive cooperative interactions with peers | |
| | Select target behavior based on individual's specific needs | Improved ratings of overall social skills | |
| | Common areas of need: cooperation, problem solving, recognizing and controlling anger, assertiveness, conversation, accepting consequences | | |
| | Modeling both inappropriate & inappropriate examples of skill | | |
| | Behavioral rehearsal (students attempt skill & receive feedback/reinforcement) | | |
| | Self-monitoring (students observe/track use of skill in natural environment) | | |
| | Reinforcement (home-school communication logs; earning points; specific praise) | | |
| | Include parent and teacher training (groups sessions, videotaped modeling, role-plays) | | |
| | Use diverse peer groups (e.g. students with and without social skills concerns) | | |
| Peer Mediated Interventions | Playground monitors to manage conflict resolution | Reductions in playground violence and negative interaction | Does not require adult presence |
| | Peer coaches to help students select daily goals, provide reminders of goals, offer feedback, and rate success | Increased use of appropriate social skills during academic and unstructured settings | Easy to use during unstructured times |
| | Peer buddies (pairing students to encourage interaction and shared time) | Higher quality friendships | Positive peer interactions |

**TABLE 3.4**
**Academic Interventions for Students with ADHD**

| Intervention type | Key Features | Outcomes | Benefits |
|---|---|---|---|
| Peer Tutoring | Steps: | Improved on-task behavior | Frequent and immediate feedback |
| | 1. Class divided into two teams and pairs within teams | Improved academic performance | Increased opportunity of active responding |
| | 2. provide academic "scripts" (e.g. questions and correct responses) | Reduced off-task behavior | One-to-one ratios |
| | 3. students take turns as tutor and tutee | | Self-paced instruction |
| | 4. praise and points for correct responses | | Continuous prompting for response |
| | 5. errors lead to immediate correction and practice of correct answer | | Added social benefits |
| | 6. teachers provide bonus points for following appropriate procedures | | Maximizes instructional time |
| | 7. team with most points "wins" and receives applause | | |
| Computer-Assisted Instruction (CAI) | Target specific instructional objectives | Increases in academic performance | Active student involvement |
| | Visually highlight key facts | Decreases in off-task and disruptive behavior | Increased student motivation |
| | Immediate feedback for response | Increased academic engagement | Minimal teacher time |
| | Provide concrete examples | | |
| | Models item completion | | |
| | Elaborating tasks through step-by-step instruction | | |
| | Shortening of assignments | | |

| | | | |
|---|---|---|---|
| Modification of Academic Tasks & Instruction | Eliminate irrelevant cues (e.g. decrease visual stimuli, work in isolated locations) Highlighting relevant information (e.g. color, bold text, animation) Global explanations on essential task elements prior to introduction of more specific details Match academic tasks to ability Interperse low interest, passive tasks with active, high interest tasks Motoric responding Breaks for physical exercise Brief academics assignments presented one at a time Frequent and active student participation e.g. Direct instruction Enthusiastic teaching style | Increased attention Greater motivation Increase alertness | Simple and cost-effective strategies Benefits both behavior and academics |
| Self-monitoring | Teach student to accurately recognize & discriminate examples and non-examples of behavior Student makes record of targeted behavior Have student self-monitor either on-task time (e.g. "Am I paying attention") or academic productivity (e.g. "Did I complete my work?") | Increases in on-task behavior, engagement, academic accuracy, work quality, & assignment completion | Inexpensive Requires minimal teacher time/ supervision Unobtrusive |

with ADHD will need intense levels of reinforcement to produce the desired social behavior, particularly in challenging settings (Barkley, 2006). Home-school communication logs offer one method for tracking and reinforcing use of specific target behaviors in school settings. Student's self-monitored ratings of behavior can earn points, which are then exchanged for reinforcers at home. Examples might include small prizes, favorite activities, and special time with friends and family (Colton & Sheridan, 1998). Specific praise for use of appropriate social skills is also reinforcing. When providing specific praise, the parent or teacher should use the child's name and clearly describe the desired behavior.

Parent and teacher trainings provide adults with the skills they need to support lessons learned in SST. Adults learn to guide and support the student's efforts to resolve social challenges. Key components of parent involvement include discussing the importance of social skills and social status, and reviewing the specific skills addressed in their child's SST (Pfiffner, Calzada, & McBurnett, 2000). This includes determining when adult intervention is needed and when students should manage difficult social situations using recently learned skills. Parents and teachers can also help students set goals for social performance. Including parents and teachers in SST may support generalization of skills to everyday social situations. Parent training might include group sessions, written materials, video-taped modeling, role-playing, and homework assignments (Colton & Sheridan, 1998).

SST incorporating parent and teacher involvement have produced positive effects on social skills in students with ADHD. Many research studies demonstrating the success of SST have been conducted in clinic-based settings. Antshel and Remer (2003) found SST led to improvements in parent and child-perceived assertion skills, but did not impact other domains of social competence. Sheridan et al. (1996) showed SST lead to gains in social entry behaviors, however, treatment effects for maintaining interactions and problem solving skills were more variable. Students enrolled in a clinic-based study featuring a home-school communication component also experienced improvements in the school setting (Pfiffner & McBurnett, 1997). Similarly, Colton and Sheridan (1998) used a conjoint behavioral consultation model, which involved collaboration between parents and teachers. Results showed increases in positive cooperative interactions with peers and improvements on SSRS ratings. Although more research is needed to demonstrate the effects of SST on school behavior, these studies suggest collaboration between parents and teachers supports greater improvements in school.

## Peer Mediated Interventions

The ultimate goal of social skills interventions is to help students with ADHD become more accepted and well-liked among peers. Thus, including peers in intervention efforts is crucial to ensuring appropriate generalization. Cunningham and Cunningham (1998) developed a peer mediated strategy in which students acted as playground monitors who managed conflict resolution sessions. Results showed reductions in playground violence and negative interactions. In addition, Plumer and Stoner (2005) investigated the effects of classwide peer tutoring with and without a peer coaching component. Classwide peer tutoring produced improvements in positive social behavior during academic activities, however, effects did not generalize to social situations. With the addition of peer coaching, students showed improvements during recess, lunch, and academic activities. During peer coaching, students were matched with a coach who generally exhibited positive social behaviors. Coaches helped students to set daily social goals, provided reminders of the goal, offered positive feedback about student efforts, and rated success in meeting the goal. This peer component extends intervention into social situations where adults are typically not present.

Another type of peer-mediated intervention focuses on helping students form dyadic friendships (Hoza, Mrug, Pelham, Greiner, & Gnagy, 2003). In this study, students enrolled in a larger summer treatment program were paired with a buddy. Buddy pairs received special privileges, and parents were encouraged to support contact with buddies outside of camp. Initial results indicated that when parents complied with the program, students experienced higher quality friendships and greater improvement in teacher ratings of social behaviors. Although this study occurred during a summer program, the strategy could be implemented in classroom settings relatively easily.

## Academic Interventions

Most children with ADHD tend to struggle academically, both in their work productivity and their academic achievement (DuPaul et al., 2004). In all, up to 80% of children with ADHD have been found to exhibit academic performance problems (Cantwell & Baker, 1991). Teachers and parents report that children with ADHD underperform relative to their own abilities as well as compared to their classmates (Barkley, 2006). This may be due, in part, to the low academic engagement rates and the inconsistent work productivity evidenced by children with ADHD (DuPaul & Stoner, 2003; Vile Junod et al., 2006). However, addressing behavioral problems alone may not result in academic improvements without interventions directly targeting academic concerns (DuPaul & Eckert, 1997). Suggested academic interventions for students with ADHD include peer tutoring, computer-assisted instruction, modifying tasks or instruction, and self-monitoring.

## Peer Tutoring

Peer tutoring is a strategy in which two students work together on an academic activity. Features of peer tutoring of include frequent and immediate feedback on performance, active responding, one-to-one student-teacher ratios, self-paced instruction, and continuous prompting for response (Pfiffner, Barkley, & DuPaul, 2006). Although various models of peer tutoring exist, research on students with ADHD has focused largely on ClassWide Peer Tutoring (CWPT) (Greenwood, Delquadri, & Carta, 1988).

Research has shown CWPT improves skills in reading, mathematics, and spelling for students at all levels of achievement (Greenwood, Maheady, & Delquadri, 2002). This peer tutoring approach consists of several key steps and characteristics. First, the class is divided into two teams and tutoring pairs are formed within each team. Students are then given academic scripts (e.g., questions with correct responses) and take turns as tutor and tutee. Throughout tutoring students deliver praise and points to their peer partner contingent on correct responses. When errors occur, students are given immediate correction and the chance to practice correct answers. Teachers monitor tutoring pairs and provide bonus points for following procedures appropriately. At the end of each tutoring session, points are totaled and students with the most points are declared the winner. Sessions total 25 minutes, with 5 minutes designated for recording student progress. Instead of exchanging points for back-up reinforcers, the team with the most points is applauded by their peers at the end of the week.

Although few empirical studies have investigated the use of CWPT with populations of students with ADHD, evidence suggests its effectiveness. DuPaul and Henningson (1993) found CWPT improved on task behavior and acquisition of mathematics skills in one student with ADHD. In a larger study, DuPaul, Ervin, Hook, and McGoey (1998) investigated results of CWPT in a sample of 18 elementary school-aged students with ADHD. A within subject, repeated measures design was used. Data on behavior and academic performance were collected across two alternating baseline and CWPT conditions. Tutoring targeted either math or spelling based on the target child's area of concern. Target students were paired with tutors who were performing on grade level in all academic subjects and exhibited appropriate classroom behavior. Results of DuPaul et al. (1998) showed a reduction in off-task behavior for most students. Additionally, CWPT lead to improvements in actively-engaged on-task behavior and academic performance on typical classroom assessments. Non-ADHD comparison students also experienced improvements in both academic performance and behavior. Plumer and Stoner (2005) also showed CWPT to be effective in improving student behavior during academic activities. In sum, research suggests CWPT is a valuable strategy for addressing not only academic concerns, but also the off-task, disruptive behavior of students with ADHD.

## Computer-Assisted Instruction

Many features of computer-assisted instruction (CAI) are well-suited to students with ADHD and may encourage increased attention and focus on academic material (Lillie, Hannun, & Stuck, 1989; Torgesen & Young, 1983). CAI offers an easy and efficient way to use multiple sensory modalities, divide academic content into smaller pieces of information, target specific instructional objectives, visually highlight key facts, and offer immediate feedback on each response (DuPaul & Weyandt, 2006). Such characteristics demand active student involvement in learning and may increase student motivation (Fitzgerald, 1994). CAI supports instructional modifications including providing concrete examples, modeling of item completion, elaborating tasks in a step-by-step fashion, and shortening assignments, all of which may benefit students with ADHD (Bender & Bender, 1996).

Few well-controlled experimental studies have examined the effectiveness of CAI in students with ADHD; many investigations have limited sample sizes, insufficient outcome measures, and poor selection procedures (Xu, Reid, & Steckelberg, 2002). However, results of three well-designed empirical studies indicate the benefits of CAI for students with ADHD. Ota and DuPaul (2002) used a multiple baseline design to examine the effects of a game-based mathematics software package (Math Blaster™) on three students with ADHD. Data on behavior and math performance were collected using direct observations and curriculum based measurement. Results showed all participants exhibited increases in math performance, with two students showing pronounced improvements. Additionally, students showed decreases in off-task and disruptive behaviors and increases in active engagement during computer-based instruction as compared to typical classroom lessons. Mautone, DuPaul, and Jitendra (2005) also demonstrated the effectiveness of CAI in improving math performance and behavior in three children with ADHD. Clarfield and Stoner (2005) investigated the benefits of a reading-based computer program (Headsprout™) in three students in ADHD. Results showed the program produced increases in both oral reading fluency and task engagement. These studies suggest CAI offers a valuable and practical tool for increasing on-task behavior, decreasing disruptive off-task behaviors, and possibly improving academic performance of students with ADHD.

## MODIFYING ACADEMIC TASKS AND INSTRUCTION

Many characteristics of academic tasks, instruction, and curriculum can be tailored to the unique needs of students with ADHD. Zentall (2005) reviewed evidence based interventions for increasing attention to academic tasks in children with ADHD. Changes in academic tasks such as eliminating irrelevant cues and highlighting relevant information can benefit children with ADHD. For example, irrelevant cues may be eliminated by decreasing visual stimuli that compete with practice or listening tasks or allowing students to work in more isolated locations during more complex tasks. Teachers may use color, bold text, animation, or verbal cues to focus attention to relevant information. It is best to add non-relevant details like color and animation after students have initial practice with main concepts, as these details may be distracting from key content (Zentall, 2005). In addition, students with ADHD benefit from global explanations and exposure to the essential elements of tasks and concepts prior to considering finer details.

Instructional format and style can also be altered to improve attention and performance in students with ADHD. Academic tasks should be carefully matched to the student's abilities and interests. Interest and motivation improve when presentation formats and tasks materials are varied, for example by interspersing low-interest, passive tasks with high-interest, active tasks (Zentall, 2005). Increasing opportunities for motoric as opposed to passive responses is also beneficial (Zentall, 1993). Similarly, planning periodic breaks for physical exercise (e.g. jumping jacks, conga lines, movement songs) throughout instruction may increase alertness and attention (Pfiffner & Barkley, 1998). Academic assignments should be brief and presented one at a time to accommodate shorter attention spans. A teaching style that is enthusiastic, task-focused, includes brief teacher-directed segments, and allows for frequent and active student participation can also enhance learning. For example, direct instruction provides multiple opportunities for students to acquire and practice new skills (DuPaul & Weyandt, 2006).

## Self-Monitoring

The strategy of self-monitoring assigns two responsibilities to individuals receiving intervention. First, they must accurately recognize and discriminate instances of their target behavior. Second, they must create a record of these occurrences (Korotisch & Nelson-Gray, 1999). In this way, self-monitoring teaches individuals to track and manage their own behavior or performance. Research has shown self-monitoring to be effective in increasing on task behavior (Edwards et al., 1995), task engagement (Dunlap et al., 1995), academic accuracy (Lam, Cole, Shapiro, & Bambara, 1994), work quality (Moore, Prebble, Alexson, Waetford, & Anderson, 2001), and assignment completion (Brooks, Todd, Tofflemoyer, & Horner, 2003). In a meta-analysis of self-regulation interventions applied to children with ADHD, Reid and colleagues (2005) concluded that self-regulation interventions can produce significant improvements in academic productivity and accuracy.

Two approaches to self-monitoring have been shown effective in increasing academic performance. Students can either monitor on-task behavior or academic productivity. Research has indicated that self-monitoring of on-task behaviors is effective in increasing time spent engaged in the academic task. However, studies also suggest that academic on-task time may not necessarily translate to improved academic performance (DiGangi, Maag, & Rutherford, 1991). Indeed, when Reid (1996) reviewed 17 studies examining self-monitoring and academic productivity he concluded the effects were "equivocal." For the purpose of intervention, practitioners should not assume that improvements in on-task time are benefiting academic outcomes. Although it is often appropriate to monitor on-task behavior alone to ensure that students are not missing academic material, alternate strategies (e.g., self-monitoring of work productivity and/or accuracy) may be needed to address academic goals. In addition, self-monitoring systems that feature either a self-reinforcement or external reinforcement component may be more effective than those without such a component.

Interventions directed toward students with ADHD often address behavioral concerns alone, because these issues are most disruptive. However, improving levels of attention and reducing levels of off-task behaviors will not necessarily lead to increased levels of academic performance. Therefore, direct academic and instructional modifications should be included in a comprehensive treatment plan. One benefit of the instructional modifications and interventions detailed above is that they are relatively simple to implement. In addition, these strategies produce academic benefits for all students, not only those with ADHD, and represent best practice in classroom instruction.

## CONCLUSIONS AND FUTURE DIRECTIONS

ADHD is a disorder of early onset that affects a significant percentage of school-aged children and adolescents in the United States. As a function of the core symptoms of ADHD, students with this disorder experience significant difficulties with academic achievement, peer relationships, and responding appropriately to authority figures. The risks associated with this disorder are particularly relevant to important school outcomes (e.g., successfully completing high school) and imply the need for multiple interventions over extended periods of time. Although psychotropic medications, particularly stimulants, are effective in reducing ADHD symptoms, this treatment approach is typically not sufficient for addressing all of the difficulties attendant to this disorder.

Over the past several decades, considerable empirical evidence has been gathered to support the use of behavioral strategies in treating students with ADHD. Effective interventions can include the modification of antecedent and/or consequent events to increase the probability of desired behaviors occurring. More recently, promising evidence has been gathered to support the use of specific strategies to enhance academic and social functioning of students with ADHD. School-based strategies are enhanced when (a) treatment decisions are made on the basis of data (e.g., functional assessment), (b) multiple mediators of intervention (e.g., teachers, peers, parents, and students themselves) participate in treatment planning and implementation, and (c) a balanced treatment plan that includes both antecedent and consequent-based interventions is used.

Significant advances in our understanding of effective school-based interventions for students with ADHD have taken place over the past two decades. Nevertheless, several key areas must be addressed by future empirical studies. First, larger scale studies must be conducted in "real world" public school settings. Most of the available research has included relatively small samples studied under very controlled conditions (e.g., summer treatment program classrooms). Thus, the degree to which these interventions are effective and feasible in general education classrooms (i.e., where most students with ADHD are placed) has not been established.

Second, more studies need to be conducted in secondary school settings as there is a critical need for middle and high school personnel to know how to address the myriad difficulties faced by students with ADHD. Currently, there are less than a dozen investigations of school-based interventions for adolescents with this disorder.

Third, little is known about how best to support students with ADHD as they make the transition from high school to college or to the workforce. This is a critical issue given that teenagers with this disorder are at higher than average risk for school drop-out and are less likely to go on to college than their peers. Further, adults with ADHD tend to complete less schooling and attain lower occupational rankings than control subjects (Mannuzza, Gittelman-Klein, Bessler, Malloy, & LaPadula, 1993). For those high school students with ADHD that do pursue a college degree, preliminary studies suggest they are at greater risk for psychological and adjustment problems, neuropsychological impairments, and problems with internal restlessness (Heiligenstein, Guenther, Levy, Savino, & Fulwiler, 1999; Weyandt, Iwaszuk et al. 2003; Weyandt, Mitzlaff, &

Thomas, 2002). Thus, specific programs to identify and address the school-to-college or school-to-work needs of students with ADHD need to be developed and evaluated.

Finally, although effective school-based interventions are available, little is known about how to help teachers and other school personnel adopt these strategies on a consistent basis in classroom and other school settings. In other words, the optimal way for school psychologists and other related services personnel to consult with teachers in order to enhance treatment acceptability and integrity is unclear. Given that relatively low rates of treatment integrity are the rule rather than the exception for school-based interventions (e.g., Gresham, Gansle, Noell, Cohen, & Rosenblum, 1993), methods to enhance the feasibility and use of effective interventions must be developed and evaluated.

## REFERENCES

Abikoff, H. B., Jensen, P. S., Arnold, L. E., Hoza, B., Hechtman, L., Pollack, S., Martin, D., et al. (2002). Observed classroom behavior of children with ADHD: Relationship to gender and comorbidity. *Journal of Abnormal Child Psychopathology, 30,* 349–360.

American Psychiatric Association (2000). Diagnostic and statistical manual of mental disorders: *DSM-IV-TR* (4th ed., text revision). Washington, DC: Author.

Ang, R. P., & Hughes, J. N. (2002). Differential benefits of skills training with antisocial youth based on group composition: A meta-analytic investigation. *School Psychology Review, 31,* 164–185.

Antshel, K. M., & Remer, R. (2003). Social skills training in children with attention deficit hyperactivity disorder: A randomized-controlled clinical trial. *Journal of Clinical Child and Adolescent Psychology, 32,* 153–165.

Barkley, R. A. (1989). Attention deficit-hyperactivity disorder. In E. J. Mash, & R. A. Barkley (Eds.), *Treatment of Childhood Disorders* (pp. 39–72). New York: Guildford.

Barkley, R. A. (1998). *Attention-deficit hyperactivity disorder: A handbook for diagnosis and treatment* (2nd ed.). New York: Guilford.

Barkley, R. A. (Ed.) (2006). *Attention-deficit hyperactivity disorder: A handbook for diagnosis and treatment* (3rd ed.). New York: Guilford.

Barkley, R. A., Copeland, A. P., & Sivage, C. (1980). A self-control classroom for hyperactive children. *Journal of Autism and Developmental Disabilities, 10,* 75–89.

Barkley, R. A., DuPaul, G. J., & McMurray, M. B. (1990). Comprehensive evaluation of attention deficit disorder with and without hyperactivity as defined by research criteria. *Journal of Consulting and Clinical Psychology, 58,* 775–789.

Bender, W. N., & Bender, R. L. (1996). *Computer-Assisted Instruction for Students at Risk for ADHD, Mild Disability, or Academic Problems.* Boston: Allyn & Bacon.

Brock, S. W., & Knapp, P. K. (1996). Reading comprehension abilities of children with attention-deficit/hyperactivity disorder. *Journal of Attention Disorders, 1,* 173–186.

Brooks, A., Todd, A. W., Tofflemoyer, S., Horner, R. H. (2003). Use of functional assessment and a self-management system to increase academic engagement and work completion. *Journal of Positive Behaviour Interventions, 3,* 144–152.

Campbell, S. B. (1994). Hard-to-manage preschool boys: Externalizing behaviour, social competence, and family context at two-year follow-up. *Journal of Abnormal Child Psychology, 22,* 247–157.

Campbell, S. B., & Ewing, L. J. (1990). Follow-up of hard to manage preschoolers; Adjustment at age nine and predictors of continuing symptoms. *Journal of Child Psychology and Psychiatry, 31,* 871–889

Cantwell, D. P., & Baker, L. (1991). Association between attention-deficit hyperactivity disorder and learning disorders. *Journal of Learning Disabilities, 24,* 88–95.

Chafouleas, S. M., Riley-Tillman, T. C., & McDougal, J. L. (2002). Good, bad, or in-between: How does the daily behavior report card rate? *Psychology in the Schools, 39,* 157–169.

Clarfield, J., & Stoner, G. (2005). The effects of computerized reading instruction on the academic performance of students identified with ADHD. *School Psychology Review, 34,* 246–254.

Colton, D. L., & Sheridan, S. M. (1998). Conjoint behavioral consultation and social skills training: Enhancing the play behaviors of boys with attention deficit hyperactivity disorder. *Journal of Educational and Psychological Consultation, 9,* 3–28.

Conners, C. K., Epstein, J. N., March, J. S., Angold, A., Wells, K. C., Klaric, J., Swanson, J. M., Arnold, L. E., Abikoff, H. B., Elliott, G. R., Greenhill, L. L., Hechtman, L., Hinshaw, S. P., Hoza, B., Jensen, P. S., Kraemer, H. C., Newcorn, J. H., Pelham, W. E., Severe, J.B ., Vitiello, B, & Wigal, T. (2001). Multimodal treatment of ADHD in the MTA: An alternative outcome analysis. *Journal of the American Academy of Child and Adolescent Psychiatry, 40,* 159–167.

Connor, D. F. (2006a). Stimulants. In R. A. Barkley (Ed.), *Attention-deficit/hyperactivity disorder: A handbook for diagnosis and treatment* (3rd ed.), (pp. 608–647). New York: Guilford.

Connor, D. F. (2006b). Other medications. In R. A. Barkley (Ed.), *Attention-deficit/hyperactivity disorder: A handbook for diagnosis and treatment* (3rd ed.), (pp. 658–677). New York: Guilford.

Cunningham, C. E., & Cunningham, L. J. (2006). Student-mediated conflict resolution programs. In R. A. Barkley (Ed.), Attention-deficit hyperactivity disorder: A handbook for diagnosis and treatment (3rd ed.), (pp. 590–607). New York: Guilford.

DeRisi, W. J., & Butz, G. (1975). *Writing behavioral contracts: A case simulation practice manual.* Campaign, IL: Research Press.

DiGangi, S. A., & Maag, J. W. (1992). A component analysis of self-management training with behaviorally disordered youth. *Behavioral Disorders, 17,* 281–290.

DiGangi, S. A., Maag, J. W., & Rutherford, R. B. (1991). Self-graphing of on-task behavior: Enhancing the reactive effects of self-monitoring on on-task behavior and academic performance. *Learning Disabilities Quarterly, 14,* 221–230.

Dunlap, G., Clarke, S., Jackson, M., Wright, S., Ramos, E., & Brinson, S. (1995). Self monitoring of classroom behaviors with students exhibiting emotional and behavioral challenges. *School Psychology Quarterly, 10,* 165–177.

Dunlap, G., DePerczel, M., Clarke, S., Wilson, D., Wright, S., White, R., & Gomez, A. (1994). Choice making to promote adaptive behavior for students with emotional and behavioral challenges. *Journal of Applied Behavioral Analysis, 27,* 505–518.

DuPaul, G. J. & Carlson, J. S. (2005). Child psychopharmacology: How school psychologists can contribute to effective outcomes. *School Psychology Quarterly, 20,* 206–221.

DuPaul, G. J. & Eckert, T. L. (1997). The effects of school-based interventions for attention deficit hyperactivity disorder: A meta-analysis. *School Psychology Review, 26,* 5–27.

DuPaul, G. J. & Ervin, R. A. (1996). Functional assessment of behaviors related to Attention-Deficit/Hyperactivity Disorder: Linking assessment to intervention design. *Behavior Therapy, 27,* 601–622.

DuPaul, G. J., Ervin, R. A., Hook, C. L., & McGoey, K. E. (1998). Peer tutoring for children with attention-deficit hyperactivity disorder: Effects on classroom behavior and academic performance. *Journal of Applied Behavior Analysis, 31,* 579–592.

DuPaul, G. J., Guevremont, D. C., & Barkley, R. A. (1992). Behavioral treatment of attention-deficit hyperactivity disorder in the classroom: The use of the attention training system. *Behavior Modification, 16,* 204–225.

DuPaul, G. J., & Henningson, P. N. (1993). Peer tutoring effects on the classroom performance of children with attention-deficit hyperactivity disorder. *School Psychology Review, 22,* 134–143.

DuPaul, G. J., & Stoner, G. (2003). ADHD in the schools: Assessment and intervention strategies (2nd ed.). New York: Guilford.

DuPaul, G. J., Volpe, R. J., Jitendra, A. K., Lutz, J. G., Lorah, K. S., & Gruber, R. (2004). Elementary school students with AD/HD: Predictors of academic achievement. Journal of School Psychology, 42, 285–301.

DuPaul, G. J., & Weyandt, L. L. (2006). School-based intervention for children with attention-deficit hyperactivity disorder: Effects on academic, social, and behavioural functioning. *International Journal of Disability, Development and Education, 53,* 161–176.

Eckert, T. L., Martens, B. K., & DiGennaro, F. D. (2005). Describing antecedent-behavior consequence relations using conditional probabilities and the general operant contingency space: A preliminary investigation. *School Psychology Review, 34,* 520–528.

Edwards, L., Salant, V., Howard, V. F., Brougher, J., & McLaughlin, T. F. (1995). Effectiveness of self-management and reading comprehension for children with *Attention Deficit Disorder. Child & Family Behavior Therapy, 17,* 1–17.

Ervin, R., A., DuPaul, G. J., Kern, L., & Friman, P. C. (1998). Classroom-based functional and adjunctive assessments: Proactive approaches to intervention selection for adolescents with attention deficit hyperactivity disorder. *Journal of Applied Behavior Analysis, 31,* 65–78.

Ervin, R. A., Ehrhardt, K. E., & Poling, A. (2001). Functional assessment: Old wine in new bottles. *School Psychology Review, 30,* 173–179.

Fergusson, D. M., & Horwood, L. J. (1995). Predictive validity of categorically and dimensionally scored measures of disruptive childhood behaviors. *Journal of the American Academy of Child & Adolescent Psychiatry, 34,* 477–485.

Fischer, M., Barkley, R., Fletcher, K., & Smallish, L. (1990). The adolescent outcome of hyperactive children diagnosed by research criteria: II. Academic, attentional, and neuropsychological status. *Journal of Consulting and Clinical Psychology, 58,* 580–588.

Fitzgerald, G. E. (1994). Using the computer with students with emotional and behavioral disorders. *Technology and Disability, 3,* 87–99.

Gentschel, D. A., & McLaughlin, T. F. (2000). Attention deficit hyperactivity disorder as a social disability: Characteristics and suggested methods of treatment. *Journal of Developmental and Physical Disabilities, 12,* 333–346.

Greenwood, C. R. Delquadri, J., & Carta, J. J. (1988). *Classwide peer tutoring.* Seattle, WA: Educational Achievement Systems.

Greenwood, C. R., Maheady, L., & Delquardi, J. (2002). Classwide peer tutoring programs. In M. R. Shinn, H. M. Walker, & G. Stoner (Eds.), *Interventions for academic and behavior problems II: Preventive and remedial approaches* (pp. 611–649). Bethesda, MD: National Association of School Psychologists.

Gresham, F. M. (2002). Teaching social skills to high-risk children and youth: Preventative and remedial strategies, In M. R. Shinn, H. M. Walker, & G. Stoner (Eds.), *Interventions for academic and behavior problems II: Preventive and remedial approaches* (pp. 403–432). Bethesda, MD: National Association of School Psychologists.

Gresham, F. M., & Elliott, S. N. (1990). *Social skills rating system.* Circle Pines, MN: American Guidance Service.

Gresham, F. M., Gansle, K. A., Noell, G. H., Cohen, S., & Rosenblum, S. (1993). Treatment integrity of school-based behavioral intervention studies: 1980–1990. *School Psychology Review, 22,* 254–272.

Heiligenstein, E., Guenther, G., Levy, A., Savino, F., & Fulwiler, J. (1999). Psychological and academic functioning in college students with attention deficit hyperactivity disorder. *Journal of American College Health, 47,* 181–185.

Hinshaw, S. P. (1992). Academic underachievement, attention deficits, and aggression comorbidity and implications for intervention. *Journal of Consulting and Clinical Psychology, 60,* 893–903

Hinshaw, S. P., & Simmel, C. (1994). Attention-deficit hyperactivity disorder. In M. Hersen, R. T. Ammerman, & L. A. Sisson (Eds.), *Handbook of aggressive and destructive behavior in psychiatric patients* (pp. 347–362) New York: Plenum.

Hoff, K. E., & DuPaul, G. J. (1998). Reducing disruptive behavior in general education classrooms: The use of self-management strategies. *School Psychology Review, 27,* 290–303.

Hoza, B., Gerdes, A. C., Mrug, S., Hinshaw, S. P., Bukowski, W. M., Gold, J. A., et. al. (2005). Peer-assessed outcomes in the multimodal treatment study of children with attention deficit hyperactivity disorder. *Journal of Clinical Child and Adolescent Psychology, 34,* 74–86.

Hoza, B., Mrug, S., Pelham, W. E., Jr., Greiner, A. R., & Gnagy, E. M. (2003). A friendship intervention for children with attention deficit/hyperactivity disorder: Preliminary findings. *Journal of Attention Disorders, 6,* 87–98.

Johnson, T. C., Stoner, G., & Green, S. K. (1996). Demonstrating the experimenting society model with classwide behavior management interventions. *School Psychology Review, 25,* 198–213.

Kehle, T. J., Bray, M. A., Theodore, L. A., Jenson, W. R., & Clark, E. (2000). A multicomponent intervention designed to reduce disruptive classroom behavior. *Psychology in the Schools, 37,* 475–481.

Kelley, M. L. (1990). *School-home notes: Promoting children's classroom success.* New York: Guilford.

Kern, L., Choutka, C. M., & Sokol, N. G. (2002). Assessment-based antecedent interventions used in natural settings to reduce challenging behavior: An analysis of the literature. *Education and Treatment of Children, 25,* 113–130.

Kern, L., Mantegna, M. E., Vorndran, C. M., Bailin, D., Hilt, A. (2001). Choice of task sequence to reduce problem behaviors. *Journal of Positive Behavior Interventions, 3,* 3–10.

Kern, L., Vorndran, C. M., Hilt, A., Ringdahl, J. E., Adelman, B. E., & Dunlap, G. (1998). Choice as an intervention to improve behavior: A review of the literature. *Journal of Behavioral Education, 8,* 151–169.

Lam, A. L., Cole, C. L, Shapiro, E. S., & Bambara, L. M. (1994). Relative effects of self-monitoring on-task behavior, academic accuracy, and disruptive behavior in students with behavior disorders. *School Psychology Review, 23,* 44–58.

Landau, S., Milich, R., & Diener, M. (1998). Peer relations of children with attention-deficit hyperactivity disorder. *Reading & Writing Quarterly: Overcoming Learning Difficulties, 14,* 83–105.

Lillie, D. L., Hannun, W. H., & Stuck, G. B. (1989). *Computers and effective instruction.* New York: Longman.

Mannuzza, S., Gittelman-Klein, R., Bessler, A., Malloy, P., & LaPadula, M. (1993). Adult outcome of hyperactive boys: Educational achievement, occupational rank, and psychiatric status. *Archives of General Psychiatry, 50,* 565–576.

Mautone, J. A., DuPaul, G. J., & Jitendra, A. K. (2005). The effects of computer-assisted instruction on the mathematics performance and classroom behavior of children with ADHD. *Journal of Attention Disorders, 9,* 301–312.

Moes, D. R. (1998). Integrating choice-making opportunities within teacher-assigned academic tasks to facilitate the performance of children with autism. *Journal of the Association for Persons with Severe Handicaps, 23,* 319–328.

Moore, D. W., Prebble, S., Alexson, J., Waetford, R., & Anderson, A. (2001). Self recording with goal setting: A self-management programme for the classroom. *Educational Psychology, 21,* 255–265.

MTA Cooperative Group. (1999). A 14-month randomized clinical trial of treatment strategies for attention-deficit/hyperactivity disorder. *Archives of General Psychiatry, 56,* 1073–1086.

MTA Cooperative Group (2004). National Institute of Mental Health multimodal treatment study of ADHD Follow-up: 24-month outcomes of treatment strategies for attention-deficit/hyperactivity disorder. *Pediatrics, 113,* 754–761.

Northup, J., & Gulley, V. (2001). Some contributions of functional analysis to the assessment of behaviors associated with attention deficit hyperactivity disorder and the effects of stimulant medication. *School Psychology Review, 30,* 227–238.

O'Neill, R. E., Horner, R. H., Albin, R. W., Sprague, J. R., Storey, K., & Newton, J. S. (1997*). Functional assessment and program development for problem behavior: A practical handbook.* Pacific Grove, CA: Brooks/Cole Publishing Company.

Ota, K. R., & DuPaul, G. J. (2002). Task engagement and mathematics performance in children with attention-deficit hyperactivity disorder: Effects of supplemental computer instruction. *School Psychology Quarterly, 17,* 242–257.

Pelham, W. E., Carlson, C., Sams, S. E., Vallano, G., Dixon, M. J., & Hoza, B. (1993). Separate and combined effects of methylphenidate and behavior modification on boys with attention deficit-hyperactivity disorder in classroom. *Journal of Consulting and Clinical Psychology, 61,* 506–515.

Pelham, W. E., Hoza, B., Pillow, D. R., Gnagy, E. M., Kipp, H. L., Greiner, A. R. et al. (2002). Effects of methyphenidate and expectancy on children with ADHD: Behavior, academic performance, and attributions in a summer treatment program and regular classroom settings. *Journal of Consulting and Clinical Psychology, 70,* 320–335.

Pelham, W. E., Wheeler, T., & Chronis, A. (1998). Empirically supported psychosocial treatments for attention deficit hyperactivity disorder. *Journal of Clinical Child Psychology, 27,* 190–205.

Pfiffner, L. J., Barkley, R. A., & DuPaul, G. J. (2006) Treatment of ADHD in school settings. In R. A. Barkley (Ed.), *Attention-deficit hyperactivity disorder: A handbook for diagnosis and treatment* (3rd ed.), (pp. 547–589) New York: Guilford.

Pfiffner, L. J., Calzada, E., & McBurnett, K. (2000). Interventions to enhance social competence. *Child and Adolescent Psychiatric Clinics of North America, 9*, 689–707.

Pfiffner, L. J., & McBurnett, K. (1997). Social skills training with parent generalization: Treatment effects for children with attention deficit disorder. *Journal of Consulting and Clinical Psychology, 65*, 749–757.

Pfiffner, L. J., & O'Leary, S. G. (1987). The efficacy of all-positive management as a function of the prior use of negative consequences. *Journal of Applied Behavior Analysis, 20*, 265–271.

Plumer, P. J., & Stoner, G. (2005). The relative effects of classwide peer tutoring and peer coaching on the positive social behaviors of children with ADHD. *Journal of Attention Disorders, 9*, 290–300.

Powell, S., & Nelson, B. (1997). Effects of choosing academic assessments on a student with attention deficit hyperactivity disorder. *Journal of Applied Behavior Analysis, 30*, 181–183.

Power, T. J., DuPaul, G. J., Shapiro, E. S., & Kazak, A. E. (2003). *Promoting children's health: Integrating health, school, family, and community systems.* New York: Guilford.

Purdie, N., Hattie, J., & Carroll, A. (2002). A review of the research on interventions for attention deficit hyperactivity disorder: What works best? *Review of Educational Research, 72*, 61–99.

Rapport, M. D., Murphy, H. A., & Bailey, J. S. (1982). Ritalin vs. response cost in the control of hyperactive children: A within-subject comparison. *Journal of Applied Behavior Analysis, 15*, 205–216.

Reid, R. (1996). Research in self-monitoring with students with learning disabilities: The present, the prospects, the pitfalls. *Journal of Learning Disabilities, 29*, 317–331.

Reid, R., Trout, A. L., & Schartz, M. (2005). Self-regulation interventions for children with attention-deficit/hyperactivity disorder. *Exceptional Children, 71*, 361–377.

Rhode, G., Jenson, W. R., & Reavis, H. K. (1993). *The tough kid book: Practical classroom management strategies.* Longmont, CO: Sopris West, Inc.

Rhode, G., Morgan, D. P., & Young, K. R. (1983). Generalization and maintenance of treatment gains of behaviorally handicapped students from resource rooms to regular classrooms using self-evaluation procedures. *Journal of Applied Behavior Analysis, 16*, 171–188.

Schnoes, C., Reid, R., Wagner, M., & Marder, C. (2006). ADHD among students receiving special education services: A national survey. *Exceptional Children, 72*, 483–496.

Semrud-Clikeman, M., Biederman, J., Sprich-Buckminster, S., Lehman, B. K., Faraone, S. V., & Norman, D. (1992). Comorbidity between ADHD and learning disability: A review and report in a clinically referred sample. *Journal of the American Academy of Child & Adolescent Psychiatry, 31*, 439–448.

Shapiro, E. S., DuPaul, G. J., Bradley-Klug, K. L. (1998). Self-management as a strategy to improve the classroom behavior of adolescents with ADHD. *Journal of Learning Disabilities, 31*, 545–555.

Sheridan, S. M., Dee, C. C., Morgan, J. C., McCormick, M. E., & Walker, D. (1996). A multimethod intervention for social skills deficits in children with ADHD and their parents. *School Psychology Review, 25*, 57–76.

Smith, D. J., Young, K. R., Nelson, J. R., & West, R. P. (1992). The effect of a self-management procedure on the classroom and academic behavior of students with mild handicaps. *School Psychology Review, 21*, 59–72.

Sprick, R. S., Borgmeier, C., & Nolet, V. (2002). Prevention and management of behavioral problems in secondary schools. In M. R. Shinn, H. M. Wallker, & G. Stoner (Eds.), *Interventions for academic and behavior problems, II: Preventive and remedial approaches* (pp. 373–401). Bethesda, MD: National Association of School Psychologists.

Stormont, M. (2001). Social outcomes of children with AD/HD: Contributing factors and implications for practice. *Psychology in the Schools, 38*, 521–531.

Stroes, A., Alberts, E., & Van der Meere, J. J. (2003). Boys with ADHD in social interaction with a nonfamiliar adult: An observational study. *Journal of the American Academy of Child & Adolescent Psychiatry, 42*, 295–302.

Torgesen, J. K., & Young, K. (1983). Priorities for the use of microcomputers with learning disabled children. *Journal of Learning Disabilities, 16*, 234–237.

U.S. Department of Education (2005). *25th annual report to Congress on the implementation of the Individuals with Disabilities Education Act.* Washington, D.C.: Author.

Vile Junod, R. E., DuPaul, G. J., Jitendra, A. K., Volpe, R. J., & Cleary, K. S. (2006). Classroom observations of students with and without ADHD: Differences across types of engagement. *Journal of School Psychology, 44,* 87–104.

Weyandt, L. L., Iwaszuk, W., Fulton, K., Ollerton, M., Beatty, N., Fouts, H., Schepman, S., & Greenlaw, C. (2003). The internal restlessness scale: Performance of college students with and without ADHD. *Journal of Learning Disabilities, 36,* 382–389.

Weyandt, L. L., Mitzlaff, L., & Thomas, L. (2002). The relationship between intelligence and performance on the Test of Variables of Attention (TOVA). *Journal of Learning Disabilities, 35,* 114–120.

Xu, C., Reid, R., & Steckelberg, A. (2002). Technology applications for children with ADHD: Assessing the empirical support. *Education and Treatment of Children, 25,* 224–248.

Zentall, S. (1993). Research on the educational implications of attention deficit hyperactivity disorder. *Exceptional Children, 60,* 143–153.

Zentall, S. (2005). Theory and evidence-based strategies for children with attentional problems. *Psychology in the Schools, 42,* 821–836.

# 4

# Disruptive Behavior

## Carl J. Liaupsin and Terrance M. Scott

It is common for teachers and other school personnel to describe challenging student behavior as one of the most significant issues in education. In fact, teachers report that challenging student behavior is the most difficult and stressful aspect of their job (e.g., Furlong, Morrison, & Dear, 1994; Kuzsman & Schnall, 1987; Safran & Safran, 1988). Further, they report that the most distracting and time-consuming problem behaviors are not necessarily the most intense, but the most frequent (Sprague & Walker, 2000). The most frequently cited problem behaviors include simple non-compliance and disrespectful interaction that disrupt the learning routine. Perhaps the most difficult type of behavior that teachers are asked to deal with are those that are considered "disruptive." These include student acts that range in severity from mild forms such as "talking-out" and "interrupting" to more serious forms such as "fighting," "theft," and "bullying." Disruptive, aggressive, and anti-social behaviors can have a range of problematic outcomes for teachers, administrators, and students.

With increasing frequency, students with emotional and behavioral disorders (EBD) are being included in general education classrooms (e.g., Cheney & Barringer, 1995; McLeskey, Henry, & Hodges 1999; Sawka, McCurdy, & Mannella, 2002). Representing only one to five percent of the student population, these students typically account for more than half of the school's discipline referrals (Sugai, Sprague, Horner, & Walker, 2000; Taylor-Greene et al., 1997) and, as this population increases, there is an increasing demand for teachers who possess the skills and abilities to effectively work with these students (Sawka et al., 2002). One thing is clear; simple inclusion in a general education classroom will not, by itself, change these students' behaviors (Cartwright, Cartwright, & Ward, 1988; Gable, McLaughlin, Sindelar, & Kilgore, 1993).

Teachers clearly find disruptive behaviors to be among the most difficult problems to manage in their daily activities. In a survey of inner-city schools, teachers identified various forms of disruptive behavior as accounting for 80% of the disciplinary and mental health problems within their schools (Walter, Gouze, & Lim, 2006). Unfortunately, teachers often report that they do not have the ability to keep defiant students involved in instruction or to prevent such behavior from disrupting the instruction (Baker, 2005). Ultimately, such problems can have the effect of forcing many teachers to leave the profession (Scheckner, Rollins, Kaiser-Ulrey, & Wagner, 2002).

Disruptive behavior can also put heavy demands on the work of school administrators. For example, aggression has been found to be the most common reason for administrators to recommend that students be suspended (Costenbader & Markson, 1994), while comparatively minor forms of disruptive behavior (e.g., lack of cooperation, insubordination, verbal abuse, and inappropriate language), tend to be the most common reason for students to be referred for administrative discipline (Skiba, Peterson, & Williams, 1997). A recent study of office referral rates found elementary schools averaging 567 office referrals per year, while middle and junior high schools averaged over 1500 office referrals (Sugai et al., 2000). One study (Scott & Barrett, 2004) found that the average office discipline referral usurped an average of 20 minutes of administrator time while suspensions averaged 45 minutes. This suggests that elementary school administrators may be expending hundreds of valuable hours each school year dealing with disruptive behavior, with middle/junior high administrators spending even larger amounts of time dealing with challenging behavior.

The effect of disruptive behavior on the students who exhibit such behavior must also be considered. The outcomes for students who exhibit disruptive and anti-social behavior in school and other environments are grim. These students are likely to have negative educational and social experiences that can lead to life-long problems. In school, they experience greater levels of negative interactions with teachers and students (Shores et al., 1993), spend less time on instructional activities (Carr, Taylor, & Robinson, 1991), spend more time in restrictive educational settings, and are at higher risk for leaving school before graduating (Snyder, 2001). Once out of school, they are at high risk for a range of negative outcomes, including unemployment, use of drugs, and high rates of criminal offending (Loeber et al., 2000).

Given the broad negative outcomes that disruptive behavior holds for students, staff, administrators, and the school as a whole, there is a need to identify interventions that have shown effectiveness in reducing disruptive behavior in schools. This chapter focuses on evidence-based interventions for students who exhibit disruptive behavior. The chapter begins by describing the range of terms and behaviors that describe and characterize children who exhibit disruptive behavior. Next, a broad range of interventions are discussed in a format that strongly suggests a multi-level preventive approach to dealing with issues of disruptive behavior.

## DEFINITIONS AND CHARACTERISTICS

This section describes a variety of terms that are used to refer to youth who exhibit disruptive behavior and delineates the specific behavioral characteristics of these students

### Emotional Disturbance

Some children who exhibit chronic disruptive behavior in school qualify to receive special education services under the *Individuals with Disabilities Education Act* or *IDEA* (U.S. Office of Education, 1976). The federal term *emotional disturbance* (ED) is a softening of the original term *seriously emotionally disturbed* that was abandoned in the 1997 reauthorization of the act. Many states have chosen to further soften the term in ways that they generally believe are less stigmatizing. The most common alternative terms for the same category are *emotional and behavioral disordered* (EBD) and *behaviorally disordered* (BD). Children in any of the 13 categories of disability defined in IDEA may display disruptive behavior at one time or another. However, children for whom behavior problems are determined to be the major cause of educational difficulties are identified in the category of ED. The definition of ED that is included in federal law is based on research originally conducted by Eli Bower in the 1950s (Bower, 1982). Other than the 1997 change in terminology, few changes have been made to the federal definition of ED since it was first included in the law in 1975. The definition of ED states:

(i)   The term means a condition exhibiting one or more of the following characteristics over

a long period of time and to a marked degree that adversely affects a child's educational performance:
(A) An inability to learn that cannot be explained by intellectual, sensory, or health factors
(B) An inability to build or maintain satisfactory interpersonal relationships with peers and teachers.
(C) Inappropriate types of behavior or feelings under normal circumstances.
(D) A general pervasive mood of unhappiness or depression.
(E) A tendency to develop physical symptoms or fears associated with personal or school problems.

(ii)    The term includes schizophrenia. The term does not apply to children who are socially maladjusted, unless it is determined that they have an emotional disturbance. (CFR §300.7 (a) 9)

As can be seen, only a few of the five characteristics of this definition are directly related to what might be considered as disruptive, aggressive, or anti-social behavior. However, it is generally accepted by researchers and school staff that disruptive, aggressive, and anti-social behaviors are more likely to result in a label of ED than behaviors typically associated with anxiety and withdrawal (Kauffman, 1997). While this may indeed be the case, recent research demonstrates that children identified as ED are likely to exhibit chronic behavior associated with all of the 5 characteristics included in the definition (Joe & Flannery, 2002).

While researchers have suggested that the actual number of children who require services in this area of special education ranges from 2% to 20% (Kauffman, 1997), children identified as ED make up 0.73% of all youth ages 6–21 and 8.16% of all children receiving special education services (U.S. Department of Education, 2004). Both gender and ethnicity appear to mediate the identification of youth in the category of ED. While few studies have found reliable gender differences regarding the characteristics of ED among school-age children (Cullinan, Evans, Epstein, & Ryser, 2003), males are more likely to be identified as ED than are females (Kauffman, 1997). Black youth are more likely to be identified as ED than are whites (Cohen & Osher, 1994) and white students are more likely to be identified as ED than are Hispanic students (Artiles, Rueda, Salazar, & Higareda, 2005). Exactly how issues of gender and ethnicity interact with the definition of ED is complex, not well understood, and continues to be explored by researchers.

The federal definition of ED has been roundly criticized for a number of reasons. First, many leaders in the field of special education have taken issue with the exclusion of *children who are socially maladjusted* from this category. This term refers to children whose behaviors manifest from a home life in which either behavioral skills have not been taught or more basic needs have interfered with acquisition of social norms. Many argue that definitions of social maladjustment are imprecise and that any child who would fit a definition of social maladjustment should also satisfy the criteria for ED (Bower, 1982; Kauffman, 1997). On the other hand, Merrell and Walker (2004) describe research suggests that it is possible to distinguish between children who are socially maladjusted and those who exhibit characteristics of ED. However, these researchers concluded that while it may be possible to make such a distinction, children with problem behaviors are best served by not distinguishing between ED and social maladjustment.

## Psychiatric Diagnoses

Psychiatrists, psychologists, and other licensed mental health professionals use the *Diagnostic and Statistical Manual of Mental Disorders, 4th edition* (*DSM-IV*; American Psychiatric Association, 1994) to diagnose the existence of mental disorders, determine effective treatment options, and gather valuable public mental health statistics. Disruptive behavior could be considered as part of the criteria in many diagnostic categories. However, youth who exhibit disruptive, aggressive, and/ or anti-social behavior are likely be diagnosed as having a conduct disorder (CD) or oppositional defiant disorder (ODD). It has been estimated that one or both of these disorders can be found in between 2% and 16% of all children in the United States (Eddy, Reid, & Curry, 2002)

The distinction between ODD and CD is generally related to the severity of behavior, with ODD representing a "milder form" of CD (Conner, 2004). ODD refers to a recurrent pattern of negativistic, defiant, disobedient, and hostile behavior toward authority figures. A youth is considered to exhibit a CD if he shows a persistent pattern of behavior that violates the basic rights of others or major age-appropriate societal norms. The criteria in the *DSM-IV* include a long list of behaviors that typify a person who exhibits a CD. These include theft, deceitfulness, physical cruelty to animals or people, destruction of property, and serious rule violations (Loeber et al., 2000). Diagnosis of both ODD and CD are not based on individual behavioral events, but when the behaviors occur over time with a significant intensity.

Two to three times more boys than girls are diagnosed with CD and ODD (Kann & Hanna, 2000). The ways in which girls and boys present characteristics of disruptive behavior disorders may be one reason for this large gender disparity (Kann & Hanna, 2000). That is, girls tend to exhibit fewer easily identifiable externalizing characteristics, such as fighting, vandalism, and destructiveness. In addition, boys are at a higher risk than girls of exhibiting both CD and Attention-Deficit Hyperactivity Disorder (ADHD) (Lumley, McNeil, Herschell, & Bahl, 2002). While these differences have been described in a number of research studies, CD in girls has not, until recently, been studied extensively and has been identified as the most common problem for clinically referred girls (Keenan, Loeber, & Green, 1999).

## Comorbidity of CD and ADHD

When a youth who is diagnosed with one disorder is found to meet the criteria for a second disorder, it is referred to as *comorbidity* (Walker, Ramsey, & Gresham, 2004). Youth with CD often also meet the criteria for another *DSM-IV* diagnosis: Attention-Deficit Hyperactivity Disorder (Hinshaw, 1987). In fact, these disorders occur together with such frequency that there has been debate regarding whether they should be classified as different disorders (e.g., Loney & Milich, 1982). Longitudinal research studies have determined that children who exhibit both CD and ADHD characteristics are at higher risk on a wide range of problematic socio-behavioral measures than children who are diagnosed with only CD or ADHD (Gresham, Lane, & Beebe-Frankenberger, 2005). Children comorbid for CD and ADHD have also been described as being particularly resistant to intervention. Lynam (1998) has suggested that youth who exhibit this combination of disorders are at critically high risk for lifelong patterns of aggressive, antisocial, and criminal behavior. In a comprehensive review of the research conducted from 1990 to 2000 related to ODD and CD, Loeber et al. (2004) note that there has been very little investigation of the comorbidity of ADHD and ODD.

## Juvenile Delinquency

Disruptive behaviors exhibited by youth are considered to be *deliquent acts* when such behaviors cause the youth to be arrested by the police and, in turn, become involved with the juvenile justice court system. Kauffman (1997) describes two key terms that are used to refer to youth who commit illegal acts of disruptive, aggressive, or anti-social behavior. *Index crimes* are acts that are illegal regardless of a person's age, such as assault, theft, and vandalism. *Status crimes* are acts that are against the law only because of the age of the person engaging in the behavior. Some common examples of status crimes are smoking, possessing alcohol, or being truant.

The level of crime in schools is difficult to assess, with most data coming in the form of self-reports from victims. During the 2002–2003 school year, students reported being the victim of non-fatal crimes in school at a rate of 72 incidents per 1,000 students (U.S. Departments of Education and Justice, 2005). Sixty-two percent of these incidents involved theft, while the remainder involved more serious acts such as assault and rape. Over a 5-year period (1999–2003), teachers reported being the victim of non-fatal crimes at a much lower, but significant rate (39 per 1,000 teachers).

A number of factors have been shown to be associated with the likelihood of youth to become involved in delinquent acts. These include school failure, early acts of delinquency, substance abuse, family history of criminality, poverty, and parental disciplinary style (e.g., Kauffman, 2004; Schumaker & Kurz, 2000; Walker, Colvin, & Ramsey, 1995). Youth who have a disability are particularly likely to become involved with the juvenile justice system (Quinn, Rutherford, Leone, Osher, & Poirier, 2005). In fact, Jay and Padilla (1987) found that approximately 70% of youth with ED are arrested within three years of dropping out of school.

Various theories have been proposed to suggest how students with disabilities develop the tendency to commit acts of delinquency and become involved with the juvenile justice system. Some researchers have suggested that the student's disability puts him or her at greater risk of school failure, leading to a negative self-image, disruptive behavior in school, and ultimately unsupervised time with other peers when they are suspended, expelled, or drop out of school (Post, 1981). Others have proposed that while students with disabilities commit similar numbers of delinquent acts as peers without disabilities, the students with disabilities tend to have developed patterns of interpersonal behavior that lead to greater levels of miscommunication with school and legal personnel (Leone & Meisel, 1997).

## Adaptive and Maladaptive Aggression

In some situations, behaviors that appear disruptive, aggressive, or anti-social are actually an appropriate or, at least, a reasonable and expected response to the environment. For instance, some people would say that fighting is a reasonable response to being attacked and cursing is a common response to accidentally hitting your hand with a hammer. To ensure proper identification and treatment of violent problem behavior, researchers and clinical professionals find it useful to distinguish between *adaptive* and *maladaptive* aggression (Conner, 2004). It is important for teachers and other personnel who work with children and youth in schools to also consider this distinction to make accurate decisions during assessment and to determine when intervention is actually necessary.

## School Violence

Perhaps the most alarming expressions of disruptive, aggressive, and anti-social behavior are the well-publicized and tragic incidents of serious violence and crime that occur in schools. Prior to the early 1990s, few efforts were made to collect reliable data on serious incidents of school violence. In fact, it was the occurrence of several high profile violent school events at that time which focused media, political, and grassroots attention on the issue of school violence (Furlong & Morrison, 2000). The U.S. Departments of Education and Justice publish a yearly compendium from several sources called the *Indicators of School Crime and Safety* (2005) that provides comprehensive data on disruptive, aggressive, and other behaviors that are considered as school violence. A review of this source and other data on school violence brings to light some interesting issues related to disruptive behavior.

Despite the media coverage given to such events, very few incidents of disruptive behavior result in fatalities or serious crimes at school. For example, data collected since 1992 demonstrate that students are 70 times more likely to die from violence away from school than at school (U.S. Departments of Education and Justice, 2005). For instance, during the 2001–2002 school year, there were 17 homicides and 5 suicides of school-age youth on school property. This represents less than 1 homicide or suicide per million students enrolled (Figure 4.1) during 2001–2002. In fact, there has been a decreasing trend in deadly school incidents from across a 10-year period from 1992–2002. Other serious disruptive, aggressive, and anti-social behaviors classified as criminal acts have also decreased over the last 10 years.

While the events of school violence seen in the media tend to hold the attention of the general public, surveys conducted with teachers, administrators, and students suggest that they may define school violence in terms that involve less serious forms of disruptive behavior. These studies have found that behaviors like cursing, grabbing, and verbal threats are considered the most prevalent forms of violence occurring on school campuses (e.g., U.S. Departments of Education and Justice, 2005; Petersen, Pietrzak, & Speaker, 1998). These results may explain why, despite overall decreases in serious violent events in schools, staff and students continue to report constant levels of concern over personal safety (Scott, Nelson, Liaupsin, 2001). This also suggests that efforts to intervene in milder forms of disruptive behavior may have the effect of reducing staff and student anxiety regarding safety in school environments.

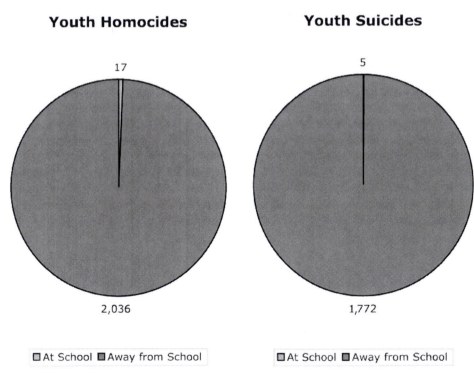

FIGURE 4.1.   Homicides and suicides at home and away from school: 2001–2002.
Adapted from *Indicators of School Crime and Safety*, U.S. Department of Education and Justice (2005).
Washington, D.C.: NCES 2006001.

## RESEARCH-BASED INTERVENTIONS

Because the projected outcomes for students with behavioral disorders are so dire, there is little room for unproven practice as every failed effort decreases the probability of future success. Still, the adversity surrounding these persons is obvious and becomes a beacon to charlatans who pedal a variety of gimmicks and programs that appeal to parents and teachers whose frustrations are transparent and understandable. Despite the existence of a growing body of unproven practices, a well-documented base of evidence-based practices for dealing with challenging behaviors does exist. According to Horner, Carr, Halle, McGee, Odom, and Wolery (2005), an educational practice can be deemed to be evidence-based when it is clearly defined, can be applied with replicable fidelity, and has been repeatedly documented to have positive effects across a number of studies, researchers, and participants.

Recent federal priorities have focused on the use of evidence-based practices to improve social outcomes for students. Although available data indicate an increased probability of life-long adjustment problems among students with significant behavioral disorders (e.g., unemployment, unwanted pregnancy, imprisonment), research has demonstrated positive outcomes associated with school-wide prevention efforts built around systemic implementation of effective instructional practices that include collaboration, consistent application, formative monitoring, and data-based decision making (e.g., Leedy, Bates, & Safran, 2004; Luiselli, Putman, & Sunderland, 2002). In fact, evidence-based practices in the area of disruptive behavior disorders can be organized into three categories: (1) those that are applied across a system (i.e., school, family, community), (2) those that are applied to smaller groups of persons who have similar issues with which to deal, and (3) individualized interventions that are designed to meet the unique needs of the individual. Consistent with more recent special education conceptualizations and legal mandates regarding identification and intervention decision-making, these three categories may be thought of as a continuum of supports that identifies students in need of more intensive intervention by their lack of response to intervention at more global levels (Gresham, 2001).

Responsiveness to intervention (RTI) is a framework for guiding the use of assessment data to evaluate the extent to which a student's achievement meets expectations in response to an intervention. The term *intervention* is used to refer to (1) the curriculum all students receive at the broadest level, and (2) progressively tailored, individualized interventions a student may receive if the student's progress is not adequate under the general education curriculum. Taking RTI to its root meaning, effective intervention begins with prevention via effective instructional practices. Then, through broad assessment, students for whom such efforts are insufficient to facilitate success are identified for more individualized and intensive instruction. In a reciprocal manner, intervention and assessment inform one another so that instruction and measurement are dynamic and individualized processes. While the concept of RTI is most often applied to students with academic problems, recent research has demonstrated the benefits for students with behavioral problems, including those who exhibit disruptive behavior. The key features of evidence-based practice at each of the three levels are discussed below.

### System-Wide Interventions

System-wide interventions are those that are applied across an entire system such as a school, family, or community. Most schools manage to function without structured system-wide programs in place; the majority of students will be successful regardless, or even in spite of, the quality of systemic efforts. However, system-wide interventions can provide an important scaffold for an environment that is organized to deal effectively with disruptive student behavior. In other words, system-wide interventions are designed to reduce the occurrence of common behavior problems, allowing scarce school resources (e.g., time, effort, specialized personnel, etc.) to be directed at the provision of small-group and individualized interventions for students who do not respond to system-wide practices. System-wide practices have been implemented effectively in school, home, and juvenile correctional environments and are often effective for a significant number of students who exhibit disruptive behavior. The emphasis of evidence-based practice at the system-wide level is on identifying predictable problems, defining and teaching expected behavior, and creating environments that effectively prompt and respond to behavior, both positive and negative (e.g., Anderson & Kincaid, 2005; Evertson & Harris, 1992; Mayer, 1995; Scott & Eber, 2003; Sprick, Sprick, & Garrison, 1992; Sugai & Horner, 1999).

*Prevention.*    A foundational principle of evidence-based practice is the concept that what can be predicted can be prevented. A number of steps can be taken at the school-wide level to predict and prevent disruptive behavior. These strategies involve the application both academic and social interventions. For example, language deficits have long been recognized as a predictor of academic and social failure; language programming at an early age has been demonstrated to be an effective prevention strategy for these students (e.g., Kaiser, Xinsheng, Hancock, & Foster, 2002; Nelson, Benner, & Cheney, 2005). Similarly, it is becoming increasingly clear that literacy deficits exhibited as early as kindergarten can predict behavior problems well into elementary school (McIntosh, Horner, & Chard, 2006) and set a pattern for continued failures into high school and beyond (Fleming, Harachi, Cortes, Abbott, & Catalano, 2004; Greer-Chase, Rhodes, & Kellam, 2002). Furthermore, evidence suggests that effective reading interventions in early elementary school may result in earlier identification of students with severe problems (e.g., Denton & Fletcher, 2003; Ikeda et al., 2002), fewer students labeled as learning disabled (e.g., O'Connor & Simic, 2002), and fewer behavior problems throughout their school career (e.g., Fleming, Harachi, Cortes, Abbott, & Catalano, 2004; McIntosh, Horner, & Chard, 2006). Marston, Muyskens, Lau, & Cantor (2003) also report that early intervention can reduce occurrence of inappropriate identification of minority students for specialized programming. A growing evidence base supports the utility of prevention strategies aimed at enhancing the social behavior of students (e.g., Biglan, 1995; Horner, Sugai, Todd, & Lewis-Palmer, 2005; Lewis & Sugai, 1999). Further, research suggests that monitoring student behavior using such simple measures as office discipline referral counts is an effective means of predicting more intense disruptive behavior problems (Tobin & Sugai, 1999) and identifying students in need of early intervention.

*Instruction.*    The importance of instruction in dealing effectively with disruptive behavior cannot be overestimated. Effective instruction has been described as the foundation and most important aspect of any intervention (e.g., Heward, 2003; Scott, Nelson, & Liaupsin, 2001). Instruction in this sense is most often considered in terms of academics but is applied to all desired skills and routines, whether academic or social in nature (Taylor-Greene et al., 1997). For example, schools that teach a simple set of school-wide behavioral expectations to students, (and establish routines for acknowledging students who follow the rules), have demonstrated reductions in the overall incidence of disruptive behavior problems (e.g., Lewis, Sugai, & Colvin, 1998; Nelson, Martella, Galand, 1998; Nelson, Martella, & Marchand-Martella, 2002).

Evidence-based instruction involves providing a clear rule relationship (e.g., "you need to do this when . . ."), offering modeling and guided practice with feedback until acquisition, and then conducting gradual fading of instruction with regular assessment for mastery (Kame'enui & Simmons, 1990). The logic behind instruction is based on the well-established fact that the more and better instruction students are exposed to and engaged with, the more they learn (Brophy, 1988; Rosenshine & Berliner, 1978). In addition, when students are engaged and experiencing success, they are less likely to make errors (academic or social) and to attempt escape from instruction (McIntosh, Horner, & Chard, 2006) and more likely to have a positive relationship with the teacher (Carr, Taylor, & Robinson, 1991). In other words, students are less likely to engage in disruptive behavior problems that evolve from their inability to engage in the required academic or social task.

In summary, the evidence-base for instruction at the system-wide level describes effective and consistent use of group instruction (e.g., Nelson, Colvin, & Smith, 1996), the use of prompts and cues to facilitate success (e.g., Colvin, Sugai, & Patching, 1993), and the development of consistent routines (e.g., Scott, 2001). The literature base suggests that there is no relevant distinction between effective instruction for academics and social behaviors; both should be planned, consistent, and facilitated in the environment. Finally, effective instruction in both academic and social behavior can have a positive effect in reducing the occurrence of disruptive behavior in schools.

*Performance Feedback.*    Performance feedback, in the forms of both reinforcement and error correction, can also serve as an effective school-wide deterrent to the occurrence of disruptive behaviors. Despite clear evidence that positive feedback is associated with increased and sustained positive performance (e.g., Cameron, Banko, & Pierce, 2001; Walker, Colvin, & Ramsey, 1995), studies suggest that teacher praise drops off as grade level increases (e.g., Baker & Zigmond, 1990; Nowacek, McKinney, & Hallahan, 1990).

It is also often the case that classroom and non-classroom school environments are not conducive to the use of appropriate social or academic behavior. For example, a child is unlikely to raise a hand in class and wait to be acknowledged during discussions if the teacher regularly calls on students who call out. From within a system-wide perspective, school staff can reduce disruptive behavior by developing environments that "trap success" so that positive feedback is warranted. Effective feedback and effective instruction have elements in common. Like effective instruction, effective feedback should be proactive, not reactive. To simply sit by and wait for a child to behave appropriately is no more effective than it would be to sit by and wait for a child to learn to read. Finally, effective feedback should be a formative activity that begins with instruction (Scott, Nelson, & Liaupsin, 2001).

Performance feedback, however, involves more than just positive reinforcement. While engineering school-wide environments for success and teaching school-wide expectations can be expected to reduce the occurrence of disruptive behavior problems, students will continue to exhibit errors for a number of reasons. To be certain, error-correction in the form of re-teaching is necessary when the error involves a skill deficit, such as when a student disrupts class because they do not know an effective skill to use to gain a teacher's attention. However, re-teaching will not be sufficient for errors that are not simply skill deficits and, in such cases, feedback may take a more punitive form. Research indicates that it is illogical and ineffective to address such errors by simply sitting by and waiting for a correct response. The goal of any negative feedback must be not only to decrease the undesired response, but also to increase the likelihood of a desired response. Thus, negative feedback should be instructional in nature and, above all, punitive consequences that do not change behavior must be recognized as ineffective and should be discarded (Kerr & Nelson, 2006).

Performance feedback can also take the form of *extinction*. Far from its common description as "ignoring" disruptive behavior until it goes away, the use of extinction should be considered as a carefully planned activity that is most effectively implemented in conjunction with positive performance feedback. For instance, it would be unwise and ineffective to only ignore the disruptive behavior of students who disrupt a class. Instead, the teacher should implement a strategy combining three elements; (a) extinction (ignoring call-outs), (b) teaching or re-teaching of appropriate behavior for gaining teacher attention, and (c) positive performance feedback for any and all correct attempts to gain teacher attention.

School-wide interventions can be effectively employed to reduce the overall occurrence of disruptive behavior. However, despite the effective use of school-wide intervention, there will always be a group of students, (among them many who display disruptive behavior), for whom these efforts are insufficient to facilitate success. These non-responders will require more intensive and individualized interventions.

## Small Group Interventions

If a student is not making progress when the curriculum is effective for most students, supplemental intervention is introduced. Intervention at this level (Figure 4.2) involves small group or simple student-based strategies that are characterized by instruction, frequent monitoring of student progress, and the promotion of self-management. Evidence-based practices such as *Check-In, Check-Out* (Hawken, 2006), social skills instructional groups (Choutka, Doloughty, & Zirkel, 2004), and *First Step to Success* (Walker, Golly, McLane, & Kimmich, 2005) can be implemented. Although differing in both content and application, each of these strategies provides small-group intervention that is individualized to meet the needs of students who have not positively responded to school-wide strategies.

*Social Skills Instruction.*    Instruction is perhaps the most effective intervention for students with behavioral disorders (Scott, Nelson, & Liaupsin, 2001). The concept of instruction puts the onus of student success squarely on the teacher and may be conceptualized by the phrase, "adult behavior change must precede student behavior change." For example, if a student was to provide the response "4" when asked to solve the problem "2 – 2," there is no reason to believe that the response would change in the absence of further instruction. Likewise, when students exhibit social failure it will be the teacher's role to provide feedback and instruction to facilitate success with the next attempt. Continued student failure should not signal teacher fault, but it does signal responsibility to continue with instruction and to use the most logical strategies available to facilitate

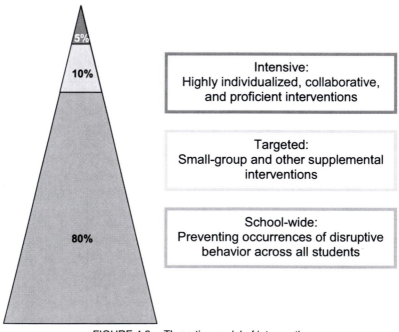

FIGURE 4.2.   Three-tier model of intervention.

success. At the second tier of intervention, prevention continues to be a priority but the focus has changed to prevent *recurrent* rather than *initial* errors. Again, effective instruction includes clear definition of positive behavior, modeling, and multiple opportunities to practice with feedback and a gradual move toward independence. Due to the intensity and individualization necessary at this level, instruction is most efficiently delivered to smaller groups. In the small group context, individualization is only as fine as the general skills necessary across the group. However, social interaction skills are fairly general across students and are seen as a key to facilitating success in the larger school environment. In fact, teachers at primary and intermediate grades report that self-control and cooperation are equally as important (Choutka, Doloughty, & Zirkel, 2004).

*Monitoring.*    As previously noted, the prognosis for students experiencing disruptive behavior and social failure is bleak and grows bleaker with each additional failure. As such, there is no room for continuation of ineffective intervention strategies and teachers must monitor intervention in a frequent and formative manner. One example of an effective monitoring procedure is *Check- in, Check-Out* (Hawken, 2006). This procedure creates a system wherein students must check-in with teachers after each class or activity and receive feedback on performance Such strategies not only provide students with multiple opportunities to receive feedback on their performance, but also allow teachers to monitor performance on a very regular basis and to evaluate the success of social skills instruction. In a sense, monitoring can be conceived of as a component of effective instruction. That is, teaching reading or any other academic skill requires curriculum-based assessment to determine whether instruction is effective. In addition, there is a well-established research base indicating that simply monitoring and charting behavior is associated with effective intervention programs (Fuchs & Fuchs, 1986). Monitoring of behavior is most effective when (1) behaviors are well defined and measured as they occur, (2) measurement takes place on a regular basis, (3) students are kept informed of their progress or even involved in the measurement, and (4) measures are used to evaluate the effectiveness of the intervention strategies in place (Kerr & Nelson, 2006).

*Self-Management.*    The ideal for any intervention is to demonstrate success and to end intervention while the student continues success without assistance. Self-management is a term that is used to describe both an intervention strategy and a student outcome. As an intervention strategy, self-management involves teaching the student to monitor his or her own behavior in concert with the teacher. Gradually, the teacher fades monitoring and students maintain management of their own behavior (Peterson, Young, Salzberg, West, & Hill, 2006). The process consists of several steps that include: (1) teaching a new behavior, (2) providing regular performance feedback, and (3) teaching the student to monitor his or her own behavior. Initial stages of self-management generally are completed in small intervals with close attention from the teacher to provide reliability and debriefing and then moving to longer intervals with less attention. Although more effective for attention than for specific academic skills (Harris, Friedlander, Saddler, Frizzelle, & Graham, 2005), self-managed increases in attention to task are associated with academic success (Lan, 2005; Mooney, Ryan, Uhing, Reid, & Epstein, 2005).

## Individualized Interventions

Effective instruction has been a part of each of the preceding two levels of intervention and will continue to be the most important component when working in the third tier with students displaying disruptive behavior for whom all other interventions have been unsuccessful. That is, students requiring the most individualized and specialized instruction are those who have not responded to school-wide or small group intervention. Too often, intervention at this level is automatically considered to include a referral for special education services. However, it is important to conceive of this top tier not as special education but as the "transition point for students who have not yet found success in school" (Brown-Cidsey & Steege, 2005, p. 3). Still, regardless of how we categorize, refer to, or see them, students at this level require intensive, individualized, and highly proficient intervention and instruction (Fuchs, Mock, Morgan, & Young, 2003).

*Collaborative Development and Implementation.*   One way of thinking about these non-responders is to consider the fact that everything the school has attempted with them has been unsuccessful. While the school will continue to be a necessary component of intervention, it must be considered insufficient as the sole agent of change. As such, the third tier of intervention will necessarily involve those outside of the school, including parents and a range of community-based professionals (e.g., physicians, mental health professionals, physical therapists, etc.). In fact, for students with oppositional defiant and conduct disorders, parent training has been found to be the single most successful treatment approach (Taylor & Biglan, 1998). Unfortunately, improvement at home has not necessarily been associated with improvement in school or with peers (Taylor & Biglan, 1998) and thus strong school involvement is critical. In the milder cases at this level, a range of stakeholders may be invited in light of the student's specific identified needs. In more intense cases, however, the fullest range of stakeholders likely will be invited from the beginning to ensure an adequate voice at the table for students who have experienced the most failure (Scott & Eber, 2003). Aside from the parents and relevant school personnel, this group may include any professionals with whom the student is involved, such as family; social workers; psychiatrists, psychologists or family counselors; court designated workers; rehabilitation counselors; and advocacy specialists. Given the range of expertise and disparate roles of such a group, the best effect can be expected when the group includes at least one member who has received training in the coordination of collaborative intervention practices.

*Function-Based Intervention.*   For students who exhibit disruptive behavior, despite appropriately implemented school-wide and targeted interventions, function-based interventions may prove to be the most effective. Function-based interventions are based on the well documented notion that disruptive behaviors are used by students to either gain something, escape from something, or to do both at the same time. Once the goal or goals of the student's disruptive behavior is identified, the task of the interventionist is to create an environment in which the student's goals can be met without the need to engage in disruptive behavior. Function-based interventions have been shown to be effective with a wide variety of disruptive behaviors and across students with a range a characteristics (Lane, Umbreit, & Beebe-Frankenberger, 1999). While the task of developing function-based interventions often falls on school personnel with specialized training, such as school psychologists, special education teachers and general education teachers can learn to effectively implement this process (Lane et al., 2006). Teaching the process of function-based intervention is, however, beyond the scope of this chapter. Those interested in implementing such interventions should seek out qualified personnel to assist them or gain the proper level of training.

The first task in implementing a function-based intervention is to determine the goal of the student's behavior. This has been referred to as a *functional assessment* or *functional analysis* (note: though many argue that these terms are not interchangeable, we will not distinguish between the two for the purposes of this explanation). Data for making this determination is generally collected via informant interviews such as the *Student Assisted Functional Assessment Interview* (Kern, Dunlap, Clarke, & Childs, 1994), brief surveys or checklists like the *Functional Assessment Checklist for Teachers and Staff* (March et al., 2000), and structured observations in the natural environment. These data are then reviewed to determine the goal or goals of the student's disruptive behavior.

Umbreit, Ferro, Liaupsin, and Lane (2007) have developed a tool called the Function Matrix (Figure 4.3) to simplify the process of making an accurate determination of function. Using the Function Matrix, the interventionist considers the collected data in light of six possible outcomes; does the behavior allow the student to (1) access attention, (2) avoid attention, (3) access tangibles or activities, (4) avoid tangibles or activities, (5) access sensory stimulation, (6) avoid sensory stimulation. One of the benefits of using such a system is that it forces the consideration that the disruptive behavior may be maintained by more than one outcome. For instance, a student who is tardy to class may not only be seeking the attention that is gained by coming late to class, but also using the behavior to avoid classroom task or activities. This becomes critically important when developing the resulting intervention, because an intervention that provides a more acceptable option for obtaining desired attention, but does not deal with the desire to escape the activity, is less likely to be completely effective in reducing the disruptive behavior.

Perhaps, the most difficult task in developing a function-based intervention is in applying the results of the functional assessment. Scott, Liaupsin, Nelson, and McIntyre, (2005) found that while school teams were likely to be accurate in determining the function of student problem behavior, they were less accurate in using the information to develop function-based intervention plans. This discontinuity may be largely due to the limited experience of school personnel in considering how to help students develop positive pro-social skills that reduce the need to engage in disruptive behavior. Applying the outcome of a functional assessment to a function-based intervention often involves identifying a new behavior the student can use (a replacement behavior) that meets the same goals as the original disruptive behavior. However, this is not always the case. In a situation where a student is destroying worksheets to gain teacher attention, the resulting intervention may focus on teaching and reinforcing a more acceptable way to gain teacher attention. However, if the goal of destroying worksheets is to avoid the given task, it may not be academically beneficial to the student to simply teach a new way to avoid the task. Instead, the focus of the intervention is likely to be one that involves teaching the skills necessary to complete the task so that there is no longer a need to use disruptive behavior to escape. In addition, the replacement behavior may be one that is entirely new to the student, such as learning an academic skill, or a behavior that is in the student's repertoire, but is not used effectively or is not actively reinforced in the environment.

Effective intervention planning involves the same set of evidence-based practices described for tiers one and two, albeit with far more collaboration, intensity, and comprehensive support. While instruction remains the key, intervention also must focus on context, consideration of the role of the environment, and how both the other humans and the physical environment may predict and maintain behavior (Lampi, Fenty, & Beaunae, 2005). A comprehensive function-based intervention designed to deal with the occurrence of disruptive behavior should include several elements that will ensure the success of the intervention. There are various models for

| | **Positive Reinforcement** (Access Something) | **Negative Reinforcement** (Avoid Something) |
|---|---|---|
| **Attention** | | |
| **Tangibles / Activities** | | |
| **Sensory** | | |

FIGURE 4.3.   Function matrix. From *Functional behavioral assessment and function-based interventions: An effective, practical approach* (p. 56), by J. Umbreit, J. Ferro, C. Liaupsin, and K. Lane, 1997. Upper Saddle River, NJ: Prentice-Hall. Reprinted with permission.

the development of function-based intervention plans (e.g., Chandler & Dahlquist, 2005; O'Neil, Horner, Albin, Storey, & Sprauge 1996; Umbreit, Ferro, Liaupsin, & Lane, 2007), but most include common elements. First, the plan should consider whether *the environment* (antecedent setting) in which the student is expected to perform is arranged to allow successful use of the new behavior. If not, the plan should include adjustments to the environment that would promote successful use of the replacement behavior. The function-based intervention plan should also include procedures to *teach and reinforce the replacement behavior*. Whether these behaviors are academic or social in nature, a direct instruction approach has demonstrated success in implementing in this portion of the function-based intervention plan. Finally, the plan should include consideration of the actions to take if the student attempts to use the problem behavior rather than the replacement behavior. As described earlier in this chapter, such error corrections can involve actively ignoring the problem behavior (*extinction*) or addressing it through negative performance feedback that includes an instructive component.

For example, Liaupsin, Ferro, Umbreit, et al. (2006) successfully implemented these common intervention elements in the development of a function-based intervention plan for a 14-year-old female student who engaged in defiance, cursing and off-task behavior in two school settings. The functional assessment revealed that the student engaged in these behaviors to escape from classroom tasks that were too difficult for her to complete due to her limited reading ability. In other words, when the student was faced with difficult reading tasks, she exhibited disruptive behaviors, was sent out of the classroom or suspended, and was therefore was not expected to complete her work tasks. The function-based intervention addressed the *environment* (antecedent setting) by altering the student's content reading and assignments so that they were on her reading level. She was also assigned a "peer buddy" to assist her with reading. The replacement behaviors, which included following directions and engaging in classroom tasks, were *reinforced* with teacher praise and by providing tokens that could be exchanged daily for simple items in the school store. In one of the settings, it was necessary for the teacher to directly *teach* reading skills so that the student could engage in the replacement behaviors. When the student engaged in instances of disruptive behavior, she was given a verbal reminder to return to her work and was not allowed to escape the task (*extinction*). Figure 4.4 shows how implementation of the function-based interventions resulted in immediate increases in the use of the replacement behaviors.

## CHAPTER SUMMARY

Disruptive behavior among school-age youth is a critical concern among teachers, administrators, other school professionals, and parents. The negative outcomes for students who exhibit disruptive behavior have been widely documented and include the likelihood of not only school failure, but failure to adjust to social norms in adulthood. The disruptive behavior may also have broader effects on schools, including higher rates of staff job dissatisfaction, and reduced perceptions of safety among both staff and students.

Behavior that is seen as disruptive ranges in severity from minor incidents of unruly classroom behavior (e.g., out of seat, talking out, cursing, and refusal) to major acts (e.g., theft, threats, and fighting). While all of these behaviors may be of concern, no single definition exists when determining whether a student has engaged in "disruptive behavior." School staff should have an understanding of the differing terminology used by school psychologists, social workers, special education personnel, juvenile justice specialists, and other professionals who work to improve the lives of students who exhibit disruptive behavior.

A wide variety of research-based practices have been identified as effective in managing disruptive behavior. Current initiatives suggest that successfully reducing the number of disruptive

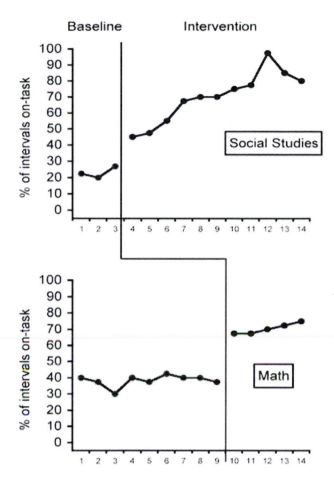

FIGURE 4.4.   Student on-task behavior. From "Improving academic engagement through systematic, function-based intervention," by C. Liaupsin, J. Ferro, J. Umbreit, A. Urso, and G. Upreti (2006). *Education and Treatment of Children, 29*, p. 585. Copyright 2006 by the Editorial Review Board, *Education and Treatment of Children*. Adapted with permission of author.

incidents in schools should involve the systematic use of research-based practices in a three-level preventive framework. This framework includes practices that are implemented (1) at the school-wide level, (2) with targeted small groups, and (3) at an intensive level with individual students who continue to exhibit disruptive behavior despite prevention efforts at the first two levels. At the school-wide level, disruptive behavior is reduced across the entire student population through the use of both high quality instruction that promotes student success and performance feedback that encourages students to engage in appropriate academic and social behavior. Small group interventions related to disruptive behavior also focus on the importance of high quality instruction, but also include practices that provide frequent monitoring of student progress, and the promotion of self-management of student behavior. Students who engage in disruptive behavior, despite the use of effective prevention practices at the school-wide and small group levels, require individualized interventions that are carefully programmed and managed. These interventions are likely to require a collaborative effort across school personnel, family members, and community resources. Parent training has been identified as a highly effective intervention for school-age youth with disruptive behavior disorders, but with effects that may not generalize to school environments. Function-based intervention planning (e.g., Chandler & Dahlquist, 2001; O'Neil, et al., 1996; Umbreit,

Ferro, Liaupsin, & Lane, 2007), has shown significant promise in dealing with disruptive behavior by combining an understanding of the goals of student problem behavior with interventions carefully designed to encourage the use of more socially appropriate alternatives.

Government initiatives, such as the establishment of the Institute for Education Sciences, are underway to support the development of new interventions and the further validation of current effective practices for students who exhibit disruptive behavior. However, the dismal outcomes for students who display disruptive behavior will never improve if we wait for the final word on effective practices. In other words, research regarding effective practice, by its very nature, will always be an on-going endeavor and never fully complete. Of even greater importance, for individuals and society at large, is the need to encourage the use of current practices that have already been identified as beneficial in working with students who display challenging behavior.

## REFERENCES

Anderson, C., & Kincaid, D. (2005). Applying behavior analysis to school violence and discipline problems: Schoolwide positive behavior support. *Behavior Analyst, 28,* 49–63.

American Psychiatric Association. (1994). *Diagnostic and statistical manual of mental disorders, 4th edition.* Washington, DC: Author.

Artiles, A., Rueda, R., Salazar, J., & Higareda, I., (2005).Within-group diversity in minority disproportionate representation: English language learners in urban school districts. *Exceptional Children, 71,* 283–300.

Baker, J. M., & Zigmond, N. (1990). Are regular education classes equipped to accommodate students with learning disabilities? *Exceptional Children, 56,* 516–526.

Baker, P. (2005). Managing student behavior: How ready are teachers to meet the challenge? *American Secondary Education, 33*(3), 51–64.

Biglan, A. (1995). Changing cultural practices: *A contextualist framework for intervention research.* Reno, NV: Context Press.

Bower, E. M. (1982). Defining emotional disturbance: Public policy and research. *Psychology in the Schools, 19,* 55–60.

Brophy, J. E. (1988). Research linking teacher behavior to student achievement: Potential implications for instruction of chapter 1 students. *Educational Psychologist 23,* 235–286.

Cameron, J., Banko, K. M., & Pierce, W. D. (2001). Pervasive negative effects of rewards on intrinsic motivation: The myth continues. *The Behavior Analyst, 24,* 1–44.

Carr, E. G., Taylor, J. C., & Robinson, S. (1991). The effects of severe behavior problems in children on the teaching behavior of adults. *Journal of Applied Behavior Analysis, 24,* 523–535.

Carr, E. G., Taylor, J. C., Robinson, S. (1991). The effects of severe behavior problems in children on the teaching behavior of adults. *Journal of Applied Behavior Analysis, 24,* 523–535.

Cartwright, G. P., Cartwright, C. A., & Ward, M. E. (1988). *Educating special learners* (2nd ed.). Belmont, CA: Wadsworth.

Chandler, L., & Dahlquist, C. (2005). *Functional assessment: Strategies to prevent and remediate challenging behavior in school settings.* Upper Saddle River, NJ: Prentice-Hall.

Cheney, D., & Barringer, C. (1995). Teacher competence, student diversity, and staff training for the inclusion of middle school students with emotional and behavioral disorders. *Journal of Emotional & Behavioral Disorders, 3,* 174–183.

Choutka, C. M., Doloughty, P. T., & Zirkel, P. A. (2004). Teacher expectations of student behavior: Social skills necessary for success in elementary school classrooms. *Journal of Special Education, 38*(2), 104–110.

Cohen, J., & Osher, D. (1994). *Race and SED Identification: An Analysis of OCR Data.* Technical paper prepared for Division of Innovation and Development, Office of Special Education Programs, U.S. Department of Education.

Colvin, G. Sugai, G., & Patching, W. (1993). Precorrection: An instructional approach for managing predictable problem behaviors. *Intervention in School and Clinic, 28,* 143–150.

Conner, D. F. (2004). *Aggression and antisocial behavior in children and adolescents: Research and treatment*. New York: Guilford.

Costenbader, V., & Markson, S. (1994). School suspension: A survey of current policies and practices. *NASSP Bulletin, 78*(564), 103–108.

Cullinan, D., Evans, C., Epstein, M., & Ryser, G. (2003). Characteristics of emotional disturbance of elementary school students. *Behavioral Disorders, 28*(2), 94–110.

Denton, C. A., & Fletcher, J. M. (2003). Scaling reading interventionsl in B. R. Foorman (Ed.), *Preventing and remediating reading difficulties: Bringing science to scale* (pp. 445–463). Timonium, MD: York Press.

Eddy, J. M., Reid, J. B., & Curry, V. (2002). The etiology of youth antisocial behavior, delinquency and violence and a public health approach to prevention. In M. Shinn, H. Walker, & G. Stoner (Eds.), *Interventions for academic and behavior problems: II. Preventive and remedial approaches* (pp. 27–51). Washington, DC, US: National Association for School Psychologists.

Evertson, C. M., & Harris, A. H. (1992). What we know about managing classrooms. *Educational Leadership, 49*(7), 74.

Fleming, C. B., Harachi, T. W., Cortes, R. C., Abbott, R. D., & Catalano, R. F. (2004). Level and change in reading scores and attention problems during elementary school as predictors of problem behavior in middle school. *Journal of Emotional and Behavioral Disorders, 12*(3), 130–144.

Fuchs, L. S., Fuchs, D. (1986). Effects of systematic formative evaluation: A meta-analysis. *Exceptional Children, 53*, 199–208.

Fuchs, D., Mock, D., Morgan, P., & Young, C. L. (2003). Responsiveness-to-Intervention: Definitions, Evidence, and Implications for the Learning Disabilities Construct. *Learning Disabilities: Research & Practice, 18*, 157–171.

Furlong, M. J., Morrison, G. M., & Dear, J. D. (1994). Addressing school violence as part of schools' educational mission. *Preventing School Failure, 38*(3), 10–17.

Furlong, M., & Morrison, G. (2000). The school in school violence: Definitions and facts. *Journal of Emotional and Behavioral Disorders, 8*(2), 71–82.

Gable, R. A., McLaughlin, V. L., Sindelar, P., & Kilgore, K. (1993). Unifying general and special education teacher preparation: Some cautions along the road to educational reform. *Preventing School Failure, 37*(2), 5–10.

Greer-Chase, M., Rhodes, W. A., & Kellam, S. G. (2002). Why the prevention of aggressive disruptive behaviors in middle school must begin in elementary school. *Clearing House, 75*(5), 242–245.

Gresham, F. (2001). Responsiveness to intervention: An alternative to the identification of learning disabilities. *Paper presented at the 2001 Learning Disabilities Summit: Building a Foundation for the Future* Retrieved March 8, 2002, from http://www.air.org/ldsummit/download

Gresham, F., Lane, K., & Beebe-Frankenberger, M. (2005). Predictors of hyperactive–impulsive–inattention and conduct problems: A comparative follow-back investigation. *Psychology in the Schools, 42*, 721–736.

Harris, K. R., Friedlander, B. D., Saddler, B., Frizzelle, R., & Graham, S. (2005). Self-monitoring of attention versus self-monitoring of academic performance: Effects among students with ADHD in the general education classroom. *Journal of Special Education, 39*(1), 145–156.

Hawken, L. (2006). School psychologists as leaders in the implementation of a targeted intervention: The Behavior Education Program, *School Psychology Quarterly, 21*(1), 91–111

Heward, W. L. (2003). *Exceptional children: An introduction to special education* (7th ed.). Upper Saddle River, NJ: Merrill/Prentice Hall.

Hinshaw, S. P. (1987). On the distinction between attentional deficits/hyperactivity and conduct problems/aggression in child psychopathology. *Psychological Bulletin, 101*, 443–463.

Horner, R. H., Carr, E. G., Halle, J., McGee, G., Odom, S., & Wolery, M. (2005). The use of single-subject research to identify evidence-based practice in special education. *Exceptional Children, 71*(2), 165–179.

Horner, R. H., Sugai, G., Todd, A. W., & Lewis-Palmer, T. (2005). School-wide positive behavior support: An alternative approach to discipline in schools. In L. M. Bambara & L. Kern (Eds.), *Individualized supports for students with problem behaviors* (pp. 359–390). New York: Guilford.

Horner, R. H., Todd, A. W., Lewis-Palmer, T., Irvin, L. K., Sugai, G., & Boland, J. B. (2004). The School-wide evaluation tool (SET): A research instrument for assessing school-wide positive behavior support. *Journal of Positive Behavior Interventions, 6*(1), 3–12.

Ikeda, M., Grimes, J., Tilly III, W. D., Allison, R., Kurns, S., & Stumme, J. (2002). Implementing and intervention-based approach to service delivery: A case example. In M. R. Shinn, G. Stoner, & H. M. Walker (Eds.), *Interventions for academic and behavioral problems II*. Bethesda, MD: National Association of School Psychologists,

Jay, D. E., & Padilla, C. L. (1987). *Special education dropouts*. Menlo Park, CA: SRI International.

Kaiser, A. P., Xinsheng, C., Hancock, T. B., & Foster, E. M. (2002). Teacher-reported behavior problems and language delays in boys and girls enrolled in head start. *Behavioral Disorders, 28*(1), 23–39.

Kame'enui, E. J., & Simmons, D. C. (1990). *Designing instructional strategies: The prevention of academic learning problems*. Columbus, OH: Merrill.

Kann, R., & Hanna, F. (2000). Disruptive behavior disorders in children and adolescents: How do girls differ from boys. *Journal of Counseling & Development, 78*(3), 267–274.

Kauffman, J.M. (2004). *Characteristics of emotional and behavioral disorders of children and youth (8th ed.)*. Upper Saddle River, NJ: Pearson Prentice-Hall.

Keenan, K., Loeber, R., & Green, S. (1999). Conduct disorder in girls: A review of the literature. *Clinical Child & Family Psychology Review, 2*(1), 3–19.

Kern, L., Dunlap, G., Clarke, S., & Childs, K. (1994). Student-assisted functional assessment interview. *Diagnostique, 19*, 29–39.

Kerr, M. M., & Nelson, C. M. (2006). *Strategies for addressing behavior problems in the classroom* (5th Ed.). Upper Saddle River, NJ: Merrill/Prentice Hall.

Kuzsman, F. L., & Schnall, H. (1987). Managing teachers' stress: Improving discipline. *The Canadian School Executive, 6*, 3–10.

Lampi, A. R., Fenty, N. S., & Beaunae, C. (2005). Making the three Ps easier: Praise, proximity, and precorrection. *Beyond Behavior, 15*(1), 8–12.

Lan, W. (2005). Self-monitoring and its relationship with educational level and task importance. *Educational Psychology, 25*(1), 109–127.

Lane, K. L., Umbreit, J., & Beebe-Frankenberger. (1999). A review of functional assessment research with students with or at risk for emotional and behavioral disorders. *Journal of Positive Behavioral Interventions, 1*, 101–111.

Lane, K., Weisenbach, J., Little, M, Phillips, A., & Wehby, J. (2006). Illustrations of function-based interventions implemented by general education teachers: Building capacity at the school site. *Education & Treatment of Children, 29*, 549–571.

Leedy, A., Bates, P., & Safran, S. P. (2004). Bridging the research-to practice gap: Improving hallway behavior using positive behavior supports. *Behavioral Disorders, 29*(2), 131–139.

Leone, P. E., & Meisel, S. (1997). Improving education services for students in detention and confinement facilities. *Children's Legal Rights Journal, 17*, 1–12.

Lewis, T. J., & Sugai, G. (1999). Effective behavior support: A systems approach to proactive schoolwide management. *Focus on Exceptional Children, 31*(6), 1–24.

Lewis, T. J., Sugai, G., & Colvin, G. (1998). Reducing problem behavior through a school-wide system of effective behavioral support: Investigation of a school-wide social skills training program and contextual interventions. *School Psychology Review, 27*(3), 446–459.

Liaupsin, C. J., Ferro, J. B., Umbreit, J., Urso, A, Upreti, G. (2006). Improving academic engagement through systematic, function-based intervention. *Education and Treatment of Children, 29*, 573–591

Loeber, R., Burke, J. D., Lahey, B.B., Winters, A., & Zera, M. (2000). Oppositional defiant and conduct disorder: A review of the past 10 years, Part I. *Journal of the American Academy of Child & Adolescent Psychiatry, 39*, 1468–1484.

Loney, J., & Milich, R. (1982). Hyperactivity, inattention, and aggression in clinical practice. In M. Wolraich & D. Routh (Eds.), *Advances in development and behavioral pediatrics* (Vol. 3, pp. 113–147). Greenwich, CT: JAI Press.

Luiselli, J. K., Putman, R. F., & Sunderland, M. (2002). Longitudinal evaluation of behavior support intervention in a public middle school. *Journal of Positive Behavior Interventions, 4*(3), 182–188.

Lumley, V., McNeil, C., Herschell, A., & Bahl, A. (2002). An examination of gender differences among young children with disruptive behavior disorders. *Child Study Journal, 32*(2), 89.

Lynam, D. R. (1998). Early identification of the fledgling psychopath: Locating the psychopathic child in the current nomenclature. *Journal of Abnormal Psychology, 107*, 566–575.

March, R. E., Horner, R. H., Lewis-Palmer, T., Brown, D., Crone, D. A., Todd, A. W., & Carr, E. G. (2000). *Functional assessment checklist for teachers and staff (FACTS).* Eugene: University of Oregon.

Marston, D., Muyskens, P., Lau, M., & Canter, A. (2003). Problem-solving model for decision-makng with high-incidence disabilities: The Minneapolis experience. *Learning Disabilities Research and Practice, 18,* 187–200.

Mayer, G. R. (1995). Preventing antisocial behavior in the schools. *Journal of Applied Behavior Analysis, 28*(4), 467–478.

McIntosh, K., Horner, R. H., & Chard, D. (2006). The use of reading and behavior screening measures to predict nonresponse to school-wide positive behavior support: A longitudinal analysis. *The School Psychology Review, 35*(2), 275–291.

McLeskey, J., Henry, D., & Hodges, D. (1999). Inclusion: What progress is being made across disability categories? *Teaching Exceptional Children, 31,* 60–64.

Merrell, K. W., & Walker, H. M. (2004). Deconstructing a definition: Social maladjustment versus emotional distrubance and moving the field forward. *Psychology in the Schools, 41*(8), 899–910.

Mooney, P., Ryan, J. B., Uhing, B. M., Reid, R., & Epstein, M. H. (2005). A review of self-management interventions targeting academic outcomes for students with emotional and behavioral disorders. *Journal of Behavioral Education, 14*(3), 203–221.

Nelson, J. R., Benner, G. J., & Cheney, D. (2005). An investigation of the language skills of students with emotional disturbance served in public school settings. *The Journal of Special Education, 39,* 97–105.

Nelson, J. R., Colvin, G., & Smith , D. J. (1996). The effects of setting clear standards on students' social behavior in common areas of the school. *The Journal of At-Risk Issues, Summer/Fall,* 10–17.

Nelson, J. R., Martella, R. M., & Marchand-Martella, N. (2002). Maximizing student learning: The effects of a comprehensive school-based program for preventing problem behaviors. *Journal of Emotional and Behavioral Disorders, 10*(3), 136–148.

Nelson, J. R., Martella, R., & Galand, B. (1998). The effects of teaching school expectations and establishing a consistent consequence on formal office disciplinary actions. *Journal of Emotional and Behavioral Disorders, 6*(3), 153–161.

Nowacek, E. J., McKinney, J. D., & Hallahan, D. P. (1990). Instructional behaviors of more and less effective beginning regular and special educators. *Exceptional Children, 57,* 140–149.

O'Conner, E., A., & Simic, O. (2002). The effect of Reading Recovery on special education referrals and placements. *Psychology in the Schools, 39*(6), 635–646.

O'Neill, R., Horner, R., Albin, R., Storey, K., & Sprauge, J. (1996). *Functional assessment and program development for problem behavior: A practical handbook.* Belmont, CA: Wadsworth.

Petersen, G.J., Pietrzak, D., & Speaker, K.M. (1998). The enemy within: A national study on school violence and prevention. *Urban Education, 33,* 331–359.

Peterson, L. D., Young, K. R., Salzberg, C. L., West, R. P., & Hill, M. (2006). Using self management procedures to improve classroom social skills in multiple general education settings. *Education and Treatment of Children, 29*(1), 1–21.

Post, C. H., (1981). The link between learning disabilities and juvenile delinquency: Cause, effect, and "present solutions." *Juvenile and Family Court Journal, 32,* 58–68.

Quinn, M. M., Rutherford, R. B., Leone, P. E., Osher, D. M., & Poirier, J. M. (2005). Youth with disabilities in juvenile corrections: A national survey. *Exceptional Children, 71,* 339–345.

Rosenshine B., & Berliner, D. C. (1978). Academic engaged time. *British Journal of Teacher Education, 4,* 3–16.

Safran, S., & Safran, J. (1988). Perceptions of problem behaviors: A review and analysis of research. In R. B. Rutherford, C. M. Nelson, & S. R. Forness (Eds.), *Bases of severe behavioral disorders in children and youth* (pp. 39–50). Boston: College-Hill.

Sawka, K., McCurdy, B., & Mannella, M. (2002). Strengthening emotional support services: An empirically based model for training teachers of students with behavior disorders. *Journal of Emotional and Behavioral Disorders, 10,* 223–232.

Scheckner, S., Rollins, S.A., Kaiser-Ulrey, C., & Wagner, R. (2002). School violence in children and adolescents: A meta-analysis of effectiveness. *Journal of School Violence, 1*, 5–34.

Schumaker, M., & Kurz, G. A. (2000). *The 8% solution; Preventing serious, repeat juvenile crime*. Thousand Oaks, CA: Sage.

Scott, T. M. (2001). Positive behavioral support: A school-wide example. *Journal of Positive Behavioral Interventions, 3*, 88–94.

Scott, T. M., & Barrett, S. B. (2004). Using staff and student time engaged in disciplinary procedures to evaluate the impact of school-wide PBS. *Journal of Positive Behavior Interventions, 6*(1), 21–28.

Scott, T. M., & Eber, L. (2003). Functional assessment and wraparound as systemic school processes: Primary, secondary, and tertiary systems examples. *Journal of Positive Behavior Interventions, 5*(3), 131–143.

Scott, T. M., Nelson, C. M., & Liaupsin, C. (2001). Effective instruction: The forgotten component in preventing school violence. *Education and Treatment of Children, 24*, 309–322.

Sugai, G. M., & Horner, R. H. (1999). Discipline and behavioral support: Preferred processes and practices. *Effective School Practices, 17*, 10–22.

Shores, R. E., Jack, S. L., Gunter, P. L., Ellis, D. N., DeBriere, T. J., & Wehby, J. H. (1993). Classroom interactions of children with behavior disorders. *Journal of Emotional and Behavioral Disorders, 1*, 27–39.

Skiba, R., Peterson, R., & Williams, T. (1997). Office referrals and suspension: Disciplinary intervention. *Education & Treatment of Children, 20*(3), 295–316.

Snyder, H. (2001). Epidemiology of official offending. In L. Loeber & D. P. Farrington (Eds.), *Child Delinquents: Development, intervention, and service needs* (pp. 25–46). Thousand Oaks, CA: Sage.

Sprague, J., & Walker, H. (2000). Early identification and intervention for youth with antisocial and violent behavior. *Exceptional Children, 66*, 367–379.

Sprick, R., Sprick, M., & Garrison, M. (1992). *Foundations: Developing positive school-wide discipline policies*. Longmont, CO: Sopris West.

Sugai, G., Horner, R.H., Dunlap, G., Hieneman, M., Lewis, T. J., Nelson, C.M., et al. (2000). Applying positive behavioral support and functional assessment in schools. *Journal of Positive Behavioral Interventions, 2*, 131–143.

Sugai, G., Sprague, J., Horner, R., & Walker, H. (2000). Preventing school violence: The use of office discipline referrals to assess and monitor school-wide discipline interventions. *Journal of Emotional & Behavioral Disorders, 8*, 94–101.

Taylor, T., & Biglan, A. (1998). Behavioral family interventions for improving child rearing: A review. *Clinical Child and Family Psychology Review, 1*(1), 41–60.

Taylor-Greene, S., Brown, D., Nelson, L., Longton, J., Gassman, T., Cohen, J., et al. (1997). School-wide behavioral support: Starting the year off right. *Journal of Behavioral Education, 7*, 99–112.

Tobin, T. J., & Sugai, G. M. (1999). Discipline problems, placements, and outcomes for students with serious emotional disturbance. *Behavioral Disorders, 24*(2), 109–121.

U.S. Department of Education. (2004). *Twenty-sixth annual report to congress on the implementation of IDEA: The individuals with disabilities education act*. Washington, D.C.

U.S. Office of Education. (1976). Education of handicapped children. *Federal Register, 41*, 52405.

U.S. Departments of Education and Justice. (2005). *Indicators of school crime and safety, 2005*. (NCES 2006001). Washington, D.C.

Umbreit, J., Ferro, J., Liaupsin, C., & Lane, K. (2007). *Functional behavioral assessment and function-based interventions: An effective, practical approach*. Upper Saddle River, NJ: Prentice-Hall

Walker, B., Ramsey, E., Gresham, F. (2004). *Antisocial behavior in school: Evidence-based practices*. Belmont, CA: Wadsworth/Thompson Learning.

Walker, H. M., Colvin, G., & Ramsey, E. (1995). *Antisocial behavior in school: Strategies and best practices*. Pacific Grove, CA: Brooks/Cole.

Walker, H. M., Golly, A., McLane, J. Z., & Kimmich, M. (2005). The Oregon first step to success replication initiative: Statewide results of an evaluation of the program's impact *Journal of Emotional & Behavioral Disorders, 13*(3), 163–172.

Walter, H. J., Gouze, K., & Lim, K. (2006). Teacher's beliefs about mental health needs in inner city elementary schools. *Journal of the American Academy of Child & Adolescent Psychiatry, 45*(1), 61–68.

# 5

# Fears and Related Anxieties[1]

## Gretchen Schoenfield and Richard J. Morris

Anxiety disorders are one of the most common types of behavior disorders in children and adolescents, with estimates ranging from 6% to 18% of the population (Costello, Egger, & Angold, 2004). Childhood anxiety disorders are associated with an elevated risk for anxiety, depression, substance abuse, and social dysfunction in adulthood (Liebowitz, Gorman, Fyer, & Klein, 1985; Wittchen, Stein, & Kessler, 1999). Anxiety disorders in children[2] can also lead to significant distress in daily functioning, resulting in considerable difficulty both academically and socially (Last, Hanson, & Franco, 1997; McGee & Stanton, 1990). For example, children with social anxiety disorder or separation anxiety may risk avoiding social interaction, attending school, and may ultimately be at risk for school failure (Albano, Marten, Holt, Heimberg, & Barlow, 1995; Beidel, Turner, & Morris, 1999). Given the challenges youth with fears and related anxieties experience during their school-age years, as well as the potentially negative consequences of such difficulties, there is a need for the development and implementation of effective interventions within multiple contexts, including school settings.

In this chapter, we discuss the major evidence-based psychosocial intervention approaches for reducing fears and related anxieties in children. In addition, we briefly review medications that have been frequently used to manage anxiety symptoms, and provide an overview of the emerging area of anxiety prevention.

## HISTORICAL PERSPECTIVES

There is a long tradition of interest in the study of childhood fears and related anxieties, dating back to the late 1890s and early 1900s (e.g., Freud, 1909; Hall, 1897; Jersild & Holmes, 1935; Jones, 1924; Jones & Jones, 1928; King, Hamilton, & Ollendick, 1988; Lapouse & Monk, 1959; Morris & Kratochwill, 1983; Winker, 1949). For example, most contemporary treatment approaches for reducing fears and related anxieties have their roots in the writings of early theorists in the areas of learning theory and behavioral psychology, such as Ivan Pavlov (1927), Edward Thorndike (1898, 1913), John B. Watson (1913, 1919), B.F. Skinner (1938, 1953), O. Hobart Mowrer (1939), and Clark Hull (1943). Though they differed in their respective approaches, each of these theorists sought to demonstrate and/or explain the process by which learning occurred and how a stimulus became connected to a particular behavior such as a fear or anxiety response.

Over time, researchers began to focus on the contribution of modeling or observational learning to the acquisition of fear responses (e.g., Bandura, 1969), as well as underlying cognitive factors (e.g., Beck, 1967; Ellis, 1962, 1973; Kendall, 1994; Meichenbaum, 1971). Information processing theories further influenced our understanding of the etiology of fears and related anxieties (e.g., Foa & Kozak, 1986; Lang, 1977). Each of these theories, as well as the psychoanalytic theory of Sigmund Freud (e.g., Freud, 1909), the individual psychology of Alfred Adler (e.g., Adler, 1964; Dreikurs & Soltz, 1964), and the phenomenological theory of Carl Rogers (e.g., Rogers, 1951, 1959), contributed substantially over the past 50 to 75 years to the development of various therapeutic approaches to treat such fears and related anxieties (e.g., Morris & Kratochwill, 1983).

More recently, however, interest in treating such behavior difficulties has shifted toward an emphasis on evidence-based interventions and prevention (or early intervention) programs. This emphasis has led researchers to begin to evaluate treatment programs using methodologically rigorous criteria (see, for example, Weisz, Hawley, & Doss, 2004 for a review). Such evidence-based intervention studies also strive to provide practitioners with treatment manuals and protocols that can be used in a variety of settings—such as the school setting—to reduce the frequency and severity of children's fears and related anxieties.

The recent emphasis on prevention and early intervention of fears and anxiety reflects a growing body of research on risk factors for developing fears and related anxieties, developmental trajectories, and treatment efficacy. Researchers suggest that addressing suspected symptoms of anxiety prior to onset of a clinical diagnosis may be a critical component to prevention of fears and anxiety, as well as comorbid symptoms or disorders (Kendall & Kessler, 2002).

## CHARACTERISTICS OF CHILDHOOD FEARS AND RELATED ANXIETIES

Most fears and related anxieties in childhood are an adaptive and integral part of normal development, are typically transitory in nature, and rarely interfere with a child's or adolescent's everyday functioning in or outside of school. However, some fears and anxieties persist over time, are out of proportion to the demands of the particular setting(s) in which they occur, and negatively impact the child's or adolescent's daily functioning (Marks, 1969; Morris & Kratochwill, 1983). It is important for school personnel such as school psychologists, social workers, counselors, and teachers to be able to differentiate between such "clinical" fears and anxieties versus "typical" or "normal" developmental fears and related anxieties, particularly when considering implementing an intervention program.

In this regard, a student's fears or related anxieties warrant intervention when they affect the person's developmental functioning (Klein & Pine, 2001). Foa, Costello, Franklin, Kagan, Kendall, Klein, et al. (2005) proposed the following heuristics for determining whether fears and related anxieties reach the threshold for them to be considered a "clinical" problem. First, is the child capable of recovering from experiencing the fear or anxiety and can she or he remain asymptomatic in the absence of the anxiety-provoking situation? Second, does the severity of the fear responses or related anxieties negatively impact the child's daily functioning? Last, is the fear or related anxiety developmentally appropriate for the child's or adolescent's age? These questions are consistent with the criteria proposed by Marks (1969) in differentiating a fear from a "clinical fear" or "phobia." Specifically, she stated that a fear becomes a phobia when it:

1. Is out of proportion to demands of the situation.
2. Cannot be explained or reasoned away.
3. Is beyond voluntary control.
4. Leads to avoidance of the feared situation.

Fears and related anxieties that are considered to be clinical in nature (i.e., those that merit professional attention and possible intervention) fall into several diagnostic categories within in the *Diagnostic and Statistical Manual of Mental Disorders* (*DSM-IV-TR*; American Psychiatric Association [APA], 2000). These are described briefly below. See Table 5.1 for common characteristics of children with fears and anxieties.

## Separation Anxiety Disorder

Separation anxiety disorder (SAD) is characterized by excessive anxiety due to separation from the home or from an attachment figure. The anxiety response exceeds what is expected for the child's developmental level, persists for a period of at least four weeks, and causes marked distress

**TABLE 5.1**
**Common Characteristics of Children with Fears and Related Anxieties**

| Anxiety disorder | Characteristics/symptoms |
| --- | --- |
| Panic disorder | Intense fear in the absence of an actual threat, accompanied by at least four of the following symptoms: palpitations, sweating, trembling, shortness of breath, feeling of choking, chest pain, nausea, dizziness or light-headedness, fear of losing control, fear of dying, and/or a burning or itching sensation. |
| Specific phobia | Persistent fear of an identifiable object or situation, typically resulting in one or more of the following anxiety responses: avoidance anticipated harm, feelings of loss of control, or a physiological response to a feared stimulus. Characteristics in young or elementary school-age children may include crying, tantrums, freezing, or clinging behaviors. |
| Social phobia | Fearful or anxious anticipation of being negatively evaluated (such as reading aloud in class, timed tests in school, or performing math problems in front of the class with the teacher watching) resulting in one or more of the following: avoidance of feared situation, headaches or stomach aches; panic attacks, and crying. |
| Generalized anxiety disorder | Excessive anxiety and worry about several events or activities, with at least one of the following symptoms: restlessness, fatigue, difficulty concentrating, irritability, perfectionism, and seeking excessive approval. |
| School refusal | Anxiety and avoidance due to the anticipation of attending school, excessive absences, leaving school early, refusing to attend, and occasionally somatic symptoms. |
| Selective mutism | Failure to speak in school or when in the company of peers, communicating through the use of gestures, head nodding, monosyllables, utterances, or a change in vocal intonation, excessive shyness, fear of embarrassment, withdrawal, clinging, compulsive tendencies, tantrums, and occasionally oppositional behaviors. |
| Separation anxiety | Excessive anxiety due to separation from the home or from an attachment figure, social withdrawal, sadness, apathy, difficulty with concentration. |

*Source*: Adapted from American Psychiatric Association. (2000). *Diagnostic and statistical manual of mental disorders* (4th ed. text revision). Washington, DC: Author.

and disruption to the child's daily functioning (APA, 2000). Children with SAD may exhibit social withdrawal, sadness, and apathy, and may have difficulty with concentration. Onset of SAD may be preschool age and can occur until 18 years of age, though occurrence of the disorder in adolescence is uncommon. Prevalence estimates of SAD are approximately 4.1% in children and young adolescents (Shear, Jin, Muscio, Walters, & Kessler, 2006).

## Selective Mutism

Selective mutism is marked by a failure to speak in specific situations, such as in school or when in the company of peers. Children demonstrating selective mutism must manifest these characteristics for at least one month and such characteristics must be a direct result of the situation in which the child is placed. Once in these situations (such as a school setting), these children often communicate acceptance or rejection of inquiries through the use of gestures, head nodding, monosyllables ("Yes," "No"), utterances ("Uh-Uh"), or a change in vocal intonation. Children with this disorder also may present with excessive shyness, fear of embarrassment, withdrawal, clinging, compulsive tendencies, tantrums, and, in some case, oppositional behaviors. This disorder is also often associated with lower academic performance and impaired social functioning. Onset of selective mutism often occurs before five years of age, although symptoms may not be evident until the child begins school. Prevalence of selective mutism is less than 1% of the school-age population (Bergman, Piacentini, & McCracken, 2002).

## Panic Disorder

A panic attack is characterized by a distinct period of intense fear in the absence of an actual threat, and is accompanied by at least four of the following physiological or cognitive symptoms: palpitations, sweating, trembling, shortness of breath, feeling of choking, chest pain, nausea, dizziness or light-headedness, fear of losing control, fear of dying, and/or a burning or itching sensation with no apparent cause. Panic disorder presents as recurrent panic attacks followed by a period of at least one month of excessive worry about having another panic attack and/or the perceived consequences, or any marked behavioral change following an attack.

Age of onset of panic disorder is typically no earlier than late adolescence. However, it should be noted that panic attacks often occur as a symptom of another anxiety disorder. The distinguishing characteristic of panic disorder versus other anxiety disorders is the unexpected nature and occurrence of the panic attack. The reported prevalence of panic attack ranges from 4% to 10% in clinically referred samples (Alessi & Magen, 1988; Hayward, Killen, Hammer, Litt, Wilson, Simmonds, et al., 1992; Last & Strauss, 1989; Masi, Favilla, Mucci, & Millepiedi, 2000), and approximately 0.6% in school-age children (Whitaker, Johnson, Shaffer, Rapoport, Kalikow, Walsh, et al., 1990).

## Specific Phobia

A specific phobia is a persistent fear of an identifiable object or situation, the exposure to which typically results in an immediate anxiety response. The anxiety response can present as avoidance of the phobic stimulus or a panic attack, and may cause considerable distress and disruption in the individual's daily functioning. In addition, the symptoms must persist for at least six months, and the fear could involve anticipated harm, feelings of loss of control, or a physiological response to a feared stimulus. Moreover, in young or elementary school-age children, the presenting characteristics may include crying, tantrums, freezing, or clinging behaviors. Reported prevalence of specific phobia ranges from 4% to 8.8% (see, for example, Ollendick, King, & Muris, 2002, for a review).

## Social Anxiety Disorder

Social anxiety disorder (or social phobia) is characterized by a persistent fear of embarrassment or being judged/evaluated in social situations or during public performances or recitations (including performances or recitals in a school or classroom setting). In addition, the child must manifest these characteristics for at least six months. The disorder may present as fearful or anxious anticipation of being placed in a setting where the person may be negatively evaluated (such as reading out aloud in class, timed tests in school, or performing math problems in front of the class with the teacher watching) or it may cause the child to avoid the situation entirely (such as in the case of school phobia or school refusal). In each instance, the anxiety response must interfere appreciably with the child's daily routine, functioning, social interactions, and/ or academic functioning. Other symptoms of social anxiety disorder may include headaches or stomach aches, panic attacks, and crying. Prevalence of this disorder among school-age children is estimated to range from 5% to 15% of school-age children (Kashdan & Herbert, 2001).

As mentioned above, social anxiety disorder may be associated in the school setting with a particular academic subject or academic skill, as well as with taking exams or performing in front of a class. For example, research suggests that a link exists between reading performance and socio-emotional difficulties in children, with an estimated 50% of children who experience difficulties in reading also experiencing socio-emotional and related behavioral difficulties (Fergusson & Lynskey, 1997). Anxiety in other aspects of a child's life has also been found to be highly correlated with reading anxiety (Tsovili, 2004). In this regard, until a child has a thorough psychological evaluation, it may be difficult to determine whether the cause of the reading-associated anxiety is learning disability-based or due to other socio-emotional factors in the child's life. On the other hand, with regard to math anxiety, little systematic research has been conducted in this area. Though math-related anxiety may be attributable to a child's learning difficulties, researchers and educators have also speculated that it may also relate to quality of instruction, a student's perception of her or his ability in this area, and/or parental and teacher attitudes towards the child (e.g., Wigfield & Meece, 1988).

In terms of writing anxiety, there is also a paucity of research in this area. The research that does exist suggests that writing anxiety may be attributable to a lack of practice and exposure to skill-building (Pajares & Viliante, 1997). Children experiencing writing anxiety may also be those who procrastinate, feel apprehension, tension, or suffer from low self-esteem and poor motivation (Shweiker-Marra & Marra, 2000). Test (or examination) anxiety is characterized by feelings of tension and apprehension, worrisome thoughts, or autonomic nervous system responses due to an evaluation of academic performance (Spielberger, 1995). Children with test anxiety often have difficulty thinking clearly, understanding questions while taking an exam, or organizing thoughts even when the person has spent considerable time preparing for the test (Goonan, 2003). Reported prevalence of test anxiety is variable, ranging from 5% to 41% of all school-age children (e.g., Ball, 1995; Beidel, 1991; Turner, Beidel, Hughes, & Turner, 1993).

## Generalized Anxiety Disorder

Generalized anxiety disorder (GAD) is excessive anxiety and worry about several events or activities, occurring more days than not for at least six months. In children, the anxious response is usually associated with at least one additional symptom such as restlessness, being easily fatigued, difficulty with concentration, irritability, and disturbed sleep patterns. The anxious response is difficult to control and usually leads to impairment in daily functioning. The child may be perfectionistic, uncertain of him- or herself, and may seek excessive approval about performance. Prevalence of GAD in school-age children is an approximately 2%–4% (Anderson, Williams, McGee, & Silva, 1987; Bowen, Offord, & Boyle, 1990).

## School Refusal

Children with school refusal (or school phobia) exhibit anxiety and avoidance due to the anticipation of attending school, and often experience somatic symptoms. The child may have excessive absences, frequently ask to leave school early, or simply refuse to attend (Kearney & Silverman, 1996). School refusal is not conceptualized as a distinct anxiety disorder, but rather a set of symptoms with variable underlying causes. Separation anxiety is a common source of school refusal in children, particularly in younger children, whereas social anxiety is a common source of school refusal for older children. Specific phobias are also potential causes of school refusal. School refusal can also occur due to conditions such as learning difficulties, bullying, or family discord (Kearney & Albano, 2004).

School refusal exists in approximately 1%–5% of all school-age children, occurring with equal frequency in males and females (Kearney & Roblek, 1998). School refusal can occur at any point throughout the school years. However, children between the ages of 5 and 6 and 10 and 11 are reportedly at higher risk, which is likely due to initial entry into school and transition from elementary to middle school (King, Heyne, Tonge, Gullone, & Ollendick, 2001).

## ASSESSMENT OF CHILDHOOD FEARS AND RELATED ANXIETIES

A multi-method and multi-informant approach to assessing behavior problems in children is often recommended. Teacher reports in particular are an invaluable source of information, as they provide context-specific examples of a child's behavioral difficulties (e.g., Fisher, Masia-Warner, & Klein, 2004). Although teachers can be a unique source of information on a student's behavioral difficulties throughout the day, research on teachers' awareness of, for example, student levels of anxiety and depression is somewhat limited (e.g., Layne, Bernstein, & March, 2006). Studies have been published evaluating teacher-reports as a source of assessment data, but these have focused primarily on inter-rater reliability between parent and/or child reports and those of teachers. In addition, some writers have suggested that teachers may be less aware of mild and moderate manifestations of children's anxieties that are not typically associated with disruptive classroom behaviors (e.g., Loeber, Green, & Lahey, 1990; Muris & Meester, 2002). On the other hand, one must also question whether teachers should be expected to be aware of (or familiar with) the symptoms of fears and related anxieties, since many teacher education programs provide little exposure to childhood behavior and affective disorders. In this regard, see Table 5.2 for a guide that teachers and other school personnel may use to determine whether a student should be referred for evaluation by a counselor, school psychologist, or other mental health professional.

Several methods are used for identifying children experiencing clinically significant fears and related anxieties within the school or classroom setting. Methods of assessment are ordered along a continuum of directness, with the least direct procedure consisting of a child's verbal recollections of clinically relevant experiences and the most direct consisting of assessment occur-

**TABLE 5.2**
**What Teachers Should Be Looking for in Deciding whether Students Should Be Referred for a Psychological Evaluation Regarding Fears and Related Anxieties**

*The behaviors, thoughts, and feelings associated with children's fears, phobias, and related anxieties typically:*

- are not proportional to situation demands in or outside of the classroom
- cannot be removed or explained on the basis of discussions with the student
- are beyond the student's voluntary control
- lead to avoidance of or escape from the anxiety-provoking situations
- are not age-appropriate
- persist of an extended period of time
- are associated with worry and related feelings whenever the student anticipates being in the anxiety-provoking situation

*Source*: Morris, Kratochwill, Schoenfield, & Auster. (in press). Fears and related anxieties. In R.J. Morris & T. R. Kratochwill (Eds.), *The practice of child therapy*. Mahwah, NJ: Erlbaum.

ring at the time that the fear or related anxiety is taking place. In this regard, interviews with the child and/or her or his parents, as well as questionnaires, are considered to be indirect sources of assessment information, whereas a child's self-monitoring observations during the time that the fear or anxiety response occurs—or the teacher's direct observation when the child's fear or anxiety response take place—is considered to be a direct observation. Physiological responses—such as heart rate and perspiration—at the time of the anxiety or fear response also represent direct assessment measures.

## Behavior Checklists and Rating Scales

Behavior checklists and rating scales offer school personnel with a means of gauging a child's level of subjective stress or anxiety, and can be used as a screening device to determine whether a particular child is at risk. Given that these self-report questionnaires are limited in the breadth and depth of information that they can provide, they are not necessarily suitable as the sole means of establishing a diagnosis for the child. Additionally, most self-report questionnaires cannot provide adequate insight into the degree of functional impairment that an individual may be experiencing (Langley, Bergman, McCracken, & Piacentini, 2004). However, there is considerable utility within a school setting when the goal of an assessment is to implement a school-wide screening procedure for determining which children are at risk for clinically-based fears and related anxieties.

The advantages of self-report checklists and rating scales are that they are relatively low in per-unit cost and are easily administered to large groups. They can be administered without much training in test administration methods, and often include a means by which a child's score can be compared to normative data. In this regard, self-report questionnaires are also useful in distinguishing between normative, developmentally appropriate fears and clinically significant fears and anxieties. Most self-report checklists and rating scales also include versions for parents and teachers.

Examples of self-report instruments that have been empirically validated include the *Screen for Child Anxiety and Related Emotional Disorders* (SCARED; Muris, 1997), *Spence Children's Anxiety Scale* (SCAS; Spence, 1998), and the *Multidimensional Anxiety Scale for Children* (MASC; March, Parker, Sullivan, Stallings, et al., 1997). These assessments identify a range of symptoms and also include components that distinguish between types of anxiety disorders.

## Direct Observation

Direct observation is useful for identifying and quantifying specific behaviors associated with particular fears and related anxieties in school settings (e.g., Johnston & Murray, 2003; Ramirez, Feeney-Kettler, Flores-Torres, Kratochwill, & Morris, 2006). Classroom teachers are directly interacting with their students throughout the day, which provides them with an opportunity to notice behavioral and affective changes over time. However, in some instances, fears and related anxiety-based behaviors may go unnoticed by a teacher, especially when such behaviors do not cause classroom disruption or otherwise draw atypical attention toward a particular child.

## Clinical Interview

Clinical interviews are a means by which more information can be gleaned regarding the nature of a child's fear and related anxieties, as well as pertinent social, medical, familial, and academic history. These interviews are typically conducted by trained mental health professionals who have received extensive training in this method. Interviews often involve not only the child but also his or her parents and siblings and often require considerable time; therefore, this technique may not always be feasible in the school environment.

The questioning format for clinical interviews can be structured, semi-structured, or informal. A commonly used structured interview technique that is based upon *DSM-IV* (APA, 2000) is the *Anxiety Disorders Interview Schedule for Children* (ADIS; Silverman & Albano, 1996). The ADIS includes an interview for children and parents, though little agreement is found between parent and child information on several of the anxiety scales (Rapee, Barrett, Dadds, & Evans, 1994).

## EVIDENCE-BASED PSYCHOSOCIAL INTERVENTIONS

Several evidence-based interventions are frequently used to treat fears and related anxieties in children, most of which have origins in various theories of learning, cognitive theory, and information processing theory (King, Muris, & Ollendick, 2005). These interventions include such behavior therapy approaches as systematic desensitization, modeling, reinforced practice, and cognitive behavioral therapy.

There is some debate in the literature regarding what constitutes "evidenced-based interventions" (EBI; Weisz, Sandler, Durlak, & Anton, 2005), and there has been a substantial effort to define and disseminate information regarding "what works" in child psychotherapy. Though proposed criteria for EBI vary in methodological rigor, the common criteria among them are that the intervention being discussed has demonstrated success in comparison to a control group (Chambless & Ollendick, 2001) and the steps in implementing the intervention have been detailed in a treatment manual. For the purposes of this chapter, we will use the term "evidence-based" to describe those treatments cited in the literature as either "well-established" or "probably efficacious," using the criteria developed by the American Psychological Association's Division 12 Task Force on "Promotion and Dissemination of Psychological Procedures" (Chambless, Baker, Baucom, Beutler, Calhoun, Crits-Cristoph, et al., 1998). As such, we limit our discussion in this chapter to those interventions that have received empirical support using the criteria described in Table 5.3.

## Cognitive Behavioral Therapy

There has been a rapid proliferation of empirical investigation into the effectiveness of cognitive behavioral treatment (CBT) approaches in ameliorating fears and related anxieties in children.

**TABLE 5.3**
**Criteria for Empirically-Validated Treatments**

*Well-established treatments*

I.  At least two good between group design experiments demonstrating efficacy in one or more of the following ways:
    A.  Superior (statistically significantly so) to pill or psychological placebo or to another treatment.
    B.  Equivalent to an already established treatment in experiments with adequate sample sizes.
Or
II.  A large series of single case design experiments (n > 9) demonstrating efficacy. These experiments must have:
    A.  Used good experimental designs and
    B.  Compared the intervention to another treatment as in I(A).

**Further criteria for both I and II:**
III.  Experiments must be conducted with treatment manuals.
IV.  Characteristics of the client samples must be clearly specified.
V.  Effects must have been demonstrated by at least two different investigators or investigating teams.

*Probably efficacious treatments*

I.  Two experiments showing the treatment is superior (statistically significantly so) to a waiting-list control group.
Or
II.  One or more experiments meeting the Well-Established Treatment Criteria IA or IB, III, and IV, but not V.
Or
III.  A small series of single case design experiments (n >3) otherwise meeting Well-Established Treatment

*Source*: Update on empirically validated therapies: II, by D. L. Chambless, M. J. Baker, D. H. Baucom, L. E. Beutler, K. S. Calhoun, P. Crits-Christoph et al., 1998, *The Clinical Psychologist, 51*, p. 4.

CBT approaches combine several components of behavior therapy and ultimately seek to manage anxiety symptoms through the cognitive channel. CBT approaches, therefore, emphasize the role of cognitions in the development of fears and anxieties with the goal of replacing these cognitions with more adaptive and realistic cognitions about those settings or situations that contribute to the fear or anxiety response. One intervention that has received considerable empirical support is the *Coping Cat* program (Kendall, 2000). This approach is considered to be a "probably efficacious" intervention for treating SAD as well as over-anxious disorder and social phobia. The *Coping Cat* program has gained empirical support for a wide age range, and can be adapted to group settings and to various cultures (e.g., Albano & Kendall, 2002; Kendall, 2000; Kendall, Hudson, Choudhury, Webb, & Pimentel, 2005). A modified version, the *C.A.T. Program* (Kendall, Choudhury, Hudson, & Webb, 2002), is an empirically supported treatment program for adolescents.

*Coping Cat* consists of 16 structured sessions that occur weekly, each lasting approximately 60 minutes The first eight sessions are devoted to education, during which the child is taught to recognize his or her own symptoms of anxiety, to engage in progressive muscle relaxation, and to identify and modify negative self-talk and cognitions. Through graduated exposure (initially imaginal and eventually *in vivo*), the child habituates to anxiety-provoking situations and learns to employ the newly acquired coping skills. The child is also given homework assignments, role-play exercises, and education regarding his or her subjective experience of anxious symptoms (Kendall et al., 2002; Kendall et al., 2005).

The primary objectives of the *Coping Cat* process are to: (1) recognize fearful/phobic feelings and somatic reactions to fears; (2) identify cognitions in fear-provoking situations; (3) develop a plan to cope with fear-provoking situations; (4) practice the coping plan via behavioral exposure techniques; (5) evaluate performance; and (6) learn self-reinforcement techniques (Kendall et al., 2005). Parental collaboration is instrumental to the treatment, and occurs in various stages of the program. Parents are encouraged to meet with the therapist throughout the program course and are directly involved in extra-session exposure practice.

*Family Anxiety Management (FAM).*    Parental involvement is an important factor in many interventions for fears and related anxieties. Parents are often responsible for implementing procedures outlined by a clinician. Additionally, children may benefit from witnessing parents engaging in adaptive coping styles. One family-based intervention that has received some empirical support is the Family Anxiety Management model (Dadds, Heard, & Rapee, 1992). This approach involves gradual relinquishing of control from clinician to parents and ultimately to the child. Self-control and self-instructional strategies are emphasized with the ultimate goal of teaching the child how to manage his or her fear or related anxiety when faced with the anxiety provoking or fear evoking setting or situation. Contingency management systems are also used to ease the child's exposure to the feared stimuli. The FAM model also addresses parental fears and anxiety, issues within in the family dynamic, as well as parent-child communication and problem-solving skills (Dadds et al., 1992; Ginsburg & Schlossberg, 2002).

There is some empirical support for FAM when used in conjunction with CBT in treating SAD, overanxious disorder, and social phobia in children. For example, Barrett, Dadds, and Rapee (1996) found significant differences between children receiving CBT+FAM treatment and children receiving CBT intervention alone, and a wait list control group. Additionally, Barrett (1998) found that group CBT+FAM was superior at one-year follow-up to group CBT alone, and to the wait list condition. Interestingly, girls were found to be more likely to demonstrate treatment gains than boys. Additionally, the family component did not seem to yield significant treatment gains in adolescents.

## Modeling

Modeling procedures have a long history in the research literature for ameliorating fears and related anxieties in children (e.g., Bandura, 1969; Bandura, Grusec, & Menlove, 1967; Fassler, 1985; Luscre & Center, 1996; Melamed, Hawes, Heiby, & Glick, 1975; Morris & Kratochwill, 1983). Modeling is a process by which an individual learns to adopt a behavior simply by observing another person while she or he engages in that behavior (Bandura, 1969). With regard to fears and anxieties, an intervention using modeling techniques involves the child observing a model engage in the desired non-fearful or anxious behavior within a familiar setting or situation that the child tends to avoid or produces anxiety. A critical component of this procedure is that child observes the model experiencing only neutral or positive consequences as she or he approaches the feared stimulus (Kazdin, 2000). Modeling typically occurs in a series of graduated steps rather than in a single session (Bandura, 1971). Three approaches to modeling have been discussed in the literature: live modeling, symbolic modeling, and participant modeling.

*Live Modeling.*    Live modeling involves a live demonstration of the graduated approach behavior of the model toward the feared or anxiety provoking stimuli. This procedure has received empirical support in treating childhood fears and related anxieties and is considered to be "probably efficacious" in the treatment of specific phobias (Chambless & Ollendick, 2001). Murphy and Bootzin (1973) investigated the effectiveness of live modeling in treating children's fear of snakes. White and Davis (1974) studied the relative effectiveness of live modeling, observation/exposure only, and a no-treatment control condition on the avoidance of dental treatment in girls ranging from 4 to 8 years of age. Treatment gains were found in both the live modeling condition and the exposure-only condition.

*Symbolic Modeling.*    Symbolic modeling differs from live modeling in that the modeling procedure is presented through film, videotape, DVD, or the person's own imagination. This procedure has received empirical support and is considered to be "probably efficacious" in treating specific phobias in childhood. Bandura and Menlove (1968) demonstrated the effectiveness of filmed modeling in treating fear of dogs in children between the ages of 3 and 5. In one condition, children observed a single model approaching a dog with increasing degrees of contact throughout several film sequences. A second condition presented several models interacting with many dogs of various sizes. Results suggested that children in both filmed modeling conditions demonstrated treatment gains superior to the control group, which consisted of children watching movies that did not depict models interacting with dogs. No significant differences existed between the two filmed treatment groups initially, but significant treatment gains were found in the multiple model condition at follow-up.

Symbolic modeling has also been used to address anxiety in children prior to undergoing elective surgical procedures (Melamed & Siegel, 1980). Children between 4 and 12 years of age were either assigned to a condition in which they viewed a film about a child who underwent a surgical procedure with no negative consequences or a control group. Children in the control group watched a film about a child taking a nature walk. Children in the experimental group exhibited significantly less situational anxiety compared to children in the control condition. Additionally, treatment gains were maintained at follow-up.

*Participant Modeling.*    In participant modeling, a child approaches the feared stimulus in a series of graduated steps, with each step first being performed by the model (typically, a peer) followed by the child performing the step. Participant modeling has received a great deal of empirical support and is considered to be a "well-established" approach to treating specific phobias in children. One example is an early study by Ritter (1968) examining the relative effectiveness of participant modeling to live modeling and a to an active treatment control group. Children in the participant modeling condition observed and then followed the model while he or she safely approached the harmless snake in a series of graduated steps. The live modeling group observed while a model safely approached the snake. Results of the study suggested that both treatment conditions were more effective in reducing avoidance behavior than a wait-list control group. However, further analysis of the data revealed that significantly more children in the participant modeling group successfully completed the behavior avoidance test than did those in the live modeling group.

## Reinforced Practice

Positive reinforcement is typically defined as an event or activity that immediately follows a behavior and results in an increase in the frequency of performance of that behavior. Thus, a positive reinforcer is something that follows a particular behavior and strengthens the number of times that behavior occurs (Morris, 1985). A reinforcer in the context of therapeutic intervention for fears and anxiety may be applied as the child practices approaching the feared stimulus in a series of graduated steps. The reinforcer is then faded and eventually withdrawn once the child has reached a point at which he or she can successfully approach the stimulus without the fear response. This particular method is considered to be "well-established" in treating childhood phobias (e.g., Chambless & Ollendick, 2001; King et al., 2005; Ollendick & King, 1998; see also, special section of *Journal of Clinical Child Psychology*, 1998).

Reinforced practice has also been found to be superior to verbal coping skills training in treating the fear of darkness in children (Leitenberg & Callahan, 1973; Sheslow, Bondy, & Nelson,

1983), and has been successfully applied within school settings to treat school refusal (Trueman, 1984; Vaal, 1973). Additionally, Menzies and Clark (1993) found that reinforced practice produced superior treatment gains when compared to a modeling approach in reducing water phobia in children between 3 and 8 years of age.

## Systematic Desensitization

Systematic desensitization, developed in the early 1950s by Joseph Wolpe, is a frequently used procedure for reducing specific fears and phobias (e.g., King et al., 2005; Labellarte, Ginsburg, Walkup, & Riddle, 1999; Morris & Kratochwill, 1983). The desensitization process involves decreasing the association between fear or anxiety provoking stimuli and the avoidance or escape responses by having the child engage in activities that are antagonistic to this response.

Relaxation training is the first step in the desensitization procedure. An adaptation of the deep muscle relaxation technique developed by Jacobson (1929, 1938, 1977) is used and is presented in Table 5.4. These relaxation skills will ultimately assist the child in coping with anxiety responses associated with exposure to the feared stimuli.

Construction of the anxiety hierarchy is the second step in the desensitization procedure and entails identifying situations or settings that are associated with the fearful response, and rank ordering them from least to most anxiety provoking. The child and therapist (as well as parents, in many cases) work together to construct and refine the anxiety hierarchy, which typically consists of 20–25 items.

Once the anxiety hierarchy has been finalized, the next phase of the desensitization process begins. In this phase, the child uses the newly acquired relaxation skills to cope with the feelings of anxiety and tension that he or she experiences as the therapist gradually presents each hierarchy scene for the child to imagine. Once the child has successfully moved through steps of the anxiety hierarchy, he or she will be encouraged to approach the feared stimulus in real life, with the aid of a therapist and/or parent. Systematic desensitization has a long history in successfully treating specific fears in children and is regarded as being "probably efficacious." Though several studies have reported its effectiveness (e.g., Bentler, 1962; Obler & Terwilliger, 1970; Barrios & O'Dell, 1989; Graziano, DiGiovanni, & Garcia, 1979; see also Morris & Kratochwill, 1983; Morris, Kratochwill, Schoenfield, & Auster, in press), there is little support for its efficacy relative to other treatment modalities. In addition, since this intervention requires that the child be able to visually imagine each item on the hierarchy, it is recommended that prior to initiating this intervention the therapist should be certain that the child has the ability to visually imagine each scene in a vivid manner.

In addition to the procedures discussed in the above section, teachers can implement the methods presented in Table 5.6. It is recommended, however, that these methods only be used in consultation with a school psychologist, counselor, or other mental health professional.

## PHARMACOLOGICAL INTERVENTIONS

Children are being prescribed psychotropic medications at an increasing rate in the United States today compared to 5 to 10 years ago (Carlson, Demaray, & Hunter-Oehmke, 2006). Many of these medications have been found to be effective in reducing the severity of various childhood emotional and behavior disorders. With respect to children's fears and related anxieties, several psychotropic medications have been found to be clinically useful in reducing the frequency and intensity of the behaviors, cognitions and/or physiologic responsivity associated with this

**TABLE 5.4**
**Relaxation Protocol**

*Steps in Relaxation*

1. Take a deep breath and hold it (for about 10 seconds). Hold it. Okay, let it out.
2. Raise both of your hands about halfway above the couch (or arms of the chair) and breathe normally. Now drop your hands to the couch (or arm).
3. Now hold your arms out and make a tight fist. Really tight. Feel the tension in your hands. I am going to count to three and when I say "three" I want you to drop your hands. One...two...three.
4. Raise your arms again and bend your fingers back the other way (toward your body). Now drop your hands and relax.
5. Raise your arms. Now drop them and relax.
6. Now raise your arms again, but this time "flap" your hands around. Okay, relax again.
7. Raise your arms again. Now relax.
8. Raise your arms above the couch (chair) again and tense your biceps. Breathe normally and keep your hands loose. Relax your hands. (Notice how you have a warm feeling of relaxation.)
9. Now hold your arms out to your side and tense your triceps. Make sure that you breathe normally. Relax your arms.
10. Now arch your shoulders back. Hold it. Make sure that your arms are relaxed. Now relax.
11. Hunch your shoulders forward. Hold it and make sure that you breathe normally and keep your arms relaxed. Okay, relax. (Notice the feeling of relief from tensing and relaxing your muscles.)
12. Now turn your head to the right and tense your neck. Relax and bring your head back into in its natural position. Turn your head to the left and tense your neck. Relax and bring your head back again to its normal position.
13. Turn your head to the left and tense your neck. Relax and bring your head back again to its natural position.
14. Now bend your head back slightly toward the chair. Hold it. Okay, now bring your head back slowly to its natural position.*
15. This time bring your head down almost to your chest. Hold it. Now relax and let your head come back to its natural resting position.
16. Now open your mouth as much as possible. A little wider, okay, relax (mouth should be partly open afterwards).
17. Now tense your lips by closing your mouth. Okay, relax.
18. Now put your tongue at the roof of your mouth. Press hard. (Pause.) Relax and allow your tongue to come to a comfortable position in your mouth.
19. Now put your tongue at the bottom of your mouth. Press down hard. Relax and let your tongue come to a comfortable position in your mouth.
20. Now just lie (sit) there and relax. Try not to think of anything.
21. To control self-verbalizations, I want you to go through the motions of singing a high note-not aloud. Okay, start singing to yourself. Hold that note. Okay, relax. (You are becoming more and more relaxed.)
22. Now sing a medium tone and make your vocal cords tense again. Relax.
23. Now sing a low note and make your vocal cords tense again. Relax. (Your vocal apparatus should be relaxed now. Relax your mouth.)
24. Now close your eyes. Squeeze them tight and breathe naturally. Notice the tension. Now relax. Notice how the pain goes away when you relax.
25. Now let your eyes relax and keep your mouth open slightly.
26. Open your eyes as much as possible. Hold it. Now relax your eyes.
27. Now wrinkle your forehead as much as possible. Hold it. Okay, relax.
28. Now take a deep breath and hold it. Relax.
29. Now exhale. Breathe all the air out...all of it out. Relax. (Notice the wondrous feeling of breathing again.)
30. Imagine that there are weights pulling on all your muscles making them flaccid and relaxed...putting your arms and body down into the couch.
31. Pull your stomach muscles together. Tighter. Okay, relax.
32. Now extend your muscles as if you were a prizefighter. Make your stomach hard. Relax. (You are becoming more and more relaxed.)
33. Now tense your buttocks. Tighter. Hold it. Now relax.
34. Now search the upper part of your body and relax any part that is tense. First the facial muscles. (Pause 3 to 5 sec.) Then the vocal muscles. (Pause 3 to 5 sec.) The neck region. (Pause 3 to 5 sec.) Your shoulders...relax any part that is tense. (Pause.) Now the arms and fingers. Relax these. Becoming very relaxed.

*(continued)*

TABLE 5.4
(Continued)

*Steps in Relaxation*

35. Maintaining this relaxation, raise both your legs (about a 45% angle). Now relax. Notice how this further relaxes you.
36. Now bend your feet back so that your toes point toward your face. Relax your mouth. Bend them hard. Relax.
37. Bend your feet the other way...away from your body. Not far. Notice the tension. Okay, relax.
38. Relax. (Pause.) Now curl your toes together as hard as you can. Tighter. Okay, relax. (Quiet- silence for about 30 seconds.)
39. This completes the formal relaxation procedure. Now explore your body from your feet up. Make sure that every muscle is relaxed. Say slowly-first your toes, your feet, your legs, buttocks, stomach, shoulders, neck, eyes, and finally your forehead-you should be relaxed now. (Quiet-silence for about 10 seconds.) Just lie there and feel very relaxed, noticing the warmness of the relaxation. (Pause.) I would like you to stay this way for about 1 minute, and then I am going to count to five. When I reach five, I want you to open your eyes feeling very calm and refreshed. (Quiet-silence for about 1 minute.) Okay, when I count to five I want you to open your eyes feeling very calm and relaxed.
40. One...feeling very calm; two...very calm, very refreshed; three...very refreshed; four...and five.

*The child or adolescent should not be encouraged to bend his or her neck either all the way back or forward.
*Source:* Adapted in part from Jacobson, 1938, Rimm (1967, personal communication), and Wolpe and Lazarus (1966). From *Treating children's fears and phobias: A behavioral approach* (p. 135) by R. J. Morris and T. R. Kratochwill, 1983, Elmsford, NY: Pergamon Press. Copyright 1983 by Pergamon Press. Reprinted by permission.

behavior problem. In particular, selective serotonin reuptake inhibitors (SSRIs) have been found to have the most empirical support, as well as FDA indications of effectiveness (Walkup, Labellarte, & Ginsburg, 2002). Specifically, there is empirical evidence to support the use of fluoxetine and fluvoxamine for effectively treating children and adolescents with separation anxiety disorder, social anxiety disorder, and generalized anxiety disorder (Birmaher, Axelson, Monk, Kalas, Clark, Ehmann, et al., 2003; Clark, Birmaher, Axelson, Monk, Kalas, Ehmann, et al., 2005; Irons, 2005; RUPP Anxiety Study Group, 2001).

Other classes of medication prescribed to manage anxiety symptoms include: anxiolytics, antidepressants, and major tranquilizers and antipsychotics (Williams & Miller, 2003). Antihistimines, antiepileptics, and β-blockers are also prescribed to treat clinical anxiety in children. Evidence supporting effective use of sertraline in children having generalized anxiety disorder also exists (Compton, Grant, Chrisman, Gammon, Brown, March, et al., 2001). Other antidepressants that may have anxiety reducing effects include the combined norepinephrine-serotonin reuptake inhibitors (NSRIs). Venlaflaxine, in particular, has been investigated in industry-sponsored trials, though the results are currently unpublished (Walkup et al., 2003). The effectiveness of benzodiazepines in treating fears and anxieties has also been investigated, but no demonstrated efficacy and yet been reported. Busiprone is also commonly prescribed for children with fears and related anxieties, though there are currently no no methodologically rigorous trials supporting its efficacy. Table 5.5 presents a list of medications prescribed to treat childhood fears and related anxieties, as well as the most common side effects.

## PREVENTION AND EARLY INTERVENTION APPROACHES

Although several psychosocial and pharmacological interventions have been proposed for reducing children's fears and related anxieties, several researchers have suggested that an alternative intervention approach involving prevention may ultimately prove to be even more effective (e.g., Barrett & Turner, 2001; Hudson, Flannery-Schroeder, & Kendall, 2004). In this regard, anxiety

**TABLE 5.5**
**Medications Commonly Prescribed to Treat Fears and Related Anxieties in Children**

| Generic name (Brand) | Possible side effects |
| --- | --- |
| Clonazapam (Klonopin) | Decreased appetite, nausea, insomnia. |
| Fluoxetine (Prozac) | Mild headaches, restlessness, insomnia, fatigue, nausea, disinhibition, decreased appetite |
| Fluvoxamine (Luvox) | Gastrointestinal symptoms, insomnia, headaches, dizziness, muscle weakness. |
| Paroxetine (Paxil) | Drowsiness, headache, nausea, dizziness, dry mouth |
| Sertraline (Zoloft) | Nausea, diarrhea, insomnia, decreased appetite, drowsiness. |

prevention programs exist along a continuum defined by levels of directness and intended population. For example, Caplan (1964) identified a three-level model, consisting of primary, secondary, and tertiary prevention. Primary prevention is designed to address concerns before symptoms of a disorder actually occur. Secondary prevention refers to interventions addressing symptoms that are identified, yet not considered to be severe. Tertiary prevention focuses on treatment of diagnosed disorders as well as relapse prevention. Due to concerns that the secondary and tertiary levels were more treatment- rather than prevention-oriented, an alternative classification system based on a continuum of risk for developing psychopathology was proposed by Gordon (1987). In this system, prevention approaches are categorized as *universal*, *selective*, and *indicated*. Universal programs target entire populations, irrespective of the presence of risk factors. Selective intervention focuses on individuals of a certain group who are believed to be at higher risk for developing psychopathology. Indicated prevention approaches are designed to address mild symptoms of behavior disorders through early intervention. Candidates for this category of prevention are considered to be at high risk. Gordon's classification system is widely used among experts in the field of prevention (e.g., Craske & Zucker, 2001; Donovan & Spence, 2000) and has been adopted by the Institute of Medicine's Committee on Prevention of Mental Disorders (Mrazek & Haggerty, 1994; Munoz, Mrazek, & Haggerty, 1996). In this regard, Table 5.6 provides a list of suggested possible procedures for reducing students' fears and anxieties in the classroom.

**TABLE 5.6**
**Suggested Procedures for Reducing Student Fears and Related Anxieties in the Classroom**

| Reducing fears and related anxieties in the classroom |
| --- |

- Model appropriate behavior for the student in anxiety-provoking situations and provide positive feedback for student success in coping with anxiety
- Relaxation training
- Make expectations clear
- Wherever possible, emphasize positive written and verbal feedback
- Encourage peer support
- Give the student sequenced activities with graduated difficulty, providing positive feedback at each level.
- When negative feedback on academic performance is necessary, it should be given in a constructive manner on a 1:1 basis. Positive comments should always be included to balance the student's perception of negative comments.
- Give extra time on timed tests when necessary
- When giving examples during instruction, incorporate desirable or familiar content
- When students express negative beliefs or expectations about themselves, teach them to say alternative, positive statements about themselves.
- If a student would feel more comfortable, allow the student to sit among familiar or preferred classmates— assuming that this will not lead to class disruption.
- Have the student practice positive self-talk

With respect to empirical research, limited support exists for universal prevention, mainly because of the difficulties associated with measuring its effectiveness. In addition, among those studies that have examined the effectiveness of universal prevention programs only a few have explicitly included fears or related anxiety symptoms as outcome measures (Hudson et al., 2004). For example, Barrett and Turner (2001) conducted a longitudinal study examining the effectiveness of school-based universal anxiety prevention program in 6th-grade children. The brief CBT-based intervention program, called *Friends for Children* (Barrett, Lowry-Webster, & Holmes, 1998), was implemented by teachers or psychologists in participating schools. The program incorporated relaxation, attentional training, cognitive restructuring, guided exposure, as well as parental and peer support. Results showed that children in the intervention conditions demonstrated significantly less self-reported anxiety symptoms when compared to a control group of children who were engaging in self-monitoring only. Despite some methodological limitations (e.g., use of self-report for measured levels of anxiety and limited sample size to examine variance between children exhibiting at-risk anxiety symptoms at pre-test versus those without symptoms), the study offered encouraging findings.

Lowry-Webster, Barrett, and Dadds (2001) conducted a similar study with children between 10 and 13 years of age. However, results of their study were inconclusive, with significant differences in self-reported anxiety symptoms found only on one of the two dependent measures. Reduced symptoms of anxiety, however, were observed among children in the study regardless of whether they reported high pretreatment levels of anxiety.

Selective prevention programs have the least empirical support. For example, Rapee (2002) evaluated the effectiveness of a selective prevention program in preventing anxiety in children between 3 and 4 years of age. The children were identified as being at-risk for anxiety disorders on the basis of rating scales completed by mothers and through direct observation of behavioral inhibition in a laboratory setting. Children were either assigned to either a treatment condition or a monitoring-only condition. Components of the treatment included education regarding the nature and symptoms of anxiety, modeling adaptive behaviors, parental anxiety management, development and use of anxiety hierarchies, and exposure techniques. Results at 12-month follow-up revealed significant decreases in mothers' reports of behavioral inhibition and decreases in reported anxiety diagnoses when compared to participants in the control condition. However, direct observation data revealed no significant differences between the treatment and the control groups.

Indicated prevention approaches are similar to individually-based treatment methods for treating children's fears and related anxieties, in that they target existing anxiety symptoms.. Support for the effectiveness of these approaches, however, in preventing onset of a clinical disorder is somewhat sparse. For example, Dadds and colleagues (1997, 1999) implemented a modified version of Kendall's *Coping Cat* program (Kendall, 2000) in a study examining the long-term effects of early intervention on children who exhibited anxiety symptoms. Results of the investigation showed significant improvement in parent and teacher-rated anxiety symptoms among the intervention groups when compared to the control condition.

In another study, La Frenière and Capuano (1997) worked with children exhibiting anxiety and withdrawal symptoms, using self-report measures of maternal stress, data on children's anxious or withdrawn symptoms when performing a problem-solving task, and teacher ratings of a children's social competence. Results using the self-reported maternal stress measure and reports of children's anxious and inhibited behaviors suggested that the intervention was successful, although teacher ratings revealed a decrease in social competence among the children in the treatment condition at posttreatment and follow up. Although this study did not specifically examine children's fears and related anxieties, the findings certainly lend justification for further investigation.

## CONCLUSIONS AND DIRECTIONS FOR FUTURE RESEARCH

In this chapter, we have reviewed empirically-supported psychosocial and pharmacologic interventions for reducing fears and related anxieties in children, and reviewed the empirical literature on anxiety prevention. The research literature has shown that those psychosocial intervention programs that are administered on a relatively short term basis are effective in treating children having a variety of fears and related anxieties. Specifically, reinforced practice and participant modeling have garnered the most empirical support in treating specific fears and phobias in children, with systematic desensitization also showing effectiveness in older children. In addition, CBT approaches have demonstrated effectiveness in treating separation anxiety, social phobia, and overanxious disorder. Less empirical information, however, is available on the long-term maintenance of treatment gains or on relapse prevention approaches. Few studies have included sufficient sample sizes of high school, middle school, elementary age, and preschool children to permit adequate comparisons across age categories of the relative effectiveness of these intervention programs. Additionally, the majority treatment effectiveness studies have included participants spanning a wide age range, or have focused exclusively on pre-adolescent children. Few studies have had an adequate samples size of adolescents such that age comparisons could be made.

Indeed, the research agenda for fears and anxiety intervention is quite extensive. More information is also needed concerning the extent to which these interventions can be generalized to the successful treatment of other anxieties that children may experience, such as more cognitively oriented fears as the fear of (or anxiety concerning) loss of control, rejection by peers, or a school shooting or school hostage situation. In addition, research is needed on the extent to which these effective interventions apply equally across gender and racial, cultural or ethnic groups, and on the potential contribution of comorbid behavioral problems—such as depression or ADHD—to the relative effectiveness of these interventions.

Although more research is needed on the treatment of fears and related anxieties in children, the majority of studies in this area have nevertheless demonstrated that the interventions discussed in this chapter are effective when compared at least to no-treatment or wait list control conditions. However, more school-based research is needed to firmly cement the effectiveness of these procedures.

Psychotropic medications are becoming a common approach to treating anxiety symptoms in children, with SSRIs having the most empirical support. Thus far, research suggests that SSRIs have demonstrated success in ameliorating symptoms associated with separation anxiety disorder, social anxiety disorder, and generalized anxiety disorder in particular. However, the effectiveness of SSRIs in treating other types of fears and related anxieties is still unknown. Several other classes of medication are also commonly prescribed to treat anxiety symptoms, though evidence supporting their effectiveness is somewhat sparse. Further investigation is needed to determine their efficacy relative to SSRIs.

With respect to prevention and early intervention programs for children who are at high risk for developing fears and related anxieties, little research literature exists that investigates the efficacy of these programs. For example, universal prevention programs require broad participation among children and families regardless of whether there are concerns on the part of parents (or teachers) about the presence of anxiety and/or fears. Determining effectiveness, therefore, of such prevention programs is difficult, given the myriad variables that cannot be accounted for in such large population research. Selective and indicated prevention programs share the same concern regarding how to recruit high-risk candidates without subjecting them to potential peer rejection, either real or imagined. In addition, all levels of prevention-based programs require longitudinal data to be gathered to assess relative effectiveness over time in preventing the occurrence of fears and related anxieties and to gather information on the characteristics of those who remain diagnosis-free versus those who do not. The programs that have shown some empirical support are quite promising and, if found in future research to be effective, could be readily implemented by school psychologists, counselors, or social workers on a school-wide basis.

## NOTES

1. Preparation of this chapter was supported, in part, by the "Project on Children's Policy Studies and Research" at the University of Arizona (Richard J. Morris, Ph.D., Project Director).
2. The term "children" or "child" will be used throughout this chapter to refer to both children and adolescents. Where it appears appropriate in terms of the research or practice literature, a distinction will be made between children and adolescents.

## REFERENCES

Adler, A. (1964). *Problems of neurosis.* New York: Harper & Row.

Albano, A. M., & Kendall, P. C. (2002). Cognitive behavioral therapy for children and adolescents with anxiety disorders: Clinical research advances. *International Review of Psychiatry, 14,* 129–134.

Albano, A. M., Marten, P. A., Holt, C. S., Heimberg, R. G., & Barlow, D. H. (1995). Cognitive-behavioral group treatment for social phobia in adolescents: A preliminary study. *The Journal of Nervous and Mental Disease, 183,* 649–656.

Alessi, N. E., & Magen, J. (1988). Panic disorders in psychiatrically hospitalized children. *American Journal of Psychiatry, 145,* 1450–1452.

American Psychiatric Association. (2000). *Diagnostic and statistical manual of mental disorders* (4th ed. text revision).Washington, D.C.: Author.

Anderson, J. C., Williams, S., McGee, R., Silva, P. A.(1987). DSM-III disorders in preadolescent children: Prevalence in a large sample from the general population. *Archives of General Psychiatry, 44,* 69–76.

Ball, S. (1995). Anxiety and test performance. In C. D. Spielberger & P. R. Vagg (Eds.), *Test anxiety: Theory, assessment, and treatment* (pp. 3–14). Washington DC: Taylor & Francis.

Bandura, A. (1969). *Principles of behavior modification.* New York: Holt, Rinehart, & Winston.

Bandura, A. (1971). Psychotherapy based upon modeling principles. In A. E. Bergin & S. L. Garfield (Eds.), *Handbook of psychotherapy and behavior change* (pp. 653–708). New York: Wile.

Bandura, A., Grusec, J., & Menlove, F. (1967).Vicarious extinction of avoidance behavior. *Journal of Personality and Social Psychology, 5,* 16–23.

Bandura, A., & Menlove, F. (1968). Factors determining vicarious extinction of avoidance behavior through symbolic modeling. *Journal of Personality and Social Psychology, 8,* 99–108.

Barrett, P. M. (1998). Evaluation of cognitive-behavioral group treatments for childhood anxiety disorders. *Journal of Clinical Child Psychology, 27,* 459–468.

Barrett, P. M., Dadds, M. R., & Rapee, R. M. (1996). Family treatment of childhood anxiety: A controlled trial. *Journal of Consulting and Clinical Psychology, 64,* 333–342.

Barrett, P. M., Lowry-Webster, H. M    , & Holmes, J. M. (1998). *Friends for children group leader manual* (2nd ed.). Brisbane, Australia: Australian Academic Press.

Barrett. P. M., & Turner, C. (2001). Prevention of anxiety symptoms in primary school children: Preliminary results from a universal school-based trial. *British Journal of Clinical Psychology, 40,* 399–410.

Barrios, B., & O'Dell, S. L. (1989). Fears and anxieties. In E. J. Mash & R. A. Barkley (Eds.), *Treatment of childhood disorders* (pp. 167–221). New York: Guilford.

Beck, A. T. (1967). *Cognitive therapy and the emotional disorders.* New York: International Universities Press.

Beidel, D. C. (1991). Social phobia and overanxious disorder in school age children. Journal *of the American Academy of Child and Adolescent Psychiatry, 30*, 545–552.

Beidel, D. C., Turner, S. M., & Morris, T. L. (1999). Psychopathology of childhood social phobia. *Journal of the American Academy of Child and Adolescent Psychiatry, 38*, 643–650.

Birmaher, B., Axelson, D. A., Monk, K., Kalas, C., Clark, D.B., Ehmann, M. et al. (2003). Fluoxetine for the treatment of childhood anxiety disorders. *Journal of the American Academy of Child & Adolescent Psychiatry, 42*, 415–424.

Bentler, P. M. (1962). An infant's phobia treated with reciprocal inhibition therapy. *Journal of Psychology and Psychiatry, 3*, 185–189.

Bergman, R. L., Piacentini, J., & McCracken, J. T. (2002). Prevalence and description of selective mutism in a school-based sample. Journal of the American Academy *Child Adolescent Psychiatry, 41*, 938–946.

Bowen, R. C., Offord, D. R., & Boyle, M. H. (1990). The prevalence of overanxious disorder and separation anxiety disorder: Results from the Ontario Child Health Study. *Journal of the American Academy of Child & Adolescent Psychiatry, 29*, 753–758.

Caplan, G. (1964). *Principles of preventative psychiatry*. New York: Basic Books.

Carlson, J. S., Demaray, M. K., & Hunter-Oehmke, S. (2006). A survey of school psychologists' knowledge and training in child psychopharmacology. *Psychology in the schools, 43*, 623–633.

Chambless, D. L., Baker, M. J., Baucom, D. H., Beutler, L. E., Calhoun, K. S., Crits-Christoph, P., et al. (1998). Update on empirically validated therapies: II. *The Clinical Psychologist, 51*, 3–16.

Chambless, D. L., & Ollendick, T. H. (2001). Empirically supported psychological interventions: Controversies and evidence. *Annual Review of Psychology, 52*, 685–716.

Clark, D. B., Birmaher, B., Axelson, D., Monk, K., Kalas, C., Ehmann, M. et al. (2005) Fluoxetine for the treatment of childhood anxiety disorders: Open-label, long-term extension to a controlled trial. *Journal of the American Academy of Child & Adolescent Psychiatry, 44*, 1263–1270.

Compton S. N., Grant P. J., Chrisman A. K., Gammon, P. J., Brown, V. L., March, J. S. et al. (2001). Sertraline in children and adolescents with social anxiety disorder: An open trial. *Journal of the American Academy of Child & Adolescent Psychiatry, 40*, 564–571.

Costello, E. J., Egger, H., & Angold, A. (2004) 10-year research update review: The epidemiology of child and adolescent psychiatric disorders: I. Methods and public health burden. *Journal of the American Academy of Child & Adolescent Psychiatry, 44*, 972–986.

Craske, M. G., & Zucker, B. G. (2001). Prevention of anxiety disorders: A model for intervention. *Applied and Preventive Psychology, 10*, 155–175.

Dadds, M. R., Heard, P. M., & Rapee, R. M. (1992). The role of family intervention in the treatment of child anxiety disorders: Some preliminary findings. *Behaviour Change, 9*, 171–177.

Dadds, M. H., Holland, D. E., Laurens, K. R., Mullins, M., Barrett, P. M., & Spence, S. H. (1999). Early intervention and prevention of anxiety disorders in children: Results at 2-year follow-up. *Journal of Consulting and Clinical Psychology, 67*, 145–150.

Dadds, M. H., Spence, S. H., Holland, D. E., Barrett, P. M., & Laurens, K. R. (1997). Early intervention and prevention of anxiety disorders: A controlled trial. *Journal of Consulting and Clinical Psychology, 65*, 627–635.

Donovan, C. L., & Spence, S. H. (2000). Prevention of childhood anxiety disorders. *Clinical Psychology Review, 20*, 509–531.

Dreikurs, R., & Soltz, V. (1964). *Children: The challenge*. New York: Hawthorn Books, Inc.

Ellis, A. (1962). *Reason and emotion in psychotherapy*. New York: Lyle Stuart.

Ellis, A. (1973). *Humanistic psychotherapy: The rational-emotive approach*. New York: Julian.

Fassler, D. (1985). The fear of needles in children. *American Journal of Orthopsychiatry, 31*, 371–377.

Fergusson, D. M., & Lynskey, M. T. (1997). Early reading difficulties and later conduct problems. *Journal of Child Psychology and Psychiatry, 39*, 721–730.

Fisher, P. H., Masia-Warner, C., & Klein, R. G. (2004). Skills for social and academic success: A school-based intervention for social anxiety disorder in adolescence. *Clinical Child & Family Psychology Review, 7*, 241–249.

Foa, E. B., Costello, E. J., Franklin, M., Kagan, J., Kendall, Klein, R., et al. (2005). Defining anxiety disorders. In Evans, D. L., Foa, E. B., Gur, R.E., Hendin, H. et al. (Eds.) *Treating and preventing adolescent mental health disorders: What we know and what we don't know* (pp. 162–182). New York: Oxford University Press.

Foa, E. B., & Kozak, M. J. (1986). Emotional processing of fear: Exposure to corrective information. *Psychological Bulletin, 90*, 20–35.

Freud, S. (1909). Analysis of a phobia of a five year old boy. *Standard edition of the complete psychological works of Sigmund Freud (volume 10)* (pp.169–306). London: Hogarth Press.

Ginsburg, G. S., & Schlossberg, M.C. (2002). Family-based treatment of childhood anxiety disorders. *International Review of Psychiatry, 14*, 143–154.

Goonan, B. (2003). Overcoming test anxiety: Giving students the ability to show what they know, In *Measuring up: Assessment issues for teachers, counselors, & administrators* (pp. 257–27). Office of Educational Research and Improvement. Washington DC: U.S. Department of Education.

Gordon, R. (1987). An operational classification of disease prevention. In J. Steinberg & M. Silverman (Eds.), *Preventing mental disorders: A research perspective* (pp. 20–26). Washington, DC: Department of Health and Human Services: National Institute of Mental Health.

Graziano, A. M., DiGiovanni, I. S., & Garcia, K. A. (1979). Behavioral treatments of children's fears: A review. *Psychological Bulletin, 86*, 804–830.

Hall, G. S. (1897). A study of fears. *American Journal of Psychology, 8*, 147–249.

Hayward C., Killen, J. D., Hammer, L .D, Litt, Wilson, D. M., Simmonds, B. et al (1992). Pubertal stage and panic attack history in sixth-and seventh-grade girls. *American Journal of Psychiatry, 149*, 1239–1243.

Hull, C. (1943). *Principles of behavior*. New York: Appleton-Century-Crofts.

Hudson, J. L., Flannery-Schroeder, E., & Kendall, P. C. (2004). Primary prevention of anxiety disorders. In J.A. Dozois & K.S. Dobson (Eds.), *The prevention of anxiety and depression: Theory, research, and practice* (pp. 101–130). Washington, DC: American Psychological Association.

Irons, J. (2005). Fluvoxamine in the treatment of anxiety disorders. *Neuropsychiatric Disease and Treatment, 1*, 289–299.

Jacobson, E. (1929). *Progressive relaxation*. Chicago: Chicago University Press.

Jacobson, E. (1938). *Progressive relaxation* (2nd ed.). Chicago: University of Chicago Press.

Jacobson, E. (1977). The origins and development of progressive relaxation. *Journal of Behavior Therapy and Experimental Psychiatry, 8*, 119–123.

Jersild, A. T., & Holmes, F. B. (1935). Children's fears. *Child Development Monographs, 1935*, No. 20.

Johnston, C., & Murray, C. (2003). Incremental validity in the psychological assessment of children and adolescents. *Psychological Assessment, 15*, 496–507.

Jones, M. C. (1924). A laboratory study of fear: The case of Peter. *Journal of Genetic Psychology, 31*, 308–315.

Jones, H. E., & Jones, M. C. (1928). Fear. *Childhood Education, 5*, 136–145.

Kashdan, T. B., & Herbert, J. D. (2001). Social anxiety disorder in childhood and adolescence: Current status and future directions. *Clinical Child and Family Psychology Review, 4*, 37–62.

Kazdin, A. E. (2000). *Behavior Modification in Applied Settings* (6th ed.). Belmont, CA: Wadsworth.

Kearney, C. A., & Albano, A. M. (2004). The functional profiles of school refusal behavior. *Behavior Modification, 28*, 147–161.

Kearney, C. A. & Roblek, T. L. (1998). Parent training in the treatment of school refusal behavior. In Briesmeister, J. M., & Schaekfer, C. E. (Eds.), *Handbook of parent training: Parents as co-therapists for children's behavior problems* (2nd ed., pp. 225–256). Hoboken, NJ: Wiley.

Kearney C. A., & Silverman, W. K. (1996). The evolution and reconciliation of taxonomic strategies for school refusal behavior. *Clinical Psychology: Science and Practice, 3,* 339–354.

Kendall, P. C. (1994). Treating anxiety disorders in children: Results of a randomized clinical trial. *Journal of Consulting and Clinical Psychology, 62*, 100–110.

Kendall, P. C. (2000). *Cognitive-behavioral therapy for anxious children: Treatment manual* (2nd ed.). Ardmore, PA: Workbook Publishing.

Kendall, P.C., Choudhury, M., Hudson, J., & Webb, A. (2002). *The C.A.T. Project manual for the cognitive behavioral treatment of anxious adolescents*. Ardmore, PA: Workbook Publishing.

Kendall, P. C., Hudson, J. L., Choudhury, M., Webb, A., & Pimentel, S. (2005). Cognitive behavioral treatment for childhood anxiety disorders. In E. D. Hibbs, & P. S. Jensen, (Eds.) *Psychosocial treatments for child and adolescent disorders: Empirically based strategies for clinical practice* (2nd ed.; pp. 47–73). Washington, DC: American Psychological Association.

Kendall, P. C., & Kessler, R. C. (2002). The impact of childhood psychopathology interventions on subsequent substance abuse: Comments and recommendations. *Journal of Consulting and Clinical Psychology, 70,* 1303–1306.

King, N. J., Hamilton, D. I., & Ollendick, T. H. (1988). *Children's phobias: A behavioral perspective.* New York: John Wiley & Sons.

King, N. J., Heyne, D., Tonge, B. J., Gullone, E., & Ollendick, T. H. (2001). School refusal: Categorical diagnoses, functional analysis, and treatment planning. *Clinical Psychology and Psychotherapy, 8,* 352–360.

King, N. J., Muris, P., & Ollendick, T. H. (2005). Childhood fears and phobias: Assessment and treatment. *Child and Adolescent Mental Health, 10,* 50–56.

Klein, R. G., & Pine, D. S. (2001). Anxiety disorders. In M. Rutter, E. Taylor, & M. Hersov (Eds.), *Child and adolescent psychiatry* (3rd ed; pp. 486–509.). New York: Blackwell Scientific.

La Frenière, P. J., & Capuano, F. (1997). Preventive intervention as a means of clarifying direction of effects in socialization: Anxious-withdrawn preschooler's case. *Development and Psychopathology, 9,* 551–564.

Labellarte, M. J., Ginsburg, G.S., Walkup, J. T., & Riddle, M. A. (1999). The treatment of anxiety disorders in children and adolescents. *Biological Psychiatry, 46,* 1567–1578.

Lang, P. J. (1977). Imagery in therapy: An information processing analysis of fear. *Behavior Therapy, 8,* 862–886.

Langley, A. K., Bergman, R. L., McCracken, J., & Piacentini, J. C. (2004). Impairment in childhood anxiety disorders: Preliminary examination of the *Child Anxiety Impact Scale–Parent Version. Journal of Child & Adolescent Psychopharmacology, 14,* 105–114.

Lapouse, R., & Monk, M. A. (1959). Fears and worries in a representative sample of children. *American Journal of Orthopsychiatry, 29,* 803–818.

Last, C. G., Hanson, C., & Franco, N. (1997). Anxious children in adulthood: A prospective study of adjustment. *Journal of the American Academy of Child and Adolescent Psychiatry, 36,* 645–652.

Last, C. G., & Strauss, C. C. (1989). Panic disorder in children and adolescents. *Journal of Anxiety Disorders, 3,* 87–95.

Layne, A. E., Bernstein, G. A., & March, J. S. (2006). Teacher awareness of anxiety symptoms in children. *Child Psychiatry and Human Development, 36,* 383–392.

Leitenberg, H., & Callahan, E. J. (1973). Reinforcement practice and reductions of different kinds of fears in adults and children. *Behaviour Research & Therapy, 11,* 19–30.

Liebowitz, M. R., Gorman, J. M., Fyer, A. J., & Klein, D. F. (1985). Social phobia: Review of a neglected disorder. *Archives of General Psychiatry, 42,* 729–736.

Loeber, R., Green, S.M., & Lahey, B.B. (1990) Mental health professionals' perception of the utility of children, mothers, and teachers as informants on childhood psychopathology. *Journal of Clinical Child Psychology, 19,* 136–143.

Lowry-Webster, H. M., Barrett, P. M., & Dadds, M. R. (2001). A universal prevention trial of anxiety and depressive symptomatology in childhood: Preliminary data from an Australian study. *Behaviour Change, 18,* 36–50.

Luscre, D. M., & Center, D. B. (1996). Procedures for reducing dental fears in children with autism. *Journal of Autism and Developmental Disorders, 26,* 547–558.

McGee, R., & Stanton, W. R. (1990). Parent reports of disability among 13-year-olds with DSM-III disorders. *Journal of Child Psychology and Psychiatry and Allied Disciplines, 31,* 793–801.

March, J. S., Parker, J. D. A., Sullivan, K., Stallings, P. et al. (1997). The *Multidimensional Anxiety Scale for Children (MASC)*: Factor structure, reliability, and validity. *Journal of the American Academy of Child and Adolescent Psychiatry, 36,* 554–565.

Marks, I. M. (1969). *Fears and phobias.* New York: Academic Press.

Masi, G., Favilla, L., Mucci, M., & Millepiedi, S. (2000). Panic disorder in clinically referred children and adolescents. *Child Psychiatry and Human Development, 31*, 139–152.

Meichenbaum, D. (1971). Examination of model characteristics in reducing avoidance behavior. *Journal of Personality and Social Psychology, 17*, 298–307.

Melamed, B. G., & Siegel, L. J. (1980). *Behavior medicine*. New York: Springer.

Melamed, B. G., Hawes, R. R., Heiby, E., & Glick, J. (1975). Use of filmed modeling to reduce uncooperative behavior of children during dental treatment. *Journal of Dental Research, 54*, 797–801.

Menzies, R.G., & Clark, J.C. (1993). The etiology of childhood water phobia. *Behaviour Research & Therapy, 31*, 499–501.

Morris, R. J. (1985). *Behavior modification with exceptional children: Principles and practices*. Glenview, IL: Scott, Foresman & Company.

Morris, R. J., & Kratochwill, T. R. (1983). *Treating children's fears and phobias: A behavioral approach*. Elmsford, NY: Pergamon Press.

Morris, R. J., Kratochwill, T. R. Schoenfield, G., & Auster, E. R. (in press). Childhood fears, phobias, and related anxieties. In R. J. Morris & T. R. Kratochwill (Eds.), *The practice of child therapy* (4th ed.). Mahwah, NJ: Lawrence Erlbaum& Associates.

Mowrer, H. O. (1939). A stimulus-response analysis of anxiety and its role as a reinforcing agent. *Psychological Review, 46*, 553–565.

Mrazek, P. J., & Haggerty, R. J. (1994). *Reducing risks for mental disorders: Frontiers for preventive intervention research*. National Academy of Sciences, Institute of Medicine, Division of Biobehavioral Sciences and Mental Disorders, Committee on Prevention of Mental Health Disorders. Washington, DC: National Academy Press.

Munoz, R. F., Mrazek, P. J., & Haggerty, R. J. (1996). Institute of Medicine report on prevention of mental disorders: Summary and commentary. *American Psychologist, 51*, 1116–1122.

Muris, P. (1997). *The Screen for Child Anxiety Related Emotional Disorders (revised version)*. Maastricht: Maastricht University, Department of Psychology.

Muris, P., & Meester, C. (2002) Symptoms of anxiety disorders and teacher-reported school functioning of normal children. *Psychological Report, 91*, 588–590.

Murphy, C. M., & Bootzin, R. R. (1973). Active and passive participation in the contact desensitization of snake fear in children. *Behavior Therapy, 4*, 203–211.

Obler, M., & Terwilliger, R. F. (1970). Test effectiveness of systematic desensitization with neurologically impaired children with phobic disorders. *Journal of Consulting and Clinical Psychology, 34*, 314–318.

Ollendick, T. H., & King, N. J. (1998). Empirically supported treatments for children with phobic and anxious disorders: Current status. *Journal of Clinical Child Psychology, 27*, 156–167.

Ollendick, T. H., King, N. J., & Muris, P. (2002). Fears and phobias in children: Phenomenology, epidemiology, and aetiology. *Child and Adolescent Mental Health, 7*, 98–106.

Pajares, F., & Viliante, G. (1997). Influences of self-efficacy on elementary student's writing. *Journal of Educational Research, 90*, 353–360.

Pavlov, I. P. (1927). *Conditioned reflexes*. Trans. G. V. Anrep. London: Oxford University Press.

Ramirez, S. Z., Feeney-Kettler, K. A., Flores-Torres, L., Kratochwill, T. R., & Morris, R. J. (2006). Fears and anxiety disorders. In G. G. Bear & K. M Minke (Eds.), *Children's needs III: Development, prevention and intervention* (pp. 267–279). Bethesda, MD: National Association of School Psychologists.

Rapee, R. M. (2002). The development and modification of temperamental risk for anxiety disorders: Prevention of a lifetime of anxiety. *Biological Psychiatry, 52*, 947–957.

Rapee, R. M., Barrett, P. M., Dadds, M. R., & Evans, L. (1994). Reliability of the DSM-III-R childhood anxiety disorders using structured interview: Interrater and parent-child agreement. *Journal of the American Academy of Child & Adolescent Psychiatry, 33*, 984–992.

Ritter, B. (1968). The group desensitization of children's snake phobias using vicarious and contact desensitization procedures. *Behaviour Research & Therapy, 6*, 1–6.

Rogers, C. (1951). Client-centered therapy: Its current practice, implications, and theory. New York: Houghton Mifflin.

Rogers, C. (1959). A theory of therapy and personality change as developed in the client-centered framework. In E. Koch (Ed.), *Psychology: A study of science*. Vol. III. (pp.184–256). New York: McGraw Hill.

Research Units for Pediatric Psychopharmacology (RUPP) Anxiety Study Group. (2001). Fluvoxamine for the treatment of anxiety disorders in children and adolescents. *New England Journal of Medicine, 344*, 1279–1285.

Shear, K., Jin, R., Muscio, A. M., Walters, E. E., & Kessler, R. C. (2006). Prevalence and correlates of estimated DSM-IV child and adult separation anxiety disorder in the *National Comorbidity Survey Replication. American Journal of Psychiatry, 163*, 1074–1083.

Sheslow, D. V., Bondy, A. S., & Nelson, R. O. (1983). A comparison of graduated exposure, verbal coping skills and their combination in the treatment of children's fear of the dark. *Child and Family Behavior Therapy, 4*, 33–45.

Shweiker-Marra, K. E., & Marra, W. T. (2000). Investigating the effects of prewriting activities on writing performance and anxiety of at-risk students. *Reading Psychology, 21*, 99–114.

Silverman, W. K., & Albano, A. M. (1996). *The Anxiety Disorders Interview Schedule for DSM-IV: Child and Parent Versions*. San Antonio, TX: Physiological Corporation.

Skinner, B. F. (1938). *The behavior of organisms*. New York: Appleton-Century.

Skinner, B. F. (1953). *Science and human behavior*. New York: Macmillan.

Spence, S. H. (1998). A measure of anxiety symptoms among children. *Behavior Research and Therapy, 36*, 545–566.

Spielberger, C. D., & Vagg, P. R. (1995).Treatment of test anxiety: Application of the transactional process model. In C. D. Spielberger and P. R. Vagg (Eds.), *Test anxiety: Theory, assessment, and treatment* (pp. 197–212).Washington, DC: Taylor and Francis.

Thorndike, E. L. (1898). Animal intelligence: an experimental study of the associative processes in animals. *Psychological Review Monograph 2* (Suppl. 8).

Thorndike, E. L. (1913). The psychology of learning. *Educational psychology* (Vol. 2). New York: Teachers College Press.

Trueman, D. (1984). What are the characteristics of school phobic children? *Psychological Reports, 5*, 191–202.

Tsovili, T. D. (2004). The relationship between language teachers' attitudes and the state-trait anxiety of adolescents with dyslexia. *Journal of Research in Reading, 27*, 69–86.

Turner, B. G., Beidel, D. C., Hughes, S., & Turner, M. W. (1993). Test anxiety in African American school children. *School Psychology Quarterly, 8*, 140–152.

Vaal, J. J. (1973). Applying contingency contracting to school phobia: A case study. *Journal of Behavior Therapy and Experimental Psychiatry, 4*, 371–373.

Walkup, J. T., Labellelarte, M. J., & Ginsburg, G. S. (2002). The pharmacological treatment of childhood anxiety disorders. *International Review of Psychiatry, 14*, 135–142.

Watson, J. B. (1913). Psychology as the behaviorist views it. *Psychological Review, 20*, 158–177.

Watson, J. B., (1919). *Psychology from the standpoint of a behaviorist*. Philadelphia: Lippincott.

Weisz, J. R., Hawley, A. J., & Doss, K. M. (2004). Empirically tested psychotherapies for youth internalizing and externalizing problems and disorders. *Child and Adolescent Psychiatric Clinics of North America, 13*, 729–815.

Weisz, J. R., Sandler, I. N., Durlak, J. A., & Anton, B. S. (2005). Promoting and protecting youth mental health through evidence-based prevention and treatment. *American Psychologist, 60*, 628–648.

Whitaker, A., Johnson, J., Shaffer, D., Rapoport, J. L., Kalokow, K., Walsh, B. T. et al. (1990). Uncommon troubles in young people: prevalence estimates of selected psychiatric disorders in a non-referred adolescent population. *Archives of General Psychiatry, 47*, 487–496.

White, W. C., & Davis, M. T. (1974). Vicarious extinction of phobic behavior in early childhood. *Journal of Abnormal Child Psychology, 2*, 25–37.

Wigfield, A., & Meece, J. L. (1988). *Journal of Educational Psychology, 80*, 210–216.

Williams, T. P., & Miller, B. D. (2003). Pharmacologic management of anxiety disorders in children and adolescents. *Current Opinion in Pediatrics, 15*, 483–490.

Winker, J. B. (1949). Age trends and sex differences in the wishes, identifications, activities and fears of children. *Child Development, 20*, 191–200.

Wittchen, H.U., Stein M. B., & Kessler, R. C. (1999). Social fears and social phobia in a community sample of adolescents and young adults: Prevalence, risk factors and comorbidity. *Psychological Medicine, 29*, 309–323.

# 6

# Depression and Related Difficulties

## Dawn H. S. Reinemann and Sarah Schnoebelen

Depressive disorders are currently conceptualized as chronic, recurrent conditions that, in most cases, have their onset during childhood or adolescence. Furthermore, research shows that the prevalence rates of depressive disorders are increasing at the same time the age of onset of mood disturbances is decreasing (Kessler, 2002). This development is especially disturbing, given that depression in childhood is associated with increased risk for developing recurrent depressive episodes in adulthood (Hammen & Rudolph, 2003). Youth who suffer from depressive disorders evidence impaired social, emotional, behavioral, and academic functioning that may lead to delays that will adversely impact their subsequent development across the lifespan. Thus, it is imperative for schools to address childhood and adolescent depression.

The ways in which schools can assist students affected with depressive disturbances are numerous including identifying students at risk or currently suffering from depression, offering classroom-based prevention and intervention services, implementing treatments in individual or small group formats, educating parents and school personnel about depressive disorders and treatment options, and consulting with community-based mental health professionals in order to coordinate care. However, many youth suffering from depression and/or other psychological problems remain unidentified and underserved. The magnitude of the problem has been illustrated by a U.S. Public Health Service Report (2001), which found that although 1 in 10 youngsters suffer from mental illness serious enough to cause functional impairment, estimates indicate that less than 1 in 5 receives any form of treatment.

Why have children with mental health problems, and particularly those with depression, been overlooked? Reasons vary but include the fact that depressed children rarely act out and often present with physical complaints that may be misleading to parents and educational professionals. Furthermore, with the exception of mental health specialists such as school psychologists, licensed psychologists, school social workers, or school counselors, most other school staff have little training regarding the ways that depressive disturbances may present themselves during childhood, which also may contribute to underidentification (Sander, Reinemann, & Herren, 2007). In addition, licensed psychologists and school psychologists who are trained to identify depressive disorders spend a majority of their time evaluating children referred for special education services. However, children who present with depression often are general education students and school personnel may not account for their specific educational needs (Reinemann, Stark, Molnar, & Simpson, 2006). While some children with severe or lengthy episodes of childhood depression may qualify for special education services under "Severe Emotional Disturbance," many students with depression do not demonstrate educational need sufficient to warrant such services (Sander et al., 2007). However, with emphasis now placed on pre-referral services, children with depression may be more likely to come to the attention of child study teams who can consider intervention options, including the development of a possible accommodation plan, if warranted, based on Section 504 of the Rehabilitation Act (1973).

It is important to note that even when children suffering from depressive disturbances are identified, most do not receive evidenced-based interventions at school or in the community. Stark and associates (2006a) point out in their review and discussion of treatments for childhood depression that the majority of depressed youth are being treated by physicians, or by community mental health providers who use an eclectic mix of treatments that lack any evidence base. This type of psychotherapy has been found to be no more effective than providing no treatment (Stark et al., 2006). In contrast, evaluations of research-based prevention and intervention programs for childhood depression are quite promising. Most of these programs are manualized (i.e., in the form of a treatment manual) and can be implemented in schools or community settings. Thus, school professionals can greatly assist their students who are at risk or suffering from depressive disturbances by gaining knowledge about and training in evidence-based interventions for childhood depression. The purpose of this chapter is to provide information about the state of the art in preventing and treating depression in youth. However, we begin with an overview of depression before turning our attention to evidence-based interventions.

## OVERVIEW OF CHILDHOOD DEPRESSION

### Definitions

Depression can be defined as a symptom, syndrome, or disorder. Clinical experience suggests that depressive disturbances frequently go unrecognized for long periods of time within the classroom due to the internalizing nature of the symptoms. This may be particularly true for those depressed children that tend to withdraw and isolate themselves as opposed to demonstrating significant irritability and acting out behaviors. Nonetheless, there are a number of academic, social, behavioral, cognitive, affective, and physical indicators of depression that are likely to manifest themselves in the classroom.

Affective symptoms in youth include sad mood, anger or irritability, anhedonia (loss of interest or pleasure), weepiness, feeling unloved, and self-pity (Stark, 1990). Along with these symptoms, educational professionals may notice a decline in academic performance and loss of interest in previously enjoyed subjects, as well as failure to complete assignments or a tendency to give up easily. Cognitive symptoms include negative self-evaluations, guilt, hopelessness, concentration difficulties, and suicidal ideation (Stark, 1990). In the classroom, these symptoms may manifest themselves in the form of indecisiveness, inattentiveness, or expectations for failure. Certainly, writing or statements that contain themes of death or suicide should be taken seriously and risk should be assessed by appropriately trained mental health professionals in order to guide intervention. Youngsters suffering from depression also may experience social and behavioral symptoms that can manifest as social withdrawal from peers and adults or engagement in behaviors which alienate others, suicidal behaviors, agitation, aggression, hyperactivity, or other disruptive behaviors. In addition, physical symptoms include fatigue, changes in appetite and weight, somatic complaints, sleep disturbances, and psychomotor retardation or agitation (Stark, 1990). For example, students may complain of fatigue or may be observed falling asleep during class. When examining these symptoms, it becomes apparent that children who suffer from depression experience symptoms or characteristics that negatively impact their academic confidence, motivation, and cognitive processing, culminating in impaired academic functioning.

A depressive *disorder* consists of a constellation of behaviors and emotions that co-occur for a minimum duration and lead to functional impairment. The *Diagnostic and Statistical Manual of Mental Disorders, Fourth Edition, Text Revision (DSM-IV-TR*; American Psychiatric Association, 2000) recognizes three major diagnostic categories of unipolar depressive disorders: Major Depressive Disorder (MDD), Dysthymic Disorder (DD), and Depressive Disorder Not Otherwise Specified (DDNOS). The primary difference between these disorders is the number, severity, and duration of depressive symptoms. Only a trained mental health professional or physician can assign the diagnosis of depression (usually based on the *DSM-IV* or a similar classification system).

The diagnostic criteria for MDD stipulate that five or more symptoms must be present over a 2-week period, including one symptom of either depressed mood, loss of interest or pleasure (anhedonia), or irritability. In addition to the mood disturbance, the syndrome also includes at least four of the following symptoms: (a) changes in weight or failure to make necessary weight gains, (b) sleep disturbance, (c) psychomotor agitation or retardation, (d) fatigue or loss of energy, (e) excessive feelings of worthlessness or guilt, (f) lack of concentration and decision-making ability, (g) suicidal ideation or attempts or plans of suicide (American Psychiatric Association, 2000).

Dysthymic Disorder is characterized by a chronic mood disturbance of either dysphoria or anger and at least two other depressive symptoms. In children, these symptoms must be present for a minimum of 1 year without more than 2 symptom-free months. Children who exhibit depressive symptoms but do not meet the diagnostic criteria for either MDD or DD may receive a diagnosis of DDNOS.

School-age youth can experience any of the three depressive disorders; however, the manner in which depressive symptoms cluster may vary as a function of development. Symptoms commonly found in children include depressed appearance, irritability, aggressive behavior, somatic complaints, and social withdrawal, preferring solitary play. These symptoms may often be mistaken for simple lack of motivation, attentional problems, or defiance. Adolescents present more often with psychomotor retardation, sleepiness or sleeping more than usual, delusions, hopelessness, and suicide ideation and attempts (American Psychiatric Association, 2000). Thus, proper identification of children suffering from depression involves a consideration of the child's development and ways in which it may affect symptom presentation.

## Prevalence

A significant number of youth experience depressive disorders at some point in time and prevalence rates increase with age. While about 1% to 3% of children evidence a depressive disorder at any given time (see, for example, Hammen & Rudolph, 2003, for a review), the percentage of adolescents with a lifetime history of major depression ranges from 9% to 21% in community samples (Hankin et al., 1998; Kessler & Walters, 1998). Fewer studies have examined the prevalence rates of DD. However, it is important to uncover the prevalence of DD because it is a serious, long-lasting disturbance that places the youngster at risk for a variety of psychosocial problems and the later development of MDD. While initial reports indicated that approximately 2.5% of children in the general population currently evidence Dysthymic Disorder (see, for example, Stark, 1990, for a review), a more recent study of a community sample of 17- to 19-year-olds indicated that 4.7% had a lifetime history of dysthymia (Jonas, Brody, Roper, & Narrow, 2003). As can be seen, youth seem to be at heightened risk for developing depressive disturbances during adolescence. Thus, middle and high school personnel may be especially likely to encounter students who are suffering from significant forms of depression and are in need of services.

## Gender Differences

During the elementary school years males and females are equally likely to develop depressive disturbances. However, beginning with the middle school years and extending through high school, the balance changes and females become twice as likely as males to develop a depressive disorder (Hankin et al., 1998; Stark, 1990). Investigators have begun to explore possible biological, psychological, and social factors that may account for the increased rates of depression in females. Although an in-depth review of this literature is beyond the scope of this chapter, a brief summary of the major findings reveals that there is little evidence that hormone levels or pubertal status directly account for the observed gender differences in rates of depression (see, for example, Nolen-Hoeksema, 2002, for a review). However, it appears that girls, especially those who mature early, are less satisfied with their bodies and physical appearance than their peers, and are at increased risk for developing psychopathology including depression (Graber, Lewinsohn, Seeley, & Brooks-Gunn, 1997).

Moreover, females are believed to have a stronger biological reactivity to stress than males, characterized by a dysregulated hypothalamic-pituitary-adrenal (HPA) axis response, in part because they are more likely to be exposed to traumatic life events which are known to impact the HPA axis (Heim et al., 2000). For example, females are more likely to experience sexual victimization which increases the risk for depression as well as Post-Traumatic Stress Disorder (PTSD; Cutler & Nolen-Hoeksema, 1991).

In addition, exposure to negative life events of an interpersonal nature may pose a particular risk for girls, due to their greater affiliative needs and emphasis on social relationships (Nolen-Hoeksema, 2002; Rudolph, 2002). This exposure, combined with a cognitive style characterized by excessive rumination, dysfunctional attitudes, and a pessimistic explanatory style, appears to contribute to higher rates of depressive disorders in females (Nolen-Hoeksema, 2002). All of the variables discussed above likely interact to increase the risk for depression in females.

## Depression in Specific Populations

The literature on ethnicity and depression suggests that some racial groups experience more severe depression, experience different symptoms, and are less likely to receive help from mental health professionals. Minority students have been found to report higher rates of depression (e.g., Roberts, Roberts, & Chen, 1997; Rushton, Forcier, & Schectman, 2003). For example, a recent meta-analysis of studies using the Children's Depression Inventory (CDI; Kovacs, 1992) revealed that Hispanic youth report higher levels of depressive symptoms than African American and Caucasian youngsters (Twenge & Nolen-Hoeksema, 2002). Research also has revealed that female African American youth have higher rates of depression than European American students (Garrison, Jackson, Marsteller, McKeown, & Addy, 1990). Other groups that may be at increased risk for developing depressive disturbances include Native American youngsters (Petersen et al., 1993), children from lower socio-economic backgrounds (Reinherz, Giaconia, Lefkowitz, Pakiz, & Frost, 1993), and gay, lesbian, and bisexual youth (Anhalt & Morris, 1998). Youth with learning disabilities also may be at greater risk for developing depressive symptomatology (Arnold et al., 2005). In addition, children who suffer from medical problems have higher rates of depression than those in the general population (see Stark, et al., 2006, for a review).

The way in which ethnic groups experience depressive symptomatology and respond to self-report measures of depressive symptoms may differ. For example, a recent investigation that used the Center for Epidemiologic Studies Depression Scale (CES-D) found that African American adolescents and adults scored high on items that inquired about somatic symptoms (Iwata,

Turner, & Lloyd, 2002). Thus, examination of specific symptom clusters may assist mental health professionals in understanding how depression is manifested in various minority populations.

Although minority students appear to experience higher rates of depression, they are less likely to receive mental health services. For example, Asian American and Native American youngsters appear less likely to receive treatment (Bui & Takeuchi, 1992). African American adolescents with psychological problems are more likely to enter the juvenile justice system than their Caucasian adolescent counterparts (Kaplan & Busner, 1992).

Numerous explanations for the lack of service utilization by ethnic minority families have been proposed, including the possibility that ethnic groups differ regarding what is perceived to be a mental health problem and how severe the problem needs to be before seeking outside assistance (see, for example, Cauce et al., 2002, for a review). Cauce and associates (2002) also indicate that poor, ethnic minority families are likely under increased stress and may be less sensitive to their child's psychological problems. When a child's problem is recognized, culture, context and development are likely to influence help-seeking. There may be a stigma to seeking treatment in some cultures such as Asian groups (Sue, 1988), while other groups such as African Americans are more likely to turn to nonprofessional resources such as churches and extended family (Zito, Safer, DosReis, & Riddle, 1998). Adolescents in general may be less likely to seek out mental health services due to the emphasis placed on autonomy and privacy, as well as the precarious nature of their self-identities during this developmental period (Cauce et al., 2002). Of importance for school mental health professionals is the finding that the majority of youth (70%) who evidence psychological disorders receive services in the school system rather than from specialty treatment providers in the community (Burns et al., 1995). Schools have become the primary providers of mental health services for youth (Hoagwood & Jensen, 1997). Thus, given the reluctance of minority families and adolescents to seek help from formal mental health treatment providers, schools are likely to be an important source for the identification and treatment of youth suffering from depression (Cauce et al., 2002). They also can play a major role in educating parents about their child's psychological disturbance, addressing the family's questions and concerns about treatment options, and connecting the family with community mental health treatment providers.

## Course and Prognosis

Childhood depressive disorders remit naturally. However, even after remission, subsyndromal levels of symptoms often persist along with continued impairment (Kovacs & Goldston, 1991). Children who have experienced an episode of depression are likely to develop a subsequent episode while still in their teens, suggesting that for many youth, depression represents a recurrent, and in some instances chronic, disorder. In fact, adolescent depression is associated with recurrent episodes in adulthood (Lewinsohn, Rohde, Klein, & Seeley, 1999). Adolescent depression also predicts adverse outcomes in adulthood, including early marriage, marital dissatisfaction, impaired occupational functioning, reduced physical well-being, and potential suicide (e.g., Lewinsohn, Rohde, Seeley, Klein, & Gotlib, 2003). Therefore, primary prevention and early intervention efforts in educational settings become an important means by which school professionals can affect the course of depression during children's formative years and throughout their lives.

## Comorbidity

Comorbidity is defined as two or more psychological disorders that co-occur more often than would be expected by chance (Mash & Dozois, 2003). Comorbidity is common in childhood, and youth who suffer from depression are likely to also evidence other psychological disturbances. For example, it has been estimated that 43% of adolescents with MDD have a lifetime comorbid psychiatric disorder, with anxiety disorders being the most common (Lewinsohn, Rohde, & Seeley, 1998). Depressed youth also often experience comorbid disruptive behavior disorders and substance abuse (Lewinsohn et al., 1998). A summary of the existing data reveals that depression co-occurs with Conduct Disorder, Oppositional Defiant Disorder, or Attention Deficit Hyperactivity Disorder (ADHD) in approximately 25% of youngsters (Nottelmann & Jensen, 1995). Of note, a diagnosis of comorbid depression plus Conduct Disorder or comorbid depression plus substance abuse also increases the risk of suicide in youth. When comorbidity occurs, depression seems to develop after the other condition in the majority of youth (Lewinsohn et al., 1998).

Apart from disorders, depressed youngsters also are likely to exhibit dysfunction in other areas that may impact their functioning, especially at school. Depressed children often exhibit social skills deficits and have been found to be less popular, less liked, and more likely to be rejected by peers than their non-disturbed counterparts (e.g., Rudolph & Clark, 2001). Depressed students also have been found to have significantly lower academic achievement than their non-depressed peers (Puig-Antich et al., 1985), and are more likely to miss school, fail to complete homework assignments, and repeat a grade than their non-depressed counterparts (Lewinsohn et al., 1994). Of major concern, depressed adolescents also appear to be at increased risk for dropping out of high school (Kessler, Foster, Saunders, & Stang, 1995). Thus, depression is often associated with difficulties in multiple domains and areas of functioning. Since comorbidity has been shown to lead to greater functional impairment and a poorer long-term prognosis (Rohde, Lewinsohn, & Seeley, 1991), proper assessment for possible co-occurring conditions in youth suffering from depression is paramount.

## Assessment of Depression

Assessing depressive disturbances requires information gathering from multiple sources, including the youth, parent(s), and teachers. Self-report measures play a crucial role in the assessment process of school-age youth, as key symptoms of depression (e.g., sadness, beliefs about self-worth and competence, etc.) involve feelings and self-perceptions which are not easily observable (Reynolds, 1994). However, there are concerns about how well these measures discriminate between different disorders and whether they specifically assess depression or psychopathology in general (Stark, 1990). As a result, self-report measures may best be used as screening devices that are part of a more comprehensive assessment.

For more specific and accurate identification of depressive disorders in youth, either an individual assessment or a multiple-stage assessment procedure is recommended (Reynolds, 1994; Stark, 1990). In order to screen for depressive disturbances in a large numbers of students, a multiple-stage procedure is recommended. This procedure involves first screening the student body using a self-report questionnaire such as the *Children's Depression Inventory* (CDI; Kovacs, 1992), *Reynolds Child Depression Scale* (RCDS; Reynolds, 1989), or the *Beck Depression Inventory for Youth* (BDI-Y; Beck, Beck, & Jolly, 2001). After the initial screening, students who scored at or above a clinical cutoff score are re-tested a short time later (1 to 2 weeks) as there is evidence that youth may score higher on the first administration of a self-report measure of depression than on a second testing (Reynolds, 1994). Those youth who continue to endorse significant levels of depressive symptomatology during the second screening are then referred for a more comprehensive assessment, which may include a diagnostic interview, such as the *Schedule for Affective Disorders and Schizophrenia for School-Age Children* (K-SADS; Orvaschel & Puig-Antich, 1994), along with information from parent and teacher questionnaires and interviews. Clinical interviews provide a more detailed examination of onset of the disturbance, specific symptoms and their severity, and may provide information regarding problems that may be contributing to the depression (Reynolds, 1994).

For a more complete picture of the scope of the child's problems, parents can provide important information regarding the child's behaviors and functioning at home that may be of concern, while teachers can provide data regarding the child's classroom behavior and academic functioning. Parents and teachers may be asked to complete a behavioral rating scale such as the *Achenbach System of Empirically Based Assessment* (ASEBA), *Child Behavior Checklist* (6–18 years) (Achenbach & Rescorla, 2001) or the *Behavior Assessment System for Children, 2nd edition* (BASC-2; Reynolds & Kamphaus, 2004), which addresses symptoms across several areas of behavioral and emotional functioning. For example, the BASC-2 self-report measure contains subscales that assess self-esteem, self-reliance, and interpersonal relations, while the BASC-2 parent and teacher reports contain subscales that assess the child's social skills, study skills, and leadership abilities. Since children with depression often present with low self-esteem, poor peer relations and social skills problems, assessment of these areas may assist school personnel in developing treatment goals and in intervention planning.

## School Factors Related to Childhood Depression

In addition to being able to identify depression in the classroom, educators need to be aware of the relationship between school factors and the emotional health of students. For example, research has suggested that at the same time that middle school students report a reduction in both teacher support and self-esteem, these students report an increase in depressive symptoms (Reddy, Rhodes, & Mulhall, 2003). Furthermore, increased perceived teacher support was linked to improvements in self-esteem and decreases in depression. Positive teacher-student relationships appear to create positive school-related emotions, self-esteem, and a sense of belonging (Hoge, Smith, & Hanson, 1990; Murray & Greenberg, 2000; Roeser, Midgley, & Urdan, 1996), and those children and adolescents who do not perceive themselves to belong are at greater risk for depression, social rejection, and school problems (Anderman, 2002). Anderman described the relationship between depression and school belonging to be moderated by aggregated sense of belonging across all the students in the school. In schools in which most of the students perceived to belong, those students who did not report this sense of belongingness were at higher risk for depressive symptoms, a finding which necessitates the importance of efforts to engage isolated students.

## EVIDENCE-BASED PREVENTION PROGRAMS FOR DEPRESSED YOUTH

Because of the chronicity, severity, long-term adverse effects, and high recurrence rate of depressive disturbances, there has been an increased interest in, and development of, prevention programs for reducing the initial onset of depressive disorders or to prevent relapse. These prevention programs typically consist of sessions that address negative cognitions that are linked to depression via teaching cognitive restructuring techniques and problem-solving. Prevention programs also may include sessions that provide assertiveness training, teach relaxation procedures, and target social skills development. Most of the evidence-based programs are in the form of a treatment manual and designed to be implemented in school settings.

Results of investigations designed to evaluate prevention programs for depressed youths have, in general, reported positive results immediately following program completion, but mixed results during subsequent follow-up evaluations. For example, the Penn Resiliency Program for Children and Adolescents (PRP-CA) is a school-based prevention program for late elementary and middle school students that has undergone empirical investigation. Jaycox, Reivich, Gillham, and Seligman (1994) reported that the 12-session prevention program, which emphasized training in cognitive and social problem-solving, reduced the severity of depressive symptoms and behavior problems in the classroom immediately following completion of the program, prevented symptoms from recurring for 6 months, and significantly prevented depressive symptomatology over 2 years. However, by year 3 results were no longer significant (Jaycox et al., 1994; Gillham & Reivich, 1999). Subsequent research on the program was conducted with groups of middle school students who were identified as being at risk for developing depressive disorders because of the chronic stress of poverty. According to the study, the program significantly reduced depressive symptoms among participants of Latino descent but not among African American participants (Muñoz, Penilla, & Urizar, 2002). These results raise important questions about the need for, and potential benefits of, developing culturally sensitive interventions.

Given the mixed results discussed above, Gillham and associates (2006) recently developed a parent component to the PRP-CA and collected pilot data on its effectiveness in preventing depression in youth. The parent intervention focuses on teaching the same cognitive and problem-solving skills to the adults so that they may serve as models for their children, as well as preventing parental depression which is a risk factor for childhood depression. In the pilot study, children's groups met weekly for eight, 90-minute sessions, while parents met for six 90-minute sessions. Results showed that in comparison to a control group, children who completed the PRP-CA with the parent component reported lower levels of depressive symptoms and anxiety symptoms at 6-month and 12-month follow-ups. Although results appear promising, it will be important for these researchers to conduct future studies that will help determine whether the inclusion of the parent component to the PRP-CA leads to significantly better outcomes than providing the program solely to the children.

Another group of researchers has developed and evaluated a series of manualized cognitive–behavioral programs for the prevention and treatment of depressive disorders in adolescents, titled Coping with Stress (CWS) and Coping with Depression (CWD), respectively (Clarke et al., 1995; Clarke, Rohde, Lewinsohn, Hops, & Seeley, 1999). Components focus on experiential learning and skills training, with attention to increasing pleasant activities, improving social interaction, and coping with maladaptive thoughts. These programs have been administered in school and clinical settings, and the materials can be downloaded at no cost for use by mental health professionals. In an evaluation, adolescents who reported subclinical levels of depressive symptoms, which placed them at risk for developing a depressive disorder, completed the 15-session CWS group prevention program (Clarke et al., 1995). When compared with a "treatment as usual" control condition, the prevention program significantly reduced the number of adolescents who developed diagnosable depressive disorders over a 12-month period. However, because a number of adolescents in the study still developed depressive disorders, additional research is needed in order to identify the variables that predict those who are resilient versus those who subsequently experience depression.

Another group of prevention programs are considered "universal" because they are implemented with entire school populations and do not select students for participation based on level of depressive symptomatology or family risk factors. These programs are typically conducted with entire classrooms and may be implemented by teachers or other school mental health personnel. Shochet and colleagues (2001) have developed an 11-session program titled the Resourceful Adolescent Program (RAP), which has been implemented by psychologists and evaluated in a school setting. The RAP focuses on promoting self-management, coping with stress, building support networks, and teaching cognitive restructuring and problem-solving skills. Similar to the recent addition of a parent component in the Penn Resiliency Program discussed above, the RAP includes a 3-session family program for parents that focuses on stress management, parenting adolescents, and family conflict resolution. In order to evaluate the program's effectiveness, students were assigned to either the adolescent program, the adolescent program plus the family component, or a control condition. Results revealed that adolescents who participated in either prevention program reported significantly lower levels of depressive symptoms and hopelessness immediately following program completion and at 10-month follow-up compared to adolescents in the control condition. However, there were no differences between those receiving only the adolescent program and those who also participated in the family program (Shochet et al., 2001).

More recently, Spence, Sheffield, and Donovan (2003, 2005) have developed a universal, school-based cognitive-behavioral program designed to prevent the development of youth depression, titled the Problem-Solving for Life program. Spence et al. specifically attempted to create a curriculum which can easily be used by classroom teachers who implement the program with all students in the class. The program consists of eight, 45- to 50-minute sessions that focus on cognitive restructuring and problem-solving skills training. Youngsters are first taught to identify thoughts, feelings, and problem situations and then are provided with training in challenging negative or irrational thoughts that contribute to the development of depression. The second part of the program emphasizes teaching life problem-solving skills and the development of a positive problem-solving orientation.

In a well-designed evaluation of the program, 8th-grade students (ages 12 to 14) who completed the program were compared to students in a monitoring-control condition. Results indicated that students who initially reported elevated levels of depression (high risk group) and who participated in the program showed a significant decrease in depressive symptoms and an increase in problem-solving skills immediately following program completion compared to control students also at high risk for depression. In addition, those students who completed the program but did not evidence initial elevated levels of depression also reported a significant decrease in depressive symptoms and an increase in problem-solving skills compared to the low-risk control students, who actually reported an increase in depressive symptomatology (Spence et al., 2003).

Subsequent follow-up evaluations were conducted to assess the long-term impact of the Problem-Solving for Life program. Results revealed that treatment gains were not maintained at 12-month follow-up. Specifically, Spence and colleagues (2003) reported that there were no significant differences between the prevention group and control group in the percentage of students who developed a depressive disorder or who exhibited elevated levels of depression. Furthermore, there were no group differences in changes from pre-intervention to 12-month follow-up on measures of depression, cognitive style, and problem-solving, among others. Likewise, re-evaluations showed no significant differences between those who completed the program and those in the control condition at 2-, 3-, and 4-year follow-up (Spence et al., 2005).

Taken together, the evidence base for various childhood depression prevention programs appears somewhat equivocal at this time. Future studies are needed to address possible factors that may influence whether prevention programs lead to long-term benefits. Examination of factors such as program length, content, mode of delivery, training of teachers, and other implementers, as well as which youth are best served by such preventive interventions may lead to improved programs that demonstrate longer-term maintenance of initial treatment gains.

## EVIDENCE-BASED INTERVENTIONS FOR CHILDHOOD DEPRESSION

### Issues in Implementation and Evaluation of School-Based Interventions

A number of evidence-based interventions for child and adolescent depression have been developed and are undergoing evaluation. Several of these evaluations have been conducted within the school setting. The provision of such services within the school offers a natural vehicle for effective service delivery. By bringing services to the place where children and adolescents spend the majority of the day, issues such as poor therapy attendance due to transportation and scheduling conflicts may be prevented. Furthermore, as Stark and colleagues (2006a) have articulated, the goals of any intervention with depressed children and adolescents extend beyond symptom reduction to improvement in functional capacity. Given the significant amount of time children spend within the school setting, it is easy to understand how quality of life is inextricably linked to a child's performance and satisfaction in the school environment. Providing services in the school also facilitates close consultation with the youngster's teachers. Such communication allows educators and therapists to collaborate to determine how to reinforce and support the specific interventions provided as part of the therapy within the classroom setting where students spend the majority of their days. From a purely pragmatic standpoint, group interventions, of which many of the published protocols employ, may be easier to manage within the school setting than the clinic because there are greater chances of identifying enough children at similar ages and grades to form more developmentally homogeneous groups. Furthermore, it is hoped that by providing services for depression within the school, the disorder is de-stigmatized and awareness is increased.

Despite the fact that many benefits exist to providing services for depressed children within the educational setting, some problems exist with this method of service delivery. For example, children and adolescents may perceive some risk to confidentiality by attending therapy with friends and classmates, even when confidentially agreements are clearly negotiated. Furthermore, efforts must be taken to avoid students feeling as though they are being clearly identified as a student who is receiving intervention services for depression, for example, when possible, avoiding the interruption of class to remind a student to attend a therapy session. Also, it is important to recognize scheduling constraints within a school and the need for students to avoid missing a significant portion of time in any one academic class.

Although many of the evaluation studies comprising the childhood depression literature have screened participants in the school and provided services there, many other issues of treatment generalizability and transportability remain. In a recent review, Weisz , Doss, and Hawley (2005) directly addressed the clinical representativeness of the literature base in terms of the manner in which participants were identified and enrolled in the studies, the characteristics and training of the service providers, and the setting in which the treatment was provided. Weisz's group found that very few depression treatment outcome studies reported information on all three of these categories. Of those studies that did provide such data, 78% of the participants were not actually seeking treatment at the time of recruitment. In terms of treatment providers, a large percentage of depressed participants (approximately 56%) were treated by practicing mental health professionals, with the remainder of services provided by researchers or graduate students. Certainly, the degree of time and resources that graduate students and individual researchers are able to devote to psychotherapy protocols may be significantly greater than that of the front-line school-based mental health provider. As Weisz and colleagues highlight, a rapid movement from initial efficacy studies to tests of interventions in ecologically valid conditions is essential. An account of the experience, including some of the challenges of transporting a specific therapy (Interpersonal Therapy for Adolescents; IPT-A) from a university-based clinic setting to school health centers, can be found in Mufson, Dorta, Olfson, Weissman, and Hoagwood (2004).

## Overview of Evidence-Based Interventions

The psychotherapeutic treatment approaches which have received the most empirical support include cognitive-behavioral therapy (e.g., Brent et al., 1997; Butler, Miezitis, Friedman, & Cole, 1980; Kahn & Kehle, 1990; Lewisohn, Clarke, Hops, & Andrews, 1990; Reynolds & Coates, 1986; Stark, Reynolds, & Kaslow, 1987; Stark, Rouse, & Livingston, 1991; Vostanis, Feehan, Grattan, & Bickerton, 1996a, 1996b; Weisz, Thurber, Sweeney, Proffitt, & LeGagnoux, 1997; Wood, Harrington, & Moore, 1996) and interpersonal therapy (e.g., Mufson et al., 1994; Mufson, Dorta, Wickramaratne, et al., 2004; Mufson & Fairbanks, 1996; Mufson, Moreau, Weissman, & Garfinkel, 1999; Rossello & Bernal, 1999). Family interventions for various mood disorders also have been described in the literature (e.g., Fristad, Goldberg-Arnold, & Gavazzi, 2002; Harrington et al., 2000; Lewinsohn et al., 1990; Miklowitz et al., 2004; Sanford et al., 2006). These intervention efforts frequently take the form of adjunctive family psychoeducation and training in communication and problem-solving which, in some cases, have had positive effects on family relationships and social functioning of depressed adolescents (e.g., Sanford et al., 2006). Unfortunately, literature regarding the efficacy of family involvement in interventions for depression is sparse. Family interventions in particular will not be described in great detail here; the interested reader is encouraged to see Sander and McCarty (2005) for a comprehensive review of the family risk factors associated in depression, as well family involvement in treatment approaches. Before presenting information regarding empirically-supported psychosocial treatments for depression, the literature regarding psychopharmacological intervention will be discussed briefly as many children receive combined treatment that includes medication and psychotherapy.

## Medication

Although tricyclic antidepressants (TCAs) formerly were utilized with frequency in the treatment of depression in youth (Stark, et al., 2006b), studies generally have not found TCAs to be effective in children (see, for example, Geller, Reising, Leonard, Riddle, & Walsh, 1999). Furthermore, these authors point out that the serious side effects, especially cardiovascular effects, must be carefully considered when using TCAs in children. Currently, the first line of antidepressant medication treatment for children consists of the selective serotonin reuptake inhibitors (SSRIs) (American Academy of Child and Adolescent Psychiatry, 1998), which include fluoxetine (Prozac), sertraline (Zoloft), paroxetine (Paxil), fluvoxamine (Luvox), citalopram (Celexa), and escitalopram (Lexapro). Fluoxetine has the greatest research support (e.g., Emslie et al., 1997, 2002) and is the only SSRI approved by the U.S. Food and Drug Administration (FDA) for the treatment of depression in children and adolescents, although the other SSRIs are frequently prescribed by psychiatrists based on their clinical experiences of safe and effective use with patients (Stark, et al., 2006). One of the most important recent studies of medication efficacy was the Treatment for Adolescents with Depression Study (TADS), a multi-site investigation comparing the effectiveness of fluoxetine alone, CBT alone, fluoxetine + CBT, and placebo (Treatment for Adolescents with Depression Study Team, 2004). The results suggested that rates of response were higher for fluoxetine alone (60.6%) than CBT alone (43.2%), the latter of which was not significantly different than pill placebo. Combined therapy resulted in a 71.0% rate of response. Patients receiving CBT, either alone or in combination with medication, demonstrated decreased suicidal ideation. The American Academy of Child and Adolescent Psychiatry (1998) has suggested that combined treatments for childhood depression are often appropriate, stating, "Given the psychosocial context in which depression unfolds, pharmacotherapy is never sufficient as the sole treatment" (p. 72S).

Other studies have provided evidence for the effectiveness of SSRIs, including sertraline (e.g., Wagner et al., 2003), citalopram (e.g., Wagner et al., 2004), and paroxetine (Keller et al., 2001), compared to placebo, although a study by Simeon, Dinicola, Ferguson, and Copping (1990) reported no statistical significance in the superiority of fluoxetine over placebo. Other medications that may be utilized to treat child and adolescent depression include bupropion (Wellbutrin), mirtazapine (Remeron), venlafaxine (Effexor), and the monoamine oxidase inhibitors (MAOIs), the latter of which are very rarely used in pediatric depression due to their significant side-effect profile (Stark et al., 2006b).

Although the SSRIs have demonstrated efficacy for depressed adolescents, their use with this age group is controversial as a 2003 report by the British Medicines and Healthcare Products Regulatory Agency (MHRA) concluded that most of the SSRIs do not show benefits that exceed their risks of suicidal ideation and thus should not be prescribed to youth (Reinemann et al., 2006). The FDA (FDA, 2004) then reanalyzed the results of existing drug studies and found that youths who took antidepressants were 78% more likely to exhibit suicidal behaviors relative to children who took a placebo. The FDA recommended that paroxetine not be used to treat depression in youth under age 18 and that caution be used when administering other antidepressants to children and adolescents. Parents should be warned of possible suicidality concerns, especially early in treatment. However, recent results from the TADS study found that treated youth actually reported less suicidal ideation. Thus, continued research is needed that addresses the potential risks and benefits of psychopharmacological treatment of depression in youth (Reinemann et al., 2006).

## Psychotherapeutic Interventions

In reviewing the evidence base for psychosocial interventions in child and adolescent depression, it is important to refer readers to previous comprehensive reviews and meta-analyses of the literature regarding intervention outcomes for a range of childhood disorders (e.g., Casey & Berman, 1985; Durlak, Wells, Cotton, & Johnson, 1995; Kazdin, 2000; Shirk & Russell, 1996; Weisz, Weiss, Alicke, & Klotz, 1987; Weisz, Weiss, Han, & Granger, 1995; Weisz et al., 2005). In their most recent review of the literature spanning from 1962 to 2002, Weisz and colleagues (2005) evaluated outcome studies addressing four major clusters of childhood disorders, including problems related to anxiety, depression, conduct, and difficulties with inattentiveness, hyperactivity, and impulsivity. Of these four domains, the depression treatment outcome research was the most recent, with 89% of the studies published in the 1990s or later, compared to 43% for anxiety outcome research, 20% for attention problems, and 33% for conduct problems. Furthermore, compared to research associated with the other disorders, Weisz and colleagues found that those studies evaluating outcomes of treatments for depression reported more systematic sample selection as well as a greater degree of pre-treatment training for clinicians, use of manualized or otherwise structured treatments, and supervision or monitoring of adherence. However, as Stark and colleagues (Stark, et al., 2006a; Stark, et al., 2006b) have noted, simple "adherence" to treatment manuals is not sufficient. Rather, Stark stresses the need for an "artistic application" of the treatment components in order to flexibly and individually relate the skills taught to working hypotheses regarding the etiological and maintenance factors underlying the child's depressive symptoms.

The Weisz et al. (2005) results reflect the increased awareness of childhood depression as well as its consequence. These authors suggest that the literature base evaluating the outcomes of depression treatment has "profited from the more rigorous methodological standards of the era," (Weisz et al, 2005, p. 350), although the more recent foray into this realm of research also results in a relatively limited number of studies on the topic. In addition to the small number of studies, most of the published evaluations are composed of small sample sizes, rendering them underpowered. Generalizability is a problem for studies of interventions for depression as well as psychotherapy outcome research in general. For example, Kazdin (2000) has commented that, for the most part, participants in currently published outcome research may experience less severe symptoms than seen in regular clinical practice. Furthermore, participants may face less severe contextual factors, such as parental psychopathology and economic disadvantage (Kazdin, 2000). Transportability is another problem. According to Weisz and colleagues (2005), approximately 1% of published youth psychotherapy outcome studies report representativeness to actual clinic populations across setting, therapist, and recruitment.

With these caveats in mind, the two psychotherapeutic modalities with the greatest empirical evidence, cognitive-behavioral therapy and interpersonal therapy, will be discussed briefly. Table 6.1 outlines the essential features and findings of the published outcome studies of outpatient treatments for youth depression. Although a number of these treatment programs have been delivered in the school setting, one particular program, the ACTION program, has been developed specifically for school-based service and will be described in greater detail.

## Cognitive-Behavioral Therapy

Cognitive-behavioral therapy (CBT) is built upon the philosophical and theoretical tenants of both behaviorism/learning theory and cognitive theory. In particular, the central components of Beck's cognitive therapy have been outlined in several sources (e.g., Alford & Beck, 1997; Clark, Beck, & Alford, 1999). Most central to Beck's form of CBT is the concept of schemata or the "meaning-making structures of cognition" (Alford & Beck, 1997). Within the cognitive paradigm, humans are active information seekers. As information is filtered through a schema, meaning is assigned to situations, which influences behavior, emotion, attention, memory, and physiology (Alford & Beck, 1997). The rules for processing information are referred to as "cognitive operations" (Hollon & Kriss, 1984) which serve to manipulate data in order to produce the "cognitive products" of attributions, decisions, images, and thoughts. Cognitive operations, however, may result in distortion or bias (Alford & Beck, 1997). Schema-consistent information processing causes an individual to selectively attend to and process information congruent with his or her beliefs. This restricted range of information serves to reinforce the schema. If the core schemata are negative, the resulting cognitive products, including negative automatic thoughts, will result in unpleasant emotional experience (Beck, 1995). Important in Beck's theoretical model is the concept of the cognitive triad, consisting of meaning constructed about the self, the world, and the future. Psychological difficulties stem from maladaptive meaning construction in any of these domains (Alford & Beck, 1997).

Cognitive-behavioral therapy attempts to restructure maladaptive cognitions and foster more balanced information processing. For example, children who possess the core belief that they are unlovable may interpret other people's behavior as reflecting this unlovability. Whereas a healthy child may attribute a teacher's short response to the teacher being busy or stressed, a depressed child may interpret this to mean that the teacher does not like him or her, producing negative automatic thoughts such as "He must hate me" and seemingly more evidence that the child is unlovable. The process of cognitive restructuring involves examining such negative thoughts to determine whether they are true or helpful. When working with depressed youth,

**TABLE 6.1**

**Characteristics and Results of Published Treatment Efficacy Studies of Childhood Depression**

| Study | Format | Participants/Setting | Interventions | Results |
|-------|--------|---------------------|---------------|---------|
| Butler et al., 1980 | Group 10 weekly one-hour sessions | 56 children 5th–6th grade school | • **Role Play** (combination of problem solving and social skills)<br>• **Cognitive Restructuring** (recognition of irrational automatic thoughts, relationship between thoughts and feelings, and restructuring to produce more adaptive alternatives)<br>• **Attention Placebo** (cooperative academic problem solving)<br>• **Classroom Controls** | • Both role play and cognitive restructuring groups showed reduction on self-report measures of depression and self-esteem, with greater improvement noted for the Role Play group<br>• A reduction in depressive symptoms on one self-report measure also was observed in the Control group, although authors noted that a subset of this group received three sessions with a "resource teacher" focusing upon self-esteem improvement<br>• Role play group also showed improvement on self-report measures of locus of control and depressive cognitive distortions |
| Reynolds & Coates, 1986 | Group 10 50-minute sessions over 5 weeks | 30 adolescents 9th–12th grades school | • **CBT** (self-control, affective education, goal setting, self-monitoring, cognitive restructuring)<br>• **Relaxation Training** (psychoeducation regarding the relationship between stress and depression; progressive muscle relaxation; direct application to stressful situations)<br>• **Waitlist Control** | • CBT and Relaxation Training were both more effective in reduction of symptoms than waitlist at immediate post-treatment and 5-week follow-up (on a self-report measure, 83% of the CBT group and 75% of the Relaxation Training group scored within normal range at post-treatment; whereas none of the waitlist group did)<br>• Differences between the two treatment groups were not significant<br>• Reductions in anxiety were noted in the Relaxation Training group and improved academic self-concept was observed in both active treatment groups |

| Study | Format | Participants/Setting | Interventions | Results |
|---|---|---|---|---|
| Stark et al., 1987 | Group 12 45-50 minute sessions over 5 weeks | 29 children 4th–6th grade school | • **Self Control** (self-monitoring of behavior and thoughts, pleasant events scheduling, self-evaluation and reward, and appropriate setting of goals and standards)<br>• **Behavioral Problem Solving** (psychoeducation, pleasant events scheduling, and interpersonal problem solving, expression of feelings)<br>• **Waitlist** | • Both treatment groups improved on interview and two self-report measures of depression<br>• Waitlist group improved significantly only on one self-report measure<br>• Self Control group only scored significantly lower than the Waitlist group on self-report questionnaire; Difference approached significance on another self-report measure<br>• Only subjects in the Self Control group reported significantly improved self-concept at post-treatment and follow-up<br>• Benefits maintained at 8-week follow-up, and the Self-Control group was less depressed than Behavioral Problem-Solving group based on interview |
| Kahn et al., 1990 | Group CBT and Relaxation Training; Individual Self-modeling; all had 12 one-hour sessions over 6-8 weeks | 68 children 6th–8th grade school | • **CBT** (downward extension of the adolescent version of the Coping with Depression course–see Lewisohn et al., 1990–comprehensive program including psychoeducation, pleasant events scheduling, cognitive restructuring, problem solving, social skills, self reinforcement)<br>• **Relaxation Training** (psychoeducation regarding stress and anxiety, progressive muscle relaxation)<br>• **Self-Modeling Treatment** (use of video recording to reinforce behaviors incompatible with depression)<br>• **Waitlist Control** | • Greatest improvement in CBT group in terms of reduction of depressive symptoms and improvement of self-esteem; but other two active treatment groups also demonstrated improvement compared to waitlist condition at immediate and one-month follow-up<br>• Participants in the active treatment groups were more likely to move into the nonclinical range on measures after treatment (from 59-88% depending on the group and measure) compared to 12-18% of the waitlist group, depending on measure |

*(continued)*

**TABLE 6.1**
**(Continued)**

| Study | Format | Participants/Setting | Interventions | Results |
|---|---|---|---|---|
| Lewisohn et al. (1990) | Group 14 two-hour sessions over 7 weeks; For adolescent + parent group, additional 7 weekly 2-hour sessions | 59 adolescents ages 14-18 setting not clearly indicated | • **Coping with Depression –Adolescent course** (Affective education, social skills, conflict resolution skills, pleasant events scheduling, relaxation techniques, goal setting, cognitive restructuring) <br> • **Coping with Depression + Parent Group** (Coping with Depression Adolescent program as described above with parent group that provided information about the same skills taught to the adolescents) <br> • **Waitlist Control** | • Compared to wait-list condition, subjects in both treatment conditions improved significantly on self-report measures of depressive symptoms, although not parent-report measures <br> • At post-treatment, 57.1% of adolescent group and 52.4% of adolescent and parent group met criteria for a depressive disorder but 95.7% of waitlist group continued to meet criteria <br> • Gains appeared to be maintained for up to 2 years follow-up <br> • Trend for greater improvement in Adolescent + Parent group over Adolescent-Only; statistically significant for only one comparison |
| Liddle & Spence (1990) | Group 8 weekly one-hour sessions | 31 children ages 7–11 school | • **Social Competence Training** (social skills training, interpersonal problem solving and adjustment of maladaptive cognitive coping styles) <br> • **Attention Placebo Control** (drama program) <br> • **No treatment control** | • Decline in self-reported depressive symptoms across all three conditions immediately and at three-months; no statistically significant difference between active treatment and placebos |
| Fine et al., 1991 | Group 12 weekly sessions | 66 adolescents ages 13-17 clinic | • **Social Skills Training** (series of skills including recognition of feelings, assertiveness, conversation, exchange of feedback, social problem solving and conflict resolution; included role plays and videotaping) <br> • **Therapeutic Support Group** (addressed self-concept through the identification and reinforcement of strengths, sharing of concerns, discussions of ways to manage concerns, mutual support) <br> *Note: A portion of both groups were receiving concurrent therapy. | • Statistically significant difference between the groups on an interview measure of depressive symptoms, with the therapeutic support group demonstrating greater improvement; trend toward greater improvement in the therapeutic support group on self-report measures of depression <br> • Trend for more adolescents in the therapeutic support group falling in the nonclinical range at immediate post-treatment, although this difference was not clinically significant <br> • Greater improvement in self-concept among adolescents in the therapeutic support group <br> • At 9-month follow-up, there was no difference between the two groups on depression measures, which the authors interpreted as the social skills group "caught up" with the therapeutic support group |

| Study | Format | Participants/Setting | Interventions | Results |
|---|---|---|---|---|
| Stark et al., 1991 | Group 24 to 26 45-50 minute sessions (2x week for 8 weeks and 1x week thereafter)monthly individual family sessions | 24 children 4th–7th grade school and home (family sessions) | • **Expanded CBT program** (including elements of both active treatments in the Stark et. al., 1987 study; self-control, assertiveness training, social skills, relaxation training and imagery, cognitive restructuring, problem solving; in family sessions, discussion of engagement in pleasant family activities and encouraging participants to apply their skills) <br> • **Traditional Counseling** (psychoeducation and supportive psychotherapy) | • Although participants in both groups reported less depressive behavior and cognitions, those in the CBT group were less depressed than participants in the Traditional Counseling group at post-treatment, as measured by a diagnostic interview and self-report measure of depressive cognitions <br> • Group differences at 7-month follow-up were not significant; however, a high attrition rate was observed with only 7 CBT and 5 Traditional Counseling participants available for follow-up assessment |
| Mufson et al., 1994; Mufson & Fairbanks, 1996 | Individual 12 45-minute weekly sessions + phone contact when indicated | 14 adolescents 11 completers clinic | • **Interpersonal Psychotherapy for Depressed Adolescents** (IPT-A addresses common developmental issues, such as separation from parents and authority in relationship to parents, development of interpersonal relationships, experience with the loss of a loved one, peer pressure, single-parent families) <br> **\*Note:** Initial open trial with no control group | • At post-treatment, no adolescents met criteria for depression on clinical interview <br> • Significant reduction in depressive symptoms on self-report and clinician rating scale <br> • Improvement in global functioning <br> • At one-year follow-up, 10 adolescents were assessed; of the 9 receiving a clinical interview, only 1 met diagnostic criteria for depressive disorder <br> • At follow-up, overall social adjustment improved since termination <br> • Worsening in clinician-rated measure of overall functioning from termination to follow-up, although authors suggest this may be a result of having a different rater at pre- and post-treatment than follow-up; no inter-rater reliability obtained |

*(continued)*

**TABLE 6.1**
**(Continued)**

| Study | Format | Participants/Setting | Interventions | Results |
|---|---|---|---|---|
| Vostanis et al., 1996ab | Individual 9 biweekly sessions | 57 youth ages 8-17 clinic | • **CBT** (recognition and labeling of emotions, social skills/problem solving, and cognitive restructuring) <br> • **Nonfocused Intervention** ("supportive therapy," review of mental state and social activities; unstructured with no therapist suggestions) | • CBT resulted in slightly higher recovery from depression (87% in CBT vs. 75% in control) <br> • No significant difference between groups on any outcome measures, including diagnostic interviews, structured social adjustment interview, and self- and parent-reports immediately after treatment (authors did indicate that only 50% of the CBT group completed the full program and a number of absences occurred during the cognitive restructuring component) <br> • No significant difference between treatment groups at 9-month follow-up; risk of recurrence was relatively high in both groups |
| Wood et al., 1996 | Individual 5-8 sessions | 48 completers ages 9–17 clinic | • **CBT** (cognitive restructuring, social problem solving, alleviation of symptoms, such as sleep difficulties and inactivity) <br> • **Relaxation Training** | • CBT significantly better in reducing depressed mood and symptoms and improving remission rates, self-image, and global functioning although no significant differences between groups were noted on measures of anxiety or conduct symptoms <br> • Differences between groups did not persist at 3- and 6-month follow-up |
| Brent et al., 1997; Birmaher et al., 2000 | Individual or family 12-16 weekly sessions, followed by 2 to 4 monthly booster sessions | 107 adolescents ages 13-18 clinic | • **CBT** (addressed autonomy and trust, affective regulation, problem solving, cognitive restructuring) <br> • **Systemic Behavior Family Therapy** (structural, behavioral family therapy; identification of dysfunctional behavior patterns; development of communication and problem solving skills; alteration of family interaction patterns) <br> • **Nondirective Supportive Therapy** (establishment and maintenance of rapport, reflective listening, empathy, discussion of patient-initiated ideas to address problems) <br> \***Note:** In all groups, patients and families received psychoeducation regarding depression and the treatment of depression | • Significantly more adolescents in CBT group met requirement for remission (absence of MDD and three consecutive low self-report depression scores, sustained through sessions). Rates of remission were 60% for CBT, 37.9% for family therapy and 39.4% for supportive therapy; CBT group also demonstrated a faster rate of symptom improvement <br> • At immediate post-treatment, there no differences between treatment groups in functional status <br> • At two-years post-treatment (Birmaher et al., 2000), no significant differences on outcome measures between the groups; most adolescents eventually recovered from depression |

| Study | Format | Participants/Setting | Interventions | Results |
|---|---|---|---|---|
| Weisz et al. 1997 | Group 8 weekly sessions (including one individual session) | 48 children 3rd–6th grade school | • **Primary and Secondary Control Enhancement Training** (PASCET; two-process model of control; primary control involves active problem solving and instrumental behavior and secondary control refers to emotion-focused coping and ability to adjust oneself)<br>• **Control Group** (No treatment) | • At immediate post-treatment and 9-month follow-up, the treatment group demonstrated significantly greater reductions in depressive symptoms on a self-report questionnaire than the control group and a trend towards such on a clinical interview<br>• At immediate post-treatment, more treated children moved into the normal range on the questionnaire measure; at follow-up, significantly more treated children fell in the normal range for both the questionnaire and interview measure |
| Clarke et al., 1999 | Group 16 two-hour sessions over 8 weeks; For adolescent + parent group, 8 additional two-hour parent sessions; participants in active treatment group randomly assigned to one of three conditions:1) booster sessions and assessments every 4 months, 2) assessments every 4 months with no booster sessions, or 3) annual assessments only with no booster sessions | 96 adolescents ages 14-18 setting not clearly indicated | • **Coping with Depression - Adolescent course** (see Lewinsohn et al., 1990)<br>• **Coping with Depression + Parent Group** (see Lewinsohn et al., 1990)<br>• **Waitlist Control**<br>• **Booster Sessions** (participants in active treatment sessions were randomly assigned to booster sessions or no booster sessions; however, attendance was less than 50%) | • Compared to wait-list condition, subjects in both treatment conditions improved on a self-report measure of depressive symptoms and clinical assessment of functioning (no significant difference between two active treatment groups), although not on parent-report measures<br>• At post-treatment, 66.7% of participants in the active treatment group demonstrated recovery from depression (defined as no longer meeting criteria for major depression or dysthymia as outlined in the DSM-III-R for the two weeks prior to the post-treatment assessment) compared to 48.1% of waitlist group; no significant difference in recovery between two active conditions<br>• Booster sessions did not appear to reduce relapse rate of those participants who had recovered during initial treatment but in the first year post-treatment may have helped those who remained depressed after treatment |
| Mufson et al., 1999 | Individual 12 weekly sessions + additional phone contact during first 4 weeks of treatment + one parent session | 48 adolescents, 32 completers ages 12–18 clinic | • **Interpersonal Psychotherapy for Depressed Adolescents** (IPT-A; see Mufson et al., 1994)<br>• **Clinical Monitoring** (30-minute monthly sessions; discussion of symptoms and functioning, supportive listening) | • Compared to the control group, adolescents in IPT-A treatment endorsed fewer depressive symptoms, in addition to improved overall social functioning and problem solving skills, at the end of treatment<br>• Significantly more IPT-A participants met criteria for recovery on clinician ratings of depression (75% vs. 46% in monitoring group)<br>• No significant group differences in clinical ratings of global functioning |

(continued)

**TABLE 6.1**
(Continued)

| Study | Format | Participants/Setting | Interventions | Results |
|-------|--------|---------------------|---------------|---------|
| Rossello & Bernal, 1999 | Individual 12 weekly 1-hour sessions | 71 adolescents ages 13–18 clinic | • **Interpersonal Psychotherapy for Depressed Adolescents** (IPT-A; see Mufson, 1994)<br>• **Cognitive Behavioral Therapy** (identification and restructuring of negative thinking; pleasant events scheduling; interpersonal relationships)<br>• **Waitlist**<br>**Note:** Active treatments were adapted for depressed Puerto Rican adolescents to provide for culturally sensitive treatment | • Compared to the waitlist condition, significant reduction in depressive symptoms for the two active treatment groups<br>• Compared to the waitlist group, IPT group showed improvements in self-esteem and social adjustment<br>• No significant differences between IPT and CBT groups at follow-up (waitlist group was provided treatment prior to follow-up evaluation so no comparisons with the waitlist group were available); however, high attrition rate for follow-up assessment |
| Mufson et al., 2004 | Individual 8 weekly 35-minute sessions followed by 4 sessions over 12 weeks | 63 adolescents, ages 12–18 school-based health clinic | • **Interpersonal Psychotherapy for Depressed Adolescents** (IPT-A; see Mufson, 1994)<br>• **Treatment as Usual** (treatment which would have been provided in the school-based setting should the study not have occurred; authors reported that, in general, such treatment resembled supportive counseling; mostly individual, some group, and some with additional family or parent sessions) | • Compared to the control group, adolescents in IPT-A treatment endorsed fewer depressive symptoms in addition to improved overall social functioning at the end of treatment<br>• More IPT-A participants met criteria for recovery on clinician ratings of depression (50% vs. 34% in treatment as usual group) and on a self-report measure (74% vs. 52%)<br>• Adolescents in the IPT-A group demonstrated significantly greater improvement in clinical ratings of global functioning |

it becomes important to provide concrete examples of how thinking affects feeling, as well as simple methods to challenge maladaptive cognition. In addition, behavioral interventions are a key component of treatment, especially for children and adolescents. Behavioral interventions include engagement in pleasant activities and training in coping strategies to improve mood, as well as direct instruction in problem solving. Kendall (2006) describes that the therapist working with children and adolescents assumes the role of a "coach" by stressing the importance of applying the skills to the real-life concerns of the children rather than merely talking about the skills in an abstract manner.

Cognitive-behavioral therapy for children is considered "possibly efficacious" (Kazdin & Weisz, 1998) according to the criteria outlined by Chambless and Hollon (1998). According to Chambless and Hollon, empirically-supported treatments are ones that have been found to have greater efficacy than no treatment, a placebo, or an alternate treatment. Furthermore, their effects are present across multiple studies conducted by different research teams. Kazdin and Weisz (1998) point out that the label of CBT as "possibly efficacious" for children is conservative and has been applied because different research teams are using various manualized programs, albeit with positive results.

An example of one such manualized CBT treatment program that has received empirical support is Clarke et al.'s (1999) Coping with Depression Course (CWDC). The program consists of 16 two-hour group meetings delivered over 8 weeks. Participants are educated about the nature of depression and are provided with a cognitive–behavioral rationale for treatment. During subsequent meetings, participants are taught a variety of behavioral and cognitive skills. Self-monitoring is used to help the participants become more aware of their moods and the strategies that they use to try to improve mood, including pleasant events scheduling. Participants are taught to identify and change negative thoughts. In addition to these core cognitive-behavioral treatment components, CWDC teaches participants social skills, skills for improving communication and decreasing conflict, and skills for reducing anxiety. The skills are taught through didactic presentations, coaching, rehearsal, and feedback and are applied through structured homework assignments. Evaluations of the CWDC have shown that recovery rates for depressed adolescents in the program were greater than for those in a wait-list control group, and improvements were maintained over 2 years (Clarke et al., 1995; Clarke et al., 1999).

## Interpersonal Psychotherapy for Adolescents

Interpersonal Psychotherapy for Depressed Adolescents (IPT-A) is an adaptation of a brief psychotherapy initially developed by Klerman and colleagues (Klerman, Weissman, Rounsaville, & Chevron, 1984) for depressed adults which has been modified for use with adolescents (Mufson, Moreau, Weissman, & Klerman, 1993). The primary goals of this form of therapy include improvement in interpersonal functioning and development of a greater understanding on the part of parents and adolescents about depression in this population, in addition to a reduction of depressive symptoms. As Mufson, Gallagher, Dorta, and Young (2004) note, "IPT-A posits that, regardless of etiology, depression occurs in an interpersonal context" (p. 221). Although initially developed as an individual therapy, it was later adapted to be used in a group format (Mufson et al., 2004). Both the individual and group forms of the treatment are divided into a number of phases, including identifying specific problem areas (i.e., mild to moderate grief, interpersonal role disputes, role transitions, interpersonal deficits, and living in single-parent families), developing an understanding of the problem area, attainment and application of skills specific to the problem area, and termination.

Treatment involves two initial individual sessions with the adolescent, as well as some parental involvement. During these individual sessions, information about the adolescents' interpersonal functioning is gathered. Also, the specific problems that will become the areas of focus are determined in these initial sessions. Next, there are 12 group therapy sessions, as well as an additional session with each participant and parent during the middle of the treatment and at the end. These individual sessions serve as a means to review progress and modify therapeutic goals as necessary. The group therapy sessions focus upon the acquisition and application of new interpersonal skills, which are practiced in vivo within the context of the interpersonal relationships existing in the group. Termination is given particular consideration as the therapists work to reinforce the group member's competence and establish an adaptive and supportive termination experience (Mufson et al., 2004). Several studies have supported the efficacy (e.g., Mufson et al., 1994; Mufson & Fairbanks, 1996; Mufson, Weissman, Moreau, & Garfinkel, 1999; Rossello & Bernal, 1999) and effectiveness of IPT-A in a school-based clinic setting (Mufson et al., 2004).

## Treatment Designed for School-Based Delivery: The ACTION Project

Stark and colleagues have developed a comprehensive school-based depression treatment program for children, entitled the ACTION Program (Stark et al., 2005a; Stark, et al., 2005b). This program currently is being evaluated by Stark and his team at the University of Texas at Austin in surrounding local schools as part of a 5-year National Institute of Mental Health (NIMH) funded study. Given the gender difference in depression that is observed after puberty, the program is targeted at females in the upper elementary and early middle school grades, although the general treatment components would be appropriate for use with males and females and across age ranges, with some modifications (e.g., Stark et al., 2006b).

The most recent version of the treatment has its roots in earlier programs developed and tested by Stark and colleagues. In 1987, Stark and colleagues randomly assigned 29 moderately to severely depressed children to a self-control training group, a behavioral problem solving group, or a waitlist condition. Both of the groups met for 12 sessions. The intervention provided in the self-control training group was reflective of the treatment model for adults outlined by Rehm, Kaslow, and Rabin (1987) and included skills such self-monitoring of behavior and thoughts, self-evaluation and reward, and appropriate attributions. The behavioral problem-solving group focused on psychoeducation, pleasant events scheduling, and interpersonal problem-solving and was similar in some respects to an adult model designed by Lewinsohn, Sullivan, and Grosscup (1980). The results suggested that both active treatment groups demonstrated reductions in depressive symptoms across more measures than those in the waitlist control group. These benefits were maintained at an 8-week follow-up.

After these initial findings, Stark and colleagues (1991) tested a treatment package which combined the skills in both of the groups described above in a comprehensive cognitive-behavioral intervention. The intervention included 24 to 26 group sessions lasting approximately 3½ months. The therapy was provided in the school, and each child also participated in monthly individual family sessions. In the control condition, students received "traditional counseling," which included psychoeducation and supportive therapy. Twenty-four 4th to 7th graders were enrolled. At immediate post-treatment evaluation, greater reductions in depressive symptoms and negative cognitions were noted in the children who had received the cognitive-behavioral treatment package versus traditional counseling. No significant group differences were noted at a 7-month follow-up; however, only seven of the CBT participants and five of the traditional counseling participants were evaluated at the time of the follow-up.

The current conceptualization and implementation strategies for the ACTION project have been described in great detail in several recent sources (Stark et al., 2006a; Stark et al., 2006b), and we refer the interested reader to these comprehensive overviews of the treatment package for further information, as well as examples of actual materials. Although the cornerstone of the ACTION program is a group cognitive-behavioral child intervention, parent training and teacher consultation are also important components of the treatment package. All of these services are provided in the school setting.

The core component of the ACTION program is the group CBT sessions for the child participants. Groups are composed of four to six girls and, in the context of the research study, led by one or two highly trained graduate student therapists. There are 20 group and 2 individual meetings that occur over an approximately 11-week period. Additional individual meetings can be scheduled if necessary. Although the core therapeutic elements are presented in a specific order within the manual, the therapists may be flexible in their teaching and application of the skills and strategies in order to address the concerns which the participants bring to the group setting. As outlined by Stark and his team (Stark et al., 2006a; Stark et al., 2006b), the primary therapeutic components include affective education, goal setting, coping skills training, training in problem-solving and cognitive restructuring, and building a positive sense of self. Homework assignments are given in order to help the children apply the skills they have learned. Forms that can be utilized in the completion of the homework are included in the published workbook (Stark et al., 2005a). In addition, the participants in the study receive "ACTION kits," which include colorful cards providing reminders about the skills taught during the sessions as well as forms which allow the participants to outline their own goals for the therapy and specific plans that can be utilized to facilitate goal attainment.

The process of conducting the therapy within the schools during school hours offers the therapists the advantage of operating within the child's major systems. Participants come directly from classes and activities and can readily bring real-life problems or concerns into group. These concerns are discussed during the meeting time, and the therapeutic skills the children learn can be immediately applied. Being situated within the school offers the additional advantage of access to school personnel for consultative services.

Teacher consultation is an important part of the overall treatment package. Consultation appears most successful when conducted in a collaborative, collegial manner (Caplan & Caplan, 1999). By providing services in the schools, therapists are able to meet directly with teachers to gain their valuable observations regarding the child's behavior within the classroom. Additionally, collaborating with teachers allows for skills being discussed in group to be generalized to the classroom. For example, depressed children often present as being socially withdrawn, often because core beliefs such as "I'm unlovable" or "I'm unlikable" prevent them from initiating social contact. However, many of these children or adolescents do desire social contact. Teachers can help implement behavior modification programs that successively encourage increased levels of social approach-related behaviors. This environmental support facilitates the development of new skills and, in turn, helps provide experiences that are contradictory to negative core beliefs. For example, the teacher and student may establish two times during the day in which the student reports to the teacher social contacts he or she has initiated, such as smiling and saying "hello," inviting a partner to work, etc. When the teacher and child have a good relationship, this established time together can be reinforcing in and of itself. If not, small tangible rewards or privileges can be provided for attempts at social interaction. In addition to strengthening the teacher-student relationship, this also serves to establish the teacher as a resource to help the student problem-solve challenging social situations. A variety of other specific classroom-based interventions which can be developed in collaboration with the therapist and teacher have been outlined by Stark and colleagues (Stark et al., 2006a).

One of the specific research questions being addressed by the current investigation conducted by Stark and his team is whether or not the addition of an eight-session parent training element (with two individual family sessions) improves treatment outcomes beyond the group therapy. One of the primary objectives of the parent training is to provide parents with ways to reinforce and support the skills the children are learning. At the same time, it is hoped that the parents will learn the skills themselves and attempt to apply them in their own lives. It is stressed that since children only meet as part of the group for a relatively short period of time, practice outside the group is essential. Furthermore, tuning the parent into the child's key negative automatic thoughts and core beliefs allows parents to be aware of any messages they send which either support or negate such maladaptive thinking. The ACTION program also teaches parents skills such as empathic listening, effective communication, positive behavior management, and conflict resolution. Half the meetings involve only parents while the other half include both the parents and the child participants in order to provide opportunities to practice skills. Finally, many of the activities included in the parent training component revolve around strengthening the relationship between parent and child, including the scheduling of pleasant family events and learning to use effective praise. Preliminary results with the first 62 participants are very promising and suggest that more children improve through treatment than from the normal passage of time (Reinemann et al., 2006).

Thus, a growing evidence base supports the use of various manualized cognitive-behavioral and interpersonal intervention programs to treat depression in youth. However, school-based professionals will likely need some additional training in order to implement these programs with their students. Likewise, it will be important for future research to examine the effectiveness of such programs when implemented by school mental health personnel. Factors that may impact treatment outcomes such as age, gender, race/ethnicity, SES, etc. of participants, along with treatment integrity, adherence, and other implementation factors also await further examination. Although much work still needs to be done, initial evidence shows that cognitive-behavioral treatments for childhood depression are effective and can be easily implemented in the school setting. It is hoped that knowledge of childhood depression and related interventions will lead to the implementation of such programs by school-based professionals. Use of evidence-based treatments will translate into more positive student outcomes in those suffering from depression and will particularly benefit those students who otherwise may remain unidentified and untreated.

## REFERENCES

Achenbach, T. M., & Rescorla, L. A. (2001). *Manual for ASEBA School-Age Forms & Profiles*. Burlington, VT: University of Vermont, Research Center for Children, Youth, & Families.

Alford, B. A., & Beck, A. T. (1997). *The integrative power of cognitive therapy*. New York: Guilford.

American Academy of Child and Adolescent Psychiatry. (1998). Summary of the practice parameters for the adolescent and treatment of children and adolescents with depressive disorders. *Journal of the American Academy of Child and Adolescent Psychiatry, 37*, 1234–1239.

American Psychiatric Association. (2000). *Diagnostic and statistical manual of mental disorders* (4th ed., text revision). Washington, DC: Author.

Anderman, E. M. (2002). School effects on psychological outcomes during adolescence. *Journal of Educational Psychology, 94*, 795–809.

Anhalt, K., & Morris, T. L. (1998). Developmental and adjustment issues of gay, lesbian, and bisexual adolescents: A review of the empirical literature. *Clinical Child and Family Psychology Review, 1*, 215–230.

Arnold, E. M., Goldston, D. B., Walsh, A. K., Reboussin, B. A., Daniel, S. S., Hickman, E., et al. (2005).

Severity of emotional and behavioral problems among poor and typical readers. *Journal of Abnormal Child Psychology, 33*, 205–217.

Beck, J. S., Beck, A. T. & Jolly, J. (2001). *Beck Youth Inventories*. San Antonio, TX: The Psychological Corporation.

Beck, J. (1995). *Cognitive therapy: Basics and beyond*. New York: Guilfords.

Birmaher, B., Brent, D. A., Kolko, D., Baugher, M., Bridge, J., Holder, D., et al. (2000). Clinical outcome after short-term psychotherapy for adolescents with major depressive disorder. *Archives of General Psychiatry, 37*, 29–36.

Brent, D. A., Holder, D., Kolko, D., Birmaher, B., Baugher, M., Roth, C., et al. (1997). A clinical psychotherapy trial for adolescent depression comparing cognitive, family, and supportive therapy. *Archives of General Psychiatry, 54*, 877–885.

Bui, K., & Takeuchi, D. T. (1992). Ethnic minority adolescents and the use of community mental health care services. *American Journal of Community Psychology, 20*, 403–417.

Burns, B., Costello, E. J., Angold, A., Tweed, D., Stangl, D., Farmer, E. M. Z., et al. (1995). DataWatch: Children's mental health service use across service sectors. *Health Affair, 14*, 147–159.

Butler, L., Miezitis, S., Friedman, R., & Cole, E. (1980). The effect of two school-based intervention programs on depressive symptoms in preadolescents. *American Educational Research Journal, 17*, 111–119.

Caplan, G., & Caplan, R. B. (1999). *Mental health consultation and collaboration*. Prospect Heights, IL: Waveland Press.

Casey, R. J., & Berman, J. S. (1985). The outcome of psychotherapy with children. *Psychological Bulletin, 98*, 388–400.

Cauce, A. M., Domenech-Rodriguez, M., Paradise, M., Cochran, B. N., Shea, J. M., Srebnik, D. et al. (2002). Cultural and contextual influences in mental health help seeking: A focus on ethnic minority youth. *Journal of Consulting and Clinical Psychology, 70*, 44–55.

Chambless, D. L., & Hollon, S. D. (1998). Defining empirically supported therapies. *Journal of Consulting & Clinical Psychology, 66*, 7–18.

Clark, D. A., Beck, A. T., & Alford, B. A. (1999). *Scientific foundations of cognitive theory and therapy of depression*. New York: Wiley.

Clarke, G. N., Hawkins, W., Murphy, M., Sheeber, L. B., Lewinsohn, P. M., & Seeley, J. R. (1995). Targeted prevention of unipolar depressive disorder in an at-risk sample of high school adolescents: A randomized trial of a group cognitive intervention. *Journal of the American Academy of Child and Adolescent Psychiatry, 34*, 312–321.

Clarke, G. N., Rohde, P., Lewinsohn, P. M., Hops, H., & Seeley, J. R. (1999). Cognitive-behavioral treatment of adolescent depression: Efficacy of acute group treatment and booster sessions. *Journal of the American Academy of Child and Adolescent Psychiatry, 38*, 272–279.

Cutler, S. E., & Nolen-Hoeksema, S. (1991). Accounting for sex differences in depression through female victimization: Childhood sexual abuse. *Sex Roles, 24*, 425–438.

Durlak, J. A., Wells, A. M., Cotton, J. K., & Johnson, S. (1995). Analysis of selected methodological issues in child psychotherapy research. *Journal of Clinical Child Psychology, 24*, 141–148.

Emslie, G. J., Heiligenstein, J. H., Wagner, K. D., Hoog, S. L., Ernest, D. W., Brown, E., et al. (2002). Fluoxetine for acute treatment of depression in children and adolescents: A placebo-controlled, randomized clinical trial. *Journal of the American Academy of Child and Adolescent Psychiatry, 41*, 1205–1215.

Emslie, G. J., Rush, A. J., Weinberg, W. A., Kowatch, R. A., Hughes, C. W., Carmody, T., et al. (1997). A double-blind, randomized, placebo-controlled trial of fluoxetine in children and adolescents with depression. *Archives of General Psychiatry, 54*, 1031–1037.

Federal Drug Administration (2004). *FDA updates its review of antidepressant drugs in children: Agency details plans to present data to advisory committees in September and seek advice on appropriate regulatory actions*. Retrieved August 28, 2004, from http://www.fda.gov/bbs/topics/ANSWERS/2004/ANS01306.html

Fine, S., Forth, A., Gilbert, M., & Haley, G. (1991). Group therapy for adolescent depressive disorder: A comparison of social skills and therapeutic support. *Journal of the American Academy of Child and Adolescent Psychiatry, 30*, 79–85.

Fristad, M. A., Goldberg-Arnold, J. S., & Gavazzi, S. M. (2002). Multifamily psychoeducation groups (MFPG) for families of children with bipolar disorder. *Bipolar Disorders, 4*, 254–262.

Garrison, C. Z., Jackson, K. L., Marsteller, F., McKeown, R., & Addy, C. (1990). A longitudinal study of depressive symptomatology in young adolescents. *Journal of the American Academy of Child and Adolescent Psychiatry, 29*, 580–585.

Geller, B., Reising, D., Leonard, H., Riddle, M. A., & Walsh, B.T. (1999). Critical review of tricyclic anti-depressant use in children and adolescents. *Journal of the American Academy of Child and Adolescent Psychiatry, 38*, 513–517.

Gillham, J. E., & Reivich, K. J. (1999). Prevention of depressive symptoms in school children: A research update. *Psychological Science, 10*, 461–462.

Gillham, J. E., Reivich, K. J., Freres, D. R., Lascher, M., Litzinger, S., Shatté, A., et al. (2006). School-based prevention of depression and anxiety symptoms in early adolescence: A pilot of a parent intervention component. *School Psychology Quarterly, 21*, 323–348.

Graber, J. A., Lewinsohn, P. M., Seeley, J. R., & Brooks-Gunn, J. (1997). Is psychopathology associated with the timing of pubertal development? *Journal of the American Academy of Child and Adolescent Psychiatry, 36*, 1768–1776.

Hammen, C., & Rudolph, K. D. (2003). Childhood mood disorders. In E. J. Mash & R. A. Barkley (Eds.), *Child psychopathology* (2nd ed., pp. 233–278). New York: Guilford Press.

Hankin, B. L., Abramson, L. Y., Moffitt, T. E., Silva, P. A., McGee, R., & Angell, K. E. (1998). Development of depression from preadolescence to young adulthood: Emerging gender differences in a 10-year longitudinal study. *Journal of Abnormal Psychology, 107*, 128–140.

Harrington, R., Kerfoot, M., Dyer, E., McNiven, F., Gill, J., Harrington, V., et al. (2000). Deliberate self-poisoning in adolescence: Why does a brief family intervention work in some cases and not others. *Journal of Adolescence, 23*, 13–20.

Heim, C., Newport, J., Heit, S., Graham, Y., Wilcox, M., Bonsall, R., et al. (2000). Pituitary-adrenal and autonomic responses to stress in women after sexual and physical abuse in childhood. *Journal of the American Medical Association, 284*, 592–596.

Hoagwood, K., & Jensen, P. S. (1997). Developmental psychopathology and the notion of culture: Introduction to the special section on "The fusion of cultural horizons: Cultural influences on the assessment of psychopathology in children and adolescents." *Applied Developmental Science, 1*, 108–112.

Hoge, D. R., Smith, E. K., & Hanson, S. L. (1990). School experiences predicting changes in self-esteem of sixth and seventh-grade students. *Journal of Educational Psychology, 82*, 117–127.

Hollon, S. D., & Kriss, M. R. (1984). Cognitive factors in clinical research and practice. *Clinical Psychology Review, 4*, 35–76.

Iwata, N., Turner, R. J., & Lloyd, D. A. (2002). Race/ethnicity and depressive symptoms in community-dwelling young adults: A differential item functioning analysis. *Psychiatry Research, 110*, 281–289.

Jaycox, L. H., Reivich, K. J., Gillham, J., & Seligman, M. E. P. (1994). Prevention of depressive symptoms in school children. *Behavior Research and Therapy, 32*, 801–816.

Jonas, B. S., Brody, D., Roper, M., & Narrow, W. E. (2003). Prevalence of mood disorders in a national sample of young American adults. *Social Psychiatry and Psychiatric Epidemiology, 38*, 618–624.

Kahn, J. S., & Kehle, T. J. (1990). Comparison of cognitive-behavioral, relaxation, and self-modeling interventions for depression. *School Psychology Review, 19*, 196–212.

Kaplan, S., & Busner, J. (1992). A note on racial bias in the admission of children and adolescents to state mental health facilities versus correctional facilities in New York. *American Journal of Psychiatry, 149*, 768–772.

Kazdin, A. (2000). *Psychotherapy for children and adolescents: Directions for research and practice.* New York: Guilford.

Kazdin, A., & Weisz, J. R. (1998). Identifying and developing empirically supported child and adolescent treatments. *Journal of Consulting and Clinical Psychology, 66*, 19–36.

Keller, M. B., Ryan, N. D., Strober, M., Klein, R. G., Kutcher, S. P., Birmaher, B., et al. (2001). Efficacy of paroxetine in the treatment of adolescent major depression: A randomized, controlled trial. *Journal of the American Academy of Child and Adolescent Psychiatry, 40*, 762–772.

Kendall, P. C. (2006). Guiding theory for therapy with children and adolescents. In P.C. Kendall (Ed.), *Child and adolescent therapy: Cognitive-behavioral procedures* (pp. 3–30). New York: Guilford.

Kessler, R. C. (2002). Epidemiology of depression. In I. H. Gotlib & C. L. Hammen (Eds.), *Handbook of depression* (pp. 23–42). New York: Guilford.

Kessler, R. C., Foster, C. L., Saunders, W. B., & Stang, P. E. (1995). Social consequences of psychiatric disorders: I. Educational attainment. *American Journal of Psychiatry, 152,* 1026–1032.

Kessler, R. C., & Walters, E. E. (1998). Epidemiology of DSM-III-R major depression and minor depression among adolescents and young adults in the National Comorbidity Survey. *Depression and Anxiety, 7,* 3–14.

Klerman, G. L., Weissman, M. M., Rounsaville, B. J., & Chevron, E. S. (1984). *Interpersonal psychotherapy of depression.* New York: Basic Books.

Kovacs, M. (1992). *Children's Depression Inventory Manual.* New York: Multi-Health Systems, Inc.

Kovacs, M., & Goldston, D. (1991). Cognitive and social cognitive development of depressed children and adolescents. *Journal of the American Academy of Child and Adolescent Psychiatry, 30,* 388–392.

Lewinsohn, P. M., Clarke, G. N., Hops, H., & Andrews, J. (1990). Cognitive-behavioral treatment for depressed adolescents. *Behavior Therapy, 21,* 385–401.

Lewinsohn, P. M., Roberts, R. E., Seeley, J. R., Rohde, P., Gotlib, I. H., & Hops, H. (1994). Adolescent psychopathology II: Psychosocial risk factors for depression. *Journal of Abnormal Psychology, 103,* 302–315.

Lewinsohn, P. M., Rohde, P., Klein, D. M., & Seeley, J. R (1999). Natural course of adolescent major depressive disorder: I. Continuity into young adulthood. *Journal of the American Academy of Child and Adolescent Psychiatry, 38,* 56–63.

Lewinsohn, P. M., Rohde, P., & Seeley, J. R. (1998). Major depressive disorder in older adolescents: Prevalence, risk factors, and clinical implications. *Clinical Psychology Review, 18,* 765–794.

Lewinsohn, P. M., Rohde, P., Seeley, J. R, Klein, D. N., & Gotlib, I. H. (2003). Psychosocial functioning of young adults who have experienced and recovered from major depressive disorder during adolescence. *Journal of Abnormal Psychology, 112,* 353–363.

Lewinsohn, P. M., Sullivan, J. M., & Grosscup, S. J. (1980). Changing reinforcing events: An approach to the treatment of depression. *Psychotherapy: Theory, Research and Practice, 17,* 322–334.

Liddle, B., & Spence, S. H. (1990). Cognitive behaviour therapy with depressed primary school children: A cautionary note. *Behavioural Psychotherapy, 18,* 85–102.

Mash, E. J., & Dozois, D. J. (2003). Child psychopathology: A developmental-systems perspective. In E. J. Mash & R. A. Barkley (Eds.), *Treatment of childhood disorders* (pp. 3–71). New York: Guilford.

Miklowitz, D. J., George, E. L., Axelson, D. A., Kim, E. Y., Birmaher, B., Schneck, C., et al. (2004). Family-focused treatment for adolescents with bipolar disorder. *Journal of Affective Disorders, 82S,* S113–S128.

Mufson, L., Dorta, K. P., Olfson, M., Weissman, M. M., & Hoagwood, K. (2004). Effectiveness research: Transporting interpersonal psychotherapy for depressed adolescents (IPT-A) from the lab to school-based health clinics. *Clinical Child and Family Psychology Review, 7,* 251–261.

Mufson, L., Dorta, K. P., Wickramaratne, P., Nomura, Y., Olfson, M., & Weissman, M. M. (2004). A randomized effectiveness trial of interpersonal psychotherapy for depressed adolescents. *Archives of General Psychiatry, 61,* 577–584.

Mufson, L., & Fairbanks, J. (1996). Interpersonal psychotherapy for depressed adolescents: A one-year naturalistic follow-up study. *Journal of the American Academy of Child and Adolescent Psychiatry, 35,* 1145–1155.

Mufson, L., Gallagher, T., Dorta, K. P., & Young, J. F. (2004). A group adaption of interpersonal psychotherapy for depressed adolescents. *American Journal of Psychotherapy, 58,* 220–237.

Mufson, L., Moreau, D., Weissman, M. M., & Garfinkel, R. (1999). Efficacy of interpersonal psychotherapy for depressed adolescents. *Archives of General Psychiatry, 56,* 573–579.

Mufson, L., Moreau, D., Weissman, M. M., & Klerman, G. L. (1993). *Interpersonal psychotherapy for depressed adolescents.* New York: Guilford.

Mufson, L., Moreau, D., Weissman, M. M., Wickramaratne, P., Martin, J., & Samoilov, A. (1994).

Modification of interpersonal psychotherapy with depressed adolescents (IPT-A): Phase I and II Studies. *Journal of American Academy of Child and Adolescent Psychiatry, 33,* 695–705.

Mufson, L., Weissman, M. M., Moreau, D., & Garfinkel, R. (1999). Efficacy of interpersonal psychotherapy for depressed adolescents. *Archives of General Psychiatry, 56,* 573–579.

Muñoz, R. F., Penilla, C., & Urizar, G. (2002). Expanding depression prevention research with children of diverse cultures. *Prevention & Treatment, 5,* Article 13. Retrieved August 16, 2004, from http://journals.apa.org/prevention/volume5/pre0050013c.html

Murray, C., & Greenberg, M. T. (2000). Children's relationship with teachers and bonds with school. An investigation of patterns and correlates in middle childhood. *Journal of School Psychology, 38,* 423–445.

Nolen-Hoeksema, S. (2002). Gender differences in depression. In I. H. Gotlib & C. L. Hammen (Eds.), *Handbook of depression* (pp. 492–509). New York: Guilford.

Nottelmann, E. D., & Jensen, P. S. (1995). Comorbidity of disorders in children and adolescents: Developmental perspectives. In T. H. Ollendick & R. J. Prinz (Eds.), *Advances in clinical child psychology* (*Vol. 17,* pp. 109–155). New York: Plenum.

Orvaschel, H. & Puig-Antich, J. (1994). *Schedule for affective disorders and schizophrenia for school-age children* (Epidemiologic version, 5th ed.). Pittsburgh, PA: Western Psychiatric Institute and Clinic.

Petersen, A. C., Compas, B. E., Brooks-Gunn, J., Stemmler, M., Ey, S., & Grant, K. E. (1993). Depression in adolescence. *American Psychologist, 48,* 155–168.

Puig-Antich, J., Lukens, E., Davies, M., Goetz, D., Brennan-Quattrock, J., & Todak, G. (1985). Psychosocial functioning in prepubertal major depressive disorders: I. Interpersonal relationships during the depressive episode. *Archives of General Psychiatry, 42,* 500–507.

Reddy, R., Rhodes, J. E., & Mulhall, P. (2003). The influence of teacher support on student adjustment in the middle school years: A latent growth curve study. *Development and Psychopathology, 15,* 119–138.

Rehabilitation Act of 1973, Section 504. (1973). 29 U.S.C. § 706, 1996; § 504 [30 C.F.R Part 104].

Rehm, L. P., Kaslow, N. J, & Rabin, A. S. (1987). Cognitive and behavioral targets in a self-control therapy program for depression. *Journal of Consulting and Clinical Psychology, 55,* 60–67.

Reinemann, D. S., Stark, K. D., Molnar, J., & Simpson, J. (2006). Depressive disorders. In G. G. Bear & K. M. Minke (Eds.), *Children's needs III: Development, prevention, and intervention* (pp. 199–210). Bethesda, MD: National Association of School Psychologists.

Reinherz, H. Z., Giaconia, R. M., Lefkowitz, E. S., Pakiz, B., & Frost, A. K. (1993). Prevalence of psychiatric disorders in a community population of older adolescents. *Journal of the American Academy of Child and Adolescent Psychiatry, 32,* 369–377.

Reynolds, C. R., & Kamphaus, R. W. (2004). *Behavior Assessment System for Children, 2nd Edition (BASC-2) Manual.* Circle Pines, MN: American Guidance Service.

Reynolds, W.M. (1989). *Reynolds Child Depression Scale.* Odessa, FL: Psychological Assessment Resources, Inc.

Reynolds, W. M. (1994). Assessment of depression in children and adolescents by self-report questionnaires. In W. M. Reynolds & H. E. Johnston (Eds.), *Handbook of depression in children and adolescents* (pp. 209–234). New York: Plenum.

Reynolds, W. M., & Coates, K. I. (1986). A comparison of cognitive-behavioral therapy and relaxation training for the treatment of depression in adolescents. *Journal of Consulting and Clinical Psychology, 54,* 653–660.

Roberts, R. E., Roberts, C. R., & Chen, Y. R. (1997). Ethnocultural differences in prevalence of adolescent depression. *American Journal of Community Psychology, 25,* 95–110.

Rohde, P., Lewinsohn. P. M., & Seeley, J. R. (1991). Comorbidity of unipolar depression: II. Comorbidity with other mental disorders in adolescents and adults. *Journal of Abnormal Psychology, 100,* 214–222.

Roeser, R. W., Midgley, C., & Urdan, T. C. (1996). Perceptions of the school psychological environment and early adolescents' psychological and behavioral functioning in school: The mediating role of goals and belonging. *Journal of Educational Psychology, 88,* 408–422.

Rossello, J., & Bernal, G. (1999). The efficacy of cognitive-behavioral and interpersonal treatments for depression in Puerto Rican adolescents. *Journal of Consulting and Clinical Psychology, 67*, 734–745.

Rudolph, K. D. (2002). Gender differences in emotional responses to interpersonal stress during adolescence. *Journal of Adolescent Health, 30*, 3–13.

Rudolph, K. D., & Clark, A. G. (2001). Conceptions of relationships in children with depressive and aggressive symptoms: Social-cognitive distortion or reality? *Journal of Abnormal Child Psychology, 29*, 41–56.

Rushton, J. L., Forcier, M., & Schectman, R. M. (2003). Epidemiology of depressive symptoms in the national longitudinal study of adolescent health. *Journal of the American Academy of Child and Adolescent Psychiatry, 41*, 199–205.

Sander, J. B., & McCarty, C. A. (2005). Youth depression in the family context: Familial risk factors and models of treatment. *Clinical Child and Family Psychology Review, 8*, 203–219.

Sander, J. B., Reinemann, D. S., & Herren, S. (2007). School-based interventions for children with internalizing disorders. In S. Goldstein (Ed.), *Understanding and managing children's classroom behavior, second edition* (pp. 361–382). Hoboken, NJ: Wiley.

Sanford, M., Boyle, M., McCleary, L., Miller, J., Steele, M., Duku, E., et al. (2006). A pilot study of adjunctive family psychoeducation in adolescent major depression: Feasibility and treatment effect. *Journal of the American Academy of Child and Adolescent Psychiatry, 45*, 386–395.

Shirk, S., & Russell, R. L. (1996). *Change processes in child psychotherapy: Revitalizing treatment and research.* New York: Guilford.

Shochet, I. M., Dadds, M. R., Holland, D., Whitefield, K., Harnett, P. H., & Osgarby, S. M. (2001). The efficacy of a universal school-based program to prevent adolescent depression. *Journal of Clinical Child Psychology, 30*, 303–315.

Simeon, J. G., Dinicola, V. F., Ferguson, H. B., & Copping, W. (1990). Adolescent depression: A placebo-controlled fluoxetine treatment study and follow-up. *Progress in Neuro-Psychopharmacology & Biological Psychiatry, 14*, 791–795.

Spence, S. H., Sheffield, J. K., & Donovan, C. L. (2003). Preventing adolescent depression: An evaluation of the Problem Solving for Life program. *Journal of Consulting and Clinical Psychology, 71*, 3–13.

Spence, S. H., Sheffield, J. K., & Donovan, C. L. (2005). Long-term outcome of a school-based, universal approach to prevention of depression in adolescents. *Journal of Consulting and Clinical Psychology, 73*, 160–167.

Stark, K. D. (1990). *The treatment of depression during childhood: A school-based program.* New York: Guilford.

Stark, K. D., Hargrave, J., Sander, J., Custer, G., Schnoebelen, S., Simpson, J., et al. (2006a). Treatment of childhood depression: The ACTION treatment program. In P. C. Kendall (Ed.), *Child and adolescent therapy: Cognitive-behavioral procedures* (pp. 169–216). New York: Guilford.

Stark, K. D., Reynolds, W. M., & Kaslow, N. J. (1987). A comparison of the relative efficacy of self-control therapy and a behavioral problem-solving therapy for depression in children. *Journal of Abnormal Child Psychology, 15*, 91–113.

Stark, K. D., Rouse, L. W., & Livingston, R. (1991). Treatment of depression during childhood and adolescence: Cognitive-behavioral procedures for the individual and family. In P.C. Kendall (Ed.), *Child and adolescent therapy: Cognitive-behavioral procedures* (pp. 165–206). New York: Guilford.

Stark, K. D., Sander, J., Hauser, M., Simpson, J., Schnoebelen, S., Glenn, R., et al. (2006b). Depressive disorders during childhood and adolescence. In E.J. Mash and R.A. Barkley (Eds.), *Treatment of childhood disorders, third edition* (pp. 336–407). New York: Guilford.

Stark, K. D., Schnoebelen, S., Simpson, J., Hargrave, J., Molnar, J., & Glenn, R.(2005). *Treating depressed children: Therapist's manual for ACTION.* Broadmore, PA: Workbook Publishing.

Stark, K. D., Simpson, J., Schnoebelen, S., Glenn, R., Hargrave, J., & Molnar, J. (2005). *Children's workbook for ACTION.* Broadmore, PA: Workbook Publishing.

Sue, S. (1988). Psychotherapeutic services for ethnic minorities: Two decades of research findings. *American Psychologist, 43*, 301–308.

Treatment for Adolescents with Depression Study (TADS) Team. (2004). Fluoxetine, cognitive-behavioral therapy, and their combination for adolescents with depression: Treatment for adolescents with depression study (TADS) randomized controlled trial. *Journal of the American Medical Association, 292,* 807–820.

Twenge, J. M., & Nolen-Hoeksema, S. (2002). Age, gender, race, sociometric status, and birth cohort differences on the Children's Depression Inventory: A meta-analysis. *Journal of Abnormal Psychology, 111,* 578–588.

U.S. Public Health Service. (2001). *Report of the surgeon general's conference on children's mental health: A national action agenda.* Washington, DC: U.S. Department of Health and Human Services.

Vostanis, P., Feehan, C., Grattan, E., & Bickerton, W.-L. (1996a). Treatment for children and adolescents with depression: Lessons from a controlled trial. *Clinical Child Psychology and Psychiatry, 1,* 199–212.

Vostanis, P., Feehan, C., Grattan, E., & Bickerton, W.-L. (1996b). A randomized controlled out-patient trial of cognitive-behavioural treatment for children and adolescents with depression: 9-month follow-up. *Journal of Affective Disorders, 40,* 105–116.

Wagner, K. D., Ambrosini, P., Rynn, M., Wohlberg, C., Yang, R., Greenbaum, M. S., et al. (2003). Efficacy of sertraline in the treatment of children and adolescents with major depressive disorder: Two randomized controlled trials. *Journal of the American Medical Association, 290,* 1033–1041.

Wagner, K. D., Robb, A. S., Findling, R. L., Jin, J., Gutierrez, M. M., & Heydorn, W. E. (2004). A randomized, placebo-controlled trial of citalopram for the treatment of major depression in children and adolescents. *American Journal of Psychiatry, 161,* 1079–1083.

Weisz, J. R., Doss, A. J., & Hawley, K. M. (2005). Youth psychotherapy outcome research: A review and critique of the evidence base. *Annual Review of Psychology, 56,* 337–363.

Weisz, J. R., Thurber, C. A., Sweeney, L., Proffitt, V. D., & LeGagnoux, G. L. (1997). Brief treatment of mild-to-moderate child depression using primary and secondary control enhancement training. *Journal of Consulting and Clinical Psychology, 65,* 703–707.

Weisz, J. R., Weiss, B., Alicke, M. D., & Klotz, M. L. (1987). Effectiveness of psychotherapy with children and adolescents: A meta-analysis for clinicians. *Journal of Consulting and Clinical Psychology, 55,* 542–549.

Weisz, J. R., Weiss, B., Han, S. S., & Granger, D. A. (1995). Effects of psychotherapy with children and adolescents revisited: A meta-analysis of treatment outcome studies. *Psychological Bulletin, 117,* 450–468.

Wood, A., Harrington, R., & Moore, A. (1996). Controlled trial of a brief cognitive-behavioural intervention in adolescent patients with depressive disorders. *Journal of Child Psychology and Psychiatry, 37,* 737–746.

Zito, J. M., Safer, D. J., DosReis, S., & Riddle, M. A. (1998). Racial disparity in psychotropic medications prescribed for youths with Medicaid insurance in Maryland. *Journal of the American Academy of Child and Adolescent Psychiatry, 37,* 179–184.

# III

# STUDENTS HAVING LEARNING CHALLENGES

# 7

# Oral Language Problems

## Kathleen R. Fahey

Research findings regarding efficacious speech and language intervention have been on the rise in recent years. Efforts have been made to link science to practice across many areas of intervention through the life span (Fey & Johnson, 1998; Hodson, 1998; Imbens-Bailey, 1998; Ingram, 1998; Wilcox, Hadley, & Bacon, 1998). Some researchers use their empirical findings to provide details regarding how clinicians and educators can adapt them to their work with students including characteristics of individuals who will benefit from such research, and what methodology needs to be utilized for implementing the interventions (Holland, 1998). Clearly, the movement for evidence-based practice is forging new and exciting connections between researchers, clinicians, and educators. In this regard, in 2005, the editors of *Topics in Language Disorders* (Butler, Nelson, Wallach, Fujiki, & Brinton) devoted the fall issue of the journal to a look at how researchers have studied the nature of language and learning disabilities, and how practitioners have worked with such students during the past 25 years. The perspective of the articles was to examine how we have changed our views based on both research and practice, but also how we have remained the same in many of our beliefs and practices across time.

The most remarkable changes in recent years regarding language learning problems have occurred in our understandings of the nature of such problems in the context of the school day and across the oral-literacy continuum, the ways in which they should be identified relative to the school curriculum and other social and vocational settings, the collaboration of professionals including general education teachers to make identification and intervention relevant for classroom learning, and the participation of the students and parents as active decision-makers in team intervention planning. These advances in our thinking and actions have led to our current interventions that are decidedly more student and curricula-centered than they have been in the past. Intervention must be focused on building a student's success in academic, social and vocational realms. Speech-language pathologists (SLPs), special educators, and classroom teachers are learning to work together toward the realization of intervention goals, which is of central importance in integrating language learning goals into the curriculum. In this regard, the recent addition of the Response to Intervention (RTI) model is an exciting avenue for strong collaboration of educators with the goal of applying interventions directly in the classroom. The core principles of RTI stress that: we can effectively teach all children; early intervention matters; a multi-tier model of service delivery provides appropriate and effective intervention; a problem-solving approach to decision-making is profitable; interventions and instructions are research-based and scientifically validated; student progress informs instruction; data is used to make decisions; and assessment is used for screening, diagnostics, and progress monitoring (National Association of State Directors of Special Education, 2005). Under this model, SLPs and related service professionals must redefine their roles to become actively engage in the general education curriculum. In addition, teachers are encouraged to take advantage of the particular and specialized education and experience of SLPs and related service providers to maximize the shared responsibility for the implementation of RTI.

The focus of this chapter is on what we know about oral language problems, how these problems are manifest in academic and social situations, and the current state of interventions available to practitioners in classrooms and through other service delivery models including collaboration, consultation, RTI, and traditional pull-out intervention strategies. In particular, the focus is on students who have language-learning problems, hereafter referred to as students with language impairment (LI). It does not include students who have speech disorders exclusively (i.e., articulation, voice, fluency) or students who have severe motor, sensory, or cognitive challenges, even though many of the interventions described herein are effective with such students.

## CHARACTERISTICS OF LANGUAGE IMPAIRMENTS

Language problems are often described according to our understanding of language as we receive it (reception) or produce it (expression) within the language skill set appropriate to the students' ages. In an attempt to study, discuss, teach, and assess language characteristics in students, professionals consider several components, including *language form* (phonology, morphology, syntax), *language content* (semantics, metalinguistics, figurative language), and *language use* (pragmatics and discourse). Students with LI may have difficulty with all or some of these components. Table 7.1 provides a detailed list of characteristics from the literature and illuminates the numerous problems students experience within the oral-written continuum of language learning

Viewing language characteristics is helpful for understanding the variety of skills involved, but it often results in a fragmented presentation of the aspects of the language leading to fragmented intervention for language problems (Wallach, 2004). Such decontextualized descriptions of language problems, as noted in Table 7.1, make it difficult for teachers, SLPs, and related service providers to consider how language problems directly affect the daily performance of students in classrooms, and most importantly, how to intervene with these children (Nelson, 2005; Simon, 1991; Ukrainetz, 2006; Wallach, 2004). Thus, the goal of the following pages is to describe language problems as they often appear in classroom contexts for children of various ages and to present interventions within the classroom setting.

It is not uncommon for teachers to say that children with LI are considerably disadvantaged in schools, especially those who participate in assessments, planning meetings, and intervention programs for school-age children with such problems. Teachers describe the language difficulties demonstrated by students in relation to their performance within the learning environment. Some examples of what teachers say regarding student difficulties include: understanding complex oral and written directions for projects and assignments; participating in activities, such as rhyming, word segmentation, and spelling; recalling information; using background knowledge to predict outcomes from discussions, debates, narratives or plays; making inferences during discussions or readings; understanding and using multiple meanings of words in conversations; developing new and expanded definitions for words, and explaining and understanding metaphors and other figurative forms as encountered in readings, discussions and social interactions. Teachers often understand how each student's language problem directly impacts the tasks that are required within the classroom, sometimes without knowing or recalling the specific results of language

TABLE 7.1
**Characteristics of Oral Language Problems**

*Articulation, Phonology, and Metalinguistics*

Delayed phonological acquisition
Articulation disorder
Phonological processing deficits result in speaking, listening, and reading problems
Ineffective access of phonological codes from working memory for rapid automatic naming
Difficulty making sound-symbol associations, sequencing sounds and syllables to decode words, encoding sound and
   syllable patterns to spell words, and comprehending rapid, distorted speech, especially in noise
Limited perception and production of complex phonemic configurations
Reduced phonological awareness
Incomplete development of sources of knowledge regarding phonemic awareness

*Morphology and Syntax*

Overall immaturity in grammatical structure with less elaboration and fewer complex forms than age peers
Difficulty with sentence repetition and completion tasks
Differences in the comprehension and production of syntax
Lack of appreciation for the morphemic structure of words
Low but significant frequency of grammatical errors, particularly in written text
Lack of later developing morphological and syntactic structures
Limited variety and combinations of verb forms, especially morphemes that mark verb tense
Limited ability to generalize morphemes to new word roots
Limited use of the copula, auxiliaries, and modals along with forms such as the perfect, progressive, and passive
   involving verb suffixes and auxiliaries
Fewer and more limited range of questions containing wh and auxiliary and modal elements
Fewer complex sentences
Limited use of later developing adverbial connectives for syntactic conjunction and discourse cohesion
Difficulty with left branching clauses and combinations of clauses
Limited production and complexity of noun phrase expansions
Continued use of spoken language forms in writing
Reduced ability to use grammatical rules to understand sentences produced by teachers
Reduced flexibility in understanding word order variations
Ineffective use of grammatical morphemes to predict words in academic tasks

*Semantics and Figurative Language*

Reduced rate and quantity of acquisition of vocabulary
Comprehension difficulties and misinterpretations of messages
Difficulty establishing new words, their definitions and their use
Limited variety and flexibility of word use
Premature decisions about a speaker's intentions
Difficulty comprehending basic classroom vocabulary and concepts
Immaturity in the acquisition and use of figurative forms including idioms, metaphors, multi-meaning words, jokes, and
   puns
Failure to interpret headings in books and newspapers
Off-target responding
Inaccurate word selection
Word-finding and recalling problems
Use of invented words and phrases (neologisms)
Rigidity in categorizing words and difficulty making rapid associations or shifts in meaning relative to context
Difficulty drawing inferences and comprehending the broader meanings of textual information
Lack of strategies for using the dictionary

*Oral and Written Discourse*

Quantity and quality differences in oral and written narrative development including less detail about characters and
   events, omission of story segments, and failure to use cohesive ties and explicit referents
Problems in the management of narratives and expository texts
Use of starters and stereotyped phrases

*(continued)*

TABLE 7.1
(*Continued*)

Inadequate or inaccurate use of pronouns for anaphoric reference
Immaturity in the comprehension and production of school discourse
Inadequate topic closure
Disorganized sentences and events in stories
Poor advanced cognitive planning and immature command of linguistic structures
Difficulty identifying misunderstandings and lack of strategies to seek clarification
Difficulty learning and applying classroom communication rules
Poor ability to express thoughts in a connected fashion

*Pragmatics*

Misinterpretation of nonverbal messages
Failure to accurately interpret facial expressions and gestures that accompany spoken messages
Significantly less eye contact
Inappropriate maintenance of distance during conversational situations
Poor use of survival language
Inappropriate interaction with peers
Limited use of style shifts to fit social situations

*Information processing*

More time necessary to process information
Slower rate of acquisition of lexical, syntactic, and morphological structures
Short-term memory difficulties
Difficulty recalling verbal facts and details from long-term memory
Failure to take an active role in learning
Reduced comprehension monitoring and question asking
Persistence of comprehension difficulties into adolescents and adulthood
Immaturity in the interpretation of events
Inadequate selection and attention to relevant information
Difficulty remembering and following directions
Ineffective use of strategies for learning, remembering, and generalizing information
Disorganization of thoughts and reduced flexibility in thinking
Ineffective and inefficient learning strategies
Reduced language processing and reading problems
Psychiatric and social problems

assessments. The specific and relevant information that teachers give regarding the language and learning demonstrations of students can serve as the basis for not only assessment, but also for intervention planning. Such information should be used in conjunction with assessment data from norm-referenced and observational data to plan intervention strategies that directly impact the student's performance within the classroom or other contexts determined by the planning team (Ukrainetz, 2006).

## PRINCIPLES THAT UNDERLIE LANGUAGE PROBLEMS

Some principles have been learned across decades of research about language and learning. The first principle is that *children do not outgrow language and learning problems*. In fact, longitudinal studies show that language problems are pervasive and change as children age (Bashir & Scavuzzo, 1992; Bashir, Conte, & Heerde, 1998; Wallach, 2004). The difficulties that children demonstrate in acquiring the language as toddlers and preschoolers do not resolve themselves with time or completely, even with intervention. Rather, such problems take on different manifestations as the demands increase and change through the curriculum. Nelson (1998) describes language as multifaceted, complex, and heterogeneous. That is, language users must have a solid and flexible system that can be adapted to suit a variety of situations and levels of complexity to meet current and future demands for learning and the application of information to familiar and new situations.

The second principle regarding students with LI is that *the context of the situation is an important variable in how the student uses language* (Nelson, 1998; Simon, 1991a). Despite decades of research to the contrary, language-learning interventions continue to be offered in a fragmented and decontextualized format with a focus on competence for single skills. When we ask only about the nature of a child's language problem, we miss the important idea that the student performs differently depending on the nature of the task at hand. The more useful question for assessment and intervention is: What is this child able to do and what is she or he having difficulty with in your classroom (or with this assignment, task, subject, etc.)? Mather and Goldstein (2001) place the learning environment among four foundational skills within their framework for understanding classroom learning and behavior. They discuss many attributes of effective teachers and offer concrete suggestions for creating optimal classroom environments, noting that what works for the majority of students require flexibility and thoughtful engineering for others. The language environment in particular is a critical component in language intervention and contextual learning is vital for students to use language within classrooms. Ukrainetz (2006) calls for "contextualized skill intervention" that emphasizes naturalistic, hybrid (blend of child and adult-centered), systematic, and explicit interventions.

*Language and learning problems in children require individualized, direct and specialized intervention.* Each student's needs must be carefully identified within the classroom and other settings to design a comprehensive plan for intervention with participation from the student, parents, teachers, and related service providers. Such a plan requires short- and long-term objectives that lead to academic, social, and/or vocational progress. Educators should together, in consultation with parents of students with LI, direct classroom-based and consultative/collaborative services that will provide maximum instructional and generalization opportunities. Short-term pull out services should primarily be used to teach new strategies and skills. Student goals and objectives should be clearly focused to improve language in all of the affected areas.

A fourth principle is that *language is not only a primary avenue for interaction with others, but it is also a primary tool for learning. Thus, students with LI have difficulty across modes.* Language competence and performance develops and is refined over many years and within overlapping modes. Thus, language must be thought of as a continuum of abilities that include speaking, listening, reading, and writing. Further, language interacts with the development of executive functions including attention, memory, critical thinking, reasoning, and problem-solving. As students encounter difficulties with learning in classrooms, it is a complex process to discover the nature of their problems and to plan appropriate evidence-based interventions.

*Students with LI are disadvantaged.* LI *interferes with academic, social and vocational success.* Children, who have enriched language backgrounds, a typical rate and sequence of acquisition, and ongoing strategies for learning, continue to gain in all of these areas. Conversely, children, who do not have adequate opportunity and show weaknesses in learning language, do not catch up and continue to get further behind across time (Aram, Ekelman, & Nation, 1984; Aram & Hall, 1989; Hall & Tomblin, 1978; King, Jones, & Lasky, 1982). Thus, those students with impoverished language and learning abilities not only continue to demonstrate these problems across the curriculum, but also show the additive effect of their depressed skills on their acquisition and use of academic knowledge and written language. Such students do not catch up to age-matched peers and may continue to have language problems as adults (Johnson & Blalock, 1987).

Early intervention is critical for students with LI. The identification of infants, toddlers and preschoolers who have communication delay leads to programs and services that are important for long-term academic and emotional health (Rossetti, 2001). Research in early childhood reveals that children of preschool age are prime for reaping long term benefits from early intervention services (Billeaud, 2003; Rossetti, 2001).

Achievements in language development (Fahey & Reid, 2000) highlight the knowledge and skills that students require to be successful across the school curriculum and socially in this environment. Preschoolers and early elementary school-age children must have solid foundations in phonology, morphology, syntax, semantics, and pragmatics. By the second grade, students advance in all areas of language and learning. They also have at least one year of experience in their home school and have learned the language and culture of the classroom and the expectations of teachers and peers. During the middle and high school years, most students achieve a high level of competence in oral language and learning skills and can navigate effectively in schools and other settings. They seek independence from adults and use listening, reading and writing as primary learning avenues. Limitations in language and learning tend to result in self-esteem and interaction difficulties with others as well as academic performance problems.

## Intervention Strategies for Increasing Language Structure

*Phonological Awareness.*    When planning effective language interventions for students with severe phonological delay as one aspect of their language disability, it is important to recognize that the speech production error patterns are overt signs of a systemic and covert problem with establishing phonological representations (Sutherland & Gillon, 2005). Thus, even with intensive intervention on sound production, it may take considerable time for students to fully internalize these sounds into their phonological system including the coding, storage, and retrieval of these sounds for all purposes in oral and written language modes. Thus, as students are learning to produce the sounds, activities to promote phonological knowledge directly improves phonological representations necessary for decoding of words for successful reading and spelling development.

Activities, such as rhyming games, breaking words into syllables, creating alliteration phrases, changing words through additions, deletions, substitutions, and rearrangement of sounds, and learning sound-symbol association, help children understand that knowledge about sound segments allows them to make meaning distinctions, classify words by sounds in the beginning, middle, and end; and represent sound segments with letters. The knowledge acquired through such activities is an important precursor to the development of proficient reading, vocabulary, and speech perception abilities (Rvachew, 2006). Thus, it is an important ingredient to include in language and literacy instruction, especially is the early grades (Ball, 1997; Blachman, 1989; Blachman, Ball, Black & Tangel, 1994; Catts, 1991; 1990; Stanovich, 2000; Tummer & Cole, 1991). Although it is not too late to begin phonological awareness training in first grade, it is more effective in preschool and kindergarten (Laing, 2006), since phonological awareness develops from infancy through 7+ years (Norris & Hoffman, 2002). However, Swanson, Hodson, and Schommer-Aikins (2005) found phonological awareness training successful even for seventh-grade poor readers from a bilingual community.

Once most children are using their phonological awareness to participate in phonics and reading activities, explicit phonological awareness activities are not often embedded in the curricula beyond the second grade. In fact, reading is the best activity to promote continued development of phonological awareness, as these skills have a reciprocal relationship (Hogan, Catts, & Little, 2005).

Researches have determined that phonological awareness tasks exist on a continuum of linguistic complexity. Ball (1997) notes students in kindergarten and first grade are successful in sound identification and letter naming, but have difficulty with segmenting sounds in words. The ability to employ manipulation of sounds in words to substitute, omit, add, and rearrange them requires even greater phonological sophistication. In addition, many types of input and levels of difficulty exist in phonemic awareness activities. Norris and Hoffman (2002) identify and discuss 10 sources of knowledge that children acquire along with the developmental progression of each source area, such as alphabet knowledge, rhyme, sound in word position, print conventions, word recognition, and developmental spelling. Common activities and the types of knowledge associated with each provide a matrix that is useful for intervention planning along the developmental continuum and the assessment of student progress in this area. Further, instruction should progress along the difficulty continuum, noting that individual children vary in their performance across tasks and difficulty level. Instruction is most effective when it is combined with instruction in sound-symbol relationships (Blachman et al., 1994), conducted individually or in small groups (Laing & Espeland, 2005; Gillon, 2005a), provided in classrooms where it is consistently part of the curriculum (Hadley, Simmerman, Long, & Luna, 2002), and the focus of instruction is during preschool and kindergarten years (Bus & Van Ijzendoorn, 1999; Gillon, 2005a).

Children who have LI, speech sound disorders, dyslexia, and specific spelling disability are particularly vulnerable to delays in phonological awareness (Larrivee & Catts, 1999; Moats & Lyon, 1996; Nathan, Stackhouse, Goulandreis, & Snowling, 2004; Raitano et al., 2004; Rvachew, 2006; Snowling, Bishop, & Stoddard, 2000; Webster & Plante, 1992) because they lack the explicit awareness of the phonemes in words resulting in an "incomplete and degraded template on which to link associations to an alphabetic writing system" (Moats & Lyon, 1996, p. 74). Therefore, language intervention must include direct and explicit teaching, intense practice, and many experiences in using phonological awareness in authentic speaking, reading, and writing situations (Moats & Lyon, 1996). Such intervention is successful in advancing speech and literacy outcomes for students (Bernhardt & Major, 2005; Gillon, 2000, 2005; Hesketh, Adams, Nightingal, & Hall, 2000; Major & Bernhardt, 1998). Tyler (2002) advocates a four component intervention model for children who have co-occurring speech and LI focusing on auditory awareness activities for increased attention to the acoustic attributes of sounds, contrasting sounds in words, practicing in drill and natural contexts, and engaging in phonological awareness activities. Justice and Ezell (2004) recommend the use of print referencing strategies in storybooks to focus student attention on the makeup of words and how printed word forms relate to meaning. The intensity of the services is critical for students with LI to make the necessary gains required for them to achieve the success needed for successful participation in the curriculum.

*Morphology and Syntax.* The complexity of oral language increases during the first five years as children elaborate on noun and verb phrases through the addition of grammatical morphemes and through the use of combinations of phrases and clauses (Owens, 1996). By school age, students have a strong command of the language to participate effectively across all modes, engage in metalinguistic analysis of oral and written forms, and manipulate language for academic and social uses. Yet, oral language sophistication continues to develop through the adolescent years and well into adulthood (Nippold, 1998)

Children with LI find the acquisition of grammatical forms challenging. Overall immaturity, lack of flexibility, and reduced use or lack of forms defines the difficulties common to these children. They are slow to acquire grammatical forms, the use of elaboration in noun and verb phrases is weak, and they have poor conjoining techniques for the creation of complex sentences. Thus, their language is immature for speaking, listening, reading, writing, thinking and reasoning. The accumulated effects of such problems can have a major impact on the academic success of students with LI as grammatical sophistication increases in classroom instruction, peer dialogue, and written texts within each grade level. Intervention should focus on the expansion of current morphology and syntactic foundation, with increased flexibility for the use of syntax in all modes across several purposes.

*Contextually-Based Approaches to Learning Grammar.*   Eisenberg (2006) provides an extensive review of the intervention studies that target grammar. Her summary concludes that most discrete skill intervention is not efficacious, however specific strategies, especially the use of imitation involving contrasting sentences and content alterations, modeling combined with production, and sentence combining activities, improve student performance on the targeted grammatical forms (Gerber, 1993). Less successful are tasks that involve grammar analysis and error detection for isolated sentences (Eisenberg, 2006). Since the efficacy of discrete skill teaching in general, however, is not particularly strong, Eisenberg recommends that the specific strategies noted above be used in conjunction with contextually-based communication activities.

Contextually-based approaches for grammar include writing as the mode of both the content of the intervention and the instructional avenue, the use of literature-based units to engage students in syntactic activities, and reading and conversational activities (Ukrainetz, 2006b). Popular interactive strategies with students include writing conferences, modeling, peer collaboration, and classroom dialogue. In these sessions grammar is worked on during the first draft so that students understand the importance of accuracy for conveying meaning, rather than as just an editing function to be focused on as the written piece is being prepared for its final copy.

Ukrainetz (2006b) advocates activities that assist students with grammar during reading of literature. They focus the student's attention on grammatical patterns that are repeated in books and she recommends sentence manipulation, matching, story retelling, and drawing pictographs to represent sentences. Grammar instruction can also be approached in conversational activities. Brinton and Fujiki offer that "conversation is the best starting point from which to approach language impairment, regardless of whether the impairment involves structural or interactional components of language" (1994, p. 60). Various genres, such as expository passages in textbooks, poems, narratives, and newspapers and magazines, provide many instances of grammatical forms appropriate to a variety of language levels. Using patterns that often appear within writings will help teachers highlight desired structures. Conversation about these forms captures the student's attention to them within the context of the passage.

*Mini Lessons.*   Five mini-lesson strategies discussed by Eisenberg (2006) reflect the emphasis on current practice of providing RISE in intervention activities: repeated opportunities, intensive, systematic support, with an explicit skill focus within a contextualized framework (Ukrainetz, 2006a). The literature supports the use of observational modeling, content alterations, contrastive modeling and imitation, sentence expanding, and sentence combining, all of which can be used separately and collectively to enhance student learning of grammatical forms. Eisenberg's detailed review of each of these instructional methods includes procedural information and easy to follow examples. Each method explicates the form for the student and then guides the student to use the form successfully in oral and written language opportunities. The forms are gradually assimilated in the classroom expectations for students, as they become a part of the language system of each student. Teachers determine which structures are needed for classroom success, the order and timing for introducing the forms, the amount and types of scaffolds each student needs, and the instructional context that will be used to learn the forms and practice them in meaningful exchanges (Eisenberg, 2006; Nelson, 1998).

Oral language competence and performance should be taught in tandem and as a bridge to the development of written language. The methods suggested above integrate oral and written language from the start, making the continuum truly operational for learning. The SLP should work closely with teachers and parents to assist them in using newly acquired skills in phonological awareness, morphology, and syntax to increase student mastery of decoding, reading fluency, reading comprehension, and spelling and writing.

## INTERVENTION STRATEGIES FOR INCREASING MEANING

There are many effective strategies for working with semantic knowledge that include aspects of thinking, and reasoning skills. Not all of them will be addressed here, but the strategies described below highlight the nature of effective language intervention for students with LI.

Students show frustration in their daily struggles in the classroom making this setting an important one for the intervention focus. Classroom-based collaborative models have become popular for providing learning strategies that enhance their student learning and success. Researchers have confirmed that the classroom teacher has a strong influence on student learning. In fact, studies show that the teacher is the most important factor for student learning (Sanders & Horn, 1994; Wright, Horn, & Sanders, 1997). All team members including parents can assist students in practicing newly acquired information, elaborating on information already learned, and preparing for new content through reading, thinking, and discussion (Foyle, 1985; Foyle & Bailey, 1988).

*Promoting Interaction for Practice, Expansion, Refinement, and Recall of Information.* Active and interactive participation with other learners and with the information at hand provides students opportunities to construct meanings from multiple avenues. Several strategies help learners focus on instructional language, which facilitates the ease in which they are able to attend to and benefit from the instruction itself (Bashir & Scavuzzo, 1992; Silliman & Wilkinson, 1991, 1994). Nelson (1989) discusses several curricula within typical classrooms requiring participation that students must negotiate. The "learning to do school" continuum includes not only the material to be learned and the background knowledge required (official and de facto curriculum), but also involves the set of implicit and explicit rules for interactions (classroom curriculum), the world knowledge that students bring from their previous experiences and background (cultural curriculum), teacher attitudes, beliefs, and practices (hidden curriculum), and the rules for social interactions from the peer group (underground curriculum). While typical students acquire knowledge about all of these curricula implicitly, as they actively engage in school activities, students with LI require much of this information to be made explicit. Thus, strategies that highlight meanings for students within all of these realms are effective in teaching such students. The three strategies summarized below are examples of ways to bring new and related background information into the spotlight. They are useful for all learners, and are especially helpful for students who have LI, because they advocate interaction about ideas and provide the necessary scaffolding for supportive learning.

*Dialogue, Cooperative Learning, and Reciprocal Teaching.* Students need to regularly converse with their peers regarding the information they are learning in school and daily experiences. Verbal interactions foster the growth of personal identity, enable sharing of different discourses, and promote the learning of critical reflection (Burbules & Rice, 1991; Nieto, 1994; Perl, 1994; Reid & Leamon, 1996) and dialogue allows negotiation to occur as all participants determine the level and types of supports individual students need to be successful. Short interchanges with teachers and peers after lectures, readings, and group discussions allow students repeated exposure to main ideas. Teachers should select dialogue partners to help students with LI to highlight ideas, report and verify their understandings, ask questions, and use the information to share with others. Modeling and practice of dialogues in a variety of situations assists students in learning slang from peers, comprehending and using words in meaningful interaction, and applying words learned from content areas to real-world contexts.

Small group cooperative learning allows students to benefit from the combined efforts of all group members, who explore ideas through sharing their insights and problem-solving strategies. A group of three or four members is the most effective size (Lou et al., 1996) and heterogeneous groups with varied abilities, skills, interests, and motivations make strong cooperative learning groups (Kagan, 1994). Learning within cooperative groups often surpasses what individuals achieve on their own (Reid & Leamon, 1996; Shachar & Sharan, 1994). The stronger students are taught to model and scaffold information from the teacher and from each other. They expand and refine their existing abilities and develop coaching skills under the direction of their teacher. Students, who have weaker abilities, learn from those who are stronger. (Brinton & Fujiki, 2006; Nelson, 1998). The purpose of the group and the group itself may change from informal to formal to base groups depending on the nature of the work to be accomplished (Johnson & Johnson, 1999; Kagan, 1994).

Small groups use reciprocal teaching to provide systematic support to peer learning by engaging members in joint problem-solving, generation of solutions, and consensus seeking through predicting, questioning, clarifying, and summarizing about a topic (Brown et al., 1991; Palinscar, 1986). The interactive steps in reciprocal teaching build in the redundancy that students need to acquire new information and to relate it to what they already know.

*Explicit Vocabulary and Concept Instruction.*   The development of the lexicon requires early and repeated exposure to words within meaningful contexts, opportunities to explore word use with feedback that enhances the learner's understandings, the use of a variety of words for a variety of purposes, and specific learning of words for use with specific topics. As children acquire vocabulary, they discover how ideas conveyed by words relate to each other in ever-expanding levels of meanings and through complex relationships. In the early years of word learning, children focus on words to express the daily use of objects and events or routines within the household (Nelson, 1985). They use social words (e.g., hi, bye-bye), functional words (e.g., up, more), names for objects, and action words within their first 50 words and then expand their networks through the addition of more word varieties, including descriptive adjectives, prepositions, adverbs, and pronouns (Gleason, 1997). Vocabulary is acquired as children are exposed to concepts, literacy terms, and stories. Students use association strategies early on to relate nouns to verbs and, by second grade, they associate words using hierarchical and categorical knowledge. The changes in word association strategies reflect a reorganization and refinement of the meaningful features of words, which some have related to the ability to understand and use figurative language forms and contribute to the ability to construct definitions (Fahey & Reid, 2000; Owens, 1992).

Semantic knowledge is vital for early learning and interactions. In fact, the single strongest predictor of social status in a preschool sample was receptive vocabulary knowledge (Gertner, Rice, & Hadley, 1994). In addition, vocabulary development has both immediate and long-term effects on the development of both oral and written language, as well as on academic success (Baddeley, Gathercole, & Papagno, 1998; Sternberg, 1987).

Word learning is highly related to reading success. In fact, receptive and expressive vocabulary size at 3½ years was predictive of decoding ability at end of second grade and both vocabulary development and the acquisition of decoding abilities lead to increased comprehension during reading (Snowling et al., 2000; Storch & Whitehurst, 2002). When basic reading skills are in place by third grade, students learn most new words through reading (Nagy & Anderson, 1984), which promotes automaticity and efficiency resulting in increased vocabulary. Thus, the reciprocal nature of vocabulary knowledge and reading ability provides continuous reinforcement and development of these areas. Oral vocabulary is essential to word-and text-level reading development.

Vocabulary deficits are evident early and preschoolers with LI have poor conceptual and semantic structures for organizing lexical information, difficulty comprehending oral language, and difficulty remembering and retrieving words. They often find it challenging to connect the meanings of new words to their stored knowledge based on a few opportunities (fast-mapping; Nelson & Van Meter, 2006), as well as gradual acquisition of deep meanings as words are used across contexts and as they relate to other words (slow mapping or extended mapping skills; Carey, 1978; Owens, 1996). Delay in vocabulary impacts reading speed, automaticity, comprehension, and overall ability to learn curriculum content. Unfortunately, vocabulary delays widen over time and influence growth in phonological awareness, because word knowledge sets the stage for phonological knowledge.

Incidental exposure to words through reading is not, however, the most effective strategy for word learning, especially for young students with low ability (Nagy & Herman, 1987; Swanborn & de Glopper, 1999). Direct instruction, even when it is minimal, increases student knowledge of words (Stahl & Fairbanks, 1986). Research also shows that: (a) students must encounter new words at least six times in order to acquire and remember their meanings (Jenkins, Stein, & Wysocki, 1984); (b) prior instruction on words increases word understandings during reading (Jenkins et al, 1984); (c) association of the word with an image increases word knowledge (Powell, 1980); and (d) content specific vocabulary instruction increases student achievement (Stahl & Fairbanks, 1986).

Ukrainetz (2006) and others advocate for an explicit and intensive skill focus in vocabulary intervention within the situations in which they occur, including the school curriculum. Students with LI need time, many opportunities (greater than the six exposures for typical learners), and resources, including teachers, peers, parents, and strategies that promote interaction and exploration, to fully learn the meanings of words in a variety of situations and applications. Direct guidance and practice in fast and slow mapping facilitates storage, organization, retrieval, and strengthening vocabulary in relation to content areas is an appropriate focus of intervention.

*Focus on Variety and Flexibility of Words.*    As discussed above, vocabulary expansion is a common goal in language intervention programs due to its importance in overall language growth and its strong relationship to academic achievement. Several developmentally appropriate principles regarding vocabulary instruction are discussed in the literature and relate to intervention to strengthen the lexical system.

- Teach a flexible system of semantic knowledge. Establish and stabilize an organized structure for understanding, remembering, retrieving, and expressing semantic information. Marzano and colleagues. (2001) recommend a five-step process for teaching new terms and phrases: (1) teacher provides brief explanation or description, (2) teacher provides non-linguistic representation, (3) students generate own explanations or descriptions, (4) students create own nonlinguistic representations, and (5) teacher asks students to review the accuracy of their explanations and representations. DeKemel (2003) includes metalinguistic aspects in teaching word meanings.

- Use multiple and authentic situations to promote fast mapping—child creates a representation of a new word on the basis of a few incidental exposures, and slow mapping—child retains lexical representation in memory, differentiates it from other words, and revises and verifies word meaning based on feedback from others in a long-term process (Carey, 1978; DeKemel, 2003).
- Include both common high frequency words and rare low frequency words in vocabulary training.
- Include specialized vocabulary taken from content area units to develop conceptual networks (Nelson & Van Meter, 2006).
- Focus on contextual information to teach multiple meanings in different contexts and across various literary genres (DeKemel, 2003) and on definitional information to teach formal categorical structures of word meanings (Anglin, 1993; DeKemel, 2003; Johnson & Anglin, 1995).
- Focus instruction on depth of semantic knowledge because it will aid in word retrieval. Depth across at least three levels includes verbal association strategies, the use of words in limited contexts, and the use of words with understanding and the ability to manipulate meaning through word relationships, such as with antonyms, compare/contrast, multiple meanings, novel uses, and similarities and differences.
- Emphasize morphologic, orthographic, and semantic association cues to aid in understandings of words (Nelson & Van Meter, 2006) and word awareness in print (Justice, 2002; Justice & Ezell, 2004; Justice, Meier, & Walpole, 2005).
- Teach dictionary and other referencing skills as a strategy for learning words within the student's curriculum including use of the alphabetical system, the pronunciation key, prototypical and alternative definitions, the origin of the word, and abbreviations (DeKemel, 2003).
- Use multidimensional approaches for vocabulary intervention including peer models.

Some factors to consider in the selection of words include: the general importance of the words in everyday use; the importance of the words in academics; the student's current knowledge of the target words; the need and motivation for the student to use the words, and the kinds of instructional techniques best suited to the words (Nelson, 2006).

*Focusing on Word Meanings and Relationships.*   As the lexicon develops from event-based learning in the early years, to a system that is organized categorically and hierarchically, students are able to use their mental processes to relate words in a variety of ways and for several purposes. For instance, the ability to identify similarities and differences requires mental operations that lead to several avenues of thought that have direct application in classrooms (Gentner & Markman, 1994; Markman & Gentner, 1993a, 1993b; Medin, Goldstone, & Markman, 1995). Direct and explicit instruction, as well as independent practice in the identification of similarities and differences enhances students' understanding and ability to use knowledge (Chen, 1996; Chen, Yanowitz, & Dachler, 1996; Flick, 1992; Gholson, Smither, Buhrman, & Duncan, 1997; Mason & Sorzio, 1996; Newby, Ertmer, & Stepich, 1995), and the use of graphic and symbolic representations assist students in their understanding (Chen, 1999; Cole & McLeod, 1999; Mason, 1994). Similarities and differences can be applied to activities involving comparing, classifying, creating metaphors, and creating analogies.

Comparison tasks, where students focus on a specific number of characteristics (Chen, 1996;

Chen et al., 1996; Flick, 1992; Ross, 1987; Solomon, 1995), can be accomplished at any grade level in oral and written activities. Word relationships are often realized through comparing words to other words. In the case of learning opposites (antonyms), the student learns polarized terms, such as *in-out, up-down, cold-hot, big-little*. Comparing also leads to the ability to use different words to convey the same meaning (synonyms), such *big-large, cold-chilly, scared-frightened*. Learners benefit from using graphic organizers as the number of characteristics and items to be compared increases (Marzano, Pickering, & Pollock, 2001). For example, students in an eighth grade classroom may be required to compare the characters from one story with the characters from another story along several dimensions such as physical attributes, background and upbringing, attitudes and beliefs, and personality traits. They may then use this information to discuss similarities and differences relative to the story plot.

Classification tasks focus on discovering and using rules that determine category membership (Chi, Feltovich, & Glaser, 1981; English, 1997; Newby et al., 1995; Ripoll, 1999). Catagorical knowledge assists students in organizing information based on similarities and differences (Marzano, Pickering, & Pollock, 2001). Graphic organizers, such as Venn diagrams, charts, and hierachical structures are helpful for students as they interact with the information and with each other.

The creation and comprehension of metaphors require the realization that there is an abstract relationship between two items (Chen, 1999; Cole & McLeod, 1999; Dagher, 1995; Gottfried, 1998; Mason, 1994, 1995). Notice that metaphors also require knowledge of similarities and differences. Metaphors are often difficult to learn, especially for students with LI. Not only does the learner have to consider the attributes of each item, but she or he must compare them in both literal and figurative meanings. For instance, the metaphor *The sea was like a sheet of glass* requires students to consider the attributes of glass (e.g., clear, completely smooth, cool, shiny) then relate them to the sea.

There are many types of analogies, but they all require knowledge about similarities and differences (Alexander, 1984; Nippold, 1998; Rattermann & Gentner, 1998; Sternberg, 1977, 1979). Analogies use the comparison of two items (A is to B) to predict the nature of the relationship between two additional items (as C is to D), one of which is not stated. For example, animal is to tiger as furniture is to _____ (couch,* porch, house, doorknob) demonstrates the supraordinate-subordinate relationships. Other analogous relationships include antonyms, synonyms, part-whole, characteristic property, familial, temporal-sequential, and causal relationships (Gallagher & Wright, 1979; Sternberg & Nigro, 1980). Analogic reasoning develops with age and experience and poses challenging problems through adolescence as difficulty increases in levels of abstraction and complexity (Crais, 1990; Nippold, 1998; Sternberg & Nigro, 1980). An 8th grade exercise may require students to practice solving later developing analogies including antonym, synonym, and sequential patterns (Nippold, 1998). For example, the analogy: surely is to amiable as gregarious is to: (a) effervescent, (b) outgoing, (c) withdrawn,* (d) agitated is likely to be difficult, not only because the vocabulary is abstract and unfamiliar, but also because the relationship between the words is not a simple polar opposite or synonym. Overall vocabulary growth should be targeted to include a full range of word relationships with students, so that analogic reasoning develops along the continuum expected for typical students.

*Using Discussion to Facilitate Word Learning.*   Dialogic reading techniques, also known as communicative reading strategies (Badon, 1993, DeKemel, 2003; Norris, 1988, 1989, 1991) are authentic and effective contextual techniques that build word and world knowledge. Rvachew (2006) recommends the use of dialogic reading to increase interactions between the student and the adult to improve vocabulary knowledge during storybook reading, thus leading to better literacy skills. Scaffolding is used to relate meaning from the text using all modalities and repeated readings of short sections of text are followed with questions to assist the student's comprehension. When working with toddlers, preschoolers, and early elementary grade students use storybooks with accompanying pictures to engage the learners in vivid descriptions of objects, events, and actions on the page. Discuss the relationship of the story to each student's own experiences and the narrative as a whole. Scripted book-sharing discussions (van Kleech, Vander Woude, & Hammett, 2006) increase both literal and inferential language skills in preschoolers with LI. During this technique, students answer questions that focus on literal information, as it is directly present within the text, as well as on information that requires students to think about unstated meanings, such as internal states and motives of characters, similarities and differences between text information and life experiences, predictions, and the meanings of new words and concepts. A book club is an effective way for students to share books with peers. High-interest reading material can be accompanied by wh-questions for new vocabulary, distancing questions to relate the story to learner experiences, and highlighted word meanings, including synonyms, antonyms, and comparisons of words. The word should then be integrated back into the context in which it was encountered and generalized to new contexts.

The use of thematic units has also shown promise in working on extending word meanings for increased text-level comprehension. DeKemel (2003) suggests the use of literature and activities, such as drama, writing, art, music, play, and food customs to help students explore a particular topic in a thorough manner. Some goals for teaching vocabulary include: analyzing word meanings in the context; using dictionaries and glossaries; analyzing words into roots, suffixes, and prefixes; creating semantic maps to understand relationships between words and concepts; noting the importance of word meanings for comprehension; and recognizing multiple word meanings. Gillam and Ukrainetz (2006) stress that thematic units help to tie language intervention sessions together toward the accomplishment of the intervention goals.

Authentic writing projects also provide an avenue for increasing word learning in an interactive environment. Curriculum-based writing projects provide social interaction as well as language comprehension and formulation opportunities. Writing can be used to activate dormant vocabulary acquisition processes by stimulating retrieval of known and new words. Nelson offers that students tend to write only the words they know how to spell, thus limiting their vocabulary diversity. She recommends that teachers encourage students to expand their semantic systems through the use of specific words and phrases necessary to convey particular meanings during writing. Her students use their own ideas and words to plan, draft, revise, edit, publish, and present writing products for peers, parents, and teachers. Writing labs can be incorporated in any environment, thereby offering a flexible and dynamic avenue for word learning. Students with LI work side-by-side with peers and benefit from scaffolding from teachers to write stories, reports, and poems. They use specific language during peer conferences and discussion of works in progress.

*Targeting Figurative Language.*    Within the day-to-day interactions of home, day care, and/or preschool, young children encounter numerous instances of figurative and nonverbal language and they experiment with these in their communications with others. Word play, name games, and invented figures of speech are used for teasing and joking. Gradually, as students advance through elementary, middle, and high school, they show increased understanding and use of riddles (Horgan, 1981; Shultz, 1974), metaphors and similes (Nippold, 1998; Polanski, 1989; Pollio & Pollio, 1974), idioms, proverbs and fables (Ackerman, 1982; Nippold, 1998; Nippold & Martin, 1989; Prinz, 1983), slang (Nelson & Rosenbaum, 1972), and awareness of multi-meaning words (Gardner, 1974).

Nippold (1998) discusses five changes that occur within students in the early elementary grades that lead to their increasing ability to interpret and use non-literal language forms. The ability to read allows students multiple avenues of information leading to knowledge about a variety of topics of their own choosing, as well as the specialized vocabulary of the curriculum. Students advancement in their metalinguistic abilities promote their thinking about the structural and meaningful aspects of language and to explore these in song, rhymes, and figurative forms. Their ability to reflect on and analyze language begins a process that will continue into adolescence. Students also gain in their ability to think abstractly, which in turn broadens understandings of concepts and the relationships between ideas and the opportunity to interpret nonliteral forms of language such as puns, idioms, metaphors, jokes, riddles, and linguistic ambiguity. Lastly, students gradually are able to take the social perspective of others, so that they respond to the thoughts and feelings expressed in daily situations. They modify the content and style of language to fit social and academic expectations and they take responsibility for their own communication behaviors.

Recall that students who have LI process figurative language like younger children. This lag sets them apart as they attempt to take part in the ever-changing demands of the social and academic contexts of school. The five changes noted above pose significant challenges for these students (Nippold & Fey, 1983; Seidenberg & Bernstein, 1986). Failure to understand and use figurative language appropriate to ones peer group may result in alienation, frustration, hurt feelings, and low self-esteem (Donahue & Bryan, 1984; Larson & McKinley, 1995). Older students with LI may demonstrate their knowledge and use of literal language and to an extent, nonliteral language in noninteractive contexts, yet as Creaghead and Tattershall (1991) point out, "... some children fail to use nonliteral language, because they cannot determine when it is appropriate, or they may use expressions inappropriately, which will make them seem odd and socially inept to their peers and to adults" (p. 118). Poor use and understanding of nonliteral language negatively impacts interaction with others. Students may have similar difficulty interpreting and using body language, thus making their demeanor seem awkward and uncomfortable.

Interventions for increasing figurative language should mirror the principles of effective vocabulary instruction including relevant and useful forms that are encountered in spoken and written language in the classroom, direct instruction that assists students with understanding the relationships of the words and ideas within the figurative form, many opportunities for practice, repeated occasions for their use, and teaching that provides scaffolded learning in multiple modalities (Lund & Duchan, 1993; Nelson, 1998; Nippold, 1998; Ukrainetz, 2006). Such strategies must provide teacher and peer modeling, opportunities for discussion about the meaning of the form and appropriate use, practice in using the form, and self-monitoring to determine the effective use of the form for the intended purpose. The use of role plays can be used to demonstrate the meaning behind idioms, similes, metaphors, riddles, jokes, and other figurative forms. Drawing pictures to illustrate figurative meanings, practicing idiomatic expressions, comprehending written material with embedded figurative language using context, and practicing communicative and classroom routines that use figurative and nonverbal language are effective in learning to use such forms (Creaghead & Tattershall, 1991).

The visual and verbal medium of television can provide a rich source of material to show how nonverbal language and figurative language are used to create drama, comedy, mystery, adventure, advertisement, and the news. Bourgault (1991) used secondary school competency guidelines, literature regarding functional communication, and surveys from secondary classroom teachers to design a pragmatic program that focuses on Halliday's communication functions. She developed language units from videotaped television programs and a process for teaching, practicing and using language competencies in speaking and writing opportunities. Bourgault (1991) provides several ideas from sitcoms, story segments, commercials, news shows, soap operas, and game shows. Students use the lessons to engage in discussions, small group activities, and individual exercises. These ideas seem particularly useful for high-school students with LI, as they involve the students in watching, listening, analyzing, discussing, modeling, and critiquing human interactions within social situations.

*Providing Structure to Aid Comprehension through Literature.*   The use of literature as a context for language intervention has become a popular and effective medium to support oral and written language development. Strong (2001) provides a detailed list of outcomes that can be realized for students in fostering meanings, structure, and purposes of language. Strong's advice regarding the benefits of using literature as the content for instruction is worth repeating here.

> Through literature-based intervention strategies, students learn new vocabulary, concepts, and figurative language. They also expand their world knowledge; discover, in context, the meanings of complex sentence patterns such as cause-effect and conditional relationships; and become familiar with the structure of stories (i.e., the cohesion and story grammar) so that they can comprehend and recall new stories. They use language for important communicative functions to predict events from picture clues, summarize a story's events, identify main ideas/ themes, compare and contrast information, share ideas, clarify subtle meanings, retell stories, or create stories. They practice turn-taking, topic maintenance, and perspective taking. Finally, as they work with diagrams, maps, and charts, students acquire strategies for organizing and remembering information. (p. 21)

Strong (2001) presents numerous suggestions for working with students to gain the most from literature in pre-story, during-story, and post-story activities. Pre-story strategies focus on activating the student's prior knowledge and using prediction skills. While students read stories, strategies are geared to promote comprehension monitoring, active thinking, and discussion of ideas. Follow-up activities engage students to reflect on information, discuss ideas for deeper understandings, and relate information in a variety of ways to maximize learning. The use of a constellation of strategies will be useful for students, as they all engage the students in their own learning, provide interaction with the teacher and other students, encourage practice, and provided repeated and meaningful exposure to information in dynamic exchanges. Most of the strategies can be easily modified for effective use with narratives or expository materials.

*Summary Frames.*   Text-level information, whether provided orally or through written text, can present challenges to students and impact their academic performance as they attempt to recall facts, discuss ideas, and retain the main ideas from instruction. When interacting with expository texts, students benefit from instruction that guides their learning. For instance, it is difficult for even advanced students to summarize, especially when oral or written text is lengthy and complex. Summarizing requires students to delete, substitute, and keep some information (Kintsch, 1979; van Dijk, 1980) through an analysis of the text (Rosenshine & Meister, 1994; Rosenshine, Meister, & Chapman, 1996). Teachers use summary frames to illuminate the structure of information, thus providing a scaffold that focuses on how information relates within the text. Some types of narrative frames include the topic-restriction-illustration frame, the definition frame, the argumentation frame, the problem/solution frame, and the conversation frame. Frame questions focus the student on accessing the relevant information for the summary (Marzano, Pickering, & Pollack, 2001). This strategy for text-level comprehension can be easily taught in classrooms, small groups and with individual students. The specific frame questions suggestions by Marzano and his colleagues for argumentation are included here as an example.

What information is presented that leads to a claim? What is the basic statement or claim that is the focus of the information? What examples or explanations are presented to support this claim? What concessions are made about the claim?

Several types of strategies exist to help students to learn a structure for topically and semantically related groups of words and to link new words and concepts with existing knowledge. Graphic organizers combine linguistic information with nonlinguistic organizational strategies to represent relationship among ideas (Hyerle, 1996; Marzano, Pickering, & Pollack, 2001). There are many different patterns that help learners visualize description, time sequence, process/cause-effect, episode, generalization/principal, problem-solution, compare/contrast, and concept. They can take various forms, such as semantic webs and maps, diagrams, decision trees, text frames (Armbruster, Anderson, & Meyer, 1987), and story graphs (Balwin & Henry, 1991; Simon, 1991a). Research indicates that the use of graphic organizers enhances understanding of content as it engages students in active generation of mental pictures through kinesthetic activities (Aubusson, Foswill, Barr, & Perkovic, 1997; Druyan, 1997), such as drawing and pictographs (Newton, 1995) and the creation of physical models (Welch, 1997). As with summary frames, graphic organizers can assist students with conceptual understanding of how words relate to each other in many different ways depending on the topic and its level of depth. The ability to create a graphic representation helps students to make explicit the meaningful links between bits of information.

## INTERVENTION STRATEGIES FOR METACOGNITIVE LEARNING AND FUNCTIONAL COMMUNICATION

### Self-Instruction and Self-Monitoring

It can be difficult for students with LI to keep pace with other students in their classrooms and such students may show confusion when given oral directions for classroom activities, projects, and assignment. Although they may listen to the directions for main ideas, the difficulty may lie with using the information to plan and carry out the activity. Thus, students with LI often appear to be in the dark about what to do and they look to other students for guidance. Confusion and frustration about how to implement the information has been characterized by some as having difficulty in "doing school" as discussed earlier (Cahir & Kivac, 1981a, 1981b; Nelson, 1998; Ukrainetz, 2006). Students may also experience text-level processing problems inherent in complex directions, and may lack metacognitive, metalinguistic, and metatextual strategies for understanding both the processes and the products of dealing with complex instructions (Nelson, 1998).

Self-instruction, also referred to as self-talk, is based on the notion that covert speech is the way learners gain voluntary control of behavior. The technique requires verbal mediation to increase the learner's perception, understanding, problem-solving, and actions (Lasky, 1991). The strategy involves a progression of steps whereby students use self-talk to guide behaviors. First, self-talk is overt and the verbalizations consist of explicit steps necessary to accomplish a task, with a gradual transition to whispered talk and then finally covert self-talk. This strategy may be useful for explicating the steps in successfully entering a group (Brinton & Fijuki, 2006), preparing for the lead role in a book discussion, facilitating a planning session for a fundraising event, or for predictable socially embedded conversations. Once students are proficient with the technique through modeling and practice, they need time and lots of opportunities to generalize the technique to academic and social contexts.

The ability to self-monitor requires that we step back from ourselves to look at and then evaluate our behaviors for accuracy, effectiveness, and appropriateness to the situation at hand. The primary way in which learners evaluate behavior is to use self-questioning. Students ask themselves whether their attempts at a task are successful. Once the evaluation takes place, they must determine to persevere in the same tactics or to change an aspect of their behavior through the use of self-correction strategies. The implementation of our decision is an outcome of self-monitoring. This metacognitive activity is considered to be a very necessary and powerful learning strategy (Polloway & Patton, 1993; Prater et al., 1991; Swanson, 1996).

Self-monitoring should be employed during the process of completing class assignments. Students should be encouraged to check with peers or the teacher on each step for completeness and accuracy. The classroom teacher, with assistance from the SLP and special educator, should also monitor student progress by checking comprehension of each facet of the project and assisting the student in self-questioning and self-monitoring as appropriate to facilitate success. Nelson (1998, p. 449) summarized Seidenberg's (1988) systematic steps for teaching cognitive strategies that provide necessary scaffolding: (1) Introduce the strategy and review the student's current performance; (2) Explain the relevance of the strategy by using real-life examples; (3) Describe the strategy and provide a "help sheet" that lists its steps; (4) Model the strategy and rehearse it with students as a group; (5) Provide opportunity to practice using controlled materials, with prompts and corrective feedback as necessary; (6) With the student, evaluate the data gathered during practice with controlled materials; and (7) Provide further practice using textbook materials drawn from the regular curriculum.

*Functional Communication in a Variety of Contexts.*   An important goal for students with LI is to become competent language users within the social realm of school, community and future work. There are several models available for viewing functional communication (Halliday, 1973; Bereiter & Engelmann, 1966; Grice, 1975). They all share the notion that communication competence has many features that allow us to operate and cooperate effectively with others. A systematic approach to teaching the variety of functions is an effective way to build "functional flexibility" for students (Simon, 1991b). Simon used Halliday's seven functions (e.g., instrumental, regulatory, interactional, personal, heuristic, imaginative, and informative) to detail intervention activities that address each area. Her ideas provide an excellent basis for direct teaching of these communicative functions. They are easily adaptable to a wide range of ages and interests.

*Situated Pragmatics.*   It is of prime importance that functional communication is viewed within a "situated pragmatic" approach (Duchan, Hewitt, & Sonnenmeier, 1994) that considers the events or discourse genres within the daily experiences of students. The situated pragmatics framework (Duchan, 1997) emphasizes the identification of "naturally occurring goals by examining the activity contexts of the child and designing interventions that would involve the child more meaningfully in his or her daily life" (p. 10). It is desirable that students work closely with the SLP and a small group of students initially to: (1) gain understanding of the function and it's practical uses, (2) observe others' use of the function in several relevant contexts, (3) practice the function in a safe and positive environment, and (4) use self-monitoring strategies to evaluate success and make appropriate modifications as necessary. Once success is seen in small groups there should be a gradual and careful plan to warrant their use in the classroom and at home. Time, care, and support should be taken to make generalization activities successful and meaningful (Bricker & Cripe, 1992; Beukelman & Mirenda, 1992; Duchan, 1994, 1997).

## SUMMARY, CONCLUSIONS, AND FUTURE DIRECTIONS FOR RESEARCH

The primary goal of this chapter regarding students with LI was to discuss research-based strategies for teaching and learning that result in positive results. Across many disciplines, research has improved and expanded on the strategies, techniques, contexts, and models educators can select and use for working directly with the students who require our assistance in effectively learning from the curriculum. Outdated and ineffective practices are being revealed and discarded, while state-of-the-art programs are being created and refined based on efficacy studies. Further, researchers are working more directly with practitioners to make experimental procedures applicable to classrooms and other intervention settings.

Intervention plans for students with LI must link language goals to scientifically-based interventions. Plans must utilize: strategies that facilitate language learning within the context of the classroom; strategies that transcend language modes to provide greater links between listening, speaking, reading, and writing; professionals who collaborate and consult with each other and parents to provide integrated language intervention for students; practices that include participation from families and their students as a part of the intervention team; and evidence-based interventions to assist students in learning

The large number of students who are identified as having LI in schools is a testament to the challenges involved in successful schooling. Thus, it is incumbent on our preservice and inservice educational programs that teachers, special educators, SLPs, related service providers, and administrators understand the complexities of developing and using language in the learning process. All educators require a solid foundation in the development of the language system. Courses in language development and its disorders should be integrated into the curricula for future educators. It is advantageous to all when courses are offered in a transdisciplinary fashion so that educators use similar terminology and have a similar perspective on language-related development, differences, and disorders (Fahey & Reid, 2000). When educators have common reference points, dialogue becomes more productive and purposeful. Such dialogue has become very important in the implementation of the Response to Intervention model. This model provides hope that educators will work collaboratively to employ the use of scientifically-based teaching practices for all students with descriptive and prescriptive outcomes for students, who are not making adequate progress in the school curriculum. This proactive approach, through a multi-tiered strategy of interventions, has great potential in providing evidenced-based instruction to all students, boosting students who need tailored and supplemental instruction, and identifying those students who need intensive interventions (National Association of State Directors of Special Education, Inc, 2005). Regardless of the intervention models used in school districts, educators need to find common ground and recognize and use each other's strengths for the benefit of their students. The approaches described in this chapter require that educators work together and with families.

There is still much to do in education as we discover what methods and practices lead to the greatest success for our students. For students with language learning problems, the matrix of strategies is not complete. We need to continue to ask questions about the strategies we are using now, and continue our efforts in determining those that work, for whom, and under what circumstances. The one-size-fits-all approach does not produce favorable outcomes. Thus, researchers and practitioners require continued and enhanced partnerships to refine our selections for individual students.

Several future directions for research will expand our current knowledge and practices (Butler et al., 2005).

- Longitudinal research to identify effective literacy programs (Whitmire, 2005)
- Effective literacy programs for middle and high school students (Whitmire, 2005)
- Systematic and controlled studies of advantages of inclusive classrooms (Nelson, 2005)
- Effects of differentiated learning within classrooms (Nelson, 2005)
- Use of peer-to-peer communication techniques (Nelson, 2005)
- Exploration of cognitive-linguistic models that integrate components of language (Nelson, 2005)
- Identification of interventions for subgroups of individuals with language impairments (Wallach, 2005)
- Integration and summarization of research across time and diagnostic labels (Wallach, 2005)
- Effective functional and contextually-based language interventions (Fujiki & Brinton, 2005)
- Determination of language abilities involved in academic tasks (Erhen & Lentz, 1989)
- Long-term follow up studies of particular interventions (Richardson & Wallach, 2005)
- Systematic evaluation of the effects of preservice and inservice training in language and literacy for practitioners (Richardson & Wallach, 2005)
- Determining outcomes of the Response to Intervention model for students with and without language learning disabilities (National Association of State Directors of Special Education, 2005)

The relationships between research and practice will no doubt continue to be the emphasis for many years to come. Thus, the practices we use across disciplines in schools will continue to evolve and our perspectives will continue to change. Our students are our best teachers, for it is in their progress and their struggles that we continue to search for more effective, efficient, and engaging strategies for learning.

## REFERENCES

Ackerman, B.P. (1982). On comprehending idioms: Do children get the picture? *Journal of Experimental Child Psychology, 33,* 439–454.

Alexander, P.A. (1984). Training analogical reasoning skills in the gifted. *Roeper Review,* 6(4), 191–193.

Anglin, J.M. (1993). Vocabulary development: A morphological analysis. *Monographs of the Society for Research in Child Development, 58*(10), 1–165.

Aram, D.M., Ekelman, B.L., & Nation, J.E. (1984). Preschoolers with language disorders: 10 years later. *Journal of Speech and Hearing Research, 27,* 232–244.

Aram, D.M., & Hall, N.E. (1989). Longitudinal follow-up of children with preschool communication disorders: Treatment Implications. *School Psychology Review, 18,* 487–501.

Armbruster, B.B., Anderson, T.H., & Meyer, J.L. (1987). Does text structure/summarization instruction facilitate learning from expository text? *Reading Research Quarterly, 22*(3), 331–346.

Aubusson, P., Foswill, S., Barr, R., & Perkovic, L. (1997). What happens when students do simulation-role-play in science. *Research in Science Education, 27*(4), 565–579.

Baddeley, A., Gathercole, S., & Papagno, C. (1998). The phonological loop as a language learning device. *Psychological Review, 105*(1), 158–173.

Badon, L.C. (1993). *Comparison of word recognition and story retelling under the conditions of contextualized versus decontextualized reading events in at-risk poor readers.* Unpublished doctoral dissertation, Louisiana Sate University, Baton Rouge.

Baker, L., & Cantwell, D.P. (1982). Psychiatric disorder in children with different types of communication disorders. *Journal of Communication Disorders, 15,* 113–126.

Baldwin, L.S. & Henry, M.K. (1991). Reading and language arts: A design for integrated instruction. In C.S. Simon (Ed.), *Communication skills and classroom success: Assessment and therapy methodologies for language and learning disabled students.* Eau Claire, WI: Thinking Publications.

Ball, E.W. (1997). Phonological awareness: Implications for whole language and emergent literacy programs. *Topics in Language Disorders, 17*(3), 14–16.

Ball, E.W., & Blachman, B. (1991). Does phoneme awareness training in kindergarten make a difference in early word recognition and developmental spelling? *Reading Research Quarterly, 26*, 49–66.

Bashir, A.S. & Scavuzzo, A. (1992). Children with language disorders: Natural history and academic success. *Journal of Learning Disabilities, 25*(1), 53–65.

Bashir, A.S., Conte, B.M., & Heerde, S.M. (1998). Language and school success: Collaboration, changes and choices. In D.D. Merritt & B. Culatta (Eds.), *Language intervention in the classroom* (pp. 1–36). San Diego, CA.: Singular.

Bereiter, B., & Engelmann, S. (1966). *Teaching disadvantaged children in the preschool.* Englewood Cliffs, NJ: Prentice-Hall.

Bernhardt, B., & Major, E.M. (2005). Speech, language and literacy skills three years later: A follow-up study of early phonological and metaphonological intervention. *International Journal of Language and Communication Disorders, 40*, 1–27.

Beukelman, D., & Mirenda, P. (1992). *Augmentative and alternative communication.* Baltimore: Paul H. Brookes.

Billeaud, F.P. (2003). Communication disorders in infants and toddlers: Assessment and intervention (Third Ed.), St. Louis, MS: Butterworth Heinemann.

Blachman, B. (1989). Phonological awareness and word recognition: Assessment and intervention. In A Kamhi & H. Catts (Eds.), *Reading disabilities: A developmental language perspective.* Boston: College-Hill.

Blachman, B., Ball, E., Black, S., & Tangel, D. (1994). Kindergarten teachers develop phoneme awareness in low-income, inner-city classrooms: Does it make a difference? *Reading and Writing: An Interdisciplinary Journal, 6*, 1–17.

Bourgault, R. (1991). Mass media and pragmatics: An approach for developing listening, speaking, and writing skills in secondary school students. In C.S. Simon (Ed.), *Communication skills and classroom success: Assessment and therapy methodologies for language and learning disabled students* (pp. 358–385). Eau Claire, WI: Thinking Publications.

Brackenberry, T., and Pye, C. (2005). Semantic deficits in children with language impairments: Issues for clinical assessment. *Language, Speech, and Hearing Services in Schools, 36*(1), 5–16.

Bricker, D., & Cripe, J. (1992). *An activity-based approach to early intervention.* Baltimore: Paul H. Brookes.

Brinton, B. & Fujiki, M. (1994). Ways to teach conversation. In J.F. Duchan, L.E. Hewitt, and R.M. Sonnenmeirer, *Pragmatics: From theory to practice* (pp. 1–9). Englewood Cliffs: NJ: Prentice-Hall, Inc.

Brinton, B., & Fujiki, M. (2006). Improving peer interaction and learning in cooperative learning groups. In T.A. Ukrainetz (Ed.), *Contextualized language intervention: Scaffolding PreK-12 Literacy Achievement* (pp. 289–318). Eau Claire, WI: Thinking Publications.

Brown, A.L., Campione, J.C., Reeve, R.A., Ferrara, R.A., & Palincsar, A.S. (1991). Interactive learning, individual understanding: The case of reading and mathematics. In L.T. Landsman (Ed.), *Culture, schooling, and psychological development* (pp.136–170). Mahwah, NJ: Erlbaum.

Burbules, N.C., & Rice, S. (1991). Dialogue across differences: Continuing the conversation. *Harvard Educational Review, 61*(4), 393–416.

Bus, A., & Van Ijzendoorn, M. (1999). Phonological awareness and early reading: A meta-analysis of experimental training studies. *Journal of Educational Psychology, 91*, 403–411.

Butler, K.G., Nelson, N.W., Wallach, G.P., Fujiki, M., & Brinton, B. (2005). Language disorders and learning disabilities: A look across 25 years. *Topics in Language Disorders, 25*(4). 287–407.

Cahir, S., & Kivac, C. (1981a). *Teacher talk works.* Washington, DC: Center for Applied Linguistics.

Cahir, S., & Kivac, C. (1981b). *It's your turn.* Washington, DC: Center for Applied Linguistics.

Carey, S. (1978). The child as word learner. In M. Halle, J. Bresnan, & G. Miller (Eds.), *Linguistic theory and psychological reality* (pp. 503–528). Cambridge, MA: MIT Press.

Catts, H. (1991). Facilitating phonological awareness: Role of speech-language pathologists. *Language, Speech, and Hearing Services in Schools, 22*, 196–203.

Chen, Z. (1996). Children's analogical problem solving: The effects of superficial, structural, and procedural similarities. *Journal of Experimental Child Psychology, 62*(3), 410–431.

Chen, Z. (1999). Schema induction in children's analogical problem solving. *Journal of Educational Psychology, 91*(4), 703–715.

Chen, Z., Yanowitz, K.L., & Dachler, M.W. (1996). Constraints on accessing abstract source information. Instantiation of principles facilitates children's analogical transfer. *Journal of Educational Psychology, 87*(3), 445–454.

Chi, M.T.H., Feltovich, P.J., & Glaser, R. (1981). Categorization and representation of physics problems by experts and novices. *Cognitive Science, 5*, 121–152.

Cohen, R., & Netley, C. (1981). Short-term memory deficits in reading disabled children, in the absence of opportunity for rehearsal strategies. *Intelligence, 5*, 19–76.

Cole, J.C., & McLeod, J.S. (1999). Children's writing ability. The impact of the pictorial stimulus. *Psychology in the Schools, 36*(4), 359–370.

Crais, E.R. (1990). World knowledge to word knowledge. *Topics in Language Disorders, 10*(3), 45–62.

Creaghead, N.A. & Tattershall, S.S. (1991). Observation and assessment of classroom pragmatic skills. In C.S. Simon (Ed.), *Communication skills and classroom success: Assessment and therapy methodologies for language and learning disabled students* (pp. 106–123). Eau Claire, WI: Thinking Publications.

Dagher, Z.R. (1995). Does the use of analogies contribute to conceptual change? *Science and Education, 78*(6), 601–614.

DeKemel, K. (2003). *Intervention in language arts: A practical guide for speech-language pathologists.* Philadelphia, PA: Butterworth Heinemann.

Donahue, M., and Bryan, T. (1984). Communicative skills and peer relations of learning disabled adolescents. *Topics in Language Disorders, 4*(2), 10–21.

Druyan, S. (1997). Effects of the kinesthetic conflict on promoting scientific reasoning. *Journal of Research in Science and Teaching, 34*(10), 1083–1099.

Duchan, J.F. (1997). A situated pragmatics approach for supporting children with severe communication disorders. *Topics in Language Disorders, 17*(2), 1–18.

Duchan, J.F. (1994). *Pragmatics: From theory to practice.* Englewood Cliffs: NJ: Prentice-Hall.

Duchan, J.F., Hewitt, L.E., & Sonnenmeier, R.M. (1994). Three themes: Stage two pragmatics, combating marginalization, and the relation of theory and practice. In J.F. Duchan, L.E. Hewitt, & R.M. Sonnenmeirer, *Pragmatics: From theory to practice* (pp. 1–9). Englewood Cliffs, NJ: Prentice-Hall.

Ehren,B.J., & Lentz, B.K. (1989). Adolescents with language disorders: Special considerations in providing academically relevant language intervention. *Seminars in Speech and Language, 3*, 193–204.

Eisenberg, S.L. (2006). Grammar: How can I say it better? In T.A. Ukrainetz, Contextualized language intervention: Scaffolding PreK-12 Literacy Achievement (pp. 145–194), Eau Claire, WI: Thinking Publications.

English, L.D. (1997). Children's reasoning in classifying and solving computational word problems. In L.D. English (Ed.), *Mathematical reasoning: Analogies, metaphors and images* (pp. 191–220). Mahwah, NJ: Erlbaum.

Fahey, K. R. & Reid, D.K. (2000). Language development, differences, and disorders: A perspective for general and special education teachers and classroom-based speech-language pathologists. Austin, TX: Pro-Ed.

Fey, M.E., & Johnson, B.W. (1998). Research to practice (and back again) in speech-language intervention. *Topics in Language Disorders, 18*(2), 23–34.

Flick, L. (1992). Where concepts meet percepts. Stimulating analogical thought in children. *Science and Education, 75*(2), 215–230.

Foyle, H.C. (1985). The effects of preparation and practice homework on student achievement in tenth-grade American history (Doctoral dissertation, Kansas State University, 1984). *Dissertation Abstracts International, 45*, 2474A.

Foyle, H.C., & Bailey, G.D. (1988). Homework experiments in social studies: Implications for teaching. Social Education, *52*(4), 292–298.

Fujiki, M., & Brinton, B. ( 2005). Forward. Part 2: Lessons from longitudinal case studies. *Topics in Language Disorders, 25*(4), 287–407.

Gallagher, J.M., & Wright, R.J. (1979). Piaget and the study of analogy: Structural analysis of items. In M.K. Poulsen & G.I. Lubin (Eds.), *Piagetian theory and the helping professions: Proceedings from the eighth interdisciplinary conference* (Vol. 2, pp. 100–104). Los Angeles: University of Southern California.

Gardner, H. (1974). Metaphors and modalities: How children project polar adjectives onto diverse domains. *Child Development, 45*, 84–91.

Gentner, D., & Markman, A.B. (1994). Structural alignment in comparison: No difference without similarity. *Psychological Science, 5*(3), 152–158.

Gerber, A. (1993). *Language-related learning disabilities: Their nature and treatment.* Baltimore: Paul H. Brookes.

Gertner, B., Rice, M., & Hadley, P. (1994). The influence of communicative competence on peer preferences in a preschool classroom. *Journal of Speech and Hearing Research, 37*, 913–923.

Gholson, B., Smither, D., Buhrman, A., & Duncan, M.K. (1997). The source of children's reasoning errors during analogical problem solving. *Applied Cognitive Psychology, 10* (Special Issue).

Gillam, R.B., & Ukrainetz, T.A. (2006). Language intervention through literature-based units. In T.A. Ukrainetz (Ed.), *Contextualized language intervention: Scaffolding PreK-12 Literacy Achievement* (pp. 59–94), Eau Claire, WI: Thinking Publications.

Gillon, G.T. (2000). The efficacy of phonological awareness intervention for children with spoken language impairment. *Language, Speech, and Hearing Services in Schools, 31*, 126–141.

Gillon, G.T. (2005). Effecting change through the integration of research findings. *Language, Speech, and Hearing Services in Schools, 36*(4), 346–349.

Gillon, G.T. (2005a). Facilitating phoneme awareness development in 3- and 4-year-old children with speech impairment. *Language, Speech, and Hearing Services in Schools, 36*(4), 308–324.

Gillon, G.T. (2005b). Prologue: Phonological awareness: Evidence to influence assessment and intervention practices. *Language, Speech, and Hearing Services in Schools, 36*(4), 281–284.

Gleason, J.B. (1997). *The development of language* (4th ed.). Needham Heights, MA: Allyn & Bacon.

Gottfried, G.M. (1998). Using metaphors as modifiers: Children's production of metaphoric compounds. *Journal of Child Language, 24*(3), 567– 601.

Hadley, P., & Simmerman, A., Long, M., & Luna, M. (2002). Facilitating language development for inner-city children: Experimental evaluation of a collaborative classroom based intervention. *Language, Speech, and Hearing Services in Schools, 31*, 280–295.

Hall, P., & Tomblin, B. (1978). A follow-up study of children with articulation and language disorders. *Journal of Speech and Hearing Disorders, 43*, 227–241.

Halliday, M.A.K. (1973). *Explorations in the functions of language.* London: Edward Arnold.

Hesketh, A., Adams, C., Nightingale, C., & Hall, R. (2000). Phonological awareness therapy and articulatory training approaches for children with phonological disorders: A comparative outcome study. *International Journal of Language and Communication Disorders, 35*, 337–354.

Hodson, B.W. (1998). Research and practice: Applied phonology. *Topics in Language Disorders, 18*(2), 58–70.

Hogan, T.P., Catts, H.W., and Little, T.D. (2005). The relationship between phonological awareness and reading: Implications for the assessment of phonological awareness. *Language, Speech, and Hearing Services in Schools, 36*(4), pp.285–293.

Holland, A.L. (1998). Some guidelines for bridging the research-practice gap in adult neurogenic communication disorders. *Topics in Language Disorders, 18*(2), 49–57.

Horgan, D. (1981). Learning to tell jokes: A case study of metalinguistic abilities. *Journal of Child Language, 8*, 217–227.

Hyerle, D. (1996). *Visual tools for constructing knowledge.* Alexander, VA: Association for Supervision and Curriculum Development.

Imbens-Bailey, A.L. (1998). Evaluating evaluations of language intervention. *Topics in Language Disorders, 18*(2), 35–48.

Ingram, D. (1998). Research-practice relationships in speech-language pathology. *Topics in Language Disorders, 18*(2), 1–9.

Jenkins, J.R., Stein, M.L., & Wysocki, K. (1984). Learing vocabulary through reading. *American Educational Research Journal, 21*(4), 767–787.

Johnson, C.J., & Anglin, J.M. (1995). Qualitative developments in the content and form of children's definitions. *Journal of Speech-Language-Hearing Research, 38*, 612–629.

Johnson, D., & Blalock, J. (1987). *Adults with learning disabilities.* New York: Grune & Stratton.

Johnson, D.W., & Johnson, R.T. (1999). *Learning together and alone: Cooperative, competitive, and individualistic learning.* Boston: Allyn & Bacon.

Justice, L.M. (2002). Word exposure conditions and preschoolers' novel word learning during shared storybook reading. *Reading Psychology, 23*, 767–787.

Justice, L.M., & Ezell, H.K. (2004). Print referencing: An emergent literacy enhancement strategy and its clinical applications. *Language, Speech, and Hearing Services in Schools, 35*, 185–193.

Justice, L.M., Meier, J., and Walpole, S. (2005). Learning new words from storybooks: An efficacy study with at-risk kindergartners. *Language, Speech, and Hearing Services in Schools, 36*(1), pp.17–32.

Justice, L.M., Skibbe, L., & Ezell, H. (2006). Using print referencing to promote written language awareness. In T.A. Ukrainetz, *Contextualized language intervention: Scaffolding PreK-12 Literacy Achievement* (pp. 389–428), Eau Claire, WI: Thinking Publications.

Kagan, S. (1994). *Cooperative learning.* California: Author.

King, R.R., Jones, C., & Lasky, E. (1982). In retrospect: A fifteen-year follow-up report of speech-language-disordered children. *Language, Speech, and Hearing Services in Schools, 13*, 24–32.

Kintsch, W. (1979). On modeling comprehension. *Educational Psychologist, 1*, 3–14.

Laing, S.P. (March, 2006). Phonological awareness, reading fluency, and strategy-based reading comprehension instruction for children with language learning disabilities: What does research show? In ASHA Division 1 *Perspectives on Language Learning and Education, 13*(1), 17–22.

Laing, S. & Espeland, W. (2005). The impact of a classroom-based preschool phonological awareness training program for children with spoken language and expressive phonological impairments. *Journal of Communication Disorders, 38*, 65–82.

Larrivee, L.S. & Catts, H.W. (1999). Early reading achievement in children with expressive phonological disorders. *American Journal of Speech-Language Pathology, 8*, 118–128.

Larson, V.L. & McKinley, M.S. (1995). *Language disorders in older students: Preadolescents and adolescents.* Eau Claire, WI: Thinking Publications.

Larson, V.L. & McKinley, N.L. (1987). *Communication assessment and intervention strategies for adolescents.* Eau Claire, WI: Thinking Publications.

Lasky, E.Z. (1991). Comprehending and processing of information in clinic and classroom. In C.S. Simon (Ed.), *Communication skills and classroom success: Assessment and therapy methodologies for language and learning disabled students* (pp. 282–297). Eau Claire, WI: Thinking Publications.

Lee, R.F. & Kamhi, A.G. (1990). Metaphoric competence in children with learning disabilities. *Journal of Learning Disabilities, 23*, 476–482.

Lou, Y., Abrami, P.C., Spence, J.C., Paulsen, C., Chambers, B., & d'Apollonio, S. (1996). Within-class grouping: A meta-analysis. *Review of Educational Research, 66*(4), 423–458.

Loban, W.D. (1976). *Language development: Kindergarten through grade twelve* (Research Report No. 18). Urbana, IL: National Council of Teachers of English.

Lund, N., & Duchan, J. (1993). *Assessing children's language in naturalistic contexts* (3rd ed.). Engelwood Cliffs, NJ: Prentice Hall.

Major, E.M., & Bernhardt, B. (1998). Metaphonological skills of children with phonological disorders befor and after phonological and metaphonological intervention. *International Journal of Language and Communication Disorders, 33*, 413–444.

Markham, A.B., & Gentner, D. (1993a). Splitting the difference: A structural alignment view of similarity. *Journal of Memory and Learning, 32*, 517–535.

Markham, A.B., & Gentner, D. (1993b). Structural alignment during similarity comparisions. *Cognitive Psychology, 25*, 431–467.

Marzano, R.J., Pickering, D.J., & Pollack, J.E. (2001). *Classroom instruction that works: Research-based strategies for increasing student achievement.* Alexandria, VA: Association for Supervision and Curriculum Development.

Mason, L. (1994). Cognitive and metacognitive aspects in conceptual change by analogy. *Instructional Science, 22*(3), 157–187.

Mason, L. (1995). Analogy, meta-conceptual awareness and conceptual change: A classroom study. *Educational Studies, 20*(2), 267–291.

Mason, L., & Sorzio, P. (1996). Analogical reasoning in restructuring scientific knowledge. *European Journal of Psychology of Education, 11*(1), 3–23.

Mather, N., & Goldstein, S. (2001). *Learning disabilities and challenging behaviors: A guide to intervention and classroom management.* Baltimore: Paul H. Brookes.

Medin, D., Goldstone, R.L., & Markman, A.B. (1995). Comparison and choice: Relations between similarity processes and decision processes. *Psychonomic Bulletin & Review, 2*(1), 1–19.

Moats, L.C., & Lyon, G.R. (1996). Wanted: Teachers with knowledge of language. *Topics in Language Disorders, 16*(2), 73–86.

Nagy, W., & Anderson, R.C. (1984). How many words are there in printed school English? *Reading Research Quarterly, 19*, 304–330.

Nagy, W.E., & Herman, P.A. (1987). Breadth and depth of vocabulary knowledge: Implications for acquisition and instruction. In M.C. McKeown & M.E. Curtis (Eds.), *The nature of vocabulary instruction* (pp. 19–36). Hillsdale, NJ: Erlbaum.

Nathan, L., Stackhouse, J., Goulandreis, N., & Snowling, M.J. (2004). The development of early literacy skills among children with speech difficulties: A test of the "critical age hypothesis." *Journal of Speech, Language, and Hearing Research, 47*, 377–391.

National Association of State Directors of Special Education, Inc. (2005). *Response to intervention: Policy considerations and implementation.* Alexandria, VA.

National Reading Panel (2000). Teaching children to read: *An evidence-based assessment of the scientific research literature on reading and its implications for reading instruction.* Washington, DC: National Institute of Child Health and Human Development.

National Research Council (1998). *Preventing Reading Difficulties in Young Children.* (Committee on the Prevention of Reading Difficulties in Young Children; C.E. Snow, M.S. Burns, and P. Griffin, Editors.) Washington, DC: National Academy Press.

National Research Council (1999). *Starting Out Right: A Guide to Promoting Children's Reading Success.* In M.S. Burns, P. Griffin, & C.E. Snow (Eds.), *Committee on the Prevention of Reading Difficulties in Young Children.* Washington, DC: National Academy Press.

Nelson, E.A., & Rosenbaum, E. (1972). Language patterns within youth subculture: Development of slang vocabularies. *Merrill-Palmer Quarterly, 18*, 273–285.

Nelson, K. (1985). *Making sense: The acquisition of shared meaning.* New York: Academic Press.

Nelson, N.W. (1989). Curriculum-based language assessment and intervention. *Language, Speech, and Hearing Services in Schools, 20*, 170–184.

Nelson, N.W. (1998). *Childhood language disorders in context: Infancy through adolescence* (2nd ed.). Needham Heights, MA: Allyn and Bacon.

Nelson, N.W. (2005). The context of discourse difficulty in classroom and clinic: An update. *Topics in Language Disorders, 25*(4), 322–331.

Nelson, N.W., & Van Meter, A.M. (2006). Finding the words: Vocabulary development for young authors. In T.A. Ukrainetz, *Contextualized language intervention: Scaffolding PreK-12 Literacy Achievement* (pp. 95–143), Eau Claire, WI: Thinking Publications.

Newby, T.J., Ertner, P.A., & Stepich, D.A. (1995). Instructional analogies and the learning of concepts. *Educational Technology Research and Development, 43*(1), 5–18.

Newton, D.P. (1995). Pictorial support for discourse comprehension. *British Journal of Educational Psychology, 64*(2), 221–229.

Nieto, S. (1994). Lessons from students on creating a chance to dream. *Harvard Educational Review, 64*(4), 392–426.

Nippold, M.A. (1990). *Idioms in textbooks for kindergarten through eighth grade students.* Unpublished manuscript, University of Oregon, Eugene.

Nippold, M.A. (1998). *Later language development.* Austin, TX: Pro-Ed.

Nippold, M.A., & Fey, S.H. (1983). Metaphoric understanding in preadolescents having a history of language acquisition difficulties. *Language, Speech, and Hearing Services in Schools, 14*, 171–180.

Nippold, M.A., & Martin, S.T. (1989). Idiom interpretation in isolation versus context: A developmental study with children and adolescents. *Journal of Speech and Hearing Research, 32*, 59–66.

Norris, J. (1988). Using communication strategies to enhance reading acquisition. *The Reading Teacher, 41*, 368–373.

Norris, J. (1991). From frog to prince: Using written language as a context for language learning. *Topics in Language Disorders, 12*(1), 1–6.

Norris, J.A. (1989). Providing language remediation in the classroom: An integrated language-to-reading intervention method. *Language, Speech, and Hearing Services in Schools, 20*, 205–218.

Norris, J.A., & Hoffman, P.R. (2002). Phonemic awareness: A complex developmental process. *Topics in Language Disorders, 22*(2), 1–34.

Owens, R. (1996). *Language development: An introduction* (4th ed.). Boston: Allyn & Bacon.

Palincsar, A.S. (1986). The role of dialogue in providing scaffolded instruction. *Educational Psychologist, 21*, 73–98.

Palincsar, A.S., & Brown, A.L. (1984). Reciprocal teaching of comprehension fostering and comprehension monitoring activities. *Cognition and Instruction, 1(2)*, 117–175.

Perl, S. (1994). Teaching and practice: Composing texts, composing lives. *Harvard Educational Review, 64*(4), 427–449.

Polanski, S. (1989). Spontaneous production of figures in writing of students: Grades four, eight, twelve, and third year in college. *Educational Research Quarterly, 13*, 47–55.

Pollio, M.R., & Pollio, H.R. (1974). The development of figurative language in school children. *Journal of Psycholinguistic Research, 3*, 185–201.

Polloway, E.A., & Patton, J.R. (1993). *Strategies for teaching learners with special needs* (5th ed.). Columbus, OH: Merrill.

Powell, G. (1980, December). *A meta-analysis of the effects of "imposed" and "induced" imaginary word recall.* Paper presented at the annual meeting of the National Reading Conference, San Diego, CA: (ERIC Document Reproduction Series No. Ed 199 644).

Prater, M.A., Joy, R., Chilman, B., Temple, J., & Miller, S.R. ((1991). Self-monitoring of on-task behavior by adolescents with learning disabilities. *Learning Disabilities Quarterly, 14*, 164–177.

Prinz, P.M. (1983). The development of idiomatic meaning in children. *Language and Speech, 26*, 263–272.

Raitano, N.A., Pennington, B.F., Tunick, B.F., Boada, R., & Shriberg, D.D. (2004). Pre-literacy skills of subgroups of children with speech sound disorders. *Journal of Child Psychology and Psychiatry, 45*, 821–835.

Rattermann, M.J., & Gentner, D. (1998). More evidence for the relational shift in the development of analogy: Children's performance on the casual-mapping task. *Cognitive Development, 13*(4), 453–478.

Reid, D.K., & Leamon, M.M. (1996). The cognitive curriculum. In D.K. Reid, W.P. Hresko, & H.L. Swanson (Eds.), *Cognitive approaches to learning disabilities* (3rd ed., pp. 401–432). Austin, TX: Pro-Ed.

Richardson, S.O., & Wallach, G.P. (2005). Pulling the pieces together: The doctor is in. *Topics in Language Disorders, 25*(4), 332–336.

Ripoll, T. (1999). Why this made me think of that. *Thinking and Reasoning. 4*(1), 15–43.

Rosenshine, B., & Meister, C.C. (1994). Reciprocal teaching: A review of the research. *Review of Educational Research, 64*(4), 479–530.

Rosenshine, B., Meister, C., & Chapman, S. (1996). Teaching students to generate questions. A review of the intervention studies. *Review of Educational Research, 66*(2), 181–221.

Ross, B.H. (1987). This is like that: The use of earlier problems and the separation of similarity effects. *Journal of Experimental Psychology, 13*(4), 629–639.

Rossetti, L.M. (2001). *Communication intervention birth to three* (2nd Ed.). Oshkosh, WC: Singular-Thompson Learning.

Rvachew, S. (2006). Longitudinal predictors of implicit phonological awareness skills. *American Journal of Speech-Language Pathology, 15*(2), 165–176.

Sanders, W.L., & Horn, S.P. (1994). The Tennessee value-added assessment system (TVAAS): Mixed-model methodology in educational assessment. *Journal of Personnel Evaluation in Education, 8*, 299–311.

Seidenberg, P.L., & Bernstein, D.K. (1986). The comprehension of similies and metaphors by learning-disabled and non-learning-disabled children. *Language, Speech, and Hearing Services in Schools, 17*, 219–229.

Shachar, H., & Sharan, S. (1994). Talking, relating, and achieving: Effects of cooperative learning and whole-class instruction. *Cognition and Instruction, 12*(4), 313–353.

Shultz, T.R. (1974). Development and appreciation of riddles. *Child Development, 45,* 100–105.

Silliman, E., & Wilkinson, L.C. (1991). *Communicating for learning: Classroom observation and collaboration.* Gaithersburg, MD: Aspen.

Silliman, E., & Wilkinson, L.C. (1994). Discourse scaffolds for classroom intervention. In G.P. Wallach & K.G. Butler (Eds.), *Language learning disabilities in school-age children and adolescents* (pp. 27–54). New York: Merrill.

Simon, C.S. (1991a). *Communication skills and classroom success: Assessment and therapy methodologies for language and learning disabled students.* Eau Claire, WI: Thinking Publications.

Simon, C.S. (1991b). Functional flexibility: Developing communicative competence in the speaker and listener roles. In C.S. Simon (Ed.), *Communication skills and classroom success: Assessment and therapy methodologies for language and learning disabled students* (pp. 298–333). Eau Claire, WI: Thinking Publications.

Snowling, M.J., Bishop, D.V.M., & Stoddard, S.E. (2000). Is preschool language impairment a risk factor for dyslexia in adolescence? *Journal of Child Psychology and Pyschiatry, 41*, 587–600.

Solomon, I. (1995). Analogical transfer and "functional fixedness" in the science classroom. *Journal of Educational Research, 87*(6), 371–377.

Stahl, S.A., & Fairbanks, M.M. (1986). The effects of vocabulary instruction: A model-based meta-analysis. *Review of Educational Research, 56*(1), 72–110.

Stanovich, K. E. (2000). *Progress in understanding reading: Scientific foundations and new frontiers.* New York: Guilford Press.

Sternberg, R.J. (1977). *Intelligence, information processing and analogical reasoning: The componential analysis of human abilities.* Hillsdale, NJ: Erlbaum.

Sternberg, R.J. (1979). Developmental patterns in the encoding and combination of logical connectives. *Journal of Experimental Child Psychology, 28*, 469–498.

Sternberg, R. J. (1987). Most vocabulary is learned from context. In M. McKeown & M. Curtis (Eds.), *The nature of vocabulary acquisition* (pp. 89–106). Hillsdale, NJ: Erlbaum.

Sternberg, R.J. & Nigro, G. (1980). Developmental patterns in the solution of verbal analogies. *Child Development, 51*, 27–38.

Storch, S.A., & Whitehurst, G.J. (2002). Oral language and code-related precursors to reading: Evidence from a longitudinal structural model. *Developmental Pyschology, 38*, 934–947.

Strong, C. (October, 2001). Literature-based language intervention. *ASHA Special Interest Division 1: Language learning and Education, 8*(2), 21–25.

Swanborn, M.S.L., & de Glopper, K. (1999). Incidental word learning while reading: A meta-analysis. *Review of Educational Research, 69*(3), 261–285.

Swanson, H.L. (1996). Information processing: An introduction. In D. K. Reid, W.P. Hresko, & H.L. Swanson (Eds.), *Cognitive approaches to learning disabilities* (3rd ed., pp. 251–283). Austin, TX: Pro-Ed.

Swanson, T.J., Hodson, B.W., & Schommer-Aikins, M. (2005). An examination of phonological awareness treatment outcomes for seventh-grade poor readers from a bilingual community. *Language, Speech, and Hearing Services in Schools, 36*, 336–345.

Tummer, W., & Cole, M. (1991). Phonological awareness and reading acquisition. In D. Sawyer & B. Fox (Eds.), *Phonological awareness in reading.* New York: Springer-Verlag.

Tyler, A. (2002). Planning and monitoring intervention programs. In A.G. Kamhi & K.E. Pollack (Eds.), *Phonological disorders in children: Clinical decision making in assessment and intervention.* Baltimore: Paul H. Brookes

Ukrainetz, T.A. (2006a). *Contextualized language intervention: Scaffolding preK-12 literacy achievement.* Eau Claire, WI: Thinking Publications.

Ukrainetz, T.A. (2006b). Assessment and intervention within a contextualized skill framework. In T.A. Ukrainetz, *Contextualized language intervention: Scaffolding PreK-12 Literacy Achievement* (pp. 7–58), Eau Claire, WI: Thinking Publications.

van Dijk, T.A. (1980). *Macrostructures.* Hillsdale, NJ: Erlbaum.

van Kleeck, A., Vander Woude, J., & Hammett, L. ( 2006). Fostering literal and inferential language skills in head start preschoolers with language impairment using scripted book-sharing discussions. *American Journal of Speech-Language Pathology, 15*(1), 85–95.

Wallach, G.P. (2004). Over the brink of the millennium: Have we said all we can about language-based learning disabilities? *Communication Disorders Quarterly, 25*(2), 44–55.

Wallach, G.P. (2005). A conceptual framework in language-learning disabilities: School-aged language disorders. *Topics in Language Disorders, 25*(4), 292–301.

Webster, P.E., & Plante, A.S. (1992). Effects of phonological impairment on word, syllable, and phoneme segmentation and reading. *Language, Speech, and Hearing Services in Schools, 23*, 176–182.

Welch, M. (1997, April). *Students' use of three-dimensional modeling while designing and making a solution to a technical problem.* Paper presented at the annual meeting of the American Educational Research Association, Chicago.

Westby, C. (2006). There's more to passing than knowing the answers: Learning to do school. In T.A. Ukrainetz, *Contextualized language intervention: Scaffolding PreK-12 Literacy Achievement* (pp. 319–379), Eau Claire, WI: Thinking Publications.

Whitmire, K.A. (2005). Language and literacy: In the age of federal incentives. *Topics in Language Disorders, 25*(4), 302–309.

Wilcox, M.J., Hadley, P.A., & Bacon, C.K. (1998). Linking science and practice in management of childhood language disorders: Models and problem-solving strategies. *Topics in Language Disorders, 18*(2), 10–22.

Wright, S.P., Horn, S.P., & Sanders, W.L. (1997). Teacher & classroom context effects on student achievement: Implications for teacher evaluation. *Journal of Personnel Evaluation in Education, 11*, 57–67.

# 8

# Teaching Younger Readers with Reading Difficulties

## Nancy Mather and Annmarie Urso

Children who struggle with the early stages of reading, particularly the development of phonological awareness and decoding, face increasing obstacles each year to their literacy development (Adams & Bruck, 1995; Juel, 1988; Torgesen & Burgess, 1998). Because they cannot pronounce words accurately or quickly, they struggle to comprehend and gain conceptual knowledge (Beck & Juel, 1995; Shaywitz, Fletcher, & Shaywitz, 1994).With each year, the gap between their reading skill and ability to meet the ever-increasing expectations for proficient literacy continues to widen and a disproportionate percentage of these students end up dropping out of school (Wagner, Blackorby, & Hebbeler, 1993). Effective reading instruction is, therefore, a critical issue for students with learning disabilities (LD) of which an estimated 80% have difficulty mastering varied aspects of reading (Wagner et al., 1993). Approximately 3.5% of children in the United States receive services for a reading disability (Snow, Burns, & Griffin, 1998); the accurate and early identification of these children is a critical concern (Lipka, Lesaux, & Siegel, 2006).

This problem is not new. Throughout the 21st century, reading experts and researchers tried to resolve the issue of the many children who had difficulty learning to read (e.g., Fernald, 1943; Hinshelwood, 1917; Monroe, 1932; Orton, 1937; Stanger & Donohue, 1937; Weisenburg & Mc-Bride, 1935). Monroe (1932) discussed the serious educational problem of those atypical children who did not learn to read as well as would be expected given their intellectual abilities and accomplishments. This characteristic of "unexpected reading failure" is often what distinguishes the child with a specific reading disability, from one who is struggling for other reasons. In many cases, oral language abilities are intact which are also reflected in early definitions of reading disability. For example, Weisenburg and McBride (1935) described "word-blindness" as a disorder in the perception or understanding of letter- or word-forms that exist apart from other language disturbances. More recently, others have explained that what distinguishes individuals with a reading disability from other poor readers is that their listening comprehension ability is higher than their ability to decode words (Rack, Snowling, & Olson, 1992). Despite a century of interest in this population, numerous children still struggle to learn to read.

Recently, the goal of reducing the number of students experiencing reading failure has become a national priority (Al Otaiba & Fuchs, 2006). Legislation has even attempted to address and enforce change. For example, Public Law 107-110, The No Child Left Behind Act (NCLB) of 2001, ushered in sweeping reforms in school accountability for student performance. Because of NCLB, all students are supposed to reach high standards, attaining a minimum proficiency or better in reading by the year 2014. As a result of this increased pressure for high standards, greater emphasis has been placed on the implementation of effective teaching methods, also referred to as *evidence-based, scientifically-based,* or *research-based* practices. In fact, implementation of evidence-based practices forms an integral part of the new evaluation procedures specified for identifying students with LD in the Individuals with Disabilities Education Act (IDEA, 2004).

## WHAT IS EVIDENCE-BASED READING RESEARCH?

To ensure that most students develop an acceptable level of reading performance, teachers need to know and use the most effective practices and procedures (Fuchs & Fuchs, 1998; Warby, Greene, Higgins, & Lovitt, 1999). Some teachers use strategies, methods, and programs that are not supported by scientifically-based research, whereas others select and use well validated practices. When making decisions about what instructional strategies, approaches, programs, and materials to adopt, educators need to have knowledge of the criteria that constitute rigorous research. The report of the *National Reading Panel: Teaching Children to Read: An Evidence-Based Assessment of the Scientific Research Literature on Reading and Its Implications for Reading Instruction* (2000) summarized the empirical findings regarding the most efficacious reading instruction.

Within this report, the term *scientifically-based reading research* was used to describe research that met the following four criteria: (a) incorporation of rigorous, systematic, and empirical methods; (b) use of adequate data analyses to test the stated hypotheses and justify the conclusions; (c) inclusion of measurements or observational methods that demonstrate a reliance on valid data across evaluators and observers and across multiple measurements and observations; and (d) acceptance by a peer reviewed journal or approval by a panel of independent experts through a comparably rigorous, objective and scientific review. Ideally, evidence of a method's effectiveness should be available across all four of the above criteria. In practice, however, the quality of evidence available on each of the four criteria varies.

The criteria used to select the programs and instructional methodology included in this chapter as evidence-based best practices were based primarily on the Florida Center for Reading Research (FCRR, Florida State University, 2002) framework, as well as the results reported in meta-analysis studies. The FCRR framework was developed to determine if a program or method met the criteria to be determined to be a best practice. The seven criteria that constitute quality research are presented in Table 8.1. Although a substantive body of research exists on some aspects of early reading development (e.g., phonological awareness), limited research exists in other areas (e.g., vocabulary).

Many programs and strategies are geared toward the provision of effective instruction in one critical aspect of reading performance, such as helping the young reader increase phonological awareness, improve decoding skills, or increase reading speed. Regardless of the skill or skills being targeted, all strategies and programs are aligned to the goal of increasing reading competence so that students can comprehend text and read effectively for a variety of purposes. Although reading is a complex process that includes the integration of many skills, this review highlights strategies and programs that integrate what is currently known about the most effective instruction for younger readers in: (a) phonological awareness, (b) decoding, (c) fluency, (d) vocabulary, and (e) reading comprehension. Findings from evidence-based research show dramatic reductions in the incidence of reading failure when students receive explicit instruction in these components (Foorman & Torgesen, 2001). In addition, the chapter includes a brief discussion of generalizations regarding instruction, an overview of a few comprehensive programs and class-

**TABLE 8.1**
**Research Criteria for Programs**

| Research Criteria | Description |
|---|---|
| Experimental Design | 1) True experimental design with random assignment of participants is preferred.<br>2) Quasi-experimental design is acceptable when any number of variables are matched in when control group and experimental group with appropriate analysis of variance statistical tests. |
| Sample | Samples should be based on a normal distribution, with a large enough size to ensure validity of statistical analyses. Unless the study designates otherwise, the sample should be heterogeneous. |
| Investigators | Studies conducted by third-party investigators are preferred to preserve objectivity. |
| Reporting of Results | Peer-reviewed journal is preferred, but does not exclude consideration of other publication sources. Question of objectivity is present in other publication sources. |
| Statistical Analysis | Statistical procedures employed must be appropriate for research question being asked and the data being analyzed. Foundational assumptions that underlie the statistically procedures should be adequately addressed |
| Method | Methodology should be described in sufficient detail for replication by other researchers. Methodology should be sound, well-constructed and comprehensive. No questions should arise as to how certain dimensions of the study were carried out. |
| Performance Measures | All measurement tools must have adequate reliability and validity. Appropriate assessment tools for the measured elements of interest should be used to evaluate growth or progress in students' performance. |

*Note.* From ©Florida Center for Reading Research (2002). *Research Criteria for FCRR Reports.* Retrieved September 3, 2004, from the Florida State University Center Web site: http://www.fcrr.org/FCRRReports/PDF/Reserach_Criteria.pdf. Reprinted with permission.

wide tutoring programs, as well as a discussion of the need for increased and enhanced teacher knowledge and preparation.

## PHONOLOGICAL AWARENESS

Phonological awareness is an oral language ability that refers to the ability to attend and manipulate to the various aspects of speech sounds. This metacognitive understanding involves the realization that spoken language is composed of a series of discrete speech sounds (phonemes) that are arranged in a particular sequence (Clark & Uhry, 1995). Although the terms *phonological awareness* and *phonemic awareness* are sometimes used interchangeably, these terms refer to two distinct aspects of oral language. Phonemic awareness refers to the ability to hear and identify the individual speech sounds or phonemes, whereas phonological awareness is a broader term that includes all types of phonological activities, such as rhyming pairs of words or counting the number of syllables in words. As young children learn to read an alphabetic language like English, a critical first step is awareness that speech can be divided and sequenced into a series of words, syllables, and phonemes.

English words have three basic units for analysis: syllables, onsets and rimes, and phonemes. Syllables are formed by single vowels or vowels with combinations of various consonants. The English syllable can then be divided into two parts: the onset and the rime. The onset refers to the initial part of the syllable (i.e., one or more consonants) that precedes the vowel in a monosyllabic word. The rime refers to the ending part. Every English syllable has a rime, but not necessarily an onset. For example, in the word "open," the first syllable /o/ is considered to be a rime, whereas the second syllable /pen/ contains both an onset /p/ and a rime /en/. The phoneme, a single speech sound, is the smallest unit of analysis. English has between 40 to 44 phonemes (dialectal differences can increase or decrease the number of speech sounds used). Awareness of these discrete speech sounds allows one to perceive and manipulate language sounds. The number of phonemes in a word is not necessarily equal to the number of letters. For example, the word "soap" has four letters but only three speech sounds: /s/, /ō/, /p/, whereas the word fox has three letters but four speech sounds: /f/, /ŏ /, /k/, /s/.

## Sequence of Development

Phonemic awareness abilities develop in a sequence that ranges from simpler to more complex tasks (Chard & Dickson, 1999; Ehri, 1991; Smith, 1997; Stanovich, 1986; Torgesen & Mathes, 2000). As a general principle, instruction begins with easier tasks, such as rhyming words or identifying the first sound of a word, to more complex tasks, such as blending and segmenting the phonemes in words (Chard & Dickson, 1999: Torgesen & Mathes, 2000). *Big Ideas in Beginning Reading* (2002–2004) presents a sequence of skill development in which the child recognizes that words can: (a) rhyme, (b) be broken into syllables, (c) be broken into onsets and rimes, (d) start and end with the same sound, (e) have the same medial sound, and (f) be broken into phonemes. A similar sequence uses the following order of phonological awareness tasks progressing from the easiest to the most difficult: (a) selecting pictures beginning with the first-sound of a word, (b) blending onset-rimes into words, (c) blending phonemes into words, (d) deleting a phoneme and pronouncing the remaining word, (e) segmenting words into phonemes, and (f) blending words into phonemes (Schatschneider, Francis, Foorman, Fletcher, & Mehta, 1999).

Once a word has been broken into phonemes, the child can then delete sounds from words to make new words, blend sounds together to pronounce words, and break the sounds in words apart (segmentation). These abilities form the foundation for the acquisition of decoding (pronouncing words) and encoding (spelling words). Thus, phonemic awareness abilities have their primary impact on the development of children's phonics skills, or their knowledge of the ways that letters represent the sounds in printed words (Torgesen & Mathes, 2000), as well as on their spelling development (Bailet, 2001).

## Research Base

A substantive body of research supports the link between phonological awareness abilities and the subsequent development of reading skill (e.g., Lyon, 1995; Perfetti, 1992; Torgesen, 1992, 1993; Wagner & Torgesen, 1987). After conducting a meta-analysis of 52 studies, the National Reading Panel (2000) presented the following conclusions: (a) phonemic awareness can be taught and learned; (b) instruction in phonemic awareness improves reading and spelling skills; (c) instruction is most effective when the focus is on one or two types of activities, rather than several types; (d) the amount of progress is enhanced when children manipulate phonemes using letters; (e) small group instruction for 30 minutes for no more than 20 hours is effective for most children; and (f) computers can be used effectively. In addition, teachers need to be able to pronounce individual phonemes correctly (Kroese, Mather, & Sammons, 2006; Moats, 2000; Torgesen & Mathes, 2000).

The various phonological awareness abilities are not of equal importance to early reading and spelling development. For example, measures of rhyme recognition (e.g., "Which word rhymes with tree: sun or me?") are less predictive of reading failure than tasks that require children to attend to the individual phonemes in words (Hoien, Lundberg, Stanovich, & Bjaalid, 1995; Torgesen & Mathes, 2000). The two most important phonological awareness abilities are blending (synthesizing sounds) and segmenting (analyzing sounds) (Ehri, 2006). For blending, children are presented with a series of sounds and then asked to push the sounds together to form a word. For segmentation, children are presented with a word and then asked to break the word apart into the individual sounds. Segmentation and blending can be taught using a variety of manipulatives, including plastic markers, poker chips, colored tiles, magnetic letters, and scrabble tiles. Different colored chips can represent the consonant and vowel sounds (e.g., consonant sounds are blue and vowel sounds are red). Using letters, the teacher can demonstrate how to pull the sounds of a word apart and then push the sounds back together again to form a word.

## Blending

The purpose of teaching blending is to help young children combine letter sounds to be able to pronounce or decode words (Ehri, 2006). Chard and Osborn (1999) recommended a three-step procedure for helping students learn to blend sounds to pronounce words more easily. In the first step, students blend sounds together as quickly as possible, rather than stopping between the sounds. In the second step, students follow the sounding out with a fast pronunciation of the word. In the third step, students discontinue sounding out words aloud. Gradually, as skill progresses, word reading changes from the overt activity of oral reading to a covert activity of silent reading. At this stage, the instructor may model the process for children by mouthing the pronunciation of words, demonstrating how words can be sounded out silently.

The difficulty level of a blending task is affected by both the length of the pause between the sounds, as well as the number of sounds that are presented in the sequence. A word that is sounded with a short pause between the sounds is much easier to blend than a word that is presented with a one-second interval between the sounds. Instruction then begins with words with two sounds (/sh/oe/), then three sounds (/c/a/t), and finally four sounds (/s/a/n/d/) (Kirk, Kirk, Minskoff, Mather, & Roberts, 2007). In addition, speech sounds that can be prolonged and sustained (e.g., /s/, /f/, /m/, /l/, /n/, /r/, /v/, /z/) are easier to blend than those that cannot (e.g., /b/, /t/) (Carnine, Silbert, Kame'enui, & Tarver, 2004). Carnine et al. described a similar procedure called *telescoping sounds* where a student transforms a series of blended sounds pronounced quickly in succession (e.g., /i/ /i/ i/ /t/ /t/ /t/) into a word (e.g., "it") said at a normal rate.

## Segmentation

Segmentation involves breaking apart the sounds of words so that children can generate more complete spellings of words (Ehri, 2006). Kirk et al. (2007) suggested the following sequence for teaching segmentation:

1. Begin with compound words (e.g., "baseball"). Say: When I say the word "baseball," how many words do you hear? If needed use pictures or hand gestures to reinforce how to break the two words apart.
2. Progress to syllable units (e.g., "car-pen-ter"). An easy way to help children learn how to count the number of syllables is to have them place their hand under their chins and then say the word aloud. The number of syllables is equal to the number of times that the chin drops. One rule of English spelling is that each syllable must have a vowel and the vowel sound forces the mouth to open.
3. Practice with onsets and rimes (e.g., "c-at").
4. Practice breaking words into individual phonemes (/c/ /a/ /t/).

Phonological awareness abilities do, however, form the foundation for the acquisition and application of phonics skills. Without appropriate intervention in important phonological abilities, such as blending and segmentation, the reading development of children with poor phonological processing skills will be impeded (Lipka et al., 2006). Phonological awareness is a necessary factor, but not the only factor that promotes good reading ability (Ehri, 2006; Torgesen & Mathes, 2000). Other factors such as phonics skills, sight word recognition, reading rate, vocabulary, and comprehension also contribute to skilled reading performance.

## DECODING

Decoding refers to the ability to use the systematic correspondences between sounds and spellings to acquire a repertoire of words that can be recognized by sight (McCardle, Scarborough, & Catts, 2001). Decoding includes both phonics and structural analysis, as well as instant recognition of sight words. Phonics is the reading method used to teach children how to identify words by pronouncing the sounds. Structural analysis involves breaking words into units, often syllables, to make longer words easier to pronounce. Sight word recognition refers to the quick pronunciation of words without analysis of word structure.

### Phonics and Structural Analysis

Several programs that have been identified as being evidence-based address the development of decoding skills, including: the *Wilson Reading System*® (Wilson, 1996), the *Lindamood Phoneme Sequencing Program for Reading, Spelling and Speech* (LiPS®, Lindamood & Lindamood, 1998), *Read, Write & Type!™, Learning System* (Herron, 2000), *DaisyQuest* (Erickson, Foster, Foster, Torgesen, & Packer, 1993) and *Reading Excellence: Word Attack and Rate Development Strategies* (REWARDS®, Archer, Gleason, & Vachon, 2000).

The *Wilson Reading System*® is a multisensory approach to teaching reading and writing, designed to teach specific strategies for decoding and encoding in a step-by-step sequential manner. This program has been part of numerous on-going empirically-based studies and is recognized by several states in their reading initiatives (Banks, Guyer, & Guyer, 1993; Bursuck & Dickson, 1999; Clark & Uhry, 1995; Moats, 1998). Originally, the *Wilson Reading System*® was intended for use with upper elementary and older students struggling with reading. More recently, *Wilson Fundations*® (Wilson Reading Systems, 2002) was added for younger readers in general education classrooms to build a foundation of skills in phonological/phonemic awareness, phonics, and spelling. Based upon the *Wilson Reading System*® principles, *Fundations*® is a prevention program designed to help reduce early reading and spelling failure.

Another program that has resulted in improved decoding for students with reading difficulties is *LiPS*®. This program teaches phonemic awareness, blending, and phoneme sequencing skills. The program is designed to stress the oral-motor characteristics of speech and is helpful for students who have severe difficulty with speech sounds. Analyses of data gathered by the Lindamood-Bell researchers at their licensed Learning Centers have demonstrated the effectiveness of this method with struggling readers (Lindamood-Bell Learning Processes, 2003).

Computers can also deliver effective instruction. The *Read, Write & Type!™ Learning System* (RWT) is a software program designed for children 6 to 9 years-of-age (Herron, 2000). By using the keyboard, children learn the 40 speech sounds and then how to build words by typing the sounds. The sequential curriculum is organized in 40 lessons, with each lesson covering four sounds. When RWT was compared to an earlier version of the *LIPs* program, at-risk first-grade readers in both instructional conditions made dramatic improvements (Torgesen, Wagner, Rashotte, & Herron, 2000). *DaisyQuest* (Erickson et al., 1993) is an inexpensive software program developed by researchers at the University of Florida for young children 3 to 7 years-of-age. Through a variety of engaging games, children can work independently at developing phonological awareness and phonics skills. Research studies on *DaisyQuest* showed significant improvement on phonological awareness and phonics skills when students participated in 15-32 sessions, each lasting 20-25 minutes (Barker & Torgesen, 1995; Foster, Erickson, Foster, Brinkman, & Torgesen, 1994; Mitchell & Fox, 2001).

*REWARDS®*, a specialized reading program designed for upper elementary and secondary school students, teaches students the use of a flexible strategy for decoding multi-syllabic words. The aim is to increase comprehension by increasing oral and silent reading fluency. Using *REWARDS®*, readers are taught an overt and a covert strategy. The overt strategy involves circling the prefixes, circling the suffixes, and underlining the vowel sound in the root word. The teacher then says: "What part? What part? What part?" while drawing scoops under the segments or decodable "chunks." Then, students are instructed to say the words quickly. Eventually, underlining the vowel and circling the word parts are eliminated, leaving the student with the covert strategy of looking for the word parts and vowel sounds, and saying the parts quickly to form a real word.

## Sight Word Recognition

Children with the most severe reading difficulties have difficulty recognizing letter sequences as decoding units and learning to read individual words by sight (Perfetti & Hogaboam, 1978; Torgesen, 2000; Torgesen, Rashotte, & Alexander, 2001). The key to skilled reading is the ability to read words by sight automatically (Ehri, 1998). Ehri indicates that skilled readers can identify different words in at least five different ways: (a) blending the sounds of letters into words, (b) pronouncing and blending spelling patterns, (c) retrieving sight words from memory, (d) making analogies to words already known by sight, and (e) using context clues to predict words. Although capable readers can use all of these strategies for word identification, the most skilled reading is based on retrieving sight words rapidly and easily from memory because all of the other cueing systems require attention and disrupt the reading process (Ehri, 1998).

Ehri (1998, 2000) also described four overlapping phases that underlie the development of a sight vocabulary: prealphabetic, partial alphabetic, full alphabetic, and consolidated alphabetic. During the *prealphabetic stage*, readers recognize words by selected visual attributes that are not connected to grapheme–phoneme relationships. In the *partial alphabetic phase*, readers make connections between some of the letters and sounds in written words. Partial-phase readers do not store sight words in memory in sufficient letter detail to recognize how they are similar yet different from other words. In the *full alphabetic stage*, students make complete connections between letters and sounds, and they are able to pronounce phonically regular words. In the *consolidated alphabetic phase*, letter patterns that occur across many words are retained. These larger units consist of morphemes, syllables, or onsets and rimes. Operating with chunks or word parts makes it easier to decode and encode multisyllabic words (Ehri, 2000). In regard to the instantaneous recognition of sight words, readers are not able to retain many sight words until they are fully alphabetic. Thus, children must know phoneme-grapheme relationships before they can develop and acquire a substantial sight vocabulary. In general, rapid word recognition develops as phonic word recognition improves (Moats, 2000). Interventions with struggling readers, however, have been more successful in improving accuracy than rate (Torgesen et al., 2001). The most promising approach to increasing sight word recognition is to first develop accuracy in word reading followed by repeated practices viewing and naming words quickly in multiple contexts. Thus, a core problem for children with reading disabilities is their lack of ability to rapidly and automatically read sight words, phrases, and sentences (Chard, Vaughn, & Tyler, 2002), an ability referred to as "reading fluency." In fact, the extent of a child's sight vocabulary is the most important factor for explaining differences in reading fluency (Torgesen et al., 2001).

## READING FLUENCY

Reading fluency encompasses both the accuracy and the speed or rate of reading, as well as the ability to read materials with expression. Meyer and Felton (1999) defined fluency as "...the ability to read connected text rapidly, smoothly, effortlessly, and automatically with little conscious attention to the mechanics of reading, such as decoding" (p. 284). Children are successful with decoding when the process used to identify words is fast and nearly effortless or automatic. This concept of "automaticity" refers to a student's ability to recognize words rapidly with little attention required to the word's appearance. Chard et al. (2002) reviewed the results of 24 studies that investigated the application of reading fluency interventions for students with reading disabilities. Their findings indicated that effective interventions for fluency include: (a) provision of an explicit model of fluent reading, (b) multiple readings of text with corrective feedback on missed words, and (c) established performance criteria to increase the difficulty level of the text. In addition, instruction and practice in processing larger orthographic units quickly seems to enhance fluency. Although additional research is needed, a few methods have been found to be effective for increasing reading fluency. These are described below.

### Repeated Readings

Ample evidence suggests that repeatedly practicing oral reading of instructional level text with a model and feedback supports growth in oral reading fluency (Denton, Fletcher, Anthony, & Francis, 2006). The use of both oral and silent repeated readings has been found to be effective for increasing reading fluency and improving comprehension (e.g., Fuchs, Fuchs, Hosp, & Jenkins, 2001; National Reading Panel, 2000; Perfetti, 1986; Shankweiler, Lundquist, Dreyer, & Dickinson, 1996). In a review of the effectiveness of repeated reading, Meyer and Felton (1999) concluded that this method improves reading speed for a wide variety of readers when used within the following context: (a) have students engage in multiple readings (three to four times); (b) use instructional level text; (c) use decodable text with struggling readers; (d) provide short, frequent periods of fluency practice; (e) provide concrete measures of progress; and (f) base the amount of teacher guidance on individual student characteristics. For students with poor reading skills, modeling and practicing specific words between readings can improve performance and reduce frustration.

Repeated reading procedures have also been used as a component of classwide peer tutoring (Mathes & Fuchs, 1993). In a study of this intervention, pairs of students in one group read continuously over a 10-minute period, whereas pairs of students in the other group read a passage together three times before going on to the next passage. Although both experimental conditions produced higher results than the typical reading instruction, no difference existed between the two procedures, suggesting that the main benefit of the intervention was the repeated practice of passages and the increased time spent reading (Mastropieri, Leinart, & Scruggs, 1999). In general, the most effective applications of the repeated reading technique seem to include: (a) reading and rereading selected text a specified amount of times, (b) providing more practice with tutors or peers, and (c) providing some type of feedback regarding accuracy and fluency (Torgesen et al., 2001).

## Commercial Programs

Commercially-based programs, such as the *Six-Minute Solution* (Adams & Brown, 2003), are based on the repeated readings of one-minute non-fiction passages with a peer-monitoring and feedback system. Two other commercially available fluency based reading programs that meet the criteria for effective practices are *Read Naturally*© (Ihnot, Mastoff, Gavin, & Hendrickson, 2001) and *Great Leaps*© (Campbell, 1998, 2005; Mercer & Campbell, 1998). The *Read Naturally*© program combines the following three evidence-based strategies to develop reading fluency: reading from a model, repeated readings, and progress-monitoring. Passages range from pre-K to eighth-grade levels. Research has documented the effectiveness of the *Read Naturally*© program at both elementary and secondary levels (Denton et al., 2006; Hasbrouck, Ihnot, & Rogers, 1999; National Reading Panel, 2000; Onken, 2002; Wahl, 2006).

*Great Leaps*© is a program developed to increase reading fluency through the development and mastery of phonics skills, sight word reading, and passage reading. The program is a one-to-one supplemental reading program that takes approximately 10 minutes per day and includes a progress-monitoring component. Daily application of this program with middle school students with LD contributed to growth in reading and an improvement in reading rate (Mercer, Campbell, Miller, Mercer, & Lane, 2000). *Great Leaps*© spans reading levels K through 8 with interest levels through adulthood. A K–2 version of this program provides a phonological awareness instruction component (Mercer & Campbell, 1998). The *Great Leaps*© program meets the criteria set forth as an effective practice (Mercer et al., 2000; Robinson, 2003; Tenenbaum & Wolking, 1989).

A new promising approach is the Retrieval, Automaticity, Vocabulary, Elaboration, Orthography (*RAVE-O*) program, a multicomponential approach to increasing fluency (Wolf, Miller, & Donnelly, 2000; Wolf et al., 2003). Although currently, the program is not being widely distributed, its availability will likely increase in coming years. With the use of computerized games and a variety of manipulative materials, the program is designed to help develop and increase accuracy and automaticity at both the sublexical and lexical levels by helping the young reader develop explicit and rapid connections among the phonological, orthographic, syntactic, semantic, and morphological systems (Wolf et al., 2003). When used as an intervention, *RAVE-O* is taught in conjunction with a program that teaches phonological awareness and blending. The program was developed from a strong research and theoretical base, and preliminary research results support its effectiveness (Lovett, Lacerenza, & Borden, 2000). The curriculum was originally designed to assist struggling second and third graders; however, successful results have been obtained with fourth-grade children (Wolf et al., 2003). Although *RAVE-O* is described as a reading fluency intervention, its goal is improvement in comprehension through use of a comprehensive, engaging, developmental approach (Wolf et al., 2003).

## Fluency and Comprehension

Fluency is often described as forming the link or the bridge between word analysis and comprehension (Chard et al., 2002). Numerous studies have investigated the role of reading fluency on comprehension (e.g., Allington, 1983; Cunningham & Stanovich, 1998; Fuchs, Fuchs, Hosp, et al., 2001; Fuchs, Fuchs, & Maxwell, 1988; Hasbrouck et al., 1999; Jenkins & Jewell, 1993; Mastropieri et al., 1999; Sindelar, Monda, & O'Shea, 1990). The rationale for increasing reading fluency and rate is that when students allocate too much attention to lower-level processes such as reading words with accuracy, not enough attentional resources are left to accomplish the higher-order linguistic processing involved in comprehension (LaBerge & Samuels, 1974; Perfetti & Hogaboam, 1975).

Some researchers have indicated that readers cannot be considered as fluent, unless they understand what they read (Wolf & Katzir-Cohen, 2001). Research has not, however, always demonstrated that interventions designed to increase fluency also enhance comprehension abilities. More complex, interventions with multiple components appear more effective for gains in both fluency and comprehension. Reading instruction that integrates teaching of the alphabetic principle, applying these skills in context, and reading the same words repeatedly in different contexts, may increase reading fluency in a way that improves reading comprehension (Berninger, Abbott, Vermeulen, & Fulton, 2006). In addition, combining the repeated reading procedures with comprehension activities appears to enhance both fluency and comprehension (Chard et al., 2002).

## VOCABULARY

As compared to other areas of reading instruction, little research exists on the effectiveness of instructional methods to improve vocabulary (Jitendra, Edwards, Sacks, & Jacobsen, 2004; National Reading Panel, 2000) and, unfortunately, current school practices appear to have little impact on vocabulary growth and development (Biemiller, 2005). One finding seems clear: for readers at all skill levels, the relationship between reading comprehension and vocabulary appears reciprocal. Vocabulary knowledge contributes to improved reading comprehension; and word knowledge increases through reading experiences (Ackerman, Weir, Metzler, & Dykman, 1996; Cunningham & Stanovich, 1991). Even the vocabulary knowledge of low readers is strongly related to the amount of reading that they do (Cunningham & Stanovich, 1998). Thus, a weakness in oral vocabulary can compromise reading comprehension (Berninger et al., 2006). In general, students with reading difficulties typically spend less time engaged in independent reading than their peers and as a result, they have less familiarity with the vocabulary used in texts and their comprehension suffers (Anderson & Roit, 1993; Bos & Anders, 1990).

Differences in the number of words that a student has learned are apparent in the first years of school. By the end of second grade, the difference in root vocabulary knowledge between children in the highest and in the lowest quartile differs by as many as 4,000 word meanings (Biemiller, 2004; Biemiller, 2005). Knowing a word's meaning, however, is not an all or nothing proposition (Beck & McKeown, 1991). Readers may have little, partial, or complete knowledge of a word. Also, a distinction exists between the breadth of vocabulary (or the size of the vocabulary or number of lexical entities), the depth of vocabulary knowledge, and the extent and depth of semantic knowledge (Ouellette, 2006). The breadth of vocabulary seems to be primarily related to decoding proficiency, whereas the depth appears more related to oral language capabilities (Ouellette, 2006).Thus, students with poor word recognition skills but good verbal ability tend to increase their vocabulary knowledge more through listening than reading (Carlisle, 1993). Effective vocabulary instruction must focus on both oral and written communications, as well as include techniques for increasing the number of words, and the extent, detail, and depth of processing of the words.

Several studies have specifically addressed methods and strategies for facilitating vocabulary acquisition in students with LD. For example, Pany and Jenkins (1978) and Pany, Jenkins, and Schreck (1982) compared several vocabulary instruction strategies to determine which methods were most effective for increasing word knowledge and comprehension in students with LD. Students read sentences containing target words and synonyms, read definitions of target words, and practiced using target words in sentences. The more the meanings of words were practiced, the higher was student performance on vocabulary measures and the better was their retention of words.

Findings from a recent review of 27 studies investigating the effects of vocabulary instruction with students with LD continue to substantiate that methods employing the direct teaching of vocabulary are effective and that systematic practice of word meanings is critical to vocabulary acquisition and maintenance (Burns, Dean, & Foley, 2004; Jitendra et al., 2004). In addition, explicit teaching of word meanings within the context of shared storybook reading is effective for young children with reading difficulties (Coyne, Simmons, & Kame'enui, 2004) and is the most powerful source of new vocabulary (Stahl & Stahl, 2004). Books should be read aloud several times to children combined with an explanation of from 8 to 10 new vocabulary words (Biemiller, 2004). In contrast, methods, such as looking up words in a dictionary and writing definitions or using context clues to determine a word's meaning, are ineffective for students with LD (Bryant, Goodwin, Bryant, & Higgins, 2003).

In addition to the need for more practice, a growing consensus exists regarding other elements of effective vocabulary instruction. In a review of four effective vocabulary programs, Foorman, Seals, Anthony, and Pollard-Durodola (2003) found that the programs were consistent on the following instructional principles: (a) introduction of approximately three words per day, or no more than 12 to 15 words per week; (b) selection of words that could be extended derivationally and conceptually through discussion; (c) location and discussion of words in engaging text; and (d) provision of contextualized definitions with practice opportunities in new and multiple contexts. In addition, words are taught in a sequence with an attempt to determine which words should be learned next. The words to target for struggling readers are usually the ones that some children of that grade level know but others do not (Biemiller, 2005). Instruction needs to focus on words that students will meet often and will be useful (McKeown & Beck, 2004). Thus, the vocabulary words being taught need to be of appropriate complexity (Stahl & Stahl, 2004).

Several effective methods for teaching vocabulary incorporate visual diagrams and support. One method is *semantic mapping* (Nagy, 1998) where the relationships among the words are visually mapped. The target word is placed in the center of a word web and the web is then expanded with related words and ideas that are connected to show relationships among the words or concepts. The benefits of graphic organizers for retaining words across several content areas (e.g., science, social studies, mathematics, Spanish as a second language), multiple grade levels (first through senior high school), and different student populations (general education and students with LD) have been supported in both experimental and quasi-experimental studies (e.g., Bos & Anders, 1992; Braselton & Decker, 1994; Bryant et al., 2003; Doyle, 1999; Meyer, 1995; Ritchie & Volkl, 2000). In addition, the process of developing and using a graphic organizer appears to enhance students' critical thinking or higher-order thinking skills (Boyle & Weishaar, 1997; DeWispelaere & Kossack, 1996; Doyle, 1999).

*Inspiration®* and *Kidspiration®* (Inspiration Software, Inc., © 2002a, 2002b) are examples of two commercially produced software programs designed to incorporate the scientifically-based research on graphic organizers. A similar strategy, semantic feature analysis, also seems to enhance vocabulary growth. For this technique, the student compares words by placing them in a grid that outlines the semantic similarities and differences (Walker, 2000). Both methods appear effective for helping students notice similarities and differences among words and ideas (Jitendra et al., 2004).

Other methods that are designed to help students recall vocabulary focus on the creation of visual images which can help students recall more difficult terminology, such as new words to be learned for a math, science, or history class. The key word method (described in detail in chapter 13 of this volume) involves tying new words to visual images to help students recall word meanings and learn new vocabulary (Mastropieri, 1988; Mastropieri & Scruggs, 1998). Findings indicate that the keyword mnemonic strategy can both increase vocabulary knowledge, as well as facilitate recall of words over time (Jitendra et al., 2004). Computer-assisted instruction also shows promise for providing independent practice opportunities for students with LD (Bryant et al., 2003; Jitendra et al., 2004).

Research highlights the need for early intervention that offers effective vocabulary instruction that begins in the preschool years, and continues through the early grades permeating the instructional day (Coyne et al., 2004; Foorman et al., 2003). With good instruction, several studies have demonstrated that primary-level children can acquire new vocabulary at a rate of two or three words a day (Biemiller, 2004). Adequate time and attention must be devoted to helping students with reading difficulties build and maintain their word knowledge through multiple exposures to words and systematic and intensive instruction. Without this type of instruction, gaps in vocabulary knowledge will continue throughout elementary school, leaving students at greater risk for continued problems with reading comprehension as they progress through school.

As described in previous sections of this chapter, successful reading comprehension is highly correlated with both oral reading fluency and vocabulary knowledge. Even so, research has shown that interventions that focus on improving fluency or vocabulary do not necessarily increase reading comprehension especially of lengthy passages (Gersten, Fuchs, Williams, & Baker, 2001). This finding calls attention to the need for instruction in specific skills and strategies that can increase the comprehension of longer text passages.

## READING COMPREHENSION

Reading comprehension is a complex skill that is dependent upon many factors, including a readers' background knowledge of facts and concepts, depth and breadth of vocabulary, familiarity with various sentence and text structures, verbal reasoning abilities, and knowledge of print and literacy conventions (McCardle et al., 2001). Today's comprehension demands far exceed the traditional poststory recall questions that were typically used in basal readers. Essentially, a student's reading comprehension will be no stronger than their comprehension of oral language (Fletcher, Lyon, Fuchs, & Barnes, 2007).

Recent research on comprehension instruction has focused on the importance of teaching the use of multiple strategies for text comprehension (e.g., Fielding & Pearson, 1994; Minskoff, 2005; Paris, Wasik, & Turner, 1991, Pressley, 2000; Rakes, Rakes, & Smith, 1995). For example, the National Reading Panel (2000) found that students' text comprehension improved when teachers demonstrated and then had students apply varied strategies, such as answering and generating questions and summarizing what was read. Similar types of interventions have also been shown to be effective for children with LD (Gersten et al., 2001); however, research findings have not yet revealed conclusive procedures for how to select methods or how to use them effectively in different types of educational environments (Dole, 2000; Vaughn, Gersten, & Chard, 2000). Recent reviews of meta-analyses of reading research, however, have highlighted the importance of specific instruction in text structure (Elbaum, Vaughn, Hughes, Moody, & Schumm, 2000; Gersten et al., 2001; Mastropieri, Scruggs, Bakken, & Whedon, 1996; Swanson, 1999; Swanson, 2001).

### Text Structure

Research has also addressed the different types of structure. The two most common types of structures are narrative, texts that tell stories that may be fiction or nonfiction, and expository, texts that include discussions of issues, events, and content area knowledge. Several strategies have been found to be effective for enhancing student understanding of both types of text (e.g., Bakken & Whedon, 2002; Boulineau, Fore, Hagan-Burke, & Burke, 2004; Dickson, 1995; Ehren, 2005; Minskoff, 2005; Williams, 2005).

*Narrative text structure* is the type of text that children are usually exposed to initially when adults read stories to them. Many children develop a natural understanding of story structure after repeated exposures to stories using this strategy. This understanding takes place in most cases even before these children learn to read, building expectations once they read independently regarding how stories should unfold and develop. One effective way to help students increase understanding of narrative text is to teach them how to recognize the components of story grammar, the underlying structure of a story. Story grammar instruction can be used as a prereading or prewriting strategy or as a postreading activity. In the early grades, a teacher can introduce the following general elements of story grammar:

1. The setting: Where and when does the story take place?
2. The main characters: Who is the story about?
3. The problem: What happens to the main character?
4. The solution: What does the main character do to solve the problem?
5. The ending: How is the story resolved? (Stein & Glenn, 1979)

As students increase their knowledge, more complex elements can be introduced using the following seven categories of story elements (Montague & Graves, 1993; Stein & Glenn, 1979):

1. Major setting: The main character is introduced.
2. Minor setting: The time and place of the story are described.
3. Initiating event: The atmosphere is changed and the main character responds.
4. Internal response: The characters' thoughts, ideas, emotions, and intentions are noted.
5. Attempt: The main character's goal-related actions are represented.
6. Direct consequence: The attainment of the goal is noted; if the goal is not attained, the changes resulting from the attempt are noted.
7. Reaction: The main character's thoughts and feelings in regard to the outcome are discussed along with the effect of the outcome on the character.

Instruction in story-grammar elements using story-mapping can help children with LD increase their ability to identify story grammar elements when reading narrative text (Boulineau et al., 2004). The key to increasing comprehension using narrative text lies in teaching both the structural knowledge of stories, as well as how to apply this knowledge when analyzing stories (e.g., Boulineau et al., 2004; Gurney, Gersten, Diminio, & Carnine, 1990; Minskoff, 2005).

Although instruction in narrative text is often an appropriate place to begin with young readers, specific instruction in expository structures is needed at all levels (Englert & Mariage, 1991). Expository text, the main type of text found in text books and non-fiction stories, also has its own unique structure. Comprehension of expository text structures begins in the elementary grades when students begin the process of reading to learn information, often through the use of content area text books. The organization of expository prose is unpredictable and often laden with syntactical complexities such as passive voice, compound and complex sentences, prepositional phrases, and embedded sentences, presenting a unique challenge for elementary students with LD (Abrahamsen & Shelton, 1989).

The most commonly cited factors that cause students to experience difficulty with expository text are: (a) limited knowledge of text structure; (b) low vocabulary knowledge; (c) insufficient prior knowledge; (d) the complexity of the ideas expressed (conceptual density); and (e) a lack of familiarity with the content. Older students with LD who have instructional reading levels between grades 2 and 6 appear to read expository text with less fluency than narrative texts, and comprehend expository text with less accuracy (Saenz & Fuchs, 2002). Students may also lack the advanced word attack skills needed to decode multi-syllabic, unfamiliar words that are typically found in expository text (Bryant, Ugel, Thompson, & Hamff, 1999).

A three-phase study by Williams (2005) explored the effects of explicitly teaching a text structure program to second-grade at-risk readers. The following components and key elements of a successful text structure program were identified: (a) instruction in clue words; (b) trade book reading and discussion to supplement expository sources (i.e. encyclopedias, text books); (c) vocabulary development; (d) reading and analysis of target paragraphs focusing on compare-contrast structure; (e) graphic organizer; (f) compare-contrast strategy questions; (g) written summaries with a paragraph frame as support; and (h) review of vocabulary and the strategies at the end of each lesson. The results suggested that when provided with highly structured and explicit instruction that focuses on text structure, children at-risk for reading failure, show gains in comprehension, including the ability to transfer what they have learned to novel texts.

In the upper elementary years, students must acquire several different types of expository styles to succeed (Westby, 1994). Many of the strategies that have been designed to assist students with expository text are based upon sound elements of effective instruction, including: (a) teacher modeling, (b) students practicing asking and answering questions, and (c) students receiving feedback on responses. One example of a content-area textbook study strategy developed by researchers at the University of Kansas is MULTIPASS (Schumaker, Deshler, Alley, Warner, & Denton, 1982). The teacher explains the steps and rationale and then demonstrates the strategy by thinking aloud. Students verbally rehearse the strategy. By using the following three steps, the student never reads the passage in its entirety.

*Survey.* The student surveys by reading the chapter title, introductory paragraph, the table of contents (in order to understand the relationship of the chapter to others in the text), subtitles, illustrations, diagrams, and summary paragraphs. The student then paraphrases all the information gained from the first pass.

*Size-Up.* The student sizes-up by reading the questions at the end of the chapter and checking off those for which he or she already knows the answer. The student then looks through the text for headings and parts of the text that are in italics, bold, or colored print in order to identify cues. The student turns each of these cues into a question and skims the text for an answer. At the end of the chapter, the student paraphrases all remembered facts and ideas.

*Sort-Out.* The student sorts out by reading the questions at the end of the chapter and marking those questions that he or she can answer immediately. If a question cannot be answered, the student attempts to locate the answer by skimming the text.

Students with LD need to be taught explicitly how to analyze text and use this analysis strategically to assist with reading comprehension (e.g., Bakken, Mastropieri, & Scruggs, 1997; Dickson, Simmons, & Kame'enui, 1998; Dimino, Taylor, & Gersten, 1995; Minskoff, 2005). Methods involving "self questioning," such as Reciprocal Teaching (Palinscar & Brown, 1984) and adaptations such as Collaborative Strategic Reading ([CSR]; Klingner & Vaughn, 1998), are also effective methods for improving comprehension. In CSR which was designed specifically for students the following four strategies are taught:

1. Preview—before reading, brainstorm about the topic and predict what will be learned;
2. Click and Clunk—identify parts of a passage that are hard to understand (clunk), then use four "fix up" strategies;

3. Get the Gist—identify the most important information in a passage; and
4. Wrap Up—ask and answer questions that demonstrate understanding and review what was learned.

The students form cooperative groups to participate in the roles of (a) the leader who determines next steps for the group, (b) the clunk expert who reminds the group of steps involved in the process, (c) the gist expert who guides the group through getting the gist, (d) the announcer who asks group members to carry out activities, and (e) the encourager who provides encouragement to group members. The teacher teaches each of the strategies and the student roles to the entire class prior to reading. The teaching process takes several days and includes identifying, in advance, the vocabulary words from the reading materials that may prove to be too difficult. Students with LD show gains in reading comprehension in studies of CSR's effectiveness (Bryant, Vaughn, Linan-Thompson, Ugel, & Hougen, 2000).

In general, this concept of "making known" the thoughts and processes involved in decision-making through the use of making predictions, self-questioning techniques, and "thinking aloud" is highly related to comprehension improvement (e.g., Gersten et al., 2001; Mastropieri et al., 1996; Swanson & Hoskyn, 1998; Swanson, Hoskyn, & Lee, 1999). Table 8.2 provides an abbreviated summary of the effective instructional practices for the major areas identified by the National Reading Panel.

## ADDITIONAL GENERALIZATIONS

In a meta-analysis of reading research spanning 25 years, Swanson (1999) examined over 90 studies involving samples of children and adolescents with LD. The results yielded important information regarding evidence-based effective instructional models, methods, and strategies for teaching word recognition and reading comprehension to children with reading disabilities. For example, direct instruction alone was found to be most effective for teaching word recognition, and a combination of direct instruction and strategy instruction was found to be most effective for

**TABLE 8.2**
**Examples of Effective Reading Strategies**

| Reading Component | Strategy |
| --- | --- |
| Phonological Awareness | Teaching students how to blend and segment speech sounds |
| **Decoding** | |
| Phonics | Teaching students directly and systematically the relationships between the speech sounds (phonemes) and letter patterns (graphemes). |
| Sight Words | Providing students with practice recognizing common morphemes and orthographic units quickly |
| Word Analysis | Teaching students how to recognize and pronounce word parts and syllables in multi-syllabic words. |
| Fluency | Having students engage in repeated readings of lists of words and connected text. |
| Vocabulary | Having students connect known words to new words with multiple exposures to words in varied, engaging contexts. |
| Comprehension | Having students ask and answer questions, summarize, make predictions, and clarify text. Teaching students about the components of various types of text structures. |

TABLE 8.3
**Evidence-Based Components of Effective Reading Instruction for Students with Learning Disabilities**

| Component | Description |
|---|---|
| Direct response/questioning | Teacher asks students questions, guides them in asking their own questions, or engages them in discussion about the subject matter. |
| Controlling task difficulty | Teacher uses short activities that move from easier to more difficult and provides students with support and demonstration. |
| Elaboration | Teacher provides additional information about the subject and/or the steps involved in accomplishing the task. |
| Modeling | Teacher demonstrates the steps required to complete the task. |
| Group instruction | Teacher provides instructions and interaction in small groups. |
| Strategy cues | Teacher reminds students to use strategies, explains the benefits of strategies or specifies steps in strategies (e.g. when the teacher encourages students to "think out loud"). |

*Note.* From "Reading Research for Students with LD: A Meta-Analysis of Intervention Outcomes," by H.L. Swanson, 1999, *Journal of Learning Disabilities, 32,* p. 522. Adapted with permission.

teaching reading comprehension. Moreover, the following six components were found to have a major impact on student performance: (a) direct response/questioning, (b) controlling task difficulty, (c) elaboration, (d) modeling, (e) small group instruction, and (f) strategy cues. Table 8.3 provides a description of these components.

In addition to strategies for teaching (i.e., elaborating, modeling, and providing strategy cues), the conditions of instruction, such as the size of the instructional group, the control of task difficulty, and the conditions and components of the interventions were found to be important for instruction in all aspects of reading.

## Instructional Group Size

From a meta-analysis of reading research, Swanson (1999) found that instruction in small, interactive groups of six or fewer tended to be the most conducive for comprehension gains. Similarly, in a meta-analysis of reading research that spanned 19 years, Elbaum et al. (2000) found that grouping children rather than teaching the whole class at once significantly improved the reading of students with LD. In addition, groups of four or fewer students were better than larger groups. After analyzing research on the best practices in reading instruction, Foorman and Torgesen (2001) identified small-group or one-to-one instruction as an evidence-based critical component for the children who are most at risk for reading failure.

Some early intervention programs, such as *Reading Recovery*®, have been designed to promote literacy learning for the most at-risk children using one-to-one instruction (Clay, 1993). Several studies have demonstrated the effectiveness of this intervention (e.g., Center, Wheldall, Freeman, Outhred, & McNaught, 1995; Pinnell, 1989; Schwartz, 2005), although some have suggested that similar types of instructional techniques based on the *Reading Recovery* format can be successfully adapted for use in pairs (Iversen, Tunmer, & Chapman, 2005) Unfortunately, the realities of classroom constraints can make the implementation of one-to-one instruction too expensive, and even small grouping formats a challenge, due to limitations in the number of teachers, classroom size, and scheduling.

## Task Difficulty

To enhance both word recognition and comprehension, control of task difficulty is another critical component of teaching reading to students who struggle (Gersten et al., 2001; Swanson & Hoskyn, 1998). Swanson and Hoskyn identified controlling task difficulty as one of the three most critical components of effective instruction, and Vaughn et al. (2000) identified control of task difficulty as a critical component of instructional scaffolding. Reading concepts and skills need to be introduced systematically, beginning with easier tasks and progressing to more difficult tasks over time. When the task difficulty is not controlled, students often exhibit behavioral and attentional difficulties in the general education classroom (Liaupsin, Umbreit, Ferro, Urso, & Upreti, 2006; Umbreit, Lane, & Dejud, 2004).

## Conditions and Components of Interventions

The conditions and components of an intervention appear as important as the selection and use of a specific evidence-based approach. Results from intervention studies seem to suggest that the nature of the program is less important than its comprehensiveness and intensity (Fletcher et al., 2007). For example, Torgesen et al. (2001) found the same positive outcomes for two different reading programs that both provided intensive, systematic one-to-one instruction. Effective instructional elements included: small group instruction with high response rates, the provision of immediate feedback, and the sequential mastery of topics, all elements of good teaching (National Joint Committee on Learning Disabilities, 2005). In addition, several instructional principles can help inform decisions regarding diverse learners and effective early literacy instruction: (a) capitalize and use instructional time efficiently; (b) provide interventions early, frequently, and strategically; (c) teach less, more thoroughly; (d) explain reading strategies in a clear, explicit manner to students; (e) provide teacher-directed and student-centered activities; and (f) evaluate the effectiveness of instructional materials and student progress frequently (Kame'enui, 1993).

## COMPREHENSIVE READING PROGRAMS

Some comprehensive reading programs address all areas of reading instruction specified by the National Reading Panel (NRP). For example, Carnine et al. (2004) developed a comprehensive model of instruction, referred to as "Direct Instruction Reading," which incorporates the five essential reading components identified by the NRP: phonemic awareness, phonics, fluency, vocabulary, and text comprehension instruction. These subcomponents are carefully sequenced to allow for fluid progression from beginning reading skills to more advanced reading skills. The Direct Instruction Reading model and teaching procedures incorporate effective instructional strategies using teaching techniques and sequences that are designed to facilitate acquisition and progression of skills.

Another example of a structured curriculum that teaches literacy explicitly is: *Language!*™ *The Comprehensive Literacy Curriculum* (Greene, 2005). This program provides sequential instruction in: (a) phonemic awareness and phonics, (b) word recognition and spelling, (c) vocabulary and morphology, (d) grammar and usage, (e) listening and reading comprehension, and (f) speaking and writing. The *Language!*™ curriculum was developed to provide differentiated instruction through explicit and direct teaching of the major components of written language. *Language!* has been shown to be effective with students who are English Language Learners and special education students in addition to delayed readers. The program uses evidence-based strategies to address the needs of students with low literacy through instruction in the reading and writing skills necessary for success. Research evaluating *Language!* has resulted in significant results across a variety of settings (e.g., Greene, 1996; Moats, 2003; Torgesen et al., 2001).

## CLASSWIDE AND PEER TUTORING PROGRAMS

Tutoring, cooperative grouping, and other peer-assisted learning situations have received considerable research attention since the 1980s. Grouping practices that allow more proficient readers to provide feedback and guide less able readers can increase reading fluency (Chard et al., 2002). Elbaum et al. (2000) found that being paired with another student in a reciprocal tutoring format was beneficial for students with LD regardless of whether the student was acting as the reciprocal tutor or as the tutee. In contrast, cross-age tutoring only had a positive impact on older students with disabilities who tutored younger students; the younger students with disabilities did not benefit from being tutored by older students with disabilities.

Empirical support is also available for ClassWide Peer Tutoring (CWPT), a program developed by Delquadri, Greenwood, Whorton, Carta, and Hall (1986) at the Juniper Gardens Project at the University of Kansas (Delquadri et al., 1986; Fantuzzo, King, & Heller, 1992; Greenwood, Delquadri, & Hall, 1989; Maheady & Harper, 1987; Maheady, Harper, & Sacca, 1988). CWPT pairs all students in a classroom to increase the time that students spend on task receiving feedback, immediate error correction, and appropriate pacing on academic content (Greenwood et al., 1989). The research on CWPT is focused on increasing the academic performance of low socioeconomic status (SES) students (Greenwood, 1991a, 1991b; Greenwood et al., 1989) and lowering the need for special services by this population (Greenwood, Terry, Utley, Montagna, & Walker, 1993).

Fuchs, Fuchs, Mathes, and Simmons (1997) extended the research on CWPT to include students with and without disabilities, across socio-economic status and achievement levels in general education classrooms. Peer-Assisted Learning Strategies (PALS) was originally designed for students in grades two through six and has since expanded to separate programs for kindergarten, first grade, and high school. A strong research base exists for the efficacy of PALS and First Grade PALS, including recognition by the Florida Center for Reading Research as an evidence-based program based on nearly 15 years of empirical research (e.g., Al Otaiba & Fuchs, 2006; Grek, 2002; Fuchs et al., 1997; Fuchs, Fuchs, Thompson, Al Otaiba, et al., 2001; Ginsburg-Block, Rohrbeck, & Fantuzzo, 2006; Maheady, Mallette, & Harper, 2006; McMaster, Fuchs, & Fuchs, 2006; Simmons, Fuchs, Fuchs, Hodge, & Mathes, 1994).

Results from two studies on Kindergarten PALS (K-PALS) found that students receiving K-PALS training and phonological awareness activities outperformed students receiving phonological awareness training alone on measures of beginning reading skills (Fuchs, Fuchs, Thompson, Svenson, et al., 2001); however, some kindergartners with disabilities who participated in the K-PALS program did not make sufficient progress (Fuchs et al., 2002).

First Grade PALS (Mathes, Howard, Allen, & Fuchs, 1998) incorporates two separate tutoring routines, namely, Sounds and Words and Partner Reading. Sounds and Words focuses on beginning decoding skills including phonological skills and word recognition skills, and Partner Reading is a fluency component designed to increase speed and accuracy. This one-to-one tutoring program incorporates partner reading, paragraph summary, prediction, and other strategies identified as evidence-based practices. Results from several research studies (Fuchs et al., 1997; Mathes et al., 1998) indicated that students receiving First-Grade PALS outperformed students who did not receive this program, and students enrolled in peer tutoring classrooms performed better than those receiving traditional instruction regardless of the type of learner (i.e., low achieving, low achieving with a disability, and average achieving).

PALS for grades 2 through 6 also incorporates partner reading, paragraph summary, prediction, and other strategies identified as evidence-based practices for improving decoding skills and reading comprehension. In addition to proving the program's efficacy, studies have shown positive social outcomes in classrooms using PALS, including greater social acceptance of students with LD and improved social and self-concept outcomes (e.g., Fuchs et al., 1997, 2002; Ginsburg-Block et al., 2006). Although implementation of PALS has resulted in positive student gains in decoding and comprehension skills across grade levels, McMaster et al. (2006) caution that this supplementary reading approach may not benefit all students. PALS interventions appear to be most effective for low-income, minority students in urban settings in grades 1 through 3 (Ginsburg-Block et al., 2006). As with all instructional techniques, teachers have to monitor students' progress carefully and modify activities to address the instructional needs of the children who do not make progress.

As another example of a successful classwide intervention, Blachman, Schatschneider, Fletcher, and Clonan (2003) used a classroom prevention model with kindergarten children, as well as with first and second grade students, and found that it was effective in advancing both reading and spelling performance as compared to control children. The 30-minute lessons replaced the basal reading program and were built around a five-step core program that involved: (1) teaching and review of sound-symbol associations by showing a child a letter card and asking for the name, the sound, and the key word for the letter; (2) practice making words by manipulating the letters using a pocket chart or scrabble tiles; (3) timed review with flash cards of the decodable words and introduction and practice reading high frequency irregular words; (4) practice reading stories; and (5) writing 4 to 6 words and a sentence from dictation, beginning with simple consonant-vowel-consonant patterns, and progressing to more complex syllable patterns. Blachman et al. noted that when teachers were provided with an understanding of scientifically based principles of reading instruction, classroom reading instruction improved and students benefited.

## TEACHER PREPARATION AND KNOWLEDGE

One major conclusion reached from the last decade of research on young children with poor reading performance is that early systematic instruction in phonological awareness and systematic phonics can improve early reading and spelling skills. This type of instruction does not completely eliminate cases of reading failure, but it does significantly reduce the number of students who are reading below expectancy level (Torgesen, 2000). Thus, to teach reading to at-risk students and students with reading disabilities, teachers need to have knowledge of English language structure as well as knowledge of how to implement systematic explicit instruction within the classroom.

Unfortunately, many elementary and special education teachers do not have the necessary preparation or expertise to provide specific reading interventions (Brady & Moats, 1997; Moats, 1994) so a substantial gap exists between the evidence-based reading instruction literature and teachers' preparedness to deliver this type of instruction (Moats & Foorman, 2003). Consistent with this view is the finding that when interventions are implemented with lower implementation fidelity in the general education classroom, more students experience an inadequate response to the intervention (Al Otaiba & Fuchs, 2006). Moreover, even instruction in special education classes may not be sufficiently explicit, systematic, and intensive to result in sustained reading growth (Denton et al., 2006). In studies examining teachers' self-perceptions and knowledge regarding the teaching of reading, the results showed that experienced special and general education teachers lack knowledge about word structure (e.g., Bos, Mather, Dickson, Podhajski, & Chard, 2001; Bos, Mather, Friedman-Narr, & Babur, 1999; Cunningham, Perry, Stanovich, &

Stanovich, 2004; McCutchen & Berninger, 1999; McCutchen, Abbott, et al., 2002; McCutchen, Harry, et al., 2002; Moats, 1994; Spear-Swerling, Brucker, & Alfano, 2005).

Research also suggests that even when teachers believe that they are well prepared in teaching certain components of reading they may, in fact, not be so prepared. For example, in one study, kindergarten to third-grade teachers rated their knowledge of children's literature, phonemic awareness, and phonics as high, but the majority demonstrated limited actual knowledge of phonemic awareness and phonics (Cunningham et al., 2004). The potential significance of this problem becomes even greater when one considers the number of teachers for whom knowledge of such skills are essential, namely, all kindergarten through third-grade teachers, as well as all special education teachers who teach children with more severe challenges such as reading disabilities. Consequently, there has been a call for increased professional development throughout the professional and educational policy literature (e.g., Brady & Moats, 1997; International Reading Association, & National Association for the Education of Young Children, 1998; Snow et al., 1998; Snow et al., 2005).

One conclusion is apparent: Teacher preparation and professional development programs need to provide instruction regarding how to improve reading performance. As noted by Lyon (1999), "Major efforts must be undertaken to ensure that colleges of education develop preparation programs to foster the necessary content and pedagogical expertise at both preservice and inservice levels" (p. 8). Because poor readers do not catch-up and continue to struggle with reading throughout school, early intervention from knowledgeable teachers is essential (Juel, 1988; Lyon, 1999; Shaywitz et al., 1994). More than 15 years ago, Liberman, Shankweiler, and Liberman (1989) expressed similar sentiments:

> In view of all the evidence that has accumulated in the past fifteen years to support the critical importance of phonological sensitivity for the attainment of literacy in an alphabetic system, one would surely expect teacher training to reflect these findings. Unfortunately, all too often it does not. Many teachers are being trained to teach reading without themselves ever having learned how an alphabetic orthography represents the language, why it is important for beginners to understand how the internal phonological structure of words relates to the orthography, or why it is hard for children to achieve this understanding. (p. 23)

With proper preparation, both general and special educators can provide informed instruction that will assist all children with reading development (Torgesen, 2000). In this regard, some research has suggested that after completion of a course followed by a year long partnership with elementary teachers, teachers can: (a) deepen their knowledge of language structure, (b) use that knowledge to change classroom practice, and (c) provide reading instruction that will improve all student learning (e.g., Bos et al., 1999; Bos et al., 2001; Mather, Bos, & Babur, 2001; McCutchen, Harry, et al., 2002). The current knowledge base gives us the responsibility to train teachers, not in how to implement one reading approach over another, but rather in how to make informed choices about which components of reading to target for which students at what point in time (Brady & Moats, 1997). Recent teacher training courses, such as the *LETRS* program (Moats, 2004) and *Mastering the Alphabetic Principle* (Podhajski, Varricchio, Mather, & Sammons, in press) may hold promise for more in-depth preservice and inservice training that will increase teacher knowledge of language structure. Any sustained change in reading instruction will require that teachers receive: (a) instruction in empirically-based reading strategies, (b) feedback from trained observers regarding how to implement these strategies and monitor student progress, and (c) information on how to individualize instruction for a variety of students (Foorman & Schatschneider, 2003). As observed by McCutchen and Berninger (1999): Those who know, teach well.

## CONCLUSION

Reading is a complex process that involves the development and consolidation of numerous skills. One cannot just teach only one aspect of reading and expect that young children will become competent readers. Phonological awareness, phonics, and fluency are all aspects of reading performance with early developmental benchmarks, whereas vocabulary and comprehension continue to improve throughout the school years. When children fail to progress in any aspect of reading, their difficulties increase each year. Whereas some children have specific reading disabilities, others struggle to learn to read because of second language issues or limited exposures to reading and literacy opportunities in the home (Carlisle & Rice, 2002).

Despite decades of progress regarding the use and implementation of evidence-based reading interventions, we are still left with the lingering problem of the treatment resisters (Al Otaiba & Fuchs, 2006; Torgesen, 2000). Even when children receive high-quality reading instruction, not all students make adequate progress (Denton et al., 2006; Torgesen, 2000). We do not yet know enough about the underlying characteristics that make it so difficult for some children to learn to read or the specific approaches that will be most effective for each child (Al Otaiba & Fuchs, 2006). These hard-to-teach children epitomize the true meaning of learning disabilities as "unexpected underachievement" (Denton et al., 2006) and suggest that, despite our best efforts and implementation of evidence-based reading interventions, some children may still be left behind. Stanovich (1986) aptly described the plight of the struggling reader:

> Slow reading acquisition has cognitive, behavioral, and motivational consequences that slow the development of other cognitive skills and inhibit performance on many academic tasks. In short, as reading develops, other cognitive processes linked to it track the level of reading skill. Knowledge bases that are in reciprocal relationships with reading are also inhibited from further development. The longer this developmental sequence is allowed to continue, the more generalized the deficits will become, seeping into more and more areas of cognition and behavior. Or to put it more simply and sadly—in the words of a tearful 9-year-old, already failing frustratingly behind his peers in reading progress, "Reading affects everything you do." (p. 390)

To meet the needs of young struggling readers, we must: (a) identify their difficulties at a young age; (b) implement targeted instruction that represents evidence-based best practices; (c) monitor their progress frequently and adjust instruction as needed; (d) ensure that intensive interventions are available and that teachers have the requisite skills and knowledge to deliver high quality instruction; and (e) provide a language rich, safe, motivating environment for learning to read. The most effective programs are comprehensive, provide instruction in the alphabetic principle, teach strategies for comprehension, and provide ample opportunities for practice (Fletcher et al., 2007).

Children who are behind in reading contend daily with the tyranny of time as the pedagogical clock continues to tick mercilessly (Kame'enui, 1993). One conclusion from research is clear: For children with learning problems, learning is hard work; for their teachers, instruction is very hard work and requires an enormous amount of training and support (Semrud-Clikeman, 2005). Children with learning difficulties benefit from the teaching of the same instructional components as peers, but the instruction needs to be more explicit, more comprehensive, and more intensive (Foorman & Torgesen, 2001). Therefore, we must be ever vigilant, persistent, and systematic in all of our efforts to help. We need to identify and intervene early with children who struggle to read to avoid the substantial social and emotional consequences (Fletcher et al., 2007). Over 160 years ago, Carlyle said that it was the business of schools to teach children to read (cited in Stanger & Donahue, 1937). It's time we get down to business.

# REFERENCES

Abrahamsen, E. P., & Shelton, K. C. (1989). Reading comprehension in adolescents with learning disabilities: Semantic and syntactic effects. *Journal of Learning Disabilities, 22,* 569572.

Ackerman, P. T., Weir, N. L., Metzler, D. P., & Dykman, R. A. (1996). A study of adolescent poor readers. *Learning Disabilities Research & Practice, 11,* 68–77.

Adams, G. & Brown, S. (2003). *Six-minute solution.* Boston: Sopris West Educational Services.

Adams, M. J., & Bruck, M. (1995). Resolving the great debate. *American Educator, 19,* 7–20.

Al Otaiba, S., & Fuchs, D. (2006). Who are the young children for whom best practices in reading are ineffective? *Journal of Learning Disabilities, 39,* 414–431.

Allington, R. (1983). Fluency: The neglected reading goal. *Reading Teacher, 36,* 556–561.

Anderson, V., & Roit, M. (1993). Planning and implementing collaborative strategy instruction for delayed readers in grades 6–10. *Elementary School Journal, 94,* 121–137.

Archer, A. L., Gleason, M. M., & Vachon, V. (2000). *Reading excellence: Word attack and rate development strategies.* Longmont, CO: Sopris West.

Bailet, L. L. (2001). Development and disorders of spelling in the beginning school years. In A. M. Bain, L. L. Bailet, & L. C. Moats (Eds.), *Written language disorders: Theory into practice* (2nd ed., pp. 1–41). Austin, TX: PRO-ED.

Bakken, J. P., Mastropieri, M. A., & Scruggs, T. E. (1997). Reading comprehension of expository science material and children with learning disabilities: A comparison of strategies. *Journal of Special Education, 31,* 300–324.

Bakken, J. P., & Whedon, C. K. (2002). Teaching text structure to improve reading comprehension. *Intervention in School and Clinic, 37,* 229–233.

Banks, S. R., Guyer, B. P., & Guyer, K. E. (1993). Spelling improvement by college students who are dyslexic. *Annals of Dyslexia, 43,* 186–193.

Barker, T., & Torgesen, J. K. (1995). An evaluation of computer-assisted instruction in phonological awareness with below average readers. *Journal of Educational Computing Research, 13*(1), 89–103.

Beck, I. L., & Juel, C. (1995). The role of decoding in learning to read. *American Educator, 8,* 21–25, 39–42.

Beck, I.. L., & McKeown, M. (1991). Conditions of vocabulary acquisition. In R. Barr, M. L. Kamil, P. Mosenthal, & P. D. Pearson (Eds.), *Handbook of reading research* (Vol. 2, pp. 789–814). New York: Longman.

Berninger, V. W., Abbott, R. D., Vermeulen, K., & Fulton, C. M. (2006). Paths to reading comprehension in at-risk second-grade readers. *Journal of Learning Disabilities, 39,* 334–351.

Biemiller, A. (2004). Teaching vocabulary in the primary grades. In J. F. Baumann & E. J. Kame'enui (Eds.), *Vocabulary instruction: Research to practice* (pp. 28–40). New York: Guilford.

Biemiller, A. (2005, July). *Teaching vocabulary in the primary and upper elementary grades.* Paper presented at the meeting of the International Dyslexia Association's Special Conference, Research to Practice, Advances in Reading and Literacy, Washington, DC.

*Big Ideas in Beginning Reading.* (2002–2004). University of Oregon Web site. Retrieved June 7, 2006, from http://reading.uoregon.edu

Blachman, B. A., Schatschneider, C., Fletcher, J. M., & Clonan, S. M. (2003). Early reading intervention: A classroom prevention study and a remediation study. In B. R. Foorman (Ed.), *Preventing and remediating reading difficulties: Bringing science to scale* (pp. 253–271). Baltimore: York Press.

Bos, C. S., & Anders, P. L. (1990). Effects of interactive vocabulary instruction on the vocabulary learning and reading comprehension of learning disabled students. *Learning Disabilities Quarterly, 13,* 31–42.

Bos, C. S., & Anders, P. L. (1992). Using interactive teaching and learning strategies to promote text comprehension and content learning for students with learning disabilities. *International Journal of Disability, Development and Education, 39,* 225–238.

Bos, C., Mather, N., Dickson, S., Podhajski, B., & Chard, D. (2001). Perceptions and knowledge of preservice and inservice educators about early reading instruction. *Annals of Dyslexia, 51,* 97–120.

Bos, C. S., Mather, N., Friedman-Narr, R. F., & Babur, N. (1999). Interactive, collaborative professional development in early literacy instruction: Supporting the balancing act. *Learning Disabilities Research & Practice, 14,* 215–226.

Boulineau, T., Fore III, C., Hagan-Burke, S., & Burke, M.D. (2004). Use of story-mapping to increase the story-grammar text comprehension of elementary students with learning disabilities. *Learning Disability Quarterly, 27,* 105–121.

Boyle, J. R., & Weishaar, M. (1997). The effects of expert-generated versus student generated cognitive organizers on the reading comprehension of students with learning disabilities. *Learning Disabilities Research & Practice, 12,* 228–235.

Brady, S., & Moats, L. C. (1997, Spring). Informed instruction for reading success: Foundations for teacher preparation. *Perspectives: A position paper of the International Dyslexia Association.* Baltimore: The International Dyslexia Association.

Braselton, S., & Decker, C. (1994). Using graphic organizers to improve the reading of mathematics. *Reading Teacher, 48,* 276–281.

Bryant, D. P., Goodwin, M., Bryant, B. R., & Higgins, K. (2003). Vocabulary instruction for students with learning disabilities. *Learning Disability Quarterly, 26,* 117–128.

Bryant , D. P., Ugel, N., Thompson, S., & Hamff, A. (1999). Instructional strategies for content-area reading instruction. *Intervention in School and Clinic, 34,* 293–302.

Bryant, D. P., Vaughn, S., Linan-Thompson, S., Ugel, N., & Hougen, M. (2000). Reading outcomes for students with and without reading disabilities in general education middle school content area classes. *Learning Disabilities Quarterly, 23,* 238–252.

Burns, M. K., Dean, V. J., & Foley, S. (2004). Preteaching unknown key words with incremental rehearsal to improve reading fluency and comprehension with children identified as reading disabled. *Journal of School Psychology, 42,* 303–314.

Bursuck, W., & Dickson, S. (1999). Implementing a model for preventing reading failure: A report from the field. *Learning Disabilities Research & Practice, 14,* 191–202.

Campbell, K. U. (1998). *Great leaps reading program* (4th ed.). Gainesville, FL: Diarmuid.

Campbell, K. U. (2005). *Great leaps reading program Grades 3–5.* Gainesville, FL: Diarmuid.

Carlisle, J. F. (1993). Selecting approaches to vocabulary instruction for the reading disabled. *Learning Disabilities Research & Practice, 8,* 97–105.

Carlisle, J. F., & Rice, M. S. (2002). *Improving reading comprehension: Research-based principles and practices.* Baltimore: York Press.

Carnine, D. W., Silbert, J., Kame'enui, E. J., & Tarver, S. G. (2004). *Direct instruction reading* (4th ed.). Upper Saddle River, NJ: Pearson.

Center, Y., Wheldall, K., Freeman, L., Outhred, L., & McNaught, M. (1995). An evaluation of Reading Recovery. *Reading Research Quarterly, 30,* 240–263.

Chard, D. J., & Dickson, S. V. (1999). Phonological awareness: Instructional and assessment guidelines. *Intervention in School and Clinic, 34,* 261–270.

Chard, D. J., & Osborn, J. (1999). Phonics and word recognition instruction in early reading programs: Guidelines for accessibility. *Learning Disabilities Research & Practice, 14,* 107–117.

Chard, D. J., Vaughn, S., & Tyler, B. J. (2002). A synthesis of research on effective interventions for building reading fluency with elementary students with learning disabilities. *Journal of Learning Disabilities, 35,* 386–406.

Clark, D. B., & Uhry, J. K. (1995). *Dyslexia: Theory and practice of remedial instruction* (2nd ed.). Timonium, MD: York Press.

Clay, M. M. (1993). *Reading Recovery: A guidebook for teachers in training.* Portsmouth, NH: Heinemann.

Coyne, M. D., Simmons, D. C., & Kame'enui, E. J. (2004). Vocabulary instruction for young children at risk of experiencing reading difficulties: Teaching word meanings during shared storybook readings. In J. F. Baumann & E. J. Kame'enui (Eds.), *Vocabulary instruction: Research to practice* (pp. 41–58). New York: Guilford.

Cunningham, A. E., Perry, K. E., Stanovich, K. E., & Stanovich, P. J. (2004). Disciplinary knowledge of K-3 teachers and their knowledge calibration in the domain of early literacy. *Annals of Dyslexia, 54,* 139–167.

Cunningham, A. E., & Stanovich, K. E. (1991). Tracking the unique effects of print exposure in children: Associations with vocabulary, general knowledge, and spelling. *Journal of Educational Psychology, 83,* 264–274.

Cunningham, A. E., & Stanovich, K. E. (1998). What reading does for the mind. *American Educator, 22*(1&2), 8–15.

Delquadri, J., Greenwood, C. R., Whorton, D., Carta, J. J., & Hall, R. V. (1986). Classwidepeer tutoring. *Exceptional Children, 52,* 535–542.

Denton, C. A., Fletcher, J. M., Anthony, J. L., & Francis, D. J. (2006). An evaluation of intensive interventions for students with persistent reading difficulties. *Journal of Learning Disabilities, 39,* 447–446.

DeWispelaere, C., & Kossack, J. (1996). *Improving student higher order thinking skills through the use of graphic organizers.* Elk Grove Village, IL: Master's Thesis, Saint Xavier University. (ERIC Document Reproduction Service No. ED400684)

Dickson, S. V. (1995). Text organization and its relation to reading comprehension: A synthesis of the research: ED/OSERS.

Dickson, S., Simmons, D. C., & Kame'enui, E. J. (1998). Text organization: Research bases. In D. C. Simmons & E. J. Kame'enui (Eds.), *What reading research tells us about children with diverse learning needs* (pp.239–277). Mahwah, NJ: Erlbaum.

Dimino, J. A., Taylor, R. M. & Gersten, R. M. (1995). Synthesis of the research on story grammar as a means to increase comprehension. *Reading and Writing Quarterly, 11,* 53–72.

Dole, J. A. (2000). Explicit and implicit instruction in comprehension. In B. M. Taylor, M. F. Graves & P. v. d. Broek (Eds.), *Reading for meaning: Fostering comprehension in the middle grades* (pp. 52–69). Newark, DE: International Reading Association.

Doyle, C. S. (1999). *The use of graphic organizers to improve comprehension of learning disabled students in social studies.* Union, NJ: M.A. Research Project, Kean University. (ERIC Document Reproduction Service No. ED427313)

Ehren, B. J. (2005). Looking for evidence-based practice in reading comprehension instruction. *Topics in Language Disorders, 25,* 310–321.

Ehri, L. C. (1991). Development of the ability to read words. In R. Barr, M. L. Kamil, P. Mosenthal, & P. D. Pearson (Eds.), *Handbook of reading research* (pp. 383–417). New York: Longman.

Ehri, L. C. (1998). Grapheme-phoneme knowledge is essential for learning to read words in English. In J. L. Metsala & L. C. Ehri (Eds.), *Word recognition in beginning literacy* (pp. 3–40). Mahwah, NJ: Erlbaum.

Ehri, L. C. (2000). Learning to read and learning to spell: Two sides of a coin. *Topics in Language Disorders, 20*(3), 19–36.

Ehri, L. C. (2006). Alphabetics instruction helps students learn to read. In R. M. Joshi & P. G. Aaron (Eds.), *Handbook of orthography and literacy* (pp. 649–677). Mahwah, NJ: Erlbaum.

Elbaum, B., Vaughn, S., Hughes, M. T., Moody, S. W., & Schumm, J. S. (2000). How reading outcomes of students with disabilities are related to instructional grouping formats: A meta-analytic review. In R. Gersten, E. P. Schiller & S. Vaughn (Eds.), *Contemporary special education research: Syntheses of the knowledge base on critical instruction issues* (pp. 105–135). Mahwah, NJ: Erlbaum.

Englert, C. S., & Mariage, T.V. (1991). Shared understandings: Structuring the writing experience through dialogue. *Journal of Learning Disabilities, 24,* 330–342.

Erickson, G. C., Foster, D., Foster, K. C., Torgesen, J. K., & Packer, S. (1993). *DaisyQuest,* Scotts Valley: Great Wave Software.

Fantuzzo, J. W., King, J., & Heller, L. R. (1992). Effects of reciprocal peer tutoring on mathematics and school adjustment: A component analysis. *Journal of Educational Psychology, 84,* 331–339.

Fernald, G. M. (1943). *Remedial techniques in basic school subjects.* New York: McGraw-Hill.

Fielding, L. G., & Pearson, P. D. (1994). Reading comprehension: What works. *Educational Leadership, 51*(5), 62–68.

Fletcher, J. M., Lyon, G. R., Fuchs, L. S., & Barnes, M. A. (2007). *Learning disabilities: From identification to intervention.* New York: Guilford.

Florida Center for Reading Research. (2002). *Research criteria for FCRR reports.* Retrieved September 30, 2004, from http://www.fcrr.org

Foorman, B. R. & Schatschneider, C. (2003). Measurement of teaching practices during reading/language arts instruction and its relationship to student achievement. In S. Vaughn & K. L. Briggs (Eds.), *Reading in the classroom: Systems for the observation of teaching and learning* (pp. 1–30). Baltimore: Paul H. Brookes.

Foorman, B. R., Seals, L. M., Anthony, J., & Pollard-Durodola, S. (2003). A vocabulary enrichment program for third and fourth grade African-American students: Description, implementation, and impact. In B. R. Foorman (Ed.), *Preventing and remediating reading difficulties: Bringing science to scale* (pp. 419–441). Baltimore: York Press.

Foorman, B. R., & Torgesen, J. K. (2001). Critical elements of classroom and small-group instruction promote reading success in all children. *Learning Disability Research & Practice, 16*, 203–212.

Foster, K. C., Erickson, G. C., Foster, D. F., Brinkman, D., & Torgesen, J. K. (1994). Computer administered instruction in phonological awareness: Evaluation of the *DaisyQuest* program. *Journal of Research and Development in Education, 2*, 126–137.

Fuchs, D., & Fuchs, L.S. (1998). Researchers and teachers working together to adapt instruction for diverse learners. *Learning Disabilities Research & Practice, 13*, 126–137.

Fuchs, L. S., & Fuchs, D., Hosp, M. K., & Jenkins, J. (2001). Oral reading fluency as an indicator of reading competence: A theoretical, empirical, and historical analysis. *Scientific Studies of Reading, 5*, 239–256.

Fuchs, L. S., Fuchs, D., Mathes, P. G., & Simmons, D. C. (1997). Peer-assisted learning strategies: Making classrooms more responsive to academic diversity. *American Educational Research Journal, 34*, 174–206.

Fuchs, D., & Fuchs, L. S. & Maxwell, L. (1988). The validity of informal reading comprehension measures. *Remedial and Special Education, 9*, 20–28.

Fuchs, D., Fuchs, L. S., Thompson, A., Al Otaiba, S., Yen, L., Yang, N., et al. (2001). Is reading important in reading-readiness programs? A randmonized field trial with teachers as program implementers. *Journal of Educational Psychology, 93*, 251–267.

Fuchs, D., Fuchs, L. S., Thompson, A., Al Otaiba, S., Yen, L., Yang, N., et al. (2002). Exploring the importance of reading programs for kindergartners with disabilities in mainstream classrooms. *Exceptional Children, 68*, 295–311.

Fuchs, D., Fuchs, L. S., Thompson, A., Svenson, E., Yen, L., Al Otaiba, S., et al. (2001). Peer-assisted learning strategies in reading: Extensions for kindergarten, first grade, and high school. *Remedial and Special Education, 22*, 15–21.

Gersten, R., Fuchs, L. S., Williams, J. P., & Baker, S. (2001). Teaching reading comprehension strategies to students with learning disabilities: A review of research. *Review of Educational Research, 71*, 279–320.

Ginsburg-Block, M. D., Rohrbeck, C. A., & Fantuzzo, J. W. (2006). A meta-analytic review of social, self-concept, and behavioral outcomes of peer-assisted learning. *Journal of Educational Psychology, 98*, 732–749.

Greene, J. F. (1996). LANGUAGE! The effects of an individualized structured language curriculum for middle and high school students. *Annals of Dyslexia, 46*, 97–121.

Greene, J. F. (2005). *LANGUAGE! The comprehensive literacy curriculum* (3rd ed.). Boston: Sopris West Educational Services.

Greenwood, C. R. (1991a). Longitudinal analysis of time engagement and academic achievement in at-risk and non-risk students. *Exceptional Children, 57*, 521–535.

Greenwood, C. R. (1991b). ClassWide Peer Tutoring: Longitudinal effects on the reading, language, and mathematics achievement of at-risk students. *Journal of Reading, Writing, and Learning Disabilities International, 7*, 105–124.

Greenwood, C. R., Delquadri, J. C., & Hall, R. V. (1989). Longitudinal effects of classwide peer tutoring. *Journal of Educational Psychology, 81*, 371–383.

Greenwood, C. R., Terry, B., Utley, C. A.., Montagna, D., & Walker, D. (1993). Achievement, placement, and services: Middle school benefits of ClassWide Peer Tutoring used at the elementary school. *School Psychology Review, 22*, 497–516.

Grek, M. L. (2002). *First grade peer-assisted literacy strategies.* Tallahassee: Florida Center for Reading Research.

Gurney, D., Gersten, R., Dimino, J., & Carnine, D. (1990). Story grammar: Effective literature instruction for high school students with learning disabilities. *Journal of Learning Disabilities, 23*, 335–348.

Hasbrouck, J. E., Ihnot, C., & Rogers, G. (1999). Read Naturally: A strategy to increase oral reading fluency. *Reading Research and Instruction, 39*, 27–38.

Herron, J. (2000). *Read, Write, & Type! Learning System.* San Rafael, CA: Talking Fingers, Inc. & California Neuropsychology Services.

Hinshelwood, J. (1917). *Congenital word blindness.* London: H. K. Lewis.

Hoien, T., Lundberg, I., Stanovich, K.E., & Bjaalid, I. (1995). Components of phonological awareness. *Reading and Writing: An Interdisciplinary Journal, 7,* 171–188.

Ihnot, C., Mastoff, J., Gavin, J., & Hendrickson, I. (2001). *Read naturally.* St. Paul, MN: Read Naturally.

Individuals with Disabilities Education Improvement Act (IDEA) of 2004, PL 108–446, 20 U. S. C. §§ 1400 *et seq.*

Inspiration Software, Inc. (2002a). Inspiration® 8. Beaverton, OR: Inspiration Software, Inc.

Inspiration Software, Inc. (2002b). Kidspiration™ 2.1. Beaverton, OR: Inspiration Software, Inc.

International Reading Association, & National Association for the Education of Young Children. (1998, July). Learning to read and write: Developmentally appropriate practices for young children. A joint position statement. *Young Children, 30*–46.

Iverson, S., Tunmer, W. E., & Chapman, J. W. (2005). The effects of varying group size on the Reading Recovery approach to preventive early intervention. *Journal of Learning Disabilities, 38,* 456–473.

Jenkins, J. R., & Jewell, M. (1993). Examining the validity of two measures for formative teaching: Reading aloud and maze. *Exceptional Children, 59*, 421–432.

Jitendra, A. K., Edwards, L. L., Sacks, G., & Jacobsen, L. A. (2004). What research says about vocabulary instruction for students with learning disabilities. *Exceptional Children, 70,* 299–322.

Juel, C. (1988). Learning to read and write: A longitudinal study of 54 children from first through fourth grades. *Journal of Educational Psychology, 80,* 437–447.

Kame'enui, E. J. (1993). Diverse learners and the tyranny of time: Don't fix blame; fix the leaky roof. *The Reading Teacher, 46,* 376–383.

Kirk, S. A., Kirk, W. D., Minskoff, E. H., Mather, N., & Roberts, R. (2007). *Phonic reading lessons: Skills.* Novato, CA: Academic Therapy.

Klingner, J. K., & Vaughn, S. (1998). Using collaborative strategic reading. *Teaching Exceptional Children, 30*(6), 32–37.

Kroese, J., Mather, N., & Sammons, J. (2006). The relationship between nonword spelling abilities of K-3 Teachers and student spelling outcomes. *Learning Disabilities: A Multidisciplinary Journal, 14,* 85–89.

LaBerge, D., & Samuels, S. J. (1974). Toward a theory of automatic processing in reading. *Cognitive Psychology, 6,* 293–323.

Liaupsin, C., Umbreit, J., Ferro, J. B., Urso, A., & Upreti, G. (2006). Improving academic engagement through systematic, function-based intervention. *Education and Treatment of Children, 29,* 573–592.

Liberman, I. Y., Shankweiler, D., & Liberman, A. (1989). The alphabetic principle and learning to read. In I. Y. Liberman & D. Shankweiler (Eds.), *Phonology and reading disability: Solving the reading puzzle* (pp. 3–33). Ann Arbor: The University of Michigan.

Lindamood-Bell Learning Processes. (2003). *2002 Clinical statistics.* Lindamood-Bell Learning Processes.

Lindamood, P. C., & Lindamood, P. D. (1998). *Lindamood phoneme sequencing program for reading, spelling and speech.* Austin, TX: PRO-ED.

Lipka, O., Lesaux, N. K., & Siegel, L. S. (2006). Retrospective analyses of the reading development of grade 4 students with reading disabilities: Risk status and profiles over 5 years. *Journal of Learning Disabilities, 39,* 364–378.

Lovett, M. W., Lacerenza, I., & Borden, S. I. (2000). Putting struggling readers on the PHAST track: A program to integrate phonological and strategy-based remedial reading instruction and maximize outcomes. *Journal of Learning Disabilities, 33,* 458–476.

Lyon, G. R. (1995). Toward a definition of dyslexia. *Annals of Dyslexia, 45,* 3–27.

Lyon, G. R. (1999). The NICHD research program in reading development, reading disorders and reading instruction: A summary of research findings. In *Keys to successful learning: A national summit on research in learning disabilities* (pp.1–5). New York: The National Center for Learning Disabilities.

Maheady, L., & Harper, G. F. (1987). A classwide peer tutoring program to improve the spelling and test performance of low-income, third- and fourth-grade students. *Education and Treatment of Children, 10,* 120–133.

Maheady, L., Harper, G. F., & Sacca, M. K. (1988). ClassWide peer tutoring programs in secondary self-contained programs for the mildly handicapped. *Journal of Research and Development in Education, 21*(3), 76–83.

Maheady, L., Mallette, B., & Harper, G. F. (2006). Four classwide peer tutoring models: Similarities, differences, and implications for research and practice. *Reading & Writing Quarterly, 22,* 65–89.

Mastropieri, M. A. (1988). Using the keyboard (sic) method. *Teaching Exceptional Children, 20*(2), 4–8.

Mastropieri, M. A., Leinart, A., & Scruggs, T. E. (1999). Strategies to increase reading fluency. *Intervention in School and Clinic, 5,* 278–284.

Mastropieri, M. A., & Scruggs, T. E. (1998). Enhancing school success with mnemonic strategies. *Intervention in School and Clinic, 33,* 201–208.

Mastropieri, M. A., Scruggs, T. E., Bakken, J. P., & Whedon, C. (1996). Reading comprehension: A synthesis of research in learning disabilities. In T. E. Scruggs & M. A. Mastropieri (Eds.), *Advances in learning and behavioral disabilities* (pp. 201–227). Greenwich, CT: JAI Press.

Mather, N., Bos, C., & Babur, N. (2001). Perceptions and knowledge of preservice and inservice teachers about early literacy instruction. *Journal of Learning Disabilities, 34,* 472–482.

Mathes, P. G., & Fuchs, L. S. (1993). Peer-mediated reading instruction in special education resource rooms. *Learning Disabilities Research & Practice, 8,* 233–243.

Mathes, P. G., Howard, J. K., Allen, S. H., & Fuchs, D. (1998). Peer-assisted learning strategies for first-grade readers: Responding to the needs of diverse learners. *Reading Research Quarterly, 33,* 62–94.

McCardle, P., Scarborough, H. S., & Catts, H. W. (2001). Predicting, explaining, and preventing children's reading difficulties. *Learning Disabilities Research & Practice, 16,* 230–239.

McCutchen, D., Abbott, R D., Green, L. B., Beretvas, S. N., Cox, S. Potter, N. S., et al. (2002). Beginning literacy: Links among teacher knowledge, teacher practice, and student learning. *Journal of Learning Disabilities, 35,* 69–86.

McCutchen, D. & Berninger, V. W. (1999). Those who know, teach well: Helping teachers master literacy-related subject-matter knowledge. *Learning Disabilities Research & Practice, 14,* 215–226.

McCutchen, D., Harry, D. R., Cunningham, A. E., Cox, S. Sidman, S., & Covill, A. E. (2002). Reading teachers' content knowledge of children's literature and phonology. *Annals of Dyslexia, 52,* 207–228.

McKeown, M. G., & Beck, I. L. (2004). Direct and rich vocabulary instruction. In J. F. Baumann & E. J. Kame'enui (Eds.), *Vocabulary instruction: Research to practice* (pp. 13–27). New York: Guilford.

McMaster, K. L., Fuchs, L. S., & Fuchs, D. (2006). Research on peer-assisted learning strategies: The promise and limitations of peer-mediated instruction. *Reading & Writing Quarterly, 22,* 5–25.

Mercer, C. D. & Campbell, K.U. (1998). *Great Leaps Reading Program Grades K-2.* Gainesville, FL: Diarmuid, Inc.

Mercer, C. D., Campbell, K. U., Miller, M. D., Mercer, K. D., & Lane, H. B. (2000). Effects of a reading fluency intervention for middle schoolers with specific learning disabilities. *Learning Disabilities Research & Practice, 15,* 177–187.

Meyer, D.J. (1995). *The effects of graphic organizers on the creative writing of third grade students.* Union, NJ: M. A. Project, Kean College of New Jersey. (ERIC Document Reproduction Service No. ED380803)

Meyer, M. S., & Felton, R. H. (1999). Repeated reading to enhance fluency: Old approaches and new directions. *Annals of Dyslexia, 49,* 283–306.

Minskoff, E. (2005). *Teaching reading to struggling readers.* Baltimore: Paul H. Brookes.

Mitchell, M. J., & Fox, B. J. (2001). The effects of computer software for developing phonological awareness in low-progress readers. *Reading Research and Instruction, 40,* 315–332.

Moats, L. C. (1994). The missing foundation in teacher education: Knowledge of the structure of spoken and written language. *Annals of Dyslexia, 44,* 81–102.

Moats, L. C. (1998). Reading, spelling and writing disabilities in the middle grades. In B. Wong (Ed.), *Learning about learning disabilities* (pp. 367–390). Orlando, FL: Academic Press.

Moats, L. C. (2000). *Speech to print: Language essentials for teachers.* Baltimore Paul H. Brookes.

Moats, L. C. (2003). *The research base and implementation results for LANGUAGE!* Longmont, CO: Sopris West.

Moats, L. C. (2004). *LETRS. Language essentials for teachers of reading and spelling.* Longmont, CO: Sopris West.

Moats, L. C. & Foorman, B. R. (2003). Measuring teachers' content knowledge of language and reading. *Annals of Dyslexia, 52,* 23–45.

Monroe, M. (1932). *Children who cannot read.* Chicago: University of Chicago Press.

Montague, M., & Graves, A. (1993). Improving students' story writing. *Teaching Exceptional Children, 25(4),* 36–37.

Nagy, W. E. (1998). *Teaching vocabulary to improve reading comprehension.* Newark, DE: International Reading Association.

National Joint Committee on Learning Disabilities. (2005, June). Responsiveness to intervention and learning disabilities. Retrieved September 6, 2006, from LD Online. Web site: http://www.ldonline.org/about/partners/njcld

National Reading Panel. (2000). *Report of the National Reading Panel. Teaching children to read: An evidence-based assessment of the scientific research literature on reading and its implications for reading instructions* (NIH Publication No. 00-4769). Washington, DC: U.S. Government Printing Office.

Onken, J. S. (2002). *The effects of the Read Naturally Program on middle school students' oral reading fluency and reading comprehension skills in a residential treatment setting.* Unpublished capstone, Winona State University.

Orton, S. T. (1937). *Reading, writing, and speech problems in children.* London: Chapman and Hall.

Ouellette, G. P. (2006). What's meaning got to do with it: The role of vocabulary in word reading and reading comprehension. *Journal of Educational Psychology, 98,* 554–566.

Palinscar, A. S., & Brown, A. L. (1984). Reciprocal teaching of comprehension-fostering and comprehension-monitoring activities. *Cognition & Instruction, 1*(2), 117–176.

Pany, D. & Jenkins, J. R. (1978). Learning word meanings: A comparison of instructional procedures. *Learning Disability Quarterly, 1,* 21–32.

Pany, D., Jenkins, J. R., & Schreck, J. (1982). Vocabulary instruction: effects on work knowledge and reading comprehension. *Learning Disabilities Quarterly, 5,* 202–215.

Paris, S. G., Wasik, B. A., & Turner, J. C. (1991). The development of strategic readers. In R. Barr, M. L. Kamil, P. B. Mosenthal & P. D. Pearson (Eds.), *Handbook of Reading Research* (Vol. II, pp. 609–640). New York: Longman.

Perfetti, C. A. (1986). Continuities in reading acquisition, reading skill and reading disability. *Remedial and Special Education, 7*(1), 11–21.

Perfetti, C. A. (1992). The representation problem in reading acquisition. In P.B. Gough, L.C. Ehri, & R. Treiman (Eds.), *Reading acquisition* (pp. 145–174). Mahwah, NJ: Erlbaum.

Perfetti, C. A., & Hogaboam, T. (1975). Relationship between single word decoding and reading comprehension skill. *Journal of Educational Psychology, 67,* 461–469.

Pinnell, G. S. (1989). Reading Recovery: Helping At-Risk Children Learn to Read *The Elementary School Journal, 90,* 161–181.

Podhajski, B., Varricchio, M., Mather, N., & Sammons, J. (in press). *Mastering the alphabetic principle: A course in how we MAP speech to print for teaching reading and spelling.* Baltimore: Paul H. Brookes.

Pressley, M. (2000). Comprehension instruction in elementary school: A quarter-century of research in progress. In B. M. Taylor, M. F. Graves & P. v. d. Broek (Eds.), *Reading for meaning: Fostering comprehension in the middle grades* (pp. 32–51). Newark, DE: International Reading Association.

Public Law 107-110, The No Child Left Behind Act of 2001. Retrieved October 3, 2004, from http://www.ed.gov/legislation/ESEA02/107-110.pdf

Rack, J. P., Snowling, M. J., & Olson, R. K. (1992). The nonword reading deficit in developmental dyslexia: A review. *Reading Research Quarterly, 27*(1), 28–53.

Rakes, G., Rakes, T. A., & Smith, L. J. (1995). Using visuals to enhance secondary students' reading comprehension of expository texts. *Journal of Adolescent & Adult Literacy, 39*(1), 46–54.

Ritchie, D., & Volkl, C. (2000). Effectiveness of two generative learning strategies in the science classroom. *School Science & Mathematics, 100*(2), 83–89.

Robinson, C. (2003). *Great Leaps.* Tallahassee: Florida Center for Reading Research.

Saenz, L. M., & Fuchs, L. S. (2002). Examining the reading difficulty of secondary students with learning disabilities. *Remedial and Special Education, 23*(1), 31–41.

Schatschneider, C., Francis, D., Foorman, B., Fletcher, J., & Mehta, P. (1999). The dimensionality of phonological awareness: An application of item response theory. *Journal of Educational Psychology, 91,* 439–449.

Schumaker, J. B., Deshler, D. D., Alley, G. R., Warner, M. M., & Denton, P. (1982). Multipass: A learning strategy for improving reading comprehension. *Learning Disabilities Quarterly, 5,* 295–304.

Schwartz, R. M. (2005). Literacy learning of at-risk first-grade students in the Reading Recovery early intervention *Journal of Educational Psychology, 97,* 257–267.

Semrud-Clikeman, M. (2005). Neuropsychological aspects for evaluating learning disabilities. *Journal of Learning Disabilities, 38,* 563–568.

Shankweiler, D., Lundquist, E., Dreyer, L. G., & Dickinson, C. C. (1996). Reading and spelling difficulties in high school students: Causes and consequences. *Reading & Writing: An Interdisciplinary Journal, 8,* 267–294.

Shaywitz, S. C., Fletcher, J. M, & Shaywitz, B. A. (1994). A conceptual framework for learning disabilities and attention deficit-hyperactivity disorder. *Canadian Journal of Special Education, 9,* 1–32.

Simmons, D. C., Fuchs, D., Fuchs, L. S., Hodge, J. P., & Mathes, P. G. (1994). Importance of instructional complexity and role reciporcity to classwide peer tutoring. *Learning Disabilities Research and Practice, 9,* 203–212.

Sindelar, P. T., Monda, L. E., & O'Shea, L. J. (1990). Effects of repeated readings on instructional- and mastery-level readers. *Journal of Educational Research, 8,* 220–226.

Smith, C. R. (1997, February). A hierarchy for assessing and remediating phonemic segmentation difficulties. Paper presented at the Learning Disabilities Association International Conference, Chicago.

Snow, C. E., Burns, M. S., & Griffin, P. (1998). *Preventing reading difficulties in young children.* Washington, DC: National Academy Press.

Snow, C. E., Griffin, P., & Burns, M. S. (2005). *Knowledge to support the teaching of reading: Preparing teachers for a changing world.* San Francisco: Wiley.

Spear-Swerling, L., Brucker, P. O., & Alfano, M. P. (2005). Teachers' literacy-related knowledge and self-perceptions in relation to preparation and experience. *Annals of Dyslexia, 55,* 266–296.

Stahl, S. A., & Stahl, K. A. D. (2004). Word wizards all! Teaching word meanings in preschool and primary education. In J. F. Baumann & E. J. Kame'enui (Eds.), *Vocabulary instruction: Research to practice* (pp. 59–78). New York: Guilford.

Stanger, M. A., & Donohue, E. K. (1937). *Prediction and prevention of reading difficulties.* New York: Oxford University Press.

Stanovich, K. E. (1986). Matthew effects in reading: Some consequences of individual differences in the acquisition of literacy. *Reading Research Quarterly, 21,* 360–406.

Stein, N., & Glenn, C. G. (1979). An analysis of story comprehension in elementary school children. In R. O. Freedle (Ed.), *New directions in discourse processes* (Vol. 2, pp. 53–120). Norwood, NJ: Ablex.

Swanson, H. L. (1999). Reading research for students with LD: A meta-analysis of intervention outcomes. *Journal of Learning Disabilities, 32,* 504–532.

Swanson, H. L. (2001). Searching for the best model for instructing students with learning disabilities. *Focus on Exceptional Children, 34,* 1–15.

Swanson, H. L., & Hoskyn, M. (1998). Experimental intervention research on students with learning disabilities: A meta-analysis of treatment outcomes. *Review of Educational Research, 68,* 277–321.

Swanson, H. L., Hoskyn, M., & Lee, C. (1999). *Interventions for students with learning disabilities: A meta-analysis of treatment outcomes.* New York: Guilford.

Tenenbaum, H. A., & Wolking, W. D. (1989). Effects of oral reading rate and inflection on intraverbal responding. *The Analysis of Verbal Behavior, 7,* 83–89.

Torgesen, J. K. (1992). Learning disabilities: Historical and conceptual issues. In B. Y. L. Wong (Ed.), *Learning about learning disabilities* (pp. 3–38). San Diego: Academic Press.

Torgesen, J. K. (1993). Variations on theory in learning disabilities. In G. R. Lyon, D. B. Gray, J. F. Kavanagh, & N. A. Krasnegor (Eds.), *Better understanding learning disabilities: New views from research and their implications for education and public policies* (pp. 153–170). Baltimore: Paul H. Brookes.

Torgesen, J. K. (2000). Individual differences in response to early interventions in reading: The lingering problem of treatment resisters. *Learning Disabilities Research & Practice, 15*, 55–65.

Torgesen, J. K., Alexander, A.W., Wagner, R. K., Rashotte, C. A., Voeller, K., Conway, T., et al. (2001). Intensive remedial instruction for children with severe reading disabilities: Immediate and long-term outcomes from two instructional approaches. *Journal of Learning Disabilities, 34*, 33–58.

Torgesen, J. K., & Burgess, S. R. (1998) Consistency of reading-related phonological processes throughout early childhood: Evidence from longitudinal-correlational and instructional studies. In J. L. Metsala & L. C. Ehri (Eds.), *Word recognition in beginning literacy* (pp. 161–188). Mahwah, NJ: Erlbaum.

Torgesen, J. K., & Mathes, P. G. (2000). *A basic guide to understanding, assessing, and teaching phonological awareness.* Austin, TX: PRO-ED.

Torgesen, J. K., Rashotte, C. A., & Alexander, A. W. (2001). Principles of fluency instruction in reading; Relationships with established empiricaloutcomes. In M. Wolf (Ed.), *Dyslexia, fluency, and the brain* (pp. 333–355). Timonium, MD: York Press.

Torgesen, J. K., Wagner, R. K., Rashotte, C. A., & Herron, J. (2000). The effectiveness of teacher supported computer assisted instruction in preventing reading problems in young children. Unpublished manuscript. Florida State University, Tallahasee.

Umbreit, J., Lane, K. L., & Dejud, C. (2004). Improving classroom behavior by modifying task difficulty: The effects of increasing the difficulty of too-easy tasks. *Journal of Positive Behavior Interventions, 6*, 13–20.

Vaughn, S., Gersten, R., & Chard, D. (2000). The underlying message in LD intervention research: Findings from research syntheses. *Exceptional Children, 67*, 99–114.

Wagner, M., Blackorby, J., & Hebbeler, K. (1993). *Beyond the report card: The multiple dimensions of secondary school performance of students with disabilities. A report from the national longitudinal study of special education students.* Menlo Park, CA: SRI International.

Wagner, R. K., & Torgesen, J. K. (1987). The nature of phonological processing and its causal role in the acquisition of reading skills. *Psychological Bulletin, 101*, 192–212.

Wahl, M. (2006). *Read Naturally..* Tallahassee, FL: Florida Center for Reading Research.

Walker, B. J. (2000). *Diagnostic teaching of reading* (4th ed.). Upper Saddle River, NJ: Prentice Hall.

Warby, D. B., Greene, M. T., Higgins, K., & Lovitt, T. (1999). Suggestions for translating research into classroom practices. *Intervention in School and Clinic, 34*, 205–211.

Westby, C. E. (1994). The effects of culture on genre, structure, and style of oral and written texts. In G. P. Wallach & K. G. Butler (Eds.), *Language learning disabilities in school-age children and adolescents* (pp. 180–218). New York: Merrill.

Weisenburg, T. H., & McBride, K. E. (1935). *Aphasia.* New York: Oxford University Press.

Williams, J. P. (2005). Instruction in reading comprehension for primary-grade students: A focus on text structure. *Journal of Special Education, 39*(1), 6–18.

Wilson, B. (1996). *Wilson reading system, instructor manual* (3rd ed.). Oxford, MA: Wilson Language Training.

Wilson Reading Systems. (2002). *Fundations.* Oxford, MA: Wilson Language Training.

Wolf, M., & Katzir-Cohen, T. (2001). Reading fluency and its intervention. *Scientific Studies of Reading, 5*, 211–239.

Wolf, M., Miller, L., & Donnelly, K. (2000). Retrieval, automaticity, vocabulary, elaboration, orthography (RAVE-O): A comprehensive fluency-based reading intervention program. *Journal of Learning Disabilities, 33*, 322–324.

Wolf, M., O'Brien, B., Donnelly Adams, K., Joffe, T., Jeffrey, J., & Lovett, M., et al. (2003). Working for time: Reflections on naming speed, reading fluency, and intervention. In B. Foorman (Ed.), *Preventing and remediating reading difficulties: Bringing science to scale* (pp. 355–379). Timonium, MD: York Press.

# 9

# Teaching Older Readers with Reading Difficulties

## Jade Wexler, Meaghan S. Edmonds, and Sharon Vaughn

Over the past 30 years, interventions that provide explicit, systematic instruction in phonological awareness, phonics, fluency, vocabulary, and comprehension have facilitated reading instruction for a significant number of students (National Reading Panel, 2000). Much of our knowledge about reading instruction comes from studies conducted with students in grade 3 and younger. Despite the large amount of knowledge regarding effective reading instruction for young, beginning readers, there are still students in grades 4 through 12 who continue to struggle with reading. Often, we borrow what we know regarding effective practices for younger readers and apply that knowledge to older, struggling readers. While many elements of reading are the same for younger and older students, our confidence about interventions improves when the practice has been implemented with students from similar grades and with similar reading difficulties.

This chapter provides an overview of the current research and practice related to instruction for older students with reading difficulties. Elements of reading instruction for older readers, including advanced word study, fluency, and comprehension, will be presented.

## ADVANCED WORD STUDY

Secondary students are expected to be skilled readers who can effortlessly and accurately read text while comprehending what they read. Because of the increasing amount of complex content and text secondary students are asked to read, they must be highly adept at all processes related to effective reading, including reading words efficiently and knowing what they mean—as well as being able to integrate and comprehend complex ideas and concepts (Nagy & Anderson, 1984). A breakdown in any of these critical reading processes makes understanding and learning from text difficult or even impossible.

One might not expect word study to be a relevant instructional element for secondary students. However, many students are reaching the upper grades deficient in the skills necessary to become competent readers, including the ability to decode text (Curtis, 2004). Often, these students have learned how to compensate for their reading deficiencies and have honed other skills, such as listening comprehension, that help them to disguise the fact that they are not effective and efficient word readers. When it becomes apparent that an older student's listening comprehension ability has surpassed his reading comprehension ability, slow decoding usually is the reason (Shankweiler, Lundquist, Katz, Stuebing, Fletcher, & Brady, 1999).

Does it make sense to provide word study for older students with reading difficulties? Some long-term studies show that older students who fall behind benefit considerably from specialized, intensive instruction aimed at improving word study (Torgesen, Alexander, Wagner, Rashotte, Voeller, & Conway, 2001). Moats (2001) states that chronological age should not be a factor in determining who receives remediation in any of the critical skills necessary to read fluently and comprehend text—including word study. In summary, although early intervention is preferable, older readers with significant reading difficulties deserve remediation efforts as much as younger, poor readers (Moats, 2001).

## What is Advanced Word Study?

Word recognition and analysis involves being skilled at phonological processing (recognizing the speech sounds in words) and having an awareness of letter-sound correspondences in words (Ehri & McCormick, 1998). As students become more mature readers, word study includes applying knowledge of phonology and orthography to read many novel, complex multisyllabic words. Typically, secondary students reading between the 2.5 and 5.0 grade levels can be characterized as those needing instruction in multisyllabic word decoding, or what we might call advanced word study (Archer, Gleason, & Vachon, 2003). Intervention focused on addressing word study instruction for older students with reading difficulties typically targets two main types of instruction: (1) word analysis instruction and (2) word recognition instruction (Curtis, 2004).

**Word analysis** instruction exposes students to information and strategies that will help them gain access to the meaning of words. This includes instruction in morphemic analysis, such as knowledge of prefixes, suffixes and roots, as well as instruction in vocabulary. In word analysis instruction, students are taught to "chunk" word parts to gain access to any known word units within the larger word, which in turn provides access to the meaning of words. For example, in the word *repossessed*, students may be taught to chunk the word into the following parts: *re–pos–sess–ed*. In this example, they can decode the word and get at the meaning quickly by associating the prefix *–re* with something that means "to go back." They will associate the base word, *possess*, with something that means "to hold onto," and the suffix *–ed* tells them that it happened in the past. Not only does this help students access the meaning of the word, but also it helps them isolate the root word and decode the word in chunks, rather than trying to read the entire word at once. As a result of this type of instruction, students learn strategies to read words part by part, while associating the word with its meaning. It is important that when educators and students use this strategy, they are flexible in their approach of dividing the word into parts.

Instruction in **word recognition** involves instruction in orthographic processing, or the ability to recognize the letter patterns in words and their corresponding sound units. Word recognition instruction at the secondary level focuses on various advanced word study components. Students might be taught how to use knowledge of the different syllable types in the English language (consonant-vowel-consonant, consonant-vowel, vowel-consonant-*e*, *r*-controlled, double vowel, and consonant-*le*) to decode words. For example, students learn that in a consonant-vowel-consonant word such as *cat,* the vowel makes a short sound.

In the previous example, students might divide the word *repossessed* differently to decode the word than they would if their goal were to access the morphemic elements in the word. Instead, they would divide the word according to syllable types. According to syllable types, a student might divide the word into the following parts to help with decoding: *re–po–ssess–ed.*

While this might not help the student access the word's meaning, it provides a way to break down and decode a multisyllabic word.

In this type of advanced word study instruction, students are taught rules that they can apply when trying to segment words based on the role of the vowel. This is often referred to as the "rules of syllabication." For example, in the word *locate*, students will learn first to try to read the word by referring to the rule that a consonant usually follows a vowel in this situation and goes with the second syllable. Therefore, the student would learn to segment and decode the word as *lo–cate*, breaking it up into an open syllable followed by a vowel-consonant-*e* syllable word part. Instruction in the syllable types gives students a pattern or rule to follow, as well as knowledge about how to pronounce the vowel sound. Students can use their knowledge of the syllable types to analyze the role of the vowels in a word which helps separate letters into chunks and understand the spelling patterns (Curtis, 2004).

## Should Educators Spend Time Trying to Improve Word Recognition?

At the secondary level, factors other than reading words accurately contribute to comprehension, such as background knowledge and knowledge of vocabulary and comprehension strategies (Kintsch & Kintsch, 2004). However, while it is necessary to focus on instruction that will improve students' comprehension through enhancing background knowledge, vocabulary, and comprehension strategies, for many older students with reading difficulties, it is still critical to build word-level skills so the students can access more difficult text. No matter how strong a student's background or vocabulary knowledge on a particular text or how developed a student's knowledge of comprehension strategies, without being able to decode fluently, reading comprehension will suffer (Archer et al., 2003; Torgesen, 2005).

There is another important reason why older students benefit from improved word reading and decoding. Students who are able to read text effortlessly are less frustrated readers and, thus, more likely to spend time reading. When students become frustrated, they read less text, and as a result, they usually fall further behind (Stanovich, 1986). Students who are frustrated because they struggle to decode are also more likely to drop out of school, have trouble finding employment, or have challenges in society in general (Biancarosa & Snow, 2004; National Association of State Boards of Education (NASBE; 2005; RAND Reading Study Group (RRSG; 2002).

Much value exists, therefore, in providing remediation for students who need help in advanced word study. Specifically, these are typically students who can decode single-syllable (e.g., *came*, *time*, *lump*) and high-frequency irregular words (e.g., *was*, *from*, *about*) but have difficulty with the pronunciation of multisyllabic words (Just & Carpenter, 1987).

## Results/Findings from Intervention Studies

The overall purpose of spending time on advanced word study instruction is to help students learn to decode text fluently and, ultimately, comprehend what they are reading. The comprehension of older, struggling readers can be improved through several types of interventions, including instruction that provides comprehension strategies, multicomponent interventions, and word-study interventions (Edmonds et al., in review).

Interestingly, word-level interventions ($N = 3$) were associated with small to moderate effects ($ES = .34$) in comprehension outcomes between treatment and comparison students. Thus, word-study interventions significantly affect comprehension. Older students who have low decoding skills and require extensive instruction in word-reading skills might benefit from word-level instruction. Therefore, using a direct approach to teaching the analysis of the structure of words (syllables and morphemes) is relatively effective for teaching struggling readers how to decode multisyllabic words (Archer et al., 2003; Lenz & Hughes, 1990).

Furthermore, several studies have evaluated the effectiveness of word study interventions that were designed to teach students to analyze words structurally. Bhattacharya and Ehri (2004) reported that teaching sixth- to ninth-grade struggling readers a multisyllabic chunking structural analysis approach yielded positive effects. Students in their study read multisyllabic words by analyzing grapho-syllabic units in the words or by reading the words as whole parts. Students who practiced reading the words in multisyllabic units orally divided the words' pronunciations into beats and then matched the pronounced form of each beat to its spelling.

In another study that applied a structural analysis approach to interventions, Abbott and Berninger (1999) studied the effect of phonics and structural analysis instruction on word reading skills of fourth- to seventh-grade low achievers. The effect was minimal; however, the contrasted condition was similar to the treatment, making it hard to discern the benefit of instruction versus no instruction. Both the treatment condition (Structural Analysis Group) and the contrasted condition (Study Skills Group) participated in an hour of a systematic intervention, including equal time training in skill areas such as orthographic skills, alphabetic skills, and oral reading. The only difference was that for 15 minutes, the students in the Structural Analysis condition were taught to check for affixes and roots, break the word into syllables, and then apply letter-sound correspondences, while the students in the Study Skills condition worked in a commercial workbook that covered topics such as outlining, writing paragraphs, and taking notes.

In 1990, Lenz and Hughes taught 12 adolescents a decoding strategy. Their approach to strategy training was based on the idea that teachers can teach students to think of word identification as a problem-solving process in which students follow a number of steps to solve a word-identification problem. The problem-solving steps included use of contextual clues as well as application of common principles of structural analysis such as isolating the prefixes and suffixes in multisyllabic words. The strategy resulted in fewer oral reading errors and increased comprehension for some students. Although some students improved their comprehension, the authors cautioned that comprehension was not improved as a direct effect of the study and that to improve comprehension, some students will need simultaneous comprehension instruction.

While the above studies examined the effects of providing a word-recognition or structural-analysis intervention, Bhat, Griffin, and Sindelar (2003) studied the effects of a phonemic awareness (PA) intervention on the PA and word-recognition skills of 40 middle school readers with learning disabilities. Results showed that the intervention had an effect on students' PA skills, but these students were not able to generalize their PA skills to word identification. Teachers of older students with reading difficulties may consider focusing their instruction on teaching letter-sound correspondences and structural-analysis training, rather than providing explicit instruction in phonological awareness.

## Implications for Practice

Several implications for practice can be gleaned from the knowledge base regarding instruction in advanced word study for older, struggling readers. Older students with reading difficulties profit from word-level interventions beyond improving their word-reading skills—they also improve their reading comprehension (Edmonds et al., in review). Most secondary students with reading difficulties would benefit from improving their knowledge and use of orthographic processing skills. Providing explicit, systematic instruction in letter-sound relationships, sight word instruction, and multisyllabic word study instruction is associated with overall improved reading performance (Curtis, 2004). Students can learn to decode multisyllabic words by breaking them

**TABLE 9.1**
**Word Study Instruction for Older Students with Reading Difficulties**

| Recommendation | Example |
|---|---|
| Teach students to look for words they know within larger words. | In the word *resubmit*, students can be taught to identify the word *submit*. |
| Help students divide large words into smaller segments so they can read the segments and, thus, the entire word. | Students can be taught to divide the word *contemplate* into *con–tem–plate* or *dissatisfy* into: <br> 1. *Dis–sat–is–fy* for word-recognition purposes using knowledge of syllable types and the role of the vowel. This divides the word into three closed syllable types and one open syllable type; OR <br> 2. *Dis–satisfy* using a word-analysis approach. Students will use the prefix *dis-* and the previously known word *satisfy* to make sense of the word and decode it. |
| Teach students to identify affixes, what they mean, and how to interpret the meaning of words that use common affixes. | Example affixes: *re-*, *un-*, *–ly*, *–ment*. |

into parts using their knowledge of the rules of syllabication, including the role the vowel plays in a word, and they can learn to identify word parts such as prefixes and suffixes to help decode multisyllabic words as well as get at the meaning of words. To help students make the connection between decoding multisyllabic words and comprehension, students can receive instruction in morphemic analysis, word relationships, and word origins.

In addition to providing students with various methods to decode words and use word parts to get at meaning, continuous and extensive opportunities to read target words in connected text are essential. Finally, students will need extensive practice applying these word-study skills so they can read text with speed and accuracy. Therefore, students must practice reading fluently (discussed in the next section). When they can decode multisyllabic and sight words fluently, students can spend less energy trying to decode and allocate more energy to comprehending the text they are reading. Table 9.1 provides recommended word study instruction for older students, as well as examples for each recommended practice.

## FLUENCY

To meet increasing accountability demands, students must be able to read and comprehend text at a rapid pace. When students exert too much effort at the word-recognition level, difficulties deriving meaning from text ensue (Samuels, 1979). Therefore, although fluency is generally regarded as a critical component of a reading intervention at the elementary level, the importance of fluency extends into the upper grades as well (Rasinski, Padak, McKeon, Wilfong, Friedauer, & Heim, 2005).

### What is Fluency?

Fluency is the ability to read text with speed, accuracy, and prosody. Since LaBerge and Samuels brought fluency to the forefront in 1974, it has been considered a critical element in the reading process. They proposed that students should be able to recognize words instantly and connect them with meaning. Chall (1983) also brought attention to the critical role of fluency as the third of six stages of becoming an efficient reader. She describes fluency as the "ungluing from print" stage. In this stage, students have already established their decoding ability and are therefore applying automaticity in print as well as making use of the prosodic features in text, such as appropriate stress and intonation in their reading. After mastering the "ungluing from print" stage, Chall suggests that it should be easier for students to read for meaning. Overall, we know that students who can decode text fluently are generally better readers because they can demonstrate an understanding of the text they read (Shinn & Good, 1992). We also know that, unfortunately, students who struggle with reading typically struggle with reading fluently and often fall behind because of their slow reading speed and a lack of motivation.

## Should Educators Spend Time Trying to Improve Fluency?

If we can assume that fluency affects a student's ability to comprehend text at the older grades as it does at the younger grades (Chard, Vaughn, & Tyler, 2002), then it becomes important for older students to practice reading text fluently as well. Scores on brief measures of oral reading fluency are highly predictive of scores on standardized tests of reading comprehension, such as the Stanford Achievement Test for students with reading disabilities in middle and junior high school (Fuchs, Fuchs, Hosp, & Jenkins, 2001); therefore, one might assume that interventions aimed at improving fluency may also improve students' comprehension. In theory, reading fluently would allow students to spend more energy comprehending text.

Fluency instruction alone, however, is likely not enough to support increased comprehension for students at the upper grades. Rasinski et al. (2005) examined the role fluency plays with a large group of ninth graders in a school that historically struggled on its high school state graduation test. After assessing the decoding (word-reading accuracy) and fluency levels (i.e., reading rate) of the students, it became apparent that the overall student word-recognition ability was quite strong, while their fluency levels were on average below the 25th percentile for eighth graders. From these findings, it would appear that fluency is indeed a factor in comprehension among older students; however, the relative causal role of improved fluency on increased comprehension of older students requires further study.

A study by Allinder and colleagues (2001) indicated that increased reading rate and accuracy did not result in improved comprehension. Kuhn and Stahl (2000) also indicated that improving fluency alone does not always foster better comprehension ability. In addition, the correlation between oral reading fluency and comprehension seems to decrease as students get older and text gets more complicated (Paris, Carpenter, Paris, & Hamilton, 2005). Background knowledge and working memory are other factors that may play a larger role in comprehending text as a student gets older. Therefore, while fluency remains an essential component of skilled reading and increases may be associated with improved comprehension, educators may want to be thoughtful of the amount of time spent trying to improve fluency alone for older, struggling readers.

In addition, fluency remains a very difficult area to improve. Improvements in decoding and word recognition have been far easier to obtain than improvements in fluency (Lyon & Moats, 1997). In intervention studies that have effectively focused on and increased other critical components of reading such as phonological awareness, fluency outcomes were not significantly affected (Lovett, Steinbach, Frijters, 2000; Torgesen, 2004).

## Results/Findings from Intervention Studies on Fluency: Elements that Affect Repeated Reading

A majority of fluency interventions can be characterized as repeated reading interventions in which students read the same text repeatedly. In addition, several elements involved in a repeated reading intervention can affect student outcomes.

*Previewing/Modeling Procedures and Feedback.*    One strong influence on the success of a repeated reading intervention is whether it incorporates a previewing/modeling procedure. Fluency outcomes are consistently improved following interventions that include a previewing/modeling procedure (Conte & Humphreys, 1989; Daly & Martens, 1994; Rose & Beattie, 1986; Rose & Sherry, 1984; Skinner, Cooper, & Cole, 1997; Strong, Wehby, Falk, & Lane, 2004). Specifically, including a previewing procedure such as having students listen to an adult, partner, or audiotape of good reading prior to reading text generally results in positive outcomes.

Another positive outcome related to repeated reading interventions is incorporating a model of good reading that also provides corrective feedback to a student (Freeland, Skinner, Jackson, McDaniel, & Smith, 2000; Mercer, Campbell, Miller, Mercer, & Lane., 2004; Scott & Shearer-Lingo, 2002; Strong et al., 2004).

*Setting a Criterion vs. Set Number of Rereads.*    Repeated reading interventions vary in the number of times a student rereads a passage. There seems to be a general consensus that setting the number of rereads in a repeated reading intervention at three or four is sufficient for students to make gains (Meyer & Felton, 1999; O'Shea, Sindelar, & O'Shea, 1987; Therrien, 2004). For example, O'Shea et al. (1987) studied the effects of having students read text one, three, and seven times. Students demonstrated more fluency (i.e., reading rate) growth on the seventh reading than the third reading and on the third reading than the first reading. However, the effects were greater from three rereads to one read than from seven reads to three reads. Keeping in mind the amount of time teachers have to dedicate to fluency practice and the potential negative effects on students' interest and motivation from seven rereads, it seems that three repeated readings may be sufficient.

Another way to conduct a repeated reading intervention is to specify a criterion students must reach before moving to the next passage or level in text difficulty. For example, a researcher might set a criterion of reaching 100 words per minute before a teacher has a student move on. Conte and Humphreys (1989) studied the effects of repeated reading with audiotaped material compared to students who received an alternative reading program. They specified a criterion that students had to read a passage without assistance of an audiotape and without hesitation at the same speed as the tape, with no oral reading errors. Students in the repeated reading condition showed significant gains in reading rate.

## Repeated Reading versus Non-repetitive Wide Reading

Although improving rate on practiced passages is encouraging, because secondary students have so much complex content to get through, it is important that gains from fluency interventions have positive effects on unpracticed passages and have a positive effect for comprehension as well. Therefore, gains from fluency interventions must be transferable and generalizable.

Unfortunately, gains from repeated reading interventions do not necessarily generalize to unpracticed passages and do not automatically improve comprehension or word recognition ability (Steventon & Frederick, 2003; Valleley & Shriver, 2003). In fact, results from intervention studies with older, struggling readers show that there may be no differential effects for repeated reading and the same amount of non-repetitive reading for increasing speed, word recognition, and comprehension (Homan, Klesius, & Hite, 1993; Rashotte & Torgesen, 1985). Reading rate improved only slightly in the study by Rashotte and Torgesen (1985), while there were no gains from the repeated reading groups in comprehension on either study. In addition, the wide reading of a variety of texts provides students with exposure to different text structures, more vocabulary, and different content areas.

Implications for Practice

Several important implications can be drawn from intervention studies that have focused on flu-ency-building practices. While it probably goes without saying that additional research is needed, our interpretation of the research on older, struggling readers is that our knowledge base about effective fluency interventions is inadequate. Repeated reading interventions may have an effect on increasing reading rate; however, the same interventions did not support the development of comprehension skills. Based on current research on fluency interventions with older, struggling readers, practitioners may want to consider incorporating the following suggestions into their instructional practices:

1. While improving reading rate may be *related* to improved comprehension, it does not necessarily *cause* improved comprehension. This may be because other factors such as working memory or background knowledge may play a larger role in comprehending text at the older grades. Therefore, to enhance comprehension, educators may want to com-bine fluency instruction with word-recognition and comprehension-strategy instruction.
2. Educators may want to consider having students practice reading the same amount of text non-repetitively (e.g., wide reading) as they would in a repeated reading intervention. Interventions that employ a component in which students read an equal amount of text non-repetitively compared to a repeated reading component show promise in terms of af-fecting word accuracy and comprehension and do not differ greatly from improvements in reading rate. In addition, reading the same amount of text repeatedly may not only sacrifice students' exposure to text structure, vocabulary, and different content matter, but there might also be an element of boredom to reading the same thing several times. Be-cause motivation at the secondary level is such an important factor (Biancarosa & Snow, 2004; National Association of State Boards of Education [NASBE], 2005), practitioners may want to consider effects of repeated reading on students' interest and motivation to read.
3. It may be useful for educators to increase the duration of fluency interventions in their classrooms. In a synthesis of 19 fluency interventions for students in grades 6–12 (Wexler, 2006), most interventions were relatively brief, with the longest intervention providing 40 sessions (Fuchs, Fuchs, & Kazdan, 1999). In general, the interventions were conducted only a few times per week and were an average of 5–20 minutes. Interventions longer in duration may lead to greater effects.
4. A majority of studies used only narrative text in their intervention, making it difficult to generalize findings to expository text. This is troublesome because secondary students tend to encounter expository text on a more regular basis. Educators may want to consider incorporating expository text into fluency interventions so students practice reading what they will realistically be faced with across all content areas.

Table 9.2 provides recommended fluency instruction for older students, as well as examples for each recommended practice.

## COMPREHENSION

For adolescents, success in school depends on their ability to learn content from a wide range of domain-specific texts. Upon entering middle and high school, proficient elementary-age readers

TABLE 9.2
**Fluency Instruction for Older Students with Reading Difficulties**

| | *Recommendation* | *Example* |
|---|---|---|
| 1. | Have students practice reading text repeatedly. | Students should read text 3–4 times or until a specified criterion is met (e.g., 100 words per minute). |
| 2. | Have students practice wide reading. | Students should have an opportunity to read the same amount of text as they would in a repeated reading intervention. |
| 3. | Provide models and feedback during fluency work. | Students can listen to an adult model of good reading (on audiotape or "live") prior to reading text. They can also receive corrective feedback from adults or partners. |
| 4. | Provide other instruction along with fluency instruction. | Remember that students will need comprehension-strategy instruction and possibly word-recognition instruction along with fluency practice. |

may experience a decline in comprehension due to the increasing demands of the text and the complexity of the vocabulary and constructs (Chall, 1983). Many students are unprepared for the sophisticated text structure and complex, content-specific vocabulary they encounter in the upper grades.

## What is Reading Comprehension?

Ultimately, reading comprehension is the process of constructing meaning by coordinating a number of complex processes, including word reading, word and world knowledge, and fluency (Anderson, Hiebert, Scott, & Wilkinson, 1985; Jenkins, Larson, & Fleischer, 1983; O'Shea et al., 1987). For some adolescent readers, competency in word-level skills provides a stumbling block that prevents them access to fluent reading and, thus, comprehension. In the last few years, students with reading difficulties were identified as having inadequate phonological awareness and decoding skills, which proved to seriously inhibit successful reading (Ball & Blachman, 1991; O'Connor & Jenkins, 1995; Vellutino & Scanlon, 1987). While there is little question that difficulties in these foundation skills impede successful growth in reading for many students, several students with reading difficulties have significant challenges understanding and learning from text even when they are able to decode adequately (Williams, 1998, 2000). Explicit and highly structured development of beginning reading skills is required along with highly structured instruction in reading comprehension (Gersten & Carnine, 1986; Gersten, Fuchs, Williams, & Baker, 2001). For many adolescent readers, word-level reading is "necessary but insufficient to engender better academic performance" (Biancarosa & Snow, 2004). To successfully read to learn, these students must be able to read with deep comprehension; that is, they must be able to go beyond simple retell and proficiently apply more complex inferential and analytical skills (Duke & Pearson, 2002; Pressley, 2000).

Kintsch's (1998) model of comprehension differentiates between garnering text-based information through word-level reading and learning from text by actively constructing meaning during reading and connecting new information with prior knowledge (Deshler & Hock, 2007; Kintsch & Kintsch, 2005). While sufficient word-level skills may engender a surface understanding of text, students who struggle to comprehend at a deeper level require explicit comprehension and vocabulary instruction as part of an effective intervention program (Deshler & Hock, 2007; Kamil, 2003; Kintsch & Kintsch, 2005).

Table 9.3 outlines the key findings from the National Reading Panel Report (NRP, 2000) on effective comprehension practices. Good readers continually evaluate their understanding, depict

**TABLE 9.3**
**Summary of National Reading Panel (2000) Report on Effective Comprehension Practices**

- Teaching students to monitor their understanding while reading and procedures for adjusting reading practices when difficulties understanding are detected.
- Using cooperative learning practices that provide interaction with peers about text understanding in the context of reading.
- Providing graphic and semantic organizers that assist students in making connections from the story.
- Teaching students to use questioning practices through asking and answering their own questions about text, interacting and obtaining feedback from students and teachers, and analyzing and responding to questions about text types.
- Teaching students to write and summarize ideas from their reading.
- Teaching students to integrate and apply multiple comprehension strategies before, during, and after reading.

the relationships among ideas in text (e.g., organize content in a graphic), evaluate the connection between new and prior knowledge, and summarize what they read (Pressley, 2001; Pressley, 2005). Many older, struggling readers read fluently but do not comprehend what they read for a variety of reasons, including problems: (a) relating content to prior knowledge, (b) monitoring understanding, and (c) applying comprehension strategies (Biancarosa & Snow, 2004; Carlisle & Rice, 2002; Kamil, 2003; RAND Reading Study Group, 2002).

### Relating Content to Prior Knowledge

Prior knowledge plays a critical role in students' ability to draw inferences and synthesize information from text, particularly texts that require students to have previous knowledge to make connections among concepts. Research has provided evidence that activating relevant knowledge prior to reading enhances understanding (e.g., Anderson, Spiro, & Anderson, 1978; Hansen & Pearson, 1983). Struggling adolescent readers often lack the necessary background knowledge that would allow them to infer information from text and connect new learning to prior knowledge. Teaching students to make connections between prior knowledge and new information in text differs from commonly used previewing activities that solicit guesses from students about what they will learn with little guidance or opportunities for feedback.

In a study examining comprehension through previewing short stories with struggling junior high students, Graves and colleagues (1983) reported that previewing significantly improved recall of information read. The previews studied differed from the "brief previewing activities typically used" by activating related knowledge through questioning and providing students with considerable information needed to comprehend the text (Graves, Cooke, & Laberge, 1983).

### Activities Related to Improving Connections between Content and Prior Knowledge

Teachers can improve connections between what students know and are learning in many ways but some of these practices are exceedingly time consuming and can actually take away valuable instructional time from other practices such as reading and discussing text. For this reason, teachers benefit from efficient and effective previewing practices such as the following.

1. Preview the material by identifying key words or concepts from the text prior to reading and discussing what students know and need to know about these key words.
2. Ask students to "put their heads together" with another student and to briefly discuss what they know about the topic.

3. Ask students to look for key words and ideas in the passage (quickly, 2–3 minutes) and to make links between what they are going to read and previous reading.

## Applying Comprehension Strategies

Results of intervention research suggest that struggling readers benefit from explicit comprehension strategy instruction (Connor, Morrison, & Petrella, 2004; Gersten et al., 2001; Kamil, 2004; Swanson, 1999). The positive effect of explicitly teaching students to learn and use cognitive and metacognitive strategies continues to be replicated in studies of older readers (Guthrie et al., 1998; Guthrie et al., 2004; Mason, 2004). Effective strategies include teaching students how to answer and generate questions as a means of monitoring understanding, summarizing, and clarifying when a breakdown in comprehension occurs.

*Questioning.*    Students who are taught to ask themselves and others questions about what they read demonstrate improved reading comprehension. However, many teachers view asking and answering questions about text as their responsibility and provide limited time for students to learn to ask and answer questions. Many teachers consider questions as a means for determining whether students truly understand and make connections with text. Smart questioning can contribute to improving teachers' knowledge of students' reading comprehension and can also extend understanding of text. However, many questions teachers ask can limit responses and critical thinking.

Students with reading difficulties benefit from instruction that teaches them how to answer and develop questions (Gall, 1984; Walsh & Sattes, 2005). Cue cards about how to ask and answer questions can be useful:

1. Listen: Ask yourself, "What was the question?"
2. Say the answer to yourself.
3. Say the answer aloud, when called upon.
4. Listen to feedback from the teacher and answers of other students and integrate with your answer.

Raphael (1986) identifies types of questions for students through Question-Answer Relationships (QARs) to teach students strategies to answer different question types. Students learn to consider the type of information needed to answer different question types. Students can use question types to determine how to answer questions from others (teacher) or to develop their own questions.

1. Right There: Answers to these literal questions are right in the text.
2. Think and Search: Answers require students to integrate information from more than one place in the text.
3. The Author and You: Answers require students to connect information from the text to what they know or have previously learned.
4. On Your Own: Answers require students to connect critical information from what they read with their own experience.

Teaching students to use questioning strategies can facilitate regulating understanding and establishing relationships among ideas in text. Features of effective questioning strategies include using text structure to assist students in answering critical questions about the passage, providing feedback, and structuring opportunities for students to *ask* and *answer* their own questions about the text.

This form of interactive questioning has been studied extensively by Beck and colleagues in their work on Questioning the Author (Beck, McKeown, Hamilton, & Kucan, 1997; Beck, McKeown, Worthy, Sandora, & Kucan, 1996), an approach that uses questioning and discussion as a means of engaging students in text rather than as a means for eliciting correct responses. Their research indicates that students engaged in interactive reading instruction tend to see reading as a process for learning new information rather than as a task or a particular activity format (e.g., reading with a partner) (Beck & McKeown, 2001; Pressley, 2001). However, because a discussion that leads to students actively constructing meaning "needs direction, focus, and movement toward a goal" (Beck & McKeown, 2001), teachers often find the approach difficult to implement. Supporting students' engagement in active questioning is a rather complex teaching task that requires considerable professional development and classroom-based support.

*Monitoring Understanding.* Metacognitive strategies include teaching students to monitor their understanding and procedures for adjusting their reading when difficulties in understanding arise. The efficacy of teaching students to monitor their comprehension has been mainly studied with expository text, particularly in science and social studies (NRP, 2000). In a synthesis of reading comprehension practices for students with learning disabilities, Gersten and colleagues (2001) speculated that comprehension difficulties may be a result of a breakdown in metacognition, not adequately monitoring understanding while reading or knowing what to do when reading progress is breaking down (e.g., monitoring understanding and determining that there is a problem with understanding). Students with learning difficulties typically are able to recall less about what they have read and are challenged to identify the most critical information in stories (Roth & Speckman, 1986). Interestingly, older students with reading difficulties may have less knowledge about story structure than younger students without reading difficulties (Cain, 1996). Table 9.4 provides examples of monitoring practices.

*Summarization.* Summarization strategies include teaching students to write important ideas about what they've read (i.e., main ideas) and to synthesize these ideas after longer passages are read. Summarization and main idea practices are typically measured on high-stakes tests and are viewed as important indicators of reading comprehension.

Summarization requires students to generate multiple main ideas from across a reading and to then combine them to form a summary. In addition, students must be able to generalize from specific examples and be able to identify when information is repeated (NRP, 2000). Learning to summarize is an effective strategy for improving comprehension for students with learning difficulties (Gajria & Salvia, 1992; Nelson, Smith & Dodd, 1992). Many summarization strategies include rules that students learn to use to write summaries. Through modeling, feedback, and many opportunities to practice, students are taught to use the following rules (NRP, 2000): (a) delete trivial and redundant information, (b) use fewer key words to replace lengthy descriptions, (c) identify topic sentences, and (d) provide a topic sentence when one is not in the text.

When we teach students strategies to summarize after reading, students learn to do the following:

- Distinguish between important information and details.
- Use key vocabulary or concepts.
- Synthesize information.
- Use their own words.
- Write only what is needed to present the main idea(s).

**TABLE 9.4**
**Comprehension Strategies and How to Teach Them**

| Name of Strategy | What Students Do | How to Teach the Strategy |
|---|---|---|
| Predicting | Students predict what they think a selection will be about or what they will learn. During reading, they can modify their predictions if they choose. After reading, they verify whether their predications were correct. | • Have students think about what they already know about the topic.<br>• Teach students to read the title, skim the text, and look at headings before making their predictions.<br>• Ask students what information they used to come up with their predictions.<br>• Have students modify their predictions as they learn new information while reading.<br>• Teach students to check whether their predictions were accurate after reading.<br>• Ask students to think about how helpful it is to predict. |
| Questioning and Answering | Students answer questions about the passage. The teacher may ask questions about the text at key points during and after reading. Or students may generate questions, either before reading, about what they would like to learn, or after reading, about key points. Students identify the question-answer relationships (Raphael, 1986) and answer the questions. | • Teach students to identify different types of questions and the strategy for finding the answer to each.<br> • "Right there" — Find the answer in one place in the book.<br> • "Think and search" — Find the answer in more than one place in the book.<br> • "Author and me" — Find the answer in the book and in your head.<br> • "On my own" — Answer the question using what you already know about the topic.<br>• Teach students how to generate questions using these same question types. |
| Visualizing | Students construct mental images that represent text content. Extension: Students construct graphic representations to represent their mental images. | • Teach students to visualize the content in a passage or to imagine what is happening.<br> • For stories, have students visualize what is happening at the beginning, middle, and end of the story.<br> • For informational text, have students think about key words and visualize the content they are learning.<br>• Ask students to explain their images.<br>• Have students compare the picture in their minds with what they are reading.<br>• Extension: Have students draw diagrams or pictures to represent their visualizations. |
| Seeking clarifications | During reading, students monitor their understanding. When the text does not make sense, the student selects a strategy to help clarify the confusing text. | • Teach students to check their understanding while reading. At first, frequently ask students, "Does this make sense?" Encourage students to do the same.<br>• Teach students to select a strategy to use to fix comprehension when breakdowns occur. These can include:<br> • Ignore and read on.<br> • Guess, using clues from the context.<br> • Reread for clarification.<br> • Look back in the text for clues that can help.<br>• Ask students to explain why they selected the strategy and whether it helped. |

*(continued)*

**TABLE 9.4**
**Continued**

| Name of Strategy | What Students Do | How to Teach the Strategy |
|---|---|---|
| Responding to text based on prior knowledge | Students make connections between the text and their background knowledge and personal experiences. | • Ask students to tell how the information from the passage relates to their own lives.<br>• Ask students how the information might be important to them and how it might help them.<br>• Encourage students to discuss their ideas with one another. Ask how considering different points of view can broaden their knowledge. |
| Summarizing | After reading, students summarize the passage. For informational text, they restate the most important ideas. For narrative text, they retell the story. Extension: For expository text, students identify the text structure (e.g., compare and contrast, sequence) and use this structure as a way to organize summaries. | • Teach students to differentiate between expository and narrative text.<br>  • When retelling a story, have students describe the setting, characters, problem, events (in order), and the solution.<br>  • For expository text, have students restate the main ideas in the passage.<br>• Extension: Teach students about different text structures (see Chapter 4) and how to use these as organizational structures for expository text summaries. |

*Note:* Used with permission from: Klingner, J. K., Vaughn, S., & Boardman, A. (2007). *Teaching reading comprehension to students with learning disabilities.* New York: Guilford.

Learning how to state or write a main idea and then to combine a series of main ideas into a summarization is challenging for most students but particularly for students with reading difficulties (Simmons, Kame'enui, & Darch, 1988). Students who are provided systematic and explicit instruction in how to identify the main idea also demonstrate improved outcomes in reading comprehension (Graves, 1986; Jenkins, Heliotis, Stein, & Haynes., 1987; Jitendra, Cole, Hoppes, & Wilson, 1998; Jitendra, Hoppes, & Xin, 2000; Wong & Jones, 1982).

In two studies of students with reading difficulties (Jenkins et al., 1987; Malone & Mastropieri, 1991), students' passage retelling and recall was improved by systematically teaching them to answer questions about what they read: (a) "Who is it about?" and (b) "What's happening?" Students with reading difficulties often benefit from strategies that involve ways to cue recall of information visually (McCormick, 1999). Baumann (1984) combined summarization instruction with visual representation with sixth-grade students, yielding improvement in students' summaries.

Jitendra and colleagues (2000) combined strategy and direct instruction to improve main idea use for students with learning disabilities. Middle school students were taught to use a main idea strategy in eight 30-minute lessons that taught students to: (a) name the subject and categorize the action, (b) model applying the strategy within a text passage, (c) demonstrate the use of a cue card, and (d) provide opportunities for guided and independent practice. Table 9.4 provides descriptions of summarization practices.

*Multiple-Strategy Interventions.*    Many of the reading comprehension strategies that have been associated with the highest effect sizes for students with reading difficulties are those that teach students to monitor and reflect before, during, and after reading. These strategies ask students to consider their background knowledge on the topic, to summarize key ideas, and to self-question while they read (e.g., Gersten et al., 2001; Jenkins, Heliotis, Stein, & Haynes, 1987; Mastropieri, Scruggs, Bakken, & Whedon, 1996; Swanson, 1999; Wong & Jones, 1982).

Multiple-strategy interventions address the many processes involved in the implementation of multiple strategies and the conditions that influence student performance on the related tasks. This strand of research represents a move away from examining the application of strategies in a technical manner to studying how the use of comprehension strategies facilitates interaction and engagement with text (Guthrie et al., 2004; Pressley, 2001). Guthrie et al. (1998) found that strategy instruction alone in the absence of opportunities to use strategies to build content and concept knowledge is insufficient. Current applications and research on multiple strategy interventions stress the process of actively gaining meaning from text over the rote application of a procedure (Beck & McKeown, 2001; Carlisle & Rice, 2002; Guthrie et al., 2004).

Several studies with older, struggling readers have employed reciprocal teaching (Palincsar, Brown, & Martin, 1987), a model that includes previewing, clarifying, generating questions, and summarizing. Reciprocal teaching has been shown to be highly effective in improving comprehension (see for review, Rosenshine & Meister, 1994). Research on the effects of such approaches with middle and high school students has been initially studied. Mason (2004) taught struggling readers an integrated self-regulation strategy throughout the reading of social studies and science texts. Students in the self-regulated, multiple-strategy condition outperformed students in the questioning condition on oral summarization tasks, but not on written comprehension tasks. Alfassi (1998) reported moderate effects from implementing a multiple-strategy intervention modeled after reciprocal teaching in a remedial high school setting, a context not typically examined in previous studies of reciprocal teaching. Table 9.4 provides descriptions of multiple-strategy intervention practices.

## Research on Reading Comprehension Interventions with Older Students with Reading Difficulties

From a recent synthesis of intervention studies ($N = 29$) conducted between 1994 and 2004 with older students (grades 6–12) with reading difficulties, a meta-analysis was conducted on a subset of treatment-comparison design studies to determine the overall effect of reading interventions on students' reading comprehension (Edmonds et al., in review). Thirteen studies met criteria for a meta-analysis, yielding $ES = .89$ for the weighted average of the difference in comprehension outcomes between treatment and comparison students. Studies were included because they had similar contrasts and measures of reading comprehension and examined the effects of a reading intervention with a comparison.

## VOCABULARY

Insufficient reading vocabularies present another barrier to comprehension for students who are otherwise fluent readers. While research has demonstrated the correlation between vocabulary size and comprehension, the premise that vocabulary instruction leads to improved comprehension has yet to be substantiated through a converging research base (Stanovich, 2000, as cited in Kamil, 2003; Kamil, 2004). However, a growing body of literature on effective vocabulary instruction provides educators with research-supported practices for building students' knowledge of word meanings. Based on existing research, we can tentatively conclude that definitional (direct) and contextual (incidental) learning of vocabulary is associated with improved reading achievement, including comprehension. We also know that pre-teaching vocabulary words and repeated exposure to new words have been found to have a positive effect on content area learning. Instruction in content area vocabulary may lead to improved comprehension and content area achievement.

Additional research has supported the efficacy of directly teaching individual words (Baumann, Kame'enui, & Ash, 2003; Blachowicz & Fisher, 2000). Cain, Oakhill, and Lemmon (2004) demonstrated that students with poor comprehension skills benefited from direct instruction in new words, however students with a double deficit of weak vocabularies and poor comprehension skills had additional difficulties learning new words.

Some research has begun to explore the effects of fostering word consciousness (Graves & Watts-Taffe, 2002; Nagy & Scott, 2000), but the relationship of this construct to improved comprehension is unclear. The area that has arguably received the most attention is the effect of morphemic and contextual analysis on vocabulary acquisition. Although results show positive effects on vocabulary, the link to improved comprehension is less convincing. Specifically, two studies of vocabulary instruction in grade 5 social studies classrooms provided evidence that morphemic and contextual analysis instruction, either in combination or alone, can improve students' vocabulary growth but not necessarily their comprehension (Baumann et al., 2002; Baumann, Edwards, Boland, Olejnik, & Kame'enui, 2003). Recent research has also provided additional evidence to support incidental learning of words through units of instruction and reading in the content areas (Carlisle, Fleming, & Gudbrandsen, 2000).

## Vocabulary Instruction

Several key ideas can help to facilitate growth in vocabulary knowledge:

- Provide instruction in the meanings of words and in word-learning strategies.
- Use oral and written language to actively involve students in linking concepts and new vocabulary.
- Provide many opportunities for students to read widely (a variety of texts).
- When defining words, use examples of what they mean and do not mean.
- Connect new words to words students already know.
- Use antonyms and synonyms to improve word meaning and to extend meaning.
- When possible, show pictures and provide examples.

## IMPLICATIONS

It appears that interventions that focus on or include single-component comprehension strategies can result in students becoming more proficient in applying learned strategies and learning taught content, but these interventions often do not result in readers who use the strategies independently and flexibly in novel contexts. While other critical factors are associated with improved reading comprehension for older students with reading difficulties (e.g., motivation and use of graphic organizers), discussion of all elements related to reading comprehension are beyond the scope of this chapter.

Despite having comprehension and vocabulary deficiencies, many older, struggling readers lack instructional opportunities designed to foster improved comprehension primarily because teaching students *how* to read is not seen as a responsibility of middle and high school teachers (Biancarosa & Snow, 2004; Kamil, 2003; RAND Reading Study Group, 2002). The RAND Reading study group (2002) highlighted upper-grade teachers' lack of preparation for teaching the components of reading. Thus, if effective instruction for older students with reading difficulties is likely to occur, additional professional development for teachers will be required.

Determining which conditions can improve comprehension, especially for expository reading, has been established as a national research priority by both the National Reading Panel (2000) and the RAND Reading Study Group (2002). Although much work remains, a foundation for effective adolescent literacy instruction has been established.

The sources of reading difficulties for older students are multiple and varied, requiring targeted and often multi-component interventions. While mastering each component discussed in this chapter is important for reading success, placing too much emphasis on any one, while neglecting others, will likely not address this population's diverse needs. Crafting a targeted intervention for older, struggling readers takes skillful teaching and access to resources such as this chapter for guidance on effective practices. While there is still a need for additional research in this area of literacy, there is a growing knowledge base educators can access to unlock the doors through which older, struggling readers must pass to achieve reading success.

## REFERENCES

Abbott, S. P., & Berninger, V. W. (1999). It's never too late to remediate: Teaching word recognition to students with reading disabilities in grades 4–7. *Annals of Dyslexia, 49,* 223–250.

Alfassi, M. (1998). Reading for meaning: The efficacy of reciprocal teaching in fostering reading comprehension in high school students in remedial reading classes. *American Educational Research Journal, 35,* 309–332.

Allinder, R. M., Dunse, L., Brunken, C. D., & Obermiller-Krolikowski, H. J. (2001). Improving fluency in at-risk readers and students with learning disabilities. *Remedial and Special Education, 22,* 48–54.

Anderson, R. C., Hiebert, E. H., Scott, J. A., & Wilkinson, A. G. (1985). *Becoming a nation of readers: The report of the commission on reading.* Washington, DC: National Institute of Education and the Center for the Study of Reading.

Anderson, R. C., Spiro, R. J., & Anderson, M. C. (1978). Schemata as scaffolding for the representation of information in connected discourse. *American Educational Research Journal, 15,* 433–440.

Archer, A. L., Gleason, M. M., & Vachon, V. L. (2003). Decoding and fluency: Foundation skills for struggling older readers. *Learning Disability Quarterly, 26,* 89–101.

Ball, E. W., & Blachman, B. A. (1991). Does phoneme awareness training in kindergarten make a difference in early word recognition and developmental spelling? *Reading Research Quarterly, 26*(1), 49–66.

Baumann, J. F. (1984, December). *Effect of restructured content textbook passages on middle grade students' comprehension of main ideas: Making the inconsiderate considerate.* Paper presented at the meeting of the National Reading Conference, St. Petersburg, FL.

Baumann, J. F., Edwards, E. C., Boland, E., Olejnik, S., & Kame'enui, E. J. (2003). Vocabulary tricks: Effects of instruction in morphology and context on fifth-grade students ability to derive and infer word meaning. *American Educational Research Journal, 40,* 447–494.

Baumann, J. F., Edwards, E. C., Font, G., Tereshinski, C. A., Kame'enui, E. J., & Olejnik, S. (2002). Teaching morphemic and contextual analysis to fifth grade students. *Reading Research Quarterly, 37,* 150–176.

Baumann, J. F., Kame'enui, E. J., & Ash, G. (2003). Research on vocabulary instruction: Voltaire redux. In J. Flood, D. Lapp, J. R. Squire, & J. Jensen, (Eds.), *Handbook of research on teaching the English Language Arts* (2nd ed.) (pp. 752–785). Mahwah, NJ: Erlbaum.

Beck, I. L., & McKeown, M. G. (2001). Inviting students into the pursuit of meaning. *Educational Psychology Review, 13*(3), 225–241.

Beck, I. L., McKeown, M. G., Hamilton, R. L., & Kucan, L. (1997). *Questioning the Author: An approach for enhancing student engagement with text.* Newark, DE: International Reading Association.

Beck, I. L., McKeown, M. G., Worthy, J., Sandora, C. A., & Kucan, L. (1996). Questioning the Author: A year-long classroom implementation to engage students with text. *Elementary School Journal, 96,* 385–414.

Bhat, P., Griffin, C. C., & Sindelar, P. T. (2003). Phonological awareness instruction for middle school students with learning disabilities. *Learning Disability Quarterly, 26,* 73–87.

Bhattacharya, A. & Ehri, L. C. (2004). Graphosyllabic analysis helps adolescent struggling readers read and spell words. *Journal of Learning Disabilities, 37,* 331–348.

Biancarosa, G., & Snow, C. E. (2004). *Reading next—A vision for action and research in middle and high school literacy: A report from Carnegie of New York.* Washington, DC: Alliance for Excellence in Education.

Blachowicz, C. L. Z., & Fisher, P. (2000). Vocabulary instruction. In M. L. Kamil, P. B. Mosenthal, P. D. Pearson, & R. Barr (Eds.), *Handbook of reading research: Vol. 3* (pp. 503–523). Mahwah, NJ: Erlbaum.

Cain, K. (1996). Story knowledge and comprehension skill. In C. Cornoldi & J. V. Oakhill (Eds.), *Reading comprehension difficulties: Processes and remediation* (pp. 167–192). Mahwah, NJ: Erlbaum.

Cain, K., Oakhill, J., & Lemmon, K. (2004). Individual differences in the inference of word meanings from context: The influence of reading comprehension, vocabulary knowledge, and memory capacity. *Journal of Educational Psychology, 96*(4), 671–681.

Carlisle, J. F., Fleming, J. E., & Gudbrandsen, B. (2000). Incidental word learning in science classes. *Contemporary Educational Psychology, 25,* 184–211.

Carlisle, J. F., & Rice, M. S. (2002). *Improving reading comprehension: Research-based principles and practices.* Baltimore: York Press.

Chall, J. S. (1983). *Stages of reading development.* New York: McGraw-Hill.

Chard, D. J., Vaughn, S., & Tyler, B. (2002). A synthesis of research on effective interventions for building reading fluency with elementary students with learning disabilities. *Journal of Learning Disabilities, 35,* 386–406.

Connor, C. M., Morrison, F. J., & Petrella, J. N. (2004). Effective reading comprehension: Examining child X instruction interactions. *Journal of Educational Psychology, 96*(4), 682–698.

Conte, R., & Humphreys, R. (1989). Repeated readings using audiotaped material enhances oral reading in children with reading difficulties. *Journal of Communication Disorders, 22,* 65–79.

Curtis, M. (2004). Adolescents who struggling with word identification: Research and Practice. In T. L. Jetton & J. A. Dole (Eds.) *Adolescent literacy research and practice* (119–134). New York: Guilford.

Daly, E. J., & Martens, B. K. (1994). A comparison of three interventions for increasing oral reading performance: Application of the instructional hierarchy. *Journal of Applied Behavioral Analysis, 27,* 459–469.

Deshler, D. D., & Hock, M. F. (2007). Adolescent literacy: Where we are, where we need to go. In M. Pressley, A. Billman, K. Perry, K. Reffitt, & J. Moorhead Reynolds (Eds.), *Shaping literacy achievement: Research we have, research we need.* New York: Guilford.

Duke, N. K., & Pearson, P. D. (2002). Effective practices for developing reading comprehension. In A. E. Farstup & S. J. Samuels (Eds.), *What research has to say about reading instruction* (pp. 205–242). Newark, DE: International Reading Association.

Edmonds, M. S., Vaughn, S., Wexler, J., Reutebuch, C. K., Cable, A., Tackett K., & Wick, J. (in review). A synthesis of reading interventions and effects on reading outcomes for older struggling readers.

Ehri, L. C., & McCormick, S. (1998). Phases of word learning: Implications for instruction with delayed and disabled readers. *Reading and Writing Quarterly: Overcoming Learning Difficulties, 14,* 135–164.

Freeland, J. T., Skinner, C. H., Jackson, B., McDaniel, E., & Smith, S. (2000). Measuring and increasing silent reading comprehension rates: Empirically validating a repeated readings intervention. *Psychology in the Schools, 37,* 415–429.

Fuchs, L. S., Fuchs, D., Hosp, M. K., & Jenkins, J. R. (2001). Oral reading fluency as an indicator of reading competence: A theoretical, empirical, and historical analysis. *Scientific Studies of Reading, 5,* 239–256.

Fuchs, L. S., Fuchs, D., & Kazdan, S. (1999). Effects of peer-assisted learning strategies on high school students with serious reading problems. *Remedial and Special Education, 20,* 309–318.

Gall, M. (1984). Synthesis of research on teachers' questioning. *Educational Leadership, 42*(3), 40–47.

Gajria, M., & Salvia, J. (1992). The effects of summarization instruction on text comprehension of students with learning disabilities. *Exceptional Children, 58*(6), 508–516.

Gersten, R., & Carnine, D. (1986). Direct instruction in reading comprehension. *Educational Leadership, 43*(7), 70–78.

Gersten, R., Fuchs, L. S., Williams, J. P., & Baker, S. (2001). Teaching reading comprehension strategies to students with learning disabilities: A review of research. *Review of Educational Research, 71*(2), 279–320.

Graves, A. W. (1986). Effects of direct instruction and metacomprehension training on finding main ideas. *Learning Disabilities Research, 1*(2), 90–100.

Graves, M. F., Cooke, C. L., & Laberge, M. J. (1983). Effects of previewing difficult short stories on low-ability junior high school students' comprehension, recall, and attitudes. *Reading Research Quarterly, 18,* 262–276.

Graves, M. F., & Watts-Taffe, S. M. (2002). The place of word consciousness in a research-based vocabulary program. In A. E. Farstrup and S. J. Samuels (Eds.), *What research has to say about reading instruction* (pp. 140–165). Newark, DE: International Reading Association.

Guthrie, J. T., Van Meter, P., Hancock, G. R., Alao, S., Anderson, E., & McCann, A. (1998). Does concept-oriented reading instruction increase strategy use and conceptual learning from text? *Journal of Educational Psychology, 90*(2), 261–278.

Guthrie, J. T., Wigfield, A., Barbosa, P., Perencevich, K. C., Taboada, A., Davis, M. H., et al. (2004). Increasing reading comprehension and engagement through concept-oriented reading instruction. *Journal of Educational Psychology, 96*(3), 403–423.

Hansen, J., & Pearson, P. D. (1983). An instructional study: Improving the inferential comprehension of good and poor fourth-grade readers. *Journal of Educational Psychology, 75,* 821–829

Homan, S. P., Klesius, J. P., & Hite, C. (1993). Effects of repeated readings and nonrepetitive strategies on students' fluency and comprehension. *Journal of Educational Research, 87,* 94–99.

Jenkins, J. R., Heliotis, J. D., Stein, M. L., & Haynes, M. C. (1987). Improving reading comprehension by using paragraph restatements. *Exceptional Children, 54*(1), 54–59.

Jenkins, J. R., Larson, K., & Fleischer, L. (1983). Effects of error correction on word recognition and reading comprehension. *Learning Disability Quarterly, 6,* 139–145.

Jitendra, A. K., Cole, C. L., Hoppes, M. K., & Wilson, B. (1998). Effects of a direct instruction main idea summarization program and self-monitoring on reading comprehension of middle school students with learning disabilities. *Reading and Writing Quarterly, 14*(4), 379–396.

Jitendra, A. K., Hoppes, M. K., Xin, Y.P. (2000). Enhancing main idea comprehension for students with learning problems: The role of a summarization strategy and self-monitoring instruction. *Journal of Special Education, 34,* 127–139.

Just, M. A., & Carpenter, P. A. (1987). *The Psychology of Reading and Language Comprehension.* Boston: Allyn & Bacon.

Kamil, M. L. (2003). Adolescents and literacy: Reading for the 21st century. Washington, DC: Alliance for Excellent Education.

Kamil, M. L. (2004). Vocabulary and comprehension instruction: Summary and implications of the National Reading Panel findings. In P. McCardle & V. Chhabra (Eds.), *The voice of evidence in reading research* (pp. 213–234). Baltimore: Brookes.

Kintsch, W. (1998). Comprehension: A paradigm for cognition. New York: Cambridge University Press.

Kintsch, W. & Kintsch, E. (2005). Comprehension. In S. G. Paris & S. A. Stahl (Eds.), *Children's reading comprehension and assessment* (pp. 71–92). Mahwah, NJ: Erlbaum.

Klingner, J. K., Vaughn, S., & Boardman, A. (2007). *Teaching reading comprehension to students with learning disabilities.* New York: Guilford.

Kuhn, M. R., & Stahl, S. A. (2000). *Fluency: A review of developmental and remedial practices* (Rep. No. 2-008). Ann Arbor, MI: Center for the Improvement of Early Reading Achievement.

LaBerge, D., & Samuels, S. J. (1974). Toward a theory of automatic information processing in reading. *Cognitive Psychology, 6,* 293–323.

Lenz, B. K., & Hughes, C. A. (1990). A word identification strategy for adolescents with learning disabilities. *Journal of Learning Disabilities, 23,* 149–158, 163.

Lovett, M. W., Steinbach, K. A., & Frijters, J. C. (2000). Remediating the core deficits of developmental reading disability: A double-deficit perspective. *Journal of Learning Disabilities, 33*, 334–358.

Lyon, G. R., & Moats, L. C. (1997). Critical conceptual and methodological considerations in reading intervention research. *Journal of Learning Disabilities, 30*, 578–588.

Malone, L. D., & Mastropieri, M. A. (1991). Reading comprehension instruction: Summarization and self-monitoring training for students with learning disabilities. *Exceptional Children, 58*(3), 270–279.

Mason, L. H. (2004). Explicit self-regulated strategy development versus reciprocal questioning: effects on expository reading comprehension among struggling readers. *Journal of Educational Psychology, 96*(2), 283–296.

Mastropieri, M. A., Scruggs, T. E., Bakken, J. P. & Whedon, C. (1996). Reading comprehension: A synthesis of research in learning disabilities. *Advances in Learning and Behavioral Disabilities, 10B*, 201–227.

McCormick, S. (1999). *Instruction students who have literacy problems* (3rd ed.). Columbus, OH: Prentice-Hall.

Mercer, C. D., Campbell, K. U., Miller, M. D., Mercer, K. D., & Lane, H. B. (2000). Effects of a reading fluency intervention for middle schoolers with specific learning disabilities. *Learning Disabilities Research & Practice, 15*, 179–189.

Meyer, M. S., & Felton, R. H. (1999). Repeated reading to enhance fluency: Old approaches and new directions. *Annals of Dyslexia, 49*, 283–306.

Moats, L. C. (2001). When older students can't read. *Educational Leadership, 58* (retrieved July 15, 2006 from http://www.cdl.org/resources/reading_room/older_read.html).

Nagy, W. E., & Anderson, R. C. (1984). How many words are there in printed school English? *Reading Research Quarterly, 19*, 304–330.

Nagy, W. E. & Scott, J. A. (2000). Vocabulary processes. In M. L. Kamil, P. B. Mosenthal, P. D. Pearson, & R. Barr (Eds.), *Handbook of reading research: Vol. III.* (pp. 269–284). Mahwah, NJ: Erlbaum.

National Association of State Boards of Education (NASBE). (2005). *Reading at risk: The state response to the crisis in adolescent literacy.* Alexandria, VA: Author.

National Reading Panel (2000). *Teaching children to read: An evidence-based assessment of the scientific research literature on reading and its implications for reading instruction*: Reports of the subgroups (NIH Publication No. 00-4754). Washington, D.C: National Institute of Child Health and Human Development.

Nelson, J. R., Smith, D. J., & Dodd, J. M. (1992). Effects of teaching a summary skills strategy to students identified as learning disabled on their comprehension of science text. *Education and Treatment of Children, 15*, 228–243.

O'Connor, R. E., & Jenkins, J. R. (1995, April). *Cooperative Learning for Students with Learning Disabilities: Teacher and Child Contributions to Successful Participation.* Paper presented at the annual conference of the American Educational Research Association, San Francisco, CA.

O'Shea, L. J., Sindelar, P., & O'Shea, D. J. (1987). Effects of repeated readings and attentional cues on the reading fluency and comprehension of learning disabled readers. *Learning Disabilities Research, 2*, 103–109.

Palincsar, A. S., Brown, A. L., & Martin, S. M. (1987). Peer interaction in reading comprehension instruction. *Educational Psychologist, 22*, 231–253.

Paris, S. G., Carpenter, R. D., Paris, A. H., & Hamilton, E. E. (2005). Spurious and genuine correlates of children's reading comprehension. In S. G. Paris & S. A. Stahl (Eds.), *Children's reading comprehension and assessment* (pp. 131–160). Mahwah, NJ: Erlbaum.

Pressley, M. (2000). What should comprehension instruction be the instruction of? In M. Kamil, P. Mosenthal, P. Pearson, & R. Barr (Eds.), *Handbook of reading research* (Vol. 3, pp. 545–562). Mahwah, NJ: Erlbaum.

Pressley, M. (2001). Comprehension strategy instruction: A turn-of the century status report. In C. Block & M. Pressley (Eds.), *Comprehension instruction: Research-based best practices.* (pp. 11–27), New York: Guilford.

Pressley, M. (2005). *Reading instruction that works: The case for balanced teaching* (3rd ed.). New York: Guilford.

RAND Reading Study Group (2002). *Reading for understanding: Toward an R&D program in reading comprehension.* Santa Monica, CA: RAND.

Raphael, T. (1986). Teaching question answer relationships, revisited. *The Reading Teacher, 39*(6), 516–522.

Rashotte, C. A., & Torgesen, J. K. (1985). Repeated reading and reading fluency in learning disabled children. *Reading Research Quarterly, 20,* 180–188.

Rasinski, T. V., Padak, N. D., McKeon, C. A., Wilfong, L. G., Friedauer, J. A., & Heim, P. (2005). Is reading fluency a key for successful high school reading? *Journal of Adolescent and Adult Literacy, 49,* 22–27.

Rose, T. L., & Beattie, J. R. (1986). Relative effects of teacher-directed and taped previewing on oral reading. *Learning Disability Quarterly, 9,* 193–199.

Rose, T. L., & Sherry, L. (1984). Relative effects of two previewing procedures on LD adolescents' oral reading performance. *Learning Disability Quarterly, 7,* 39–44.

Rosenshine, B. & Meister, C. (1994). Reciprocal teaching: A review of the research. *Review of Educational Research, 64*(4), 479–530.

Roth, F. P., & Speckman, N. J. (1986). Narrative discourse: Spontaneously generated stories of learning-disabled and normally achieving students. *Journal of Speech-Language-Hearing Pathology, 51,* 8–23.

Samuels, S. J. (1979). The method of repeated readings. *The Reading Teacher, 32,* 403–408.

Scott, T. M., & Shearer-Lingo, A. (2002). The effects of reading fluency instruction on the academic and behavioral success of middle school students in a self-contained EBD classroom. *Preventing School Failure, 46,* 167–173.

Shankweiler, D., Lundquist, E., Katz, L., Stuebing, K. K., Fletcher, J. M., and Brady, S. (1999). Comprehension and decoding: Patterns of association in children with reading difficulties. *Scientific Studies of Reading, 3*(1), 69–94.

Shinn, M. R., & Good, R. H. (1992). Curriculum-based measurement of oral reading fluency: A confirmatory analysis of its relation to reading. *School Psychology Review, 21,* 459–479.

Simmons, D., Kame'enui, E., & Darch, C. (1988). The effect of textual proximity on fourth-and fifth-grade LD students' metacognitive awareness and strategic comprehension behavior. *Learning Disability Quarterly, 11,* 380–395.

Skinner, C. H., Cooper, L., & Cole, C. L. (1997). The effects of oral presentation previewing rates on reading performance. *Journal of Applied Behavior Analysis, 30*(2), 331–333.

Stanovich, K. E. (1986). Matthew effects in reading: Some consequences of individual differences in the acquisition of literacy. *Reading Research Quarterly, 21*(4), 360–407.

Stanovich, K. E. (2000). *Progress in understanding reading: Scientific foundations and new frontiers.* New York: Guilford.

Steventon, C. E., & Frederick, L. D. (2003). The effects of repeated readings on student performance in the corrective reading program. *Journal of Direct Instruction, 3,* 17–27.

Strong, A. C., Wehby, J. H., Falk, K. B., & Lane, K. L. (2004). The impact of a structured reading curriculum and repeated reading on the performance of junior high students with emotional and behavioral disorders. *School Psychology Review, 33,* 561–581.

Swanson, H. L. (1999). Reading research for students with LD: A meta-analysis of intervention outcomes. *Journal of Learning Disabilities, 32,* 504–532.

Therrien, W. J. (2004). Fluency and comprehension gains as a result of repeated reading. *Remedial and Special Education, 25,* 252–261.

Torgesen, J. K. (2004). Lessons learned from research on interventions for students who have difficulty learning to read. In P. McCardle & V. Chabra (Eds.), *The voice of evidence in reading research* (pp. 355–382). Baltimore: Brookes.

Torgesen, J. K. (2005, September). *Multiple tiers of instruction and intervention: What it will take to leave no child behind in reading.* Report presented at the Nebraska Reading Conference, Lincoln, NE.

Torgesen, J. K., Alexander, A. W., Wagner, R. K., Rashotte, C. A., Voeller, K. K. S., & Conway, T. (2001). Intensive remedial instruction for children with severe reading disabilities: Immediate and long-term outcomes from two instructional approaches. *Journal of Learning Disabilities, 34,* 33–58.

U.S. Department of Education, NCES. (2003a). *International comparisons in fourth-grade reading literacy:*

*Findings from the progress in international reading literacy study (PIRLS) of 2001* (NCES 2003-073). Washington, DC: U.S. Government Printing Office.

Valleley, R. J., & Shriver, M. D. (2003). An examination of the effects of repeated readings with secondary students. *Journal of Behavioral Education, 12*(1), 55–76.

Vellutino, F. R., & Scanlon, D. M. (1987). Phonological coding, phonological awareness, and reading ability: Evidence from a longitudinal and experimental study. *Merrill-Palmer Quarterly, 33*(3), 321–370.

Walsh, J. A., & Sattes, B. D. (2005). *Quality questioning: Research-based practice to engage every learner.* Thousand Oaks, CA: Corwin Press.

Wexler, J., Vaughn, S., Edmonds, M., & Reutebuch, C. K. (in press). A synthesis of fluency interventions for secondary struggling readers. *Reading and Writing: An Interdisciplinary Journal.*

Williams, J. P. (1998). Improving comprehension of disabled readers. *Annals of Dyslexia, 68,* 213–238.

Williams, J. P. (2000). Strategic processing of text: Improving comprehension for students with learning disabilities. *ERIC Clearinghouse on Disabilities and Gifted Education. Council for Exceptional Children.*

Wong, B. Y. L., & Jones, W. (1982). Increasing metacomprehension in learning disabled and normally achieving students through self-questioning training. *Learning Disability Quarterly, 5,* 228–240.

# 10

# Written Language Instruction during Early and Middle Childhood

## Virginia W. Berninger

This chapter is organized into four parts. Part 1 begins with a brief historical overview of the field of writing instruction. Two themes are emphasized: the changing developmental focus and the diverse perspectives on what counts as evidence. In this chapter, evidence will be discussed that resulted from research using paradigms considered to be scientific by mainstream cognitive, educational, and developmental psychology and neuroscience. Part 2 describes the characteristics of writing and of writers. The characteristics of writing are described in reference to the cognitive processes involved, comparison of the simple and not-so simple views of writing, the relationship of writing to reading, listening, and speaking, and stages of writing development. Characteristics of writers are discussed in reference to whether they are typically developing, at-risk, or learning disabled. Part 3 provides an overview of a programmatic line of research that evaluated the effectiveness of specific kinds of writing instruction for writers that met researcher-defined criteria: (a) early intervention for at-risk writers in the primary grades and at the critical third- to fourth- grade transition, (b) supplementary instruction to increase the number of students passing high stakes tests in writing, and (c) specialized instruction in writing for students with dyslexia who struggle with writing as well as reading. Part 4 explores future directions, with focus on the need for evidence about effective writing instruction for students with specific learning disabilites, importance of generalizing results of research only to the population sampled in a research study, and the limitations of meta-analyses in fully capturing effective writing instruction for the complexities of the writing process, the normal variation among writers, and developmental changes in writing.

## PART 1: HISTORICAL PERSPECTIVES

Recent federal initiatives call for schools to use scientifically supported reading instruction (SSRI), science based reading instruction (SBRI), or evidence-based reading instruction (EBRI) and provide financial incentives if schools do. Curiously missing from these initiatives that focus on reading is a similar focus on writing.

Writing neglect may be due to the myth that children first learn to read during the elementary years and then learn to write during the secondary years. Because of this widely held myth, most research on writing instruction focused on grades 6 and above until the process writing movement in the last two decades of the 20th century (Hillocks, 1986). Clay (1982), Graves (1983), and Calkins (1986) brought to educators' attention the importance of including writing activity in the primary grades—not just penmanship and spelling but written expression of ideas for authentic social communication. This "process writing" movement made a major contribution in shifting the developmental focus of writing instruction from the upper grades to the beginning of formal schooling.

Yet, "process writing" downplayed the role of formal pedagogy in teaching writing. Rather the goal was to engage young children in the writing process in a way that is analogous to professional writers at work. Children learned to use graphic organizers to plan, produce multiple drafts, and revise their writing on the basis of peer feedback and teacher feedback. Peers offered constructive suggestions for improving the writing during author's chair. Teachers did not grade the first product but rather provided ideas during writers' workshop for improving the writing and graded only the final product after many revisions. The social nature of writing was emphasized—not only do writers write for an audience, but also they perform social acts (Britton, 1978) as they create authentic communications within a social community (Englert, 1992).

Although the process writing movement exerted great influence on instructional practices in writing, it is not an evidence-based approach to writing instruction. It is an approach based on teacher philosophy and belief. According to Applebee (2000), 51% of teachers in a national survey report using process writing instruction; if so, then surely this instructional practice during early childhood and middle childhood warrants experimental evaluation of its effectiveness, but this evaluation has not been done. However, many of the innovations introduced by process writing teachers were incorporated by researchers who gathered evidence on the effectiveness of specific instructional practices in writing (e.g., Englert, Raphael, Anderson, Anthony, & Stevens, 1991; Graham & Harris, 2005; Traweek and Berninger, 1997; Wong, Butler, Ficzere, & Kuperis, 1996, 1997; also studies in Table 10.1).

Another factor stimulating research on early writing was the emergence of research oriented to preventing learning disabilities rather than treating chronic learning disabilities (e.g., Berninger & Whitaker, 1993). Early intervention for students at-risk for handwriting and spelling difficulties prevents more serious writing disabilities later in schooling (e.g., Berninger & Amtmann, 2003). Beginning writers can also benefit from composing practice and explicit composition instruction (Englert et al., 1991; studies in Table 10.1).

Although research on writing instruction during the elementary school years was sparse throughout the 20th century, spelling during the elementary grades was the focus of earliest application of the scientific method to evaluate effective instructional methods. Rice (1913) evaluated the optimal instructional time based on student response to spelling instruction in a large scale study including samples throughout the United States. She found that children who received 15 minutes of spelling instruction a week achieved significantly higher spelling test scores than those who were drilled for an hour or more a week. This finding may be counter-intuitive to many who assume that more is necessarily better—but not if students habituate due to monotony and do not benefit from the instruction. During the middle of the 20th century educational psychologists published many studies supporting the value of distributed instruction—short lessons distributed over time—rather than massed practice—intensive instruction over a relatively short period of time. Experimental research that tests hypotheses by gathering data (evidence) that may confirm or disconfirm a working hypothesis is important because evidence does not always support teacher philosophy or belief or the researcher's hypotheses.

Important advances in writing since that pioneering study of effective spelling instruction during early childhood and middle childhood are best understood in reference to what writing is and what the characteristics of the writers are in a particular research study. Characteristics of writing and writers are considered next.

## PART 2: CHARACTERISTICS OF WRITING AND WRITERS

### Writing

*Cognitive Processes.* Hayes and Flower (1980) asked college students who were skilled writers to think aloud while composing. Three cognitive processes were identified in the protocols—planning, translating, and revising. These three processes did not fully explain the writing of children during early and middle childhood (Berninger & Swanson, 1994). For one thing, research showed that translation of beginning writers consisted of two independent components—text generation (translating ideas into language in the mind) and transcription (translating mental language representations in the mind into written symbols in the external environment; Berninger, Yates, Cartwright, Rutberg, Remy, & Abbott, 1992). Also working memory (Swanson & Berninger, 1996a) as well as short-term and long-term memory contributed to the writing of children. Furthermore, children showed intraindividual differences in levels of text generation—at the word, sentence, and text levels (Whitaker, Berninger, Johnston, & Swanson, 1994). In addition, children showed evidence of two kinds of planning—planning in advance and planning on line—and two kinds of revising—on-line and post-translating—each of which has its own developmental trajectory (Berninger & Swanson, 1994). Like good writers, both Hayes (1996, 2000) and the University of Washington research team (e.g., Berninger & Winn, 2006) have revised their models of writing for adults and children, respectively, as new studies with new evidence became available.

*Simple and Not So Simple Views of Reading and Writing.* Gough and Hillinger (1980) proposed a simple view of reading that involved only word reading and listening comprehension. Evidence from the programmatic research at the University of Washington over the last decade indicates that this simple model is probably an oversimplification of the developmental stepping stones in learning to read. For example, in the beginning stages, reader profiles show interindividual and intraindividual differences (relative strengths and weaknesses) in the following skills some of which are directly linked to each other and some of which are not: (a) orthographic and phonological awareness, (b) knowledge of the alphabetic principle (phonemes that correspond to graphemes [1- or 2-letter spelling units]), (c) application of alphabetic principle to decoding unknown words, (d) automatic recognition of single words, (e) oral reading accuracy for single words and text, (f) oral reading fluency (speed and smooth coordination) for text, and (g) reading comprehension at the word vocabulary, sentence, and discourse levels (e.g., Berninger, Abbott, Vermeulen, & Fulton, 2006).

Likewise, Berninger et al. (2002) initially proposed a simple view of writing in which transcription skills and executive functions at the base of the writing triangle support the text generation process. However, based on accumulating research evidence, Berninger and Winn (2006) revised this model and called it the not-so-simple view of writing. In the revised model, the text generation process, which is supported by transcription and executive functions, occurs in a working memory environment through which ideas flow in the cognitively engaged writer (see Kellogg, 1994). The working memory system, which has links to incoming information from the external environment through short-term memory and to existing knowledge stored in long-term memory, consists of a three word-form storage system (phonological, morphological, and orthographic), a time-sensitive phonological loop, and a set of executive functions (Berninger, Abbott, & Thomson, et al., 2006). These executive functions, which account for much of the not-so-simple view of writing, regulate the writing process and include, but are not restricted to (a) selecting, maintaining, and switching focus (supervisory attention); (b) managing levels of consciousness (awareness, presence, and engagement); (c) setting goals; (d) generating ideas and plans; (e) self-monitoring and updating (reviewing); (f) repairing (revising); (g) reflecting; and (h) adapting to the audience. It is this last executive function that underlies knowledge transforming that distinguishes the expert writers from the knowledge tellers who are novice writers (Scaradamalia & Bereiter, 1983).

*Levels of Language.*    Writing draws upon at least three separable skills that represent different levels or units of language: handwriting (*letter* formation) or keyboarding (*letter* selection), spelling (*word* formation), and composition (*text* formation) (Abbott & Berninger, 2003). Although they are separable at one level of analysis, at another level they function together in a system. When the various cognitive processes and levels of language are coordinated in real time in goal-driven working memory, the writing system is functional. Temporal coordination is as essential to working memory as is capacity limitations related to resources or workspace (Berninger, 1999).

*Connections between Writing and Reading, Listening, and Speaking.*    Writing is language by hand. It is one of four functional language systems that develop because language has no end organs of its own and teams up with sensory and motor systems to receive and transmit information to the environment (Liberman, 1999). The other language systems are language by ear (listening), language by mouth (speaking), and language by eye (reading). These systems have their own developmental trajectories, beginning during infancy and the preschool years and continuing through the adult years, but also interact with one another throughout the life span (Berninger, 2000a; Berninger & Richards, 2002; Berninger, Abbott, & Thomson, et al., 2006). For example, children's first written productions are often letter-like stimuli in imitation of letter symbols they have seen in books read to them; and their first spellings reflect their early understandings of how the spelling system represents speech (Traweek & Berninger, 1997). Later in schooling they learn to write narrative structures based on stories they have listened to and books they have read. Oral discussion during the brain storming phase of writing develops planning skills for writing expository text, and oral feedback during author's chair and teacher's workshops develops revising skills.

*Stages of Writing Development.*    Writing, like other human behaviors, develops not in discrete, insular stages but rather in discontinuous phases that sometimes show forward, upward change, but sometimes show receding regression, and sometimes flatline for a period of time. Yet patterns emerge from this developmental change that can be described, are reasonably predictable, and have instructional implications: the early emergent writing phase in preschool and kindergarten; the early conventional phase in the primary grades; the developing phase during upper elementary and middle school years; and the maturing phase during high school and college and beyond. See Berninger, Abbott, & Thomson, et al. (2006, Figures 1, 2, and 3) for stepping stones in writing development for transcription and composition; Berninger, Fuller, and Whitaker (1997) for Fuller's dissertation research on the development of the compositional algorithms for writing the next relevant sentence during the school years and Whitaker's dissertation research on the process of learning to write profession-specific genre in adult writers; Wong (1997) for the development of discourse genre in school-age years; Wong and Berninger (2004) for instructional approaches for each of the developmental phases; and Berninger and Richards (2002, chapters 6 and 9) for the relationship between brain development and writing development.

## Writers

*Typically Developing Writers.* Variation in spelling (and reading) skill development is normal when children enter first grade (Berninger, 1986). Some of this normal variation is due to biological differences (genetic and neurological), some of it is due to cultural and home differences, and some of it is due to differences in prior engagement in literacy activities in home or preschool. Reading and writing skills, like other human abilities such as athletic, artistic, musical, etc., distribute along a normal curve; only a few individuals fall outside the normal range that is characterized by variation, that is, individual differences. Beginning writers show normal variation in their handwriting, spelling, and composition skills and relative strengths in their profiles across each of these three writing skills and related processes (Berninger, Abbott, & Thomson, et al., 2006). Only recently have researchers begun to investigate the most effective match between these patterns of normal variation and instructional approaches for written language (e.g., Connor, Morrison, & Katch, 2004). See Wong (1989) for conceptual and practical considerations in dealing with individual differences among writers in the general education classroom.

Gender differences, favoring girls over boys, occur in typically developing writers, but are related to automatic recall and writing of letters in alphabetic order rather than to motor skills per se (Berninger & Fuller, 1992). Controlling for individual differences in automatic production of alphabet letters from memory eliminated gender differences, favoring girls over boys, in quality of writing in junior high writers in grades 7 to 9 (Berninger, Whitaker, Feng, Swanson, & Abbott, 1996).

The best predictors of handwriting skills of typically developing writers in the elementary grades (Berninger et al., 1992) are (a) orthographic coding of written words into memory and analyzing the letter patterns in them (Berninger, Yates, & Lester, 1991; Abbott & Berninger, 1993), and (b) planning sequential finger movements (e.g., Berninger & Rutberg, 1992). The best predictor of composition length and quality of typically developing writers in the elementary grades (Graham, Berninger, Abbott, Abbott, & Whitaker, 1997; Jones, 2004), middle and high school (Jones, 2004), and college (Connelly, Campbell, MacLean, & Barnes, 2006) and of note taking in lectures in college (Peverley, 2006) is automatic letter writing. Good writers tend to use a mix of manuscript and cursive and to increase handwriting speed as they progress across grade levels 1 to 9 (Graham, Berninger, & Weintraub, 1998; Graham, Berninger, Weintraub, & Schafer, 1997). Typically developing writers in grades 1 to 9 tend to reverse j and z, low frequency letters, rather than b, d, p, q, and g (Graham, Weintraub, & Berninger, 2001). Students with dyslexia reverse these letters as well as b, d, p, and q (Brooks, 2003). Working memory, verbal reasoning, and language skills such as vocabulary knowledge, syntax construction, and discourse organization also contribute to compositional quality (e.g., Berninger, Cartwright, Yates, Swanson, & Abbott, 1994). The best predictors of spelling of typically developing writers are (a) orthographic coding (holding written words in memory while analyzing all the letters in the word or letter segments called graphemes), (b) phonological coding (holding spoken words into memory while analyzing the sound segments called phonemes that correspond to graphemes), and (c) vocabulary (verbal intelligence) (Berninger et al., 1992, 1994). Reading ability of typically developing writers does not fully explain their writing ability (Swanson & Berninger, 1996b).

*At-Risk Writers.*    Gough and Hillinger (1980) also proposed that reading was an unnatural act compared to talking, which is a natural act. This claim does not mesh with the fact that many preschoolers require individual speech and language therapy from highly trained specialists to learn to talk intelligibly, grammatically, and fluently. Nor does this claim fit with the findings of Connor et al. (2004) who documented that some students, who enter school with more advanced literacy skills, learn written language as naturally as they learned oral language and benefit from self-directed, engagement in literacy activities rather than teacher-led instruction in decoding. Likewise, some beginning writers appear to learn to write naturally by engaging in the writing process, but others require explicit, systematic, and sustained instruction in writing. School practitioners can turn to the research literature on individual differences in writing to screen children early in schooling to determine which students are most likely to benefit from which approach to writing instruction: (a) engagement in the writing process because their writing skills are already grade-appropriate, or (b) explicit, systematic, and sustained writing instruction because their writing skills and related processes are not yet grade-appropriate. Most students will probably benefit from both approaches to some extent—but the relative mix that optimizes their writing achievement may vary. However, many students may not make adequate progress in writing without the explicit, systematic, and sustained instruction tailored to their individual profiles of writing, reading, listening, and speaking abilities. Gifted students may have transcription problems that mask superb oral text generation (Yates, Berninger, & Abbott, 1994). Skills to target in early intervention for all at-risk writers include (a) handwriting (forming letters automatically and retrieving them quickly from memory), and (b) conventional spelling (phoneme awareness and syllable awareness; teaching alphabetic principle in phoneme-to-grapheme direction; the six syllable types in English spelling) (Berninger & Amtmann, 2003).

*Third-to-Fourth Grade Transition.*    Students who learn to read relatively easily and can meet the writing requirements in the primary grade classroom, first surface as having writing difficulties at the transition from the primary to intermediate grades. One reason for these later emerging writing disabilities is that the writing requirements in some primary grade classrooms (e.g., the 49% who do not teach process writing) are minimal—for example, filling in blanks in independent work sheets, writing spelling words from dictation, and completing handwriting assignments that require copying letters legibly. Even in those classrooms including some process writing activities, writing products are often not graded on the basis of the conventions of writing, which become increasingly important in the grading of writing in the upper grades and in high-stakes writing assessment. Building-wide screenings, based on research-supported, grade-appropriate measures for identifying at-risk writers, should be conducted not only in the early grades (1 to 2) but also during this important third to fourth grade transition when intervention may be needed that is geared to (a) integrating low-level transcription and high-level composition skills (Berninger, Abbott, Whitaker, Sylvester, & Nolen, 1995), writing text of varied genre (Berninger et al., 2002), and integrating reading and writing (Altemeier, Jones, & Berninger, 2006). Altemeier and colleagues showed that individual differences in the executive functions of writers play an important role in integrating reading and writing to complete written assignments during this transition in the middle of the elementary grades. Hooper, Swartz, Wakely, de Kruif, and Montgomery (2002) showed that executive functions contribute to difficulties in written expression of fourth- and fifth- students.

*Older, Struggling Writers.*    If earlier problems in transcription and executive functions are not treated effectively, they pose ongoing challenges as students are confronted with ever more complex writing assignments that require increasingly longer stretches of time to complete.

For example, middle school teachers request help with teaching grade-appropriate composing to students whose transcription skills are well below grade level (Troika & Maddox, 2004). In middle school and high school, individual differences in time management become critically important as students are expected to complete such complex, long-term writing assignments (for instructional approaches for dealing with this challenge, see Wong & Berninger, 2004). Another challenge for older students and their teachers is learning to integrate technology and writing instruction. Wong and colleagues developed teacher-friendly, research-based models for integrating *process writing, teacher and peer feedback* (Wong, Butler, Ficzere, Kuperis, & Corden, 1994; Wong, Wong, Darlington, & Jones, 1991), *explicit and systematic writing instruction, goal-setting, computer technology,* and *general education curriculum and long-term writing assignments* in school settings for students who struggle in writing for a variety of reasons, including English language learning, learning disabilities, and socioeconomic differences (Wong et al., 1996, 1997). Such comprehensive instructional models are an excellent match with the characteristics of preadolescent and adolescent writers.

*Students with Dyslexia.*    One of the unexpected findings of the decade-long family genetics study of dyslexia at the University of Washington was that dyslexia is not only a reading disorder but also a writing disorder (Berninger, Abbott, & Thomson, et al., 2006; Berninger, Nielsen, et al., 2007a). After the children with dyslexia learned to decode and read words reasonably well, they invariably had ongoing spelling problems; whether the spelling problems resolved or persisted was a matter of not only instructional programs but also gender differences. Boys with dyslexia were more likely to be impaired in all writing skills than girls with dyslexia, and mothers who still showed markers of dyslexia (rate of real word or pseudoword reading) were more likely to compensate in spelling than fathers with those same dyslexia markers. The genetic pathway to spelling problems in dyslexia was pinpointed to phonological memory as assessed by repeating aurally presented pseudowords without meaning clues (Wijsman et al., 2000). Children with dyslexia varied as to whether they also had handwriting automaticity problems.

## PART 3: EFFECTIVE TREATMENT

### Design Experiments and Randomized Controlled Studies

Initially, the University of Washington research team conducted design experiments (Brown, 1992) to evaluate effectiveness of instructional protocols that provided explicit writing or reading-writing instruction to bring about desired writing outcomes (e.g., Abbott, Reed, Abbott, & Berninger, 1997). Abbott et al. found that at-risk second graders responded more quickly to explicit instruction in integrated reading-writing in their reading, handwriting, and composing than spelling skills. Brooks, Vaughan, and Berninger (1999) found that fourth to sixth graders with dyslexia responded more quickly to explicit instruction in handwriting, spelling, and composition in their handwriting and composing than spelling skills and that response to spelling instruction depended on initial reading achievement level. Spelling did not respond to treatment until it was taught in the direction of spoken word-to-written word, instead of using written word strategies exclusively, in the at-risk writers and students with dyslexia. These phonological strategies included counting syllables and phonemes in spoken words and classifying syllables according to syllable type in English (see Berninger et al., 2000).

Subsequently, large-scale, randomized controlled studies in school settings were conducted for students at risk in specific writing skills (e.g., handwriting, spelling, or compositional fluency). Specific theory-driven treatments were compared to each other and to a contact control treatment. In addition, randomized, controlled instructional studies were also conducted at the university for students with persisting learning disabilities.

Table 10.1 summarizes some of these studies for students who were at-risk for writing on specific writing skills (first six studies) or had a specific learning disability (e.g., dyslexia with persisting writing problems, last study). Collectively, these studies illustrate research supported developmental principles in planning and implementing evidence-based instruction in writing, as is discussed next. Most of these studies organized the lessons to overcome temporal limitations in working memory by combining *within the same lesson close in time* instructional activities at the subword level (initially), followed by word level (to promote transfer of subword skills to word context), and culminating in text level (to promote transfer of word-level skills to text context). All treatments taught strategies for self-regulating the writing process during independent composing. To avoid habituation, instructional activities lasted 10 minutes or less; to capitalize on distributive learning, lessons were spaced in time across four months on average and took place twice a week in 20- to 30- minute sessions in groups of three or two students (first four studies in Table 10.1). The fifth and seventh were conducted during the summer and the sixth lasted about seven months. Each published, peer reviewed study was translated into lesson plans teachers can use (Berninger & Abbott, 2003).

### Early Intervention for At-Risk Primary Grade Writers

*Handwriting and Composing.* Whole classrooms were screened to find the children lowest in writing letters legibly and automatically. Five instructional methods were compared to each other and to a contact control (phonological awareness training): copying letters from models with no cues; imitating the teacher's modeling of motor movements in making letters; copying letters from models with numbered arrow cues showing component strokes and their order; writing letters from memory; and combined numbered arrow cues and writing letters from memory. All treatment groups had an opportunity to compose for 5 minutes and share their compositions with peers, that is, to engage in the writing process. The combined numbered arrow cues + writing from memory treatment was the front runner for improving automatic legible letter writing and for transfer to compositional fluency (timed composing) (Berninger et al., 1997); see first study in Table 10.1. That treatment was also more effective than the phonological control treatment in reducing letter reversals as demonstrated by Brooks in her dissertation research (see Berninger et al., 2006). Graham, Harris, and Fink (2000) and Jones and Cristensen (1999) also showed that early intervention in handwriting is effective and leads to improved composing. Rutberg' s dissertation research (Berninger, 2006, study 1) showed that motor control training and orthographic coding training, when coupled with direct instruction in letter writing improved legibility of writing in at-risk handwriters, but that direct instruction in letter writing including numbered arrow cues and writing letters from memory improved automaticity of legible letter writing.

*Spelling and Composing.* Whole classrooms were screened to find second-grade children who were the lowest in spelling words from dictation. Eight methods that varied strategy for making connections between units of written words and units of spoken words were compared to each other and to a phonological contact control treatment: connections between phonemes and graphemes in alphabetic principle, connections between onset-rimes in spoken and written words, connections between naming the spoken word and naming all the letters in a written word, each of three combinations of two of these connections, and the combination of all

TABLE 10.1
Research-Supported Integrated Writing Instruction Organized Developmentally[a]

| Writing Domain and Grade | Skills Taught |
| --- | --- |
| Handwriting and Composing (grade 1)[b] Lesson Set 3[a] | Practicing each alphabet letter once by studying numbered arrow cues; covering letter and holding it in mind's eye, and writing letter from memory after increasing delays in time; transfer of automatic letter writing by word writing (3 words), and composing for 5 minutes about composition topics provided as prompts. Compositions are shared by reading them to peers. |
| Spelling and Composing (grade 2)[c] Lesson Set 4[a] | Alphabetic principle in isolation (phonemes to letters ); transfer of alphabetic principle to spelling monosyllabic real words; transfer of alphabetic principle to spelling real words during composing when given prompts and high frequency words to include. |
| Spelling and Composing (grade 3)[d] Lesson Set 5[a] | Alphabetic principle in isolation (phonemes to letters ); transfer of alphabetic principle to spelling polysyllabic real words and spelling dictated sentences; transfer of alphabetic principle to spelling real words during composing when given phrase prompts. |
| Spelling and Composing (grade 3)[e] Lesson Set 7[a] | Word sorts for substitutions (alternative spellings for the same phoneme); transfer to spelling structure and content words; explicit modeling of planning, translating, and reviewing/revising processes in composing informational and persuasive essays. |
| Writers' Workshops transcription + composition (beginning grade 4 and above)[f] Lesson Set 8[a] | Automatic handwriting warm-ups; spelling strategies; explicit modeling and scaffolding of planning, translating, and reviewing/revising for narrative and expository genre. |
| Writers' Clubs to meet writing standards (grade 4)[g] Lesson Set 10[a] | Humor and play with language (riddles and jokes; morphological searches; bingo for structure words); automatic handwriting, spelling strategies, essay writing, and newspaper writing |
| Writing in Content Areas (grades 4-8)[h] Lesson Sets 13--14[a] | Humor and play with language (riddles and jokes), alphabetic principle and decoding, reading fluency, reading in content area, and integrating talking and writing with reading comprehension activities |

*Note:* [a]Refers to Lesson Set in Berninger, V., & Abbott, S. (2003). *PAL Research-supported reading and writing lessons.* San Antonio, TX: Harcourt.
[b]Berninger, V., Vaughan, K., Abbott, R., Abbott, S., Brooks, A., Rogan, L., Reed, E., & Graham, S. (1997). Treatment of handwriting fluency problems in beginning writing: Transfer from handwriting to composition. *Journal of Educational Psychology, 89,* 652–666.
[c]Berninger, V., Vaughan, K., Abbott, R., Brooks, A., Abbott, S., Reed, E., Rogan, L., & Graham, S. (1998). Early intervention for spelling problems: Teaching spelling units of varying size within a multiple connections framework. *Journal of Educational Psychology, 90,* 587–605.
[d]Berninger, V., Vaughan, K., Abbott, R., Brooks, A., Begay, K., Curtin, G., Byrd, K., & Graham, S. (2000). Language-based spelling instruction: Teaching children to make multiple connections between spoken and written words. *Learning Disability Quarterly, 23,* 117–135.
[e]Berninger, V., Vaughan, K., Abbott, R., Begay, K., Byrd, K., Curtin, G., Minnich, J. , & Graham, S. (2002). Teaching spelling and composition alone and together: Implications for the simple view of writing. *Journal of Educational Psychology, 94,* 291–304.
[f]Berninger, V., Abbott, R., Whitaker, D., Sylvester, L., & Nolen, S. (1995). Integrating low-level skills and high-level skills in treatment protocols for writing disabilities. *Learning Disability Quarterly, 18,* 293–309.
[g]Berninger, V., Rutberg, J., Abbott, R., Garcia, N., Anderson-Youngstrom, M., Brooks, A., & Fulton, C. (2006). Tier 1 and Tier 2 early intervention for handwriting and composing. *Journal of School Psychology, 44,* 3–30. Study 4.
[h]Berninger, V., Abbott, R., Abbott, S., Graham, S., & Richards, T. (2002). Writing and reading: Connections between language by hand and language by eye. *Journal of Learning Disabilities, 35,* 39–56. Study 3.

three connections. Each of the treatment groups was shown how to apply the taught strategy to spelling *monosyllabic* words. All treatments composed for 5 minutes and read their compositions to peers, that is, they engaged in the writing process. Results showed that (a) both the onset-rime and the whole word treatments were the most effective in achieving transfer across word contexts from taught to untaught words; and (b) the phoneme-to-grapheme strategy was the most effective in generating correctly spelled words during composing in the pretest, midtest, and posttest (Berninger et al., 1998). However, rapid automatic naming (RAN) predicted the three classes of responders (initially slow and slow growth; initially slow and fast growth; initially fast but slow growth) during the 24 lessons over four months in producing correctly spelled words during independent composing in writing lessons (Amtman, Abbott, & Berninger, in press). Collectively, these results for the second study in Table 10.1 point to the effectiveness of teaching students multiple spelling strategies for making connections between spoken and printed words and also screening those at-risk for spelling for the RAN deficit that may impede transfer of spelling knowledge to independent composing.

The evidence for multiple strategies (Berninger et al., 1998) replicated the earlier dissertation research of Hart (Hart, Berninger, & Abbott,1997) showing that learning phonological decoding benefited from multiple strategies including phoneme-grapheme relationships but also other connections between units of written and spoken words. Graham, Harris, and Fink-Chorzempa (2002) also showed that early intervention in spelling is effective and leads to improved composing and other literacy skills.

Another study screened whole classrooms for third graders low in spelling (third study in Table 10.1) and evaluated the relative effectiveness of adding phonological awareness training for syllables and syllable types in English to the kind of spelling instruction in the second study in Table 10.1. Some evidence for the added advantage of the phonological awareness training for syllables was found for learning to spell *polysyllabic* words. Daily sentence dictation was also found to be effective for word-specific spelling; but short-term mastery required 24 repeated dictations in different sentence contexts (see Berninger et al., 2000).

Yet another study screened whole classrooms to find the lowest spellers in third grade (fourth study in Table 10.1). One treatment taught alphabetic principle with an emphasis on the alternations (alternative graphemes for spelling the same phoneme in English) and transfer to spelling structure words (prepositions, conjunctions, pronouns, and articles) that have no meaning of their own but "glue" together other words to create meaningful sentences and to spelling content words (nouns, verbs, adjectives, and adverbs). One treatment taught planning, translating, and reviewing/revising strategies explicitly for writing informational and persuasive essays; that is, students not only engaged in the writing process but also they received explicit instruction in each of the cognitive processes for different genres. One treatment received both spelling and composing instruction equated for instructional time. The contact control received only a phonological and orthographic awareness control treatment. Results showed that the spelling instruction was effective in improving the spelling of the structure words, to which alphabetic principle cannot always be applied to each letter in the word, and of the content words, to which alphabetic principle can usually be applied to each letter in the word. Also, the students who received composition instruction, whether or not it was combined with spelling instruction, improved in composition (see Berninger et al., 2002).

## The Third to Fourth Grade Writing Transition

The fifth study in Table 10.1 screened for the lowest writers at the end of the school year in all third grades in two school systems and invited them to the university for a summer program in the form of a three-week writers' workshop that offered a daily one-hour individual tutorial. All children received explicit instruction in planning, writing, reviewing, and revising (PWRR strategy) in which the tutors, who were supervised by the author behind a one-way mirror, modeled each of the processes before the children engaged in each of the processes as they composed. In addition, the tutor scaffolded the writing process (provided teacher guidance) as the children planned, wrote, and reviewed and revised their daily compositions. Children chose their favorite composition to publish in a book with all students' contributions at the end of the writers' workshop. Half the children were randomly assigned to extra orthographic coding training (Looking Games that encourage careful attention to and memory for letter patterns in written words; and the Before and After game for writing letters that come before and after others in the alphabet). Half were assigned to extra practice in composition. All participating children showed faster growth in handwriting automaticity and composing than the untreated controls, who were only tested at the same pretest, midtest, and posttest occasion. Only the lowest spellers showed spelling improvement. Gains in handwriting, spelling, and composing were maintained at follow-up. The children who received extra orthographic coding training improved more in spelling. The children who received more practice in composing improved more in handwriting on a copy task (see Berninger et al., 1995).

Strategy instruction has been shown effective in developing executive self-regulation of the writing process (e.g., Graham & Harris, 2005; Troia, & Graham, 2002; Troia, Graham, & Harris, 1999; Wong, 1994, 1998, 2000, 2001). Metacognitive training (planning, translating, and reflecting) improved spelling (Hooper, Wakely, de Kruif, & Schwartz, 2006). Chenault's dissertation research showed that students who received attention training rather than reading fluency training prior to composition training improved significantly more in composing once explicit composition instruction (planning translating, and revising) was introduced (Chenault, Thomson, Abbott, & Berninger, 2006).

## Meeting Writing Standards and Passing High Stakes Tests

The sixth study in Table 10.1 used an extended school day model to offer writing clubs before or after school to help students prepare for the states' high stakes test in writing. All third graders in a school district were given a screening measure designed by the same testing company that developed the writing test for the state. Those who fell in the at-risk range as defined by the state were invited to participate in the study. Half of the schools were randomly assigned to the club treatment and half to an untreated control group that received only the regular program and were tested at the same time as the club children. The clubs met twice a week for an hour before or after school for most of the school year beginning before the winter holidays. The treatment was designed to be a like a real club with a healthy dose of Writers' Play (e.g., morphological awareness games called Mommy Longwords with rewards given by "Dr.-Mrs. Seuss-Goose"; jokes, puns, riddles; and bingo words for structure words) and writing for authentic purposes (published a newspaper *Kids Writing for Kids* that was disseminated periodically throughout the schools). Other instructional activities validated in the first, second, third, fourth, and fifth studies in Table 10.1 served as Writers' Work in the clubs. Results showed that more students in the clubs met state standards in writing and improved on a standardized measure of writing fluency than students in the control group. (Berninger, Rutberg, et al., 2006, Study 4).

## Specialized Writing Instruction for Students with Dyslexia

*Effective Instructional Treatments for Students.* Two writers' workshops have also been held at the university for students with dyslexia in grades 4 to 9 (summer 2002, Mark Twain Writers' Workshop, Berninger & Hidi, 2006; Berninger, Nunn, et al., 2007, Study 1) and in grades 4 to 6 (summer 2004, John Muir Science Writing Workshop, Berninger et al., in press, Study 2). Results of the first study showed that two orthographic strategies—photographic leprechaun and proofreaders' trick— along with games such as anagrams were more effective than morphological strategies—word building and word dissecting—along with morphological spelling rules in improving the spelling of real words at a behavioral level and normalizing brain activation (Richards et al., 2005, 2006). Both orthographic strategies required students to hold the written word in their mind's eye with their eyes closed. For the photographic leprechaun, the teacher asked students to name one or more letters in a word-specific position in polysyllabic words that could not be recovered solely on the basis of sound (e.g., the third letter and the seventh and eighth letters in elevator). For the proofreaders' trick, students spelled words forwards and then backwards. Results of the second study showed that phonological treatment improved pseudoword spelling (and pseudoword reading and oral repetition of aural pseudowords). Comparing the two studies at the behavioral and brain levels of analyses showed that real word spelling improved only if orthographic and morphological treatment were added to phonological treatment (e.g., Berninger, Winn, et al., 2007), consistent with triple word form theory (Berninger, Abbott, & Thomson, et al., 2006).

*Sustaining Intervention by Educating Teachers about Specialized Instruction for Students with Dyslexia.*   Federal initiatives for reading improvement assume that teachers who were not trained to be critical consumers of educational research can implement research-informed practices without substantial training in the nature and findings of scientific research related to learning written language (and other areas of the curriculum) at the pre-service level. These initiatives also assume that the link between research findings in controlled settings generalize neatly and simply to real world school settings, which is unlikely given the normal variation in learners and complexity of school learning environments.

Teacher training workshops have been conducted for the teachers who will work with the students with dyslexia who attended the summer programs. The goal is to sustain the intervention by increasing teacher knowledge of specialized instruction for dyslexia. The good news is that at pretest most teachers showed some degree of knowledge of phonological awareness. The bad news was that they showed virtually no knowledge of morphological awareness, which is related to literacy skills in at-risk writers in fourth grade (Nagy, Berninger, Abbott, Vaughan, & Vermeulen, 2003) and spelling in fourth to ninth graders (Nagy, Berninger, Abbott, 2006). For example, they could not give examples of inflectional suffixes, which mark tense and number, or derivational suffixes, which mark part of speech. Participants in the summer 2004 workshop showed most growth at posttest in morphological awareness, probably because they were at floor at pretest (unpublished data). However, they also made some progress in their phonological awareness as a result of participation in the workshop. These results show that even the most motivated teachers who voluntarily participate in continuing education can still benefit from professional development in understanding linguistic awareness.

## Transfer of Writing Instruction to Reading

Because the writing and reading system are separable but interrelated systems, teaching to one may lead to generalization (transfer) to the other. First, evidence of transfer from writing instruction to reading is examined. In the first grade handwriting treatment study (Table 10.1, first study), all treatment groups improved over time in accuracy of phonological decoding, perhaps because better letter formation facilitates learning of the alphabetic principle or application of it to the decoding process. In the second grade spelling treatment study (Table 10.1, second study) all treatment groups improved significantly over time in accuracy of real word reading (1/5 standard score gain), although the size of the gain was greater for spelling (1/3 standard score gain) that was directly trained. In the third grade spelling treatment study (Table 10.1, third study), transfer from spelling treatment to word reading (raw scores) was also observed; only raw scores, not standard scores, were analyzed because of the shorter duration of this third grade study than the second grade study. In the study comparing spelling only, composition only, and combined spelling and composing instruction (Table 10.1, fourth study), spelling instruction that emphasized alternative ways of spelling the same sound (e.g., c, k, or ck for /k/) transferred to improved accuracy of phonological decoding but not real word reading. In a study that taught handwriting with and without extra motor or orthographic training (Berninger et al., 2006, Study 2), children improved in real word reading (1/3 standard deviation gain).

This evidence for transfer from writing instruction to improved reading must be qualified with other null findings. The comprehensive writing instruction during the third to fourth grade transition (Table 10.1, fifth study) did not show transfer to rate of growth in real word or pseudoword reading. The comprehensive writing instruction in the clubs (Table 10.1, sixth study) did not show transfer to improved reading on the state high stakes test or an individually administered test of reading comprehension. Also, Brooks et al. (1999) did not find transfer from writing instruction to improved real word reading in intermediate grade students with dyslexia.

## Transfer of Reading Instruction to Writing

Results for transfer from reading instruction to writing are also mixed. Students with dyslexia in grades 4 to 6 given comprehensive reading instruction improved significantly in reading skills but not in writing skills (handwriting, spelling, and compositional quality and fluency; Berninger, 2000b). However, Abbott's dissertation research showed that students with dyslexia in grades 4 to 7 given comprehensive reading instruction, with either a structural analysis (syllable and phonemes for words of different word origin) or a study skills component, showed significant improvement in spelling on intercept and slope of growth curves for two spelling measures, but the improvement was not related to the component that varied between groups (Abbott & Berninger, 1999).

In a study that taught reading with and without a multisensory component (pairing handwriting instruction with phonics) to first graders who were already behind in reading and had a family history of reading and writing disabilities, the children receiving phonics instruction without the multisensory component improved significantly more in their reading skills and two writing skills (alphabet writing from memory and a copy task) than those given phonics instruction with the multisensory component (Berninger, Rutberg, et al., 2006). These at-risk students may benefit from both phonics and handwriting instruction, but the two do not necessarily have to be taught together. For example, low achieving first graders given both handwriting and reading lessons, either at different times of the day or sequenced in time over the school year, improved significantly more in real word reading and orthographic coding than did those given only additional practice in the regular code-oriented curriculum, to equate for instructional time. Both groups improved in phonological decoding (see Berninger, Dunn, Shimada, & Lin, 2004).

In another study (Table 10.1, seventh study), students with dyslexia given comprehensive reading instruction but no spelling instruction improved in number of correctly spelled words in their compositions significantly more than the wait-listed control did; although one group completed all comprehension activities with oral discussion and the other with written composition, both groups improved significantly in composition length (Berninger et al., 2002). Thus, on balance, reading instruction does appear to transfer to some improvement in writing in students with dyslexia, but this issue requires more research attention and researchers should give writing as well as reading measures in instructional studies for reading.

## PART 4: CONCLUSIONS, CAVEATS, AND CALL FOR
## FUTURE RESEARCH DIRECTIONS

### Writing Instruction for Different Specific Learning Disabilities

In this chapter we made a clear distinction among the various student populations studied for all of which researcher-defined inclusion criteria were used (see published studies for details) rather than samples of convenience. One of the issues holding back development of evidence-based practices in writing is that research samples are often not described in sufficient detail to know to whom results can be generalized. Although the federal special education laws have one umbrella category for learning disabilities, 25 years of research and clinical experience of this author point to the conclusion that this approach is overly simplistic and interfering with a scientifically grounded approach to assessment and treatment of writing disabilities (e.g., Berninger, 2004, 2006, in press; Berninger, Nagy, Richards, & Raskind, in press). Although it is widely assumed that all students respond well to the same instruction, the fact is this working hypothesis of many researchers and trainers has never been put to rigorous experimental test. This assumption also flies in the face of teachers at work in classrooms who understand the reality of normal varia-tion among learners and the results of intervention studies showing remarkable normal variation in not only pretreatment assessment (e.g., Berninger et al., 1995) but also response to the same instruction (e.g., Abbott et al., 1997). At the very least, studies are needed to evaluate response to writing instruction for the following specific learning disabilities that differ as to whether only writing or writing plus reading or writing plus reading and oral language are impaired.

*Dysgraphia.*    Some students have specific writing problems without motor, oral language, or reading disabilities (Berninger, 2004, in press). These students tend to be impaired most in orthographic coding and grapho-motor planning of sequential finger movements (Berninger, in press). They may have a deficit in the orthographic loop of working memory that coding on the *Wechsler Intelligence Scale for Children, 4th Edition* (WISC IV, Psychological Corporation, 2003), which loads on the working memory factor, may assess; specifically coding assesses ability to engage in associative learning with the orthographic loop. Effective writing instruction for these students may require specialized instruction in orthographic coding and integration of orthographic coding with grapho-motor planning for sequential finger movements within the context of the instructional protocols for writing already shown to be effective in teaching handwriting, spelling, or composing (see Table 10.1). Students who have primary motor disabilities, acquired or of developmental origin, will undoubtedly have handwriting problems. Nevertheless, many students with handwriting problems do not have primary motor problems. They are more likely to have problems in orthographic coding with and without grapho-motor control and/or planning problems (Berninger, 2004).

*Dyslexia.*    Some students have specific reading and spelling problems without oral language disabilities other than phonological memory and awareness (Berninger 2006, in press; Berninger et al., 2006). These students tend to be most impaired in phonological, orthographic, and rapid automatic naming (Berninger, Abbott, Thomson, Raskind, 2001; Berninger, Abbott, & Thomson, et al., 2006) and have phonological core deficits within components of working memory (Berninger, Abbott, & Thomson, et al., 2006). RAN may be an index of the time-sensitive phonological loop in working memory. Effective instruction may require specialized instruction in (a) phonological awareness (e.g., beginning with the spoken not written word, Berninger et al., 2000; Berninger, Rutberg, et al., 2006, Study 3; Berninger et al., 2007, Study 2), (b) orthographic awareness (e.g., Looking Games, Berninger et al., 2006, Study 3), and (c) phonological-loop through teacher-guided oral reading with turn switching at sentence punctuation and strategic decoding of unknown words (e.g., Berninger et al., in press, Study 2). This instruction should take place in the context of all the instructional components research has shown to be necessary to develop fully functional reading systems and competent readers: decoding, automatic word reading, oral reading fluency for passages, silent reading fluency, and reading comprehension (e.g., Abbott & Berninger, 1999). However, some additional adjustments for the working memory inefficiency may also be necessary (e.g., the timing of the instructional components as discussed in this chapter).

*Language Learning Disability.*    Some students have a history of and current problems in oral language in addition to their problems in reading and writing; they may or may not also have motor disabilities that are often observed in populations with oral language impairments. However, they tend to have not only decoding/word reading problems but also reading comprehension problems, morphological and syntactic awareness problems, semantic retrieval problems, and working memory problems (Berninger, in press). They probably need specialized instruction directed to morphological and syntactic awareness in spoken and written language and semantic retrieval/vocabulary within the context of instructional protocols shown to be effective for teaching students with dyslexia (see above section). Without the added attention to morphological and syntactic awareness and semantic retrieval/vocabulary related to reading comprehension and written expression, however, their reading and writing progress may be stymied.

## Generalization of Research Findings

The following point is repeated for the purpose of highlighting it. Participants in writing research need to be described carefully and results should be generalized only to the population studied. The population studied may be typically developing students or those with specific learning disabilities. A trend in applying research to practice is that findings based on learning disabled samples are often generalized to typically developing students or vice versa. For example, research has shown that students with specific reading disabilities need more explicit and intensive instruction in phonics than do their classmates, but this finding is often translated to mean all students need such explicit and intensive phonics instruction, when probably they do need some instruction in decoding but not to the same degree—unless their career goal is to become a reading or writing teacher. Often research is done on samples of convenience without adequate attention to detail in describing the characteristics of the participants. The net result is that it is difficult to know the population of students to which results may appropriately generalize.

## Caveats about Meta-Analyses

Considering that there has been less research on the writing than reading, it may be premature to conduct large scale meta-analyses of writing unless those who conduct them carefully take into account the aspect of writing that a specific study investigated and the specific population of writers studied (e.g., typically developing, at-risk, specific learning disability diagnosis, stage of writing development). Only studies comparing the same aspect of writing, the same population of writers, and the same stage of writing development should be compared in a meta-analysis. Writing is a very complex process with many different aspects to it. Normal variation in typically developing writers is enormous both in pretreatment assessment and response to instruction. Target skills for instruction and assessment change across writing development. If practitioners are to apply results of meta-analyses meaningfully to real world classrooms and individual students, it is important not to lose sight of these issues in the quest for What Works in Writing? The quest for a short list of What Works in Reading? may have been short-sighted. Evidence-based practice ultimately depends on what works for individual students in real school settings and not just in controlled laboratory research.

Another issue to be considered in conducting meta-analyses is what the working hypotheses of the researcher were. Research results usually cannot be interpreted meaningfully apart from the conceptually driven research hypotheses motivating the study. Meta-analyses often disregard the scientific purpose generating the research results when they combine results in an atheoretical fashion and the results could therefore lead to misleading conclusions.

## Cutting-Edge Research

We end where writing begins—in the preschool years. The cutting edge in literacy research in general and writing in particular is moving downward developmentally to the preschool years. Two research studies are representative of this new trend to understand early writing and early intervention to prevent writing problems. The first study found that letter naming and letter writing are highly related in four-year-olds, providing clues for future assessment and treatment studies (Molfese, Beswick, Molnar, & Jacobi-Vessels, 2006). The second study showed that early spelling ability in five-year-olds was related to their ability to analyze sound sequences in spoken words and letter sequences in written words and fast map these sequences across written and spoken words (Apel, Wolter, & Masterson, 2006). Writing instruction may begin when infants and toddlers first learn that writing instruments leave marks on the external world and parents discourage their further use until children have the cognitive and linguistic understanding of how to use those marks to communicate with others in a prosocial way. Yet, much of that important writing instruction during early childhood may occur in the home or the preschool before a child begins formal schooling. Researchers are just beginning to tackle these intriguing issues.

## ACKNOWLEDGMENTS

The author thanks, in alphabetic order, her former doctoral students in school psychology who contributed greatly to the programmatic research on writing discussed in this chapter: Dr. Sylvia Abbott for her work in the early design experiments and later randomized controlled studies in school settings and university settings; Dr. Allison Brooks for her assistance with early intervention studies in schools and specialized treatment at the university and work on letter reversals as indicators of working memory inefficiency; Dr. Belle Chenault for her work showing that prior attention training enhances response to composition training in students with dyslexia; Dr. Frances Fuller for her work on gender differences in writing and algorithms developing writers use in deciding what to write next; Dr. Terry Hart for her work on teaching multiple connections between units of written words and units of spoken words to improve reading and spelling; Dr. Judith Rutberg for her assistance in the cross-sectional studies, particularly related to finger function, and her dissertation research on teaching handwriting to at-risk writers; Dr. Dean Traweek for her work on the early development of writing in classrooms and comparison of instructional programs that did and did not integrate reading and writing; Dr. Cheryl Yates for her assistance in the early cross-sectional studies, particularly related to orthographic coding, and research on writing disabilities in gifted children; and Dr. Diane Whitaker for her work on levels of language in translation, branching diagnosis in writing disabilities, and the process by which adult writers learn to write psychological reports.

## REFERENCES

Abbott, R., & Berninger, V. (1993). Structural equation modeling of relationships among developmental skills and writing skills in primary and intermediate grade writers. *Journal of Educational Psychology, 85*, 478–508.

Abbott, S., & Berninger, V. (1999). It's never too late to remediate: A developmental approach to teaching word recognition. *Annals of Dyslexia, 49*, 223–250.

Abbott, S., Reed, L., Abbott, R., & Berninger, V. (1997). Year-long balanced reading/writing tutorial: A design experiment used for dynamic assessment. *Learning Disability Quarterly, 20*, 249–263.

Altemeier, L., Jones, J., Abbott, R., & Berninger, V. (2006) Executive factors in becoming writing-readers and reading-writers: Note-taking and report writing in third and fifth graders. *Developmental Neuropsychology, 29*, 161–173.

Amtmann, D., Abbott, R., & Berninger, V. (in press). Identifying and predicting classes of response to explicit, phonological spelling instruction during independent composing. *Journal of Learning Disabilities.*

Apel, K., Wolter, J., & Masterson, J. (2006). Effects of phonotactic and orthotactic probabilities during fast mapping on 5 year-olds in learning to spell. *Developmental Neuropsychology, 29*, 21–42.

Applebee, N. (2000). Alternate models of writing development. In R. Indrisano, & J. Squire (Eds.), *Perspectives on writing* (pp. 90–111). Newark, DE: International Reading Association.

Berninger, V. (1986). Normal variation in reading acquisition. *Perceptual and Motor Skills, 62*, 691–716.

Berninger, V. (1999). Coordinating transcription and text generation in working memory during composing: Automatized and constructive processes. *Learning Disability Quarterly, 22*, 99–112.

Berninger, V. (2000a). Development of language by hand and its connections to language by ear, mouth, and eye. *Topics in Language Disorders, 20*, 65–84.

Berninger, V. (2000b). Dyslexia an invisible, treatable disorder: The story of Einstein's Ninja Turtles. *Learning Disability Quarterly, 23*, 175–195.

Berninger, V. (2004). Understanding the graphia in dysgraphia. In D. Dewey & D. Tupper (Eds.), *Developmental motor disorders: A neuropsychological perspective* (pp. 328–350). New York: Guilford.

Berninger, V. (2006). A developmental approach to learning disabilities. In I. Siegel & A. Renninger (Eds.), *Handbook of Child Psychology*, Vol. IV, *Child Psychology and Practice* (pp. 420–452). New York: Wiley.

Berninger, V. (in press). Defining and differentiating dysgraphia, dyslexia, and language learning disability within a working memory model. To appear in M. Mody & E. Silliman (Eds.), *Language impairment and reading disability-interactions among brain, behavior, and experience*. New York: Guilford.

Berninger, V., Abbott, R., Abbott, S., Graham, S., & Richards, T. (2002). Writing and reading: Connections between language by hand and language by eye. *Journal of Learning Disabilities, 35*, 39–56.

Berninger, V. Abbott, R., Jones, J., Wolf, B., Gould, L., Anderson-Youngstrom, M., Shimada, S., & Apel, K. (2006). Early development of language by hand: Composing-, reading-, listening-, and speaking- connections, three letter writing modes, and fast mapping in spelling. *Developmental Neuropsychology, 29*, 61–92.

Berninger, V., Abbott, R., Thomson, J., & Raskind, W. (2001). Language phenotype for reading and writing disability: A family approach. *Scientific Studies in Reading, 5*, 59–105.

Berninger, V., Abbott, R., Thomson, J., Wagner, R., Swanson, H. L., Wijsman, E. & Raskind, W. (2006). Modeling developmental phonological core deficits within a working-memory architecture in children and adults with developmental dyslexia. *Scientific Studies in Reading, 10*, 165–198.

Berninger, V., Abbott, R., Vermeulen, K., & Fulton, C. (2006). Paths to reading comprehension in at-risk second grade readers. *Journal of Learning Disabilities, 39*, 334–351.

Berninger, V., Abbott, R., Whitaker, D., Sylvester, L., & Nolen, S. (1995). Integrating low-level skills and high-level skills in treatment protocols for writing disabilities. *Learning Disability Quarterly, 18,* 293–309.

Berninger, V., & Abbott, S. (2003). *PAL Research-supported reading and writing lessons.* San Antonio, TX: Harcourt.

Berninger, V., & Amtmann, D. (2003). Preventing written expression disabilities through early and continuing assessment and intervention for handwriting and/or spelling problems: Research into practice. In H.L . Swanson, K. Harris, & S. Graham (Eds.), *Handbook of Research on Learning Disabilities* (pp. 345–363). New York: Guilford.

Berninger, V., Cartwright, A., Yates, C., Swanson, H. L., & Abbott, R. (1994). Developmental skills related to writing and reading acquisition in the intermediate grades: Shared and unique variance. *Reading and Writing: An Interdisciplinary Journal, 6,* 161–196.

Berninger, V., Dunn, A., Lin, S., & Shimada, S. (2004). School evolution: Scientist-practitioner educators creating optimal learning environments for ALL students. *Journal of Learning Disabilities, 37,* 500–508.

Berninger, V., & Fuller, F. (1992). Gender differences in orthographic, verbal, and compositional fluency: Implications for diagnosis of writing disabilities in primary grade children. *Journal of School Psychology, 30,* 363–382.

Berninger, V., Fuller, F., & Whitaker, D. (1996). A process approach to writing development across the life span. *Educational Psychology Review, 8,* 193–218.

Berninger, V., & Hidi, S. (2006). Mark Twain's writers' workshop: A nature-nurture perspective in motivating students with learning disabilities to compose. In S. Hidi, & P. Boscolo (Eds.), *Motivation in writing* (pp. 159–179). Amsterdam: Elsevier.

Berninger, V., Nagy, W., Richards, T., & Raskind, W. (in press). Developmental dyslexia: A developmental neurolinguistic approach. To appear in G. Rickheit and Hans Strohner (Eds.) *Communicative Competence of the Individual* Handbook of Applied Linguistics (HAL). New York: de Gruyter.

Berninger, V., & Richards, T. (2002). *Brain literacy for educators and psychologists.* New York: Academic.

Berninger, V., & Rutberg, J. (1992). Relationship of finger function to beginning writing: Application to diagnosis of writing disabilities. *Developmental Medicine & Child Neurology, 34,* 155–172.

Berninger, V., Rutberg, J., Abbott, R., Garcia, N., Anderson-Youngstrom, M., Brooks, A., & Fulton, C. (2006). Tier 1 and Tier 2 early intervention for handwriting and composing. *Journal of School Psychology, 44,* 3–30.

Berninger, V., & Swanson, H.L. (1994). Modifying Hayes & Flower's model of skilled writing to explain beginning and developing writing. In E. Butterfield (Ed.), *Children's writing: Toward a process theory of development of skilled writing* (pp. 57–81). Greenwich, CT: JAI Press.

Berninger, V., Vaughan, K., Abbott, R., Abbott, S., Brooks, A., Rogan, L., Reed, E., & Graham, S. (1997). Treatment of handwriting fluency problems in beginning writing: Transfer from handwriting to composition. *Journal of Educational Psychology, 89,* 652–666.

Berninger, V., Vaughan, K., Abbott, R., Begay, K., Byrd, K., Curtin, G., Minnich, J., & Graham, S. (2002). Teaching spelling and composition alone and together: Implications for the simple view of writing. *Journal of Educational Psychology, 94,* 291–304.

Berninger, V., Vaughan, K., Abbott, R., Brooks, A., Abbott, S., Reed, E., Rogan, L., & Graham, S. (1998). Early intervention for spelling problems: Teaching spelling units of varying size within a multiple connections framework. *Journal of Educational Psychology, 90,* 587–605.

Berninger, V., Vaughan, K., Abbott, R., Brooks, A., Begay, K., Curtin, G., Byrd, K., & Graham, S. (2000). Language-based spelling instruction: Teaching children to make multiple connections between spoken and written words. *Learning Disability Quarterly, 23,* 117–135.

Berninger, V., & Whitaker, D. (1993). Theory-based, branching diagnosis of writing disabilities. *School Psychology Review, 22,* 623–642.

Berninger, V., Whitaker, D., Feng, Y., Swanson, H.L., & Abbott, R. (1996). Assessment of planning, translating, and revising in junior high writers. *Journal of School Psychology, 34,* 23–52.

Berninger, V., & Winn, W. (2006). Implications of advancements in brain research and technology for writing development, writing instruction, and educational evolution. In C. MacArthur, S. Graham, & J. Fitzgerald (Eds.), *Handbook of Writing Research* (pp. 96–114). New York: Guilford.

Berninger, V., Winn, W., Stock, P., Abbott, R., Eschen, K., Cindy Lin, Noelia Garcia, Marcy Anderson-Youngstrom, Heather Murphy, Lovitt, D., Trivedi, P., Jones, J., Dagmar Jones, & Nagy, W. (in press). Tier 3 specialized writing instruction for students with dyslexia. *Reading and Writing. An Interdisciplinary Journal.*

Berninger, V., Yates, C., & Lester, K. (1991). Multiple orthographic codes in acquisition of reading and writing skills. *Reading and Writing. An Interdisciplinary Journal, 3,* 115–149.

Berninger, V., Yates, C., Cartwright, A., Rutberg, J., Remy, E., & Abbott, R. (1992). Lower-level developmental skills in beginning writing. *Reading and Writing. An Interdisciplinary Journal, 4,* 257–280.

Britton, J. (1978). The composing processes and the functions of writing. In C. Cooper & D. Odell (Eds.), *Research on composing: Points of departure* (pp. 13–28). Urbana, IL: National Council of Teachers of English.

Brooks, Allison D. (2003). Neuropsychological processes related to persisting reversal errors in dyslexia and dysgraphia. *Dissertation Abstracts International, 63*(11-A), p. 3850.

Brooks, A., Vaughan, K., & Berninger, V. (1999). Tutorial interventions for writing disabilities: Comparison of transcription and text generation processes. *Learning Disability Quarterly, 22,* 183–191.

Brown, A. (1992). Design experiments. Theoretical and methodological challenges in creating complex interventions in classroom settings. *The Journal of the Learning Sciences, 2,* 141–178.

Calkins, L. (1986). *The art of teaching writing.* Portsmouth, NH: Heinemann.

Chenault, B., Thomson, J., Abbott, R., & Berninger, V. (2006). Effects of prior attention training on child dyslexics' response to composition instruction. *Developmental Neuropsychology, 29,* 243–260.

Clay, M. (1982). Research update on learning and teaching writing: A developmental perspective. *Language Arts, 59,* 65–70.

Connelly, V., Campbell, S., MacLean, M., & Barnes, J. (2006). Contribution of lower-order skills to the written composition of college students with and without dyslexia. *Developmental Neuropsychology, 29,* 175–196.

Connor, C., Morrison, F., & Katch, L. (2004). Beyond the reading wars: Exploring the effect of child-instruction interactions on growth in early reading. *Scientific Studies of Reading, 8,* 305–336.

Englert, C. S. (1992). Writing instruction from a sociocultural perspective: The holistic dialogue, and social enterprise of writing. *Journal of Learning Disabilities, 25,* 153–172.

Englert, C.S., Raphael, T., Anderson, L., Anthony, H., & Stevens, D. (1991). Making strategies and self-talk visible: Writing instruction in regular and special education classrooms. *American Educational Research Journal, 28,* 337–372.

Gough, P., & Hillinger, M (1980). Learning to read: An unnatural act. *Bulletin of the Orton Society, 30,* 179–196.

Graham, S., Berninger, V., Abbott, R., Abbott, S., & Whitaker, D. (1997). The role of mechanics in composing of elementary school students: A new methodological approach. *Journal of Educational Psychology, 89*(1), 170–182.

Graham, S., Berninger, V., & Weintraub, N. (1998). But they use both manuscript and cursive letters—A study of the relationship of handwriting style with speed and quality. *Journal of Educational Research, 91,* 290–296.

Graham, S., Berninger, V., Weintraub, N., & Schafer, W. (1997). The development of handwriting speed and legibility in grades 1 through 9. *Journal of Educational Research, 92,* 42–52.

Graham, S., & Harris, K. (2005). *Writing Better. Effective Strategies for Teaching Students with Learning Difficulties.* Baltimore: Paul H. Brookes.

Graham, S., Harris, K., & Fink, B. (2000). Is handwriting causally related to learning to write? Treatment of handwriting problems in beginning writers. *Journal of Educational Psychology, 92,* 620–633.

Graham, S., Harris, K., & Fink-Chorzempa, B. (2002). Contributions of spelling instruction to the spelling, writing, and reading of poor spellers. *Journal of Educational Psychology, 94,* 669–686.

Graham, S., Weintraub, N., & Berninger, V. (2001). Which manuscript letters do primary grade children write legibly? *Journal of Educational* Psychology, 93, 488–497.

Graves, D. (1983). *Writing: Teachers and children at work.* Exeter, NH: Heinemann.

Hart, T., Berninger, V. & Abbott, R. (1997). Comparison of teaching single or multiple orthographic-phonological connections for word recognition and spelling: Implications for instructional consultation. *School Psychology Review,26,* 279–297.

Hayes, J. R. (1996). A new framework for understanding cognition and affect in writing. In C. M. Levy, & S. Randall (Eds.), *The science of writing: Theories, methods, individual differences, and applications* (pp. 1–27). Mahwah, NJ: Erlbaum.

Hayes, J. R. (2000). A new framework for understanding cognition and affect in writing. In R. Indrisano, & J. R. Squire (Eds.), *Perspectives on writing* (pp. 6–44). Newark, DE: International Reading Association.

Hayes, J., R., & Flower, L. S. (1980). Identifying the organization of writing processes. In L. W.Gregg, & E. R. Steinberg (Eds.), *Cognitive processes in writing* (pp. 3–30). Hillsdale, NJ: Erlbaum.

Hillocks, G. (1986). *Research on written composition: New directions for teaching.* Urbana, IL: National Conference on Research in English.

Hooper, S.R., Swartz, C., Wakely, M.B., de Kruif, R.E., & Montgomery, J. (2002). Executive functions in elementary school children with and without problems in written expression. *Journal of Learning Disabilities, 35*(1), 57–68.

Hooper, S., Wakely, M., de Kruif, R., & Schwartz, C. (2006). Aptitude-treatment interactions revisited: Effect of metacognitive intervention on subtypes of written expression in elementary school students. *Developmental Neurospsychology, 39,* 217–242.

Jones, D. (2004, December). *Automaticity of the transcription Process in the production of written text.* Doctor of Philosophy Thesis, Graduate School of Education, University of Queensland, Australia.

Jones, D., & Cristensen, C. (1999). The relationship between automaticity in handwriting and students' ability to generate written text. *Journal of Educational Psychology, 91,* 44–49.

Kellogg, R. (1994). *The psychology of writing.* New York: Oxford University.

Liberman, A. (1999). The reading researcher and the reading teacher need the right theory of speech. *Scientific Studies of Reading, 3,* 95–111.

Molfese, V., Beswick, J., Molnar, A., & Jacobi-Vessels, J. (2006). Alphabet skills in preschool: A preliminary study of letter naming and letter writing. *Developmental Neuropsychology, 29,* 5–19.

Nagy, W., Berninger, V., & Abbott, R. (2006). Contributions of morphology beyond phonology to literacy outcomes of upper elementary and middle school students. *Journal of Educational Psychology, 98, 134–147.*

Nagy, W., Berninger, V., Abbott, R., Vaughan, K., & Vermeulen, K. (2003). Relationship of morphology and other language skills to literacy skills in at-risk second graders and at-risk fourth grade writers. *Journal of Educational Psychology, 95,* 730–742.

Peverley, S. (2006). The importance of handwriting speed in adult writing. Implications for automaticity and working memory. *Developmental Neuropsychology, 29,* 197–216.

Psychological Corporation. (2003). *Wechler Individual Intelligence Test for Children, 4th Edition.* San Antonio, TX: Psychological Corporation.

Rice, J. M. (1913). *Scientific management in education.* New York: Hinds Noble & Eldredge.

Richards, T., Aylward, E., Berninger, V., Field, K., Parsons, A., Richards, A., & Nagy, W. (2006). Individual fMRI activation in orthographic mapping and morpheme mapping after orthographic or morphological spelling treatment in child dyslexics. *Journal of Neurolinguistics, 19,* 56–86.

Richards, T., Berninger, V., Nagy, W., Parsons, A., Field, K., Richards, A. (2005). Brain activation during language task contrasts in children with and without dyslexia: Inferring mapping processes and assessing response to spelling instruction. *Educational and Child Psychology, 22*(2), 62–80.

Scardamalia, M., & Bereiter, C. (1983). The development of evaluative, diagnostic,and remedial capabilities in children's composing. In M. Martlew (Ed.), *The psychology of written language: Development and educational perspectives* (pp. 67–95). London: Wiley.

Swanson, H.L., & Berninger, V. (1996a). Individual differences in children's working memory and writing skills. *Journal of Experimental Child Psychology, 63,* 358–385.

Swanson, H.L., & Berninger, V. (1996b). Individual differences in children's writing: A function of working memory or reading or both processes? *Reading and Writing. An Interdisciplinary Journal, 8,* 357–383.

Traweek, D., & Berninger, V. (1997). Comparison of beginning literacy programs: Alternative paths to the same learning outcome. *Learning Disability Quarterly, 20,* 160–168.

Troia, G., & Graham, S. (2002). The effectiveness of a highly explicit, teacher-directed strategy instruction routine: Changing the writing performance of students with learning disabilities. *Journal of Learning Disabilities, 35,* 290–305.

Troia, G., Graham, S., & Harris, K. (1999). Teaching students with learning disabilities to mindfully plan when writing. *Exceptional Children, 65,* 235–252.

Troia, G. A., & Maddox, M. E. (2004). Writing instruction in middle schools: Special and general education teachers share their views and voice their concerns. *Exceptionality, 12,* 19–37.

Whitaker, D., Berninger, V., Johnston, J., & Swanson, L. (1994). Intraindividual differences in levels of language in intermediate grade writers: Implications for the translating process. *Learning and Individual Differences, 6,* 107–130.

Wijsman, E., Peterson, D., Leutennegger, A., Thomson, J., Goddard, K., Hsu, L., Berninger, V., & Raskind, W. (2000). Segregation analysis of phenotypic components of learning disabilities I. Nonword memory and digit span. *American Journal of Human Genetics, 67,* 631–646.

Wong, B. Y. L. (1989). Critical knowledge and skills required in effective teaching and management of individual differences in the general education classroom. *Teacher Education and Special Education, 12,* 161–163.

Wong, B. Y. L. (1994). Instructional parameters promoting transfer of learned strategies in students with learning disabilities. *Learning Disability Quarterly, 17,* 110–120.

Wong, B. Y. L. (1997). Research on genre-specific strategies for enhancing writing in adolescents with learning disabilities. *Learning Disability Quarterly, 20,* 140–159.

Wong, B. Y. L. (1998). Analyses of instrinsic and extrinsic problems in use of the scaffolding metaphor in learning disabilities intervention research: An introduction. *Journal of Learning Disabilities 31,* 340–343.

Wong, B. Y. L. (2000). Writing strategies for instruction for expository essays for adolescents with and without learning disabilities. *Topics in Language Disorders, 20:* 29–44.

Wong, B. Y. L. (2001). Pointers for literacy instruction from educational technology and research on writing instruction. *The Elementary School Journal, 101,* 359–369.

Wong, B. Y. L., Butler, D. L., Ficzere, S. A., & Kuperis, S. (1996). Teaching adolescents with learning disabilities and low achievers to plan, write, and revise opinion essays. *Journal of Learning Disabilities, 29,* 197–212.

Wong, B. Y. L., Butler, D. L., Ficzere, S. A., & Kuperis, S. (1997). Teaching adolescents with learning disabilities and low achievers to plan, write, and revise compare- and contrast- essays. *Learning Disabilities Research & Practice, 12,* 2–15.

Wong, B. Y. L., Butler, D. L., Ficzere, S. A., Kuperis, S., & Corden, M. (1994). Teaching problem learners revision skills and sensitivity to audience through two instructional modes: Student-teacher versus student-student interactive dialogues. *Learning Disabilities Research & Practice, 9,* 78–90.

Wong, B.Y. L., Wong, R., Darlington, D., & Jones, W. (1991). Interactive teaching: An effective way to teach revision skills to adolescents with learning disabilities. *Learning Disabilities Research & Practice, 6,* 117–127.

Yates, C., Berninger, V., & Abbott, R. (1994). Writing problems in intellectually gifted children. *Journal for the Education of the Gifted, 18,* 131–155.

# 11

# Effective Mathematics Instruction

## Marjorie Montague and Delinda van Garderen

Students in our nation's schools consistently perform poorly on state (e.g., Florida Comprehensive Assessment Test; FCAT), national (e.g., National Assessment of Educational Progress, NAEP, 2003), and international mathematics tests (e.g., Third International Mathematics and Science Study; Beatty, 1997). The National Council of Teachers of Mathematics (NCTM) first responded to the poor performance of students in 1989 with the publication of *Curriculum and Evaluation NCTM Standards for School Mathematics* (NCTM, 1989) and again in 2000 with the revised *Principles and NCTM Standards for School Mathematics* (NCTM, 2000). NCTM called attention to the dismal mathematics performance of students and called for a more meaningful approach to teaching and learning mathematics. While these standards have helped educators generally to improve many students' mathematics learning, they have had little impact on mathematics instruction for students with learning and behavioral disorders, who represent a significant challenge for teachers.

These students fare much worse than their peers in most academic areas, but particularly in mathematics, putting them at great risk for school dropout and poor post-secondary outcomes. There has been a persistent performance gap in mathematics between students with and without disabilities (NAEP, 2003). For example, NAEP 2003 results indicated that 71% of students with disabilities contrasted with 27% of students without disabilities scored below the basic level. In keeping with the No Child Left Behind Act (NCLB, 2001), all students, including students with disabilities, must meet high standards in mathematics as measured by state-administered achievement tests. To meet these standards in mathematics, students with disabilities, who vary considerably in ability, achievement, and motivation, must develop the necessary mathematical concepts, skills, and applications needed not only to perform well on mathematics assessments but also to apply these skills successfully in real world settings. Contributing to the problem is that teachers often do not have the necessary content or pedagogical knowledge or understanding in how to teach mathematics, especially when students have diverse learning and behavioral needs. With the current move toward full inclusion in our schools, it is critical that teachers become familiar with proven instructional practices and procedures for teaching students with special learning and behavioral needs. Curricular materials and teaching methodology consistent with the NCTM *Standards* need adaptation if these students are to be successful (Woodward, 2006). Typical mathematics curricula and instructional practice reflective of the *Standards* have been found to be too complex, unstructured, and confusing for most students with learning and behavioral problems (Baxter, Woodward, & Olson, 2001; Woodward & Baxter, 1997).

Fortunately, researchers have been conducting intervention research, primarily in reading, for the past 25 years to identify the most effective instructional practices to address the myriad characteristics of students with learning and behavioral disorders. For example, Swanson's (1999) meta-analysis of intervention studies in learning disabilities (LD) found direct instruction and cognitive strategy instruction, approaches that have many commonalities, to be the most powerful interventions for students with LD. Both approaches can be used across domains, including mathematics. Both approaches incorporate numerous research-based practices and procedures such as cueing, modeling, verbal rehearsal, and feedback. Instruction is highly structured and organized with appropriate cues and prompts built in, leading to mastery of new concepts, skills, and applications and eventual automaticity of responses.

Direct instruction typically focuses on basic skills and utilizes scripted lessons that are teacher-directed and fast-paced. In contrast, cognitive strategy instruction focuses on teaching students the process of learning (e.g., Montague, 2003). The instructional method underlying cognitive strategy instruction is explicit instruction, which is more interactive than direct instruction. In essence, students learn to think and behave like proficient learners as they apply various cognitive processes and self-regulation strategies. To illustrate, for mathematical problem solving, students learn to read, analyze, evaluate, and verify math problems using comprehension processes such as paraphrasing, visualization, and planning as well as self-regulation strategies including self-instruction, self-questioning, and self-checking (Montague, 2006).

In their meta-analysis, Kroesbergen and Van Luit (2003) reviewed mathematics interventions for elementary school children with special educational needs, i.e., across disabilities. Corroborating Swanson's findings, they concluded that self-instruction, a self-regulation strategy and component of cognitive strategy instruction, is the most effective method for teaching math problem solving; direct instruction is most effective for teaching basic skills; and both are superior to mediated/assisted instruction, i.e., peer tutoring or computer-assisted instruction, for teaching mathematics generally. A review specifically of self-management intervention studies targeting academic outcomes for students with emotional and behavioral disorders (EBD) included 22 studies, 11 focused on mathematics and 10 of the 11 on math calculation skills. Self-monitoring interventions predominated in these studies. A large positive effect size was found for the math interventions and improved performance seemed to maintain over time, indicating self-monitoring may be an effective intervention for learning and maintaining basic mathematics skills (Mooney, Ryan, Uhing, Reid, & Epstein, 2005).

Another review of math interventions for students with EBD included 13 studies conducted between 1985 and 2005 (Hodge, Riccomini, Buford, & Herbst, 2006). Of these, 10 focused on basic math computation skills and used student-directed interventions (i.e., self-monitoring, self-management, or self-regulated strategies such as rehearsal or mnemonics). The authors caution that self-regulation techniques are most appropriate when students have already learned the target skills. Teacher-directed instruction that is clear and includes corrective feedback and ample opportunities for practice may be necessary initially to improve students' academic performance.

The purpose of this chapter is to review evidence-based practices for teaching mathematics to students with learning and behavioral disorders. First, however, cognitive and behavioral characteristics of children and adolescents with learning and behavioral problems that may interfere with successful performance in mathematics will be described. Second, instructional practices and procedures will be discussed as they relate to levels of instruction; that is, research focusing on children in primary and intermediate elementary school as well as middle and secondary school will be described. Studies will be described, explicit examples of best practice will be provided, and conclusions will be drawn regarding "best practice." Intervention research aimed at improving mathematics performance of students with learning and behavioral disorders is very limited. The majority of the studies at the elementary level have focused on improving computation skills of students with learning and behavioral disorders. The few studies conducted with middle and secondary school students focus primarily on improving problem solving skills. Despite the paucity of research, several conclusions can be drawn regarding effective instruction in mathematics for students with learning and behavioral disorders.

## COGNITIVE AND BEHAVIORAL CHARACTERISTICS THAT INTERFERE WITH MATHEMATICS PERFORMANCE

There are a variety of cognitive characteristics that interfere with successful performance in mathematics. Geary (1993, 2003) proposed that children with mathematical disability (MD) have one or more of three subtypes of the disorder. The first subtype is deficient semantic memory. These children typically have difficulty retrieving mathematical facts or answers to simple arithmetic problems, make more errors when they do, and vary considerably on reaction time for correct retrieval. Semantic memory deficits appear to be relatively stable over time and seem to be associated with a developmental difference in that children with this deficit differ in cognitive and performance features from younger, academically typical children. The second subtype is procedural. Children with procedural deficits frequently use developmentally immature procedures similar to those used by younger, academically typical children. Procedural deficits may represent a developmental delay as they tend to improve over time. These children have difficulty retaining information in working memory and are unable to monitor their counting processes. The third subtype is visuospatial. Children with visuospatial problems have difficulties in spatially representing numerical relationships and other types of mathematical information. They frequently misinterpret or misunderstand spatially represented information. Typical problems are an inability to align and rotate numbers as well as problems in measurement, place value, and geometry.

There is consensus about the role of memory, both working memory and long-term memory, in mathematics development (Swanson & Jerman, 2006). The inability to retrieve arithmetic facts from long-term memory and the inability to store numbers in working memory has an impact on the ability to calculate, do algorithmic procedures, and solve mathematical problems. Children with MD characteristically do not show the shift from direct counting procedures to recall of the arithmetic combinations from memory (Swanson & Rhine, 1985). They do not remember certain combinations and that these combinations yield certain results, do not access certain arithmetic facts from long-term memory, and, thus, have considerable difficulty calculating.

Students with MD also have considerable difficulty translating and transforming numerical and linguistic information in mathematical word problems (Montague & Applegate, 1993). They differ significantly from nondisabled peers in their ability to represent problems, which is a critical stage in the problem solving process. Successful problem execution depends on successful problem representation. Many students with MD have serious perceptual, memory, language, and/or reasoning problems that interfere with mathematical problem solving. That is, students may have trouble reading and understanding the problem, attending to the information in the problem, identifying important information and representing that information, developing a plan to solve the problem, and computing. Even though students may have acquired the basic knowledge and skills in reading and mathematics and, therefore, should be able to carry out these cognitive activities, they often do not because of these problems. Additionally, these students often experience significant self-regulation problems that interfere with problem solving.

Students with learning and behavioral disorders characteristically are deficient in the ability to select appropriate strategies to use and to regulate themselves during academic tasks (Wong, Harris, Graham, & Butler, 2003). That is, they have self-regulation problems that prevent successful completion of tasks. These students are typically disorganized, do not know where or how to begin, lack enabling strategies, and do not evaluate what they do. The ability to regulate one's cognitive activities underlies the executive processes associated with metacognition (Flavell, 1976). Metacognition consists of both knowledge and awareness of one's cognitive strengths and weaknesses and self-regulation, the ability to coordinate that awareness with appropriate action (Wong, 1999). Metacognition develops in young children from an early age and matures during early adolescence, sometime between the ages of 11 and 14 years. Metacognitive ability is essential for successful academic performance across domains, including mathematics (Montague, 1998).

In addition to cognitive characteristics, there is a multitude of behavioral characteristics that interfere with successful math performance. For example, the behavioral symptoms of attention deficit hyperactivity disorder (ADHD) interfere with mathematics learning even for children who may have the skills but do not necessarily produce what is expected. The three symptoms associated with ADHD are inattention, impulsivity, and hyperactivity. Inattention means that an individual has difficulty sustaining attention when effort is required. Behaviors associated with inattention include carelessness, difficulty staying on task, not listening, disorganization, failure to finish schoolwork and chores, distractibility, losing things, and forgetfulness. Inattention may be less or more noticeable depending on contextual factors. Impulsive individuals seem unable to control their behaviors and appear to act without thinking. Impulsivity implies a problem with self-regulation. Hyperactivity implies an inordinate activity level. Hyperactive and impulsive behaviors include fidgeting and squirming, constant movement, inability to stay seated for a reasonable time, talking excessively, difficulty waiting or taking turns, and interrupting and intruding on others.

Finally, there are other behavioral characteristics that impact on academic performance. These characteristics, generally speaking, differentiate good and poor problem solvers and strategic learners (Montague, 2006). Students with MD typically have a limited repertoire of strategies for completing math tasks effectively and efficiently, are poorly motivated and indecisive, cannot monitor their performance by detecting and self-correcting errors, and are poor at generalizing learning across situations and settings.

## PRIMARY SCHOOL MATHEMATICS INSTRUCTION

### Computation, Number Concept, Math Fact Interventions

Failure to rapidly recall basic facts is a characteristic often associated with mathematics difficulties (Miller & Mercer, 1997). One approach for improving recall and automaticity of facts is through drill and practice. The primary advantage of such an approach is that it provides an appropriate level of challenge and time on task with plenty of opportunities for the student to respond (Burns, 2005). This is particularly important as it has been suggested that students with disabilities do not get enough opportunities to practice, which is a crucial aspect of academic remediation (Fuchs & Fuchs, 2001). Various rehearsal drill models exist, one of which has been demonstrated to work with students with disabilities at the primary level. Burns (2005) examined the effectiveness of an Incremental Rehearsal drill approach with three students with LD in the third grade to learn multiplication facts. This model uses a gradually increasing ratio of known to unknown items with the final stage of implementation at 90% known to 10% unknown. In this approach, facts are written on index cards and presented one at a time. The first unknown fact is presented. If the student answers this correctly, it is then considered a known fact. A new unknown fact is then presented. This is then followed by the known fact. This procedures repeats until all the facts, typically 10, are introduced. If the student cannot provide the correct answer within two seconds, does not know the answer, or provides an incorrect answer, the fact continues to be identified as unknown and is taught to the student.

One concern associated with the drill and practice approach is that students with disabilities often do not generalize what they have learned to other facts. It has been suggested that poor number sense, a difficulty many students with disabilities have, could be a contributing factor (Gersten & Chard, 1999). Understanding of number is a fundamental skill needed to learn topics like addition and subtraction (Woodward, 2006). Funkhouser (1995), before working on basic fact knowledge, used concrete manipulatives to develop number sense specifically to recognize the number of objects in a set without counting them. Twelve students in grades K–1 were provided a vertical display of rectangles divided into five equal squares with dots or jellybeans placed within the squares representing the numbers 0 through 5. The students represented the configurations using the jellybeans and verbally identified each by a numeral. This was then followed by discussing different combinations that could be made using the configuration. Eventually, the students were introduced to the use of the "+" symbol to produce the basic addition facts and to begin memorizing them.

Strategy instruction has also been examined as a way of teaching number concepts, basic facts, and computation. As Tournaki (2003) found in a study comparing the effectiveness of strategy instruction to drill and practice, when given a problem, even a simple basic fact, it cannot be assumed that students with disabilities have a strategy in place in order to solve it. Neither can it be assumed that strategies will change as a result of practice. Therefore, instruction should also focus on teaching students strategies for problem solving. Tournaki (2003) focused on teaching students with LD a *minimum addend* strategy. This strategy involves determining the larger addend and counting on from that cardinal value the number of units specified by the smaller addend; for example, in $4 + 5 =$, the students starts from the 5 and adds 4 more units. Students who were taught the strategy improved significantly compared to those who learned basic facts through drill and practice and a control group. Furthermore, the students with LD who learned the strategy were able to transfer what they had learned to a task that involved adding three single-digits together. Students with disabilities often do not transfer what they have learned from one task to another.

A substantial body of research exists that supports the use of the concrete-representational-abstract (C-R-A; sometimes known as concrete-semiconcrete-abstract: C-S-A) sequence for teaching primarily students with LD at the elementary school level place value (Peterson, Mercer, & O'Shea, 1988), coin sums (Miller, Mercer, & Dillon, 1992), basic facts (Mercer & Miller, 1992), and multiplication (Harris, Miller, & Mercer, 1995; Miller, Harris, Strawser, Jones, & Mercer, 1998). The first level of instruction, concrete, involves the use of three-dimensional manipulative devices to demonstrate specific mathematical concepts. When understanding of the concept at the concrete level is demonstrated, the instruction shifts to the second level of instruction, representation. At this level, students use visual depictions to represent the mathematical concept introduced at the concrete level. Again, the goal at this level like the first level is to promote conceptual understanding of the concept being presented. Finally, once conceptual understanding is obtained, the instruction shifts to the abstract level of instruction. This involves the solving of problems using number symbols without using manipulative devices or pictorial representations. At this level, students are to memorize the facts with fluency (Hudson & Miller, 2006). The C-R-A teaching sequence is taught using a four-step lesson format. The four steps include providing an advance organizer (connect the lesson to a previous lesson, identify the lesson skill, and provide a rationale for the skill being learned), demonstrating the desired skill for the student, providing guided practice with feedback, and allowing the student time for independent practice (Morin & Miller, 1998).

Self-regulation enhances learning by helping students to take control of their actions and move toward independence as they learn. Various self-regulation techniques have been researched at the primary level. Self-instruction was the foundation for a comprehensive program for improving multiplication and division skills (Van Luit & Naglieri, 1999). Participants in this study included 42 elementary school students with LD. The instruction, the MASTERS Training Program, involves an introductory phase, group practice phase, and an individual practice phase. Central to the instruction is discussion among the teacher and students of the possible solution procedures and strategies that could be used to solve the problems. Time is also spent guiding the students towards identifying various strategies and determining which will be the most effective for solving the problems. Self-instruction is built into the program throughout, for example, by teacher modeling. Results indicated a significant improvement compared with the general instructional program. The students with LD generalized the self-instruction procedure to more difficult problems.

In another study, Kroesbergen and Van Luit (2002) worked on multiplication facts with 75 students, 27 with a disability, aged 7 to 13 years. Some students received the instruction using the MASTERS Training Program or guided instruction. Others had more structured instruction which differed from the guided instruction in that the children did not actively contribute to the lessons but were required to use the procedures the teachers taught them. In the structured instruction, self-instruction is promoted by means of a strategy decision sheet that contains various questions (e.g., What is the multiplication problem? Do I know the answer if I reverse the problem?) used by students as they learn the different strategies. Students in both instructional programs improved compared to those who received instruction based on the regular curriculum method. Further, students in the guided instruction group did perform better than the students in the other groups on a task that required them to transfer what they have learned. Overall, however, the students without disabilities were found to benefit most from the guided instruction while the students in special education programs benefited more from the structured instruction.

Three studies (Fuchs, Fuchs, Hamlett, Phillips, & Bentz, 1994; Fuchs, Fuchs, Karns, Hamlett, Phillips, & Dukta, 1997; Fuchs, Fuchs, Phillips, Hamlett, & Karns, 1995) examined the effectiveness of using peer assisted learning strategies (PALS) with elementary students with and without disabilities (grades 2–5) in math computation and concept/application. PALS effectiveness was also examined with first-grade students with LD and ADHD with respect to mathematical development in number concept and basic facts (Fuchs, Fuchs, Yazdian, & Powell, 2002). PALS is a classwide peer-tutoring structure that involves students within a classroom working in dyads. A PALS session consists of coaching and independent practice. During coaching, the stronger math student coaches a lower ability student in solving problems. Roles are reversed at some point during each session. During the coaching, the tutor assists the student through each step of a problem, thereby providing immediate feedback and prompting when the student is having difficulty. As the tutees are solving problems, they are required to think aloud to help the tutor clarify as needed. Following coaching, the students solidify the new material learned through independent practice. The teacher monitors and awards points for cooperation and for following the verbal routines. Curriculum-based measurement (CBM) is used in conjunction with PALS. CBM is used to assist the teacher in tracking student progress, providing concrete recommendations for instruction, matching the students in the tutor-tutee dyads, and to provide the students feedback on their progress (Baker, Gersten, Dimino, & Griffiths, 2004).

Another form of tutoring is cross-age peer tutoring where an older, skill-competent student works with a younger student. Beirne-Smith (1991) investigated the effectiveness of cross-age peer tutoring for 20 students with LD from six to ten years in age to solve single-digit addition facts. The tutoring sessions involved presentation of a fact by the tutor which is then repeated by the tutee. The tutor then presented all the problems without the answers and instructed the tutee to read the problems and give the answers first in order and then in random order. The session ended with drill and practice using flashcards. The tutors were also trained to record the number of correct and incorrect responses during the flashcard review to determine which problems they would work on in the next session.

Overall, these peer-tutoring formats were found to be beneficial for all students, including students with disabilities, for increasing number sense, basic facts, math computation and math concepts/applications ability. However, to ensure the effectiveness of the tutoring, particularly for students with disabilities, it is recommended that the students are taught to work with each other. Peer explanations and support have been found to be more effective when the student's interactions are guided and structured (e.g., structured question sheet). In addition, teachers may need to adopt cooperative/competitive group reward structures. Finally, while students with LD have benefited from the intervention, they have not necessarily made the same gains as their peers without disabilities. Students with LD may benefit from supplemental activities focusing on the concepts being taught (Fuchs, Fuchs, Hamlett, Phillips, Karns, & Dukta, 1997; Fuchs et al., 1995).

## Mathematical Word Problem Solving Interventions

Wilson and Sindelar (1991), using a direct instruction approach, taught 62 students with LD in second to fifth grades to solve addition and subtraction word problems. The instruction was more effective when students were taught both a sequence for solving word problems and a strategy to determine when to add or subtract. During the strategy instruction, the students were told that "when the big number is given, subtract" and "when the big number is not given, add." Sequence instruction involved the use of questions such as "What numbers are given in the problem?" or "What are we supposed to find?" to prompt the students to see the information in the problem.

Marsh and Cooke (1996) taught three third-grade students with LD to use manipulatives (Cuisenaire rods) to solve one-step arithmetic word problems. Initially, the students were given a procedure to use to analyze and solve word problems. Following this, the students reviewed the Cuisenaire rod terms such as the word "set" where the students were to show "two sets of five." Using a word problem, they represented any numerical value with rods. Students were then guided to position the rods to show what the problem was asking them to do. The students then held up a flashcard indicating which operation they had to use to solve the problem. If correct, the student recorded the numbers on a worksheet along with the symbol for the operation to solve it. All the students improved in their ability to solve arithmetic word problems. Interestingly, the findings of this study suggest that it may not be necessary to use all three levels of instruction as presented in the C-S-A/C-R-A approach. The students in this study were able to move from concrete to abstract without requiring intermediate training with semi-concrete representations.

Cassel and Reid (1996) taught two students with LD and two students with mild mental retardation in the third and fourth grade to solve addition and subtraction word problems using a strategy combined with self-generated instructions presented based on principles of strategy instruction recommended by Harris and Graham (1993). The steps of the strategy, "FAST DRAW," were: (a) read the problem out loud (b) find and highlight the question and write the label, (c) ask what are the parts of the problem and circle the numbers needed, (d) set up the problem by writing and labeling the numbers; (e) re-read the problem and tie down the sign, (f) discover the sign—recheck the operation, (g) read the number problem, (h) answer the number problem, and (i) write the answer and check by asking if the answer makes sense. As the students used the strategy, they referred to a check list of self-generated instructions: (a) problem definition, "What is it I have to do?"; (b) planning, "How can I solve this problem?"; (c) strategy use, "FAST DRAW will help me organize my problem solving and remember all the things I need to do"; (d) self-monitor, "To help me remember what I have done, I can check off the steps of the strategy as they are completed"; (e) self-evaluation, "How am I doing? Did I complete all the steps?"; and (f) self-reinforcement, "Great, I'm half way through the strategy." All the students were able to learn and implement the strategy with improved performance for all students in solving word problems.

Owen and Fuchs (2002) examined the effects of a strategy to solve mathematical word problems that required third-grade students with LD in mathematics to find half of a particular number. The strategy the students were taught involved six steps which required the student to read the problem, generate a representation (e.g., circles of the number for which you will find half), and to use the representation to solve the problem. Instruction began in a large-group followed by the students working with a partner (high achieving and low achieving student) on practice problems. Compared with a control group, the students who received the entire intervention improved in both number of problems solved and accuracy of those solved.

In an attempt to move beyond typical textbook problems, Fuchs, Fuchs, Hamlett, and Appleton (2002) taught 62 students with LD in mathematics how to solve story problems, transfer story problems, and real-world math problems. Students who received an intervention got either tutoring and/or computer assisted practice. As a part of the intervention, the students were taught underlying concepts and rules for solving problems and given explicit instruction on transferring skills learned. Each session began with teacher demonstration and guided practice followed by peer-tutoring. The tutoring format involved pairing a stronger student with a weaker student. The computer assisted practice focused on solving real-life problems. Guided feedback in the form of tips was provided throughout to help improve their responses. Overall, improvements were noted for the students who received the tutoring or tutoring with computer assisted practice to solve story problems and transfer story problems. Improvements were not found in solving real-world math problems. Interestingly, while students who received the computer practice instruction alone did improve, overall, the computer-assisted practice added little extra value. It is possible that the software needed further work to incorporate more and better elaborated instruction. What the computer assisted practice may be best for, however, is reducing the amount of teacher time required to enhance problem solving.

## INTERMEDIATE ELEMENTARY MATHEMATICS INSTRUCTION

### Computation and Math Fact Interventions

As with younger students, drill and practice can be used with older students. Cooke and Reichard (1996) examined the effectiveness of the Interspersal Drill Ratio approach with six fifth-grade students with LD or EBD to learn multiplication and division facts. This approach involves using a predetermined ratio of known (e.g., 70%) to unknown facts (e.g., 30%). Initially, the teacher determines what facts the students do and do not know. Using that information, two groups of facts are written on flashcards and divided into two piles based on a predetermined ratio. Individually, the facts are presented to the student who is given two seconds to respond with the answer. Depending on the response, corrective feedback or praise is given. When the set is completed, the cards are shuffled and another round begins. At the end of the session, a mastery test is given. Each flashcard is shown to the student, again for two seconds. If the response is correct, the card is placed in the pile of known facts. The ratio of known to unknown facts may differ for each student; however, Cooke and Reichard did find that the majority of students were able to master the facts at a faster rate where 70% were unknown and 30% were known. An additional element in this study was the use of a peer tutor. Peer-tutors, prior to the tutoring sessions, were trained via role-plays on how to present the flashcards and provide corrective feedback or praise.

Originally developed to improve spelling performance, Cover, Copy, and Compare (CCC), a memorization technique, has also been shown to increase mathematics accuracy, fluency, and maintenance of math facts with 12 students with EBD at the intermediate level (Skinner, Bamberg, Smith, & Powell, 1993; Skinner, Ford, & Yunker, 1991; Skinner, Turco, Beatty, & Rasavage, 1989). The basic steps of the strategy involve having students look at an item and solution, cover the item and solution, write the item and solution, and compare their written response to the original example. If the written response matches the sample, the student then moves on to the next problem (Skinner et al., 1991). The written response could also be combined with a verbal response, or could be a verbal response alone. This strategy has also been found to be effective with students in higher grade levels (e.g., 10th grade) (Skinner et al., 1989. Mnemonic techniques have been found to be effective for memorizing multiplication facts for students with LD in fourth grade and up (Greene, 1999; Wood, Frank, & Wacker, 1998). These include:

1. Pegwords or pegword phrases: With this technique, numbers are connected to a pegword such as 6 = sticks, 7 = heaven, 42 = warty two. Students are to learn a pegword for all the corresponding numbers that will be used. Following this, math facts are then written on a flashcard with a pegword phrase and a picture that matches the phrase (e.g., "$6 \times 7 = 42$; sticks in heaven with a warty shoe") (Greene, 1999).

2. Visual mnemonic for doubles: Picture flashcards of objects are used for two-times math facts. For example, a skateboard—two sets of two wheels; a six-pack of pop—two sets of three cans; a toy spider—two sets of four legs. To use this mnemonic, first find the two in the math fact and then remember the double picture related to the other number that would provide the answer (Wood, Frank, & Wacker, 1998).

3. Mnemonic for fives: This strategy works for students who can count by fives. The students are then given simple steps to follow: first identify the fact as a fives fact and then count by fives to solve the problem (Wood, Frank, & Wacker, 1998).

4. Linking strategy: this strategy can be used for facts in the nines category. Students are first shown which numbers from 1 through 8 are linked: 1-8, 2-7, 3-6, 4-5. When they have memorized this, they are first taught to identify if the math fact presented is in the nines category. Then they are to take the number the 9 is being multiplied by and subtract one. This is then placed in the tens column. The number linked to that number is then placed in the ones column. For example, for $9 \times 5$, subtract 1 from the 5 and write then answer in the tens column (i.e., 4). Then, identify the linking number with the 4 (i.e., 5) and write it in the ones column. The answer is then 45 (Wood, Frank, & Wacker, 1998).

Even though use of mnemonics can be effective, they can take time to learn and use. For example, Wood et al. used an instructional package to teach the students the various mnemonic techniques. This included: (a) presentation of the facts in a structured sequence (e.g., facts involving zero and ones were taught first followed by doubles, and so on); (b) teaching students how to classify the facts into one of six categories (e.g., zeros, ones, doubles, fives, nines, and the remaining facts); (c) introduction to the mnemonic procedures, (d) learning the various steps for each mnemonic, and (e) using self-instruction in selecting and executing the strategies. Unlike the more "traditional" classroom methods, the mnemonic techniques were effective in helping students who had difficulty with fact recall.

Several studies at the intermediate level have focused on using self-instructions to complete addition and subtraction computation problems. Wood, Rosenberg, and Carran (1993) taught nine students with LD, 8 to 11 years old, to use step-by-step instructions (e.g., Step 1: First, I have to point to the problem. Step 2: Second, I have to read the problem. Step 3: Third, I have to circle the sign). They recorded their visualizations and played them as they solved problems. Dunlap and Dunlap (1989) gave three students with LD (1 in 5th grade and two in 6th grade) individualized self-monitoring checklists based on errors they made when solving the problems. The checklists contained specific reminders (e.g., I copied the problem correctly. All the numbers on the top are bigger than the numbers on the bottom.), which the students would reference and check off as they complete each problem. Jolivette, Wehby, and Hirsch (1999) taught three students with EBD in fourth grade three of six possible strategies to solve subtraction problems. The strategies were: (1) Bottom First—a visual cue to being in the ones column with the bottom number; (2) Permanent Model—a visual model of a correctly solved problem with regrouping; (3) Say It Before You Do It—verbal phrase (e.g., "If the bottom number is bigger than the top number, then regroup."); (4) Visual Organizer—a visual prompt such as a slash mark appearing above the column to regroup; (5) Right is Correct—visual cue to begin in the ones column and work left; and (6) Bigger on Top—verbal prompt (e.g., "Bigger on top.") to regroup so that the top number is larger than the bottom for each column. Each strategy took less than five minutes to be taught. All the students in the various studies dramatically improved in performance.

Naglieri and Gottling (1997) taught twelve 9- to 12-year-old students with LD how to use self-reflection to aid in planning and utilization of an efficient strategy to complete subtraction and multiplication problems. The students were encouraged to determine how to complete the worksheets, verbalize and discuss their ideas, explain which methods that did and did not work well to solve the problems, and be self-reflective. Students, to achieve self-reflection, were asked questions (e.g., What could you have done to get more correct?) by an instructor, to which they responded (e.g., I have to keep the columns straight). Not only did the students improve in their performance, they improved in their ability to make a plan a solution to solve a problem.

Self-monitoring of behavior as an intervention offers an alternative to other often more intrusive procedures to improve performance particularly as it requires less direct teacher intervention (Maag, Reid, & DiGangi, 1993). Several studies have focused on using self-monitoring applied to either academic or attention responses with students with LD, ADHD and/or EBD at the intermediate level in math computation (Maag et al., 1993; McDougall & Brady, 1998).Typically, students are taught to monitor either their levels of attention (e.g., on or off-task, Am I paying attention?), productivity (e.g., Am I working quickly? or number of problems completed), or accuracy (number of problems completed correctly). Students are taught to note on a form or checklist their behavior when given a cue during a math session. McDougall and Brady (1998) also taught their students to graph how many correct and incorrect digits they had computed and determine if their math fluency was improving. For improved fluency the students determined how many token points they had earned which were then exchanged for reinforcers such as sugarless gum, a blank audio cassette, or an announcement on the school intercom system about improved performance. In all the studies, the students were able to effectively and independently use the self-monitoring techniques and improved in performance to some degree. A consistent finding across the three studies is students can learn to self-monitor their productivity and accuracy.

Some researchers have used computers to teach math facts to students with LD and EBD in grades 3 through 5 (Koscinski & Gast, 1993; Landeen & Adams, 1988; Wilson et al., 1996).

In all three studies, the students who received computer instruction improved in their math fact knowledge. However, use of CAI needs further research as students who received teacher-directed instruction also improved (Landeen & Adams, 1988; Wilson et al., 1996). It is possible that "relatively simple procedures … may be more powerful when a task is less complex or when a student's needs are straightforward" (Harris, Graham, Reid, McElroy, & Hamby, 1994, p. 137). This does not necessarily mean that CAI should be ruled out. Wilson et al. point out, with the move toward inclusion in general education classrooms, teachers may have limited time to provide appropriate individualized instruction to meet their students needs. CAI instruction may be a more feasible option when students are working individually. Another issue related to CAI that needs further research is the efficacy of the specific programs used. It is unclear if a game-like format (e.g., Math Blaster) is more effective than a "paper and pencil" format. Students with disabilities seem to find the game-like programs more motivating.

## Mathematical Word Problem Solving Interventions

Of the various word problem solving procedures available, a well-researched and documented approach is schema-based strategy instruction. Schema-based strategy instruction has been shown to work with students with disabilities, including students with learning and emotional disorders in grades 2 through 8 to solve arithmetic word problems (Jitendra, Griffen, McGoey, Gardill, Bhat, & Riley, 1998; Jitendra & Hoff, 1996; Jitendra, Hoff, & Beck, 1999; Jitendra, DiPipi, & Perron-Jones, 2000; Xin, Jitendra, & Deatline-Buchman, 2005). The goal of the instruction is to help the student identify the schema, "a general description of a group of problems that share a common underlying structure" (Xin & Jitendra, 2006, p. 53), and to use that information to solve the problem.

The schema-based problem-solving model contains four separate but interrelated procedural steps: identification, representation, planning, and solution (Xin & Jitendra, 2006). Corresponding to those steps are areas of conceptual knowledge that the student will use to solve the problem: schema knowledge, elaboration knowledge, strategic knowledge, and execution knowledge. First, the student reads the problem and uses that information to identify the problem schema based on knowledge of problem schemas that exist. For example, the key phrase "3 times as many as" is a "compare" problem. Second, the student generates a schematic diagram (representation) appropriate for the schema identified. Specifically, this involves elaborating on the main features of the schema. For example, "Peter has 2 cats. Julia gave him 3 more. How many cats does Peter have now?" represents a change problem. The student will then map out the information: "2 cats" and "3 cats" and "? cats." The diagram depicts the details of the problem. Third, once the problem is represented, the student plans how to solve the problem. Planning involves setting up the final goal (what is being solved for) and, if appropriate, the subgoals (to get the answer, what else needs to be solved), selecting the appropriate operation(s), and writing the math sentence or equation. This step draws on the student's strategic knowledge, for example "when the total amount is unknown, we add to find the total." The fourth step of the model is to carry out the plan. This involves using execution knowledge techniques such as performing a skill (e.g., addition) or following an algorithm (Xin & Jitendra, 2006).

Case, Harris, and Graham (1992) worked with four students with LD in fifth and sixth grade to improve their ability to solve one-step addition and subtraction word problems. They were taught a five-step procedure for solving word problems: (a) read the problem out loud, (b) look for important words and circle them, (c) draw pictures to tell what is happening, (d) write down the math sentence, and (e) write down the answer. As part of the instruction, the students self-generated instructions to use when solving the problem to guide and direct behavior: (a) problem definition (e.g., "What is it I have to do?"), (b) planning (e.g., "How can I solve this problem?"), (c) strategy use (e.g., "The five-step strategy will help me look for important words."), (d) self-evaluation (e.g., "How am I doing?"), and (e) self-reinforcement (e.g., "I did a nice job."). To teach the students how to use the strategy and self-regulate their performance, the instructors introduced the steps and then modeled the procedures using a think aloud strategy, had the students rehearse the strategy until memorized, provided guided practice with corrective feedback and reinforcement, provided independent practice, and reminded the students to use the strategy whenever they solved word problems in other classroom situations. All students improved in performance for both addition and subtraction problems. Further, the students generalized what they had learned to other classroom settings.

The majority of research using computers in math with students with disabilities has focused on basic math facts. Shiah, Mastropieri, Scruggs, and Mushiniski Fulk (1995), however, examined the effectiveness of a computer-assisted tutorial program to learn math problem-solving with 30 students with LD in grades one to six. The computer program incorporated a seven-step strategy for solving word problems: (a) read the problem, (b) think about the problem, (c) decide the operation sign, (d) write the math sentence, (e) do the problem, (f) label the answer, and (g) check every step. The tutorial program involved several parts: a demonstration how to solve a word problem using the seven-steps, guided practice, and independent practice. The students worked thorough the problems presented at their own pace. The program prompted the students what to do and to make changes when and where necessary. The findings in this study supported the use of CAI instruction for students with LD as all the students improved in their performance to solve word problems. One concern in this study was the lack of transfer from computer to paper and pencil tasks.

## MIDDLE SCHOOL MATHEMATICS INSTRUCTION

Only eight studies with middle school students were located. Three of these used direct instruction to teach computation skills (Rivera & Smith, 1988; Scarlato & Burr, 2002; Witzel, Mercer, & Miller, 2003), and five employed strategy instruction to improve problem solving performance (Jitendra, DiPipi, & Perron-Jones, 2002; Jitendra et al., 1999; Xin et al., 2005, Montague, 1992; Montague, Applegate, & Marquard, 1993). As noted previously, direct instruction and cognitive strategy instruction were found to be the most effective interventions for students with LD across domains (Swanson, 1999).

Rivera and Smith (1988) devised an instructional routine, termed *Demonstration Plus Permanent Model*, for teaching long division to eight students with LD. In this routine, the teacher first demonstrated the steps in the algorithm as she solved a simple long division problem and then used this correct solution as the permanent model. The teacher then provided corrective feedback as students imitated the teacher demonstration with similar problems. After solving a problem correctly, students were allowed to work additional problems independently. The same procedure was used with more difficult long division problems until mastery was achieved on problems with and without remainders. All students improved substantially in minimal time (2 to 9 days). Scarlato and Burr (2002) based their instructional routine on Stein, Silbert, and Carnine's (1997) model of direct instruction to teach four seventh-grade students with LD fraction and decimal skills. Again, effective instructional practices associated with direct instruction were incorporated, i.e., modeling, guided and independent practice, cumulative review, multiple examples, immediate and corrective feedback, and mastery criteria. Following 20 weeks of instruction, the students outperformed a comparison group on both standardized and informal assessments.

Witzel et al. (2003) used the concrete-to-representational-to-abstract (C-R-A) sequence described earlier in the chapter to teach students with LD or at risk how to solve algebraic transformation equations. Thirty-four pairs of middle school students were matched on achievement score, age, pretest score, and class performance. Half the students received typical textbook instruction, while the other half received C-R-A instruction. Each lesson had four steps: introduce the lesson, model the new procedure, guide students through procedures, and have students work independently. These steps were followed for instruction at each level of the C-R-A model. At the concrete level, manipulatives were used, at the representational level, pictures were used, and at the abstract level, symbols only. Students who received C-R-A instruction significantly outperformed peers on both the posttest and follow-up test, each requiring solutions to 27 algebraic transformation equations.

Jitendra's model, Schema-Based Strategy Instruction, was the intervention for two single-subject studies and one group study to improve math problem solving for middle school students with LD (Jitendra et al., 2002; Jitendra et al., 1999; Xin et al., 2005). Jitendra's model, as described in the elementary school section of this chapter, was effective in teaching young students to solve various types of addition and subtraction problems. In her middle school studies, students were taught the schemata for multiplication and division problems, i.e., the multiplicative compare problem schema and the proportion problem schema. The following problem is an example of a multiplicative compare problem: Juan earned $15 raking leaves. This was one-third as much as Jennifer made. How much did Jennifer earn? Students learned that a multiplicative compare problem always includes a referent set, a compared set, and a statement that relates the compared set to the referent set. In this problem, the compared set is $15, one-third is the relation, and the referent set is unknown. Prompt sheets are provided initially and then faded as students learn to recognize the schema and apply the strategy. The first of five strategy steps asks students to identify and underline the relational statement in the problem. The second step requires students to identify the referent (unknown) and the compared and map the information onto the schema diagram provided. For the third step, students must map the relation onto the diagram, and the fourth instructs students how to transform the information in the diagram into a math equation, e.g., 12 over ? equals one-third. Finally, students compute, write the answer, and check the accuracy of the diagrammatic representation and the computation.

The students in these studies showed marked improvement in solving multiplication and division word problems. Students maintained strategy use and performance between two and 10 weeks, and showed generalization of strategy use to novel problems.

Montague's intervention, the *Solve It!* curriculum, was the foundation for a single subject study and a group study with middle school students with LD (Montague, 1992; Montague et al., 1993). In the single-subject study, the two sixth-grade students did not reach criterion for mastery, indicating that younger students may need adaptations to benefit from the intervention. The students with LD in the group study, following about three weeks of instruction, performed at the same level as their average-achieving peers on a test of math problems. Students declined in performance after two months. However, a booster session consisting of one day of review and one day of practice was provided, and students met criterion on the problem solving test. *Solve It!* incorporates the following cognitive processes.

1. Reading the problem (reading, rereading, identifying relevant/irrelevant information).
2. Paraphrasing (translating the linguistic information by putting the problem into one's own words without changing the meaning of the "story" or "situation").
3. Visualizing (transforming the linguistic and numerical information to form internal representations in memory through a drawing or image that shows the relationships among the components of a problem).

4. Hypothesizing about problem solutions (establishing a goal, looking toward the outcome, and setting up a plan to solve the problem by deciding on the operations that are needed, selecting and ordering the operations, and transforming the information into correct equations and algorithms).
5. Estimating the outcome or answer (validating the process as well as the product by predicting the outcome based on the question/goal and the information presented).
6. Computing the outcome or answer (recalling the correct procedures for the basic operations needed for solution—calculator skills are taught/reinforced here).
7. Checking (students become aware of problem solving as a recursive activity and learn how to check both process and product by checking their understanding and representation as well as the accuracy of the process, procedures, and computation).

Students are also taught to use self-regulation strategies, i.e., self-instruct or tell themselves what to do, self-question or ask themselves questions as they solve problems, and self-monitor or check themselves throughout the problem solving process. Self-instruction involves providing one's own prompts and talking oneself through the problem solving routine. Self-instruction combined with self-questioning is very effective for guiding learners through the problem solving process. Students are taught specific questions to ask and are provided ample practice as they solve problems. For example, after formulating a visual representation of the problem, they ask themselves, Did the picture fit the problem? and Did I show the relationships among the problem parts? Self-checking helps students review and reflect on the problem and ensure that the solution path is appropriate and correct as well as check the procedures and computations for mistakes. Each phase and process of the problem solving routine has a corresponding self-regulation strategy (a SAY, ASK, CHECK procedure). That is, students learn to check that they understand the problem, check that the information selected is correct and makes sense, check that the schematic representation reflects the problem information and shows the relationships among the problem parts, check that the solution plan is appropriate, that they used all the important information, and check that the operations were completed in the correct sequence, and, finally, check that the answer is correct. To do this, the following routine (see Figure 11.1) is used. If they are unsure at any time as they solve the problem, they tell themselves to return to the problem to recheck or ask for help. Students are taught how to decide if they need help, whom to ask, and how to ask for help.

Scripted lessons with proven procedures associated with explicit instruction provided the teaching/learning structure. These procedures, incorporated into the scripts, include verbal rehearsal, process modeling, visualization, performance feedback, mastery learning, and distributed practice. When students first learn a strategy, they must first memorize a sequence of activities for the cognitive routine. Students are cued and prompted until they can recite the salient steps of the strategy from memory. Acronyms can be used to remind students of the sequence. For example, RPV-HECC (read, paraphrase, visualization, hypothesize, estimate, compute, check) helps students remember the cognitive processes taught with *Solve It!* Process modeling is simply thinking aloud or saying everything one is thinking and doing while solving problems. First, the teacher models use of the strategy solving actual problems. As students become familiar with the routine, they can exchange roles with the teacher and model problem solving for other students. Visualization, the basis for understanding the problem, is a problem representation process. Students learn how to construct a schematic or relational image, either mentally or on paper, of the problem. Positive and corrective feedback is provided by teachers and peers throughout the acquisition and application phases of instruction. Mastery learning implies meeting a preset performance criterion, e.g., 7 problems correct out of 10 over four consecutive tests of 10 one-, two-, and three-step problems. Distributed practice is necessary if students are to maintain use of the strategy and performance levels.

**READ** (for understanding)
**Say:** Read the problem. If I don't understand, read it again.
**Ask:** Have I read and understood the problem?
**Check:** For understanding as I solve the problem.

**PARAPHRASE** (your own words)
**Say:** Underline the important information. Put the problem in my own words.
**Ask:** Have I underlined the important information? What is the question? What am I looking for?
**Check:** That the information goes with the question.

**VISUALIZE** (a picture or a diagram)
**Say:** Make a drawing or a diagram. Show the relationships among the problem parts.
**Ask:** Does the picture fit the problem? Did I show the relationships?
**Check:** The picture against the problem information.

**HYPOTHESIZE** (a plan to solve the problem)
**Say:** Decide how many steps and operations are needed. Write the operation symbols (+, -, x, and /).
**Ask:** If I …, what will I get? If I …, then what do I need to do next? How many steps are needed?
**Check:** That the plan makes sense.

**ESTIMATE** (predict the answer)
**Say:** Round the numbers, do the problem in my head, and write the estimate.
**Ask:** Did I round up and down? Did I write the estimate?
**Check:** That I used the important information.

**COMPUTE** (do the arithmetic)
**Say:** Do the operations in the right order.
**Ask:** How does my answer compare with my estimate? Does my answer make sense? Are the decimals or money signs in the right places?
**Check:** That all the operations were done in the right order.

**CHECK** (make sure everything is right)
**Say:** Check the plan to make sure it is right. Check the computation.
**Ask:** Have I checked every step? Have I checked the computation? Is my answer right?
**Check:** That everything is right. If not, go back. Ask for help if I need it.

FIGURE 11.1    Math problem solving processes and strategies. From Montague (2003). Copyright by Exceptional Innovations. Permission to photocopy this figure is granted for personal use only.

## SECONDARY SCHOOL MATHEMATICS INSTRUCTION

Six studies conducted with students with LD are described. The first utilized manipulatives to improve performance on area and perimeter problems (Cass, Cates, Smith, & Jackson, 2003). Geoboards and a model house were used to teach three high school students to solve area and perimeter problems. Instruction incorporated proven practices such as modeling, prompting, guided practice, and independent practice. Students were actively involved and showed improvement in five to seven days and maintained performance levels over a two-month period. The second study investigated the effects of peer-assisted learning strategies (PALS) and curriculum-based measurement (CBM) on the mathematics performance of 92 students in grades nine through twelve (Calhoon & Fuchs, 2003). Students in the intervention group received training in tutoring and CBM and were paired with a classmate. Tutoring dyads changed every two weeks. Following 15 weeks of PALS/CBM twice weekly, students who received the intervention scored significantly higher on a test of computation than the control group students. However, no significant difference between groups was found on the concepts and application math test.

Two studies used the C-R-A model to improve performance on algebra problems (Maccini & Hughes, 2000; Maccini & Ruhl, 2000). Maccini's model is an instructional strategy using the C-R-A graduated teaching sequence moving from the concrete to semiconcrete to abstract representations and solutions with problems involving addition, subtraction, multiplication, and division of integers. Her "STAR" strategy utilizes manipulatives and a systematic sequence of steps:

S = Search the word problem (Read; Ask yourself questions, i.e., What facts do I know? What do I need to find?; Write down facts).

T = Translate the words into an equation in picture form (Choose a variable; Identify the operations; Represent the problem using concrete, semi-concrete, and abstract representations).

A = Answer the problem using cues and a work mat.

R = Review the solution (Reread the problem; Ask the question, i.e., Does the answer make sense? Why?; Check the answer).

In both studies, students with LD improved their ability to represent algebraic problems, were more accurate in solving simple algebraic word problems, maintained improved performance over time, and generalized strategy use in both near- and far-transfer tasks.

The final two studies used cognitive strategy instruction to improve students' problem solving (Hutchinson, 1993; Montague & Bos, 1986). Montague's *Solve It!* model, described in the last section, was the basis for an intervention study with six secondary school students with LD (Montague & Bos, 1986). All students improved to criterion, maintained the strategy and

---

**Self-Questions for Representing Algebra Word Problems**

1. Have I read and understood each sentence? Are there any words whose meaning I have to ask.
2. Have I got the whole picture, a representation, for the problem?
3. Have I written down my representation on the worksheet? (goal, unknown(s), known(s), type of problem, equation
4. What should I look for in a new problem to see it is the same kind of problem?

**Self-Questions for Solving Algebra Word Problems**

1. Have I written an equation?
2. Have I expanded the terms?
3. Have I written out the steps of my solution on the worksheet? (collected like terms, isolated unknown(s), solved for unknown(s), checked my answer with the goal, highlighted my answer)
4. What should I look for in a new problem to see if it is the same kind of problem?

FIGURE 11.2   Self-question prompt card for solving algebra problems

Goal: _____

What I don't know: _____

What I know:

I can write/say this problem in my own words. Draw a picture.

Kind of problem: _____

Equation:

Solving the equation:

Solution:

Compare to goal:

Check:

FIGURE 11.3    Structured worksheet for solving algebra problems

performance level over time, and generalized strategy use to more difficult problems. Hutchinson's (1993) intervention targeted algebra problems. The strategy included a set of self-questions on prompt cards for the problem representation and solution phases and a structured worksheet (See Figure 11.2 and Figure 11.3).

Hutchinson taught three types of algebra problems: relational problems (e.g., Eddie walks 6 miles farther than Amelia. If the total distance walked by both is 32 miles, how far did each walk?); proportion problems (e.g., On a map a distance of 2 inches represents 120 miles. What distance is represented on this map by 5 inches?); and two-variable two-equation problems (e.g., Sam traveled 760 miles, some at 80 miles per hour and some at 60 miles per hour. The total time taken was 8 hours. Find the distance Sam traveled at 80 miles per hour). Scripted lessons guided instruction. Students with LD who received cognitive strategy instruction outperformed a comparison group of peers with LD on the posttest, which consisted of 5 problems of each type. Maintenance and transfer effects were evident.

## CONCLUSION

There is clearly a need for research to identify more precisely what constitutes effective, scientifi-cally-based practice in teaching mathematics to students with learning and behavioral disorders. What we have learned is that students with these special needs fall further behind in mathematics as they progress through school. Geary (2004) estimated the prevalence of mathematical learning disabilities at between 5% and 8% of the school-age population, similar to the estimated preva-lence of reading disabilities. However, unlike reading, low achievement and underachievement in mathematics actually may increase as children progress through school due to the nature of mathematical learning. Mathematics requires that learners acquire and apply multiple concepts and skills to be successful across the numerous topics in mathematics (e.g., geometry, algebra). Dietz (2006), in a study of disorders in adolescents ($n = 165$), found that between 10% and 13% of the students qualified as having learning disabilities in mathematics using stringent researcher criteria, while 40% were achieving at least one standard deviation below the mean on a standard-ized math test. Additionally, to further exacerbate matters, some students will evidence disabili-ties in both reading and mathematics.

As noted, the majority of intervention studies in mathematics in special education have fo-cused on teaching basic skills, primarily math facts and algorithmic procedures, generally with-out providing any conceptual foundation for learning these skills. If students are to be successful in mathematics, they need to understand the concepts underlying even these seemingly simple skills, i.e., they need to gain conceptual knowledge. Further, problem solving is the centerpiece of mathematics instruction in most mathematics classrooms, a result of curricular recommenda-tions in the NCTM *Standards* (NCTM, 2000). To be successful problem solvers, students must also acquire and apply strategic knowledge for solving math problems and this instruction should begin early in elementary school.

Based on findings from the intervention research in mathematics conducted so far, we can draw some conclusions about effective instruction. First, as in other academic domains, principles and practices associated with direct instruction and cognitive strategy instruction are components of most of the intervention "packages" that characterize the research across grade levels. These principles and practices include demonstration and modeling, verbal rehearsal, guided practice, corrective and positive feedback, independent practice, mastery, and distributed practice. Many studies have not been replicated and, thus, are limited in advancing knowledge of effective prac-tice. Several researchers, however, have conducted a series of studies using a particular approach or model (e.g., Jitendra's schema-based problem solving model, which further substantiates the effectiveness of the approach with different groups of students under different conditions). This perhaps is the most promising avenue if we are to identify what works, with whom the interven-tion works, and under what conditions it works. In conclusion, the limited research in mathemat-ics interventions for students with learning and behavioral disorders does indeed provide a base for moving to the next level. This next level of scientifically-based research will provide further understanding of the development of mathematical learning disabilities and, most importantly, will identify effective interventions that address and remedy the problems in mathematics that so many students manifest.

## REFERENCES

Baker, S., Gersten, R., Dimino, J. A., & Griffiths, R. (2004). The sustained use of research-based instruc-tional practice: A case study of peer-assisted learning strategies in mathematics. *Remedial and Special Education, 25,* 5–24.

Baxter, J., Woodward, J., & Olson, D. (2001). Effects of reform-based mathematics instruction in five third-grade classrooms. *Elementary School Journal, 101,* 529–548.

Beatty, A. (1997). *Learning from TIMSS: Results of the third international mathematics and science study.* Washington, DC: National Academy of Sciences.

Beirne-Smith, M. (1991). Peer tutoring in arithmetic for children with learning disabilities. *Exceptional Children, 57,* 330–339.

Burns, M. K. (2005). Using incremental rehearsal to increase fluency of single-digit multiplication facts with children identified as learning disabled in mathematics computation. *Education and Treatment of Children, 28,* 237–249.

Calhoon, M. B., & Fuchs, L. (2003). The effects of peer-assisted learning strategies and curriculum-based measurement on the mathematics performance of secondary students with disabilities. *Remedial and Special Education, 24,* 235–245.

Case, L. P., Harris, K. R., & Graham, S. (1992). Improving the mathematical problem-solving skills of students with learning disabilities: Self-regulated strategy development. *The Journal of Special Education, 26,* 1–19.

Cass, M., Cates, D., Smith, M., & Jackson, C. (2003). Effects of manipulative instruction on solving area and perimeter problems by students with learning disabilities. *Learning Disabilities Research & Practice, 18,* 112–120.

Cassel, J., & Reid, R. (1996). Use of a self-regulated strategy intervention to improve word problem-solving skills of students with mild disabilities. *Journal of Behavioral Education, 6,* 153–172.

Cooke, N. L. & Reichard, S. M. (1996). The effects of different interspersal drill ratios on acquisition and generalization of multiplication and division facts. *Education and Treatment of Children, 19,* 124–143.

Dietz, S. (2006). *Comorbidity of learning disabilities, attention-deficit disorder, and emotional and behavioral disorders in adolescents.* Manuscript submitted for publication.

Dunlap, L. K., & Dunlap, G. (1989). A self-monitoring package for teaching subtraction with regrouping to students with learning disabilities. *Journal of Applied Behavior Analysis, 22,* 309–314.

Flavell, J. H. (1976). Metacognitive aspects of problem solving. In L. B. Resnick (Ed.), *The nature of intelligence* (pp. 231–245). Mahwah, NJ: Erlbaum.

Fuchs, L. S., & Fuchs, D. (2001). Principles for the prevention and intervention of mathematics difficulties. *Learning Disabilities Research and Practice, 16,* 85–95.

Fuchs, L. S., Fuchs, D., Hamlett, C. L., & Appleton, A. C. (2002). Explicitly teaching for transfer: Effects on the mathematical problem-solving performance of students with mathematics disabilities. *Learning Disabilities Research and Practice, 17,* 90–106.

Fuchs, L. S., Fuchs, D., Hamlett, C. L., Phillips, N. B., & Bentz, J. (1994). Classwide curriculum-based measurement: Helping general educators meet the challenge of student diversity. *Exceptional Children, 60,* 518–537.

Fuchs, L. S., Fuchs, D., Hamlett, C. L., Phillips, N. B., Karns, K., & Dukta, S. (1997). Effects of task-focused goals on low-achieving students with and without learning disabilities. *American Educational Research Journal, 34,* 513–543.

Fuchs, L. S., Fuchs, D., Phillips, N. B., Hamlett, C. L., & Karns, K. (1995). Acquisition and transfer effects of classwide peer-assisted learning strategies in mathematics for students with varying learning histories. *School Psychology Review, 24,* 604–620.

Fuchs, L. S., Fuchs, D., Yazdian, L., & Powell, S. R. (2002). Enhancing first-grade children's mathematical development with peer-assisted learning strategies. *School Psychology Review, 31,* 569–583.

Funkhouser, C. (1995). Developing number sense and basic computational skills in students with special needs. *School Science and Mathematics, 95,* 236–239.

Geary, D. C. (2004). Mathematics and learning disabilities. *Journal of Learning Disabilities, 37,* 4–15.

Geary, D. C. (1993). Mathematical disabilities: Cognitive, neuropsychological, and genetic components. *Psychological Bulletin, 114,* 345–362.

Geary, D. C. (2003). Math disabilities. In H. L. Swanson, K. R. Harris, & S. Graham (Eds.), *Handbook of learning disabilities* (pp. 199–212). New York: Guilford.

Gersten, R., & Chard, D. (1999). Number sense: Rethinking arithmetic instruction for students with mathematical disabilities. *The Journal of Special Education, 44,* 18–28.

Greene, G. (1999). Mnemonic multiplication fact instruction for students with learning disabilities. *Learning Disabilities Research and Practice, 14,* 141–148.

Harris, C. A., Miller, S. P., & Mercer, C. D. (1995). Teaching initial multiplication skills to students with disabilities in general education classrooms. *Learning Disabilities Research and Practice, 10,* 180–195.

Harris, K., & Graham, S. (1993). *Helping young writers master the craft: Strategy instruction and self-regulation in the writing process.* Boston: Brookline.

Harris, K., Graham, S., Reid, R., McElroy, K., & Hamby, R. S. (1994). Self-monitoring of attention versus self-monitoring of performance: Replication and cross-task comparison of studies. *Learning Disability Quarterly, 17,* 121–139.

Hodge, J., Riccomini, P. J., Buford, R., & Herbst, M. H. (2006). A review of instructional interventions in mathematics for students with emotional and behavioral disorders. *Behavioral Disorders, 31,* 297–311.

Hudson, P., & Miller, S. P. (2006). *Designing and implementing mathematics instruction for students with diverse learning needs.* Boston: Allyn and Bacon.

Hutchinson, N. L. (1993). Effects of cognitive strategy instruction on algebra problem solving of adolescents with learning disabilities. *Learning Disability Quarterly, 16,* 34–63.

Jitendra, A., DiPipi, C. M., & Perron-Jones, N. (2002). An exploratory study of schema-based word-problem-solving instruction for middle school students with learning disabilities: An emphasis on conceptual and procedural understanding. *The Journal of Special Education, 36,* 23–38.

Jitendra, A. K., Griffin, C. C., McGoey, K., Gardill, M. C., Bhat, P., & Riley, T. (1998). Effects of mathematical word problem solving by students at risk or with mild disabilities. *The Journal of Educational Research, 91,* 345–355.

Jitendra, A. K., & Hoff, K. (1996). The effects of schema-based instruction on the mathematical word-problem-solving performance of students with learning disabilities. *Journal of Learning Disabilities, 29,* 422–431.

Jitendra, A. K., Hoff, K., & Beck, M. M. (1999). Teaching middle school students with learning disabilities to solve word problems using a schema-based approach. *Remedial and Special Education, 20,* 50–64.

Jolivette, K., Wehby, J. H., & Hirsch, L. (1999). Academic strategy identification for students exhibiting inappropriate classroom behaviors. *Behavioral Disorders, 24,* 210–221.

Koscinski, S. T., & Gast, D. L. (1993). Computer-assisted instruction with constant time delay to teach multiplication facts to students with learning disabilities. *Learning Disabilities Research and Practice, 8,* 157–168.

Kroesbergen, E. H., & Van Luit, J. E. H. (2002). Teaching multiplication to low math performers: Guided versus structured instruction. *Instructional Science, 30,* 361–378.

Landeen, J. J., & Adams, D. A. (1988). Computer assisted drill and practice for behaviorally handicapped learners: Proceed with caution. *Education and Treatment of Children, 11,* 218–229.

Maag, J. W., Reid, R., & DiGangi, S. A. (1993). Differential effects of self-monitoring attention, accuracy, and productivity. *Journal of Applied Behavior Analysis, 26,* 329–344.

Maccini, P., & Hughes, C. A. (2000). Mathematics interventions for adolescents with learning disabilities. *Learning Disabilities Research and Practice, 15,* 10–21.

Maccini, P., & Ruhl, K. L. (2000). Effects of a graduated instructional sequence on the algebraic subtraction of integers by secondary students with learning disabilities. *Education and Treatment of Children, 23,* 465–489.

Marsh, L. G., & Cooke, N. L. (1996). The effects of using manipulatives in teaching math problem solving to students with learning disabilities. *Learning Disabilities Research and Practice, 11,* 58–65.

McDougall, D., & Brady, M. P. (1998). Initiating and fading self-management interventions to increase math fluency in general education classes. *Exceptional Children, 64,* 151–166.

Mercer, C. D., & Miller, S. P. (1992). Teaching students with learning problems in math to acquire, understand, and apply basic math facts. *Remedial and Special Education, 13,* 19–35.

Miller, S. P., Harris, C., Strawser, S., Jones, W. P., & Mercer, C. (1998). Teaching multiplication to second graders in inclusive settings. *Focus of Learning Problems in Mathematics, 20,* 50–70.

Miller, S., & Mercer, C. (1997). Education aspects of mathematics disabilities. *Journal of Learning Disabilities, 30,* 47–56.

Miller, S. P., Mercer, C. D., & Dillon, A. (1992). Acquiring and retaining math skills. *Intervention, 28,* 105–110.

Montague, M. (1992). The effects of cognitive and metacognitive strategy instruction on the mathematical problem solving of middle school students with learning disabilities. *Journal of Learning Disabilities, 25,* 230–248.

Montague, M. (1998). Research on metacognition in special education. In T. Scruggs & M. Mastropieri (Eds.), *Advances in learning and behavioral disabilities.* (Vol. 12, pp. 151–183), Greenwich, CT: JAI Press.

Montague, M. (2006). Self-regulation strategies for better math performance in middle school. In M. Montague & A. Jitendra (Eds.), *Teaching mathematics to middle school students with learning difficulties* (pp. 89–107). New York: Guilford.

Montague, M. (2003). *Solve It! A mathematical problem solving instructional program.* Reston, VA: Exceptional Innovations.

Montague, M., & Applegate, B. (1993). Mathematical problem-solving characteristics of middle school students with learning disabilities. *Journal of Special Education, 27,* 175–201.

Montague, M., Applegate, B., & Marquard, K. (1993). Cognitive strategy instruction and mathematical problem-solving performance of students with learning disabilities. *Learning Disabilities Research and Practice, 29,* 251–261.

Montague, M., & Bos, C. (1986). The effect of cognitive strategy training on verbal math problem solving performance of learning disabled adolescents. *Journal of Learning Disabilities, 19,* 26–33.

Mooney, P., Ryan, J.B., Uhing, B.M., Reid, R., & Epstein, M.H. (2005). A review of self-management interventions targeting academic outcomes for students with emotional and behavioral disorders. *Journal of Behavioral Education, 14,* 203–221.

Morin, V. A., & Miller, S. P. (1998). Teaching multiplication to middle school students with mental retardation. *Education and Treatment of Children, 21,* 22–37.

Naglieri, J. & A., & Gottling, S. H. (1997). Mathematics instruction and PASS cognitive processes: An intervention study. *Journal of Learning Disabilities, 30,* 513–520.

National Assessment of Educational Progress (2003). *NAEP 2002 mathematics report card for the nation and the states.* Princeton, NJ: Educational Testing Service.

National Council of Teachers of Mathematics (1989). *Curriculum and evaluation NCTM Standards for school mathematics.* Reston, VA: The National Council of Teachers of Mathematics, Inc.

National Council of Teachers of Mathematics (2000). *Principles and NCTM Standards for school mathematics.* Reston, VA: The National Council of Teachers of Mathematics, Inc.

No Child Left Behind Act. Reauthorization of the Elementary and Secondary Education Act. Pub. L. 107-110 2102(4) (2001).

Owen, R. L., & Fuchs, L. S. (2002). Mathematical problem-solving strategy instruction for third-grade students with learning disabilities. *Remedial and Special Education, 23,* 268–278.

Peterson, S. K., Mercer, C. D., & O'Shea, L. (1988). Teaching learning disabled students place value using the concrete to abstract sequence. *Learning Disabilities Research and Practice, 4,* 52–56.

Rivera, D., & Smith, D.D. (1988). Using a demonstration strategy to teach midschool students with learning disabilities how to compute long division. *Journal of Learning Disabilities, 21,* 77–81.

Scarlato, M.C., & Burr, W.A. (2002). Teaching fractions to middle-school students. *Journal of Direct Instruction, 2,* 23–38.

Shiah, R., Mastropieri, M. A., Scruggs, T. E., & Mushiniski Fulk, B. J. (1995). The effects of computer-assisted instruction on the mathematical problem solving of students with learning disabilities. *Exceptionality, 5,* 131–161.

Skinner, C. H., Bamberg, H. W., Smith, E. S., & Powell, S. S. (1993). Cognitive cover, copy and compare: Subvocal responding to increase rates of accurate division responding. *Remedial and Special Education, 14,* 49–56.

Skinner, C. H., Ford, J. M., & Yunker, B. D. (1991). A comparison of instructional response requirements on the multiplication performance of behaviorally disordered students. *Behavioral Disorders, 17,* 56–65.

Skinner, C. H., Turco, T., Beatty, K., & Rasavage, C. (1989). Cover, copy, and compare: A method for increasing multiplication performance. *School Psychology Review, 18,* 412–420.

Stein, M., Silbert, J., & Carnine, D. (1997). *Designing effective mathematics instruction: A direct instruction approach.* Upper Saddle River, NJ: Prentice-Hall.

Swanson, H. L. (1999). Instructional components that predict treatment outcomes for students with learning disabilities: Support for a combined strategy and direct instruction model. *Learning Disabilities Research & Practice, 16,* 109–119.

Swanson, H. L., & Jerman, O. (2006). Math disabilities: A selective meta-analysis of the literature. *Review of Educational Research, 76,* 249–274.

Swanson, H.L., & Rhine, B. (1985). Strategy transformations in learning disabled children's math performance: Clues to development of expertise. *Journal of Learning Disabilities, 18,* 409–418.

Tournaki, N. (2003). The differential effects of teaching addition through strategy instruction versus drill and practice to students with and without learning disabilities. *Journal of Learning Disabilities, 36,* 449–458.

Van Luit, J. E. H., & Naglieri, J. A. (1999). Effectiveness of the MASTER program for teaching special children multiplication and division. *Journal of Learning Disabilities, 32,* 98–107.

Wilson, C. L., & Sindelar, P. T. (1991). Direct instruction in math word problems: Students with learning disabilities. *Exceptional Children, 57,* 512–520.

Wilson, R., Majsterek, D., & Simmons, D. (1996). The effects of computer-assisted versus teacher-directed instruction on the multiplication performance of elementary students with learning disabilities. *Journal of Learning Disabilities, 29,* 383–390.

Witzel, B. S., Mercer, C. D., & Miller, M. D. (2003). Teaching algebra to students with learning difficulties: An investigation of an explicit instruction model. *Learning Disabilities Research & Practice, 18,* 121–131.

Wood, D. K., Frank, A. R., & Wacker, D. P. (1998). Teaching multiplication facts to students with learning disabilities. *Journal of Applied Behavior Analysis, 31,* 323–338.

Woodward, J. (2006). Making reform-based mathematics work for academically low-achieving middle school students. In M. Montague & A. Jitendra (Eds.), *Teaching mathematics to middle school students with learning difficulties* (pp. 29–50). New York: Guilford.

Woodward, J., & Baxter, J. (1997). The effects of an innovative approach to mathematics on academically low-achieving students in inclusive settings. *Exceptional Children, 63,* 373–388.

Wong, B. Y. L. (1999). Metacognition in writing. In R. Gallimore, L. P. Bernheimer, D. L. MacMillan, D. L. Speece, & S. Vaughn (Eds.), *Developmental perspectives on children with high-incidence disabilities* (pp. 183–198). Mahwah, NJ: Erlbaum.

Wong, B. Y. L., Harris, K. R., Graham, S., & Butler, D. (2003). Cognitive strategies instruction research in learning disabilities. In H. L. Swanson, K. R. Harris, & S. Graham (Eds.). *Handbook of learning disabilities* (pp. 383–402). New York: Guilford.

Wood, D.A., Rosenberg, M. S., & Carran, D. T. (1993). The effects of tape-recorded self-instruction cues on the mathematics performance of students with learning disabilities. *Journal of Learning Disabilities, 26,* 250–258.

Xin, Y. P. & Jitendra, A. K. (2006). Teaching problem-solving skills to middle school students with learning difficulties: Schema-based strategy instruction. In M. Montague & A. Jitendra (Eds.), *Teaching mathematics to middle school students with learning difficulties* (pp. 51–71). New York: Guilford.

Xin, Y. P., Jitendra, A. K., & Deatline-Buchman, A. (2005). Effects of mathematical word problem-solving instruction on middle school students with learning problems. *Journal of Special Education, 39,* 181–192.

# 12

# Cognitive Processing Deficits

## Milton J. Dehn

Information processing analyses of mental abilities may enable us to diagnose and eventually remediate deficiencies in intellectual function at the level of process, strategies, and representations of information. (Sternberg, 1981, p. 1186)

More than 25 years after Sternberg's optimistic statement, we still have a long way to go. The whole notion of attempting to remediate a cognitive processing deficit remains quite controversial, and many psychologists and educators will simply not accept it. Early attempts to establish evidence-based procedures often met with failure or were at best equivocal (Kavale, 1990; Loarer, 2003), and reliable and valid processing assessment tools were unavailable until recently (Dehn, 2006). Nevertheless, recent advances in neuroscience and neuropsychology have expanded our knowledge of how the brain functions during academic learning (Berninger & Richards, 2002), and, as a result, efficacious neuropsychological treatments (Eslinger, 2002) are emerging. In addition, a substantial amount of educational research literature has documented a range of effective interventions for at least some of the cognitive processes that are essential for academic learning. Given the renewed emphasis on educational interventions designed to prevent and remediate learning problems (Brown-Chidsey & Steege, 2005), processing interventions, at the very least, deserve another look.

Many educators and psychologists have the impression that there is a dearth of evidence-based interventions for cognitive processing problems. To the contrary, not only is the literature replete with documentation of effective interventions but most educators frequently utilize variations of substantiated methods (often unknowingly) that reduce the deleterious effects of deficient cognitive processes. To espouse the view that no effective interventions exist for processing deficits is analogous to saying that no educational interventions exist for improving the learning and functioning of individuals with mental retardation. Nonetheless, direct instruction is widely recognized for its significant positive impact on the academic learning of children with mental retardation (Gersten & Keating, 1987). The fact that direct instruction fails to raise IQ does not diminish its acceptance or efficacy. So why do many educational professionals demand that processing interventions directly ameliorate what are often immutable brain-based processes? Once we acknowledge the value of compensatory strategies, as we do for most learning difficulties, we will discover an ample selection of scientific-based interventions for several of the processes that underlie intellectual functioning and academic learning. Gaining more knowledge about cognitive processes and implementing processing interventions will benefit all students, especially those who struggle with learning.

## HISTORY OF PROCESSING INTERVENTIONS

Within the field of special education, processing interventions have a long and controversial history. Prior to 1990, recognized processing interventions were usually referred to as "process training" and consisted mainly of modality training, perceptual-motor training, and psycholinguistic training. Modality training was based on the presumption that matching instructional strategies to individual modality preferences (either auditory, visual, or kinesthetic) would enhance learning. Perceptual-motor training focused on the integration of visual-perceptual and motoric functioning, using such techniques as Doman-Delacato psychomotor patterning. Psycholinguistic training emphasized training in discrete language production subcomponents, such as auditory reception, which could be assessed with subtests from the Illinois Test of Psycholinguistic Abilities (Kirk, McCarthy, & Kirk, 1968). These three types of process training were the subject of numerous investigations (e.g., Hammill, Goodman, & Weiderholt, 1974; Hammill & Larsen, 1974) that mostly found these methods to be ineffective (see Kavale, 1990, for a detailed review. Vigorous attacks on process training began as early as the 1960s, and Mann (1979) expressed frustration with process training's resistance to extinction, despite an overwhelming amount of empirical evidence documenting its failure. By 1990 it was clear that modality training and perceptual-motor training did not improve processes or enhance academic learning (Kavale, 1990). However, contradictory findings, including meta-analytic results, on psycholinguistic training continued to fuel the controversy surrounding it. Despite the intuitive appeal of these three early types of processing interventions, the empirical evidence was at best equivocal.

### Contemporary Approaches

Contemporary interventions for processing difficulties should not be associated with these early failed types of process training. Recent research on processing interventions has gone beyond modality, perceptual-motor, and psycholinguistic training. Interventions for several types of cognitive processing deficits now have a scientific track record of success, or at the every least, emerging support. Led by advances in neuroscience (Berninger & Richards, 2002) and applied research in pediatric neuropsychology, the nature of processing interventions has changed. This is not a case of old ideas and methods masquerading as something new, as was once suggested by Mann (1979). To begin with, advances in neuroimaging and psychometrics allow us to better measure, identify, and differentiate the neurological and cognitive processes and subprocesses involved in learning (Feifer & DeFina, 2000, 2002, 2005; Schrank, 2006). Current processing interventions are distinct from the early discredited approaches; for example, interventions for planning deficits (Naglieri & Gottling, 1997) and memory limitations (Ritchie & Karge, 1996) have nothing in common with obsolete process training. In general, contemporary, evidence-based processing interventions tend to focus on higher-level cognitive processes, such as working memory and executive functioning. Recent neuropsychological research has even discovered that processes once considered immutable might be ameliorated through specific cognitive training (Klingberg, Forssberg, & Westerberg, 2002; Olesen, Westerberg, & Klingberg, 2004). Despite recent advances, neuropsychological findings can be difficult to apply in an educational environment (Work & Choi, 2005). Hopefully, the growing interest in school neuropsychology (e.g., D'Amato, Fletcher-Janzen, & Reynolds, 2005; Hale & Fiorello, 2004) may further develop the bridge between beneficial interventions in related fields and those needed in the educational environment.

## History of Strategy Training

Cognitive strategy training, much of it directed towards processing deficiencies, especially deficiencies in memory and executive functioning, has been researched and applied in educational settings for the past 30 years. Strategy instruction and interventions, which were full-fledged by the 1980s, are based on the information processing model and are designed to teach individuals to more efficiently utilize their cognitive processing resources, such as short-term and long-term memory. Research has found strategy training to be particularly advantageous for children with learning disabilities (Swanson, 2001; Turley-Ames & Whitfield, 2003), given that they seldom independently learn and use strategies (Carlson & Das, 1997). Strategy training can lead to improved processing performance; for example, encoding strategies that add meaning to new information have been shown to increase retention and retrieval of information (Banikowski & Mehring, 1999). Unlike the classic process training, strategy training has not been limited to individuals with disabilities; there is also a history of attempts to incorporate strategy training into the general education curriculum. For example, Conway and Ashman (1989) proposed the implementation of the Process-Based Instruction (PBI) model. Although the bulk of the research on strategy training has been favorable, with significant improvements in targeted processes and academic performance (Pressley & Woloshyn, 1995), lack of maintenance and generalization remains a concern (Carlson & Das; Conway & Ashman; Deshler & Schumaker, 1993).

## PROCESSING THEORIES

The construct of cognitive processing is nearly as controversial as that of intelligence (Floyd, 2005). Despite the discord, most psychologists and educators would agree that processing involves the complex integration and interaction of many interrelated functions spread throughout the brain and that cognitive processing refers to mental operations by which sensory input is perceived, manipulated, transformed, stored, and retrieved. As we learn or accomplish a behavioral task, several processes are involved; a neural network of distributed, coordinated activity is occurring in many regions of the brain. Neuropsychologists often focus on the elemental and discrete subprocesses in the brain that underlie observable behavior and cognition; for example, there are many subprocesses involved in retrieving verbal knowledge. In contrast, a more applicable model in the educational environment is that which emphasizes the higher level and broader cognitive processes that are more readily observable and measurable and have known relationships with academic learning. Examples of such theoretical models are the classic information processing theory (Gagne, Yekovich, & Yekovich, 1993) and the PASS (Planning, Attention, Simultaneous, and Successive) processing theory (Das, Naglieri, & Kirby, 1994).

## INFORMATION PROCESSING THEORY

Information processing theory uses the computer as a metaphor for human mental processing (Gagne et al., 1993). The model describes an input-output flow of information in which the main components are the senses, immediate memory, working memory, long-term memory, executive control, and muscles that produce a response. The main processes are selective perception, encoding, retrieval, response organization, and executive functioning. Working memory is a core component in this model, as it processes most incoming and outgoing information. Working memory is also a central process because all higher level processes interact with or are embedded in working memory (see working memory section for more details). Executive processes are another crucial element, as they serve a governing function, controlling and regulating all other processes.

Information processing theory has evolved along with our understanding of cognition, learning, and brain functioning, leaving the computer metaphor and the notion of information transmission outdated. Human information processing is no longer viewed as static, passive, linear, or mechanistic. Contemporary views of information processing emphasize the executive processes because efficient processing is self-directed. A constructivist interpretation of information processing has also gained acceptance (Mayer, 1996). In this view, processing involves an active search for understanding in which incoming information is restructured and integrated with stored knowledge.

## PASS Theory

Luria (1970) proposed a theory of cognitive processes associated with three functional brain units: (1) cortical arousal and attention; (2) simultaneous and successive information processes; and (3) planning, self-monitoring, and structuring of cognitive activities (Naglieri & Gottling, 1997). PASS theory, which stands for Planning, Attention, Simultaneous, and Successive processing, is an adaptation of Lurian theory (Das et al., 1994). Planning, an essential component of executive processing, encompasses mental processes by which the individual determines, selects, applies, and evaluates solutions to problems. Attention is a mental process by which the individual selectively focuses on particular stimuli while inhibiting responses to competing stimuli (Naglieri, 1999). Simultaneous processing involves the integration of separate stimuli into a single whole or group, usually a spatial group, and being able to recognize patterns in a group, for example, seeing patterns in numbers. Successive processing, also referred to as sequential processing, is the integration of stimuli into a specific serial order whereby each link is related only to the next stimulus in the chain; for example, successive processing is used when readers blend sounds to form words (Naglieri & Pickering, 2003).

## CHC Theory

In addition, several other cognitive processes have been associated with academic learning, including auditory processing, processing speed, visual processing, phonological processing, and linguistic processing. One theoretical model that encompasses many of these cognitive processes—Cattell-Horn-Carroll (CHC) theory (Carroll, 1993; Horn & Blankson, 2005; McGrew, 2005)—is actually a theory of cognitive abilities. The theory is applicable to processing because most of the theory's cognitive abilities can be directly linked with cognitive processes. The well known Woodcock-Johnson III (WJ III) assessment battery (Woodcock, McGrew, & Mather, 2001) operationalizes CHC theory. Schrank (2006) recently added further clarification regarding the cognitive processes and subprocesses involved in performance on each WJ III test.

## Other Processes

Evidence-based interventions currently exist for only some of the processes that are identified in processing theories and brain-based research. Fortunately, several processes that are essential for academic learning have well established interventions; for example, phonological processing (necessary for reading and spelling words) programs are clearly efficacious, whereas the treatment literature on visual processing has a low correlation with academic learning (Mather &

Wendling, 2005; McGrew & Woodcock, 2001). Sensory and motoric processes also have weak relationships with learning and higher cognitive processes; thus, sensory-motor interventions will not be discussed in this chapter, although they can be beneficial for improving handwriting. Also, the reader is referred elsewhere for processing interventions related to speech/language production (e.g., Mitchum & Berndt, 1995; Robey, 1998).

## ASSESSMENT AND DIAGNOSIS OF PROCESSING DEFICITS

Selecting an intervention that matches the needs of the learner begins with an assessment of the learner's cognitive processes. Processing assessment is also controversial, with part of the current debate arising from ongoing misconceptions about what processing assessment entails. Contemporary processing assessment has nothing to do with modalities or learning styles. Rather, it is based on neuropsychology and empirically supported cognitive theories, and it consists of using recently developed standardized tests with reputable technical properties (Dehn, 2006).

Standardized testing is an essential component of processing assessment and should take precedence over informal methods. Informal processing assessment procedures are fraught with inherent reliability and validity problems. Informal processing assessment is particularly challenging because most cognitive processes are not directly observable and because many processes underlie a typical educational task, such as the many processes involved in following directions. Thus, some standardized testing of processes should be conducted whenever a student is referred for a possible learning disability or whenever a processing intervention is being considered. Fortunately, there are many technically adequate processing measures to select from. Even the most traditional intellectual instrument, the Wechsler Intelligence Scale for Children-Fourth Edition (WISC-IV), has recently added a processing supplement (Wechsler et al., 2004).

Testing of cognitive processes should be hypothesis-driven and selective, combining subtests and factors in a cross-battery fashion. Examiners need not administer entire time-consuming comprehensive batteries. Analysis and interpretation of test results should focus on significant intra-individual strengths and weaknesses across batteries, in addition to identifying normative strengths and weaknesses. Furthermore, the assessment data should be interpreted from an actuarial and a clinical perspective, with an eye towards convergent data that support or do not support processing hypotheses. See Dehn (2006) for more details and recommendations on conducting and interpreting a processing assessment.

When deliberating a processing deficit diagnosis, several factors need to be considered. First, examiners should avoid using subtest scatter to identify the learner's processing deficits. Rather, a process score should be considered indicative of a deficit only when it is *both* a statistically significant intra-individual weakness *and* below the average range (Dehn, 2006; Naglieri, 1999). Second, the learner's developmental level and the degree of process or skill automaticity will also impact test performance. Automaticity is acquired through practicing skills to an overlearned state, thereby reducing the cognitive processing and interval required for their execution (Farquhar & Surry, 1995). Awareness of the role of automaticity and knowledge of the individual's level of specific skill mastery is important when conducting an evaluation so as to avoid attributing poor performance to insufficient capacity when it may actually result from lack of automaticity. Third, what appears to be a capacity deficit might actually be a strategy deficit instead, a strategy deficit being the undirected, inefficient use of cognitive resources. The consistent use of effective strategies is thought to impact performance on measures of information processing; that is, individuals who strategically and efficiently allocate their processing resources will perform better (Turley-Ames & Whitfield, 2003). Finally, effective utilization of processing potential depends on adequate executive functioning and metacognition, the awareness and regulation of one's cognitive resources (Pressley & Woloshyn, 1995). Processing deficits are the observable indications of brain impairment. When these impairments disrupt or interfere with some aspect of functioning, the result is often the diagnosis of a disability.

## COGNITIVE PROCESSES AND ACADEMIC LEARNING

A learning difficulty or a learning disability (LD) is often due to a deficiency in one or more processes, incomplete development of processes, or inefficient (non-strategic) use of processes. Research in a variety of fields has identified several processing impairments that are correlated with specific learning disabilities, the most common ones being attentional, memory, linguistic, phonological, perceptual, and executive processing deficits. At times, learning may be impaired because of a single deficient process; at other times, the impairment may result from several weak processes. Working memory, which plays a crucial role in all types of academic learning, is the process most frequently implicated in the research (Gathercole, 1999; Minear & Shah, 2006; Pickering, 2006; Swanson, 2000; Wechsler, 2003b). Students with LD are especially deficient in the auditory component of working memory. Other processing-learning connections are also well known; for example, hardly anyone would dispute the strong connection that phonological processing has with basic reading skills (National Reading Panel, 2000) or argue that learning is not highly dependent on long-term memory storage and retrieval. Research (Evans, Floyd, McGrew, & Leforgee, 2002; Floyd, Evans, & McGrew, 2003) continues to identify the relationships various broad processes have with specific types of learning (see Table 12.1).

## APPROACHES TO PROCESSING INTERVENTIONS

In the educational environment, cognitive processing interventions refer to various treatments and interventions that involve the development of specific cognitive and metacognitive abilities and skills, with the goal of optimizing academic learning outcomes. Interventions for cognitive processing deficiencies have mostly been researched and developed within the fields of neuropsychology, cognitive psychology, educational psychology, and speech/language therapy. After introducing the construct of information processing decades ago, cognitive psychologists (Anderson, 1976; Gagne, 1974; Gagne et al., 1993) were instrumental in early research on compensatory strategies for working memory and other processing limitations. Educational psychologists followed with investigations into how effective teaching practices enhance encoding and retrieval

**TABLE 12.1**
**Cognitive Processes Highly Related with Types of Academic Learning**

| Reading | Mathematics | Written Language | Reading Comprehension |
|---|---|---|---|
| Working Memory | Working Memory | Working Memory | Working Memory |
| Auditory Processing | Fluid Reasoning | Executive Processing | Executive Processing |
| Phonological Processing | Planning | Planning | Fluid Reasoning |
| Long-Term Retrieval | Visual Processing | Auditory Processing | Long-Term Retrieval |
| Successive Processing | Processing Speed | Processing Speed | |
| Visual Processing | | | |

of information (Rosenshine & Stevens, 1986). More recently, neuroscientists have been using neuroimaging technology to reveal the various brain processes involved in learning (Berninger & Richards, 2002), and neuropsychologists have been developing treatments and interventions for processing deficits resulting from acquired brain injury (Eslinger, 2002). In the educational environment, improved academic learning and performance are the ultimate objectives of processing interventions. Consequently, the determination of effectiveness should be based on measurement of related academic skills, as well as measurement of the cognitive processes involved. For instance, some studies have found no post-intervention improvement in cognitive processes but have found improvement in related areas of achievement (Leasak, Hunt, & Randhawa, 1982).

Three general approaches to intervention have been used for processing problems—remedial, compensatory, and a combination of the two. Remedial interventions have a deficit-based focus, with the goal of improving processing weaknesses and deficiencies. Compensatory interventions utilize the individual's cognitive strengths and assets, in an effort to bypass the deficit, thereby reducing its impact on learning and performance. For example, training in the use of cognitive strategies, such as mnemonics, is a common compensatory intervention. Many interventions, however, combine these two approaches, utilizing the individual's strengths to remedy his or her deficits. For example, instruction that addresses working memory limitations may be both compensatory and remedial in nature, with the goal of more efficiently using the individual's working memory resources. Most effective interventions reported in the literature are multidimensional in nature, and most psychologists and educators would agree that a unified approach, with the potential of additive effects from multiple methods, has the best chance of success (Work & Choi, 2005). Consequently, the primary focus of this chapter will be on evidence-based compensatory interventions and interventions that combine a remedial and compensatory approach.

## Remedial Interventions

Past attempts to address processing deficits through a remedial approach alone have generally been unsuccessful (Lee & Riccio, 2005). This is not surprising, given that the capacities of various cognitive processes have traditionally been thought to be constant. Perhaps, another reason for the failure is that an exclusive emphasis on a specific processing impairment ignores intact functions. Recent studies suggest that some processes, and sometimes related processes, can be improved through remedial training (Olesen et al., 2004). However, the extent of this research is limited. Interestingly, the brain's response to direct remedial treatment appears to be compensatory in nature; remedial neurological investigations have discovered that the brain may compensate for functional loss by using other regions not normally involved in the behavior (Berninger & Richards, 2002), thereby improving cognitive functioning that is not normally associated with these other brain regions (Wilson, 1987). The fact that intact, associated neurological processes are able to perform the function of a damaged or poorly developed process is testimony to the plasticity of the brain (Shaywitz, 2003). It is also a compelling reason for attempting processing interventions.

## Compensatory Interventions

Compensatory approaches entail methods that bypass the deficient processes (Glisky & Glisky, 2002) and typically involve strategy training (see later discussion) that incorporates processing strengths. Compensatory approaches may also include external aids, accommodations, or substitute methods of reaching the same goal. Given the complexity of processing and involvement of several cognitive processes in any given academic learning task, compensatory interventions may succeed because they tend to be broad based and focus on higher-level processes. For example, a performance problem on a measure of working memory may be due to an impairment in executive processing. Thus, a top-down, broad-based treatment approach is often selected instead of focusing on a specific processing domain. Such an approach is more likely to promote generalization (Levine et al., 2000) and may additionally remediate unidentified processing deficits.

## Combined Interventions

In contrast to the lack of empirical support for remedial interventions alone, a growing body of scientific evidence supports combined interventions. For example, within the field of neuropsychology, empirical evidence in support of cognitive training, or retraining, is increasing (Eslinger, 2002; Lee & Riccio, 2005). Most research on cognitive retraining has been with individuals who have sustained a traumatic brain injury (TBI) but the methods also apply to other neurologically based cognitive processing deficits, such as the developmental processing deficits possessed by individuals with Attention Deficit Hyperactivity Disorder (ADHD) and by students with learning disabilities (Lee & Riccio, 2005).

With the combined approach, the goal of focusing on the deficient process is not to improve the process but rather to optimize its use (Lee & Riccio, 2005). The desired outcome of such an approach is more efficient use of existing processing capabilities. Typically, individuals are taught strategies that improve functioning of the targeted process. In fact, for some individuals, poor processing performance in an area such as working memory may be due to a lack of strategy knowledge or limited use of known strategies, rather than a lack of processing ability per se (Kar, Dash, Das, & Carlson, 1993). Even when individuals with learning disabilities possess a repertoire of cognitive strategies, they seldom select and apply an effective strategy when the situation warrants its use (Pressley & Woloshyn, 1995).

## Cognitive Strategy Interventions

Cognitive strategy interventions are designed to improve performance through compensatory procedures or through more efficient functioning of weak or deficient processes. Strategy training can be incorporated into classroom instruction or conducted with an individual student. Mnemonic training, which is designed to increase encoding and retrieval of information, is the most common and most effective application, with a strong effect size of 1.6 (Lloyd, Forness, & Kavale, 1998). Another major type is self-instruction training. Over the past 30 years, self-instruction training has been successfully applied to executive processing deficits and other cognitive processing impairments, such as attention and memory (Lee & Riccio, 2005). Other types of strategy training often involve a metacognitive element, and some strategy interventions are entirely metacognitive.

## GENERAL STRATEGY TRAINING PROCEDURE

Acquiring and utilizing a cognitive strategy requires more than knowledge of a skill; knowing how to select and use the best procedures is also a critical aspect of strategy application. The success of strategy training depends on adherence to evidence-based training procedures. In general, strategy training should be explicit and intensive over an extended period of time until strategy use becomes automatic. Deshler and Schumaker (1993), Mastropieri and Scruggs (1998), and Pressley and Woloshyn (1995) all provide details on strategy training procedures. The essential steps and caveats in the strategy training process are:

1. Teach only one strategy at a time, at least until the student is familiar with the idea of strategy use.
2. Inform the student about the purpose and rationale for the strategy. Explain the benefits and how it will result in better performance.
3. Explain and demonstrate the strategy, with special attention to aspects of strategy use that generally are not well understood.
4. Model all steps and components of the strategy while thinking aloud.
5. Explain to the student when, where, and why to use the strategy.
6. Provide plenty of practice with corrective feedback, first with external guidance, then with the student thinking aloud, and finally while encouraging the student to internalize the strategy, such as having the student whisper the steps while enacting them.
7. Give the student reinforcement for and feedback on the use of the new strategy so that the student understands the personal efficacy of strategy use.
8. Encourage the student to monitor and evaluate strategy use and to attribute his or her success to strategy use.
9. Encourage generalization by discussing applications of the strategy and practicing the strategy under different situations.

## The Good Information Processor

The overall goal of strategy training is not to teach just one strategy but to help the learner develop into a "good" information processor. The essential characteristics of a good information processor, according to Pressley and Woloshyn (1995), include:

1. Possessing numerous strategies for accomplishing a variety of goals.
2. Being aware of one's cognitive strengths and weaknesses.
3. Using efficient processes to accomplish a task.
4. Knowing where and when to use a particular strategy.
5. Monitoring the use of a strategy to determine if the goal is being accomplished.
6. Being able to coordinate strategies to accomplish complex goals.
7. Having developed strategies that are efficient, automatic, and flexible.
8. Engaging in reflective thinking.

## Selection and Range of Interventions

Of course, success is not guaranteed, even with well established, evidence-based interventions. One determinant of success is how well an intervention matches the needs of the learner, the academic task, and the environmental demands. Interventions for processing problems should be closely tailored to the cognitive or neurodevelopmental profile of the student, thereby increasing the likelihood of positive outcomes (Feifer & DeFina, 2000). However, selecting an intervention that focuses on an isolated process may not be the most appropriate choice, given the interactive nature of processing components during cognitive activity (Swanson, Hoskyn, & Lee, 1999). It is also frequently the case that a student has impairments in several cognitive processes. Thus, broad based, higher level processing interventions are often appropriate. Because a disability is the product of an interaction between the individual and the environment, procedures that modify the environment also constitute interventions, for example, effective instructional practices that reduce the demands on learners' processing.

## THE IMPORTANCE OF EARLY INTERVENTIONS

Education's renewed emphasis on early interventions is consistent with the brain-based research on the importance of early interventions. Just like academic interventions, some processing interventions are more effective at earlier ages; for example, there are diminishing returns on phonological processing interventions as students progress through elementary school (National Reading Panel, 2000). Processing interventions, especially those of a remedial nature, need to occur before the maturing of the specific brain regions where the process of concern is located. The key to successfully educating and retraining the brain is enrichment and treatment at critical developmental stages (Feifer & DeFina, 2000). Change is more difficult once neural structures are established and myelination is complete. The windows of opportunity for most basic processes are in early childhood and early elementary; however, higher-level cognitive processes, in particular planning, reasoning, and executive processing, continue to develop into adolescence.

### Providing Processing Interventions in Educational Settings

For the most part, classroom teachers, special education teachers, school psychologists, and other educational staff can provide the interventions reviewed in this chapter. None of the practices require the completion of a special training course. Rather, independent study of the methods involved should suffice. When implementing the intervention, it is important to faithfully adhere to the procedural details recommended in research literature and other sources. The interventions reviewed in this chapter are primarily intended for those students who have learning challenges or are already identified as LD. However, even successful students may benefit from exposure to these interventions. Most of the interventions can be adapted for individual, group, or classroom use.

## PHONOLOGICAL PROCESSING INTERVENTIONS

Phonological processing is the manipulation of the phonemes that comprise words (Gillon, 2004). One of the most important phonological processes is phonemic awareness—the understanding that words, spoken and written, can be divided into discrete sounds. The importance of phonological processing and phonemic awareness to reading decoding and spelling has been extensively documented (Kamhi & Pollock, 2005; National Reading Panel, 2000). Children who are better at detecting phonemes learn to decode words more easily. Research has clearly established that a deficit in phonological processing is a common factor among individuals with early reading problems (Mather & Wendling, 2005). In fact, some experts argue that there is enough evidence to conclude that a phonological processing deficit is a primary cause of reading disabilities (Bus & Van Ijzendoorn, 1999). Given the fundamental role of phonological processing, it is alarming that one-third of middle-class first graders fail to fully recognize the phonemic structure of words, with an even higher proportion of phonemic awareness weaknesses among disadvantaged children (Brady, Fowler, Stone, & Winbury, 1994).

Of all the evidence-based processing interventions for academic learning, phonemic awareness training has the most consistent track record of success. Phonological processing deficiencies can be ameliorated through training (Hurford et al., 1994). Numerous studies have also unequivocally shown that explicit phonological processing or phonemic awareness training has significant positive transfer effects on reading, spelling, and other linguistic processes (Bus &

Van Ijzendoorn, 1999). Of the phonemic awareness studies reviewed by the National Reading Panel (2000), the overall effect sizes were .86 for phonemic awareness outcomes, .53 for reading outcomes, and .59 for spelling outcomes.

Several commercially available scientifically-based phonological awareness training programs are intended for classroom use (e.g., Adams, Foorman, Lundberg, & Beeler, 1998), and the teaching of phonemic awareness skills is often incorporated into effective reading curricula. Although a variety of approaches exist, including computer delivered instruction (Moore, Rosenberg, & Coleman, 2004), phonemic awareness programs address varied skills, including: (1) rhyming; (2) isolating phonemes; (3) identifying phonemes; (4) deleting phonemes; (5) categorizing common phonemes; (6) segmenting phonemes that comprise words; (7) and blending phonemes into words. Because the ability to segment words into phonemic units is the hallmark of phonological awareness, it should be the focus of any phonological awareness training. A major difference among phonological awareness programs is whether or not they include a linkage with written letters and words. Programs that directly connect phonological processing with reading are generally more effective (Bus & Van Ijzendoorn, 1999). Chapters 7 and 8 of this volume provide further information on teaching phonological awareness.

## WORKING MEMORY INTERVENTIONS

Working memory is defined as the limited capacity to retain information while simultaneously manipulating the same or other information for a short period of time (Swanson, 2000). Working memory evolved from the earlier concept of short-term memory; both working and short-term memory involve short-term preservation of information. Thus, the constructs are often viewed as interchangeable, or one is considered a subtype of the other. Working memory is distinct from short-term memory in that working memory involves active manipulation of information, whereas short-term memory is more static in nature. The classic WISC-IV Digit Span subtest (Wechsler, 2003a) illustrates the difference—responding correctly to Digits Forward requires only rote short-term memory while responding correctly to Digits Backward demands the manipulation that is the hallmark of working memory. In this chapter, the term "working memory" includes short-term memory; thus, interventions for working memory apply to short-term memory as well.

Working memory can be divided into four main subprocesses—auditory, visual-spatial, executive, and the episodic buffer. The classic three-part model (which excludes the episodic buffer) of working memory, first proposed in 1974 by Baddeley and Hitch, has withstood research and controversy and is currently compatible with neuropsychological evidence (Baddeley, 2006). The executive part of working memory has the central role of controlling the other three subsystems and regulating the cognitive processes involved in working memory performance, such as allocating limited attentional capacity. Because of its association with the frontal lobes, full development of the executive component occurs later than the auditory, visual-spatial, and episodic components (Gathercole, 1999). Auditory working memory (also known as the phonological loop) is divided into two subcomponents—a temporary phonological store and a subvocal rehearsal process (Minear & Shah, 2006). Visual-spatial working memory (also known as the visuo-spatial sketchpad) is divided into the same two subcomponents and involves short-term memory for objects and their location. The episodic buffer is a temporary storage system, consciously accessible, that interfaces with long-term memory and constructs integrated representations based on the information from long-term memory and the other working memory subsystems (Baddeley).

The capacity of working memory is quite restricted, even in individuals with normal working memory capacity. The typical individual can manage only five to nine pieces of information at a time. Unless the information is being manipulated, it will only remain in working memory for a short interval, typically a maximum of 20 to 30 seconds. Given the inherent limitations of working memory, efficient utilization of its resources is important for all individuals, not just those with working memory deficits or those with learning disabilities.

Working memory plays a critical, integral role in most higher-level cognitive activities, including reasoning, comprehension, learning, and academic performance (Dehn, 2006; McNamara & Scott, 2001). The cognitive processes that are closely linked with working memory include executive functioning, fluid reasoning, processing speed, and long-term memory encoding and retrieval (McNamara & Scott). For example, working memory interacts with long-term memory by manipulating incoming information and linking it with related prior knowledge and also by retrieving and evaluating stored knowledge. Consequently, adequate working memory processes are essential for cognitive performance and learning; working memory capacity sets limits on related higher-level processes (Conners, Rosenquist, & Taylor, 2001). In regards to academic learning, reading decoding, reading comprehension, math reasoning, and written expression all depend heavily on the adequate functioning of working memory; the strong relationships between academic functioning and working memory are well established (Berninger & Richards, 2002; Swanson, 2000; Swanson & Berninger, 1996).

Research has consistently found students with learning difficulties to display poor working memory performance, especially in auditory working memory (Swanson & Berninger, 1996). For example, in a WISC-IV standardization study (Wechsler, 2003b), children with reading disabilities obtained their lowest mean on the Working Memory Index. The differences between skilled readers and those with a reading disability are often attributed to deficiencies in working memory (Swanson, 2000). Adequate working memory capacity allows the reader to fluently decode and to complete more complex cognitive processes, such as reading comprehension (McNamara & Scott, 2001). As reading decoding becomes automated, more working memory resources become available for comprehension. Some researchers (Swanson, 2000) theorize that a working memory deficit is not entirely a capacity deficit. For some students with learning disabilities, a working memory problem is primarily a strategy deficit. That is, students with LD often possess sufficient working memory resources and the ability to apply effective strategies but fail to use these strategies spontaneously. Other populations with learning challenges are also known to have weaknesses in working memory relative to their other cognitive abilities, among them children with Down Syndrome (Comblain, 1994) and children with a language impairment (Gill, Klecan-Aker, Roberts, & Fredenburg, 2003). Children with ADHD are another group who typically demonstrate a deficit in working memory (Klingberg et al., 2002).

Developmentally, working memory span expands two- to three-fold between the ages of four and 14, with more gradual improvement after age eight (Gathercole, 1999). Longer working memory spans may be due to more than increased working memory capacity. For example, increases in processing speed, retrieval speed, and speech rate may account for some of the improvement (Henry & Millar, 1993). Moreover, executive processes and strategy use develop and increase with age (Andreassen & Waters, 1989); thus, increased use of strategies, such as verbal rehearsal and chunking, is at least partially responsible for the apparent expansion in working memory (Minear & Shah, 2006). Also, acquiring automaticity will free up working memory resources, giving the appearance of increased working memory capacity.

## Evidence-Based Working Memory Interventions

Practitioners need to be mindful of the diverse functions of working memory when assessing working memory and selecting interventions. A thorough assessment might help determine whether the learner's working memory weakness is primarily auditory, visual, or executive (Dehn, 2006;

Pickering & Gathercole, 2001). Children with learning disabilities are more likely to possess a deficit in auditory and executive working memory than in visual working memory (Swanson, 2000). The consensus among theorists is that the main source of individual differences in working memory is usually the amount of working memory capacity (Minear & Shah, 2006), although knowledge, experience, strategy use, and the degree of automaticity also impact performance on specific tasks. Moreover, disorganized information in long-term memory may exacerbate an already weak working memory. Failure to use efficient and appropriate strategies may also impair performance in an otherwise normal working memory (McNamara & Scott, 2001).

Some recent studies suggest that working memory capacity, especially working memory span, can be increased through training (Comblain, 1994; McNamara & Scott, 2001; Minear & Shah, 2006) and that the improvement generalizes to untrained tasks (Klingberg et al., 2002). For instance, Olesen et al. (2003) found that brain activity related to working memory increased after working memory training. Thus, there are many possibilities for intervention, not all of them strategic or compensatory.

Most interventions for working memory involve the teaching of a strategy. Research has found that most individuals naturally employ some type of strategy, typically a subvocal rehearsal strategy, during working memory tasks, and that strategic individuals recall more information than individuals who are non-strategic (McNamara & Scott, 2001). Strategy use is the result of experience and practice and is usually domain specific (Ericsson & Chase, 1982). Unless the trainee is encouraged to apply the strategy to different situations, generalization of strategy use seldom occurs. Some studies (Klingberg et al., 2002), however, have found generalization to untrained working memory tasks and related cognitive processes, such as reasoning. Continued strategy use may also depend on the individual's awareness of the benefits of strategy use.

*Rehearsal.*   The development of subvocal verbal rehearsal strategies is thought to be at least partially responsible for increased working memory span as children develop (Minear & Shah, 2006). Although children may begin using a simple rehearsal strategy as early as 5 or 6 years of age, rehearsal is not a widespread strategy until the age of 10 (Gill et al., 2003). Rehearsal, a serial repetitive process, allows information to be maintained in working memory for a longer period of time (Gathercole, 1999), thus facilitating long-term storage encoding. Children with disabilities often fail to develop or use verbal rehearsal strategies. Several studies have found explicit rehearsal training to significantly improve the working memory performance of children, with and without disabilities (Comblain, 1994; Conners et al., 2001). Adults with low working memory spans have also shown improvement after training in simple rote rehearsal strategies (McNamara & Scott, 2001; Turley-Ames & Whitfield, 2003). Moreover, there is evidence for the maintenance and durability of rehearsal training, especially when extensive practice and overlearning are provided during the initial training phase (Broadley, MacDonald, & Buckley, 1994). Rehearsal strategies have even been shown to be more effective than more elaborate memory strategies (Turley-Ames & Whitfield). Perhaps, this is because their simplicity is less demanding of already limited working memory resources or because more complicated strategies introduce interference.

Rehearsal strategies involve repetition of verbal stimuli, such as saying over and over again a list of words to be remembered. The teacher should instruct the learner to say the to-be-remembered words aloud as many times as possible during the procedure. If one word is introduced at a time, then that word should be repeated continually until the next is added, and then the new word along with the previous words should be repeated (Turley-Ames & Whitfield, 2003). At first, students should be directed to say the stimuli aloud, but as the intervention progresses they may whisper the words or subvocalize. The difficulty level can be adjusted by increasing the number of stimuli.

Several other rehearsal techniques also have been shown to be effective. Elaborative rehearsal (Banikowski & Mehring, 1999) involves associating the new information with prior knowledge. The association helps keep the information active in working memory without repetition and also facilitates moving the information into long-term memory (see the long-term memory interventions section for more details on elaboration). Once learners engage in auditory rehearsal with minimal cuing, they can be taught to visualize the instructions as a way of keeping the information active. For example, encourage students to rehearse instructions while they visualize or imagine themselves carrying out the instructions. Gill and colleagues (2003) discovered that adding a visualization component to the rehearsal strategy increased its effectiveness and long-term application. Another approach is to simply have students repeat instructions, which can be paraphrased, until they have completed the task (Gill et al., 2003).

*Chunking.*    Chunking refers to the pairing or association of different items into units that are remembered as a whole, thereby facilitating short-term retention and encoding into long-term storage. For example, instead of separately remembering the digits "8, 6, 5" it is easier to recall them grouped as the multidigit number 865. Chunking develops naturally as children develop automatized reading decoding skills, e.g., the three phonemes in "cat" become one unit instead of three, thereby freeing up working memory resources. In instances where the chunking strategy needs to be taught, follow the steps summarized by Parente and Herrmann (1996): (1) require the student to group single digits into a larger unit; (2) require the student to group a longer list of digits into multiple units; (3) continue training with commonly used numbers, such as phone numbers for practice; (4) continue practicing until the chunking is performed consistently and automatically; and (5) convince the student that the strategy is effective by reporting baseline and post-intervention data.

*Span Tasks.*    A few recent investigations indicate that directed efforts to increase working memory span may actually increase working memory capacity (Klingberg et al., 2002; Oleson et al., 2003). Daily practice of span activities, such as a backwards digit span task or a letter span task, over a period of several weeks may increase working memory capacity and result in improvement of even non-trained activities (Oleson et al.). Klingberg and colleagues lengthened span and improved working memory by using computerized software with a group of ADHD subjects.

## Interventions for Related Processes

When considering and implementing interventions for working memory, bear in mind that reciprocal relationships exist among working memory and other essential cognitive processes. Boosting capacity and performance of related processes may have a collateral affect on working memory performance. For example, refining and solidifying the concepts in long-term memory may reduce some of the encoding and retrieval burdens on working memory (Henry & Millar, 1993). Also, phonological awareness training is thought to lead to improvements in working memory (Minear & Shah, 2006). Furthermore, executive processing is known to be intertwined with working memory. Consequently, interventions designed to strengthen executive functioning should be incorporated into working memory interventions (Swanson, 2000).

## Classroom Instruction Strategies

In the educational environment, teachers can use effective instructional practices and accommodations to manage and reduce the working memory demands placed on learners (Mather &

Wendling, 2005). These practices are designed for use with an entire classroom or for use as individualized compensatory interventions. Instructional practices for working memory limitations include: brief and linguistically simple directions; frequent repetitions of instructions and new information; child repetition of crucial information; graphic organizers; external memory aides; and other methods that reduce the processing load of the task (Gathercole, Lamont, & Alloway, 2006). Helping students acquire mastery in basic skills also alleviates impositions on limited working memory resources.

In general, effective teaching practices, such as organized presentations, guided practice, and frequent review, also prevent frequent and extensive overloading of working memory (Farquhar & Surry, 1995). Many evidence-based reading, math, and written language curricula have embedded instructional procedures and strategies for working memory limitations (Chittooran & Tait, 2005). In fact, documented effective teaching models, such as direct instruction (Gersten & Keating, 1987), may be successful primarily because they address learners' working memory shortcomings (Rosenshine & Stevens, 1986).

## LONG-TERM MEMORY INTERVENTIONS

Unlike working memory, long-term memory is capable of storing a vast amount of information for a relatively long period of time. Many different kinds of long-term memory storage systems are distributed throughout the brain, and the same information can be stored in multiple ways with multiple retrieval cues (Berninger & Richards, 2002). Despite this diversity and flexibility, information is generally stored as visual images, verbal units, or both. Long-term memory is often divided into semantic, episodic, and visual (Banikowski & Mehring, 1999). Semantic memory contains facts and general knowledge, organized into networks of connected ideas called schemata. Episodic memory is autobiographical, like a video of experiences, and visual memory consists of visual images.

Cognitive psychologists also divide semantic memory according to the two major classifications of learning—declarative (factual knowledge) and procedural. Procedural memory is a store of the steps required to complete various tasks; for example, a math algorithm may be stored as procedural memory. Academic learning requires a well organized semantic memory for declarative knowledge, as well as adequate procedural memory. Learning difficulties that are attributed to weak long-term semantic memory are more likely due to poor encoding of new information, rather than to actual difficulties retrieving stored information. Thus, the majority of memory interventions focus on properly moving information into long-term semantic storage.

Substantial literature documents the efficacy and benefits of long-term memory interventions, especially with normal populations and with individuals who have mild to moderate memory impairments (Glisky & Glisky, 2002). Because direct remedial improvement of severely impaired memory functioning is considered unrealistic (Glisky & Glisky) and because poor memory performance is often a strategy deficiency, the general approach is to rely on mnemonics and other types of strategies. Mnemonics, which originated with the ancient Greeks and have been used in schools for over 250 years, are strategies for associating relatively meaningless input with more meaningful images or words already stored in long-term memory. Over the past 30 years, an abundance of empirical evidence supports the finding that the use of mnemonic strategies improves long-term memory performance (Eslinger; 2002; Levin, 1993; Mastropieri & Scruggs, 1991). In a meta-analysis of 34 studies involving the use of mnemonic strategies with LD students, the overall effect size was a very strong 1.62 (Mastropieri, Sweda, & Scruggs, 2000). For example, the effectiveness of the mnemonic known as the keyword method (described in The Keyword Method section) has been demonstrated across a variety of instructional settings and subject areas (Levin).

Most memory strategies are designed to provide a more efficient and more meaningful way of encoding information, such as associating it with existing knowledge, and to teach a way to use cues to facilitate retrieval. Long-term memory interventions can be classified under four general categories—rehearsal, organization, elaboration, and visualization. With long-term memory, rehearsal includes practice techniques, such as distributed practice and frequent review, not just immediate repetition. Organizational strategies support and align with the structure of semantic long-term memory, which is thought to be organized into hierarchical schemata (Gagne et al., 1993). Elaboration is a process of enhancing meaningfulness by relating the new information to existing schemata. And, visualization involves connecting auditory or verbal input with a visual image that will cue the correct verbal response. The choice of memory strategy should depend on the learner's profile and the learning requirements; for example, if a memory deficit is confined to the auditory/verbal domain, then visual strategies are most likely to be effective (Glisky & Glisky, 2002). Similarly, children with a specific language impairment are known to have difficulty encoding and retrieving auditory/verbal information. Consequently, the use of visual imagery may tap the strength of the child with a language impairment (Gill et al., 2003). Due to the integral relationship between long-term memory and working memory, long-term memory interventions may produce collateral improvement in working memory. Likewise, the success of long-term memory interventions depends on an adequately functioning working memory.

## Rehearsal

Rehearsal, commonly referred to as repetition, is the first approach most individuals will attempt when memorization is required. Studies have shown that even children in the first grade can be taught to use sophisticated rehearsal strategies (Rafoth, Leal, & DeFabo, 1993). Although it is a rote strategy that does not promote meaningful processing of information, rehearsal does result in learning information required for academics. However, there is no long-term or general benefit in terms of improving long-term memory functioning (Glisky & Glisky, 2002). Nevertheless, rehearsal is a crucial step because without rehearsal it would not be possible to maintain information in working memory long enough (see discussion in working memory section) to encode it into long-term memory (Parente & Herrmann, 1996).

## Practice and Review Techniques

Distributed practice, in which several short intervals of instruction or self-study are separated by other activities, has been found to result in greater long-term retention of skills and knowledge than massed practice. The positive effects of distributed practice have been demonstrated with a variety of academic subjects, settings, and tasks, as well as with various learners with special needs (Crawford & Baine, 1992; Swanson, 2001). Spaced retrieval, a distributed practice technique in which there are gradually increasing intervals between rehearsal, has even been found to be effective for severely memory impaired individuals (Eslinger, 2002). In the classroom, distributed practice requires a teacher to periodically review previously taught material, with a gradual increase in the intervening intervals. Distributed practice is consistent with the literature on effective teaching, and it is incorporated into structured methodologies, such as direct instruction.

## Organizational Methods

Another class of strategies involves the organization of information into natural groupings or categories. These methods are particularly relevant for encoding information into and retrieving information from semantic memory, such as when studying an academic subject. For instance, when learning a list of items, it is worthwhile to group the items into categories and then later try to recall them by category (Parente & Herrmann, 1996). To teach an organizational strategy, follow these steps: (1) present a list of about 15 items to memorize; (2) have the student separate the list of words into structural categories; (3) require the student to recall the categories first, then the individual items; (4) demonstrate to the student that this method works by comparing results with a pretest completed before the strategy was taught; (4) continue practicing until the student can generalize the strategy; and (5) for students unable to form semantic categories, try more concrete categories, such as acoustic similarities. During classroom instruction, effective teachers can facilitate long-term encoding and retrieval through organized presentations and by grouping information items categorically.

## Elaboration

While simple repetitive practice has long been known to be an ineffective way to ensure retention of information over the long term (Glisky & Glisky, 2002), making information meaningful is more likely to be successful (Levin & Levin, 1990). The process of making information meaningful is accomplished by relating new information to already stored information, a strategy known as elaboration (Gagne et al., 1993). Elaboration occurs when a learner brings associated or related knowledge from long-term semantic memory into working memory and constructs a verbal or visual memory link between that knowledge and the information to be learned (Ritchie & Karge, 1996). To complete the elaboration process, the learner needs to thoughtfully pause in order to create a meaningful link, such as an inference, with prior knowledge.

If conducted correctly, elaboration actually adds to the incoming information. At the encoding level, elaboration improves retrieval through associating and storing related facts and concepts together. The elaboration process can also facilitate retrieval directly—thinking about what you know about a general topic often leads to recall of the specific information needed. In addition to long-term storage and retrieval, elaboration improves comprehension and learning (Levin & Levin, 1990).

General training steps for the elaboration strategy include: explain what elaboration is and why it helps memory; teach how and when to use it; and provide plenty of practice during both encoding and retrieval (Gagne et al., 1993). Without explicitly training the strategy, instructors may facilitate elaboration by modeling it, by prompting students to do it, and by allowing time for it. The general approach is to instruct students to think about what they already know about the new material. Examples of specific prompts include directions to paraphrase, summarize, draw inferences, or generate questions (Ritchie & Karge, 1996). In general, effective teaching practices, such as providing advance organizers, support elaborative thinking. Teachers may also suggest specific links between new information and prior knowledge. Because children do not spontaneously elaborate until about 11 years of age, young children remember more when teachers provide elaborations (Rafoth et al., 1993). On the other hand, adolescents may benefit more from self-constructed associations.

## Visual Imagery

Visual imagery can be used in a variety of ways; it involves more than just creating a visual image of the item to be learned. It is especially applicable with students who have deficits in auditory or verbal memory or have language disorders. The method creates associations between unrelated words and objects, thereby instilling meaning into these arbitrary relationships and prompting recall of the verbal information. Imagery procedures are most effective when the images are created by the student and when parts of the image interact (Ritchie & Karge, 1996). Several approaches can be used to teaching mental imagery. Whichever is selected, it is important to demonstrate the power of a visual image by first having the student try to recall a list of words through rote memorization and then directing the student to form a visual image of each word and comparing recall with that of rote memorization. An example of a visual imagery mnemonic is the rhyming pegword method, whereby the numbers from one to ten are associated with rhymes (e.g., "one-bun," "two-shoe," etc.). The first item to be remembered is visually linked with a bun, the second with a shoe, and so on (Wilson, 1987).

## The Keyword Method

The keyword method, a mnemonic that incorporates elaboration, paired association, and visual imagery, can be used when learning a variety of content areas but is especially effective when learning new vocabulary words (Mastropieri & Scruggs, 1998). The keyword method, perhaps the most researched and effective mnemonic strategy, consists of two stages. During the first stage, the acoustical link stage, the learner selects or is given a concrete word (the keyword) that sounds like the stimulus word. In the second stage, the learner is provided with or creates an image of the keyword interacting with the appropriate definition or response word. For example, in learning the Spanish word "pato" (duck), the learner decides that it reminds him or her of the keyword "pot" and then creates an image, such as a duck with a pot on its head. When retrieving, students think of the keyword, remember the association, and then retrieve the definition (Mather & Wendling, 2005). Researchers have reported that while students with LD can generate their own keywords and interactive images, their retrieval is better when they are provided with the keywords and interactive mnemonic pictures (Scruggs & Mastropieri, 1990).

Different variations of the keyword approach exist, including keyword-mediated instruction, which has been found superior to direct instruction (Pressley, Johnson, & Symons, 1987). Also, Bulgren, Hock, Schumaker, and Deshler (1995) expanded the keyword method into a comprehensive strategy referred to as Paired Associates Strategy (PAS) and provided empirical evidence for its use. In addition to keyword pairing and mental imagery, the PAS method has students put the informational pairs on study cards, draw the visual image, and do a self-test.

## Other Mnemonics

In addition to the keyword technique, there are several other evidence-based mnemonic techniques, many of which are quite familiar to teachers and students. These include acrostics and acronyms, which make use of first letter cueing, and are especially helpful when it is necessary to recall already known material in the correct order (Wilson, 1987). For example, the colors of the rainbow can be remembered by the acrostic "*R*ichard *O*f *Y*ork *G*ives *B*attle *I*n *V*ain." Other mnemonics involve the creation of visual images or a rhyme or song (Frender, 2004). Mnemonics are thought to work successfully because they allow previously isolated items to become integrated with each other (Wilson).

## EXECUTIVE AND METACOGNITIVE INTERVENTIONS

One reason students with learning problems seldom utilize strategies that would improve the functioning of their cognitive processes is that they are deficient in metacognition, a prominent aspect of executive processing (Wynn-Dancy & Gillam, 1997). Metacognition oversees cognition; cognitive strategy selection, usage, and monitoring are the primary functions of metacognition. Metacognition consists of two major components—the individual's self-awareness of his or her cognitive processes and the self-directed control and regulation of one's cognitive processing. Self-regulation is the essence of executive processing (Dawson & Guare, 2004). Interventions to improve an individual's self-regulatory functioning through self-instruction training go back more than 30 years (Meichenbaum & Goodman, 1971). The effectiveness of self-instruction training, also known as verbal mediation training, has consistently been supported in the literature (Cicerone, 2002). Specific metacognitive strategies, such as self-monitoring, can also be taught and typically result in significantly improved metacognitive functioning and cognitive strategy use and performance (Moreno & Saldana, 2004; Swanson, 2001; Wynn-Dancy & Gillam, 1997).

To encourage internalization of regulatory behavior, three stages of self-instruction training are involved: the student first learns to verbalize or think aloud; the student then whispers to herself or himself while engaging in self-regulatory behavior; and finally the student talks silently to himself or herself before and during actual task performance. Self-instruction training is often paired with learning a problem-solving algorithm, such as goal management training (Levine et al., 2000).

Metacognitive strategy training typically involves the teaching of strategies relating to a specific cognitive, behavioral, or academic task (Graham & Harris, 1989; Loarer, 2003); for example, poor readers are often taught metacognitive strategies concerning reading comprehension. Key aspects of metacognitive interventions include teaching the individual: to become aware of processing deficits and strengths; how to select an appropriate strategy for the task at hand; to self-monitor progress towards an objective; to revise or change strategies when necessary; and to self-evaluate.

Metacognitive or executive strategy training is often selected even when there is no presumption of a metacognitive or executive processing deficit. This is because high level strategic thinking permits more effective use of underutilized or impaired processes. Educators might also select executive strategy training when students fail to spontaneously use or maintain strategies they have learned for other process deficits (Lawson & Rice, 1989). When executive or metacognitive processing is itself the underdeveloped process, then the intervention should include self-instruction training because self-regulation depends on internal self-talk. When considering executive and metacognitive interventions, developmental factors need to be taken into account, as executive processing is one of the last cognitive functions to fully develop.

## INTERVENTIONS FOR PLANNING

Planning, a key component of executive processing, is a higher-level cognitive process that is essential for academic learning and performance. Numerous studies have documented the efficacy of educational interventions designed to facilitate planning (Conway & Ashman, 1989; Cormier, Carlson, & Das, 1990; Kar et al., 1993; Naglieri & Gottling, 1997) and have reported effect sizes as large as 1.4 (Naglieri & Johnson, 2000). Following intervention, students perform better on planning tasks, with poor planners improving more than good planners (Naglieri & Johnson). Teachers can provide strategy instruction designed to facilitate planning to individuals, groups, or entire classrooms. The instruction should be explicit and include: teaching students about plans and strategy use; discussing how planning helps students be more successful; explaining why some methods work better than others; requiring students to verbalize their planning process, and encouraging students to develop, use, and evaluate their own planning strategies (Naglieri

& Pickering, 2003). The technique does not entail using teacher scripts or rigidly formatted procedures.

## Planning Interventions Involving Mathematics

Planning is the foundation of problem-solving, a requisite process for mathematics; for example, poor planning may result in selecting the wrong math operation or failure to check work. Consequently, planning interventions have often involved mathematics activities. In studies involving math, math performance improved after instruction that facilitated planning (Naglieri & Gottling, 1997; Naglieri & Johnson, 2000). The procedure begins with students spending about 10 minutes completing a math worksheet. The teacher then engages the students in a discussion about how they completed the problems, which methods worked well and which worked poorly, and how they might accomplish the task more successfully in the future. For example, the teacher might ask, "Is there a better way, or is there another way to do this?" The initial purpose of this self-reflection session is to facilitate the students' understanding of the need to be planful and to utilize an efficient strategy when completing math problems (Naglieri & Gottling, 1997). The long-term goal is to help the children engage in self-reflective planning processes. See chapter 11, this volume, regarding other effective techniques for improving math performance.

## Strategy Verbalization

Requiring students to verbalize their planned strategies can be implemented with any task, not just math activities, and it can be done prior to completing the task. For example, the teacher might ask the student to explain how she or he is going to proceed with each step of the task. The teacher should require the student to explain the reason for each strategy he or she plans to employ. Verbalization tends to be successful because of the interrelationship between verbalization and the planning process. One function of verbalization is the formulation and generation of sequential plans of action (Kar et al., 1993). Overt verbalization makes elements of planning explicit and guides the problem solving activity. Thus, verbalization is a strategy that augments the planning process.

## INTERVENTIONS FOR ATTENTION DEFICITS

Attention is a fundamental process on which many higher-level processes depend (Manly, Ward, & Robertson, 2002). For instance, attentional processes are intimately related with self-regulatory executive processes, such as planning. In fact, deficient executive processing, rather than limited attentional capacity, may account for attention problems. According to Barkley (1997), problems with sustaining attention are caused by difficulties with inhibitory control, an executive function. Given the prevalence of diagnosed attention disorders and their detrimental impact on academic learning and performance, treatment for attention problems should be a priority in school systems. Pharmacological treatment is usually the treatment of choice for individuals diagnosed with attentional deficits. Despite the prevalent use of medication, most research on ADHD interventions concludes that a multimodal approach, a combination of medication, behavior modification, and school accommodations, is the most effective (Miranda, Jarque, & Tarraga, 2006). From a cognitive processing perspective, self-regulatory training should be another component of treatment, as medication combined with self-regulation may be more effective than medication alone (Reid, Trout, & Schartz, 2005). Also, many behavior modification procedures for attention problems include self-regulatory strategies (Miranda et al.). For more information, see chapter 3 of this volume on ADHD interventions.

## Self-Monitoring Training

Self-monitoring is a critical inhibitory process; thus, many interventions for attention deficits involve training in self-monitoring strategies. Several studies have found self-monitoring of attention to be effective in helping children with ADHD increase attending behaviors and academic productivity and decrease inappropriate behavior (Reid, 1999; Shimabukuro, Prater, Jenkins, & Edelen, 1999), with the majority of effect sizes in the moderate to large range of .6 or greater (Reid et al., 2005). Self-monitoring training with LD students has been associated with improved performance on measures of reading, attention, and inhibitory control (Brown & Alford, 1984). Self-monitoring training, a subtype of cognitive self-instruction, should be implemented in the general education classroom during common learning activities (Harris, Friedlander, Saddler, Frizzelle, & Graham, 2005). Wearing headphones, the student listens to taped tones that occur at random intervals, ranging from 10 to 90 seconds. The student is taught to self-assess by asking, "Was I paying attention?" immediately upon hearing a taped tone. The student then self-records whether he or she was on task when the tone sounded, and tally sheets are collected daily. A high degree of accuracy is not necessary for the effects of self-monitoring to occur. Students may also be taught to self-monitor their academic performance, such as recording the number of times information was correctly practiced, the amount of work completed, and the accuracy of the work (Harris et al., 2005; Shimabukuro et al., 1999). Whenever observable behaviors are being monitored, teachers may provide an external check on the accuracy of the student's recordings (Reid et al., 2005). Student graphing of on-task behavior or academic performance measures is another option (Shimabukuro et al, 1999).

## Computerized Interventions

Some interventions for attentional dysfunctions have used computer technology, which makes long periods of inexpensive, systematic training possible. Computerized programs are often designed to increase the duration of sustained attention and the efficiency of selective attention, through such tasks as the color-word Stroop task. Manly and colleagues (2002) report studies of computerized interventions that not only improved attentional capacity but also resulted in generalization and maintenance.

## VISUAL AND AUDITORY PROCESSING INTERVENTIONS

As stated earlier in the historical review section, past and recent attempts to ameliorate what are considered general visual or auditory processing deficits have generally met with failure (Friel-Patti, 1999; Wood & Fussey, 1987). Whereas modality training is clearly ineffective, interventions for specific subprocesses in the auditory domain, such as phonological processing and auditory short-term memory, have been very successful. Regarding visual processing, only recently have there been a few reports of successful treatment, often limited to those with acquired brain injury. Perhaps the problem with the constructs of visual and auditory processing is that they are too broad, similar to a right-brain, left-brain division; as suggested by Berninger and Richards (2002), the focus should be on component or subprocesses. Also, poor performance on modality measures may be due to interaction with other processes, such as working memory or attention

(Friel-Patti). Nevertheless, the broad visual and auditory processes should not be ignored entirely because they obviously involve critical brain functions and because one or the other can play an important intervention role as a strength serving a compensatory function.

Studies examining compensatory interventions for visual processing deficits have sometimes been successful, especially those using computerized visual information (Dirette & Hinojosa, 1999). Although much of the research has been done with subjects who have acquired brain injury, positive results have been obtained with normal students as well (Dirette & Hinojosa). A commonly used compensatory strategy for visual processing weaknesses is verbalization—orally repeating information gathered visually so as to enhance processing and recall. However, the positive evidence for verbalization or other forms of linguistic coding of visual information, especially in an educational environment, is limited (Anderson, 2002; Dirette & Hinojosa). Consequently, educational interventions for broad visual processing deficits are not recommended at this time. Fortunately, recent research has indicated that there is not a strong relationship between visual-spatial processing and academic performance (Evans et al., 2002; Floyd et al., 2003). Nevertheless, when visual processing is a strength, as it often is for individuals with learning disabilities, it can be incorporated into interventions; for instance, visual imaging has been successfully employed during compensatory interventions for long-term verbal memory weaknesses.

## SIMULTANEOUS AND SUCCESSIVE PROCESSING INTERVENTIONS

### PREP: A PASS Remedial Program

The purpose of PREP (Process-Based Reading Enhancement Program) is to remediate successive and simultaneous processing deficiencies, with the ultimate goal of improving reading decoding (Carlson & Das, 1997). During twice weekly sessions for about 16 weeks, learners are trained in global processes in a manner that encourages internalization, along with subsequent generalization and transfer. Children become aware of the underlying cognitive processes through guided discussion of what they are doing during and following the tasks. The tasks include procedures such as rehearsal, categorization, monitoring of performance, and prediction. The program consists of four successive and four simultaneous processing modules, with scripted instructions for each task. The tasks are divided into three levels of difficulty. Each task has a global component that fosters the development of successive or simultaneous processing and a bridging component that extends the task to a particular academic area. For example, for one simultaneous global component, the child selects which of two or three similar pictures is best described by a passage. For the related bridging component, the child selects which of three or four sentences best describes a single picture. PREP avoids explicit teaching of specific reading skills. Detailed descriptions of the procedures can be found in the appendix to Das, Mishra, and Pool (1995). Several studies, for example Das, Mishra, and Pool, have found PREP, which was first introduced in 1976, to be effective at improving reading decoding and reading comprehension. The success of PREP may also result from enhancement of related processes, such as planning and short-term memory.

### Simultaneous Processing

Another method for improving simultaneous processing is to provide learners with practice in forming verbal and nonverbal relationships by having them link items of information into a surveyable array (such as mapping a story on the board) and making inferences from the whole (Leasak et al., 1982). Other approaches to developing simultaneous processing are: matching and categorizing items; having the student supply missing details in a story; teaching the student how to summarize a written passage; and having the student create and use maps, both geographical and contextual (Naglieri & Pickering, 2003).

## Processing Speed

Processing speed, the speed and efficiency with which simple cognitive tasks are executed over a sustained period of time, is a strong correlate of basic academic skills (Fuchs et al, 2006; Mather & Wendling, 2005). Processing speed is also closely interrelated with other key cognitive processes, mainly working memory and long-term retrieval. The quick and fluent processing of information frees up limited resources so that higher level processing can occur. To date, no successful remedial or compensatory interventions for slow processing speed have been published. Nevertheless, accommodations, such as extended test time, may be appropriate (Mather & Wendling, 2005).

## Fluid Reasoning

Fluid reasoning is a higher level cognitive process that involves solving novel problems using inductive and deductive reasoning. Although most tasks used to assess fluid reasoning are of a nonverbal nature, fluid reasoning also includes verbal reasoning. Along with executive processing, it is one of the last cognitive processes to fully develop. Fluid reasoning ability is predictive of performance in mathematical reasoning and reading comprehension (Mather & Wendling, 2005). Interventions that directly improve fluid reasoning are non-existent. However, students with low fluid reasoning can be taught mathematical problem-solving strategies that improve their math performance (Owen & Fuchs, 2002), and planning interventions (see previous section) are also likely to have a collateral effect. Furthermore, many of the well documented reading comprehension strategies, such as elaboration, identifying the main idea, and self-questioning, are effective with learners with low fluid reasoning (Pressley & Woloshyn, 1995). Finally, effective instructional techniques also have a positive impact on the academic learning of those with fluid reasoning weaknesses and deficits (Swanson, 2001).

## RECOMMENDATIONS

Educators considering processing interventions should keep the following conclusions and recommendations in mind:

1. Educational interventions for processing deficiencies should avoid efforts that focus on remediation only, except for those processes, such as phonological processing, where research supports the likelihood of improvement. Until brain research clarifies the actual outcomes of neurological interventions, a compensatory approach that includes strategy training is the most defensible. The primary goal of interventions for processing deficits should be improved memory, academic learning, and academic performance, not the amelioration of a specific process per se.
2. Because of the interrelated functioning of cognitive processes, processing interventions should be top-down, especially when it is unclear which processes may account for poor performance. A top-down approach focuses on, or at least includes, executive processing interventions, providing the learner with self-regulatory strategies that will allow for

more efficient utilization of existing resources across a variety of processes.

3. What often appears as a processing deficit may actually be a performance deficit, resulting from a lack of strategy application. Thus, the teaching of cognitive strategies is a very appropriate processing intervention. Students who have not developed strategies independently will benefit the most from strategy instruction.

4. In the classroom, a variety of cognitive strategies should be taught routinely and explicitly, beginning in early elementary. The teaching of strategies should be embedded into routine instruction in most content areas; for example, keyword associations and images should be provided whenever new vocabulary is introduced or facts need to be memorized.

5. Educational interventions that are directed towards developing academic skills may be enhanced by the inclusion of a processing component. For instance, most effective early reading programs already include phonological processing training. Academic skills programs might also include interventions for working memory, long-term memory, planning, and executive processing, as these are inherent weaknesses among those with learning challenges.

6. Classroom instructional practices should support the information processing limitations that all learners experience. First and foremost, teachers need to avoid overloading learners' working memory. Secondly, elementary teachers should support executive processes that are not fully developed, such as providing cues that sustain attention.

7. For maintenance and generalization to occur, especially with strategy training, the intervention should include: explicit teaching of the method; student practice until there is overlearning; practice in a variety of settings and situations; feedback that demonstrates the self-efficacy of the method; and imparting when and where to use the method.

8. Many neuropsychological interventions that have been successful with acquired brain injured individuals are applicable to students with developmental and learning disabilities, typically with little adaptation. Hopefully, educational personnel with an interest in school neuropsychology will help to bridge the gap from clinic to school setting.

## DIRECTIONS FOR FUTURE RESEARCH

Some processing interventions, such as phonological interventions, already have more than adequate substantiation, but much remains to be accomplished before processing interventions will gain wide acceptance and implementation. Future studies should:

1. Develop and test standardized treatment protocols that consistently adhere to core aspects of the intervention. This allows for replication studies and facilitates correct usage of the intervention once it is validated.

2. Test how well clinic-developed treatments can be applied in an educational environment. In these instances, teachers and other school personnel should be the experimental trainers.

3. Assess whether improved performance actually results from changes in the targeted process. For example, when phonemic awareness improves, might it be due to improved attention or memory?

4. Continue to identify the specific subprocesses that comprise broader processes and then develop and test more narrowly focused interventions.

5. Investigate the learner characteristics that predict success, including such factors as age, severity of impairment, and number of deficient processes.

6. Examine more methods designed to increase maintenance and generalization once treatment is terminated.

7. Continue to study the relationships between specific processes and specific types of academic learning. Also, assess response to processing interventions with academic skills and performance measures, in addition to processing instruments.

## CONCLUSION

Rejuvenated by neuroscience research on learning and neuropsychological interventions research, processing interventions once again hold promise for struggling learners. Children with learning problems and learning disabilities typically have one or more underlying cognitive processing weaknesses or deficits. Some processes have strong relationships with specific areas of academic learning, whereas other processes play a critical role in all aspects of learning. Academic interventions and instructional approaches can be more successful when they address students' processing deficiencies. Moreover, directed efforts to improve cognitive processing performance are appropriate in an educational environment. While currently evidence-based interventions for only a few cognitive processes exist, these effective interventions can lead to improved learning and academic performance. As new interventions continue to emerge and become established in the educational environment, the foundation of processing interventions—cognitive strategy training—remains the method of choice for higher-level cognitive processing problems.

## REFERENCES

Adams, J. A., Foorman, B. R., Lundberg, I., & Beeler, T. (1998). *Phonemic awareness in young children: A classroom curriculum*. Baltimore: Brookes.

Anderson, J. R. (1976). *Language, memory, and thought*. Hillsdale, NJ: Erlbaum.

Anderson, S. W. (2002). Visuoperceptual impairments. In P. J. Eslinger (Ed.), *Neuropsychological interventions: Clinical research and practice* (pp. 163–181). New York: Guilford.

Andreassen, C., & Waters, H. S. (1989). Organization during study: Relationships between metamemory, strategy use, and performance. *Journal of Educational Psychology, 81,* 170–191.

Baddeley, A. D. (2006). Working memory: An overview. In S. J. Pickering (Ed.), *Working memory and education* (pp. 1–31). Burlington, MA: Academic Press.

Baddeley, A. D., & Hitch, G. J. (1974). Working memory. In G. A. Bower (Ed.), *Recent advances in learning and motivation. Vol. 8,* (pp. 47–89). New York: Academic Press.

Banikowski, A. K., & Mehring, T. A. (1999). Strategies to enhance memory based on brain-research. *Focus on Exceptional Children, 32,* 1–16.

Barkley, R. A. (1997). Behavioral inhibition, sustained attention and executive functions: Constructing a unifying theory of ADHD. *Psychological Bulletin, 121,* 65–94.

Berninger, V. W., & Richards, T. L. (2002). *Brain literacy for educators and psychologists.* San Diego: Academic Press.

Brady, S., Fowler, A., Stone, B., & Winbury, N. (1994). Training phonological awareness: A study with inner-city kindergarten children. *Annals of Dyslexia, 44,* 26–59.

Broadley, I., MacDonald, J., & Buckley, S. (1994). Are children with Down's syndrome able to maintain skills learned from a short-term memory training programme? *Down Syndrome: Research and Practice, 2,* 116–122.

Brown, R. T., & Alford, N. (1984). Ameliorating attentional deficits and concomitant academic deficiencies in learning disabled children through cognitive training. *Journal of Learning Disabilities, 17,* 20–26.

Brown-Chidsey, R., & Steege, M. W. (2005). *Response to Intervention: Principles and strategies for effective practice.* New York: Guilford.

Bulgren, J. A., Hock, M. F., Schumaker, J. B., & Deshler, D. D. (1995). The effects of instruction in a paired associate strategy on information mastery performance of students with learning disabilities. *Learning Disabilities Research & Practice, 10,* 22–37.

Bus, A., & Van Ijzendoorn, M. (1999). Phonological awareness and early reading: A meta-analysis of experimental training studies. *Journal of Educational Psychology, 91,* 403–414.

Carlson, J. S., & Das, J. P. (1997). A process approach to remediating word-decoding deficiencies in Chapter 1 children. *Learning Disability Quarterly, 20,* 93–102.

Carroll, J. B. (1993). *Human Cognitive Abilities: A survey of factor-analytic studies.* New York: Cambridge University Press.

Chittooran, M. M., & Tait, R. C. (2005). Understanding and implementing neuropsychologically based written language interventions. In R. C. D'Amato, E. Fletcher-Janzen, & C. R. Reynolds (Eds.), *Handbook of school neuropsychology* (pp. 777–803). Hoboken, NJ: Wiley.

Cicerone, K. D. (2002). The enigma of executive functioning. In P. J. Eslinger (Ed.), *Neuropsychological interventions: Clinical research and practice* (pp. 3–15). New York: Guilford.

Comblain, A. (1994). Working memory in Down syndrome: Training the rehearsal strategy. *Down Syndrome: Research and Practice, 2,* 123–126.

Conners, F. A., Rosenquist, C. J., & Taylor, L. A. (2001). Memory training for children with Down syndrome. *Down Syndrome: Research and Practice, 7,* 25–33.

Conway, R. N., & Ashman, A. (1989). Teaching planning skills in the classroom: The development of an integrated model. *International Journal of Disability, Development and Education, 36,* 225–240.

Cormier, P., Carlson, J. S., & Das, J. P. (1990). Planning ability and cognitive performance: The compensatory effects of a dynamic assessment approach. *Learning and Individual Differences, 2,* 437–449.

Crawford, S. A. S., & Baine, D. (1992). Making learning memorable: Distributed practice and long-term retention by special needs students. *Canadian Journal of Special Education, 8,* 118–128.

D'Amato, R. C., Fletcher-Janzen, E., Reynolds, C. R. (Eds.). (2005). *Handbook of school neuropsychology.* Hoboken, NJ: Wiley.

Das, J. P., Mishra, R. K., & Pool, J. E. (1995). An experiment on cognitive remediation of word-reading difficulty. *Journal of Learning Disabilities, 28,* 66–79.

Das, J. P., Naglieri, J. A., & Kirby, J. R. (1994). Assessment of cognitive processes: The PASS theory of intelligence. New York: Allyn & Bacon.

Dawson, P., & Guare, R. (2004). *Executive skills in children and adolescents.* New York: Guilford.

Dehn, M. J. (2006). *Essentials of processing assessment.* Hoboken, NJ: Wiley.

Deshler, D. D., & Schumaker, J. B. (1993). Strategy mastery by at-risk students: Not a simple matter. *The Elementary School Journal, 94,* 153–167.

Dirette, D. K., & Hinojosa, J. (1999). The effects of compensatory intervention on processing deficits of adults with acquired brain injuries. *Occupational Therapy Journal of Research, 19,* 223–240.

Ericsson, K. A., & Chase, W. G. (1982). Exceptional memory. *American Scientist, 70,* 607–615.

Eslinger, P. J. (Ed.). (2002). *Neuropsychological interventions: Clinical research and practice.* New York: Guilford.

Evans, J. J., Floyd, R. G., McGrew, K. S., & Leforgee, M. H. (2002). The relations between measures of Cattell-Horn-Carroll (CHC) cognitive abilities and reading achievement during childhood and adolescence. *School Psychology Review, 31,* 246–262.

Farquhar, J. D., & Surry, D. W. (1995). Reducing impositions on working memory through instructional strategies. *Performance and Instruction, 34* (8), 4–7.

Feifer, S. G., & DeFina, P. D. (2000). *The neuropsychology of reading disorders: Diagnosis and intervention workbook.* Middletown, MD: School Neuropsych Press.

Feifer, S. G., & DeFina, P. D. (2002). *The neuropsychology of written language disorders: Diagnosis and intervention.* Middletown, MD: School Neuropsych Press.

Feifer, S. G., & DeFina, P. D. (2005). *The neuropsychology of mathematics: Diagnosis and intervention.* Middletown, MD: School Neuropsych Press.

Floyd, R. G. (2005). Information-processing approaches to interpretation of contemporary intellectual assessment instruments. In D. P. Flanagan & P. L. Harrison (Eds.), *Contemporary intellectual assessment: Theories, tests, and issues* (2nd ed., pp. 203–233). New York: Guilford.

Floyd, R. G., Evans, J. J., & McGrew, K. S. (2003). Relations between measures of Cattell-Horn-Carroll (CHC) cognitive abilities and mathematics achievement across the school age years. *Psychology in the Schools, 60,* 155–171.

Frender, G. (2004). *Learning to learn: Strengthening study skills & brain power* (rev. ed.). Nashville, TN: Incentive Publications.

Friel-Patti, S. (1999). Clinical decision-making in assessment and intervention of central auditory processing disorders. *Language, Speech, and Hearing Services in Schools, 30,* 345–352.

Fuchs, L. S., Fuchs, D., Compton, D. L., Powell, S. R., Seethaler, P. M., Capizzi, A. M., et al. (2006). The cognitive correlates of third-grade skills in arithmetic, algorithmic computation, and arithmetic word problems. *Journal of Educational Psychology, 98,* 29–43.

Gagne, E. D., Yekovich, C. W., & Yekovich, F. R. (1993). *The cognitive psychology of school learning* (2nd ed.). New York: HarperCollins College.

Gagne, R. M. (1974). *Essentials of learning for instruction.* New York: Holt, Rinehart, and Winston.

Gathercole, S. E. (1999). Cognitive approaches to the development of short-term memory. *Trends in Cognitive Sciences, 3,* 410–419.

Gathercole, S. E., Lamont, E., & Alloway, T. P. (2006). Working memory in the classroom. In S. J. Pickering (Ed.), *Working memory and education* (pp. 219–240). Burlington, MA: Academic Press.

Gersten, R., & Keating, T. (1987). Long-term benefits from direct instruction. *Educational Leadership, 44,* 28–29.

Gill, C. B., Klecan-Aker, J., Roberts, T., & Fredenburg, K. A. (2003). Following directions: Rehearsal and visualization strategies for children with specific language impairment. *Child Language Teaching & Therapy, 19,* 85–104.

Gillon, G. T. (2004). *Phonological awareness.* New York: Guilford.

Glisky, E. L., & Glisky, M. L. (2002). Learning and memory impairments. In P. J. Eslinger (Ed.), *Neuropsychological interventions: Clinical research and practice* (pp. 137–162). New York: Guilford.

Graham, S., & Harris, K. R. (1989). Component analysis of cognitive strategy instruction: Effects on learning disabled students' compositions and self-efficacy. *Journal of Educational Psychology, 81,* 353–361.

Hale, J. B., & Fiorello, C. A. (2004). *School neuropsychology: A practitioner's handbook.* New York: Guilford.

Hammill, D. D., Goodman, L, & Weiderholt, J. L. (1974). Visual-motor processes: Can we train them? *Reading Teacher, 27,* 469–478.

Hammill, D. D., & Larsen, S. C. (1974). The effectiveness of psycholinguistic training. *Exceptional Children, 41,* 5–14.

Harris, K. R., Friedlander, B. D., Saddler, B., Frizzelle, R., & Graham, S. (2005). Self-monitoring of attention versus self-monitoring of academic performance: Effects among students with ADHD in the general education classroom. *The Journal of Special Education, 39,* 145–156.

Henry, L. A., & Millar, S. (1993). Why does memory span improve with age? A review of the evidence for two current hypotheses. *European Journal of Cognitive Psychology, 5,* 241–287.

Horn, J. L., & Blankson, N. (2005). Foundations for better understanding of cognitive abilities. In D. P. Flanagan & P. L. Harrison (Eds.), *Contemporary intellectual assessment: Theories, tests, and issues* (2nd ed., pp. 41–68). New York: Guilford.

Hurford, D., Johnston, M., Nepote, P., Hampton, S., Moore, S., Neal, J., et al. (1994). Early identification and remediation of phonological-processing deficits in first-grade children at risk for reading disabilities. *Journal of Learning Disabilities, 27,* 647–659.

Kamhi, A. G., & Pollock, K. E. (2005). *Phonological disorders in children: Clinical decision making in assessment and intervention.* Baltimore: Brookes.

Kar, B. C., Dash, U. N., Das, J. P., & Carlson, J. (1993). Two experiments on the dynamic assessment of planning. *Learning and Individual Differences, 5,* 13–29.

Kavale, K. A. (1990). Effectiveness of special education. In T. B. Gutkin & C. R. Reynolds (Eds.), *The handbook of school psychology* (2nd ed., pp. 868–898). Hoboken, NJ: Wiley.

Kirk, S. A., McCarthy, J. J., & Kirk, W. D. (1968). *The Illinois Test of Psycholinguistic Abilities* (rev. ed.). Urbana: University of Illinois Press.

Klingberg, T., Forssberg, H., & Westerberg, H. (2002). Training of working memory in children with ADHD. *Journal of Clinical and Experimental Neuropsychology, 24,* 781–791.

Lawson, M. J., & Rice, D. N. (1989). Effects of training in use of executive strategies on a verbal memory problem resulting from a closed head injury. *Journal of Clinical and Experimental Neuropsychology, 11,* 842–854.

Leasak, J., Hunt, D., & Randhawa, B. S. (1982). Cognitive processing, intervention, and achievement. *The Alberta Journal of Educational Research, 28,* 257–266.

Lee, D., & Riccio, C. A. (2005). Understanding and implementing cognitive neuropsychological retraining. In R. C. D'Amato, E. Fletcher-Janzen, & C. R. Reynolds (Eds.), *Handbook of school neuropsychology* (pp. 701–720). Hoboken, NJ: Wiley.

Levin, J. R. (1993). Mnemonic strategies and classroom learning: A twenty-year report card. *The Elementary School Journal, 94,* 235–244.

Levin, M. E., & Levin, J. R. (1990). Scientific mnemonics: Methods for maximizing more than memory. *American Educational Research Journal, 27,* 301–321.

Levine, B., Robertson, I. H., Clare, L., Carter, G., Hong, J., Wilson, B. A., et al. (2000). Rehabilitation of executive functioning: An experimental-clinical validation of goal management training. *Journal of the International Neuropsychological Society, 6,* 299–312.

Lloyd, J. W., Forness, S. R., & Kavale, K. A. (1998). Some methods are more effective than others. *Intervention in School and Clinic, 33,* 195–200.

Loarer, E. (2003). Cognitive training for individuals with deficits. In R. J. Sternberg, J. Lautrey, & T. I. Lubart (Eds.), *Models of intelligence: International perspectives* (pp. 243–260). Washington, DC: American Psychological Association.

Luria, A. R. (1970). The functional organization of the brain. *Scientific American, 222,* 66–78.

Manly, T., Ward, S., & Robertson, I. (2002). The rehabilitation of attention. In P. J. Eslinger (Ed.), *Neuropsychological interventions: Clinical research and practice* (pp. 105–137). New York: Guilford.

Mann, L. (1979). *On the trail of process.* New York: Grune & Stratton.

Mastropieri, M. A., & Scruggs, T. E. (1991). *Teaching students ways to remember: Strategies for learning mnemonically.* Cambridge, MA: Brookline Books.

Mastropieri, M. A., & Scruggs, T. E. (1998). Enhancing school success with mnemonic strategies. *Intervention in School and Clinic, 33,* 201–208.

Mastropieri, M. A., Sweda, J., & Scruggs, T. E. (2000). Putting mnemonic strategies to work in an inclusive classroom. *Learning Disabilities Research & Practice, 15,* 69–74.

Mather, N., & Wendling, B. J. (2005). Linking cognitive assessment results to academic interventions for students with learning disabilities. In D. P. Flanagan & P. L. Harrison (Eds.), *Contemporary intellectual assessment: Theories, tests, and issues* (2nd ed., pp. 269–298). New York: Guilford.

Mayer, R. E. (1996). Learners as information processors: Legacies and limitations of educational psychology's second metaphor. *Educational Psychologist, 31,* 151–161.

McGrew, K. S. (2005). The Cattell-Horn-Carroll theory of cognitive abilities. In D. P. Flanagan & P. L. Harrison (Eds.), *Contemporary intellectual assessment: Theories, tests, and issues* (2nd ed., pp. 136–182). New York: Guilford.

McGrew, K. S., & Woodcock, R. W. (2001). *Woodcock-Johnson III Technical manual.* Itasca, IL: Riverside.

McNamara, D. S., & Scott, J. L. (2001). Working memory capacity and strategy use. *Memory & Cognition, 29,* 10–17.

Meichenbaum, D., & Goodman, J. (1971). Training impulsive children to talk to themselves: A means of developing self-control. *Journal of Abnormal Psychology, 77,* 115–126.

Minear, M., & Shah, P. (2006). Sources of working memory deficits in children and possibilities for remediation. In S. J. Pickering (Ed.), *Working memory and education* (pp. 273–307). Burlington, MA: Academic Press.

Miranda, A., Jarque, S., & Tarraga, R. (2006). Interventions in school settings for students with ADHD. *Exceptionality, 14,* 35–52.

Mitchum, C. C., & Berndt, R. S. (1995). The cognitive neuropsychological approach to treatment of language disorders. *Neuropsychological Rehabilitation, 5,* 1–16.

Moore, D. R., Rosenberg, J. F., & Coleman, J. S. (2004). Discrimination training of phonemic contrasts enhances phonological processing in mainstream school children. *Brain and Language, 94,* 72–85.

Moreno, J., & Saldana, D. (2004). Use of a computer-assisted program to improve metacognition in persons with severe intellectual disabilities. *Research in Developmental Disabilities, 26,* 341–357.

Naglieri, J. A. (1999). *Essentials of CAS assessment.* New York: Wiley.

Naglieri, J. A., & Gottling, S. H. (1997). Mathematics instruction and PASS cognitive processes: An intervention study. *Journal of Learning Disabilities, 30,* 513–520.

Naglieri, J. A., & Johnson, D. (2000). Effectiveness of a cognitive strategy intervention to improve arithmetic computation based on the PASS theory. *Journal of Learning Disabilities, 33,* 591–597.

Naglieri, J. A., & Pickering, E. B. (2003). *Helping children learn: Intervention handouts for use in school and home.* Baltimore: Brookes.

National Reading Panel (2000). *Teaching children to read: An evidence-based assessment of the scientific literature on reading and its applications for reading instruction.* Washington, DC: National Institute of Child Health and Human Development (NICHD).

Olesen, P. J., Westerberg, H., & Klingberg, T. (2004). Increased prefrontal and parietal activity after training of working memory. *Nature Neuroscience, 7,* 75–79.

Owen, R. L., & Fuchs, L. S. (2002). Mathematical problem-solving strategy instruction for third-grade students with learning disabilities. *Remedial and Special Education, 23,* 268–278.

Parente, R., & Herrmann, D. (1996). Retraining memory strategies. *Topics in Language Disorders, 17,* 45–57.

Pickering, S. J. (Ed.). (2006). *Working memory and education.* Burlington, MA: Academic Press.

Pickering, S. J., & Gathercole, S. E. (2001). *Working Memory Test Battery for Children.* London: Psychological Corporation Europe.

Pressley, M., Johnson, C. J., & Symons, S. (1987). Elaborating to learn and learning to elaborate. *Journal of Learning Disabilities, 20,* 76–91.

Pressley, M., & Woloshyn, V. (1995). *Cognitive strategy instruction that really improves children's academic instruction* (2nd ed.). Cambridge, MA: Brookline Books.

Rafoth, M. A., Leal, L., & DeFabo, L. (1993). *Strategies for learning and remembering: Study skills across the curriculum.* Washington, DC: National Education Association.

Reid, R. (1999). Attention deficit hyperactivity disorder: Effective methods for the classroom. *Focus on Exceptional Children, 32,* 1–20.

Reid, R., Trout, A. L., & Schartz, M. (2005). Self-regulation interventions for children with attention deficit/hyperactivity disorder. *Exceptional Children, 71,* 361–377.

Ritchie, D., & Karge, B. D. (1996). Making information memorable: Enhanced knowledge retention and recall through the elaboration process. *Preventing School Failure, 41,* 28–33.

Robey, R. R. (1998). A meta-analysis of clinical outcomes in the treatment of aphasia. *Journal of Speech, Language & Hearing Research, 41,* 172–187.

Rosenshine, B., & Stevens, R. (1986). Teaching functions. In M. C. Wittrock (Ed.), *Handbook of research on teaching* (3rd ed. pp. 376–391). Washington, DC: American Educational Research Association.

Schrank, F. A. (2006). Specification of the cognitive processes involved in performance on the Woodcock-Johnson III. *Woodcock-Johnson III assessment service bulletin number 7.* Itasca, IL: Riverside Publishing.

Scruggs, T. E., & Mastropieri, M. A. (1990). The case for mnemonic instruction: From laboratory research to classroom applications. *The Journal of Special Education, 24,* 7–32.

Shaywitz, S. E. (2003). *Overcoming dyslexia: A new and complete science-based program for overcoming reading problems at any level.* New York: Knopf.

Shimabukuro, S. M., Prater, M. A., Jenkins, A., & Edelen, P. (1999). The effects of self-monitoring of academic performance on students with learning disabilities and ADD/ADHD. *Education and Treatment of Children, 22,* 397–414.

Sternberg, R. (1981). Testing and cognitive psychology. *American Psychologist, 36,* 1181–1189.

Swanson, H. L. (2000). Are working memory deficits in readers with learning disabilities hard to change? *Journal of Learning Disabilities, 33,* 551–566.

Swanson, H. L. (2001). Research on interventions for adolescents with learning disabilities: A meta-analysis of outcomes related to higher-order processing. *Elementary School Journal, 101,* 331–348.

Swanson, H. L., & Berninger, V. W. (1996). Individual differences in children's working memory and writing skill. *Journal of Experimental Child Psychology, 63,* 358–385.

Swanson, H. L., Hoskyn, M., & Lee, C. (1999). *Interventions for students with learning disabilities: A meta-analysis of treatment outcomes.* New York: Guilford.

Turley-Ames, K. J., & Whitfield, M. M. (2003). Strategy training and working memory task performance. *Journal of Memory and Language, 49,* 446–468.

Wechsler, D. (2003a). *Wechsler Intelligence Scale for Children—fourth edition.* San Antonio, TX: The Psychological Corporation.

Wechsler, D. (2003b). *WISC-IV technical and interpretative manual.* San Antonio, TX: The Psychological Corporation.

Wechsler, D., Kaplan, E., Fein, D., Kramer, J., Morris, R., Delis, D., et al. (2004). *Wechsler Intelligence Scale for Children Fourth Edition—Integrated.* San Antonio, TX: Psychological Corporation.

Wilson, B. A. (1987). *Rehabilitation of memory.* New York: Guilford.

Wood, R. L. I., & Fussey, I. (1987). Computer-based cognitive retraining: A controlled study. *International Disabilities Studies, 9*(4), 149–153.

Woodcock, R. W., McGrew, K. S., & Mather, N. (2001). *Woodcock-Johnson III Tests of Cognitive Abilities.* Itasca, IL: Riverside Publishing.

Work, P. H. L., & Choi, H. (2005). Developing classroom and group interventions based on a neuropsychological paradigm. In R. K. D'Amato, E. Fletcher-Janzen, & C. R. Reynolds (Eds.), *Handbook of school neuropsychology* (pp. 663–683). Hoboken, NJ: Wiley.

Wynn-Dancy, M. L., & Gillam, R. B. (1997). Accessing long-term memory: Metacognitive strategies and strategic action in adolescents. *Topics in Language Disorders, 18,* 32–44.

# 13

# Effective Learning Strategy
# Instruction

## Patricia Gildroy and Donald Deshler

*Give a man a fish and you feed him for a day.*
*Teach a man how to fish and you feed him for a lifetime.*
(Chinese Proverb)

This familiar Chinese proverb speaks to the purpose of teaching cognitive strategies to students with learning and behavioral challenges. Typical classes focus on teaching the knowledge and skills needed to complete assignments due today and tomorrow, far fewer teach students *how to learn.* While successful students develop strategies for learning, students who struggle in school tend to have few effective strategies for learning. Teaching cognitive or learning strategies to students with learning and behavioral disorders can help them achieve success in school and to become life-long learners.

Simply showing or telling how to use a complex cognitive strategy is insufficient for students with learning and behavioral challenges. Teaching cognitive strategies requires an approach much like that of a master and his or her apprentice. In medicine, the arts, the sciences, business, and even in manual labor fields, masters of complex skills sets have and continue to take on apprentices. Through watching and assisting, the apprentices see and hear how the experts use complex skills sets and strategies for analyzing, planning, adapting, implementing, monitoring, refining, and evaluating their work. Through extensive coaching and practice, successful apprentices may build on and extend what they learned, also becoming masters in their fields. Helping students with learning and behavioral disorders become master learners, requires teaching them how to utilize a repertoire of effective learning strategies to take in, remember, and demonstrate what they learned.

This chapter begins with a definition and an example of a cognitive strategy for learning. A brief history of several bodies of research that greatly influenced the development and research on cognitive strategies follows. The chapter continues with a discussion of the principles that guide the design and the instruction of effective learning strategies sentence needs revising help to compensate for students' potential problems with information processing. This chapter concludes with a discussion of the most effective intervention components that increase the achievement of students with learning disabilities.

## WHAT ARE LEARNING STRATEGIES?

Meichenbaum (1990) described human behavior from the social-cognitive theoretical perspective as "self-regulated, where individuals anticipate, plan, and reflect on their own behavior, thoughts and feelings" (p. 97). Being able to do this well enables people to reach their goals successfully. Students with learning challenges, however, often have difficulty with the information processing demands required for self-regulation in learning that would enable them to plan, select strategies for, and reflect on the effectiveness of their learning.

In their work on cognitive strategy instruction, Deshler and Schumaker (1986) defined a learning strategy as "how a person thinks and acts while planning for, completing, and evaluating performance on a learning task. Learning strategy instruction teaches students how to learn and perform specific tasks" (p. 52). Cognitive and learning strategies consist of a sequence of steps that cue the cognitive and overt behaviors needed to access, store, and demonstrate knowledge related to complex learning tasks. Learning strategies in particular address academic skills that students may have difficulty with such as decoding multisyllabic words, reading comprehension, studying, completing assignments, taking tests, solving word problems, and producing written or other types of products that demonstrate knowledge.

For example, one important strategy for academic success and personal communication is paraphrasing. As students progress in school, their assignments require them to paraphrase increasingly complex material. Yet, paraphrasing can be difficult for students with learning challenges. The Paraphrasing Strategy (Schumaker, Denton, & Deshler, 1984) (see Figure 13.1) has many applications for school as well as across the life span. While paraphrasing may seem simple, it has high language demands and can be complex for students, particularly those with limited academic language skills.

To paraphrase, students must first read a paragraph and identify the main idea. If the main idea appears in the first sentence, identifying it is relatively easy; however, it is more difficult when the main idea appears later, is inferred, or is missing, as is sometimes the case. After identifying the main idea, students need to distinguish important versus less important details. To do this well, many students with learning challenges need explicit modeling and much coaching to learn to make these distinctions. Finally, the third step requires students to make up a good sentence that tells about the paragraph in their own words. This requires vocabulary and syntax knowledge, as well as pragmatics to reflect the tone of the paragraph. In order to teach this and other learning strategies to mastery, both the design of the strategy and the instructional procedures need to follow the principles discussed later in this chapter.

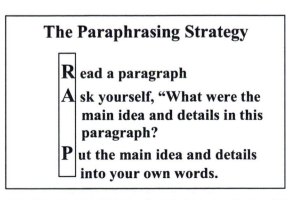

FIGURE 13.1   The Paraphrasing Strategy. From Schumaker, Denton, & Deshler (1984).

Students with learning challenges typically use the same ineffective strategies regardless of the task. For instance, when given a reading assignment, a commonly used strategy is to start reading the first page of the assignment and try to read to the end of the assignment. In contrast, comprehension and recall of what is read is much more effective when a set of reading strategies is used including previewing the assignment, reflecting on what is already known about the topic, using formatting cues and the text structures to identify what is important to remember, and paraphrasing mentally or for writing notes. Although teaching individual strategies can be powerful, the goal is for students to independently select and adapt the most appropriate strategies from a repertoire of effective strategies to meet the demands of the specific task.

## A BRIEF HISTORY OF RESEARCH LEADING TO LEARNING STRATEGIES

In the early 20th century, Luria and others began moving away from the prevailing theories that human learning was primarily associative in nature and began looking at the role of social interactions in learning. Building on Chomsky's work of examining correlations among socialization and language development, Luria examined cognitive development in relation to socio-historical contexts and the use of increasingly complex language structures (see Luria, 1976). The aspect of his research most directly related to strategy research was his insight into children's internalization and adaptation of adult speech to regulate their own behavior.

Vygotsky also explored the relationships between language and cognitive development independently as well as in collaboration with Luria (see Vygotsky, 1978). Among other contributions to strategy research was Vygotsky's theory of proximal development. Through his work, he showed that children were capable of learning complex tasks just beyond their capacities when adults provided modeling and the needed levels of support or scaffolding required for children to complete the targeted tasks. While children were in the initial stages of learning, the adults provided greater levels of support and guidance to complete the task. As children gained proficiency, the adult phased out their support until the children were able to complete the tasks independently. The rate at which the children became independent directly related to the match among the students' skill level, the task difficulty, and the level of the scaffolding provided.

Building on this research and other cognitive scientists, Meichenbaum's research on cognitive-behavior modification incorporated the development of inner speech to help children become more self-regulating. As described in chapter 13 of this volume, Meichenbaum and Goodman (1971) taught impulsive second-grade boys to use self-regulatory strategies to better control their behavior. The five steps of the instructional sequence began with the teacher modeling the covert actions of self-regulatory behavior while simultaneously thinking aloud to reveal the covert self-regulatory thoughts that guided the behavior. During the second step, the teacher provided the self-regulatory language as the student displayed the overt behaviors. For the third step, the student used the self-regulatory language aloud while practicing the overt behaviors. The fourth step began the transition of moving from speaking aloud to using internal speech as the student whispered the self-regulatory thoughts. Finally, the child practiced self-regulatory behavior while guiding behavior with the internal speech that he or she had developed to improve impulse control.

Building on these three lines of research, cognitive and learning strategy research began in earnest during the mid-1970s with the recognition of a range of characteristics that made learning difficult for a subset of low achievers, newly classified as students with learning disabilities (LD). Previously thought to be passive learners, researchers later attributed their learning difficulties with weaknesses in information processing (Swanson, 1991a; Torgesen, 1994). Swanson (1991a) described the theoretical model of *information processing* as "how sensory input is transformed, reduced, elaborated, stored, retrieved, and used" (p. 132).

## Matching Strategy Design and Instruction to Learner Characteristics

As discussed in other chapters in this text, students with learning and behavioral disorders often have limited repertoires of strategies for learning, which requires recognizing important information, organizing it, encoding it, and rehearsing it to improve long-term memory and retrieval. To address these issues, educational researchers analyzed the types of learning tasks students are asked to do in school and worked to develop effective strategies students could employ to not only meet the task demands but to also become independent learners.

Because students with learning challenges tend to have weaknesses in information processing, it is helpful to review the theory (see Figure 13. 2). Familiarity of these processes enables developers, researchers, and teachers to understand the importance of the design principles and teaching sequence of effective learning strategy instruction.

While most students without sensory impairments perceive stimuli well, the breakdown for students with learning disabilities occurs in working memory (Swanson & Siegel, 2001). Working memory is a workspace or cognitive processing center for manipulating and temporarily storing information (Alloway, 2006). Students with learning difficulties may have challenges across several aspects of working memory including listening comprehension (Catts & Kamhi, 1999), making inferences (Ellis, Deshler, & Schumaker, 1989), and identifying important information (Swanson, 1999). In a simultaneous and continuous process, learners must attend to, identify, encode, and rehearse the codes to move information into long-term memory (Swanson, 1991a, 1991b, Swanson & Cooney, 1991). If learners miss any of these steps, the likelihood of remembering new information is minimal. Therefore, the principles for the design and instruction of learning strategies need to include the scaffolding needed to move the strategies into long-term memory and enable fluent recall.

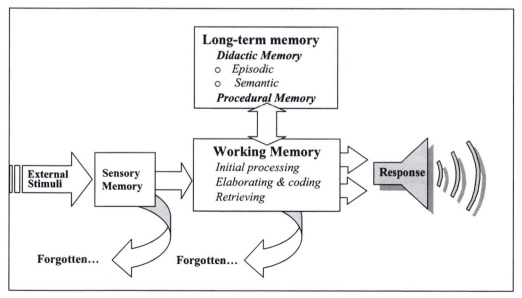

FIGURE 13.2   The Information Processing Model

## Learning Strategy Design Principles

Selecting a learning strategy to teach begins with identifying a current learning task with which students have difficulties. The strategy should be immediately applicable and have a component that enables students and teachers to compare performance prior to and after students apply the strategy. Motivation to continue to use strategies relates directly to seeing socially significant gains (e.g., improved grades and products) resulting from strategy use (Borkowski, Levers, & Gruenenfelder, 1976).

Understanding effective learning strategy design can help in the selection of effective strategies. Learning strategy design begins with a task analysis of learning tasks that are difficult for students. A detailed sequence of the overt and cognitive behaviors required to perform the learning task is then developed. The behaviors are sequenced and segmented into seven or fewer major steps, as working memory's capacity is generally five to nine items at a time (see chapter 14). Some of the major steps may involve several sub-steps or have smaller strategies embedded within them. Each of the steps is then labeled (encoded) with a short phrase or sentence that begins with an action verb to prompt the appropriate behaviors (e.g., **R**ead the paragraph, **A**sk yourself...**P**ut it, etc.). Using the first letter of each step to form a mnemonic also adds a memory device (e.g., **RAP**).

The combination of a careful task analysis, using student friendly language with action verbs to label each of the seven or fewer steps, and adding the memory device all help to reduce the information processing load so there is more likelihood that students will remember and recall the steps of the strategy. This allows more cognitive effort to be devoted to the learning task (e.g., comprehending, writing paragraphs, learning the material).

*Cautions.*    Even with this careful design, strategies can still be ineffective and inefficient. Strategies must be versatile enough to apply or be adapted easily to a range of learning tasks that students need to do on a frequent basis. The wording of the strategies must be clear, concise, and student friendly to avoid any confusion. The wording should prompt the overt and the cognitive behaviors. The strategies also should not contradict what students will learn in the future (e.g., strategies for working with positive integers should not contradict working with negative integers in the future).

Because strategy instruction can be complex and require a significant commitment of instructional time, it would benefit teachers to take a course or receive high-quality professional development in strategy instruction. Until teachers are proficient with teaching students to master and generalize learning strategies, they should only teach research-validated strategies (Harris & Graham, 1996; Pressley & Woloshyn, 1995). Once teachers have mastered strategy instruction, they will be better able to design or co-construct a strategy with an individual student that needs to refine a strategy he or she already uses.

## Learning Strategy Instructional Principles

While the various researchers developing learning strategies may use slightly different instructional sequences, most are similar to the Stages of Instruction from the University of Kansas Center for Research on Learning (CRL) Strategic Instruction Model (SIM) strategies (see Figure 13.3). This instructional sequence has eight stages that begins with assessing students' skills and ends with working on generalization of the strategy. A discussion of each of these stages follows.

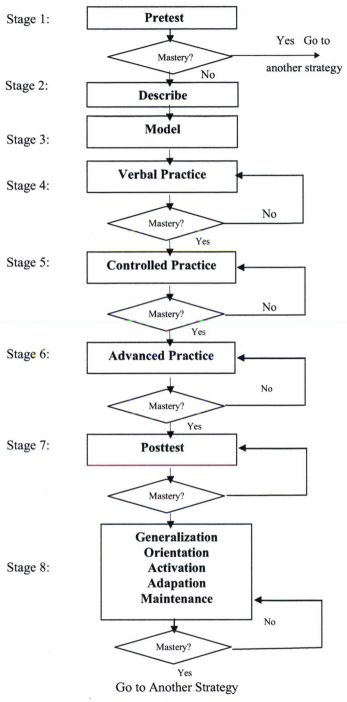

FIGURE 13.3    Stages of Instruction

*Stage 1: Pretest and Commitment.*   In the SIM model, the Pretest stage of instruction helps determine if students need to learn the strategy and provides data and products for a comparison with post-test data to show students how their performance improved through strategy use. Determining if students have the pre-skills needed for the strategy allows the teacher to pre-teach skills if needed rather than having to interrupt the flow of strategy instruction to teach component skills (e.g., how to use the index for the "Answering Written Questions" strategy (Archer & Gleason, 2003).

Following the pre-test, students review the results individually with the teacher to examine specific patterns that help or hinder learning and achievement. After the individual conferences, the teacher explains her commitment to work in partnership with students to help them achieve their learning goals through strategy instruction (e.g., improve writing skills, reading skills, raise grades). The teacher then solicits verbal commitments from students to learn the strategy as a means to reach the learning goal. When older students make verbal commitments to master the strategy, average proficiency levels are higher than when verbal commitments are not given (Ellis, 1986).

*Stage 2: Describe.*   The Describe stage focuses primarily on didactic knowledge, but also continues to develop conditional knowledge. During this stage, teachers explain more about the strategy including the purpose, the types of activities students will be involved in during instruction, the steps of the strategy, as well as the learning and classroom behaviors expected during strategy instruction.

Once students understand more about t the strategy, they continue to build conditional knowledge through sharing ideas about how and when they could use the strategy both in and outside of school. For instance, paraphrasing is useful for writing notes from reading or classroom instruction, for answering chapter questions, writing answers to essay questions, and writing letters, e-mails, and reports. Paraphrasing can also be adapted for telling about movies, television shows, or conversations. During and after strategy instruction, the teacher continues to prompt students to use the strategy and asks them how and when they have used the strategies out side of the class.

*Stage 3: Modeling.*   Modeling is the heart of strategy instruction. Teachers may need to instruct students in cognitive behaviors as well as in overt physical acts needed to perform a given task. The model step of instruction is fundamental for teaching and demonstrating these cognitive behaviors (Schumaker, 1990, p.1).

Bruner pointed out, the goal of modeling is not to have students imitate the modeled behavior, but to internalize and adapt the language and principles of the use of the strategy to meet new task demands (1966).

The modeling stage is the most difficult stage of strategy instruction. Learning from modeling can be difficult for all learners. Even experienced teachers benefit from seeing multiple models of cognitive strategy modeling and participating in coaching to help refine modeling skills.

Learning from modeling requires sustaining attention, listening comprehension, identifying important verbal information and overt physical behaviors, encoding the important information, rehearsing it, and then applying it to similar tasks. Learning from modeling requires the same information processing skill sets that are most challenging for students with learning and behavioral disorders. Therefore, the modeling must be precise, reiterative, and engage students as much as possible.

Because students may not understand the purpose for modeling, clear expectations need to be set for attending to what the teacher says and does so students can learn to do the same things

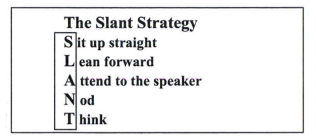

FIGURE 13.4    The Slant Strategy for Attending to Classroom Instruction

they observe. Throughout the modeling, additional cueing (telling students what to pay attention to) helps students recognize what is most important. Though attention is critical, student engagement is more highly correlated to achievement (Gerber, 1986).

Spending more than a few minutes modeling at a time can erode students' attention; engaging students by asking questions for which they have prior knowledge helps them begin to think about and use elements of the strategy. For instance, when modeling the steps in the Slant Strategy (see Figure 13.4), teachers can ask; "What would attending to the speaker look like? Show me! What does attending to the speaker feel like?"

Sometimes a quick initial model of the strategy helps give students the "big picture" of what they will learn to do. The main emphasis of the initial model is on using the steps of the strategy and not the content of the learning task (e.g., the steps of the Paraphrasing Strategy, not comprehension of the paragraph). Students should be told that the purpose of the initial model is so they can see how all of the steps of the strategy work together, they will then learn how to do each step before putting all of the steps together.

The complexity of the Modeled Strategy and the language used during the model impacts the learner's ability to benefit from the model. Increased language loads (e.g., long or complex sentence, the number of idea units, and the level of vocabulary) can affect the ability to take in and process new information. The integrity of the remembered information can also be affected by how organized it is when presented (Baker Kameenui, & Simmons, 1998; Swanson, Hoskyn, & Lee, 1999; Vaughn, Gersten, & Chard, 2000) as well as the semantic organization and meaningfulness of the information (Gagné, 1985). While good learners may compensate for poor modeling, naïve learners or students with learning difficulties may not. For these students, a poor model can be worse than no model at all (Pearson & Dole, 1988).

For simple strategies such as SLANT, teachers can model all of the steps and have students practice them during one lesson. Strategies that are more complex require modeling and mastery of individual or even subcomponents of steps, prior to synthesizing the steps (Gildroy, 2001).

Below is an example of what a teacher might say to model identifying the main idea in the Paraphrasing Strategy.

Teacher: Now that you understand a little bit about the Paraphrasing Strategy, I'm going to show you how I use it to find the main idea in a paragraph. Listen carefully, I expect you to *watch me* closely, and *pay attention to what I say and do*, because I *expect you* to learn to follow these same steps to find the main ideas in paragraphs. I'll be thinking out loud so that you can learn to use this kind of thinking to find the main ideas of paragraphs on your own. Remember, watch, and listen carefully.

First, I read over the Paraphrasing Strategy to make sure I'm familiar with the steps. Look up here at the screen. Let's read the first two steps together…(Step 1: Read a paragraph. Step 2:

Ask yourself, "What were the main idea and details in this paragraph.) Good. I put a passage up on the screen. Who will read it aloud for us?"

> Harriet Beacher Stow has left us no record of her meeting with President Lincoln at Washington in 1862. Her youngest son, Charley, was with her, and to him we are indebted for a report of the momentous occasion. It was a striking picture—the tall, rawboned man and the tiny little wisp of a woman who had undoubtedly been partly responsible for his nomination to the presidency. He held out his hand to her, looking down at her from his great height. "So, this is the little lady who made this big war!" (Allen, 1944, p. 182)

Thank you. Now, to continue with the Paraphrasing Strategy. We completed the first step, Read the paragraph. We need to do the second step. I'm going to look at my cue card that tells me questions to ask and places to look to find the main idea (see Figure 13.5).

The questions will help me think about what I need to find. Class, looking up at the screen, what question should I ask myself? Yes, "What is this paragraph about?" When I know, I should be able to finish this sentence (point) "This paragraph is about…"

OK, to be able to finish that statement, I need to figure out the clues that tell me what the paragraph is about. Show me on your papers, where it tells me where to look in the paragraph. Great! I need to look in the first sentence of the paragraph to try to find the main idea.

The first sentence says, "Harriet Beecher Stowe has left us no record of her meeting with President Lincoln at Washington in 1862." This sentence mentions two related things about Harriet Beecher Stowe, the first is that she didn't write about meeting the president, the second is that she met President Lincoln in Washington in 1862. I have to figure out which part could be the main idea. After reading the rest of the paragraph I know that her son wrote about what happened when she met President Lincoln, because he was there too. So it's not very important that Harriet Beecher Stowe did not write about the meeting. I think meeting the President of the United States is important, and the rest of the paragraph tells about the meeting, so I think that's what

---

**The Paraphrasing Strategy**

**FINDING THE MAIN IDEA
QUESTIONS TO ASK**

• **What is this paragraph about?**
  ○ **This paragraph is about _____.**
• **What does it tell me about?**
  ○ **It tells me _____**
  **_____**

**PLACES TO LOOK**
1. **Look in the first sentence of the paragraph.**
2. **Look for repetitions of the same word or words in the whole paragraphs.**

FIGURE 13.5    A Cue Card for the Paraphrasing Strategy

the paragraph is about. Class, do you agree? Now I can finish this statement: "This paragraph is about" what happened when Harriett Beecher Stowe met President Lincoln.

To review, I used the first part of the Paraphrasing Strategy. After we read the paragraph together, I looked at the cue card for finding the main idea. I read and thought about the questions I should ask myself and I re-read the first sentence. When I wasn't sure what information was the main idea, I thought about what the rest of the paragraph talks about. That gave me the clues I needed to come up with the main idea. Then I finished the statement that answers, "What is this paragraph about?"

In a few minutes, we'll work together to practice identifying the main ideas in more paragraphs about Harriet Beacher Stow. Right now, we'll practice saying the steps of the Paraphrasing Strategy so we all know them by memory.

*Stage 4: Verbal Rehearsal.*    Although the design and instructional sequence all help to compensate for weak working memory processes, this step requires students to overtly practice saying the steps of the strategy until they can say them fluently by memory. That way, when they are applying the strategy, little cognitive energy needs to be devoted to remember the strategy and students can concentrate on using the strategies to learn the content of the materials they are using.

Because the goal is to have students internalize the self-regulating behavior that is guided by the steps of the strategies, it is important to consistently use and have students use the correct wording for the steps. If the teacher or students use different words for the steps, the power of the strategy may be lost when students have difficulty recalling the steps of the strategy.

During this stage, students practice saying the names of the steps—often in a game-like activity—until they can say them with no errors. Explaining the reasons for the various instructional steps helps students remain motivated to be engaged in activities that otherwise might be seen as incongruous with the images students try to project among their peers. Tossing a soft ball randomly from one student to the other and requiring the catcher to say the next step helps everyone stay engaged in trying to remember the strategy. This even works in graduate school! The intensity and quality of rehearsal of the codes or names of the steps directly affect recall (Swanson, 1991b). Even when students master saying the steps, there should be opportunities to practice saying the steps over time to ensure retention. Once students master saying the steps fluently, they move on to controlled practice.

*Stage 5: Controlled Practice.*    During this stage, students receive coaching as they apply the strategy to material below their instructional levels. Using easier materials reduces the cognitive load and allows students to concentrate on the strategy rather than devoting energy to understanding the content with which they are working. Some learning strategy instructional materials include all of the materials needed for controlled practice and for scoring the quality of strategy use. This gives students and the teacher a criterion for evaluating student use of the strategy and helps students monitor their progress.

During the controlled practice stage, students receive elaborated feedback on their use of the strategy (Kline, Schumaker, & Deshler, 1991). First, after reviewing the students' work and observing students using the strategy, the teacher gives individualized feedback that begins with specific positive comments about what went well (e.g., "Terrific! You wrote down the mnemonic for the strategy so you could remember the steps of the strategy"). Second, the teacher identifies and gives concise and specific feedback on one or two elements that need strengthening. The teacher may provide a mini-model of the step with which the student is having difficulty. Next, the teacher asks the student to perform the difficult part of the strategy. Through coaching, the student is able to refine his or her performance. Finally, the student and teacher set goals for continued improvement in performance.

*Stage 6: Advanced Practice.* Once students master the strategy with controlled materials, they begin to apply it to grade level materials. As the strategy may change with use of more difficult materials, the teacher may model adapting the strategy to meet specific task demands. Again, the teacher coaches students as needed to help them refine their performance with the higher level of materials.

*Stage 7: Post-test.* The primary purpose of the post-test is to compare pre-test products with post-test products to show students how much improvement they made from their efforts to learn the strategy. After the post-test, students are asked to record their scores and to compare their performance prior to and after learning the strategy. If students do not see a significant improvement from learning the strategy, they may not remain motivated to use the strategy.

*Stage 8: Generalization.* During this stage, students receive assignments that require using the new strategy; ideally assignments will be for the class in which they learned the strategy and in others as well. However, without planning for and monitoring generalization of the strategy, it is unlikely students will continue to use the strategy. . Occasionally scoring the use of the strategy can help to retain mastery. A common phenomenon is that after the post-test, students continue to increase the quality of their performance in using the strategy. Seeing continued improvement again reinforces students for using the strategy.

If students know several strategies, the teacher can model using the different strategies while performing a learning task, much like the Palinscar and Brown (1984) model of reciprocal teaching. Students learn to select the best strategies to use for different assignments and can practice using them with other students as they collaborate to complete assignments (e.g., self-questioning, visualization, and paraphrasing are all appropriate for increasing reading comprehension).

## Strategy Instruction Research

Prior chapters referred to many validated strategies that can benefit students with learning and behavioral challenges. Swanson and his colleagues conducted a meta-analysis of over 931 research studies on interventions with students with learning disabilities (Swanson, 1999). Through coding the types of instructional methods used, they found that the combination of strategy instruction and direct instruction produced the highest effect sizes (M = .84). Below are the nine instructional components that produced the highest effect sizes and a discussion of how these components are incorporated into effective cognitive strategy instruction.

1. *Sequencing.* This involves breaking the task into component parts, providing step-by step prompts, and fading prompts or cues. This is the task analysis component with the naming of the steps, as well as the instructional sequence.
2. *Drill-repetition & practice-review.* Distributed short practice and review sessions over time with feedback contribute to learning and retention. In strategy instruction, students practice to mastery and then incorporate the strategy into regular assignments as well as to assignments in other classes. Regular reviews maintain mastery.

3. *Segmentation.* This involves breaking the task (or strategy) into component parts for instruction and synthesizing the parts into a whole for student mastery. Teaching preskills and difficult portions of the strategy prior to synthesization allows success at every stage of instruction.

4. *Direct questioning and responses.* This addresses engaging students in answering "process-related" and/or "content related" questions requiring discussion. This is a critical component in strategy instruction. Students need to understand how and why the arrived at their conclusions.

5. *Controlling difficulty or processing demands of a task.* By utilizing the design principles for strategy development and instruction, the load on working memory is reduced so that more cognitive energy can be devoted to the content to which the strategy is applied. Having students learn how to use the strategies with easier materials and moving to grade level materials as they master the strategy also controls task difficulty and processing demands.

6. *Technology and Visuals.* This includes using structured materials including graphic organizers. Most strategy instruction provides posters and handouts for students with the steps of the strategies and may include cue cards for remembering how to use parts of the strategy.

7. *Group instruction.* This involves small group instruction. With strategy instruction, both some small group and individualized instruction may be necessary to meet the individual needs all learners.

8. *A supplement to teacher and peer involvement.* This addresses having students apply what they learn in other contexts including homework or in other classes.

9. *Strategy cues.* This involves teachers' cuing students to use the strategy, think-aloud modeling with problem solving, and reflecting on the benefits of the learning.

The strategy design and instructional principles are well established in the literature.

## SUMMARY

Currently, a number of powerful research-validated cognitive and learning strategies exist across content areas that focus on helping students become more independent and successful learners. Using the design principles of effective learning strategies can help in the selection of validated strategies to meet specific students' immediate and long-term needs. Although only a few researchers have been able to provide the needed assessments and materials required to help students attain mastery of the strategies, following the instructional principles can help students achieve mastery.

The power of strategy instruction is equally beneficial to average achievers as well as low achievers. Some school districts have adopted sets of strategies (i.e., the Strategic Instruction Model (SIM) strategies) and developed a scope and sequence across grade levels from upper elementary through high school. Focused strategy instruction takes place in specific classes, with teachers in other classes reinforcing strategy use. Professional development for teachers is ongoing with school coaches. Nearly all students are able to facilitate their own parent-teacher conferences, and students with IEPs facilitate their own Individual Education Plans (IEP) meetings (Lancaster, Schumaker, & Deshler, 2002). Through a concerted effort, overall achievement in these districts has risen and their students are graduating with the strategies to develop and attain their own learning goals. This type of success is immeasurable in the lives of students.

# REFERENCES

Allen, J. (1944). (Ed.) *One hundred great lives.* New York: The Journal of Living Publishing Company;

Alloway, T. P. (2006). How does working memory work in the classroom. *Educational Research and Reviews, 1*(4), 134–139

Archer, A. L., & Gleason, M. M., (2003). *Skills for School Success: Completing daily assignments.* North Billerica, MA: Curriculum Associates.

Baker, S. K., Kameenui, E. J., & Simmons, D. C. (1998). Characteristics of students with diverse learning and curricular needs. In E. J. Kameenui, & D. S., Carnine (Eds.) *Effective teaching strategies that accommodate diverse learners* (pp. 19–44) Columbus, OH: Prentice Hall.

Borkowski, J. G., Levers, S., Gruenenfelder, T. M., (1976). Transfer of mediational strategies in children: The role of activity and awareness during strategy acquisition [Electronic version]. *Child Development, 47*, 779–786.

Bruner, J. S. (1966). *Toward a theory of instruction.* Cambridge, MA: Belkapp Press,

Catts, H. W., & Kamhi, A. G., (1999). *Language and reading disabilities.* Normal Heights, MA: Allyn & Bacon.

Deshler, D. D., & Schumaker, J. B. (1986). Learning strategies: An instructional alternative for low-achieving adolescents. *Exceptional Children, 52*, 583–590.

Ellis, E. S., (1986). The role of motivation and pedagogy on the generalization of cognitive strategy training. *Journal of Learning Disabilities, 19*(2), 66–70.

Ellis, E. S., Deshler, D. D., & Schumaker, J. B., (1989). Teaching adolescents with learning disabilities to generate and use task-specific strategies. *Journal of Learning Disabilities, 22*(2), 109–130.

Gangné, R. M. (1985). *The conditions of learning and the theory of instruction.* (4th ed). New York: Holt, Rinehart, and Winston.

Gerber, M. M. (1986). Cognitive-behavioral training in the curriculum: Time, slow learners and basic skills. *Focus on Exceptional Children, 18*(6), 1–12.

Gildroy, P. G. (2001)..Development and validation of an instructional modeling routine for students with learning disabilities. Unpublished doctoral dissertation. University of Kansas, Lawrence.

Harris, K. R., & Graham, S. (1996). *Making the writing process work: Strategies for composition and self-regulation.* Cambridge, MA: Brookline Books.

Kline, F. M., Schumaker, J. B., & Deshler, D. D. (1991). The development and validation of feedback routines for instructing students with learning disabilities. *Learning Disabilities Quarterly, 14*(3), 191–207.

Lancaster, P. E., Schumaker, J. B., & Deshler, D. D. (2002). The development and validation of an interactive hypermedia program for teaching a self-advocacy strategy to students with disabilities. *Learning Disability Quarterly, 25*(4) 277–302.

Luria, A. R. (1976). *Cognitive development: Its cultural and social foundations.* [Electronic version]. Cambridge, MA: Harvard University Press.

Meichenbaum, D. (1990) Paying homage: Providing challenges. *Psychological Inquiry, 1*, 96–100.

Meichenbaum, D. & Goodman, J. (1971). Training impulsive children to talk to themselves: A means of developing self-control. *Journal of Abnormal Psychology, 77*, 115–126.

Palinscar, A. S., & Brown, A. L, (1984). Reciprocal teaching of comprehension fostering and comprehension-monitoring activities. *Cognition & Instruction, 1*(2), 117–176.

Pearson, P. D., & Dole, J. A. (1988). Explicit comprehension instruction: A review of research and a new conceptualization of instruction. Technical Report No. 427.

Pressley, M., & Woloshyn, V. (1995). *Cognitive strategy instruction that really improves children's academic performance.* Brookline Books: Cambridge, MA.

Schumaker, J. B. (1990). Modeling, the heart of the Strategy Instruction Model. *Strategram.* Lawrence, KS: Center for Research on Learning.

Schumaker, J.B., Denton, P.H., Deshler, D. D. (1984). The Paraphrasing Strategy. Lawrence: The University of Kansas.

Swanson, H. L., (1991a). Learning disabilities and memory. In d.? Kim Reid, W. P. Hresko, & H. L. Swansons (Eds.), *A cognitive approach to learning disabilities* (2nd ed.; pp. 131–158). Austin, TX: Pro-Ed.

Swanson, H. L. (1991b) Information processing: An introduction. In D. Kim Reid, W. P. Hresko, & H. L. Swanson (Eds.), *A cognitive approach to learning disabilities* (2nd ed.; pp. 131–182). Austin, TX: Pro-Ed.

Swanson, H. L. (1999). Instructional components that predict treatment outcomes for students with *learning disabilities*: Support for a combined strategy and direct instruction model. *Learning Disabilities Research & Practice, 14*(3), 129–140.

Swanson, H. L., & Cooney, J. B. (1991).Learning disabilities and memory. In B.L.Y. Wong (Ed.) *Learning about learning disabilities* (pp. 103–127). San Diego: Academic Press.

Swanson, H. L., Hoskyn, M., & Lee, C. (1999). *Interventions for students with learning disabilities: A meta-analysis of treatment outcomes.* New York: Guilford.

Swanson, H. L., Siegel, L. (2001). Learning disabilities as a working memory deficit. *Issues in Education, 7*(1), 1–49.

Torgesen, J. K. (1994). Studies of children with learning disabilities who perform poorly on memory span tasks. *Journal of Learning Disabilities, 21*(10), 605–612.

Vaughn, S., Gersten, R., Chard, D. J. (2000). The underlying message in LD intervention research: Findings from research synthesis. *Exceptional Children, 67*(1), 99–114.

Vygotsky, L. S. (1978). *Mind and society: The development of higher mental processes.* Cambridge, MA: Harvard University Press.

# 14

# Accommodation of Instructional and Testing Situations

## Noel Gregg and Jennifer H. Lindstrom

Shamelka, a third grader, has significant problems in the area of reading and writing. Her learning disabilities in the areas of phonological and orthographic awareness make learning in an inclusive classroom challenging both for her and the classroom teacher. Shamelka's Individual Educational Plan (IEP) documents her right to specific accommodations in the classroom and in testing situations. These accommodations include extra time on tests that require reading or writing, alternative media (e-text read-alouds), and a word processor (Alpha Smart) for content area coursework (science, math, and history).

David, a senior in high school, was diagnosed with Aspergers in the fourth grade. Since that time, he has received the following instructional and testing accommodations: extra time on tests, use of a word processor for tests and assignments requiring written expression, a private testing room, and a personal assistant during testing to help manage potential emotional meltdown(s).

The accommodation of instructional and testing situations for students like Shamelka and David who receive special education services has led to a great deal of debate in the literature and within professional associations in terms of various methodological, policy, and legal issues (Sireci, Li, & Scarpati, 2003). In this regard, one of the most significant barriers facing students qualified to receive specific accommodations is the lack of professional knowledge pertaining to the issues surrounding such accommodations (Gregg, Morgan, Hartwig & Coleman, in press). Cursory understanding of the complex issues influencing accommodation selection can lead to under, over, or misuse of them. For example, research on the effects of different accommodations on the performance of students with disabilities has changed the mindset of most professionals in the field from the view that "one shoe fits all sizes" to the importance of "tailoring" an accommodation plan to the specific needs of each student.

An apprehension frequently voiced by the public is whether an accommodation is truly fair—that is, does it level the playing field or tilt it for a select few who qualify as disabled? Understanding the issues surrounding the use of accommodations begins with each of us reflecting upon our own perspectives as they relate to the meanings of constructs such as reading, writing, merit, equality, or fairness, especially as they pertain to modifying standardized approaches to accessing and demonstrating knowledge. For example, do we consider speed essential to measuring high school writing competency? Or, is allowing some students to use alternative media (electronic text/read-alouds) to access science, math, and history books fair to the other students in the classroom? Technologies such as word processing, audio books, e-text, or podcasts have certainly influenced our traditional definitions of reading and writing. Yet, one still hears professionals protest that to read a book one "must" read with one's eyes not ears (e.g., read-alouds) or that only a student with visual impairments should receive access to screen readers or audio texts. Moreover, on many high-stakes tests, students are required to write an essay using pencil-and-paper rather than a computer, regardless of the fact that the majority of the school writing curriculum is done on a computer. Challenging old definitions of reading and writing is a very concrete yet necessary initial step toward equity for all students with special needs.

Greater dialogue and sharing of knowledge are needed between professionals across the disciplines who work with elementary, secondary, and postsecondary students. In fact, there exists a great disconnect between the K–12 and postsecondary accommodation practices and what appears in the research literature (Gregg, Morgan, Hartwig, & Coleman, in press; Thurlow, 2006). However, it is not possible within one chapter to review all of this literature. In this regard, the purpose of this chapter is to provide professionals who work with the K–12 population information on the research and best practices literature on accommodations associated with instructional and testing situations for those students receiving special education services. We will not include a discussion of the postsecondary literature or the literature on English Language Learners (ELL) and their specific accommodation needs (see Abedi, Courtney, & Leon, 2003, for an in-depth review of this literature).

## RATIONALE FOR ACCOMMODATIONS

Accommodations adjust the manner in which instruction or testing situations are presented and/or evaluated so that students with disabilities can either access and/or demonstrate knowledge in a fair and equitable fashion. An accommodation should not change the content (i.e., knowledge) being learned or tested nor should it provide unfair advantage to the individual using it. Shamelka's case illustrates the importance for students with disabilities to receive appropriate accommodations. Her phonological and orthographic deficits significantly influence her ability to decode and spell words. However, she demonstrates above average listening comprehension and verbal reasoning skills. It is imperative that Shamelka be provided access to learning information that other students receive through reading printed text so that her knowledge base is not impacted by her poor reading decoding and spelling abilities. Using alternative media (e.g., e-text and screen readers) to learn new content (e.g., science, social studies, and math) provides her equal access to information. In a testing situation, if we are assessing math knowledge, the only equitable solution is to provide Shamelka with read-alouds and other assistive technologies that allow her to demonstrate her abilities in math. The construct being tested is math knowledge, not her ability to read or spell.

The rights provided to students with disabilities for accessing accommodations is built upon legislative precedence (e.g., 14th Amendment; Title VI of the Civil Rights Act of 1964; Equal Educational Opportunities Act of 1974; Section 504 of the 1993 Rehabilitation Act; Americans with Disabilities Act; Individuals with Disabilities Education, 1997, 2004; and No Child Left Behind). The 2004 Individuals with Disabilities Education Improvement Act (IDEA; 2004) requires that students with disabilities be provided appropriate accommodations across both instructional and testing situations. Students who are determined eligible for special education services (under IDEA) must have their accommodation needs specified in their Individualized Education Program (IEP). The IEP Team (by law) includes at least one general educator, at least one special educator, a representative of the local educational agency (LEA), and the parents. The IEP Team determines, if appropriate, the need for reasonable accommodations that are consistent with federal and state guidelines. However, a student's right to use an accommodation is not generalizable throughout his or her lifespan, or across different settings or situations. The individual, context, and accountability system requires ongoing professional decision making and re-evaluation.

The No Child Left Behind Act (NCLB) of 2001 requires states to measure student proficiency in "mathematical and reading or language arts" to determine if schools are making "adequate yearly progress" (AYP) toward academic proficiency for all students, including students with disabilities. The issues surrounding the accommodation of instruction and testing for students with disabilities are certainly not novel to the field of special education. However, as a result of the mandatory, standards-driven reform of NCLB, this group of learners has begun "to be acknowledged fully" and "schools and school districts [are being] forced to confront the conceptual and technical issues inherent in implementing reforms" (McLaughlin, Embler, & Nagle, 2004, p. 2).

Federal legislation does caution, however, that only "appropriate accommodations, where necessary" (IDEA), and "reasonable accommodations necessary to measure academic achievement" (NCLB) be provided to students. Identifying "reasonable" and "appropriate" accommodations requires professional judgment as these accommodations must be examined separately for each student. The challenge rests with the provision and implementation of accommodations. Who resolves the question of which accommodations should be provided and under what circumstances? Far too often a single accommodation is used across a variety of settings (e.g., extra time is granted for instructional and testing situations in reading, mathematics, science, etc.) with little thought given to whether this compromises the purpose of the learning task.

While accommodation rights are specified by federal legislation, the states are left with the responsibility of determining how the rules for ensuring valid and reliable decision making remain consistent with professional and technical standards. It is the responsibility of each state to develop policies clearly identifying allowable accommodations (reflecting adequate reliability and validity), decision-making criteria, and training for educators on how best to select appropriate accommodations. Without clear and consistent accommodation guidelines from the state, potential problems in the decision-making process can occur at the school level. These problems may include offering too many or too few accommodations, mismatches between instructional and testing assessments, lack of documentation for decision making, and treating accommodations and modifications synonymously.

The *Standards for Educational and Psychological Testing* (*Standards*; American Educational Research Association [AERA], American Psychological Association, and National Council on Measurement in Education, 1999), while not legally binding, are a widely respected guide to the best practices that have evolved over several decades (Koenig & Bachman, 2004). The *Standards* provide significant guidance to professionals in developing appropriate accommodation policies and procedures, although interpretation of their specific application continues to be debated in the courts (Phillips, 1994; Sireci & Green, 2000). The *Standards* encourage professionals to make accommodation decisions based on existing research (*Standards* 10.2 and 10.8), and to consistently follow clearly delineated policy describing the rationale and procedures for accommodation decision making, as well as possible limits on the validity of inferences that can be made (*Standards* 10.4 and 10.5).

One positive outcome of the NCLB Act (2001) is an increase toward proficiency on statewide assessments for students with disabilities (Thompson, Johnstone, Thurlow, & Altman, 2005). According to data that has been collected, the trend has been influenced by the following factors: development of policy for participation in testing, alignment of students' IEPs with curriculum standards, ongoing professional development, development and provision of accommodation policies and procedures, increased access to standards-based instruction, and improved data collection (see, for example, Thompson, Johnstone, Thurlow, & Altman, 2005, for an in-depth discussion). According to this report, states identified the following as emerging needs related to providing accommodations to students with disabilities: technical assistance on appropriate instructional and/or testing accommodations; professional development, particularly for general education; and federal guidance on the degree of specificity required in state guidelines. After a long and arduous battle in the courts, the state of Oregon developed a juried process (i.e., a panel that includes researchers, administrators, classroom teachers, and experts in testing, disabilities, and academic content) for identifying appropriate accommodations and/or modifications for instruction or assessment (see, for example, Almond & Karvonen, 2006, for an in-depth discussion). Oregon appears to have translated measurement theory and federal guidelines into sound practice. Clearly, the policy and procedures developed by states, guided by evidence-based research, are critical for students accessing appropriate and effective accommodations for instruction and assessment.

## MODIFICATIONS AND ALTERNATE ASSESSMENTS

The majority of students with mild/moderate learning and behavioral disorders receive accommodations rather than modifications or alternate assessments. Unlike an accommodation, a modification represents significant change to the instructional method or curriculum (e.g., instructional level, content, or performance criteria). The IDEA (2004) discontinued the use of the word modification as it pertains to testing because of the requirements established in the NCLB Act (2001) to include all students in school accountability systems.

Alternate assessments are developed to measure the performance of students who are unable to participate in general state assessments even with accommodations. Such alternate measures involve changes in test construction, administration, response, or scoring which, in turn, alters the nature of the constructs being measured (Hollenbeck, 2002). Many states are developing innovative means to preserve the construct validity of alternate assessment measures (e.g., New Hampshire Enhanced Assessment Initiative, National Alternate Assessment Center). Approximately half of the states report alternate assessments using a portfolio framework or other bodies of student performance evidence (Gong & Marion, 2006). As Gong and Marion note, "There is no question that NCLB has ratcheted up the pressure on states to compare validly the scores derived from alternate assessments to common content and achievement standards" (p. 2). Alternate assessments are more often appropriate for students with significant cognitive disabilities who demonstrate the most profound learning challenges. Table 14.1 provides definitions for the words used in the adaptation of testing or instructional content, as well as the principle markers differentiating each term.

## DECISION MAKING LEADING TO ACCOMMODATION SELECTION

One key component to the provision of accommodations is utilization of the information discussed during the student's eligibility meeting and/or included in the psychological report. Drawing upon the student's unique profile when selecting accommodations enhances the probability of their effectiveness. In addition to recognizing individual differences (e.g., cognitive, affective, and linguistic processes), it is important to consider the task format (e.g., degree of structure, modality) and the response choices (e.g., written, oral) during the decision-making process. Whether an accommodation is effective is dependent upon a professional's knowledge of specific

**TABLE 14.1**
**Definitions and Markers for Testing and Instructional Adaptations**

| Term | Markers |
|---|---|
| Instruction | Methods of teaching;<br>Activities used for student learners;<br>Activities of both teachers and students; |
| Assessment | Means to measure learning outcome;<br>Means to measure the learner |
| Accommodations | Constructs not altered;<br>Changes to instructional time or testing time, presentation, response, participation, and/or level of support;<br>Inferences from student performance the same across accommodation/non-accommodation situations; |
| Instructional Modifications | Instructional standards and pedagogy significantly altered;<br>Validity of instructional methodology altered; |
| Alternate Assessment | Test construction, administration, response, or scoring significantly altered;<br>Constructs measured significantly alter meaning;<br>Inferences from student performance not equal across altered/non altered assessment;<br>Validity of measure altered |

cognitive, affective, and linguistic processes impacting different types of learning demands. For instance, a student's underachievement on reading measures might be more directly related to problems with reasoning or strategic planning than with phonological awareness. Understanding the reason(s) for the underachievement should influence the type of accommodation(s) chosen. As with assessment, the accommodation process requires professionals to use a "reasoning from evidence" approach (Pelligrino, Chudowksy, & Glaser, 2001). Such an approach depends on the integration of multiple data sources, particularly: (a) the individual's profile, (b) the task demands (skills/content), and (c) the interpretive methodologies used to analyze the data.

Consistent and reliable professional judgment is essential to the accommodation process (Fuchs, Fuchs, Eaton, Hamlett, Binkley, & Crouch, 2000; Hollenbeck, Tindal, & Almond, 1998). Recently, researchers have been working on developing theory-driven guidelines for matching individual student profiles with accommodations (Elliott, 2006; Helwig & Tindal, 2003; Kopriva, 2002; Siskind, 2004). However, the focus of this research continues to remain predominately on the selection of testing accommodations rather than instructional accommodations.

Focusing primarily on testing accommodations is a concern if one considers the outcomes from *The Rhode Island 2002 and 2003 Assessment Accommodation Study*. Ewing (2006) reported findings from this study in which the accommodation-related decisions made by professionals were investigated across instructional and assessment situations. Ewing identified five specific testing accommodations which were most often provided to students with disabilities regardless of the learner's profile or information provided by the IEP Team. These accommodations included alternate location, oral administration of directions, clarified and repeated directions, extended time, and frequent breaks. In addition, the testing location, rather than the student's IEP, dictated the type of recommended accommodation. Interestingly, Ewing found that instructional accommodations were much more detailed and individualized than testing accommodations. Unfortunately, general educators were rarely participants in the decision making for either assessment or instructional accommodations and follow-through on assessment accommodations was almost always the responsibility of the special educator. The relationship between the accommodations students with disabilities received during instruction did not parallel those received during assessment; students consistently received far fewer and less individualized assessment accommodations compared to those received during instruction. This outcome has grave implications when one considers the weight given to high-stakes assessment for the progress and monitoring of student performance. It appears that more attention is given by professionals in the field to instructional accommodations while researchers continue to focus primarily on testing accommodations. Instead, testing accommodations should be determined based on which instructional accommodations have been found to be appropriate and effective for the individual student.

Accommodations relate to the changes in time, presentation, response, participation, and level of support necessary for a student with special needs to learn and demonstrate knowledge across instructional and/or testing situations. Unfortunately, as previously mentioned, the vast amount of research related to accommodations focuses on testing rather than instructional accommodations. As concern over high-stakes tests dominates the political, social, and educational mindset in today's schools, this is not surprising. While accommodations can benefit students across both testing and learning situations, the requirements and purpose of testing and learning are not always identical. Therefore, professional judgment is again central to the validity of using accommodations across multiple settings.

Rather than discussing test or instructional accommodations in isolation, in this chapter we will view both together under the rubric of the accommodation process. Since the whole is greater than the sum of its parts, each component of the accommodation process should influence and guide the others in a bidirectional rather than a unidirectional manner. For instance, the questions and concerns surrounding the validity of testing accommodations are equally relevant to instructional accommodations.

Borrowing from the Pellegrino et al. (2001), discussion on the design of scientifically-based assessment measures, as well as the ongoing instructional validity research of the *National Alternate Assessment Center* (NAAC Advisory Board, 2006), we developed a *Formative Accommodation Process* model to be used in identifying and supporting accommodation decisions for either instructional or testing situations at the state, school, and classroom level (see Figure 14.1). Unfortunately, the accommodation policies and procedures used by states for their high-stakes achievement testing are often not used by teachers for classroom instruction or testing situations. This practice leads to "idiosyncratic decision-making" (Tindal & Ketterlin-Gellor, 2004).

**Step One** of the *Formative Accommodation Process* includes careful review of a student's profile. This requires consideration of the individual's cognitive, behavioral/affective, and academic strengths and weaknesses for selection of specific accommodations across settings. Achievement performance alone should not be the sole basis for accommodation selection. For example, a student's low reading comprehension scores could be the result of deficits in phonological and orthographic awareness influencing reading fluency and comprehension. However, the poor reading performance might also be the result of executive processing deficits influencing adequate comprehension monitoring. The type of accommodation(s) for these two situations is not identical. It is imperative that professionals give equal consideration to a student's history and experiences along with academic content and classroom environment.

**Step Two** pertains to the evaluation of the content either being tested or taught. Identification of the specific skills (e.g., fractions) being measured rather than ancillary requirements of the task (e.g., reading) are identified. In addition, recognition of the stages of learning that are to be measured (i.e., acquisition, proficiency, maintenance, generalization, and adaptation) should be clearly identified by the team of professionals who work with the student.

**Step Three** requires careful professional evaluation of the task and setting requirements. The degree of structure required by the task or setting, including cues/prompts, response types,

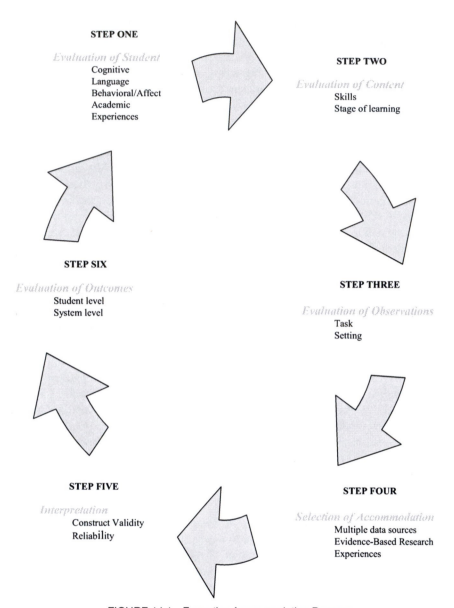

STEP ONE

*Evaluation of Student*
Cognitive
Language
Behavioral/Affect
Academic
Experiences

STEP TWO

*Evaluation of Content*
Skills
Stage of learning

STEP SIX

*Evaluation of Outcomes*
Student level
System level

STEP THREE

*Evaluation of Observations*
Task
Setting

STEP FIVE

*Interpretation*
Construct Validity
Reliability

STEP FOUR

*Selection of Accommodation*
Multiple data sources
Evidence-Based Research
Experiences

FIGURE 14.1   Formative Accommodation Process.

and modalities for the acquisition and/or production of learning are compared at this point to the student's learning profile (Step One).

**Step Four** is the point at which specific accommodations are selected based on multiple data sources (Steps One–Three) and available evidence-based research. The IEP Team would then make decisions using both their observations (Steps One–Three) and available research to determine the most appropriate instructional and test accommodation(s) for a specific student.

**Step Five** is the point at which the construct validity and the reliability of a chosen accommodation are evaluated. For standardized testing accommodations, the literature provides professionals with a great deal of valuable resources to help guide this process (see below; *Measurement Issues and Test Accommodations,* page 20 ).

**Step Six** (the final step) is time at which the professional develops a standardized and systematic method to record the effectiveness of specific instructional and/or test accommodations for each student. At any given time, an outside reviewer should be able to evaluate the progress a student is making when specific accommodations are provided.

## UNIVERSAL DESIGN FOR LEARNING (UDL)

Creating universally designed learning environments is central to any discussion of accommodating testing and learning environments for students with special needs.

Universal design is commonly associated with the movement to ensure physical environments that are accessible to all individuals (e.g., curb cuts). UDL extends universal design from a physical space to a pedagogical space. IDEA (2004) defines UDL as "a concept or philosophy for designing and delivering products and services that are usable by people with the widest possible range of functional capabilities, which include products and services that are directly accessible (without requiring assistive technologies) and products and services that are interoperable with assistive technologies" (Section 611, 16[E]). Therefore, UDL is a philosophy written into law that supports equal access to learning for all individuals.

The philosophy behind UDL encourages professionals to provide better access to learning opportunities for everyone, not just students with disabilities. UDL practices are inherently flexible so as to support all learners, thereby reducing the need for modifications and accommodations in either testing or instructional situations. Accommodations in UDL should be seamlessly integrated across all situations. According to Dolan and Hall (2006, March), the goal of UDL is to "reduce accommodations as retrofits." However, empirical-based research documenting the effectiveness of UDL has been limited both in rigor, specificity, and quantity of studies.

### Types of Accommodations

As mentioned earlier, accommodations can be classified under one of five different categories: presentation, response, scheduling/timing, setting, and behavioral. These categories can be applied to either testing or instructional accommodations. Since the early 1990s, the National Center on Educational Outcomes (NCEO) has been federally funded to maintain a systematic database on the participation of students with disabilities in large-scale testing programs. The NCEO Web site (http://www.education.umn.edu/NCEO/) provides professionals with a wealth of state-level data and other resources pertaining to state compliance and the accommodation of high-stakes testing.

*Presentation Accommodations.* Presentation accommodations provide the student access to academic information by alternative means (e.g., screen reader, access assistants [reader, sign language interpreter], alternative media [e-text, audio books, Braille], language structures (e.g., simplified language), font format (e.g., large print, type or color of font), and instructional methodology (e.g., cooperative learning, computer-assisted). Oral presentation (read-alouds) is one of the most frequently investigated and used testing accommodations across disabilities (Sireci et al., 2003; Thompson, Blount, & Thurlow, 2002). The majority of the research within this category pertains to a variety of oral presentations accommodating testing situations (Sireci et al., 2003; Thompson et al., 2002). The types of oral presentation methods most often studied include teacher reading, student/peer reading, and screen reading software.

The effectiveness of oral presentation of content during testing or instruction is not supported by any conclusive evidence (Calhoon, Fuchs, & Hamlett, 2000; Fuchs et al., 2000; Johnson, 2000; Kosciolek & Ysseldyke, 2000; Meloy, Deville, & Frisbee, 2002; Sireci et al., 2003; Thompson et al., 2002; Tindal, Heath, Hollenbeck, Almond, & Harness, 1998). It is likely that further research examining the effectiveness of oral presentation as an accommodation will reveal that read-aloud applications are only one of several variables directly and indirectly influencing student performance. For instance, researchers identified that students with disabilities often do better on constructed-response items than multiple choice across different read-aloud formats—the read aloud was not the critical variable but rather the type of task format (Calhoon et al., 2000; Sireci et al., 2003).

Read-alouds for accommodating instructional practice have primarily focused on improving reading or spelling performance for students with disabilities (Graham, MacArthur, & Schwartz, 1995; Handley-More, Deitz, Billingsley, & Coggins, 2003; Higgins & Raskin, 2000; MacArthur, 1998, 1999, 2000; MacArthur & Cavalier, 2004; MacArthur, Graham, Haynes, & De La Paz, 1996; Raskind & Higgins, 1999). However, what is lacking in the research is evidence of the effectiveness of read-alouds for accommodating student progress within the standard curriculum.

Computer-based instruction and testing has also been advocated by many as the solution to accommodating students with disabilities. However, Thompson, Thurlow, Quenemoen, and Lehr (2002) present an in-depth review of the positive and negative aspects related to computer-based testing for students with disabilities. As they note, "Often, the approach has simply been to take the paper-and-pencil test and put it onto the computer" (p. 1). This same conclusion can certainly be generalized to a great deal of computerized instruction. However, technologies are contributing to the development of classroom-based monitoring of learning progress. According to Pellegrino et al. (2001), "A possibility for the future arises from the projected growth across curricular areas of technology-based assessment embedded in instructional settings" (p. 10). Application of this type of systematic monitoring of instructional outcomes has great potential for measuring the effectiveness of instructional accommodations.

*Response Accommodations.*    Response accommodations allow for the student to demonstrate his or her knowledge using alternative forms (e.g., writing directly on test booklets, oral response, sign language), accessing assistants (scribes), using assistive technologies (voice-to-text), or other tools (word processor, calculator). The most common types of response accommodations (using technology) include word processors with spell check, proofreading assistance, abbreviation expanders (programs that allow students to type abbreviations for frequently used words or phrases and press the space bar/mouse to select the complete word or phrase), and outlining software programs (Day & Edwards, 1996).

The effectiveness of word processors for accommodating the responses of students with disabilities for either testing or instruction has been inconclusive (Cahalan-Laitusis, 2003). For instance, MacArthur and Graham (1987) found no differences between the quality scores for handwritten or computer written essays of middle school students with learning disabilities. Interestingly, Hollenbeck, Tindal, Harness, and Almond (1999) found that students with disabilities performed worse when they used computers on high-stakes tests. One needs to be very careful, however, when interpreting some of the research pertaining to word processing and writing competence for students with disabilities. The majority of the studies failed to control for the amount of instructional time that was provided to students on word processing skills prior to documenting its effectiveness for increasing writing quality.

However, research supports the use of scribes as a very effective accommodation for students with disabilities during testing situations (Trimble, 1998). Interestingly, Raskind and Higgins

(1999) found the use of text-to-speech as an effective means for helping students with learning disabilities edit their own written compositions. Again, however, application of this research to standard curriculum experiences is necessary to evaluate the effectiveness of its use as an instructional accommodation.

*Scheduling/Timing Accommodations.* Scheduling and timing accommodations are adjustments to the time provided to complete learning tasks and respond to academic content (e.g., extended time, unlimited time, frequent breaks, testing over multiple days). Researchers have explored the accommodation of extra time in testing situations more than any other scheduling/timing accommodation (Chi & Pearson, 1999; Sireci et al., 2003; Thompson et al., 2002). Unfortunately, in a great deal of current research extra time and other accommodations, in particular read-alouds, were not studied as separate variables influencing performance.

The overall conclusion of the accommodation literature points toward the effectiveness of extra time for students with disabilities across testing and instructional settings. Sireci (2004) concluded that flexible time limits reduced unintended speededness effects and did not alter the construct validity of tests. However, several researchers have pointed out that extended time alone will not improve a student's performance. The student must first acquire, by means of direct instruction, the knowledge being tested (Fuchs et al., 2000). Mandinach, Bridgeman, Cahalan-Laitusis, and Trapani (2005) investigated the interaction of extended time and a modified schedule. They concluded that (a) lower ability students were not aided by extended time, (b) section breaks helped all students, and (c) extended time helped the medium to higher ability students more significantly than low ability students. These findings highlight the fact that the accommodation should never be seen as replacing instruction, but rather facilitating access or production of knowledge.

*Setting Accommodations.* Alterations to the academic environment (e.g., private room, small group setting) as an accommodation during testing has not been empirically studied in isolation. While it is standard practice for many students with disabilities, the effectiveness of this accommodation consists mainly of anecdotal evidence to support its use in practice.

*Behavioral Accommodations.* Facilitation of appropriate behavioral responses to academic learning (e.g., personal assistant, time-out area, breaking tasks down into smaller units, reinforcement systems) is a common practice in special education classrooms. Again, while the literature has supported the need for these adaptations in teaching, empirical research documenting their use for accommodating tests and/or as a standard classroom accommodation is limited. Support for behavioral accommodations rests mainly with professional judgment.

## MEASUREMENT ISSUES AND TEST ACCOMMODATIONS

Test accommodations are designed to promote fairness in testing and lead to more accurate interpretations of examinees' tests scores (Sireci & Pitoniak, 2006). Although accommodations (e.g., extended time) are intended to provide equal access by removing unnecessary challenges (e.g., construct irrelevant variance), some types of accommodations may change the test's construct, thus altering the comparability of scores derived from the accommodated test. Preservation of construct validity allows for score comparability across individuals with and without accommodations.

Most accommodations do not appear to alter the validity of the test, so the interpretation of test scores is not influenced. For instance, a reading test written in large print should not change the underlying construct the test was intended to measure because the skill of reading is still being assessed. Several accommodations, however, are thought to change the construct of some tests. For instance, there is some debate regarding the impact of extended time on the validity of tests that are speeded. Extra time allows students to reach questions at the end of a speeded test that they may not have attempted under standard timing conditions, but no general consensus has been reached regarding the degree to which extended time changes what the test purports to measure or its impact on the comparability of tests scores across various groups of examinees (Camara & Schneider, 2000).

Phillips (1994) argues that measurement specialists should consider the impact of accommodations on the test's construct validity. He contends that any changes to testing conditions should be avoided if the change would (a) alter the skill being measured, (b) preclude the comparison of scores between examinees who received the extended time and those who did not, or (c) allow examinees without disabilities to benefit if they were granted the same accommodation. This last criterion is contentious and recently several researchers have argued that accommodations should only be provided if they offer a "differential" boost to students with disabilities (Fuchs & Fuchs, 1999; & Pitoniak & Royer, 2001).

Psychometric issues in test accommodations stress the need to remove construct-irrelevant barriers to test performance while maintaining the integrity of the construct being measured by the test (Sireci et al., 2003). For example, a student who learned Spanish as her first language may do worse on a math test administered in English (her second language). In this case, English proficiency may be considered extraneous to the math construct targeted by the test, but would certainly affect her test performance on the English language version of the test. Removing these barriers, which is analogous to accommodating the administration, is thus seen as removing construct-irrelevant variance and strengthening the validity of test scores.

Paradoxically, accommodations may also introduce construct-irrelevant variance if the accommodation itself changes the construct being measured. If the construct intended to be measured by a test changes, and the new characteristics measured represent a different and unintended construct, then construct-irrelevant variance is also present (Sireci, 2005). Furthermore, if the accommodation removes or replaces portions of the test content, construct-under-representation may result. Therefore, although accommodations are designed to promote fairness in testing, the degree to which the accommodation(s) strengthens validity is directly related to the degree to which the accommodation alters the construct being measured (Sireci, 2005).

The issue of score comparability merits a brief discussion as well. Despite its common use in the *Standards* (AERA/APA/NCME, 1999; Standard 10.11) and elsewhere, the term *score comparability* is not defined anywhere in the *Standards*. This lack of clear definition has led many researchers to define score comparability in the limited framework of differences in mean scores across groups. In fact, for many years, researchers assumed that to appropriately measure these differences one must simply administer a measure across different testing situations and/or different groups and compute the difference between the two (or more) observed scores (Cronbach & Furby, 1970). However, a number of potentially problematic issues in the use of difference scores have been identified (see, for example, Cronbach, 1992; Edwards, 1994). To get an adequate assessment of these differences when comparing mean scores across groups, it is essential that the measure is perceived to be used in the same way by individuals. In other words, it is necessary to show that the two measurements are psychometrically equivalent to make valid comparisons across groups of respondents (Horn & McArdle, 1992).

A test fulfills *measurement equivalence/invariance* when it is shown to measure the same attribute under different conditions (Meade & Lautenschlager, 2004). These different conditions may include the stability of measurement across different populations (e.g. individuals with and without disabilities) and/or different methods of test administration (e.g., extended time administration vs. standard time administration). Under such conditions, tests of equivalence/invariance are typically conducted via confirmatory factor analysis (CFA) methods (Meade & Lautenschlager, 2004), thus allowing researchers to determine the extent to which test scores across groups and/or conditions are comparable.

Another measurement issue involves the concept of *speededness*. The degree to which educational tests are speeded has a direct bearing on the issue of score comparability because the accommodation of extended time changes the construct measured on a speeded test, but not on a test that is not speeded (e.g., a power test). According to the *Standards*, speededness is "a test characteristic, dictated by the test's time limits, that results in a test taker's score being dependent on the rate at which work is performed as well as the correctness of the responses...Speededness is often an undesirable characteristic" (p. 182). In general, on a pure *speed* test, individual differences depend entirely upon the speed of performance and the items are relatively easy; on *power* tests, the differences are not contingent on speed and the items increase in difficulty (Ofiesh, Mather, & Russell, 2005). If speed of responding plays a significant role in determining scores on power tests, and speed is not part of the intended construct, then the validity of the assessments is threatened (Bridgeman, Trapani, & Curley, 2003).

The validity and reliability of *nonstandardized assessments and instruction* provide professionals a greater challenge. Single-subject methodology is one solution to ongoing validity checks, particularly for curriculum-based assessments and instruction. In addition, professional judgment can be used in determining the appropriateness of accommodations. However, ongoing accountability measures will require some of the same validity tools being designed for alternate assessments. The importance of valid and reliable measures cannot be stressed enough; they provide the accountability for the ongoing instructional and testing accommodations in the classroom.

## MEASUREMENT ISSUES AND INSTRUCTIONAL ACCOMMODATIONS

As one reviews the accommodation literature for students with disabilities, it is apparent that the primary focus of research has been on investigating the accommodation of standardized assessments, particularly statewide high-stakes tests. In comparison, the accommodation of the standard curriculum has received far less attention. However, if a student with disabilities is not able to access or demonstrate knowledge using evidence-based accommodations, the individual's performance on high-stakes tests, with or without accommodations, will be below standards. Therefore, professionals working with individuals with disabilities must begin to focus more closely on the effectiveness of instructional accommodations for different types of learners within the general education curriculum.

Encouragingly, the methodologies that are currently available can be used to guide professionals in selecting and monitoring the effectiveness of instructional accommodations. For instance, *The Learning Strategies Curriculum* developed at the University of Kansas has a wealth of evidence-based research documenting the acquisition, storage, and demonstration of learning strategies for a student's success in the classroom. The *Learning Strategies Curriculum* has been field-tested in hundreds of schools to show its effectiveness; long-term research provides evidence of its usefulness with standard curriculum when "consistent, intensive, explicit instruction and support are key ingredients" (Lenz, Deshler, & Kissam, 2004, p. 358). Obviously, one of the problems of strategy instruction has been lack of generalization to the regular classroom (Ellis,

1993). However, many innovative means to evaluate, maintain, and record the generalization of learning strategies to standard curricula have been developed by the professionals who developed the *Learning Strategies Curriculum* (Deshler, 2003; Deshler, Schumaker, Lenz, Bulgren, Hock, & Knight, 2001; Ellis, 1993, 1997; & Lenz, Deshler, & Kissam, 2004). Their research has focused primarily on adolescents with learning disabilities and their acquisition or generalization of learning strategies. However, we do not need to reinvent the wheel. The principles, knowledge, and methodologies gained from this significant body of research can provide guidance to state policymakers, school personnel, and teachers in better documenting the effectiveness of learning accommodations.

Learning accommodations are not synonymous with instructional strategies or methodologies for teaching; they are the means by which professionals adapt a learning task or curriculum to provide equal access to students with disabilities. Some learning strategies must be adapted or individualized to a specific learner just as instructional methodologies must be adapted or individualized to a specific teacher. This is the fundamental and guiding principle for special education decision making. The key is to apply this principle to ensure valid and reliable practice. Due to the lack of evidence-based research in this area, many of the decisions surrounding learning or testing accommodations are dependent upon professional judgment. At times, using professional observation and judgment to evaluate the effectiveness of accommodations on learning is more appropriate than empirical-based research. However, there continues to be a need for more evidence-based research to support decision making related to testing and instructional accommodations.

## PAST, PRESENT, AND FUTURE

The use of accommodations in both instructional and testing situations is contributing significantly to the increased success of students with disabilities on national and state assessments (Thompson et al., 2005). In this regard, it is most appropriate to view accommodations as simply leveling the playing field; they do not supply the knowledge necessary to pass tests. While accommodations are tools for accessing or demonstrating knowledge, they should never replace ongoing, direct instruction. For instance, Cohen, Gregg, and Deng (2005) found that the cause of differential performance for students with and without learning disabilities on a high-stakes mathematics test did not appear to be due to receipt of extended time but rather the individual's knowledge of the content. Mathematics competency differentiated the groups of student learners regardless of their accommodation and/or reading levels. Accommodations are not the source of differential performance; they simply mediate learning.

Unfortunately, focusing primarily on testing rather than instructional accommodations has diverted professional attention away from the main goal of special education: equal access to, and demonstration of learning for all students. Accommodating the instructional environment will provide students with special needs the knowledge necessary for success across the curriculum—not just during testing situations. Instructional accommodations must receive the same considerations as those given to testing situations. For example, the validity and reliability issues surrounding the provision of test accommodations should be considered for instructional accommodations as well. In addition, research on validating alternate instruction has the potential to help guide instructional accommodation decision making. As Sireci et al. (2003) note, "The literature is clear that accommodations and students are both heterogeneous" (p. 48). Success of students with disabilities with learning the standard curriculum in the general education classroom is dependent upon professionals making informed decisions based on evidence-based practice and research. At times, informed professional judgment will be the most valid and reliable source for decision making. However, this requires that professionals use a systematic method for decision making that is both reliable and valid.

Shamelka and David, the two students with disabilities discussed at the beginning of this chapter, require both testing and instructional accommodations. Decisions on the appropriateness and effectiveness of their accommodations should be based upon multiple data sources. In addition, systematic monitoring of the effectiveness of Shamelka's and David's accommodations will contribute to their success on high-stakes testing and proficiency across the standard curriculum. Accommodations are not ancillary to learning for these two students; rather, they are the heart and soul of special education.

## REFERENCES

Abedi, J., Courtney, M., & Leon, S. (2003). *Research supported accommodations for English language learners in NAEP.* (CSE Technical Report 586). Los Angeles: University of California, Center for Research on Evaluation, Standards and Student Testing.

Almond, P. & Karvonen, M. (2006). *The use of accommodations for a K-12 standardized assessment: Practical consideration from a state perspective 1999 through 2004.* Paper presented at the 2006 Educational Testing Service symposium on Accommodating Students with Disabilities on State Assessments.

American Educational Research Association, American Psychological Association, & National Council on measurement in Education. (1999). *Standards for educational and psychological testing.* Washington, DC: American Educational Research Association.

Bridgeman, B., Trapani, C., & Curley, E. (2003). *Impact of fewer questions per section on SAT I scores.* (College Board Research Report No. 2003-2). New York: College Board.

Cahalan-Laitusis, C. (2003). Accommodations on high stakes writing tests for students with disabilities. Retrieved January 2004 from http://www.ets.org/accommodationsconference/

Calhoon, M.B., Fuchs, L.S., & Hamlett, C.L., (2000). Effects of computer-based test accommodations on mathematics performance assessments for secondary students with learning disabilities. *Learning Disability Quarterly, 23* 271–282.

Camara, W. & Schneider, D. (2000). *Testing with extended time on the SAT® I: Effects for students with learning disabilities.* (College Board Research Report No. RN-08). New York: College Board.

Chi, C.W.T. & Pearson, P.D. (1999, June). *Synthesizing the effects of test accommodations for special education and limited English proficient students.* Paper presented at the National Conference on Large Scale Assessment, Snowbird, UT.

Cohen, A., Gregg, N., Deng, M. (2005). The role of extended time and item content on a high-stakes mathematics test. *Journal of Learning Disabilities Research and Practice, 20,* 225–233

Cronbach, L.J. (1992). Four *Psychological Bulletin* articles in perspective. *Psychological Bulletin, 112,* 389–392.

Cronbach, L.J. & Furby, L. (1970). How should we measure "change": Or should we? *Psychological Bulletin, 74,* 68–80

Day, S. L., & Edwards, B. J. (1996). Assistive technology for postsecondary students with learning disabilities. *Journal of Learning Disabilities, 29,* 486–492.

Deshler, D. (2003). Intervention research and bridging the gap between research and practice. *Learning Disabilities: A Contemporary Journal, 1*(1), 1–7.

Deshler, D. D., Schumaker, J.B., Lenz, B.K., Bulgren, J.A., Hock, M.F., Knight, J., & Ehren, B. (2001). Ensuring content-area learning by secondary students with learning disabilities. *Learning Disabilities Research and Practice, 16,* 96–108.

Dolan, R., & Hall, T. (2006, March). *Developing accessible tests with universal design and digital technologies.* Paper presented at the 2006 Educational Testing Service symposium on Accommodating Students with Disabilities on State Assessments.

Edwards, J.R. (1994). The study of congruence in organizational behavior research: Critique and proposed alternative. *Organizational Behavior and Human Decision Processes, 58*, 141–155.

Elliott, S. (2006). *Selecting accommodations wisely: Facilitating test access and enhancing implementation integrity.* Paper presented at the 2006 Educational Testing Service Symposium on Accommodating Students with Disabilities on State Assessments.

Ellis, E.S. (1993). Integrative strategy instruction: A potential model for teaching content area subjects to adolescents with learning disabilities. *Journal of Learning Disabilities, 26*, 358–383.

Ellis, E.S. (1997). Watering up the curriculum for adolescents with learning disabilities: Goals of the knowledge dimension. *Remedial & Special Education, 18*, 326–346.

Ewing, J.L. (2006). *IEP team and assessment accommodation decisions: Recommended vs. implemented.* Paper presented at the 2006 Educational Testing Service symposium on Accommodating Students with Disabilities on State Assessments.

Fuchs, L.S. & Fuchs, D. (1999). Fair and unfair testing accommodations. *School Administrator, 56*, 24–29.

Fuchs, L.S., Fuchs, D., Eaton, S.B., Hamlett, C.B., Binkley, E., & Crouch, R. (2000). Using objective data sources to enhance teacher judgments about test accommodations. *Exceptional Children, 67*(1), 67–81.

Gong, B., & Marion,S. (2006). *Dealing with flexibility in assessments for students with significant cognitive disabilities (synthesis Report 60).* Minneapolis: University of Minnesota, National Center on Educational Outcomes. Retrieved August 10, 2006, from http://education.umn.edu/NCEO/OnlinePubs/Synthesisis60.html.

Graham, S., MacArthur, C.A., & Schwartz, S.S. (1995). The effects of goal setting and procedural facilitation on the revising behavior and writing performance of students with writing and learning problems. *Journal of Educational Psychology, 87*, 230–240.

Gregg, N., Morgan, D., Hartwig, J., & Coleman, C. (in press). Accommodations: Research to practice. In L.E. Wolf, H. Scribner, & J. Wasserstein (Eds.), *Adults with Learning Disorders: Contemporary Issues, Neuropsychology Handbook Series.*

Handley-More, D., Deitz, J., & Billingsley, F.F., & Coggins, T.E. (2003). Facilitating written work using computer word processing and word prediction. *American Journal of Occupational Therapy, 57*, 139–151.

Helwig, R., & Tindal, G. (2003). An experimental analysis of accommodation decisions on large-scale mathematics tests. *Exceptional Children, 69*, 211–225.

Higgins, E. L. & Raskind, M. H. (2000). Speaking to read: The effects of continuous vs. discrete speech recognition systems on the reading and spelling of children with learning disabilities. *Journal of Special Education Technology, 15* (1), 19–30.

Hollenbeck,K. (2002). Determining when test alterations are valid accommodations or modifications for large-scale assessment. In G. Tindal & T.M. Haladyna (Eds), *Large-scale assessment programs for all students* (pp. 395–426). Mahwah, NJ: Erlbaum.

Hollenbeck, K., Tindal, G., & Almond, P. (1998). Teachers' knowledge of accommodations as a validity issue in high-stakes testing. *Journal of Special Education, 32*(3), 175–183.

Hollenbeck, K., Tindal, G., Harniss, M., & Almond, P. (1999). Reliability and decision consistency: An analysis of writing mode at two times on a statewide test. *Educational Assessment, 6* (1), 23–40.

Horn, J.L., & McArdle, J.J. (1992). A practical and theoretical guide to measurement invariance in aging research. *Experimental Aging Research, 18,* 117–144.

Johnson, E. (2000). The effects of accommodations on performance assessments. *Remedial and Special Education, 21,* 261–267.

Koenig, J.A., &Bachman, L.F. (Eds). (2004). Keeping score for all: The effects of inclusion and accommodation policies on large-scale educational assessments. National Research Council. Washington, DC: The National Academic Press.

Kopriva, R. (2002). *Taxonomy for Testing English Language Learners.* Funded proposal to the U.S. Department of Education, Grants for Enhanced Assessment instruments Program.

Kosciolek, S., & Ysseldyke, J.E. (2000). Effects of a reading accommodation on the validity of a reading test (*Technical Report 28*). Minneapolis: University of Minnesota, National Center on Educational

Outcomes. Retrieved May 2006, from http://education.umn.edu/NCEO/OnlinePubs/Technical28.htm

Lenz, B.K., Deshler, D.D. & Kissam, B.R. (2004). *Teaching content to all: Evidence-Based inclusive practices in middle and secondary schools.* Boston: Pearson Education, Inc.

MacArthur, S.A. (1998). Word processing with speech synthesis and word prediction: Effects on the dialogue journal writing of students with learning disabilities. *Learning Disability Quarterly, 21,* 1–16.

MacArthur, S.A. (2000). New tools for writing: Assistive technology for students with writing difficulties. *Topics in Language Disorders,* 20, 85–100.

MacArthur, S.A. (2004). Dictation and speech recognition technology as accommodations in large-scale assessments for students with learning disabilities. *Exceptional Children, 71,* 43–58.

MacArthur, C.A., & Cavalier, A. (2004). Dictation and speech recognition technology as accommodations in large-scale assessments for students with learning disabilities. *Exceptional Children, 71,* 43–58.

MacArthur, C., & Graham, S. (1987). Learning disabled students' composing under three methods of text production: Handwriting, word processing, and dictation. *Journal of Special Education, 21,* 22–42.

MacArthur, C.A., Graham, S, Haynes, J.A., & De La Paz, S. (1996). Spelling checkers and students with learning disabilities: Performance comparison and impact on spelling. *Journal of Special Education, 30,* 35–57.

Mandinach, E.B., Bridgeman, B., Cahalan-Laitusis, C., & Trapani, C. (2005). *The impact of extended time on SAT test performance.* College Board Research Report Number 2005-8. New York: College Board.

McLaughlin, M.J., Embler, S., & Nagle, K. (2004). Students with disabilities and accountability: the promise and the realities should there be alternatives. Prepared for Center on Education Policy. Retrieved August 1, 2006, from http://www.ncrel.org/sdrs/areas/issues/methods/technlgy/te8refer

Meade, A.W. & Lautenschlager, G.J. (2004). A Monte Carlo study of confirmatory factor analytic tests of measurement equivalence/invariance. *Structural Equation Modeling, 11*(1), 60–72.

Meloy, L.L., Deville, C., & Frisbee, D.A. (2002). The effect of a read aloud accommodation on test scores of students with and without a learning disability in reading. *Remedial and Special Education, 23,* 248–255.

National Alternate Assessment Advisory Board (2006). March 2006 advisory board meeting. Retrieved August 2006 from www.naacpartners.org/Products/AdvisoryboardPresentations/Advisory%20Board %20Meeting%20Presentation.ppt

Ofiesh, N., Mather, N., & Russell, A. (2005). Using speeded cognitive, reading, and academic measures to determine the need for extended test time among university students with learning disabilities. *Journal of Psychoeducational Assessment, 23,* 35–52.

Pelligrino, J.W., Chudowsky, N., & Glaser, R. (Eds). (2001). *Knowing what students know: The science and design of educational assessment.* Center for Education, National Research Council. Retrieved August 1, 2006, from http://www.napedu/catalog/10019.html

Phillips, S. E. (1994). High-stakes testing accommodations: Validity versus disabled rights. *Applied Measurement in Education, 7,* 93–120.

Pitoniak, M., & Royer, J. (2001). Testing accommodations for examinees with disabilities: a review of psychometric, legal, and social policy issues. *Review of Educational Research. 71*(1), 53–104.

Raskind, M. H. & Higgins, E. L. (1999). Speaking to read: The effects of speech recognition technology on the reading and spelling performance of children with learning disabilities. *Annals of Dyslexia, 49,* 251–281.

Sireci, S. (2005). Unlabeling the disabled: A psychomtric perspective on flagging scores from accommodated test administrations. *Educational Researcher, 24*(1), 3–12.

Sireci, S. G., (2004). Validity Issues in Accommodating NAEP Reading Tests. NAGB Conference on increasing the participation of SD and LEP Students in NAEP. Retrieved July 25, 2006, from http://www.nagb.org/pubs/conferences/sierci.co

Sireci S. G., & Green, P. C. (2000). Legal and psychometric criteria for evaluating teacher certification tests. *Educational Measurement: Issues and Practice, 19* (1), 22–31, 34.

Sireci, S., Li, S., & Scarpati, S. (2003). *The effects of test accommodation on test performance: A review of the literature.* (Center for Educational Assessment Research Report No. 485). Amherst: School of Education, University of Massachusetts.

Sireci, S. G. & Pitoniak, M. (2006). *Assessment accommodations: What have we learned from research?* Paper presented at the 2006 Educational Testing Service symposium on Accommodating Students with Disabilities on State Assessments.

Siskind, T. (2004). *Achieving accurate results for diverse learners: Accommodations and access-enhanced formats for English language learners and students with disabilities.* Funded proposal to the U.S. Department of Education, Grants for Enhanced Assessment Instruments Program.

Thompson, S., Blount, A., & Thurlow, M. (2002). *A summary of research on the effects of test accommodations: 1999 through 2001* (Technical Report 34). Minneapolis: University of Minnesota, National Center on Educational Outcomes, Retrieved January 4, 2004, http://www.education.umn.edu/NCEO/OnlinePubs/Technical34.htm.

Thompson, S.J., Johnstone, C.J., Thurlow, M.L., & Altman, J.R. (2005). *2005 State special education outcomes: Steps forward in a decade of change.* Minneapolis: University of Minnesota, National Center on Education Outcomes. Retrieved August 1, 2006, from http://education.umn.edu/NCEO/OnlinePubs/2005StateReprot.htm/

Thompson, S.J., Thurlow, M.L., Quenemoen,R.F., & Lehr, C.A. (2002). Access to computer-based testing for students with disabilities (Synthesis Report 45). Minneapolis, MN: University of Minnesota, National Center on Educational Outcomes. Retrieved May 2006, from http://education.lumn.edu/NCEO/OnlinePubs/Synthesis45.html

Thurlow, M. (2006). *Accommodations in state policies: What a wonderful world of diversity: Issues and implications.* Paper presented at the 2006 Educational Testing Service symposium on Accommodating Students with Disabilities on State Assessments.

Tindal, G., Heath, B., Hollenbeck, K., Almond, P., & Harniss, M. (1998). Accommodating students with disabilities on large-scale tests: An empirical study of student response and test administration demands. *Exceptional Children, 64,* 439–450.

Tindal, G., & Ketterlin-Geller, L.R. (2004). *Research on Mathematics Test Accommodations Relevant to NAEP Testing.* NAGB Conference on increasing the participation of SD and LEP Students in NAEP. Retrieved July, 2006, from http://www.nagb.org/pubs/conferences/tindal

Trimble, S. (1998). *Performance trends and use of accommodations on a statewide assessment (State Assessment Series).* Minneapolis, MN: National Center on Educational Outcomes.

# IV

# ISSUES RELATED TO TEACHING STUDENTS HAVING LEARNING AND BEHAVIORAL CHALLENGES

# 15

# Issues Unique to English Language Learners

## Samuel O. Ortiz and Agnieszka M. Dynda

*Those who cannot remember the past are condemned to repeat it.*
Santayana, 1905

## INTRODUCTION

Some may wonder whether the introductory quote for this chapter was selected intentionally with an eye toward irony. After all, Santayana was a Spanish American and the use of his ethnicity, not just his words, to highlight the thematic element of this chapter would certainly qualify as an additional twist to the problem of providing evidence-based interventions for English language learners. But the quote stands on its own merit, irrespective of the author's heritage, and truly sets the stage for understanding the issues relevant to language minority children being served and educated presently in U.S. public schools. These issues form a clear pattern, one that has repeated itself continuously throughout the history of this country, and is based on assumptions that although wrong, are still pervasive in the schools and society and especially in the minds of policy makers who hold sway over the education of all children, including English language learners.

The structure and focus of this chapter are likely to appear different than others contained in this book. The reason for this has more to do with what is known and not known about evidence-based interventions with English language learners. The fact is, there is virtually no literature base on this topic; providing a review of what there is would make this an exceedingly short chapter. And what research there is suffers from flaws that render them rather useless. To provide a discussion that is of practical significance to practitioners looking to provide effective, responsive, and appropriate interventions with English language learners requires more of a "what do we know" than a simple "what works" approach. In the final analysis, what interventions work with English language learners must necessarily be those that are based on what we know. It has been precisely this problem, a failure to apply the knowledge base regarding the learning needs and patterns of English language learners, that has doomed previous efforts in developing evidence-based interventions.

Because decisions regarding education and intervention attempts are often based on intuitive reasoning and culturally-bound beliefs rather than on empirical data, it is necessary to begin by revealing how such ideas and attitudes developed and how they have become entrenched in the educational practices of our school systems. Indeed, practitioners have little chance of developing appropriate interventions, evidence-based or not, if they are unable to recognize the manner in which their own personal and professional biases affect decisions regarding the nature of an intervention as well as the anticipated progress and expected outcome. The next section will turn to issues regarding development. This may seem unnecessary at first given that psychologists and practitioners in educationally-related fields are usually well versed in such matters. However, when it comes to English language learners, the manner in which cultural and linguistic differences affect development and how they interact with instructional practices to produce quite different learning trajectories is not nearly as well known. The chapter will conclude with a discussion regarding instructional and intervention practices and how they may be designed in accordance with the developmental principles outlined in the previous section. Practical guidelines will be offered so that professionals may be able to design and implement interventions to meet the needs of English language learners that are based on the best available science about "what works."

### English Language Learners in Historical Context

Perhaps more misconceptions exist regarding the history of schooling English language learners in the United States than in any other area. In addition, it is likely that no topic suffers more from "euphoric recall," which is the tendency to remember only the good or positive about the past and not the bad. For example, a common refrain heard often in discussions about language and education invariably sounds something like this: "my great-grand parents came to this country and they learned English immediately and succeeded, so why can't current immigrants just do the same?" Many Americans hold the belief that immigrant achievement was better in the "good old days" despite the evidence that this is far from the truth (Rothstein, 1998). When it comes to the reality about the history of achievement of English learners in this country, what is often believed to be true, is not. The cultural and linguistic assimilation and educational attainment of our immigrant populations have improved considerably over the last century yet it appears as if this phenomenon has gone largely unnoticed (Rothstein, 1998). Misconceptions continue to abound at every level of education and in the minds and gut instincts of the policy makers who determine educational practices broadly. There are many reasons for these mistaken beliefs, some of which will be discussed here, but the reader is admonished to consider that these misconceptions are so common and prevalent that they persist in policies evident in education to the present day.

*English Only.* English has been accorded special and favored status in the United Stated for quite some time, not necessarily because of any constitutional or legislative protections accorded by the founding fathers, but primarily by default. The large British population who later became American simply dominated society and English naturally became most associated with the United States despite the presence of other popular languages (e.g., German and French). After some time, however, public sentiment began to associate English with patriotism and national identity and the fervor took hold in the science of the early 20th century that began to suggest that certain immigrant populations were mentally inferior and perhaps ought to be excluded from entry (Brigham, 1923; Gould, 1996). This worry is illustrated poignantly in the case of a parochial school teacher in Hamilton County, Nebraska, by the name of Robert Meyer (see Crawford, 1992 for a detailed discussion). It seems that Mr. Meyer was found guilty of violating a 1919 statute that mandated English-only instruction in all public and private schools in the state of Nebraska (a law not unlike many that have been passed recently by other states). Mr. Meyer was apparently attempting to teach a bible story to a 10-year-old student using German which violated the 1919 statute which also specified that foreign language instruction could begin only after a pupil had reached and passed eighth grade. Upon appeal, the Nebraska Supreme Court upheld the conviction and issued the following ruling in support of its decision:

> The salutary purpose of the statute is clear. The Legislature had seen the baneful effects of permitting foreigners, who had taken residence in this country, to rear and educate their children in the language of their native land. The result of that condition was found to be inimical to our own safety. To allow the children of foreigners, who had emigrated here, to be taught from early childhood the language of the country of their parents was…to educate them so that they must always think in that language, and, as a consequence, naturally inculcate in them the ideas and sentiments foreign to the best interests of this country. (262 U.S. 390)

Fortunately for Mr. Meyer, the U.S. Supreme Court disagreed with this line of reasoning and reversed the decision upon appeal by a seven-to-two decision. The majority decision, rendered by Justice James C. McReynolds on June 4, 1923, focused on issues of liberty, control of education by parents, and the lack of evidence regarding harm to America from the use of foreign languages. The court noted that:

> The challenged statute forbids the teaching in school of any subject except in English; also the teaching of any other language until the pupil has attained and successfully passed the eighth grade, which is not usually accomplished before the age of twelve. The Supreme Court of the state has held that "the so-called ancient or dead languages" are not "within the spirit or the purpose of the act." Latin, Greek, Hebrew are not proscribed; but German, French, Spanish, Italian, and every other alien speech are within the ban. Evidently the Legislature has attempted materially to interfere with the calling of modern language teachers, with the opportunities of pupils to acquire knowledge, and with the power of parents to control the education of their own. (262 U.S. 390)

The decision clearly reinforced the rights of parents to decide matters regarding the education of their children. But the justices went further to emphasize the discriminatory implications of xenophobic attitudes, particularly when not supported by any scientific evidence. They added:

> No emergency has arisen which renders knowledge by a child of some language other than English so clearly harmful as to justify its inhibition with the consequent infringement of rights long freely enjoyed. We are constrained to conclude that the statute as applied is arbitrary and without reasonable relation to any end within the competency of the state. As the statute undertakes to interfere only with teaching which involves a modern language, leaving complete freedom as to other matters, there seems no adequate foundation for the suggestion that the purpose was to protect the child's health by limiting his mental activities. It is well known that proficiency in a foreign language seldom comes to one not instructed at an early age, and experience shows that this is not injurious to the health, morals or understanding of the ordinary child. (262 U.S. 390)

The decision appears to strike a blow for the freedom to educate children in any language or even more than one language, but that momentum has never truly caught on in the U.S. mainstream. The rights of children and their parents regarding the intersection between language and education have always been protected. Yet the reasons for that protection have been relatively thin and conditional. Moreover, whereas we aspire to place a great deal of trust in the wisdom of our Supreme Court justices, the fact of the matter is they are not often educators, psychologists, or experts in the topics they must examine critically. They, like all Americans, are subject to their own personal biases and sometimes even they are not aware of their own prejudices that stem from mistaken beliefs that have little basis in science or pedagogy.

Consider the 1974 landmark case of *Lau v. Nichols* in which the Supreme Court heard the case involving a class-action suit brought by non-English-speaking Chinese students and their parents against San Francisco Unified School District. The children and parents sought relief from English-only instruction (the same instruction given to all students by the district irrespective of native language) under the argument that it effectively created unequal educational opportunities that violate the Fourteenth Amendment.

Interestingly, the court did not apply the equal protection clause in this case and in finding for Lau, instead relied upon Title VI of the Civil Rights Act of 1964 that prohibited discrimination by any agencies receiving government funding on the basis of race, color, or national origin. The court delivered a unanimous opinion delivered by Justice William O. Douglas which concluded in part:

> Under these state-imposed standards there is no equality of treatment merely by providing students with the same facilities, textbooks, teachers, and curriculum; for students who do not understand English are effectively foreclosed from any meaningful education. Basic English skills are at the very core of what these public schools teach. Imposition of a requirement that, before a child can effectively participate in the educational program, he must already have acquired those basic skills is to make a mockery of public education. We know that those who do not understand English are certain to find their classroom experiences wholly incomprehensible and in no way meaningful. (414 U.S. 563)

The upshot of the decision was the creation of the "Lau Remedies," part of which included a short questionnaire sent home to all students who enroll in a new school for the first time. The parent's responses to the questions determine if the child will or will not receive some type of special linguistic program to prevent the discriminatory effect of being instructed in a language the child does not understand. Over the years, the type of program that has been most commonly implemented to comply with the Lau decision has been some form of ESL (English as a Second Language) service. Such a program has, unfortunately, fared little better than the alternative it was intended to replace (i.e., immersion or "sink or swim") despite the fact that it complies with the decision (Lindholm-Leary & Borsato, 2006; Ramirez, Wolfson, Talmadge, & Merino, 1986; Thomas & Collier, 2002).

A closer look at the decision in Lau reveals a much less sympathetic and insightful thought process on the part of the justices. First, two esteemed members of the court, Justice Harry Blackmun joined by Chief Justice Warren Burger, presented a caveat to clarify the reasons for the decision. Rather than strictly an issue of protecting discrimination against an individual, they made it clear that the case revolved around numbers. They stated:

> I merely wish to make plain that when, in another case, we are confronted with a very few youngsters, or with just a single child who speaks only German or Polish or Spanish or any language other than English, I would not regard today's decision…as conclusive upon the issue whether the statute and the guidelines require the funded school district to provide special instruction. For me, numbers are at the heart of this case and my concurrence is to be understood accordingly. (414 U.S. 563)

Had there been fewer plaintiffs in the case, it is unlikely that the court would have viewed the issue in the manner in which it did and the strong precedent for the educational rights of language minority students would not exist. Second, and perhaps even more alarming, are the comments by these two justices which reveal their thinking and expectations regarding the manner in which immigrants should be instructed and learn English. In the decision, they state:

Against the possibility that the Court's judgment may be interpreted too broadly, I stress the fact that the children with whom we are concerned here number about 1,800. This is a very substantial group that is being deprived of any meaningful schooling because the children cannot understand the language of the classroom. We may only guess as to why they have had no exposure to English in their preschool years. *Earlier generations of American ethnic groups have overcome the language barrier by earnest parental endeavor or by the hard fact of being pushed out of the family or community nest and into the realities of broader experience.* (414 U.S. 563; italics added for emphasis)

It would seem that even those in whom we put the utmost faith in demonstrating Solomon-like wisdom fall prey to the same misconceptions as the rest of us. It is not difficult to understand why the justices fail to comprehend the reason that children raised by non-English speaking parents would have little or no exposure to English in their preschool years. Such ethnocentric thinking notwithstanding, the comment at best minimizes the impact of early language learning in the home for language minority children. But it is the second comment that is shocking and difficult to believe that it comes from individuals whom we expect are extremely well studied and education. The principle of euphoric recall is again illustrated all too clearly in Justice Blackmun's reference to "earlier generations of American ethnic groups" and how it was simply being pushed out of the nest that facilitated their learning of English and presumably their success. Our ancestors did not simply overcome the language barrier by being immersed in mainstream society. We tend to forget immigrant portal communities, such as Little Italy or Chinatown, which provided a means for arriving families to assimilate slowly and allow the process of acculturation to unfold in its usual manner (Rothstein, 1998). We also tend to forget the educational support provided in these communities that invariably was in the native language as well as English and which across four generations or so, resulted in the monolingual English-speaking, mainstream American that forms the ideal expectation for immigrants to the United States (Rothstein, 1998; Valdés & Figueroa, 1994).

## English Language Learners and the Present Context

There is no debate that students in public schools, irrespective of their native language, should learn and need to become English literate. There is no sense in providing children an education in a language that will not serve them well in the very society in which they will attempt to establish a life and career, unless instruction in another language can be used to facilitate literacy in English. Few argue that the basic goal in the education of language minority children is in fact English literacy. Consequently, the common knee-jerk reaction is to provide a sink-or-swim program in English because "we all know the best way to learn a language is by being immersed in it." But such a notion reflects an inadequate understanding of the educational needs, or, more accurately, the course of development of English learners because it presumes that simply learning to speak a language ensures academic success in that language when this is far from the reality (Cummins, 1984; Danoff, 1978; Genesee, Lindholm-Leary, Saunders, & Christian, 2006; Lindholm-Leary & Borsato, 2006; Ramirez, Yuen, & Ramey, 1991; Thomas & Collier, 1997, 2002).

Nevertheless, there are significant factors in the present which continue to reflect the very same mistaken assumptions that have permeated U.S. educational policy for at least a century. Perhaps the most visible example of the pressures facing educators to get language minority children to succeed in school is the recent reauthorization of the Elementary and Secondary Education Act (ESEA), now known as No Child Left Behind (NCLB). Provisions in the legislation related to English learners have been formed within the context of popular ideals related to "high expectations" and "raising the bar" with respect to educational standards. For example, a recent statement by the U.S. Department of Education, citing provision in NCLB, indicated that language minority children must be tested in English on state-mandated tests after only one year of continuous enrollment in the public school system. Whereas it appears that the intent of NCLB is to promote the rapid acquisition of English, the legislation effectively ignores the path of development for English learners which is quite different than that for native English speakers. The failure to appreciate the differences in developmental paths for bilinguals versus monolinguals invariably leads to calls to abolish native language instruction in favor of English only which proponents believe will allow language minority students to "catch up" (Crawford, 1992).

*Language and Instruction.*    As noted previously, there is a natural tendency to think that learning to speak a language ensures academic success in that language. It is a thought that seems so intuitive, so obvious, that it must be true. Of course, the veracity of the assumption rests upon how one wishes to define academic success. If the goal is merely to have the student conversationally proficient in the language, then some degree of academic success might ensue solely on the basis of better comprehension. But to what degree? The answer to this question has been examined many times and the results continue to be consistent and clear—when students receive primary language instruction for at least 4 to 7 years, they typically succeed or fail at the same rates as that of their monolingual English-speaking peers (Genesee et al., 2006; Lindholm-Leary & Borsato, 2006; Ramirez et al., 1986, 1991; Thomas & Collier, 1997, 2002). When given programs that use English-only, including those that provide ESL services, the academic success of language minority students is considerably less than that of their monolingual English speaking peers.

The various patterns of achievement and development are illustrated best in Figure 15.1. This figure, using data from the 1997 longitudinal study on bilingual education by Thomas and

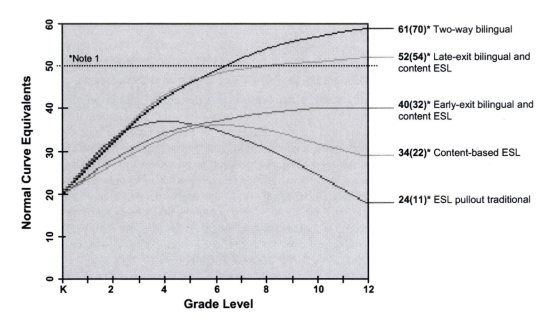

*Note 1: Average performance of native-English speakers making one year's progress in each grade. Scores in parentheses are percentile ranks converted from corresponding NCEs.

FIGURE 15.1    Data from the Thomas and Collier (1997) Study on English Learner Achievement on Standardized Tests of Reading in English

Collier, represents the average levels of academic achievement on standardized tests of reading (in English) for English learners from kindergarten through 12th grade. Of particular note in the figure is the point around 4th grade where the learning patterns of all but two programs begin to plateau. Except for the two-way developmental bilingual education and the one-way developmental bilingual education (with content ESL), all other forms of education produce results that are below that for native English speakers, in some cases substantially below. Even programs that provide native language instruction in the early grades, but then force students into English only by the third grade (transitional bilingual education with content ESL) produce achievement at the 40th/35th Normal Curve Equivalent (NCE; 32nd/23rd percentile ranks) as compared to the 50th NCE (50th percentile rank) for native English speakers. The worst outcomes occur for children who are given ESL pullout taught traditionally (i.e., English taught without the use of curriculum materials or subject content or vocabulary). This type of program is the most common one provided to children and is the minimum allowed under the Lau Remedies, but results in reading achievement at the 24th NCE (11th percentile rank) for English learners. This indicates that as a group, English learners receiving ESL, achieve at a level that is about one and one-third standard deviation below the mean of their monolingual English speaking peers. One could hardly construe this as any degree of equity in education. These findings demonstrate that conversational proficiency in English alone is entirely insufficient to ensure the kind of academic success expected for language minority children.

The instructional implications of longitudinal studies (e.g., Thomas & Collier, 1997, 2002) are important, not only in terms of understanding what may be expected academically from a given student, but also in terms of what type of instruction will work best. Unfortunately, because language is a developmental process, and because it is heavily influenced by the type of educational program being received, it is not easy to remedy academic problems once they have been solidly reinforced over the years. Figure 15.1 makes it clear that the type of education provided has a profound and long-lasting effect on academic performance. Nevertheless, there are important points that need to remain front and center regarding "what works" with English learners.

First, when bilingual education students are tested in English, they typically reach and surpass native English speakers' performance across all subject areas after 4 to 7 years in a quality bilingual program. Because they have not fallen behind in cognitive and academic growth during the 4 to 7 years that it takes to build academic proficiency in English, bilingually schooled students typically sustain this level of academic achievement and outperform monolingually schooled students in the upper grades (Lindholm-Leary & Borsato, 2006; Ramirez et al., 1986, 1991; Thomas & Collier, 1997, 2002).

Second, in terms of instruction, there are several key predictors of academic success. They include: a) cognitively complex academic instruction through the student's first language for as long as possible, and through the second language (English) for a part of the school day; b) use of current approaches to teaching the academic curriculum through first and second language through active, discovery, cognitively complex learning; and c) changes in the sociocultural context of schooling, such as integration with English-speaking peers, in a supporting, affirming environment for all students, an additive bilingual context, in which bilingual education is perceived as a "gifted and talented" program for all students, and the transformation of majority and minority student relations in a school to a positive school climate for all students regardless of language and cultural background (Thomas & Collier, 1997, 2002).

Third, at least three key instructional factors promote learning and lead to better outcomes for English learners, including: a) teaching learning strategies, in English, needed to develop thinking skill and problem solving activities; b) implementing approaches that emphasize prior knowledge; and c) maintaining respect for home language and culture (Genesee et al., 2006).

In short, there can be no substitute for good teaching. No interventions can be applied post-hoc or concomitantly with particular types of educational programs (e.g., ESL-only) that will lead to the kind of academic success or amelioration that would be expected for children who are native English speakers. Nothing is more important in determining whether a student is likely to display learning or behavioral challenges than the very education they are receiving. Whereas English-only is entirely appropriate, from a developmental perspective, for native English speaking students, those for whom English is a second or third language are set up for eventual academic failure through no fault of their own. It is not difficult to imagine that such will be the children at-risk for the development of learning difficulties and behavioral problems that result not from lack of ability, effort, or motivation, but only from dealing with the impossible task of trying to keep up academically in a language that is not well or completely understood (Ortiz, 2006).

## EVIDENCE-BASED INTERVENTION

One of the more visible trends in education, particularly in the realm of pre-referral interventions and instructional modifications, has been the movement toward evidence-based interventions and practices. Nowhere is this better exemplified than in the rapid and unprecedented adoption of response-to-intervention (RTI) models that are now codified in federal legislation, notably the Individuals with Disabilities Education Act (IDEA 2004). It seems probable that one of the reasons for its relatively quick acceptance and institutionalization is the fact that RTI provides a process for engaging in intervention activities that are presumably based on actual research and that have established empirical support. Another reason for their popularity may also rest on the notion that RTI, or more precisely the use of methods to document academic progress in an RTI framework (e.g., Curriculum Based Measurement; CBM), have often been touted as being more culturally and linguistically fair. For example, Kovaleski and Prasse (2004) stated that one of the potential benefits of RTI included *"increased fairness in the assessment process, particularly for minority students"* (emphasis added). Yet a close look at some of this research indicates that use of CBM, even within the context of an RTI framework is not necessarily less discriminatory than traditional methods of evaluation and assessment.

Baker and Good (1995) investigated the reliability, validity, and sensitivity of English CBM passages with bilingual Hispanic students and concluded that it was as reliable and valid for them as for native English speakers *despite the presence of differential growth rates.* That differential growth rates are present suggests that some factor is affecting the performance of one or the other group. It is likely that in this case, limited English proficiency and perhaps limited acculturation, are changing the expected trajectory of learning for the Hispanic students. If this influence is not identified and understood, the expectations for growth for Hispanic students may well prove discriminatory.

Gersten and Woodward (1994) suggested that CBM could be used to develop growth rates for English learners, but erroneously concluded that such *students generally continue to make academic progress toward grade-level norms* whereas English learners with a learning disability (LD) do not. This study was conducted prior to the release of the findings from the Thomas and Collier (1997) investigation so it may be excused to a certain extent. It is clear that English learners do not in fact generally continue to make academic progress toward grade-level norms if they are in English-only programs. They will plateau long before they reach grade level and do not "catch up" as is stated here. Moreover, English learners with LD will fare even worse than those without LD because of the "double whammy" effect of linguistic differences and the presence of a disability.

Again, such research tends to mislead practitioners to believe that CBM is much more fair than it actually is. This concern was recently espoused in a position statement by the National Center for Culturally Responsive Educational Systems (NCCRESt), where they state:

> We are concerned that if we do not engage in dialogue about how culture mediates learning, RTI models will simply be like old wine in a new bottle, in other words, another deficit-based approach to sorting children, particularly children from marginalized communities. (2005)

Because RTI is a measurement paradigm, it is subject to some of the same potential sources of bias that one finds in the use of other measurement paradigms (e.g., psychometrics). The very same questions come up in both cases, such as what constitutes sufficient opportunity to learn, what works, and with *whom,* what makes an intervention culturally or linguistically appropriate, and what research guides intervention programs. These are not easy questions and in the final analysis, practitioners must remain aware of the problems that may plague any attempts to measure the academic progress or response-to-intervention in English learners.

One problem revolves around the fact that the most common type of instruction given in schools today, ESL, creates an artificial linguistic "handicap" that puts otherwise capable children at levels far below their age and grade related peers in school achievement. What is "effective instruction" for the average third grader may be totally inappropriate for the average ELL who, nonetheless, is in third grade. Another problem is that unless measurement methods used in RTI, whether CBM or otherwise, account for the differential rates of development that are occurring in the processes related to native language acquisition, English acquisition, and acculturation to the mainstream, there is no guarantee that results will be any more "fair." Finally, all assessments, including CBM, should be selected and administered so as not to be discriminatory on a racial or cultural basis. The use of CBM, as with any assessment tool or procedure, should be designed to reduce threats to the reliability and validity of inferences that may arise from language (and cultural) differences.

## Instructional Interventions: What Works?

English learners with learning challenges will respond to interventions when those interventions are based on solid, research based pedagogy. Currently, there are no stand alone instructional programs that have been demonstrated empirically to be effective for English learners of all types. Many attempts to create such programs group English learners by ethnicity, mistakenly assuming such classification is sufficient to control for the variable that affects performance differentially. As such, practitioners will need to make independent determinations regarding the appropriateness of an intervention that targets instruction for English learners on the basis of what is known about their learning needs and development.

First and foremost, it is clear that all students benefit from strong cognitive and academic instruction conducted in their first language. The longer that English learners are provided instruction in their native language, the better the prognosis for their achievement (Krashen, 1985). Building upon the development that a student brings with them (the native language, in this case) is the only mechanism by which instruction can be viewed as effective and appropriate as well as evidence-based. The literature is clear in that English learners benefit from on-grade-level academic instruction in their first language. These benefits begin in the first years of schooling, and if such instruction is sustained, the benefits are cumulative. English learners whose schooling develops them academically and cognitively, using their first language, are more successful in English-based instruction by the end of their school years than those students who are not provided such first-language instruction. These effects presume that they also receive on-grade-level academic instruction in and through English for part of the school day, and throughout the school year.

Four to seven years of such combined high-quality instruction appear to ensure that by the end of high school, typical English learners will perform as well as typical native speakers of English. The more years in which first-language-based plus English-language-based instruction are present, the greater is the eventual English-based achievement. In short, whenever development is allowed to continue unabated, school success will follow. When development is interrupted or inhibited, academic achievement will suffer accordingly.

The design of programs for English language learners should be responsive to the needs and strengths of local communities, student populations, and available resources. Conventional program labels (such as first-language immersion, transitional, sheltered and content instruction in English, or English as a Second Language) are not useful in predicting school success. However, all effective programs share crucial features including but not limited to: 1) understanding students' language knowledge and needs, 2) planning and delivering instruction that meets those needs, and 3) assessing whether students have comprehended well the instruction.

For good student achievement, effective teaching methods must be employed by well-prepared teachers. Effective teaching methods have been identified by research, but are not in widespread use in English-mainstream or in bilingual/ESL classrooms. Effective approaches include students and teachers working together, in discovery processes and supportive interaction across the curriculum, developing language through dialogue, and making school meaningful by connecting instruction to students' strengths and everyday experiences in their homes and communities.

An effective model for instructional intervention may be gleaned from the Five Standards for Effective Pedagogy advanced by Tharp, Estrada, Dalton, and Yamauchi (1999). Based on the large body of empirical evidence regarding "what works" for English learners, they propose their standards as critical for improving learning outcomes for all students, and especially those of diverse ethnic, cultural, linguistic, or economic backgrounds. The Standards are defined as follows:

Standard I. Teachers and Students Producing Together. The point of this standard is to facilitate learning through joint productive activity among teacher and students. The collaborative nature of the process is an important component in helping students succeed by providing sufficient scaffolding to assist with comprehension and affirmation to keep motivation high.

Standard II. Developing Language and Literacy Across the Curriculum. The intent of this standard is to develop competence in the language and literacy of instruction across the curriculum. The focus is not merely on basic language "proficiency" in which the student learns to speak, but more on advanced levels of proficiency (e.g., cognitive-academic language proficiency) that is essential for school success. Children may learn to speak well, and young children will have no trouble achieving accent-free pronunciation when schooled in English but the focus for effective intervention must be geared toward the development of all forms of literacy across all subject areas of the curriculum.

Standard III. Making Meaning; Connecting School to Students' Lives. To ignore the language that student's bring in, when that language is not English, effectively undermines the ability to rely on one's experiences in the context of learning new material. Instructional interventions that are effective are those that contextualize teaching and curriculum in the experiences and skills of students' homes and communities. Being able to access a student's prior knowledge and experiences will go a long way toward increasing the success of any instructional intervention.

Standard IV. Teaching Complex Thinking. It is often thought that children either possess or do not possess certain cognitive abilities as a function of inherent individual differences. Although there is some truth to this assumption, it is also true that English learners often do not have the types of experiences that foster and facilitate the development of cognitive skills that are essential to school success. That is, they do not lack the ability because of intrinsic reasons, but more because of extrinsic factors. As such, English learners should be challenged to develop cognitive complexity and thinking strategies in formal, direct ways. It cannot be presumed that such strategies or ways of thinking will come along as a function of their general life experiences.

Standard V. Teaching Through Conversation. The teaching of English often takes on a de-contextualized form. That is, English is often taught as if it bore little relationship to the concepts being taught in the classroom. Instead, English learners can acquire English-speaking skills through conversations that involve the very concepts, content, and vocabulary that form the focus of instruction in the classroom. Thus, students can be engaged through dialogue, especially conversations where the point is not simply to communicate about anything in general, but to communicate about the content and subject matter that forms the basis of current instruction.

Although these standards do not represent the full range of tasks and intervention activities that are helpful in promoting the academic success of English learners, they nonetheless provide a solid foundation for the design of effective instructional interventions. When considered carefully and applied thoughtfully, it is highly likely that practitioners will be able to develop interventions that have a high probability of success and are appropriate to the cultural and linguistic needs of English learners.

## Behavioral Interventions: What works?

Intervention for behavioral challenges frequently rest upon the collection of a wide variety of data including observation, interview, behavioral scales and questionnaires, and so forth. For the most part, the collection of data will guide the types of decisions that will be made regarding the nature and form of intervention. It is then on the basis of the outcomes from such interventions, that is, the student's response to the intervention, that will determine their effectiveness. Such feedback may then be used to guide additional forms of treatment or intervention that may prove effective or appropriate. To ensure that this process is successful for English learners, practitioners will need to understand well the cultural and linguistic implications of any information they might obtain.

The potential influence of cultural and linguistic factors on data collection is substantial. Figure 15.2 provides an example regarding the manner in which behaviors of English learners might appear to be quite dysfunctional, even mimicking the characteristics of Attention-Deficit Hyperactivity Disorder (ADHD). Because English learners may not fully comprehend the language, they are often at a loss regarding what to do, what to pay attention to, what is being asked of them, what the rules of the moment are, and in so doing, may engage in a host of behaviors that are considered inappropriate, including disrupting other children, becoming easily distracted, and failing to start or complete assignments.

It is not difficult to recognize that data are not gathered in a cultural vacuum or immune to all sorts of bias. According to Ortiz (2006), "the very nature of the data collection process represents

| Characteristics and behaviors often associated with various learning problems | Common manifestations of English Language Learners (ELLs) during classroom instruction that may mimic various disorders or cognitive deficits. |
|---|---|
| **Slow to begin tasks** | ELLs may have limited comprehension of the classroom language so that they are not always clear on how to properly begin tasks or what must be done in order to start them or complete them correctly. |
| **Slow to finish tasks** | ELLs, especially those with very limited English skills, often need to translate material from English into their native language in order to be able to work with it and then must translate it back to English in order to demonstrate it. This process extends the time for completion of time-limited tasks that may be expected in the classroom. |
| **Forgetful** | ELLs cannot always fully encode information as efficiently into memory as monolinguals because of their limited comprehension of the language and will often appear to be forgetful when in fact the issue relates more to their lack of proficiency with English. |
| **Inattentive** | ELLs may not fully understand what is being said to them in the classroom and consequently they don't know when to pay attention or what exactly they should be paying attention to. |
| **Hyperactive** | ELLs may appear to be hyperactive because they are unaware of situation-specific behavioral norms, classroom rules, and other rules of social behavior. |
| **Impulsive** | ELLs may lack the ability to fully comprehend instructions so that they display a tendency to act impulsively in their work rather than following classroom instructions systematically. |
| **Distractible** | ELLs may not fully comprehend the language being spoken in the classroom and therefore will move their attention to whatever they can comprehend appearing to be distractible in the process. |
| **Disruptive** | ELLs may exhibit disruptive behavior, particularly excessive talking—often with other ELLS, due to a need to try and figure out what is expected of them or to frustration about not knowing what to do or how to do it. |
| **Disorganized** | ELLs often display strategies and work habits that appear disorganized because they don't comprehend instructions on how to organize or arrange materials and may never have been taught efficient learning and problem solving strategies. |

FIGURE 15.2  Common Behavioral Manifestations of English Learners in the Classroom due to Limited English Comprehension

a core set of values that may affect both the manner in which information is collected but also what information is collected and how such information is interpreted subsequently" (p. 34). Sandoval (1998) describes the process wherein practitioners unconsciously allow their preconceived notions to enter into the evaluation process and affect the type of data gathered as well as the meaning assigned to the data. This process is known as confirmatory bias and if a practitioner is unable to recognize it or is unaware of it, there is little chance that intervention attempts will be fair or responsive to the individual's cultural or linguistic needs as they pertain to instructional or behavioral needs. This is not an easy thing to accomplish given that practitioners are trained in a culture of assessment that does not often include or accommodate cultural factors relevant to understanding a student's behavior. To this end, Ortiz and Flanagan (2002) provide various principles that are designed to help practitioners avoid errors in practice and improve the cultural responsiveness of intervention attempts. These principles include:

1. *Establish rapport and build trust.* Use the knowledge bases regarding displays of respect, and appropriate greeting behavior and exiting behavior. Help the family to feel at ease, respected, and provide the opportunity for the family members to fully participate and contribute to the process of service delivery. Use interpreters/translators as necessary but make sure they are appropriately trained and consult with individuals who are familiar with the culture and languages relevant to the purposes of service delivery.
2. *Identify the presenting problem.* School psychologists should listen carefully to the family's perception of any suspected problem and attempt to understand it from their perspective. They may feel there is no problem at all. It is also necessary to determine the family's past efforts to resolve the problem and to elicit their present understanding of new intervention strategies and goals. Once these issues have been clarified, the school psychologist will be in a much better position to negotiate intervention strategies.
3. *Learn the family system.* The structure of the family system must be assessed and determined to the maximum extent possible. Particularly important to evaluate are the areas related to family composition, family members' roles and responsibilities, family's interactional patterns, family's support system, family's childrearing practices, and the family's beliefs about the student's suspected handicapping condition and its source. Knowledge of the relevant aspects of the structure of the family system provides the basis for interventions that are appropriate and individually tailored to the particular needs and resources of the family (p. 354).

## SUMMARY

It seems that because each of us has learned at least one language, and because that language was learned so easily and transparently even before we were aware that we had learned it, we fall prey to a variety of misconceptions regarding the relationship between language and education. Perhaps the most egregious of these mistaken beliefs is the one that leads us to conclude that immersion in English is the best way to learn the language and once the language is learned, all things educational become equal. The research, of course, shows us that this is not correct. As much as it may be politically or economically convenient to view the educational needs of English learners as rectified easily by conversational proficiency, the reality is that much more is involved if we truly desire to ensure their future academic success. English learners are different than native speakers by the very fact that they are bilingual (sometimes even trilingual). Even without additional instruction in the native language, there is a dual-language influence that must be considered, and this influence is not temporary in any way: Once a bilingual, always a bilingual. Simply because an individual has become English dominant does not mean that he or she has ceased to be bilingual (Bialystok, 1991). The effects of culture and language on the design and implementation of instructional and behavioral interventions are indelible and not erased by efforts designed to promote English at the complete exclusion of the native language.

At this time, there is virtually no research concerning specific evidence-based interventions to meet the instructional and behavioral needs of English learners. Rather, there is much empirical evidence about "what works" in both cases and what does not. Therefore, there is no simple prescription for practitioners to follow and instead, it will be necessary to first learn the nature and extent of the dynamics and complexities involved in the education of English learners and apply that knowledge to the development of interventions that may prove effective and appropriate. This chapter provided a discussion of the knowledge base that currently exists relative to instruction and intervention with English learners. Although the issues appear complex at the outset, they can be rather easily managed and scaled to make them applicable to individual situations and needs.

At the very least, practitioners will find that being flexible, open, and willing to implement new ideas and engage in new behaviors that were neither demonstrated nor taught in their training programs are the keys to successful instructional and intervention attempts with English learners and other individuals from diverse cultural, ethnic, and linguistic backgrounds. In the end, the very success of any intervention attempt may rest more on the efforts made by practitioners to be culturally responsive and linguistically appropriate which demonstrates an implicit respect for an individual's culture and experiences. This point has been articulated well by Ortiz and Flanagan (2002):

> Intervening effectively with students and families will come more from a genuine respect of their native values, beliefs, and attitudes than anything else that might be said or done, especially when their views run counter to beliefs that may be held so dearly. In such cases it must be remembered that school psychologists are not often in positions where they are designing interventions for themselves. Rather, the intervention is for others and they will only be successful in so far as they are culturally relevant to the children and families for whom they are intended. (p. 353)

## REFERENCES

Baker, S. K., & Good, R. H. (1995). Curriculum-based measurement of English reading with bilingual Hispanic students: A validation study with second-grade students. *School Psychology Review, 24*, 561–578.

Bialystok, E. (1991). *Language processing in bilingual children.* New York: Cambridge University Press.

Brigham, C. C. (1923). *A study of American intelligence.* Princeton, NJ: Princeton University Press.

Cummins, J. C. (1984). *Bilingual and special education: Issues in assessment and pedagogy.* Austin, TX: PRO-ED.

Crawford, J. (1992). *Language loyalties: A source book on the official English controversy.* Chicago: Chicago University Press.

Danoff, M. (1978). *Evaluation of the impact of ESEA Title VII Spanish/English bilingual education programs: Overview of study and findings.* Palo Alto, CA: American Institutes for Research (ERIC Document Reproduction Service No. ED 154634).

Genesee, F., Lindholm-Leary, K., Saunders, W. M., & Christian, D. (2006). *Educating English language learners: A synthesis of research evidence.* New York: Cambridge University Press.

Gersten, R. & Woodward, J. (1994). The language minority student and special education: Issues, trends, and paradoxes. *Exceptional Children, 60*, 310–322.

Gould, S. J. (1996). *The Mismeasure of Man*. New York: W.W. Norton

Kovaleski, J. F., & Prasse, D. P. (2004, February). Response to instruction in the identification of learning disabilities: A guide for school teams. *NASP Communiqué, 32*(5), insert.

Krashen, S. D. (1985). *Inquiries and insights: second language teaching, immersion and bilingual education, literacy*. Englewood Cliffs, NJ: Alemany Press.

Lindholm-Leary, K. & Borsato, G. (2006). Academic Achievement. In F. Genesee, K. Lindholm-Leary, W. M. Saunders, & D. Christian, D. (Eds.), *Educating English Language Learners: A Synthesis of Research Evidence*. New York: Cambridge University Press.

NCCRESt (2005). Position Statement on RTI. [Electronic version] Retrieved March 1, 2006 from: http://www.nccrest.org

Ortiz, S. O. (2006). Multicultural Issues in Working with Children and Families: Responsive intervention in the educational setting. In R. B.Menutti., A. Freeman, & R. W. Christner (Eds.), *Cognitive behavioral interventions in educational settings: A handbook for practice* (pp. 21-36). New York: Brunner-Routledge Publishing.

Ortiz, S. O. & Flanagan, D. P. (2002). Best Practices in Working with Culturally Diverse Children and Families. In A. Thomas & J. Grimes (Eds.) *Best practices in school psychology IV* (pp. 337–351). Washington, DC: National Association of School Psychologists.

Ramirez, J. D., Wolfson, R., Talmadge, G. K., & Merino, B. (1986). *First year report: Longitudinal study of immersion programs for language minority children* (Submitted to U.S. Department of Education, Washington, DC). Mountain View, CA: SRA Associates.

Ramirez, J. D., Yuen, S. D., & Ramey, D. R. (1991). *Final report: Longitudinal study of structured English immersion strategy, early-exit and late-exit transitional bilingual education programs for language-minority children: Executive summary*. San Mateo, CA: Aguirre International.

Rothstein, R. (1998). *The way we were?: The myths and realities of America's student achievement*. New York: The Century Foundation Press.

Sandoval, J. (1998). Test interpretation in a diverse future. In J. Sandoval, C. L. Frisby, K. F. Geisinger, J. D. Scheuneman, & J. R. Grenier (Eds.), *Test interpretation and diversity: Achieving equity in assessment* (pp. 387–401). Washington, DC: American Psychological Association.

Santayana, G. (1905). *Life of reason, reason in common sense, Vol. 1*. New York: Charles Scribner Sons, Inc.

Tharp, R. G., Estrada, P., Dalton, S. S., & Yamauchi, L. (1999). *Teaching transformed: Achieving excellence, fairness, inclusion and harmony*. Boulder, CO: Westview Press

Thomas, W. & Collier, V. (1997). *Language minority student achievement and program effectiveness*. Washington, DC: National Clearinghouse for Bilingual Education.

Thomas, W. & Collier, V. (2002). *A national study of school effectiveness for language minority student's long-term academic achievement*; retrieved September 4, 2002, from http://www.crede.uscu.edu/research/llaa1.html.

Valdés, G. & Figueroa, R. A. (1994). *Bilingualism and testing: A special case of bias*. Norwood, NJ: Ablex.

# 16

# Serving Gifted Students

## Steven I. Pfeiffer and Samara Blei

This chapter addresses unique challenges facing students who are gifted. Although no research evidence suggests that the gifted, as a group, have a higher incidence or prevalence of learning or behavioral problems (Neihart, Reis, Robinson, & Moon, 2002), the gifted are not immune to the academic and social challenges that all children and youth face. In addition, the gifted, as a group, face a set of unique challenges that increase their vulnerability to and risk for learning and behavioral challenges (Pfeiffer, 2001b; Pfeiffer & Stocking, 2000). The most frequently cited risks associated with the gifted are asynchronous development, difficulties with affect regulation related to over-excitability, unrealistic parental and teacher expectations, peer relation problems, and perfectionism (Mendaglio & Peterson, 2007; Robinson, 2002). In addition, an appreciable but as yet unknown number of gifted children suffer from troubling, often undiagnosed, disabilities such as Attention Deficit Hyperactivity Disorder (ADHD), Asperger's disorder, learning disabilities (LD), eating disorders, and mood disorders (Webb, Amend, Webb, Goerss, Beljan, & Olenchak, 2005). In the gifted literature, these children are referred to as "twice exceptional." This chapter provides a brief history of the gifted field, including a concise discussion of who are gifted students. The chapter then describes some of the types of learning and behavioral difficulties that gifted children face and concludes with a *best practices guide* consisting of eight guidelines for serving gifted students.

## BRIEF HISTORY OF THE GIFTED FIELD

Awareness of gifted children began with the recognition of differences amongst individuals within in the general population. Although Galton never offered a formal definition of giftedness, his theory of fixed intelligence emphasized a hereditary basis of intelligence and stressed an individual's innate sensory acuity, which was thought to have survival value (Galton, 1869). Galton first attempted to assess intelligence by measuring physical characteristics, such as height, weight, and head diameter, sensory acuity, motor strength, reaction time, and visual judgments (Galton, 1869, 1888; Wasserman & Tulsky, 2005). Although he did not measure mental ability or various talent areas that are now included in many definitions of giftedness (e.g., Pfeiffer & Jarosewich, 2003, 2007), Galton established the foundation for a psychometric approach to gifted identification, which still dominates the gifted field today.

With the emergence of Binet's important work in Paris, identification procedures changed from Galton's emphasis on "measurement of the body and of the senses," to focus on the measurement of "higher mental processes" (Binet, 1903; as cited in Wasserman & Tulsky, 2005). Binet introduced the field to the concept of mental age. The notion that even young children may intellectually be far ahead of their peers held profound implications for the identification of the gifted (Binet & Simon, 1903; as cited in Colangelo & Davis, 1997). Lewis Terman extended Binet's work in developing the *Stanford Binet Intelligence Scale*, which remains one of the most popular measures of intelligence today (Clark, 1997).

To many, Terman is considered the "father of the gifted education movement." He coined the term *gifted child* and developed one of the first tests to measure intelligence. In his momentous and often cited longitudinal study, Terman identified 1,528 gifted children and defined anyone scoring above 135 on the 1916 version of the Stanford Binet test as a genius (Terman, 1925). Terman's pioneering work played an important role in reifying the Intelligent Quotient (IQ) to the central role that it still enjoys in defining, identifying, and even conceptualizing the construct of giftedness. The IQ has become representative of traditional psychometric gifted identification procedures (Pfeiffer, 2001b).

## WHO ARE THE GIFTED?

One of the first federal definitions of giftedness appeared in The Education Amendment of 1969, (US Congress, 1970) which specified that

> ...the term "gifted and talented children" means in accordance with objective criteria prescribed by the Commissioner, children who have outstanding intellectual ability or creative talent, the development of which requires special activities or services not ordinarily provided by local education agencies.

The initial U.S. Office of Education definition expanded on the latter definition by including six different gifted areas: general intellectual ability, specific academic aptitude, creative or productive thinking, leadership ability, ability in the visual or performing arts, and psychomotor ability (Marland, 1972). *The Jacob K. Javits Gifted and Talented Students Education Act of 1988* (U.S. Congress, 1988) broadened the definition of giftedness to include the term *capability*; those students who display evidence of high performance *capability or potential* in intellectual, creative, artistic, or leadership would be given the opportunity to fully develop such capabilities.

A recent definition issued by the U.S. Department of Education (1994) suggests that in identifying "children with outstanding talent," students should be compared to others of the same age, experience, or environment. Pfeiffer and his colleagues (Pfeiffer & Jarosewich, 2007) remind us that society plays an important role in defining what is meant by giftedness. Different cultures value different *gifts*. In the United States, for example, our present educational system values intellectual and academic prowess, creative problem solving, and leadership ability (Pfeiffer & Jarosewich, 2003).

Authorities in the gifted field have crafted definitions that support, modify, expand and, in some instances, oppose, the federal definitions. Consistent among the federal definition and recent and emerging definitions is the recognition that gifted and talented students have *exceptional abilities and potential for outstanding performance* (Pfeiffer, 2002a). Most authorities agree that the unfolding of a child's potential does not necessarily occur on its own; optimizing one's special talent requires a supportive family climate and a stimulating, challenging, and high quality learning environment (Ericsson, Krampe, & Tesch-Römer, 1993; Johnsen, 1997; Zigler & Heller, 2000).

## THE GIFTED: VULNERABILITIES AND UNIQUE CHALLENGES

During the late 1800s, the general consensus was that giftedness increased a child's vulnerability to adjustment difficulties (Lombroso, 1889). This view was challenged by Terman's longitudinal study (1925, 1937, 1947), which found that people of high ability experienced a lower-than-expected incidence of mental illness or other psychological problems. However, the suicide of a gifted high school student in 1981 abruptly challenged the view that gifted students, as a group, were impervious to psychological problems. This event represented a turning point in research on the gifted; a number of investigators (and educators and clinicians) began exploring the social and emotional needs of the gifted and asking research questions about the social and emotional adjustment of these children (Freeman, 1979; Lejoie & Shore, 1981; Pfeiffer & Stocking, 2000). The field now recognizes that the gifted, as a group, do *not* have a higher incidence or prevalence of learning or psychiatric problems compared to regular education students (Neihart, Reis, Robinson, & Moon, 2002). The gifted field also recognizes that a significant, although as yet unknown number of gifted students are neither immune nor impervious to the many social and emotional challenges that all children and youth face growing up. In addition, research has identified unique challenges that increase the vulnerability of the gifted to learning and behavioral problems (Neihart et al., 2002; Pfeiffer & Stocking, 2000). As mentioned in the Introduction, challenges facing the gifted are related to their asynchronous development, difficulties with affect regulation related to over-excitability, unrealistic parental and teacher expectations, peer relation problems—specifically feelings of peer rejection and alienation, and perfectionism (Mendaglio & Peterson, 2007; Robinson, 2002). Finally, some gifted students suffer from troubling, often undiagnosed, disabilities including ADHD, Asperger's syndrome, learning disabilities, eating disorders and mood disorders (Neihart, in press; Webb et al., 2005). These uniquely distinctive gifted children are known as *twice exceptional.* What next follows is a brief discussion of a few of the types of gifted children with learning and behavior challenges. Because of space limitations, we are unable to discuss all of the various types of psychological and academic problems that gifted children might face.

### Gifted Children with Learning Disabilities

Gifted students with a learning disability (LD) face unique problems. The strengths of a gifted child with LD may serve as both an enabling and crippling force within their academic environment. Due to exceptional performance in specific academic areas, the gifted student's learning disability is often overlooked. As a result, the gifted child is rarely identified as LD at an early age because his/her gifts often mask a learning disability (Vialle & Baldwin, 1999). Ferri, Gregg, and Heggoy (1997) found that approximately 41% of gifted students with learning disabilities remain undiagnosed until college. This twice exceptional student with *advanced academic ability and subtle learning disabilities* represents one of four types of gifted LD students (Baum, Owen, & Dixon, 1991; Brody & Mills, 1997; Gunderson, Maesch, & Rees, 1987). Typically, this student participates in gifted programs, but may experience periods of underachievement (Ferri et al., 1997).

Many of these twice exceptional students are placed in gifted programs and silently suffer within a challenging environment, without appropriate resources. LD students typically develop unrealistic expectations, and believe that they should excel in academic areas in spite of their learning disability. Resulting frustration is often expressed through decreased or variable motivation and disruptive or withdrawn behavior. A qualitative study, examining perceptions of academically talented students with LD in relation to their elementary school years, revealed that negative experiences revolved around social and emotional development. The dynamic interplay of high ability and learning disability may cause confusion and create social, emotional and/or behavioral challenges as the student struggles to comprehend why they know an answer but are unable to say it or write it correctly (Olenchak, 1995).

Another category of gifted LD students are those that are *identified as gifted and LD*. However, the prevalence of students within this category is far lower due to stringent eligibility requirements of gifted LD and the tendency of educators and school psychologists to not identify the LD, due to the child's extraordinary gifts (Gardynik & McDonald, 2005). Even if the child's learning problem is identified and is classified according to the eligibility criteria (IDEA 1997, 2004), many schools do not consider or qualify gifted students as LD. Many states and counties do not acknowledge a learning disability if the child's IQ score is above a certain cut point (typically a 130, which would be set by the school district) (McCoach, Reis, & Moon, 2004). Classification of LD in gifted students remains a challenge for educators and school psychologists.

Regardless of the identification model used, school districts are unlikely to incorporate enough flexibility and clinical judgment to recognize both gifts *and* learning disabilities. There exists a third type of twice exceptional gifted-LD student, the *child who remains unidentified as either learning disabled or gifted*. These students are often considered average by their teachers (Baum et al., 1991; Gunderson et al., 1987). McCoach et al. (2004) proposed a comprehensive eight-step system for identifying gifted students as gifted and learning disabled. Unfortunately, the feasibility of a school district adopting this comprehensive system—including behavioral classroom observations, multiple cognitive processing tests and achievement measures, is unlikely because of the time and cost involved.

The fourth category of gifted LD represents *those who are recognized for their LD as opposed to their giftedness*. The learning disability of a student who has not yet been identified as gifted often disguises or masks their gifts. Instead of focusing on the development of the child's gifts, teachers focus exclusively on remediating the LD. A focus on student deficits, as opposed to student strengths or assets, is not unusual in today's schools (Pfeiffer & Reddy, 1998). The result, unfortunately, of focusing exclusively on a student's weaknesses can adversely impact a youngster's self-esteem, motivation and interest in academics, and emotional vibrancy (Baum, Emerick, Herman, & Dixon, 1989; Pfeiffer & Stocking, 2000).

Bianco (2005) investigated the effect of the disability labels of LD and emotional and behavioral disorders (EBD) on public school teachers' willingness to refer students to gifted programs. Results indicated that both general and special education teachers were significantly influenced by LD and EBD labels when making referrals to gifted programs. As compared to identically described gifted students, teachers were much less willing to make referrals for gifted consideration for those students with LD.

Gifted students and twice exceptional gifted students with LD face many similar problems. Although a child with LD is likely to experience academic failure (Gardynik & McDonald, 2005) and a gifted student is likely to demonstrate advanced academic or intellectual performance, both the gifted student and the twice exceptional gifted student struggle to find a peer group to share their unique experiences with. The sense of isolation that students with LD experience is further compounded when twice exceptional—feeling alone and estranged because of both their gifts and their LD. Waldron (1987) found that students who were twice exceptional gifted-LD were more likely to develop low self-esteem and have feelings of rejection than normally achieving gifted students.

School psychologists need to help inform teachers about the unique interaction between a student's abilities and disabilities. A twice exceptional child with reading or math disability may demonstrate any of the following characteristics: high verbal aptitude, boredom with grade level or below grade level work in their area of disability, variable scores on achievement tests in their area of disability, improved performance with compensation strategies, low tolerance for frustration with rote-drill reading or math drills, and/or possible inattention and unrealistically high or low self-concept (Hishinuma & Tadaki, 1996). Irrespective of the child's label, the student's strengths and weaknesses need to be recognized and addressed to provide appropriate services.

## Gifted Children and Underachievement

LD is not the only source of academic underachievement for gifted students. Underachievement may stem from a number of different factors (Reis & McCoach, 2000) that include, but are not limited to environmental causes, such as chronically underchallenging, slow moving classroom experiences (VanTassel-Baska, in press; Whitmore, 1986); unrealistic family expectations (Rimm, 1995); peer pressure to conform; and intra-individual causes, such as depression, anxiety, rebelliousness, and attention deficit hyperactivity disorder (Baum, Olenchak & Owen, 1998); failure to set realistic goals (Van Boxtel & Monks, 1992); and social immaturity. Regardless of the origin, gifted underachievement is recognized as a discrepancy between expected achievement (typically measured by standardized testing) and actual achievement (measured by grades and performance in the classroom and teacher evaluations) (Baum, Renzulli, & Hebert, 1995; Boyd, 1990; Rimm, 1997). The current section will highlight a few causes of underachievement.

Underachievement in gifted students may develop when the student lacks motivation, demonstrates boredom, and does not display interest in the subject matter. By the end of seventh grade, many gifted students report that they are bored and lack intrinsic motivation for classroom work due to a lack of interest, enthusiasm, or excitement in the curriculum (Boyd, 1990). Based on a sample of 92 children identified as academically talented fifth graders (top 5% of class), over 3% of these students dropped out of school before the eleventh grade. As indicated by their responses to a *Feelings about School Life* questionnaire, the students who dropped out of school felt that school was unrewarding.

Low motivation due to boredom and a lack of interest has been identified as a cause of underachievement for many gifted students (Boyd, 1990; Emerick, 1992). Thirteen percent of gifted students who obtained grades below the top quartile for the State of New South Wales in England indicated that they lost excitement for school learning because lessons were not applicable to the real world. They also felt a lack of purpose in completing routine assignments. Boyd (1990) concluded that gifted students are not typically provided with special attention, and opportunities to encourage and nurture their advanced intellectual abilities. Emerick (1992) found that underachieving gifted students were most likely to develop achievement oriented behaviors when stimulated in class and provided opportunities to pursue topics of high interest.

Underachievement of gifted students can also be attributed to maladaptive motivational characteristics (Reis, Neu, & McGuire, 1995). Cultural beliefs and related family values, social-peer group dynamics, and gender are factors that can adversely impact academic motivation and contribute to a gifted student's underachievement. In a longitudinal study of 35 culturally diverse, gifted urban students, Reis et al. (1995) found that after controlling for poverty, parental divorce, and family size, the only differences between high and low achieving students were attitude toward achievement and learning and familial support and encouragement. Academically successful gifted students received support and encouragement from each other and supportive adults, such as teachers, guidance counselors, coaches, and mentors. In contrast, gifted underachieving students did not demonstrate characteristics associated with resilience or coping mechanisms to overcome negative experiences within their families, schools, and communities. Additional research suggests that attending to the student's strengths and interests demonstrates support and encouragement, motivating students to reverse academic underachievement (Renzulli & Reis, 1997).

Culturally diverse gifted students face unique challenges in achieving academically. One reason is because of the value placed on achievement within their culture (Diaz, 1998; Fernandez, Hirano-Nakanish, & Paulsen, 1989). For many cultures, achievement is not necessarily defined as excelling academically in school. Students from these cultures may not receive encouragement, positive reinforcement, and support from family members for academic excellence; rather, they will be rewarded for exhibiting culturally valued behaviors—for example, cooperation and respect for authority (Barona & Pfeiffer, 1991). High ability minority students risk rejection from family if they assertively develop their cognitive abilities and succeed in the majority culture (Robinson & Noble, 1991).

Peer issues oftentimes influence adolescent behavior and can lead to academic underachievement when negative peer attitudes are encountered (Brown & Clasen, 1985). According to Clasen and Clasen (1995), 66% of underachieving gifted students reported that negative peer influence has the strongest force impeding their achievement. Berndt Hawkins, and Jiao (1999) found that the grades of gifted students were more likely to drop from the fall to spring term if their friends had lower grades in the fall. In addition, gifted students typically do not spend significant time interacting with like peers who share their unique intellectual interests and curiosities (Boyd, 1990; Pfeiffer & Stocking, 2000).

Another category of gifted underachievers includes students who possess multiple talents (in the gifted field, these students are labeled "multi-potentiality"). Gifted students who are talented in many areas often need help or guidance with their decision-making skills. Indecision regarding career choice options is common among gifted students because of the pressure they feel to make a perfect career choice, and, in turn, to please significant others. Far too many gifted students delay decisions concerning their career path, change majors, and even drop out of college. Baker, Bridger, and Evans (1998) found that underachieving gifted children have deficits in behavioral control, organizational skills, strategic problem solving skills, and coping skills. These results are also supported by other investigations of gifted underachievement (e.g., Baum et al., 1998; Gallagher, 1991; Muir-Broadus, 1995). One implication is that gifted students need to be provided with services that assist them in narrowing down, prioritizing, and identifying specific career options (Boyd, 1990; Sampson & Chason, in press).

Unfortunately, teachers focus most often on students in their class who are significantly behind academically compared to course, grade and age expectations, and tend to overlook the gifted student who may be falling behind relative to her/his potential, but not necessarily on those factors related to the *No Child Left Behind Act of 2001*. Educators typically identify underachievers by finding that the child is behind in at least one major subject area. However, the majority of gifted underachievers are not achieving a full grade below expectancy and may go unidentified as underachievers for years (Mandel & Marcus, 1995). Educators are required to have access to information regarding the special needs of students with learning disabilities; however, they are not provided with guidelines for the evaluation and planning for underachieving gifted students. As long as curriculum and instructional methodologies are geared toward the needs and learning styles of the average student, many gifted students will remain vulnerable to academic underachievement.

## Gifted Children and Attention Deficit Hyperactivity Disorder

Gifted students with academic and/or behavioral problems may have clinical or sub-clinical Attention Deficit Hyperactivity Disorder (ADHD). Baum et al. (1998) categorize gifted students who exhibit ADHD behaviors into the following three groups: gifted students whose learning and/or attention problems stem from an actual neurophysiologic disorder; gifted students whose

ADHD symptoms are precipitated and reinforced by the classroom learning environment; and, gifted students who demonstrate ADHD characteristics due to *both* an actual neurophysiologic disorder *and* a less-than-supportive learning environment. It is important diagnostically to distinguish between gifted students with an actual clinical diagnosis of ADHD and those with ADHD-like behaviors or characteristics but *not* clinically diagnosed ADHD. There are very different treatment implications for these two groups of gifted students—the most obvious being the recommendation for a trial of psychostimulant medication for the twice-exceptional gifted/ADHD student.

Gifted children may be misidentified as ADHD due to specific environmental factors that can cause or exacerbate ADHD-like behaviors among high ability students (Baum et al., 1998; Pfeiffer & Stocking, 2000). Some writers in the field propose that the reported increased incidence of hyperactivity and attention problems among gifted students stems primarily from under-challenged and unchallenging learning environments (e.g., Webb & Latimer, 1993). Gifted students, for example, often spend a quarter to half of the school day waiting for their classmates to catch up (Webb & Latimer, 1993). It is hard to imagine how this would not create boredom, restlessness, and difficulty with focused or sustained attention, particularly among young children who have not yet developed specific coping skills (Pfeiffer & Stocking, 2000). Gallagher, Harradine, and Coleman (1997) interviewed 800 gifted students and reported that the majority of their struggles stem from a slow instructional pace, an emphasis on facts rather than critical and divergent thinking, and excessive repetition of already-mastered skills. The often observed inattention of gifted students may, in many instances, be due to boredom resulting from an unchallenging classroom environment (Gallagher, in press; Hartnett, Nelson & Rimm, 2004).

Although under-challenging academic environments can contribute to ADHD-like behaviors in gifted children, the gifted literature suggests that gifted children—especially the creatively gifted—display an innate characteristic that mimics ADHD, namely, "overexcitability." Some gifted authorities suggest that overexciteabilities (OE) are inborn propensities to respond to stimuli in a heightened and intensive fashion. This increased sensitivity and awareness are purported to manifest themselves in five areas of intensity: psychomotor, sensual, intellectual, imaginational, and emotional. *Psychomotor overexcitability* among the gifted is heightened excitability of the neuromuscular system and is often displayed as a surplus of energy, rapid speech, enthusiasm, intense physical activity and the need for action (Piechowski, 1991). Gifted children with this OE may talk compulsively, act impulsively, misbehave and act out, display nervous habits, and be overly competitive (Lind, 2001). One can readily see the overlap of symptoms and the potential for misdiagnosis as ADHD.

The gifted child with *sensual overexcitability* can experience heightened sensual pleasure or displeasure from any of the five senses. Some gifted children may feel overstimulated or uncomfortable with sensory input (e.g., find clothing, noise, or odors excessively distracting). Others may overeat, go on buying sprees, or inappropriately seek out physical sensation (Piechowski, 1991).

The gifted child with *intellectual overexcitability* often displays an unrelenting thirst for knowledge, information, and truth. Typical characteristics of these gifted children are an intense curiosity, avid reading, exceptionally high concentration threshold, and seeming preoccupation with important moral and ethical issues. These gifted children often display or broadcast their intellectual passion in inappropriate and even rude ways.

The gifted child with *imaginational overexcitability* seems to the uninformed observer preoccupied with their imagination and inner world. Gifted children typically express imagination OE through fantasy, intense visualization, and dramatizations. These gifted children often find it difficult to stay on task or pay attention to a teacher lecture, since their rich imaginational world is more interesting and pulls them away from the more mundane environment of the classroom

The gifted child with *emotional overexcitability* displays heightened and intense emotions and emotional responses to events and experiences. Due to their tendency to develop strong attachments to people, places, and things, children with OE have the capacity for great emotional depth. Although these children are sometimes accused of overreacting or being melodramatic, their genuine behavior is often manifested because of the deep concern they have for others, as well as self-criticism and anxiety (Piechowski, 1991).

When viewing such creative giftedness, one finds, interestingly enough, characteristics often associated with the expression of creative talent, similar to behaviors representative of ADHD. Characteristics of the creative gifted, consistent across multiple studies, include adventuresome, self-assertive, and nonconforming (Andreason, 1989). Although there is a paucity of research on creativity and affective disorders in children, a handful of clinical case studies and empirical research has verified a link between creativity and affective disorders, particularly bipolar disorder. Adolescents with bipolar disorder often display characteristics of ADHD; educators, school psychologists, and parents need to be cognizant of this link between creativity and bipolar disorder, which could appear to the uninformed as ADHD (Biederman, Russell, Soriano, Wozniak, & Faraone, 1998; Wilens, Biederman, & Spencer, 1999). Behaviors to watch out for include poor judgment, distractibility, inattention, irritability, hyperactivity, anger, poor impulse control, demanding behaviors, and the tendency to jump from one topic or activity to another (Geller & Luby, 1997).

As mentioned above, many of the behavioral characteristics of ADHD displayed by gifted children are likely to be precipitated by boredom as well as excitement and intellectual passion. Learning environments that match well with the student's intellectual ability and thirst for knowledge enable gifted children to focus their mental resources in a goal-directed and successful manner. Within intellectually stimulating classroom environments, the passionate and focused high energy level of the gifted student can be rather easily diagnostically differentiated from the random, unfocused, hyperactive behaviors seen among non-gifted students with ADHD (Clark, 1997).

Gifted children who are deprived of a rich curriculum that is commensurate with and matches their ability level are likely to express their energy through behaviors that mimic ADHD-driven hyperactivity. The hyperactivity observed in a student with ADHD is often expressed as random energy, such as psychomotor agitation (Parker, 1992). A gifted student's high activity level, on the other hand, is generally focused and goal directed. Although the gifted student may display poor impulse control by excitedly shouting out an answer in a classroom, the gifted student's answer is likely to be correct, whereas the child with ADHD tends to guess incorrectly (Lovecky, 1994).

Although gifted students who are not placed in appropriate learning environments that challenge their intellectual curiosity are at risk for developing disruptive, inattentive classroom behaviors, the unidentified twice exceptional gifted/ADHD student is at heightened risk for *academic* and behavior problems (Moon, 2002). Even when the curriculum and instructional methodology are geared toward the gifted learner, the presence of ADHD will render the gifted student vulnerable (Pfeiffer & Stocking, 2000). A gifted student with ADHD can easily become discouraged and develop a low self-concept due to an inability to control disorganized behaviors (Leroux & Levitt-Perlman, 2000). The oppositional behaviors, daydreaming, social immaturity, and disorganization displayed by gifted children with ADHD are often triggered by their frustration (Leroux & Levitt-Perlman, 2000).

Not surprisingly, disruptiveness of the gifted student with ADHD often results from difficulty regulating emotions (Moon, Zentall, Grdkovic, Hall, & Stormont-Spurgin, 2001) and can lead to socially inappropriate behaviors and ongoing peer rejection. Due to these behaviors that are uncharacteristic for a gifted child, some children are diagnosed with ADHD without being accurately identified as gifted. Even if a child with ADHD is suspected of being gifted, and is administered an IQ test, cognitive processing inefficiencies and attentional difficulties will lead to IQ test scores that are typically 5-10 points lower than other children of the same ability level (Castellanos, 2000).

Since symptoms of ADHD are likely to overlap with giftedness, it is crucial for teachers, school psychologists, school counselors, and administrators to be cognizant of ADHD-like behaviors that gifted children may exhibit. Developing the ability to distinguish between ADHD and the innate behavioral characteristics a gifted child may display, or that stem from inadequate environmental stimulation, is necessary for appropriate intervention.

## Gifted Children and Peer Relation Problems

Many gifted children experience uneven or asynchronous development. Although there are many characteristics of uneven or asynchronous development among the gifted, the most problematic is when there is a significant disparity between intellectual, physical, and social development (Silverman, 1993). For example, an 11-year-old with an IQ of 160 is in all probability on the same intellectual level as a high school student, but is unlikely to have acquired an equivalent developmental level of emotional, social, and physical development (Burks, Jensen & Terman, 1930; Pfeiffer & Stocking, 2000). For example, the first author recently worked with the family of an exceptionally gifted young child who frustrated his parents and teachers with his "grossly immature behaviors." In reality, his social intelligence was, more or less, age appropriate. What was perplexing to others was that his social skills and interpersonal savvy, although developmentally normal, were absurdly incongruous with his extraordinarily stellar intellectual abilities.

Gross (1989) has poignantly written how mental age effects friendship choices among highly gifted children. Because of their asynchronous development, gifted students have a need for "true peers" because they are often unable to relate to peers with average abilities (Osborn, 1996). Highly gifted children prefer close, intimate relationships, but they have few peers with whom they can share their level of understanding, awareness, and resulting feelings of isolation and loneliness (Brody & Benbow, 1987). In many instances gifted students tend to more closely resemble older, non-gifted students and adults rather than students of the same age.

When gifted students are not interacting with other gifted children, they are at risk for feeling alienated and misunderstood, and for developing social deficits and low self-esteem (Pfeiffer & Stocking, 2000). Loneliness, social isolation, and even moderate to severe levels of depression may result when a school district is unwilling or unable to provide gifted students access to peers of similar intellectual and psychosocial development (Schneider, Ledingham, Crombie, & Clegg, 1986).

In one study, gifted children and adolescents who were interviewed expressed their need to be accepted, rather than rejected by other children for their talents. They also expressed a need to socialize with other children who share similar interests and abilities (Osborn, 1996). Although gifted children describe feeling more socially at ease, comfortable, and accepted when placed in educational programs that include other gifted students, most schools do not cater to gifted students' needs by forming compatible groups of students (Rimm, 2002, in press). During the first author's tenure as Executive Director of Duke University's pre-collegiate gifted program, he interviewed hundreds of gifted students attending the highly competitive Duke summer residential program. A recurring comment voiced during dozens of focus groups was that, for the great majority of these gifted children, the summer gifted program was the first time that they felt socially comfortable. There is growing evidence that positive peer interaction contributes to preventing and reversing underachievement, and that negative peer attitude impedes academic achievement (Clasen & Clasen, 1995; Weiner, 1992). Since social perceptions affect how students learn in school, Porath (1996) suggests assessing gifted students' perceptions of social acceptance at the elementary school level as a form of prevention.

Dauber and Benbow (1990) found that extremely gifted students (as measured by "out-of-level" SAT scores taken by seventh graders) were more likely to experience feelings of social incompetence than moderately gifted students. Extremely gifted students reported that they were more introverted, less socially adept, more inhibited, and that peers viewed them as less popular, less socially active, and less athletic. Gifted students scoring particularly high in verbal ability reported the lowest social status and lowest feeling of importance. Switatek (1995) also found that verbally precocious gifted students perceived themselves as less accepted than mathematically gifted students. Social acceptance tends to be a greater problem for students with unusually high IQ as compared to the moderately gifted. Gross (1993) found that 80% of students with IQs greater than 160 reported that they experienced intense social isolation in the classroom, and felt the need to conform to match the expectations of their average classmates.

In comparing two groups of high ability students, Cross, Coleman, and Stewart (1995) found that 94 out of the 473 gifted students reported perceiving themselves as similar to their peers, whereas 379 of the sample reported feeling different from their peers. The gifted students who reported feeling different from their peer group acknowledged that they had experienced stigmatizing situations. However, regardless of the gifted adolescents' true social standing, Coleman and Cross (1988) asserted that gifted students often express feelings of difference or perceived stigma that results from the gifted label (Rimm & Rimm-Kaufman, 2000).

In addition to a lack of companionship that may impede and adversely affect the gifted student's social-emotional functioning, gifted students are also more likely to experience frequent and intense bullying. In the first major study of bullying of gifted students, it is reported that by eighth grade, more than two-thirds of gifted students have been victims of bullies. Four-hundred-thirty-two gifted eighth graders from 11 states were interviewed; 67% had experienced bullying by the eighth grade. Name calling was the most common form of bullying, followed by teasing about appearance, intelligence and grades, and pushing and shoving. Teasing about appearance was reported to create the most negative emotional effect (Peterson & Ray, 2006). Thirty-seven percent of girls and 23% of boys reported "violent thoughts" as a result of the bullying, which ranged from kicking to bringing a gun to school.

Twice exceptional gifted children who have Asperger's disorder (AD), which is a pervasive developmental disorder characteristic of a dysfunction in social interaction, are even more likely to suffer from bullying and social isolation (Gallagher & Gallagher, 2002). There are four diagnostic criteria indicative of individuals with AD: impaired social functioning, restricted and stereotyped behaviors or interests, average or above average language development, and average or above average cognitive/intellectual development. It is important to note that *not* all children with AD are gifted. At the same time, a gifted child can suffer from AD. The first author has worked with a number of twice exceptional gifted children with AD and their families. He has also consulted on a number of cases in which children of average intellectual ability with AD were incorrectly diagnosed as twice exceptional gifted/AD. It is easy to understand why a parent of a child with AD might want to view their loved one as being gifted.

Since some of the behavioral characteristics of highly gifted children are similar to those behaviors characteristic of children with AD, it can be difficult to differentially diagnose the two. Educators and clinicians must keep in mind that an AD diagnosis is only warranted when the behaviors are extreme, inflexible, and resistant to behavioral intervention. Distinguishing AD and highly gifted children is often a matter of degree. Some gifted children may present as socially inept and isolated, and tend to avoid interaction with their same age peers. However, with strong incentives and encouragement, they can rather easily make the necessary social adjustments and no longer appear socially incompetent. Children with AD, display awkward and inflexible social interactions that are notoriously resistant to behavioral or environmental interventions.

Giftedness has the potential to exacerbate symptoms of AD. The heightened emotional sensitivity, constant questioning, and independent thinking associated with giftedness compounds the problems children with AD face. The twice exceptional gifted child with AD can appear socially inattentive, clumsy, and yet highly verbally adroit. The twice exceptional gifted/AD child may be aware that s/he is quite different from other children, which can fuel a deepening sense of isolation, low self-esteem, and depression.

The heightened emotional overexcitability associated with giftedness is exacerbated when children have a co-morbid disability (Sword & Hill, 2002). This is true not only for the twice exceptional gifted child with AD, but for many gifted students who may feel a heightened sense of alienation and sensitivity to being different, compared to their same age non-gifted peers. Gifted students struggle to understand and make sense of the unkindness, taunting, and derision that they too often experience from non-gifted students. Gifted children are prone to be hypercritical in their self-appraisals, which can create feelings of inadequacy and inferiority. Schneider et al. (1986) found that gifted students in the fifth, eighth and tenth grades reported less favorable self-perceptions, compared to non-gifted peers. Older gifted children reported having fewer friends compared to younger gifted children (Roedell, 1985). One possible explanation may be that gifted children, especially those who are older, hold more mature and sophisticated concepts of friendship, and are disappointed when their relationships lack the depth or intimacy that they would like.


## GIFTED CHILDREN AND SPECIFIC SOCIAL-EMOTIONAL PROBLEMS

### Gifted Children and Perfectionism

Although research is limited in the area of perfectionism among gifted students, studies indicate that it is a relatively common characteristic among gifted students, and that gifted students are more perfectionistic than their average-ability peers. However, gifted students' personal interpretation dictates whether their pursuit of perfection contributes to academic acceleration, creativity, and empowerment, or creates intense frustration and even paralysis (Burns, 1980; Schuler, 2002).

Due to experiences that gifted students encounter relating to their exceptional abilities, perfectionism in gifted students tends to create more anxiety than in their average ability peers. Gifted students' anxiety often stems from their strong need for personal excellence, which can result in unhealthy perfectionism and intense, debilitating emotions. Twice exceptional students are specifically vulnerable to unhealthy perfectionism because of their unrealistic expectations of themselves in areas in which they have disabilities (Vespi & Yewchuck, 1992). A general lack of self-confidence due to their disability is likely to interfere with their persistence in accomplishing their goals. Unrealistic expectations of teachers and parents, coupled with excessive and unnecessary praise of accomplishments, fuel unrealistically high expectations that gifted students calibrate for themselves (Pfeiffer & Stocking, 2000).

According to Silverman (1989), perfectionistic behaviors in gifted students may stem from standards they set that are appropriate for their mental age, and commensurate with older peers, but disharmonious in relation to their other abilities. In addition, gifted students tend to be failure avoidant because they have succeeded in the majority of areas within their under challenged environments (Dweck, 2000). Willings and Arseneault (1986) used Rollo May's existential view to epitomize a gifted child's perfectionist attitude which states "I am without significance unless I am on top; unless I am the superstar…I am nothing unless I am seen to be achieving something spectacular" (Willings & Arseneault, 1986). Therefore, unhealthy perfectionism, or an inability to be satisfied with a product can lead to intense frustration, and result in a general lack of motivation (Silverman & Golon, in press), learned helplessness, and disruptive or withdrawn behavior and low self-esteem.

Research suggests that perfectionism, specifically experienced during adolescence also increases the gifted child's vulnerability to patterns associated with eating disorders (Gardner, 1991). Dally and Gomez (1979) reported that 90% of their patients with eating disorders had an IQ of 130 or more, and Rowland (1970) found that 30% of his patients with eating disorders had IQs of 120 and a higher. Parent expectations of their child identified as gifted are likely to contribute to perfectionist behaviors, often demonstrated through competitiveness and the need for high performance. Although many gifted students display adaptive forms of perfectionism that encourage and support high achievement, it is important to be aware of maladaptive perfectionism that is associated with clinical depression and suicide (Schuler, 2000).

## Gifted Children and Suicide

Maladaptive perfectionism is one of the many vulnerabilities of gifted children that may be associated with contemplation of suicide. Negative or neurotic perfectionism has been suggested to be a risk factor that contributes to depression (Schuler, 2000). Unrealistic negative self-evaluations and exaggerated failure, on top of parental and societal pressure to excel, may lead to depression and suicidal ideation. Farrell (1989) asserted that a gifted child's ability to cope is compromised by perfectionism, stressful parental societal pressures to achieve, pressures of multiple potentiality, and distorted perceptions of failure.

A wide range of associated emotional problems may precede suicide attempts. Those that are salient to gifted children and adolescents include: inadequate social support; relationship failure with peers; self-derogation (Dubow, Kausch, Blum, Reed, & 1989); isolation, related to extreme introversion (Kaiser & Berndt, 2004); and unusual oversensitivity (Dixon & Scheckel, 1996).

Dixon and Scheckel (1996) asserted that overexcitabilities including psychomotor (e.g., fast games, sports, acting out, impulsive actions), sensual (e.g., sensory pleasure, sexual overindulgence), intellectual (e.g., introspection, avid reading, curiosity), imaginational (e.g., fantasy, animistic and magical thinking, mixed truth fiction, and illustrations), and emotional (e.g., strong affective memory, concern with death, depressive and suicidal moods, sensitivity in relationships, feelings of inadequacy, and inferiority) are of special concern when considering the possibility of suicide in gifted children.

Suicide has been linked to depression which can be identified in three stages of adolescence (Golombek & Kutcher, 1990; Sargent, 1984). In early adolescence depression may be marked by anger and disorganized, erratic behavior. Exaggerated, angry outbursts and autonomy may be expressed in mid-adolescence, the typical stage of rebellion. More "typical" depression may be observed in late adolescence, in which emotions are more self-directed in the form of sadness or guilt.

Some warning signs of depression and suicide among gifted students are lack of friendships, self-depreciation, sudden shift in school performance, total absorption in schoolwork, and frequent mood shifts (Delisle, 1986). Social isolation, in particular, is associated with depressed mood in gifted children and adolescence. Highly gifted children are at higher risk for social isolation, especially when surrounded by average peers and unchallenging learning environments (Gross, 1993). Depression, however, may precede the social isolation, or be associated with premature existential depression, characterized by advanced moral reasoning and heightened sensitivity, which is likely to resemble isolative behavior.

## PROPOSED GUIDELINES FOR SERVING THE GIFTED WITH LEARNING AND BEHAVIORAL CHALLENGES

The preceding section provided a brief discussion of a variety of social, emotional, and academic challenges that some gifted children may face. The next section presents a set of guidelines to consider when working with gifted students with learning and behavioral challenges. The seven guidelines were developed as a result of the first author's clinical experience working with this unique population over the past 30 years and supported, where noted, by findings from the empirical research literature. Our intention, therefore, is to provide a scholarly perspective on current practice guidelines when working with gifted students with learning and behavioral challenges.

### Guideline 1: Parent Involvement

The first principle is almost too obvious to state, but nonetheless is a core principle in effectively helping gifted students with learning or behavior problems. It is critically important to involve the gifted student's parents in any planned interventions. Classroom teachers, psychologists, and counselors (and in some instances, even the principal) need to reach out to the family and nurture a collaborative partnership. This is not always easy. There will be times when the parents have adopted, for a myriad of reasons, an adversarial or even intimidating posture in advocating for their gifted child. In these particularly challenging instances, the following suggestions are important to remember:

- The student's welfare is the central issue
- Most parents are well-intentioned and have their child's best interests at heart
- Be supportive, understanding, encouraging, and respectful, even if you disagree with the parents
- If you disagree with the family, communicate your viewpoint in a courteous, deferential, and non-emotional manner

Research indicates that the great majority of families of gifted children are child-centered, close, nurturing, and supportive (Keiley, 2002). On average, parents of gifted children invest more time and effort than do parents of non-gifted students in engaging their children in learning activities and introducing them to potential talent areas (Robinson, 2002).

However, when things are not going well academically or behaviorally for their gifted child, families will require assistance, guidance, encouragement, and or support. In some instances, the parents or family may need counseling. Parents often seek psychological services to confirm their child's giftedness; guide them in parenting (Pfeiffer, 2002b, 2003), determine an educational path and locate available resources (VanTassel-Baska & Stambaugh, in press), obtain early career information (Sampson & Chason, in press), and obtain assistance with specific issues, such as underachievement, peer relation problems or sibling conflict, depression, and negative perfectionism (Neihart, in press; Silverman & Golon, in press). Even if the issue facing the gifted student appears to be exclusively an academic problem, a parental partnership is important for two reasons: One, the home is the child's first school and can and should continue to play an important role in the student's learning and attitude toward academics and achievement. Two, all meaningful learning includes an affective component. When a student is not doing well, whatever the reason, one can and should expect an emotional reaction that is best addressed with parental involvement.

## Guideline 2: Standard of Excellence

The principle of setting a standard of excellence, like the above principle, may seem too obvious to state. However, we have encountered many parents and teachers in gifted workshops nationwide who believe that gifted children should not be encouraged to work hard. There are many underlying reasons for this belief. Some parents and educators contend that the gifted student should benefit from learning that comes easy and that the gifted learner should not have to put forth extra effort. Others believe that gifted children should not be "pushed" for fear of doing irreparable harm to their gift or creativity (Pfeiffer & Blei, 2007).

Whatever the reason, we believe that this attitude is dangerous, potentially harmful and misguided. Research has consistently shown that the development of talent and the attainment of expertise and expert performance in one's profession—whatever the area might be—requires considerable effort. Irrespective of one's innate ability, the learner must willingly, in extensive direct instruction, receive well-timed feedback, and engage in considerable deliberate practice—upwards of a few thousand hours of practice if they hope to attain expertise in a field (Ericsson, 1996; Sternberg, 2000). If one of the goals of the educational system is to provide all students—gifted and non-gifted alike—with the opportunity to reach their potential and fully actualize their gifts, then it becomes important to reinforce an attitude of the pursuit of excellence. This, in fact, is one reason why there is a measure of student motivation included on the *Gifted Rating Scales* (Pfeiffer & Jarosewich, 2003).

## Guideline 3: Appropriate Academic Fit/Academic Accommodations

It is almost universally accepted by experts in the field that gifted students need an advanced curriculum targeted toward their unique needs; time to develop talents and pursue in-depth interests; to be grouped with like intellectual peers in order to develop close peer relationships with others who are at similar developmental stages; and an enriched curriculum that excites, stimulates, and challenges their passion for learning (e.g., Olszewski-Kubilius, Limburg-Weber, & Pfeiffer, 2003; Robinson, Shore, & Enersen, 2007; VanTassel-Baska & Stambaugh, in press).

A number of research studies have documented that when things go awry academically or behaviorally for gifted students, the culprit, all too often, is the lack of an appropriately challenging curriculum or unsuitable instruction. An appropriate academic fit should take into account what we know about gifted students: they learn at faster rates (Colangelo, Assouline, & Gross, 2004), solve problems more readily (Sternberg, 1981), and manipulate abstract ideas and make creative connections more easily (VanTassel-Baska and Stambaugh, in press).

When things are not going well academically or behaviorally for the gifted child, it is important to determine whether the curriculum and instructional plan are appropriately matched for the student. This, in fact, is one of the first things areas that the educator or mental health professional should explore when consulting on referral problems for underachievement, poor motivation, inattentiveness or distractibility, unsatisfactory peer relationships, loneliness, and depression. In the first author's clinical experience, all too often a gifted child's social, emotional, or behavioral problem is the result of chronic and unrelenting boredom and frustration in a classroom environment that is poorly matched to his/her gifts.

In some instances, academic accommodations may have to be created for the gifted student or sought outside of the child's local school. Examples include: youth symphony orchestras, debate teams, and service learning opportunities, Saturday and summer gifted educational programs, online and home study gifted distance learning courses, and mentorships (see below for a more complete discussion of mentorship).

The research literature indicates that an important component in educating gifted students with learning or social, emotional or behavioral problems is providing instruction in the student's areas of strength (Emerick, 1992; Baum et al.,1995; Baum & Owen, 2004; Newman, 2004; Olenchak, 1995; Renzulli, 1977).The evidence conclusively supports interventions that focus on the gifted child's strengths, not his/her weaknesses. Emphasizing the gifted student's strengths, for example, can include praising a perfectionist child for a project that they did not believe to be adequate or noticing the gifts of a twice exceptional gifted child with LD. Consistent with the tenets of applied behavior analysis (Malott, Malott & Trojan, 2000), it is important to reward the gifted student's effort, and not focus excessively on the outcome. Teaching to a student's abilities increases self-concept, motivation, and task completion (Nielsen & Mortoroff-Albert, 1989).

## Guideline 4: Mentorship

Mentoring as an intervention for the gifted student is highly regarded for both its psychosocial and vocational benefits. There are no published reports of mentoring relationships leading to negative outcomes; in fact, the extant research literature reports only positive outcomes (Johnson & Ridley, 2004). The origins of mentoring can be traced to classical Greek mythology (Robinson, Shore, & Enersen, 2007).

The basic elements of mentoring include a responsible and trusted adult in the community (the mentor) with expertise in a vocational domain who is willing to spend one-on-one time with a gifted adolescent (the protégé). Mentorship is essentially an extension of an important aspect of the parenting role; the mentor introduces the gifted adolescent to a domain of expertise in which they both share a passion.

Mentorship is not classroom pedagogy. Mentoring relationships often need to be established by a parent, psychologist, or counselor outside of the purview of the school. One cautionary note is the importance of careful recruitment, matching, and supervision to ensure ethical conduct and congruent goals between the gifted student and mentor.

## Guideline 5: Balance in the Gifted Student's Life

Promoting balance in a gifted student's life means that the parent (and teacher) need to protect the child (and themselves) from getting caught up in focusing excessively on the student's special gifts to the neglect of other important developmental considerations. Parents of gifted children can be tempted to provide their child with *every* available opportunity and resource (Pfeiffer, 2003). Of course, nurturing a child's special gift is important—as we emphasized in guideline #2. However, when the scales tip to place *excessive* emphasis—in terms of time, emotional energy, travel, rearranged schedules, stretched financial resources, family activities—on promoting the special talent, the gifted child can miss out on important socialization experiences, and even feel guilty about the excessive attention. This can inadvertently create social, emotional, and behavioral problems such as perfectionism and rebelliousness (Pfeiffer, 2003).

The lesson underlying the guideline of promoting balance is that sometimes too much of a good thing in the pursuit of excellence—tutoring, private lessons, practice that is excessive, special classes, after-school programs, summer camps—can be detrimental to a gifted child's overall psychological health. Even highly gifted students need social and recreational activities and simple down-time to relax and unwind (Pfeiffer, 2003).

## Guideline 6: Social Intelligence and Intellectual Giftedness

Intellectual giftedness does not guarantee advanced or even adequate social skills. By social skills we mean: being courteous, a good listener, likable, helpful, trustworthy, a team player, able to get along well with others, and empathic. These important social and interpersonal skills have been variously labeled aspects of emotional intelligence, social competence, social maturity, and interpersonal intelligence (Gardner, 1983; Goleman, 1995, 2006; Pfeiffer, 2001a).

The publication of *Emotional Intelligence* (Goleman, 1995) made popular the recognition that IQ is not enough to guarantee success. Important social skills such as being able to rein in an emotional impulse, accurately read social cues and other people's feelings, delay the need for immediate gratification, tolerate frustrating situations and events, and handle interpersonal relationships smoothly are all important for success inside *and* outside of the classroom (Pfeiffer, in press).

A number of intellectually gifted children do *not* demonstrate equally well-developed social intelligence. Many extraordinarily bright children are ill at ease with peers and adults, lack self-confidence, and are unable to tolerate stressful situations (Pfeiffer, 2003). They lack the ability to present themselves as friendly, interested, and interpersonally attractive. As you might expect, this puts them at risk for academic, social, emotional, and behavioral problems.

Whenever one encounters a referral for a gifted student with learning or behavioral challenges, it is advisable to evaluate the adequacy of the child's social skills. This may provide valuable clues to help explain the reason for the problem, as well as fruitful strategies for intervention (Pfeiffer, 2003). As the reader is well aware, there is ample empirical evidence supporting the efficacy of social skills intervention programs (Pfeiffer & Reddy, 2001).

## Guideline 7: Counseling: Prevention and Intervention

As this chapter has emphasized, gifted children and adolescents, as a group, are different from their non-gifted peers in important ways. These differences can create both typical and unique stresses and challenges. When these stresses and challenges exceed the student's ability to effectively cope, the youngster and his/her parents may benefit from counseling (Peterson & Moon, in press). A search of journal abstract search service, *PsychInfo,* identified over 300 published articles using the search terms *gifted and counseling.* However, very few of the articles were empirically-based; the great majority of counseling papers were anecdotal case studies. In truth, much of what is written about counseling the gifted is based on clinical experience, pragmatic opinion, and empirically-based research from the non-gifted guidance, counseling, and psychotherapy literature. A useful resource is *Models of Counseling Gifted Children, Adolescents, and Young Adults,* edited by Mendaglio and Peterson (2007). This volume compares the major counseling models, techniques and therapeutic processes used with gifted clients and their families.

Although there is a dearth of empirically-supported research on the efficacy of specific psychotherapeutic interventions with the gifted (Emerick, 1992; Peterson & Moon, in press; Reis & McCoach, 2002), those who work with gifted children maintain that counseling is often a powerful intervention for these individuals. In our experience, psycho-educational curriculum, preventive guidance, and counseling/psychotherapy are effective interventions with the follow-ing issues: peer rejection; teasing and bullying; frustration related to ADHD, learning disabilities, and shyness; feelings of weirdness and being different; fear of failure; social skill deficits; peer pressure to "dummy-down"; and maladaptive motivation. We have found bibliotherapy to be a particularly powerful adjunctive technique for the parents of gifted students. For example, *Parenting Gifted Kids* (Delisle, 2006) and *Early Gifts: Recognizing and Nurturing Children's Talents* (Olszewski-Kubilius, Limburg-Weber, & Pfeiffer, 2003) are two excellent resources written to assist with parenting issues.

## CONCLUSION

This chapter has examined a number of typical and unique challenges facing the gifted student. The majority of gifted students are well adjusted, and the great majority of gifted students enjoy academic success and satisfactory social lives. However, a significant number of them encounter difficulties navigating the challenges of school, peer group, and home life. In some instances, the problem is a developmental challenge—for example, asynchronies in different domains or deficits in social skills. In some instances, the problem is a disability that co-exists with being gifted—the twice exceptional student who is struggling with a learning disability, ADHD, mood disorder, Asperger's disorder, physical disability, etc. Finally, in some instances, the problem is the result of being gifted in today's anti-elitist culture and results in suffering, teasing and peer rejection, difficulty making friends, peer pressure to hide or suppress one's gift, and painful bore-dom in the classroom. These many factors can contribute to learning and behavioral challenges that require well-conceived, thoughtful, and carefully monitored interventions. The goal of this chapter has been to introduce the reader to the special needs of the gifted and identify key guide-lines important in providing services to serving this unique population.

## REFERENCES

Andreason, N. (1989). Bipolar affective disorder and creativity: Implications and clinical management. *Comprehensive Psychiatry, 29,* 207–217.

Baker, J.A., Bridger, R., & Evans, K. (1998). Models of underachievement among gifted preadolescents: The role of personal, family, and school factors. *Gifted Child Quarterly, 42,* 5– 14.

Barona, A. & Pfeiffer, S. I. (1991). Effects of test administration procedures and acculturation level on achievement test scores. *Journal of Psychoeducational Assessment, 10,* 134– 132.

Baum, S., Emerick, L.J., Herman, G.N., & Dixon, J. (1989). Identification programs and enrichment strate-gies for gifted learning disabled youth. *Roeper Review, 12,* 48– 53.

Baum, S., Owen, E., & Dixon, H. (1991). *To be gifted and learning disabled.* Mansfield, CT: Creative Learning Press.

Baum, J., Renzulli, J., & Hebert, T. (1995). Reversing underachievement: Creative productivity as a system-atic intervention. *Gifted Child Quarterly, 39,* 224–235

Baum, S.M., Olenchak, F.R., & Owen, S.V. (1998). Gifted students with attention deficits: Fact and/or fic-tion? Or, can we see the forest for the trees? *Gifted Child Quarterly, 42,* 96–1 04.

Baum, S., M. & Owen, S.V. (2004). *To be gifted and learning disabled: Strategies for helping bright stu-dents with LD, ADHD, and more.* Mansfield Center, CT: Creative Learning Press.

Berndt, T., Hawkins, J.A., & Jiao, Z. (1999). Influences of friends and friendships on adjustment to junior high school. *Merrill-Palmer Quarterly, 45,* 13–41.

Bianco, M. (2005). The effects of disability labels on special education and general education teachers' referrals for gifted programs. *Learning Disability Quarterly, 28,* 285–293.

Biederman, J., Russell, R., Soriano, J., Wozniak, J., & Faraone, S. (1998). Clinical features of children with both ADHD and mania: Does ascertainment source make a difference? *Journal of Affective Disorders, 51*, 101–112.

Boyd, R. (1990). Academically talented underachievers at the end of high school. *Gifted Education International, 7*, 23–26.

Brody, L. & Benbow, C. (1987). Persson Accelerative Strategies: How effective Are they for the gifted?. *Gifted Child Quarterly, 31*, 105–110.

Brody, L. & Mills, C. (1997). Gifted children and learning disabilities: A review of theissues. *Journal of Learning Disabilities, 30*, 282–296.

Brown, B. & Clasen, D. (1985). The multidimensionality of peer pressure in adolescence. *Journal of Youth and Adolescence, 14*, 451–468.

Burks, B.S., Jensen, D.W. & Terman, L.M. (1930). *Genetic studies of genius: Volume 3. The promise of youth: Follow-up studies of a thousand gifted children.* Palo Alto, CA: Stanford University Press.

Burns, D.D. (1980). The perfectionist's script for self-defeat. *Psychology Today*, 70–76.

Castellanos, X. (2000). ADHD or gifted: Is it either/or? Paper presented at the annual meeting of the National Association for Gifted Children, Atlanta, GA.

Clark, S. (1997). Social Ideologies and Gifted Education in Today's Schools. *Peabody Journal of Education, 72*, 81–100.

Clasen, D.R., & Clasen, R.E. (1995). Underachievement of highly able students and peer society. *Gifted and Talented International, 10*, 67–75.

Colangelo, N., Assouline, S. G., & Gross, M. (2004). A nation deceived: How schools hold back America's brightest students. *The Templeton National Report on Acceleration, 1.* The University of Iowa, Iowa City: The Connie Belin & Jacqueline N. Blank International Center for Gifted Education and Talent Development.

Colangelo, N. & Davis, G. (1997). Introduction and overview. In N. Colangelo & G. A. Davis (Eds.), *Handbook of gifted education* (2nd ed., pp. 3–9). Boston: Allyn & Bacon.

Coleman, L.J. & Cross, T.L. (1988). Is being gifted a social handicap? *Journal for the Education of the Gifted, 11(4)*, 41–56.

Cross, T. Coleman, L. & Stewart, R. (1995). A Psychosocial diversity among gifted adolescents: An exploratory study of two groups. *Roeper Review. 17*, 181–185.

Dally, P. & Gomez, J. (1979). Psychometric rating in the assessment of progress in anorexia nervosa . *British Journal of Psychiatry, 136*, 290–296.

Dauber, S. & Benbow, C. (1990). Aspects of personality and peer relations of extremely talented adolescents. *Gifted Child Quarterly, 34*, 10–15.

Delisle, J. (1986). Death with honors: Suicide among gifted adolescents. *Journal of Counseling and Development, 64*, 558–560.

Delisle, J. (2006). *Parenting gifted kids.* Waco, TX: Prufrock Press.

Diaz, E.I. (1998). Perceived factors influencing the academic underachievement of talented students of Puerto Rican descent. *Gifted Child Quarterly, 42*, 105–122.

Dixon, D.N. & Scheckel, J.R. (1996). Gifted adolescent suicide. The empirical base. *The Journal of Secondary Gifted Education, 7*, 386–392.

Dubow, E., Kausch, D., Blum, M. & Reed, J. (1989). Correlates of suicidal ideation and attempts in a community sample of junior high and high school students. *Journal of Clinical Child Psychology, 18*, 158–166.

Dweck, C.S. (2000). *Self-theories: Their role in motivation, personality, and development.* Philadelphia: Taylor & Francis.

Emerick, L. (1992). Academic underachievement among the gifted: Students' perceptions of factors that reverse the pattern. *Gifted Child Quarterly, 36*, 140–146.

Ericsson, K.A. (Ed). (1996). *The road to excellence.* Mahwah, NJ: Erlbaum.

Ericsson, K. A., Krampe, R. T., & Tesch-Römer, C. (1993). The role of deliberate practice in the acquisition of expert performance. *Psychological Review, 100*, 363–406.

Farrell, D.M. (1989). Suicide among gifted students. *Roeper Review, 11*, 134139.

Fernandez, R., Hirano-Nakanish, M. & Paulsen, R. (1989). Dropping out among Hispanic youth. *Social Science Research, 18,* 21– 52.

Ferri, B, Gregg, N., & Heggoy, S. (1997). Profiles of college students demonstrating learning disabilities with and without giftedness. *Journal of Learning Disabilities, 30,* 552–559.

Freeman, J. (1979). *Gifted Children.* Baltimore: University Park Press.

Gallagher, J. (1991). Personal patterns of underachievement. *Journal for the Education of the Gifted, 14,* 221–233.

Gallagher, J. (in press). Psychology, psychologists and gifted students. In S. I. Pfeiffer (Ed.), *Handbook of the gifted: A psychological perspective.* New York: Springer Publishers.

Gallagher, S. & Gallagher, J. (2002). Giftedness and Asperger's Syndrome: A new Agenda for Education. *Understanding Our Gifted 14,* 7–12.

Gallagher, J., Harradine, C., & Coleman, M. (1997). Challenge or boredom? Gifted students' views on their schooling. *Roeper Review, 19,* 132–141.

Galton, F. (1869). *Hereditary genius: An inquiry into its laws and consequence.* London: Macmillan.

Galton, F. (1888). Co-relations and their measurement, chiefly from anthropometric data. *Proceedings of the Royal Society, London, 45,* 135–145.

Gardner, H. (1983). *Frames of mind: The theory of multiple intelligences.* New York: Basic Books.

Gardner, H. (1991). The tensions between education and development. *Journal of Moral Education, 20,* 113–25.

Gardynik, U. & McDonald, L. (2005). Implications of risk resilience in the life of the individual who is gifted/learning disabled. *Roeper Review, 27,* 206–214.

Geller, B. & Luby, J. (1997). Child and adolescent bipolar disorder: A review of the past 10 years. *Journal of the American Academy of Child & Adolescent Psychiatry, 36,* 1168–1176.

Goleman, D. (1995). *Emotional intelligence.* New York: Bantam Books.

Goleman, D. (2006). *Social intelligence.* New York: Bantam Books.

Golombek, H. & Kutcher, S. (1990). Feeling states during adolescence. *Psychiatric Clinics of North America, 13,* 443–454.

Gross, M.U.M. (1989). The pursuit of excellence or the search for intimacy? The forced-choice dilemma of gifted youth. *Roeper Review, 11,* 189–193.

Gross, M.U.M. (1993). *Exceptionally gifted children.* London: Routledge.

Gunderson, C., Maesch, C., & Rees, J. (1987). The gifted learning disabled student. *Gifted Child Quarterly, 31,* 158–160.

Hishinuma, E. & Tadaki, S. (1996). Addressing diversity of the gifted/at risk: Characteristics for identification. *Gifted Child Today, 19,* 20–25, 28–29, 45, 50.

Individuals with Disabilities Education Act. (1997). Public Law 105-117.

Individuals with Disabilities Education Act. (2004). Public Law 108–446.

Johnsen, S. (1997). Assessment beyond definitions. *Peabody Journal of Education, 72,* 136–152.

Johnson, W. B., & Ridley, C. R. (2004). *The elements of mentoring.* New York: Palgrave Macmillan.

Kaiser, C. & Berndt, D. (2004). Predictors of Loneliness in the Gifted Adolescent. In S. M. Moon (Ed). *Social/emotional issues, underachievement, and counseling of gifted and talented students. Essential readings in gifted education* (pp. 43–50). Thousand Oaks, CA: Corwin Press.

Keiley, M. K. (2002). Affect regulation and the gifted. In M. Neihart, S. M. Reiss, N. M. Robinson, & S. M. Moon (Eds.), *The social and emotional development of gifted children: What do we know?* (pp. 41–50). Waco, TX: Prufrock Press.

Lejoie, S.P. & Shore, B.M. (1981). Three myths? The overrepresentation of the gifted among dropouts, delinquents and suicides. *Gifted Child Quarterly, 26,* 138–143.

Leroux, J. & Levitt-Perlman, M. (2000). The gifted child with attention deficit disorder: An identification and intervention challenge. *Roeper Review, 22,* 171–176.

Lind, S. (2001). Overexcitability and the gifted. Supporting emotional needs of the gifted. *SENG Newsletter, 1,* 3–6.

Lombroso, C. (1889). *L'Homme de genie.* Paris: Alcon.

Lovecky, D.V. (1994). Gifted children with Attention Deficit Disorder. *Understanding Our Gifted, 6*, 7–10.

Malott, R., Malott, M. & Trojan, E. (2000). Elementary principle of behavior (4th ed.). Upper Saddle River, NJ: Prentice Hall.

Mandel, H.P., & Marcus, S.I. (1995). *Could do better*. New York: Wiley.

Marland, S.P. (1972). *Education of the gifted and talented* (Vol. 1). [Report to the U.S. Congress by the U.S. Commissioner of Education.] Office of Education (DHEW). Washington, DC.

McCoach, D., Reis, S. & Moon, S. (2004). The Underachievement of gifted students: What do we know and where do we go? *Social/emotional issues, underachievement, and counseling of gifted and talented students. Essential readings in gifted education.* (pp. 181–212). Thousand Oaks, CA: Corwin Press.

Mendaglio, S., & Peterson, J.S. (Eds.) (2007). *Models of counseling gifted children, adolescents, and young adults*. Waco, TX: Prufrock Press.

Moon, S.M., Zentall, S., Grskovic J., Hall, A.S., & Stormont-Spurgin, M. (2001). Emotional, social, and family characteristics of boys with AD/HD and giftedness: A comparative case study. *Journal for the Education of the Gifted, 24*, 207–47.

Moon, S. M. (2002). Gifted children with Attention-Deficit/Hyperactivity Disorder. In M. Neihart, S.M. Reis, N.M. Robinson, & S.M. Moon (Eds.), *The social and emotional development of gifted children: What do we know?* (pp. 13–18). Waco, TX: Prufrock Press.

Muir-Broadus, J.E. (1995). Gifted underachievers: Insights from the characteristics of Strategic functioning associated with giftedness and achievement. *Learning & Individual Differences, 7*, 189–206.

Neihart, M. (in press). Identifying and providing services to twice exceptional children. In S.I. Pfeiffer (Ed). *Handbook of the gifted: A psychological perspective*. New York: Springer Publishers.

Neihart, M., Reis, S. M., Robinson, N.M., & Moon, S.M. (Eds) (2002). *The social and emotional development of gifted children: What do we know?* Waco, TX: Prufrock Press.

Newman, C. (2004). Suicidality. In S.L. Johnson, R.L. (Eds) *Psychological treatment of bipolar disorder*. (pp. 265–285). New York: Guilford.

Nielsen, M. & Mortoroff-Albert, S. (1989). The effects of special education service on the self-concept and school attitude of learning disabled/gifted students. *Roeper Review, 12*, 29–36.

No Child Left Behind Act. (2002). P.L. 107–110. Available at http://ww.nochildleftbehind.gov/

Olenchak, F.R. (1995). Effects of enrichment on gifted/learning disabled students. *Journal for Education of the Gifted, 18*, 385–399.

Olszewski-Kubilius, P., Limburg-Weber, L., & Pfeiffer, S.I. (2003). (Eds.), *Early gifts: Recognizing and nurturing children's talents*. Waco, TX: Prufrock Press.

Osborn, J. (1996). Special education needs of gifted and talented children. *Youth Mental Health Update, 8*, 2–7.

Parker, H. (1992). Children with attention deficit disorders. ADD fact sheet. Children with Attention Deficit Disorders, Plantation, FL.

Peterson, J.S., & Moon, S.M. (in press). Counseling the gifted. In S I. Pfeiffer (Ed.), *Handbook of the gifted: A psychological perspective*. New York: Springer Publishers.

Peterson, S.K. & Ray, K. (2006). Bullying and the gifted: Victims, perpetrators, prevalence and effects. *Gifted Child Quarterly, 50*, 148–168.

Pfeiffer, S.I. (2001a). Emotional intelligence: Popular but elusive construct. *Roeper Review, 23*, 138–142.

Pfeiffer, S.I. (2001b). Professional psychology and the gifted: Emerging practice opportunities. *Professional Psychology: Research & Practice, 32*, 175–181.

Pfeiffer, S.I. (2002a). Identifying gifted and talented students: Recurring issues and promising solutions. *Journal of Applied School Psychology, 1*, 31–50.

Pfeiffer, S.I. (2003). Psychological considerations in raising a healthy gifted child. In Olszewski-Kubilius, P., Limburg-Weber, L., & Pfeiffer, S. I. (Eds.), *Early gifts: Recognizing and nurturing children's talents* (pp. 173–185). Waco, TX: Prufrock Press.

Pfeiffer, S. I. (Ed.) (in press). *Handbook of the gifted: A psychological perspective*. New York: Springer Publishers.

Pfeiffer, S.I., & Blei, S. (2007). The unique socio-emotional needs of the gifted student. *Maryland School Psychologists Association Protocol, 27*, 1–9.

Pfeiffer, S.I., & Jarosewich, T. (2003). *Gifted rating scales*. San Antonio, TX: Harcourt Assessment.

Pfeiffer, S.I., & Jarosewich, T. (2007). The Gifted Rating Scales-School Form: An analysis of the standardization sample based on age, gender, race, and diagnostic efficiency. *Gifted Child Quarterly, 51*, 39–50.

Pfeiffer, S.I., & Reddy, L.A. (1998). School-based mental health programs in the U.S.: Present status and a blueprint for the future. *School Psychology Review, 27*, 84–96.

Pfeiffer, S. I., & Reddy, L.A. (2001). *Innovative mental health interventions for children: Programs that work*. New York: The Haworth Press.

Pfeiffer, S.I. & Stocking, V.B. (2000). Vulnerabilities of academically gifted students. *Special Services in the Schools, 160*, 83–93.

Piechowski, M.M. (1991). Emotional development and emotional giftedness. In N. Colangelo & G. Davis (Eds.), *Handbook of gifted education* (pp. 285–306) Needham Heights, MA: Allyn & Bacon.

Porath, M. (1996). Affective and motivational considerations in the assessment of gifted learners. *Roeper Review, 19*, 13–17.

Reis, S.M., & McCoach, D.B. (2000). The underachievement of gifted students: What do we know and where do we go? *Gifted Child Quarterly, 44*, 152–170.

Reis, S., & McCoach, D.B. (2002). Underachievement in gifted students. In M. Neihart, S.M. Reis, N.M. Robinson, & S.M. Moon (Eds.),*The social and emotional development of gifted children: What do we know?* (pp. 81–91). Waco, TX: Prufrock Press.

Reis, S., Neu, T.W., & McGuire, S.M. (1995). *Talents in two places: Case studies of high ability students with learning disabilities who have achieved* (Research Monograph 95114). Storrs, CT: The National Research Center on the Gifted and Talented, University of Connecticut.

Renzulli, J. (1977). The enrichment triad Mmdel: A plan for developing defensible programs for the gifted and talented. *Gifted Child Quarterly, 21*, 227–233. Renzulli, J.S., & Reis, S.R. (1997). The schoolwide enrichment model: A how-to guide for educational excellence. Mansfield Center, CT: Creative Learning Press.

Rimm, S. (1995). *Why bright kids get poor grades and what you can do about it*. New York: Crown Trade Paperbacks.

Rimm, S. (1997). Why bright kids get poor grades and what you can do about it. New York: Crown Trade Paperbacks.

Rimm, S. (in press). Underachievement and the gifted. In S. I. Pfeiffer (Ed.), *Handbook of the gifted: A psychological perspective*. New York: Springer Publishers.

Rimm, S.B. & Rimm-Kaufman, S. (2000). *How Jane won: Profiles of successful women*. New York: Crown.

Rimm, S. (2002). Peer pressures and social acceptance of gifted students. In M. Neihart, S.M. Reis, N.M. Robinson, & S.M. Moon (Eds.), *The social and emotional development of gifted children: What do we know?* (pp. 13–18). Waco, TX: Prufrock Press.

Robinson, A., Shore, B. M., & Enersen, D.L. (2007). *Best practices in gifted education: An evidence-based guide*. Waco, TX: Prufrock Press.

Robinson, N.M. (2002). Introduction. In M. Neihart, S.M. Reis, N.M. Robinson, & Moon, S M. (Eds.),*The social and emotional development of gifted children: What do we know?* (pp. xi–xxiv). Waco, TX: Prufrock Press.

Robinson, N.M., & Noble, K. (1991*)*. Social-emotional development and adjustment of gifted children.. In M.C. Wang, M.C. Reynolds, & H.J. Walberg (Eds.), *Handbook of special education: Research and practice* (pp. 57–76). Elmsford, NY: Pergamon Press.

Roedell, W.C. (1985). Developing social competence in gifted preschool children. *Remedial and Special Education, 6*, 6–11.

Rowland, C. (1970). Anorexia nervosa: A survey of the literature and review of 30 cases. *International Psychiatry Clinics, 7*, 37–137.

Sampson, J. & Chason, A. (in press). Career planning for gifted children and youth. In S. I. Pfeiffer (Ed.) (in press). *Handbook of the gifted: A psychological perspective.* New York: Springer Publishers.

Sargent, M. (1984). Adolescent suicide: Studies reported. *Child and Adolescent Psychotherapy, 1,* 49–50.

Schneider, B.H., Ledingham, J., Crombie, G., & Clegg, M. (1986). *Social self-concepts of gifted children: Delusions of ungran*eur, Presented at the annual meeting of the American Psychological Association, Washington, D.C.

Schuler, P. (2000). Perfectionism and gifted adolescents. *Journal of Secondary Gifted Education, 11,* 183–196.

Shucler, P. (2002).Perfectionism in gifted children and adolescents. In M. Neihart, S. M. Reis, N. M. Robinson, & S. M. Moon (Eds.), *The social and emotional development of gifted children: What do we know?* (pp. 13–18). Waco, TX: Prufrock Press.

Silverman, L.K. (1989). Invisible gifts, invisible handicaps. *Roeper Review, 22,* 34–42.

Silverman, L.K. (1993). Counseling the needs and programs for the gifted. In K.A. Heller, F.J. Monks, & A.H. (Eds.), International handbook of research and development of giftedness and talent (pp. 631–647). Oxford, England: Pergamon.

Silverman, L.K., & Golon, A.S. (in press). Clinical practice with gifted families. In S. I. Pfeiffer (Ed). *Handbook of the gifted: A psychological perspective.* New York: Kluwer Academic/Plenum Publishers.

Sternberg, R. (1981). A componential theory of intellectual giftedness. *Gifted Child Quarterly, 25,* 86–93.

Sternberg, R. (2000). Giftedness as developing expertise. In K. A. Heller, F. J. Mönks, R. J. Sternberg, & R. F. Subotnik (Eds.), *International handbook of giftedness and talent.* (pp. 55–66). Oxford, England: Elsevier Science.

Swiatek, M.A. (1995). An empirical investigation of the social coping strategies used by gifted adolescents. *Gifted Child Quarterly, 39,* 154–161.

Sword, C. & Hill, C. (2002). Creating mentoring opportunities for youth with disabilities: Issues and suggested strategies. *Issue Brief), 1(4),* 8–19.

Terman, L.M. (Ed.) (1925–1959). *Genetic studies of genius* (Vols. 1–5). Stanford, CA: Stanford University Press.

U.S. Congress, Public Law 91-230, April, 1970.

U.S. Congress, Public Law 100-297, April, 1988.

U.S. Congress Department of Education (1994). *National excellence: A case for developing America's youth.* Washington, DC: U.S. Government Printing Office.

Van Boxtel, H.W., & Monks, F.J. (1992). General, social, and academic self-concepts of gifted adolescents. *Journal of Youth and Adolescence, 21,* 169–186.

VanTassel-Baska, J., & Stambaugh, T. (in press). Curriculum and instructional considerations in programs for the gifted. In S. I. Pfeiffer (Ed.), *Handbook of the gifted: A psychological perspective.* New York: Kluwer Academic/Plenum Publishers.

Vespi, L. & Yewchuck, C. (1992). A phenomenological study of the social/emotional characteristics of gifted learning disabled children. *Journal for the Education of the Gifted, 16,* 55–72.

Vialle,W. & Baldwin. (1999). Identification of Giftedness in Culturally Diverse Groups. *Gifted Education International, 13,* 250–57.

Waldron, K. (1987). Learning disabilities and giftedness: Identification based on self-concept, behavior, and academic patterns. *Journal of Learning Disabilities, 207,* 422–27.

Wasserman, J. & Tulsky, D. (2005). The origins of intellectual assessment. In D. P. Flanagan & P. L. Harrison (Eds.), *Contemporary intellectual assessment* (2nd ed., pp.1–23). New York: Guilford.

Webb, J.T., Amend, E.R., Webb, N.E., Goerss, J., Beljan, P., & Olenchak, F.R. (2005). *Misdiagnosis and dual diagnoses of gifted children and adolescents.* Scottsdale, AZ: Great Potential Press.

Webb, J.T., & Latimer, D. (1993). ADHD and children who are gifted (ERIC Document No. EDO-EC-93-5). Reston, VA: Council for Exceptional Children.

Weiner, B. (1992). *Psychological disturbances in adolescence* (2nd ed.). New York: Wiley.

Whitmore, J.R. (1986). Understanding a lack of motivation to excel. *Gifted Child Quarterly, 30,* 66–69.

Wilens, T., Biederman, J., & Spencer, T. (1999). Attention deficit/hyperactivity disorder in youth. *Disruptive behavior disorders in children and adolescents, 18, (2)*. Review of psychiatry series. (pp. 1–45). Washington, DC, US: American Psychiatric Association.

Willings, D. & Arseneault, M. (1986). Attempted suicide and creative promise. *Gifted Education International, 4,* 10–13.

Ziegler, A. & Heller, K.A. (2000). Conceptions of giftedness from a meta-theoretical perspective. In K.A. Heller, F.J. Mönks, R.J. Sternberg, & R.F. Subotnik (Eds). *International handbook of giftedness and talent.* (pp. 3–21). Oxford, England: Elsevier.

# 17

# Effective Service Delivery Models

## James M. Kauffman, Devery R. Mock, Melody Tankersley, and Timothy J. Landrum

Among the most contentious issues of the late twentieth and early twenty-first centuries involving students with learning and behavioral difficulties is the matter of how services should be delivered to them. Service delivery models may be described in a variety of ways (Smith & Fox, 2003). All of the following might be considered: programs, resources, policies, and services. In our view, the various alternative models are distinguished as well by questions that are perpetual in special and general education:

- What *language* should we use to designate students and interventions?
- Who should have the *authority* to designate which students receive services and to designate or approve the persons who provide services?
- How should we *group* students for service delivery?
- In what *place* are services best delivered to students?

*Language* refers to labeling students and the service(s) given to those designated. *Authority* means giving power to a person or to persons to say that a student should be identified as having difficulty, to provide special services, or to say who should provide the services and what training or competencies they should have. *Grouping* students means deciding whether students should be treated individually or congregated heterogeneously or homogeneously for services. *Place* is the issue of where services should be delivered, whether in settings considered general or special. We acknowledge that these are overlapping questions or issues, but we believe they can be most clearly discussed separately.

We have organized our discussion of effective service delivery models around these four ongoing issues. Our assumption throughout is that the services delivered will be the evidence-based practices discussed in previous chapters in sections II and III of this book, and that effective service delivery will also address matters discussed in other chapters in this section. To the greatest extent possible, we attempt to make both a logical and an evidence-based case for service delivery. We acknowledge, however, that for some issues reliable evidence is nonexistent or nearly so. We also acknowledge that effective service delivery might vary with the age of the student and the nature of the problem that makes special services necessary. To illustrate, following a comprehensive review of empirical research, Smith and Fox (2003) concluded, "We found little empirical research of the effectiveness of systems of service delivery for young children with or at risk of challenging behavior" (p. 8). In the absence of data on which to base our case, we make no apologies for relying on logical argument.

## HISTORICAL PERSPECTIVE

All questions about how best to deliver services to students have a very long history. However, Bateman (1994) was perhaps the first to describe certain issues in learning disabilities as perpetual—existing from the beginning of special education and unlikely ever to be fully resolved. Bateman described them as the questions Who? How? and Where? Kauffman and Landrum (2006) described perpetual issues and their historical roots in the education of students with emotional or behavioral disorders, among them inclusion, a continuum of alternative placements, and personnel preparation. In fact, most of the issues we discuss in this chapter have been concerns for many years and are unlikely ever to be fully resolved, simply because reliable evidence for a position on them is extremely difficult to obtain. Furthermore, they are matters of intense belief for many individuals regardless of any evidence presented.

The words used to describe children—labels—have been a matter of debate at least since special education became common in public schools. Labels have been a contentious issue in all professions dealing with deviance, but they have been a particular problem for special educators (Burbach, 1981). At the first meeting of the Council for Exceptional Children in 1923, delegates had an extended discussion of labels for categories and other issues of language (see Kauffman, 1981). Over the years, the term *handicap* turned to *disability*; *mental retardation* was changed to *intellectual or developmental disability*; *disorder* became *challenge*, and so on. In the process of changing the terminology used to designate differences that are perceived as problems, arguments have been made for and against specific labels. Some have expressed distaste for all labels in special education that are the basis for identification and grouping or that have negative connotations. Some writers consider all such labels as demeaning, unnecessary impediments to school reform (e.g., Lilly, 1992; Reynolds, 1991). Others have argued that labels for disabilities are essential, that euphemisms are counterproductive, and that resistance to labeling anything considered undesirable merely stifles prevention and appropriate services to students with disabilities (e.g., Kauffman, 1999, 2003; Kauffman & Hallahan, 2005a; Kauffman & Konold, 2007).

Controversy about whom should be given power to identify individuals as having particular conditions—psychologists, educational specialists, psychiatrists, or other physicians, for example—and what training they should have to designate individuals as needing particular educational or psychological services or to deliver those services goes back centuries (see Kauffman, 1976; Kauffman & Landrum, 2006; Kazdin, 1978; Reisman, 1976; Rie, 1971). Ray (1852) commented in the mid-nineteenth century on the difficulty of finding good attendants for institutions serving persons we would now say have mental illness. A century later, Stullken (1950) and Hobbs (1966) described the difficulty of finding and training good special educators for emotionally disturbed youngsters. In fact, just about everyone who has written about special education has commented on the difficulty of finding and training good personnel and on the controversies about what constitutes appropriate training and demonstrated competence in identifying and serving students with particular characteristics (e.g., Brownell, Rosenberg, Sindelar, & Smith, 2004).

Grouping students for instruction is a contentious contemporary issue, but the homogeneous versus heterogeneous question has been in dispute since schooling began. In the late twentieth century, Oaks (1992) argued that homogeneous grouping (or *tracking*, as she referred to it) is discriminatory. Others (e.g., Engelmann, 1997; Grossen, 1993) contended that homogeneous grouping is necessary for effective instruction and that heterogeneous grouping is a form of educational malpractice. Of course, the placement of students with disabilities in general education classes increases the heterogeneity of the groups with which teachers must contend.

Place has always occupied a central position in discussions of special education, but it became a matter of particularly hot debate in the 1980s (Crockett & Kauffman, 1999). Concern for the issue known since the 1990s as *inclusion* was obvious at least as early as the 1930s. However, proposals for a merger or integration of general and special education were popularized in the 1980s and 1990s (e.g., Goodlad & Lovitt, 1993). The more extreme advocates of full inclusion proposed abandoning pull-out models of service (i.e., removing the student from his or her regular classroom) of all types, calling programs involving any separation of students for instruction "segregated" (e.g., Stainback & Stainback, 1991). What was known first as the *Regular Education Initiative* (REI; see Lloyd, Repp, & Singh, 1991) in later years was called the *full inclusion movement* (FIM; see Fuchs & Fuchs, 1994). The probable effects of the REI and the FIM on teachers and students with and without disabilities became matters of great controversy. Many special educators expressed considerable skepticism about the feasibility of the REI and the FIM (Braaten, Kauffman, Braaten, Polsgrove, & Nelson, 1988; Fuchs & Fuchs, 1994, 1995; Kauffman, 1989, 1991, 1995, 1999; Kauffman, Gerber, & Semmel, 1988; Kauffman & Hallahan, 1993, 2005a, 2005b; Kauffman, Lloyd, Baker, & Riedel, 1995; Mock & Kauffman, 2005; Walker & Bullis, 1991; Warnock, 2005).

Given the concern in the late twentieth and early twenty-first centuries for inclusion, some may be surprised to find that these concerns have long historical roots. All of the basic issues of segregation versus integration and the relationship between general and special education were raised many decades ago (e.g., Baker, 1934; Berry, 1936; Postel, 1937; Rautman, 1944; Tenny, 1944; Stullken, 1950). Horn's (1924) observation that variability in the student population is the most basic problem of special education and that special education is designed to reduce the variability with which a teacher must contend has been echoed by Singer (1988) and Kauffman and Hallahan (2005a). Furthermore, as Zigmond (2003) noted, *where* students should be taught is, perhaps, the wrong question to ask (the better or more important question being *how* should they be taught).

Advocates for students and teachers who face special challenges have thought long and hard about all aspects of service delivery for many decades. We shall marshal what evidence we can and use our best logical analyses to make our case on four perpetual issues in service delivery, realizing that the case we make will not resolve these issues for all readers.

## LANGUAGE

Language reveals much about how we think about things, and our thinking is reflected in our language. The reciprocal influence of language and thinking on each other was described by George Orwell, who wrote:

> But an effect can become a cause, reinforcing the original cause and producing the same effect in an intensified form, and so on indefinitely. A man may take a drink because he feels himself to be a failure, and then fail all the more completely because he drinks. It is rather the same thing that is happening to the English language. It becomes ugly and inaccurate because our thoughts are foolish, but the slovenliness of our language makes it easier for us to have foolish thoughts. The point is that the process is reversible. (1954, p. 163)

The idea that language and thought can be analyzed as behavioral chains and that what is antecedent and what is consequence depends on how the chain is analyzed seems to anticipate

Skinner's (1957) behavioral analysis of verbal behavior. The last sentence in our quotation of Orwell above provides hope that a fine-grained analysis of language and thought can make both what we say and what we think about learning and behavior better—certainly more accurate, perhaps less ugly as well.

Orwell (1954) described how language is used for political purposes and wrote, "if thought corrupts language, language can also corrupt thought" (p. 174). Euphemisms not only become jokes (Carlin, 2004) but are regularly used to mislead people, to distort their thinking about many things, including special education (Kauffman, 2003; Lakoff, 2004; Orwell, 1954). Euphemisms and dense, confusing language are used not only to confuse voters in elections to government office but as well to fool stockholders in business reports when companies are doing poorly (Tong, 2006).

The legitimate uses of language to influence thinking and the abuse of language are difficult to specify. However, we believe that when language is impenetrable, unnecessarily confusing, relies on pointless words and phrases strung together in meaningless ways, or is misleading about the true nature of an intention, event, or condition, it is abusive. Writing that cannot be deciphered logically or that is not simple and straightforward is not helpful, in our opinion. Writers and speakers who cannot be easily understood probably have either nothing worthwhile to say or something to hide. We need clearer, less confusing, simpler, more interpretable language describing the students about whom we are concerned and about how we teach them.

Euphemism, abstraction, and generalization are among the political strategies of language identified by Orwell (1954), but they have been used with devastating effect in education. In special education and related professions, euphemism, abstraction, and generalization are frequently used to hide unpleasant realities (Kauffman, 2002, 2003). The terminology some have used to describe special education is nothing short of scathing (see paragraph two of Cook & Schirmer, 2006b, for examples). Moreover, *radical reform*, *restructuring*, *transformation*, and similar terms referring to revolutionary change are often proposed without defining these terms or specifying how we would know they have been achieved. Thus, someone can call for an integration of special and general education without stating the criteria for judging whether they have been integrated. We might ask how we would know when special education and general education have been integrated. Would integration mean that no one could identify teachers as general educators or special educators? Would special education and general education be indistinguishable in an integrated system? Would budgets for general and special education be seen as beside the point if integration became a reality? Will students with disabilities be indistinguishable from those without disabilities when integration is a reality? To us, these seem reasonable questions to ask of the person who proposes an integration of special and general education.

Even some of those who apparently see the risks associated with integration of various entities or enterprises have supported integration of general and special education. For example, Goodlad (1990) suggested that teacher education becomes derelict when it loses its boundaries, budget, and other indications of separateness as an enterprise. It simply cannot be fully or completely integrated into the general mission of a university without becoming lost. What, then, we might ask, do we expect to happen to special education if it is integrated into the mission of general education (Kauffman & Hallahan, 1993)? The answer, we feel, is obvious—it will be derelict, lost as an enterprise. But abstraction, generalization, and euphemism are perceived as admirable by those who are willing to sacrifice principle or reality to politically or professionally advantageous language. His knowledge of what happens to teacher education when it is integrated into the more general mission of higher education did not prevent Goodlad from proposing that special education be integrated with general education (Goodlad & Lovitt, 1993).

The sharpest issue of language in service delivery involves labels for disabilities. We have frequently heard colleagues suggest that services should be provided without labels for students, and some have written about avoiding labels in schooling (Biklen, 1992). However, we are unable to figure out how avoiding labels would actually be feasible. The suggestion that services can be provided without labels seems to us an evasion of reality (Kauffman, 2002; Kauffman & Konold, 2007).

The labels may not be those in current use for specific disabilities, but a label is necessary to designate the matter of concern. In our view of language, avoidance of labels merely makes the matter of concern unmentionable—or, ironically, all the more visible. Some have attempted to avoid labels by suggesting, for example, that "We do not believe a person *has* an intellectual disability; rather, the person is *defined* by others as having the condition" (Kliewer, Biklen, & Kasa-Hendrickson, 2006, p. 188). This puts the onus of naming the problem on others. In our view, such language reflects the pretense that definitions of disabilities and the words used to describe disabilities are inappropriate constructions of realities.

Another gambit for avoiding labels for students is to suggest labeling only the special service that they receive (e.g., positive behavioral intervention and support). However, a label for a service necessarily attaches to those who receive it (Kauffman & Konold, 2007). Still another tactic in attempts to avoid labels for disabilities or make them less unpleasant is using general, less specific language. Thus, the more general term *developmental disability*, which lumps disabilities of all kinds together, is perceived by some as more appropriate. Nevertheless, insistence on general language seems to be antithetical to scientific advancement. As a field of study matures, its language gets more specific, not less. Less specific language or more general terms without an increase in more specific subterms is a reliable indication of regression, not advances, in any field of work. Ultimately, if a term can hide the difference of an individual from the general population altogether while still acknowledging intraindividual differences—a term such as *individual with differing abilities*, which actually applies to everyone—it may be seen as achieving the goal of a label carrying no stigma. It is, nonetheless, useless in describing disabilities. Clarity, specificity, and efficiency in communication, not to mention appropriate responses, are sacrificed by more general terms. Supposing that a mechanic were allowed only to request a *tool* or were precluded from asking for anything more specific than a *wrench*, or that a farmer were not to label anything more specifically than *animal* (or *cow*), one can see the point about the need for more specific labels.

Organizations and individuals have struggled to overcome stigma by changing labels, assuming that the stigma of disability lies in a word or phrase commonly used to signify a particular problem. Thus, the American Association on Mental Deficiency became the American Association on Mental Retardation and, more recently, the American Association on Intellectual and Developmental Disabilities. Others have pointed out that stigma has been more effectively reduced through public education of the meaning of the words used to label conditions than in changing words (e.g., Kauffman, 2002, 2003).

We certainly understand the concept of the epithet, and we do not defend the use of words intended only to hurt the self-image or social status of others. However, we do think that language should reflect our willingness to face realities, even unpleasant ones, and that euphemisms, circumlocutions, and other contrivances of language are not helpful in the long run. In fact, changing terminology makes people stop and think about the referent, and once they understand what is being referred to they are even more likely to see the referent as an object of jest. Just where realism turns to brutality or kindness turns to euphemism is a difficult matter of judgment. In our view, the labels commonly used today by professionals are not brutalities, and the terms that are the most straightforward and understandable by the general public are most appropriate. Being identified as needing *special education* or as having a *behavioral disorder* or a *learning disability* is shameful only to those who make it so by their derogation of these terms or their referents (Kauffman & Hallahan, 2005a). Certainly, few people would choose to be called *retarded* (see Kliewer & Biklen, 1996), but we could say the same of any social designation carrying negative connotations (e.g., *obese, frail, antisocial,* or *incompetent*).

Changing the word we use to designate a reality does not change the reality. We do not agree with the assertion that "Philosophers have shown that words and sentences do not represent ideas or objects" (Smith, 1999, p. 131; see Blackburn, 2005 for refutation of Smith's view). If we are interested in changing the social perception of a reality, the best way to do so is to teach people more about that reality, including the meaning of the words we use to describe it. Changing a word alone is unlikely to have a good long-term effect, although changing a word may in fact fool people at least temporarily into believing that the reality is something it is not, and a change in wording may thus "frame" an issue for political advantage. If it is advisable to change words for political advantage, such that a different "frame" is provided, then our recommendation is that such "reframing" be described as such without the pretense that the underlying reality has some-how been changed and with the understanding that any change in perception of the reality will be temporary. Finally, as Dawkins (2006) notes regarding the use of language associated with femi-nism, the use of particular words may, indeed, raise consciousness in a very good way about an important issue. Nevertheless, he also suggests that silly changes in language are hardly justified because they do not really change the matter about which consciousness has been raised.

## AUTHORITY

We recognize that the authority to designate a student as needing special education is controver-sial. Controversy is sparked not only about the individuals who should be involved in identifica-tion (i.e., who should be the decision makers) but the criteria these individuals should apply in making their decisions (e.g., discrepancy between expected and actual achievement, response to intervention). However, in our view the most important question regarding authority is the train-ing and qualifications of the individuals who teach students after they have been identified as hav-ing unusual learning or behavioral difficulties. Thus, we focus our attention here on the training of special education teachers to obtain authority for instructing students with special needs.

The Individuals with Disabilities Education Act (IDEA; 2004) mandates that students with disabilities receive free and appropriate public educations. Local education agencies are charged by this law with providing educational services more specialized than those offered by general educators. Thus, the authority of special education is derived in part from law.

Nevertheless, the *specialness* of special education has repeatedly come under fire. Some writers have expressed the opinion that special education is nothing more than good teaching, that it is not truly special or even that it is counterproductive, making things worse rather than bet-ter for students (Cook & Schirmer, 2006b). *Good teaching is good teaching*, regardless where or by whom—presumably as if good teaching is all that is required to accommodate all learners, re-gardless of any variation among students—is a mantra of which reformers are fond (see Audette & Algozzine, 1997; Samuels, 2006). Others have noted that although special education does, indeed, need improvement, it also is teaching that is specialized along multiple dimensions (e.g., Cook & Schirmer, 2006a; Heward, 2003; Kauffman & Hallahan, 2005a; Kauffman & Landrum, 2007; Zigmond, 1997). Furthermore, many of the recommendations of would-be reformers (e.g., Audette & Algozzine, 1997) do not actually address the problems of labels, categories, and the unavoidably arbitrary designation of individuals as needing special education (see Kauffman & Konold, 2007).

The idea is sometimes advanced that "a completely new conception of teacher education is needed... a conception that is anchored in completely new ways of preparing teachers" (Pugach, 1992, p. 266). Precisely what the completely new conception of teacher education is or what the completely new ways of preparing teachers are and how these are different from what is now offered have not, to our knowledge, been explained. Moreover, the argument is sometimes made that general teacher training should be enhanced so that all teachers are trained in special education. This is the suggestion that for most students, if not for all, collaboration and consultation of their general and special education teachers should be sufficient (Zigmond, 2007). Special education teachers should be given training that general educators do not have, but their services should be delivered through collaboration and consultation with general educators, so some argue.

Sapona, Etienne, Bauer, Fordon, Johnson, Hendricks-Lee, and Vincent (2006) described merging their university's special and general education teacher training. They noted that this required not only structural but philosophical changes—specifically, adoption of the notion that "individuals with disabilities should be viewed as learners who demonstrate variations in development" (p. 5). In explaining the rationale for this change, Sapona et al. (2006) wrote:

> A major challenge for the special education faculty was how to prepare teachers and other educational personnel to meet the needs of all children in the next millennium. Our practice had been successful with children in self-contained, isolated settings but would not meet diverse children's needs in settings such as general education classrooms. The faculty was charged to identify a vision within and across special education certification areas, and for services to children across the developmental contexts. (p. 2)

The needs of *all* children are assumed to be addressed by this preparation, which does not explicitly target a special population. However, effective service delivery for children with unusual learning and behavioral difficulties rests on the authority of *special* educators. Those who argue for unifying the training of special and general educators (e.g., Pugach, 1996; Sapona et al., 2006; Schrag, 1993) seem to suggest that educators can be both effective specialists *and* generalists. Teachers cannot be at once special educators and general educators, for reasons that we explain further (see also Zigmond, 2007).

The 2001 reauthorization of the federal Elementary and Secondary Education Act—also known as No Child Left Behind (NCLB)—required that by 2006 all teachers be *highly-qualified*. To be *highly qualified* under the law, teachers need to: (a) hold at least a bachelor's degree, (b) have full state certification or licensure, and (c) demonstrate that they know each subject they teach. In short, to be in compliance with NCLB, school districts must eliminate teacher shortages while increasing teacher standards. Although special education has faced persistent teacher shortages since 1975, NCLB requires the same *highly qualified* status for all special educators. Many school districts cannot comply with the law for purely pragmatic reasons.

Beyond the pragmatic issues are echoes of the logic that equates the generalist with the specialist. At first blush, *highly qualified* seems to distinguish the generalist from the specialist. However, NCLB also includes provisions for entering teaching via an alternative to traditional teacher training. NCLB allows individuals with no training in *pedagogy* to receive *highly qualified* status. That is, knowledge of content, not pedagogy, can result in a teacher's being considered *highly qualified*. Thus, a *highly qualified teacher* by NCLB standards may actually possess no training in instruction, merely training in the subject matter to be taught.

Data do not support the idea that someone can be *highly qualified* as a teacher without training in instruction. Growing evidence indicates that teaching authority is developed via specific training (e.g., Berliner, 2000, 2004; Berliner & Laczko-Kerr, 2002; Darling-Hammond, Holtzman, Gatlin, & Heilig, 2005; Gage, 1984; Laczko-Kerr & Berliner, 2003; Sanders, 1998;

Tuerk, 2005). The notion that teachers can be *highly qualified* without any training in pedagogy has stimulated considerable research regarding the factors that account for teacher efficacy and consequent authority. Data show a positive correlation between teacher training and student achievement. Teachers who have received specific training in both pedagogy and content effect higher student achievement than do teachers without such training. This holds true across subject-matter domains (Laczko-Kerr & Berliner, 2002), years of service (Darling-Hammond et al., 2005), and geographic location (Tuerk, 2005).

Darling-Hammond and colleagues (2005) used regression analyses to investigate the relationship between student achievement and teacher training (i.e., certification) over a six-year period. They found that certified teachers consistently produced stronger student achievement gains than uncertified teachers. Darling-Hammond et al. (2005) then controlled for teacher experience, educational degrees, and student characteristics. They concluded that teacher effectiveness appears strongly related to teacher training.

Laczko-Kerr and Berliner (2002) conducted a similar study comparing the achievement of students instructed by certified and uncertified primary school teachers. They found that the students of certified teachers out-performed students of uncertified teachers across all three subtests of the Stanford Achievement Test (SAT9). The same researchers went on to conduct another study in which they calculated that the advantage provided to students by having a certified teacher versus an uncertified teacher was worth about two months progress on a grade-equivalent scale (Laczko-Kerr & Berliner, 2003). Thus, students taught by uncertified teachers paid a penalty in academic growth for their teacher's lack of training. In this study, Laczko-Kerr and Berliner (2003) concluded that teachers without specific training in pedagogy actually "do harm" (p. 35).

Empirical studies have suggested that teacher effects on student achievement seem to be as strong as the effects of student characteristics such as socio-economic status (Wenglinsky, 2002). The implication from this finding is that teaching skill can offset the potentially negative effects of home and community environments. The flip side of this coin is that although teacher effects appear to be cumulative, effective teachers in later grades are unlikely to undo the effects of less skilled teachers in earlier grades (Sanders & Horn, 1998). The results of all of these studies consistently document an important correlation between teacher training and student achievement. Thus, if teaching authority is measured via student achievement, we can conclude that teaching authority seems to be a function of teacher training. In other words, teacher training seems to produce differences in teaching skill.

Additional studies have investigated the relationship between teacher training and teacher attrition. Beginning teachers are at high risk for attrition (Miller, Brownell, & Smith, 1999; National Commission on Teaching and America's Future, 2003). Because of attrition, the teaching force is becoming increasingly bimodal in years of service (Darling-Hammond, 2006). Henke, Chen, Geis, and Knepper (2000) found that teachers who entered the classroom without specific training and supervision in pedagogy left the profession at nearly twice the rate of those who had completed such training. This relationship suggests that teacher training also plays a role in the goodness of fit between teacher and profession. Teacher training not only affects student achievement, but seems to increase the likelihood that teachers will remain in their jobs long enough to become something more than novices.

If teaching authority is conceptualized as the power to make and implement instructionally effective decisions specific to students and content areas, then the data suggest that teaching authority is derived from the type of training offered in teacher education. Indeed, the data suggest that if one is to be considered a highly qualified teacher—that is, a teacher who improves student achievement—then one must work to possess many of the qualifications provided through teacher training. Qualifications beget qualified status, and training begets differences in teaching authority. Effective service delivery rests upon the qualifications of the teacher delivering services.

For reasons detailed by Zigmond (2003, 2007), a teacher cannot offer both special and general education at the same time. The sine qua non of special education is "individually planned, specialized, intensive, and goal-directed instruction" (Heward, 2003, p. 38). Without this focus, special education ceases to be special, and students with disabilities are thereby denied the free and appropriate education guaranteed to them under IDEA (Kauffman & Hallahan, 2005a; Kauffman & Landrum, 2007). In order to prepare teachers to deliver this type of specialized instruction, special educators regularly proceed through university teacher education programs. There, they gain proficiency in the core areas that constitute most teacher training programs: (a) Knowledge of learners; (b) Understanding of curriculum content and goals; and (c) Understanding of and skills for teaching (National Academy of Education Committee on Teacher Education, 2005). What makes special education training different from elementary education training or science education training is the focus provided in each of the three core areas. The special educator will learn much about the characteristics of students who have at least one, if not more, of the thirteen disabilities defined in IDEA.

The special educator will also learn of specialized curricula designed to raise the achievement of students with disabilities. Such curricula may include but would not be limited to functional assessment (Horner & Carr, 1997), First Step to Success (Golly, Stiller, & Walker, 1998), Peer Assisted Learning Strategies (Fuchs & Fuchs, 2005), Positive Behavior Supports (Horner, Sugai, Todd, & Lewis-Palmer, 1999–2000), and mnemonic instruction (Scruggs & Mastropieri, 2000). It could encompass instructional issues such as the most effective class size for remedial instruction (Vaughn, Gersten, & Chard, 2000) as well as the limited usefulness of cooperative learning among students with disabilities (McMaster & Fuchs, 2002). It might also give specific focus to teaching various academic content areas, as well as basic skill development, most notably in reading, mathematics, and written language. Finally, special educators would learn to develop and apply teaching skills in contexts that include: self-contained classrooms, resource rooms, inclusive classrooms, residential schools, separate schools, and homebound instruction. In each of these contexts, they would develop proficiency in direct teaching, paperwork, collaboration, and consultation.

Berliner (2004) has argued that teaching expertise is specific to context and is developed "over hundreds and thousands of hours" (p. 201). The training offered in teacher education programs accounts for approximately 1,000 hours of supervised experience as a student teacher or classroom aide (Berliner, 2000). For those who would become what Berliner would call *expert* special educators, Berliner estimated that such individuals have spent a minimum of 7,000 hours in classrooms as a teacher.

Individuals such as Sapona et al. (2006) have suggested that in order to meet the needs of students in schools, special educators need to be integrated with general educators in both training and delivery of services. The authors reasoned that the blending of the two professions would result in an overall increase in teacher effectiveness that would benefit all students. We are skeptical.

In his eloquent treatise evaluating the feasibility of identifying disabilities via student response to teacher instruction, Gerber (2005) examined teaching and learning using an economic model. He posited that classroom instruction is an interaction in which students bring competing demands for teacher effort (i.e., supply). In this environment, similar teaching effort results in different student outcomes according to student ability. Because teacher effort is a limited resource, student outcomes are necessarily limited. Moreover, because students are competing for teacher effort, there exists "a line of maximum efficiency where increasing the achievement of one student results in the decreasing of achievement for another "(Gerber, 2005, p. 518). The more varied the students' responses to instruction, the larger the trade-off in teacher effort and student achievement.

If Gerber is correct, and we believe that he is, then the laws of supply and demand place upper limits on what any teacher can hope to accomplish in any classroom. Even if the teacher were an experienced, well-trained specialist, he or she would be unable to offer optimum intensive, specialized instruction in a general classroom. The competing demands for teacher effort would dramatically limit the possible range of student achievement. "Knowing what is needed to help students is not the same thing as being able to provide it" (Kauffman et al., 1995, p. 544), and teachers in general education classrooms may be unable to provide what they know students need. Teacher effort is a limited resource. When it is shared by an increased number of students, everyone receives less. Thus, as Kauffman and Hallahan (2005a) suggest, education offered in a general education setting can at best be *sort of* special, but not the highly specialized, intensive education envisioned by Heward (2003), Heward and Silvestri (2005), Kauffman and Landrum (2007), Zigmond (1997, 2007), and others.

Teachers can work in contexts in which demands nullify the advantages of their training. Furthermore, teachers, like students, vary in their skills. Just as students vary in reading levels, teachers vary in instructional finesse. If all teachers are to demonstrate the same level of proficiency, that level of proficiency must become the lowest common denominator. As Gerber (2005) has cautioned, "Teachers can not be made identical unless professional standards are pegged low" (p. 520).

In short, if special education involves nothing special—no specialized training, merely good teacher education—then there is no need for IDEA. But special education is more than good general education. Special educators derive their authority from training that is specific to learners, content, and context. Such teachers are qualified because they have sought out and acquired the qualifications that make them so. To suggest that there is no important difference between an individual who is a qualified special educator and one who is not is to discount the considerable data demonstrating the correlation between teacher training and student achievement.

General educators should, indeed, be taught that students demonstrate variations in development. However, pretending that general educators can accommodate all variations in development is tantamount to suggesting that one variation is no more significant than another and requires no more expertise than another. We do not tolerate such nonsense about variations in gardening, law, mechanics, medicine, music, or any other line of work in which specialization is necessary. Effective delivery of special education services rests on the specialized training of teachers as well as the contexts that permit specialized instruction. Special education, including the preparation of teachers to be special educators, is different from general education and should become even more so with evidence-based practices (see Cook & Schirmer, 2006a).

## GROUPING

The move toward more inclusive placements for students with disabilities in recent years has resulted in even greater academic and social diversity in classrooms, giving decisions about instructional grouping greater import. *Grouping* students refers to decisions teachers must make about how teaching and learning can occur most efficiently and effectively. On the surface, it is easy to conclude that whole class or large group instruction offers the greatest efficiency. Teacher time is saved, and evidence suggests that teachers spend more time actually teaching—demonstrating, modeling, explaining, and providing corrective feedback—when they instruct large groups (Ellis & Worthington, 1994). But questions remain about the extent to which struggling learners benefit from large-group or whole-class instruction.

Ample research supports the conclusion that individual instruction can be a highly effective means of teaching struggling learners (e.g., Elbaum, Vaughn, Hughes, & Moody, 2000; Wasik & Slavin, 1993). Moreover, individual instruction, at least for brief periods during the school day, is a defining characteristic of special education (e.g., Lerner, 2003; Zigmond, 1997, 2007). Indeed the concept of individualized instruction—specially designed instruction matched to an individual child's learning and behavioral characteristics—can be traced to special education's roots at least as far back as the early nineteenth century (Hallahan & Kauffman, 2006; Kauffman & Landrum, 2006).

Note that we make a distinction between *individualized* instruction and *individual* instruction. *Individualized* instruction refers to the extent to which instruction (materials, assignments, sequencing of skills to be taught, nature and level of support, etc.) is matched specifically to a child's identified strengths and needs. In contrast, *individual* instruction refers simply to one-on-one teaching. Special education needs to be individualized, something that can be accomplished in a variety of instructional grouping arrangements but may be substantially more feasible in smaller than in larger groups.

The question that must be answered in the initial decision about grouping for effective service delivery of special education is simple: Can students be taught individually, or must they be grouped in some way to receive instruction? The finite number of teachers in a school building and hours in a school day mean that individual instruction is simply not possible on any significant scale for the majority of students. Zigmond (2003) contends that general educators rarely plan or deliver individual instruction, and for good reason: It is not feasible when a teacher has responsibility for twenty-five or more students. But even smaller groups and limited time for instruction seem to preclude individualization. Vaughn, Moody, and Schumm (1998) examined the nature of instructional grouping in resource rooms, theoretically designed to provide greater opportunities for more focused instruction with individuals or small groups. They found that one-on-one instruction was implemented infrequently with students with learning disabilities (arguably those who need it most), and even when implemented lasted only a few minutes. From their observational study of fourteen special education teachers across thirteen schools, Vaughn et al. (1998) concluded that teachers in resource rooms "are struggling to provide individualized instruction to students when they are responsible for teaching 8 or more students at a time" (p. 222).

The larger question is how instructional groups are best formed, and the key dimension to consider in such decisions is heterogeneity versus homogeneity. It is surprising to us that instructional grouping remains the subject of controversy and disagreement. At a fundamental level, few educators would argue against the notion that good instruction meets students where they are—that is, few would argue that teachers need not find out through careful observation and assessment what children know and what they need to learn next. Tailoring instruction to specifically identified needs produces obvious benefits to students, just as instruction poorly matched to students' ability levels offers little promise of instructional benefit. Further, a poor match is likely to be detrimental to future success when students are bored because the task is too easy or are frustrated because it is too difficult. As Kauffman, Landrum, Mock, Sayeski, and Sayeski (2005) suggested, "If instruction is to be effective, good teaching requires congregating students of comparable performance for instruction in particular skills. This is something we have known for decades, not a new insight or finding" (p. 3).

Several alternative instructional grouping arrangements are possible (see Vaughn, Bos, & Schumm, 2007). These include whole-class or whole-group instruction, which necessarily means teaching a heterogeneous group (and the larger the group, the more heterogeneous it will be); small group instruction, which can be same- or mixed-ability grouping (and the smaller the group, the more homogeneous it *can* be); learning pairs or partners; and individual or one-on-one instruction. Undoubtedly, each instructional arrangement provides some benefit to some students, but even with limited research to guide teachers in grouping decisions, two elements seem critical regardless of which arrangement is chosen: instructional match and flexibility in grouping. Both elements of effective teaching demand that teachers attend carefully to assessment data. Ensuring a proper instructional match demands that teachers preassess skill areas before instruction so that proper materials can be chosen and the nature, structure, and pacing of lessons can be preplanned. Frequent ongoing assessment of some type is also necessary so that teachers can document the effects of instruction and modify methods or materials as needed. Ongoing assessment highlights the need for grouping. When particular students are observed to move through material more rapidly than expected, or to struggle to master concepts, the effective teacher naturally modifies his or her instruction to meet these needs. *Flexible* instructional groups provide the means to do this; students are grouped according to specific skills they need to learn, but are expected to flow into and out of different instructional groups as they master material at different rates. It is perhaps the historic concept of rigid, inflexible instructional groups, in which students were essentially tracked for entire school years (e.g., *redbird* or *bluebird* reading groups, likely formed on the basis of a single, beginning-of-year assessment, and unlikely to change throughout a school year) that has generated a negative connotation of the very concept of same-ability grouping. Nonetheless, fluid, flexible, instructional groups are consistent with good practice in special education and with existing research on effective teaching (e.g., Vaughn, Hughes, Moody, & Elbaum, 2001).

## PLACE

Unfortunately *where* students are taught tends to take priority over questions of how they are taught, by whom, and for what purposes. Indeed, place may have been given unwarranted space in discussions of service delivery (see Crockett & Kauffman, 1999; Zigmond, 2003; Warnock, 2005). Educational placements for students with learning and behavioral problems have historically been provided under the assumption that a variety of options are necessary to meet the students' diverse needs. The continuum of alternative placements (CAP) required by IDEA reflects this array of placement options that vary in degree of restrictiveness.

One of the basic tenets of IDEA is that service delivery occurs in the least restrictive environment (LRE) possible for a particular student's needs. As Crockett and Kauffman (2001) argue, restrictiveness is often erroneously judged by location alone, with placement in general education classrooms considered always the LRE. However, analysis of restrictiveness requires consideration of students' learning and behavioral characteristics (i.e., establishing *how* they might be taught most effectively), and their curricular needs (i.e., establishing *what* they need to be taught).

Too often, placement questions are answered first—or not even considered when thinking about services. Indeed, for many students with learning and behavioral disabilities the only placement option is the general education classroom. In a recent focus group interview, special education teachers reported that their students had no alternatives—the general education classroom was the only placement available (Tankersley, Niesz, Cook, & Woods, in press). What these teachers saw lacking were the hallmarks of special education—specific, intense, explicit instruction that is supportive, individualized, and carefully monitored but extremely unlikely or impossible in a general education classroom (Heward, 2003; Heward & Silvestri, 2005; Kauffman,

Bantz, & McCullough, 2002; McCray, Vaughn, & Neal, 2001; Zigmond, 2003). Moreover, what Tankersley et al. found is simply the reverse of the days in which the special self-contained class was all that was offered—a situation antithetical to the CAP now required by IDEA.

The extent to which different placement options can provide the kind of individualized instruction and support that students with learning and behavior difficulties need has not been determined. Few rigorous studies have been done to date, although researchers have been trying to investigate the effectiveness of one type of placement over another for more than thirty years. The cumulative results support no simple or unequivocal answers. In a review of studies assessing the efficacy of placements, Zigmond (2003) reached the conclusion that investigations to date provide "no compelling research evidence that place is the critical factor in the academic or social progress of students with mild/moderate disabilities" (p. 195).

The majority of early studies showed that students who received instruction in the general education classroom tended to be lower in academic achievement than those who received special education services in resource or self-contained classrooms (e.g., Carlberg & Kavale, 1980; Leinhardt & Pallay, 1982; Madden & Slavin, 1983; Sindelar & Deno, 1978). However, these early studies typically compared general education placements in which no individualized approaches or supports were provided to the students with disabilities to resource or self-contained classrooms in which specialized services were provided by trained special educators (Zigmond, 2003). More recently, research has compared student outcomes in general education that incorporated supports for students with disabilities to other placement options. Still, the results are equivocal. For some students with mild disabilities, full-time placement in general education inclusive classrooms has resulted in some academic gains comparable to those made by their peers without disabilities (e.g., Banerji & Dailey, 1995) or better than their peers with learning or behavioral problems in placements outside the general education classroom (e.g., Baer & Proctor, 1990). Nevertheless, other studies showed that many students with mild disabilities in inclusion classrooms (a) failed to achieve at a level commensurate with that of typically developing peers (e.g., Baer & Proctor, 1990); (b) experienced social difficulties (e.g., Vaughn, Elbaum, & Boardman, 2001); and (c) did not receive specialized instruction (e.g., Fox & Ysseldyke, 1997). In fact, Zigmond et al. (1995) reported the combined results of longitudinal studies that supported three full inclusion programs with tremendous amounts of financial and professional resources, showing that in relation to academic achievement, 40 percent of the students with learning disabilities in those placements "were slipping behind at what many would consider a disturbing rate" (p. 539).

The lack of clear, positive outcomes for students with learning and behavioral difficulties in particular placements has led researchers to conclude that no one place can fit the needs of all students. Indeed, after reviewing the outcomes of research on inclusionary practices, Hocutt (1996), Manset and Semmel (1997), Waldron and McLeskey (1998), Murawski and Swanson (2001), and Zigmond and Magiera (2002) all concluded that not all students with learning or behavioral difficulties can benefit from receiving educational services in one type of placement. Instead, as Zigmond (2003) noted in her summary of three decades of research investigating the efficacy of the various educational placements in which students with disabilities received their special services, "what goes on in a place, not the location itself, is what makes a difference" (p. 198).

## CONCLUSIONS

We recommend using the clearest and most efficient language possible in describing learning and behavioral difficulties and the special services needed to address them. Neither individuals with disabilities nor their teachers will be well served by assuming that people with disabilities are indistinguishable from the general population or that their education is like that designed for the majority of students. Kauffman and Hallahan (2005a) and Kauffman and Landrum (2007) have noted how special education differs along several dimensions from general education: pacing or rate, intensity, relentlessness, structure, reinforcement, pupil-teacher ratio, curriculum, and monitoring or assessment. These are matters of degree, not essentially different dimensions of teaching, but the degree of difference is extremely important. Other chapters in this book give more specifics about how education must be different from the typical to meet the needs of students who experience difficulties in learning.

The authority that we ascribe to special educators is rooted in research documenting the relationship between teacher training and student achievement. It is also based on the logical consideration of the limited teaching resources and the demands of instructional contexts. If such evidence and logic are not sufficient to document the necessity for specialized teacher training, then we urge the reader to consider special education law. For over thirty-five years, the federal government has required that schools provide specialized instruction to students with disabilities. Of course, we could return to the era in which whatever is provided in general education by a general education teacher (who has been taught that there are variations in human development but has not been fully trained as a special educator) is judged sufficient and appropriate. We do not recommend that return.

Although certainly more research is required on the effects of grouping for instruction on student achievement, the available research suggests that, short of individual instruction, flexible homogeneous instructional groups formed on the basis of specifically identified instructional needs seem best suited to promoting student success. Whether the needed instruction can be provided consistently in general education classrooms for students with disabilities remains doubtful (Zigmond, 2003).

We cannot say that one type of placement will lead to improved outcomes for students with learning and behavioral difficulties, but we can definitely identify practices that are effective for addressing these students' needs. There is no doubt that the field of special education has established educational practices and interventions that have been shown to be effective for addressing many of the learning and social needs of students who experience extraordinary difficulty in school. However, not all educational placements are conducive to incorporating these approaches into teaching and learning. Zigmond (1996), for example, found that general education environments are not supportive places in which to implement many effective teaching practices for students who have extraordinary difficulty. The structure, intensity, precision, and relentlessness with which teachers must deliver, monitor, and adapt instruction for many students with disabilities is surely beyond that which is possible in a general education classroom (Kauffman et al., 2002; Kauffman & Hallahan, 2005a; Zigmond, 2003).

The most effective service delivery system probably cannot be defined totally in the abstract, for it likely depends on the characteristics of the student (e.g., age, type and severity of disability), the qualifications of the teacher(s) who will provide instruction, other students with whom a student will be grouped, and features of the placement. Our view is that there is probably not a single, best delivery system, but a variety of arrangements suited to make maximum use of the student's abilities. Those who propose a single best solution in all cases (e.g., self-contained special class, inclusion in general education with collaboration and consultation of all concerned parties) are, in our opinion, misguided. In our opinion, it is incumbent on all concerned parties to try to find the use of language, authority, grouping, and place that will produce the optimum academic and social development of the student. This will require the use of admittedly less than perfect human judgment of all the factors involved, giving up the notion that one best plan for all students exists, and keeping the welfare of the student foremost.

# REFERENCES

Audette, B., & Algozzine, B. (1997). Re-inventing government? Let's re-invent special education. *Journal of Learning Disabilities, 30*, 378–383.

Baer, G. G., & Proctor, W. A. (1990). Impact of a full-time integrated program on the achievement of non-handicapped and mildly handicapped children. *Exceptionality, 1*, 227–238.

Baker, H. J. (1934). Common problems in the education of the normal and the handicapped. *Exceptional Children, 1*, 39–40.

Banerji, M., & Dailey, R. (1995). A study of the effects of an inclusion model on students with specific learning disabilities. *Journal of Learning Disabilities, 28*, 511–528.

Bateman, B. D. (1994). Who, how, and where: Special education's issues in perpetuity. *Journal of Special Education, 27*, 509–520.

Berliner, D. C. (2000). A personal response to those who bash teacher education. *Journal of Teacher Education, 51*, 358–371.

Berliner, D. C. (2004). Describing the behavior and documenting the accomplishments of expert teachers. *Bulletin of Science, Technology & Society, 24*, 200–212.

Berry, C. S. (1936). The exceptional child in regular classes. *Exceptional Children, 3*, 15–16.

Biklen, D. (1992). *Schooling without labels: Parents, educators, and inclusive education.* Philadelphia: Temple University Press.

Blackburn, S. (2005). *Truth: A guide.* New York: Oxford University Press.

Braaten, S. R., Kauffman, J. M., Braaten, B., Polsgrove, L., & Nelson, C. M. (1988). The regular education initiative: Patent medicine for behavioral disorders. *Exceptional Children, 55*, 21–28.

Brownell, M. T., Rosenberg, M. S., Sindelar, P. T., & Smith, D. D. (2004). Teacher education: Toward a qualified teacher in every classroom. In A. M. Sorrells, H. J. Reith, & P. T. Sindelar (Eds.), *Critical issues in special education: Access, diversity, and accountability* (pp. 243–257). Boston: Allyn & Bacon.

Burbach, H. J. (1981). The labeling process: A sociological analysis. In J. M. Kauffman & D. P. Hallahan (Eds.), *Handbook of special education* (pp. 361–377). Englewood Cliffs, NJ: Prentice-Hall.

Carlberg, C., & Kavale, K. (1980). The efficacy of special versus regular class placement for exceptional children: A meta-analysis. *The Journal of Special Education, 14*, 295–309.

Carlin, G. (2004). *When will Jesus bring the pork chops?* New York: Comedy Concepts.

Cook, B. G., & Schirmer, B. R. (Eds.). (2006a). *What is special about special education? Examining the role of evidence-based practices.* Austin, TX: Pro-Ed.

Cook, B. G., & Schirmer, B. R. (2006b). Conclusion: An overview and analysis of the role of evidence-based practices in special education. In B. G. Cook & B. R. Schirmer (Eds.), *What is special about special education? Examining the role of evidence-based practices* (pp. 175–185). Austin, TX: Pro-Ed.

Crockett, J. B., & Kauffman, J. M. (1999). *The least restrictive environment: Its origins and interpretations in special education.* Mahwah, NJ: Erlbaum.

Crockett, J. B., & Kauffman, J. M. (2001). The concept of the least restrictive environmnet and learning disabilities: Least restrictive of what? Reflections on Cruickshank's 1977 guest editorial for the *Journal of Learning Disabilities.* In D. P. Hallahan & B. K. Keogh (Eds.), *Research and global perspectives in learning disabilities: Essays in honor of William M. Cruickschank* (pp. 147–166). Mahwah, NJ: Erlbaum.

Darling-Hammond, L. (2006). Construction of 21st century teacher education. *Journal of Teacher Education, 57*, 300–314.

Darling-Hammond, L., Holtzman, D. J., Gatlin, S. J., & Heilig, J. V. (2005). Does teacher preparation matter? Evidence about teacher certification, Teach for America, and teacher effectiveness. *Education Policy Analysis Archives, 13*(42). Retrieved November 4, 2005, from http://epaa.asu.edu/epaa/v13n42/.

Dawkins, R. (2006). *The god delusion.* Boston: Houghton Mifflin.

Engelmann, S. (1997). Theory of mastery and acceleration. In J. W. Lloyd, E. J. Kameenui, & D. Chard (Eds.), *Issues in educating students with disabilities* (pp. 177–195). Mahwah, NJ: Erlbaum.

Elbaum, B., Vaughn, S., Hughes, M., & Moody, S. W. (2000). How effective are one-to-one tutoring programs in reading for elementary students at risk for reading failure? A meta-analysis of the intervention research. *Journal of Educational Psychology, 92,* 605–619.

Ellis, E., & Worthington, L. A. (1994). *Research synthesis on effective teaching principles and the design of quality tools for educators.* Technical Report #5. National Center to Improve the Tools of Educators. University of Oregon.

Fox, N. E., & Ysseldyke, J. E. (1997). Implementing inclusion at the middle school level: Lessons from a negative example. *Exceptional Children, 64,* 81–98.

Fuchs, D., & Fuchs, L. S. (1994). Inclusive schools movement and the radicalization of special education reform. *Exceptional Children, 60,* 294–309.

Fuchs, D., & Fuchs, L. S. (1995). Special education can work. In J. M. Kauffman, J. W. Lloyd, D. P. Hallahan, & T. A. Astuto (Eds.), *Issues in educational placement: Students with emotional and behavioral disorders* (pp. 363–377).Mahwah, NJ: Erlbaum.

Fuchs, D., & Fuchs, L. S. (2005). Peer-Assisted Learning Strategies: Promoting word recognition, fluency, and reading comprehension in young children. *The Journal of Special Education 39,* 34–44.

Gage, N. L. (1984). What do we know about teaching effectiveness? *Phi Delta Kappa, 66,* 87–93.

Gerber, M. M. (2005). Teachers are still the test: Limitations of response to instruction strategies for identifying children with learning disabilities. *Journal of Learning Disabilities, 38,* 516–524.

Golly, A., Stiller, B., & Walker, H. M. (1998). First Step to Success: Replication and social validation of an early intervention program. *Journal of Emotional and Behavioral Disorders 6,* 243–250.

Goodlad, J. I. (1990). *Teachers for our nation's schools.* San Francisco: Jossey-Bass.

Goodlad, J. I., & Lovitt, T. C. (Eds.). (1993). *Integrating general and special education.* Upper Saddle River, NJ: Merrill/Prentice Hall.

Grossen, B. (1993). Focus: Heterogeneous grouping and curriculum design. *Effective School Practices, 12*(1), 5–8.

Hallahan, D. P., & Kauffman, J. M. (2006). *Exceptional learners: Introduction to special education* (10th ed.). Boston: Allyn & Bacon.

Henke, R., Chen, X., & Geis, S. (2000). *Progress through the teacher pipeline: 1992–93 college graduates and elementary/secondary school teaching as of 1997.* Washington, DC: U.S. Department of Education, National Center for Education Statistics.

Heward, W. L. (2003). *Exceptional children: An introduction to special education* (7th ed.). Upper Saddle River, NJ: Merrill/Prentice Hall.

Heward, W. L., & Silvestri, S. M. (2005). The neutralization of special education. In J. W. Jacobson, J. A. Mulick, & R. M. Foxx (Eds.), *Fads: Dubious and improbable treatments for d evelopmental disabilities* (pp. 193–214). Mahwah, NJ: Erlbaum.

Hobbs, N. (1966). Helping the disturbed child: Psychological and ecological strategies. *American Psychologist, 21,* 1105–1115.

Hocutt, A. M. (1996). Effectiveness of special education: Is placement the critical factor? The *Future of Children, 6,* 77–102.

Horn, J. L. (1924). *The education of exceptional children: A consideration of public school problems and policies in the field of differentiated education.* New York: Century.

Horner, R. H., & Carr, E. G. (1997). Behavioral support for students with severe disabilities: Functional assessment and comprehensive intervention. *The Journal of Special Education, 31,* 84–104.

Horner, R. H., Sugai, G. Todd, A. W., & Lewis-Palmer, T. (1999–2000). Elements of behavior support plans: A technical brief. *Exceptionality, 8,* 205–216.

Kauffman, J. M. (1976). Nineteenth century views of children's behavior disorders: Historical contributions and continuing issues. *Journal of Special Education, 10,* 335–349.

Kauffman, J. M. (1981). Introduction: Historical trends and contemporary issues in special education in the United States. In J. M. Kauffman & D. P. Hallahan (Eds.), *Handbook of special education* (pp. 3–23). Englewood Cliffs, NJ: Prentice-Hall.

Kauffman, J. M. (1989). The regular education initiative as Reagan-Bush education policy: A trickle-down theory of education of the hard-to-teach. *Journal of Special Education, 23,* 256–278.

Kauffman, J. M. (1991). Restructuring in sociopolitical context: Reservations about the effects of current reform proposals on students with disabilities. In J. W. Lloyd, A. C. Repp, & N. N. Singh (Eds.), *The regular education initiative: Alternative perspectives on concepts, issues, and methods* (pp. 57–66). Sycamore, IL: Sycamore.

Kauffman, J. M. (1995). Why we must celebrate a diversity of restrictive environments. *Learning Disabilities Research and Practice, 10*, 225–232.

Kauffman, J. M. (1999). Commentary: Today's special education and its messages for tomorrow. *The Journal of Special Education, 32*, 244–254.

Kauffman, J. M. (2002). *Education deform: Bright people sometimes say stupid things about education.* Lanham, MD: Rowman & Littlefield Education.

Kauffman, J. M. (2003). Appearances, stigma, and prevention. *Remedial and Special Education, 24*, 195–198.

Kauffman, J. M., Bantz, J., & McCullough, J. (2002). Separate and better: A special public school class for students with emotional and behavioral disorders. *Exceptionality, 10*, 149–170.

Kauffman, J. M., Gerber, M. M., & Semmel, M. I. (1988). Arguable assumptions underlying the regular education initiative. *Journal of Learning Disabilities, 21*, 6–11.

Kauffman, J. M., & Hallahan, D. P. (1993). Toward a comprehensive service delivery system. In J. I. Goodlad & T. C. Lovitt (Eds.), *Integrating general and special education* (pp. 73–102). Upper Saddle River, NJ: Merrill/Prentice Hall.

Kauffman, J. M., & Hallahan, D. P. (2005a). *Special education: What it is and why we need it.* Boston: Allyn & Bacon.

Kauffman, J. M., & Hallahan, D. P. (Eds.) (2005b). *The illusion of full inclusion: A comprehensive critique of a current special education bandwagon* (2nd ed.). Austin, TX: Pro-Ed.

Kauffman, J. M., & Konold, T. R. (2007). Making sense in education: Pretense (including NCLB) and realities in rhetoric and policy about schools and schooling. *Exceptionality, 15*, 00–00.

Kauffman, J. M., & Landrum, T. J. (2006). *Children and youth with emotional and behavioral disorders: A history of their education.* Austin, TX: Pro-Ed.

Kauffman, J. M., & Landrum, T. J. (2007). Educational service interventions and reforms. In J. W. Jacobson, J. A. Mulick, & J. Rojahn (Eds.), *Handbook of intellectual and developmental disabilities* (pp. 173–188). New York: Springer.

Kauffman, J. M., Landrum, T. J., Mock, D., Sayeski, B., & Sayeski, K. L. (2005). Diverse knowledge and skills require a diversity of instructional groups: A position statement. *Remedial and Special Education, 26*, 2–6.

Kauffman, J. M., Lloyd, J. W., Baker, J., & Riedel, T. M. (1995). Inclusion of all students with emotional or behavioral disorders? Let's think again. *Phi Delta Kappan, 76*, 542–546.

Kazdin, A. E. (1978). *History of behavior modification: Experimental foundations of contemporary research.* Baltimore: University Park Press.

Kliewer, C., & Biklen, D. (1996). Who wants to be retarded? In W. Stainback & S. B. Stainback (Eds.), *Controversial issues confronting special education: Divergent perspectives* (2nd ed., pp. 83–95). Boston: Allyn & Bacon.

Kliewer, C., Biklen, D., & Kasa-Hendrickson, C. (2006). Who may be literate? Disability and resistance to the cultural denial of competence. *American Educational Research Journal, 43*, 163–192.

Laczko-Kerr, I., & Berliner, D. C. (2002). The effectiveness of "Teach for America" and other under-certified teachers on student academic achievement: A case of harmful public policy," *Educational Policy Analysis Archives, 10*(37). Retrieved November 4, 2005, from http://epaa.asu.edu/epaa/v10n37/.

Laczko-Kerr, I., & Berliner, D. C. (2003). In harm's way: How undercertified teachers hurt their students. *Educational Leadership, 60*(8), 34–39.

Lakoff, G. (2004). *Don't think of an elephant: Know your values and frame the debate.* White River Junction, VT: Chelsea Green.

Leinhardt, G., &Pallay, A. (1982). Restrictive educational settings? Exile or haven. *Review of Educational Research, 52*, 557–578.

Lerner, J. W., (2003). *Learning disabilities: Theories, diagnosis, and teaching strategies* (9th ed.). Boston: Houghton Mifflin.

Lilly, M S. (1992). Labeling: A tired, overworked, yet unresolved issues in special education. In W. Stainback & S. B. Stainback (Eds.), *Controversial issues confronting special education: Divergent perspectives* (pp. 85–95). Boston: Allyn & Bacon.

Lloyd, J. W., Singh, N. N., & Repp, A. C. (Eds.). (1991). *The Regular Education Initiative: Alternative perspectives on concepts, issues, and models.* Sycamore, IL: Sycamore.

Madden, N. A., & Slavin, R. E. (1983). Mainstreaming students with mild handicaps: Academic and social outcomes. *Review of Educational Research, 53,* 519–569.

Manset, G., & Semmel, M. I. (1997). Are inclusive programs for students with mild disabilities effective? A comparative review of model programs. *The Journal of Special Education, 31,* 155–180.

McCray, A. D., Vaughn, S., & Neal, L. (2001). Not all students learn to read by third grade: Middle school students speak out about their reading disabilities. *Journal of Special Education, 35,* 17–30.

McMaster, K. N., & Fuchs, D. (2002). Effects of cooperative learning on the academic achievement of students with learning disabilities: An update of Tateyama-Sniezek's review. *Learning Disabilities: Research & Practice, 17,* 107–117.

Miller, M.D., Brownell, M. T., & Smith, S. W. (1999). Factors that predict teachers staying in, leaving, or transferring from the special education classroom. *Exceptional Children, 65,* 201–218.

Mock, D. R., & Kauffman, J. M. (2005). The delusion of full inclusion. In J. W. Jacobson, J. A. Mulick, & R. M. Foxx (Eds.), *Fads: Dubious and Improbable Treatments for Developmental Disabilities* (pp. 113–128). Mahwah, NJ: Erlbaum.

Murawski, W. W., & Swanson, H. L. (2001). A meta-analysis of co-teaching research. *Remedial and Special Education, 22,* 258–267.

National Academy of Education Committee on Teacher Education. *A good teacher in every classroom: Preparing the highly qualified teachers our children deserve.* L. Darling-Hammond & J. Baratz-Snowden, (Eds.). San Francisco: Jossey-Bass.

National Commission on Teaching and America's Future (2003). *No dream denied: A pledge to America's children.* Washington, DC: Author.

Oakes, J. (1992). Can tracking research inform practice? Technical, normative, and political considerations. *Educational Researcher, 21*(4), 12–21.

Orwell, G. (1954, original essay 1946). Politics and the English language. In *A collection of essays by George Orwell* (pp. 162–177). New York: Doubleday Anchor.

Postel, H. H. (1937). The special school versus the special class. *Exceptional Children, 4,* 12–13, 18–19.

Pugach, M. C. (1992). Unifying the preservice preparation of teachers. In W. Stainback & S. B. Stainback (Eds.), *Controversial issues confronting special education: Divergent perspectives* (pp. 255–269). Boston: Allyn & Bacon.

Pugach, M. C. (1996). Unifying the preparation of prospective teachers. In W. Stainback & S. Stainback (Eds.), *Controversial issues confronting special education: Divergent perspectives* (2nd ed., pp. 239–252). Boston: Allyn & Bacon.

Rautman, A. L. (1944). Special class placement. *Exceptional Children, 10,* 99–102.

Ray, I. (1852, May 18). On the best methods of saving our hospitals for the insane from the odium and scandal to which such institutions are liable, and maintaining their place in the popular estimation: including the consideration of the question, how far is the community to be allowed access to such hospitals? Paper presented at a meeting of the Association of Medical Superintendents of American Institutions for the Insane. New York: Reprinted in *American Journal of Insanity, 9,* 36–65.

Reisman, J. M. (1976). *A history of clinical psychology* (enlarged edition). New York: Irvington.

Reynolds, M. C. (1991). Classification and labeling. In J. W. Lloyd, N. N. Singh, & A. C. Repp (Eds.), *The regular education initiative: Alternative perspectives on concepts, issues, and models* (pp. 29–41). Sycamore, IL: Sycamore.

Rie, H. E. (1971). Historical perspective of concepts of child psychopathology. In H. E. Rie (Ed.), *Perspectives in child psychopathology.* Chicago: Aldine Atherton.

Samuels, C. A. (2006, March 8). Intervention method is topic A at meeting of disabilities group. *Education Week, 25*(26), 8.

Sanders, W., & Horn, S. (1998). Research findings from the Tennessee Value-Added Assessment System database: Implications for educational evaluation and research. *Journal of Personnel Evaluation in Education, 12,* 138–151.

Sapona, R., Etienne, J., Bauer, A., Fordon, A.E., Johnson, L. J., Hendricks-Lee, M., & Vincent, N. C. (2006). Teacher education reform within university special education programs. *Focus on Exceptional Children, 38*(5), 1–12.

Sanders, W., & Horn, S. (1998). Research findings from the Tennessee Value-Added Assessment System database: Implications for educational evaluation and research. *Journal of Personnel Evaluation in Education, 12,* 138–151.

Schrag, J. A. (1993). Restructuring schools for better alignment of general and special education. In J. I. Goodlad & T. C. Lovitt (Eds.), *Integrating general and special education* (pp.203–228). New York: MacMillan.

Scruggs, T. E., & Mastropieri, M. A. (2000). The effectiveness of mnemonic instruction for students with leaning and behavior problems: An update and research synthesis. *Journal of Behavioral Education, 10,* 163–173.

Sindelar, P. T., & Deno, S. L. (1978). The effectiveness of resource programming. *The Journal of Special Education,* 12, 17–28.

Singer, J. D. (1988). Should special education merge with regular education? *Educational Policy, 2,* 409–424.

Skinner, B. F. (1957) *Verbal behavior.* Englewood Cliffs, NJ: Prentice-Hall.

Smith, B. J., & Fox, L. (2003). *Systems of service delivery: A synthesis of evidence relevant to young children at risk of or who have challenging behavior.* Tampa: University of South Florida, Center for Evidence-Based Practice: Young Children with Challenging Behavior.

Smith, P. (1999). Drawing new maps: A radical cartography of developmental disabilities. *Review of Educational Research, 69,* 117–144.

Stainback, W., & Stainback, S. (1991). A rationale for integration and restructuring: A synopsis. In J. W. Lloyd, N. N. Singh, & A. C. Repp (Eds.), *The Regular Education Initiative: Alternative perspectives on concepts, issues, and models* (pp. 226–239). Sycamore, IL: Sycamore.

Stullken, E. H. (1950). Special schools and classes for the socially maladjusted. In N. B. Henry (Ed.), *The education of exceptional children.* Forty-ninth Yearbook of the National Society for the Study of Education (Part 2, pp. 281–301). Chicago: University of Chicago Press.

Tankersley, M., Niesz, T., Cook, B. G., & Woods, W. (in press). The unintended and unexpected side effects of inclusion of students with learning disabilities: The perspectives of special education teachers. *Learning Disabilities: A Multidisciplinary Journal.*

Tenny, J. W. (1944). Adjustment of special class pupils to regular classes. *Exceptional Children, 10,* 139–145.

Tong, S. (2006, September 27). Straight talk equals good business. Market Place report. Retrieved Sept. 28, 2006, from http://marketplace.publicradio.org/shows/2006/09/27/PM200609276.html.

Tuerk, P. W. (2005). Research in the high-stakes era: Achievement, resources, and No Child Left Behind. *American Psychological Society, 16,* 419–425.

Vaughn, S., Bos, C., & Schumm, J. S. (2007). *Teaching Students who are exceptional, diverse, and at risk in the general education classroom* (4th ed.). Boston: Pearson.

Vaughn, S., Elbaum, B. E., & Boardman, A. G. (2001). The social functioning of students with learning disabilities: Implications for inclusion. *Exceptionality, 9,* 47–65.

Vaughn, S., Gersten, R., & Chard, D. J. (2000). The underlying message in LD intervention research: Findings from research syntheses. *Exceptional Children. 67,* 99–114.

Vaughn, S., Hughes, M. T., Moody, S. W., & Elbaum, B. (2001). Instructional grouping for reading for students with LD: Implications for practice. *Intervention in School and Clinic, 36,* 131–137.

Vaughn, S., Moody, S. W., & Schumm, J. S. (1998). Broken promises: Reading instruction in the resource room. *Exceptional Children, 64,* 211–225.

Waldron, N. L., & McLeskey, J. (1998). The effects of an inclusive school program on students with mild and severe learning disabilities. *Exceptional Children, 64,* 395–405.

Walker, H. M., & Bullis, M. (1991). Behavior disorders and the social context of regular class integration: A conceptual dilemma? In J. W. Lloyd, N. N. Singh, & A. C. Repp (Eds.), *The regular education initiative: Alternative perspectives on concepts, issues, and models* (pp. 75–93). Sycamore, IL: Sycamore.

Warnock, M. (2005). *Special educational needs: A new look. Impact No. 11*. London: Philosophy of Education Society of Great Britain.

Wasik, B. A., & Slavin, R. E. (1993). Preventing early reading failure with one-to-one tutoring: A review of five programs. *Reading Research Quarterly, 28*, 178–200.

Wenglinsky, H. (2002). How schools matter: The link between teacher classroom practices and student academic performance. *Education Policy Analysis Archives, 10*(12). Retrieved November 4, 2005 from http://epaa.asu.edu/epaa/v10n12.

Zigmond, N. (1996). Organization and management of general education classrooms. In D. Speece & B. Keogh (Eds.), *Research on classroom ecologies: Implications for inclusion of children with learning disabilities* (pp. 163–190). Mahwah, NJ: Erlbaum.

Zigmond, N. (1997). Educating students with disabilities: The future of special education. In J. W. Lloyd, E. J. Kameenui, & D. Chard (Eds.), *Issues in educating students with disabilities* (pp. 377–390). Mahwah, NJ: Erlbaum.

Zigmond, N. (2003). Where should students with disabilities receive special education services? Is one place better than another? *The Journal of Special Education, 37*, 193–199.

Zigmond, N. (2007). Delivering special education is a two-person job: A call for unconventional thinking. In J. B. Crockett, M. M., Gerber, & T. J., & Landrum (Eds.), *Achieving the radical reform of special education: Essays in honor of James M. Kauffman* (pp. 115–137). Mahwah, NJ: Erlbaum.

Zigmond, N., Jenkins, J., Fuchs, L. S., Deno, S., Fuchs, D., Baker, J., Jenkins, L., &Couthino, M. (1995). Special education in restructured schools: Findings from three multi-year studies. *Phi Delta Kappan, 76*, 531–540.

Zigmond, N., & Magiera, K. (2002). Co-teaching. *Current Practice Alerts, 6*, 1–4.

# V

# COMMENTARY ON TEACHING STUDENTS HAVING LEARNING AND BEHAVIORAL CHALLENGES

# 18

# Perspective and Commentary: The Power of Mindsets, Creating Classrooms that Nurture Resilience

## Robert B. Brooks and Sam Goldstein

The transition to evidence-based teaching practices must not be constricted by a narrow perspective focusing only on academics. The study of effective teaching practices must also encompass the social, emotional, and ethical goals of education as well. Cohen (2006) points out that we have failed to substantially integrate these goals into our curriculum and yet we are increasingly aware that these form the essential foundations for psychological and emotional well being (for review see Goldstein and Brooks, 2005). Generating evidence that addressing these goals leads to lifelong resilience will require creative, longitudinal studies. Emotional health, psychological well being, empathy, altruism, and connections with others are after all much more difficult to define and measure than reading and math grade levels, but yet they are equally important factors in assessing classroom environments and the learning process.

In this chapter, we draw upon a diverse literature including ethnographic studies and case material to provide evidence that educators must devote equal attention to social, emotional, and ethical goals as to academics if they are to adequately prepare students for the transition to and journey through, adulthood.

## TWO DIFFERING MINDSETS

### The Case of John

Parents of a high school student, John, contacted us[1] several years ago. They asked that we serve as consultants to his school program. John had been diagnosed with learning disabilities and was experiencing difficulty academically. We met with John and his teachers and asked each to describe him. One teacher immediately responded, "John is one of the most defiant, oppositional, lazy, irresponsible students we have at this school!" Another teacher looked surprised at this assessment. In a manner that was respectful of her colleague's opinion she said, "I have a different view. I think John is really struggling with learning and we should figure out the best ways to teach him." In a brief moment we heard two markedly contrasting descriptions of the same student from two adults who were interacting with him on a daily basis in school. It seemed as if they were talking about two different students. After the school meeting, we interviewed John and asked him to describe his teachers, not revealing what they had said about him. In describing the teacher who portrayed him very harshly, John said, "She hates me, but that's okay because I hate her. And I won't do any work in her class." Before we could even ask John to elaborate upon his obviously strained relationship with this particular teacher or to question the wisdom of his refusal to meet her class requirements, he blurted, "And don't tell me that I'm only hurting myself by not doing work (we assumed he was given that advice on numerous occasions). What you don't understand is that in her eyes I am a failure. Whatever I do in her class is never going to be good enough. She doesn't expect me to pass, so why even try?" He added that from the first day of class he experienced "angry vibes" from her.

"She just didn't like me and soon I didn't like her. I could tell she didn't want me in her class just by the way she spoke with me. Right away she seemed angry with me. I really don't know why she felt that way. So, after a while, I knew there was no way I could succeed in her class; so, I just decided that I wouldn't even try. It would just be a waste of time. She told me I was lazy, but if she was honest she would have to admit that she doesn't think I could ever get a good grade in her class."

John's face lit up as he described the teacher who thought that the primary issue that should be addressed was his struggle with learning. He said, "I love her. She went out of her way the first week of school to tell me something. She said that she knew I was having trouble with learning, but she thought I was smart and had to figure out the best way to teach me. She said that one of the reasons she became a teacher was to help all students learn. She's always there to help."

After hearing John's views of these two teachers, we could understand why he was a discipline problem with the first teacher but not the second. His behavior with each of them reflected what he believed to be their expectations for him. We recognize that it typically takes "two to tango" and most likely at some point John was responsible for adding fuel to the "angry vibes," thereby confirming the first teacher's negative perceptions of and expectations for him. However, as we will emphasize in this chapter, if we wish children and adolescents to change their attitudes and behaviors, the adults in their lives must have the courage and insight to change theirs first. This is important in raising or teaching all children, but perhaps more so for children beset by learning and behavioral problems who are often burdened by feelings of failure and defeatism.

### The Case of Lisa

Lisa, a nine-year-old girl, was referred by her pediatrician when she was about two months short of completing in her fourth-grade year. Her parents were concerned about "her moodiness, her tendency to be demanding, and her stubbornness." She demonstrated difficulty shifting from one activity to another and tolerating limits that were set. An earlier evaluation had led to a diagnosis of bi-polar disorder and attention deficit hyperactivity disorder. In school, Lisa often refused to do her work. Lisa's parents commented that they did not want to make excuses for her behavior, but they felt that her teacher "dismissed" her diagnosis. Her teacher told them, "The simple truth is Lisa is lazy. She could do the work if she wanted to. Also, she has to learn that she can't get her way and that you can't give in to her." They reported that the teacher recommended that they work with a behavioral specialist who could help them to become more "effective disciplinarians."

Similar to John's negative perception of one of his teachers, Lisa correctly felt her teacher did not like her. It was obvious that Lisa was a challenging child to both her parents and her teacher. When we first began to work with her, it was difficult for her to appreciate the ways in which her behaviors impacted on the teacher's negative judgments. She was prone to blame others, often using the word "unfair" to describe her lot in life. In our initial meeting with Lisa's parents, we asked them to identify Lisa's strengths. They responded that although she did like school and could be oppositional, she enjoyed reading, especially to younger children with whom she related more comfortably than with children her own age group. They added that, in general, Lisa liked to "help others out." They emphasized that if you told her to help out, she was quick to say no, but that if you said you needed her assistance, she was more likely to cooperate.

Given this description, we believed that if Lisa were involved in activities in which she helped out in school, she would feel more comfortable there, more likely to do her work, and less prone to engage in problematic behaviors. When we raised this possibility with her teacher, we were taken aback by the teacher's response. She angrily retorted that our "philosophy was to spoil children." She added that the only way she would permit Lisa to help out was if she first proved herself by doing all of her homework, meeting all of the school requirements, and not being "oppositional." The teacher said, "Lisa has to prove herself first, then I will let her help out." The remainder of the year was characterized by ongoing struggles between Lisa and her teacher with Lisa becoming increasingly sullen and resistant.

We do not wish to infer that Lisa was an easy child. As we have noted, she was not. We knew that she could easily anger people. We were also aware that engaging in a power struggle with her, which unfortunately had occurred with her fourth-grade teacher, did not motivate her to be more disciplined and cooperative, but rather prompted her to be more angry and inflexible. We wanted to lessen the probability that the same negative dynamic would emerge with her fifth-grade teacher. Consequently, we arranged to meet with her new teacher the week before the new school year began.

As we began the meeting, we were quite certain Lisa's reputation had preceded her. It had, but we were pleasantly surprised when her teacher began the meeting with the statement, "I know that Lisa has had difficulty in school. I also know that she is bright child. I'm curious what suggestions you have for making this year successful." The contrast between being told our "philosophy was to spoil children" with a request for suggestions to make the fifth-grade year successful was striking. The tension that had permeated the school meetings at the end of the fourth grade was replaced with an atmosphere of respect and a common goal of helping Lisa to feel more comfortable in school. We believed that a feeling of comfort would lessen her provocative behavior and improve her learning.

Several steps were instituted. Lisa's teacher scheduled a meeting with Lisa two days before classes began. With knowledge of Lisa's interests and strengths, she told Lisa that she could be very helpful if she were willing to assist the librarian an hour a week. She also informed Lisa that she had spoken with the kindergarten teacher who wondered if Lisa would be willing to read to kindergarten children once or twice a week for about 15 minutes. Lisa requested more information about these activities, which her teacher provided. Lisa enthusiastically accepted her teacher's requests.

The teacher then initiated a discussion that could be subsumed under the category of "crisis prevention." She said to Lisa that sometimes students don't agree with the requests that she makes about behavior in the classroom or the amount of homework she assigns. She added, "There are some rules that students have to follow so we can have a classroom where everyone feels comfortable and can learn. But if you ever feel I am being unfair or if you don't understand why I am asking you or the class to do something, I would like you to talk with me about it. I plan to tell the entire class this on the first day of school, but as long as you are here today, I wanted to mention it to you."

This very perceptive teacher then asked, "Lisa, do you know why I want students to feel comfortable to speak with me about things they may not understand or may disagree with me about?" Lisa shrugged, seeming a little hesitant to answer. Her teacher replied, "I've found that when students understand the reasons for my requests or what I am expecting in class, they are more cooperative and when students are more cooperative there are fewer problems. I really want all students to feel comfortable in school and to learn. I think you and I are going to have a good year together." Lisa's teacher told us that after she offered this comment, Lisa smiled and simply said, "Me too."

The teacher's prediction of a good year together and Lisa's affirmation of this prediction were realized. Lisa's oppositional behavior and her refusal to do work rarely appeared. Her teacher had masterfully provided Lisa with an opportunity to display her strengths and, as importantly, had provided a safety net should Lisa question the demands of the classroom. Rather than resort to an "I won't do the work" position, Lisa (as well as all of her classmates) was invited to speak with the teacher about the classroom requirements. This fifth-grade teacher's expectations were as high as those of the fourth-grade teacher, but the ways in which she communicated these expectations and the style with which she related to her students, established the foundation for Lisa to thrive in that classroom and become more resilient.

## THE POWER OF MINDSETS

The experiences of John and Lisa with their different teachers illustrate what may seem obvious but in many ways is not, namely, that we all possess different mindsets or assumptions about ourselves and others (Brooks, 2001a, b, 2004; Brooks & Goldstein, 2001, 2003, 2004; Goldstein & Brooks, 2007). These assumptions, which we may not even reflect upon or be aware of, play a significant role in determining our expectations and behavior. Even seemingly hidden assumptions have a way of being expressed to others. Not surprisingly, people begin to behave in accord with the expectations we have of them and when they do, we are apt to interpret this as a sign that our expectations are accurate. What we fail to appreciate is the extent to which our expectations subtly or not-so-subtly shape the behavior of others. This dynamic was vividly observed with both John and Lisa. Their teachers got what they expected.

If we examine the school environment, it should not be surprising to learn that educators possess many different assumptions about the process of education and about students with learning and behavioral problems. These assumptions, as was evident with John and Lisa, will determine whether at-risk students overcome adversity and are successful and resilient in school or if they continue on a downward spiral of frustration, unhappiness, and failure.

Given the power of mindsets, an important question can be raised, namely, "What is the mindset (or expectancies and assumptions) of educators who truly touch the minds and hearts of students with learning and behavior challenges and reinforce their motivation, hope, and resilience?" In our work with teachers, school administrators, and other school staff, we have found many who appreciate the need to focus not only on nurturing the intellectual lives of students but also their emotional lives, and who, through their words and actions, demonstrate a profound commitment to creating classroom environments in which all students will thrive.

These talented educators possess a mindset that directs their teaching style and their interactions with students, a mindset that strengthens a love of learning, even in those students struggling in school. The more aware educators are of the tenets of this mindset, the more they can adhere to constructive, realistic guideposts in their work with students and the more they can create resilient, sustainable classrooms (Goldstein & Brooks, 2007).

## THE ASSUMPTIONS AND MINDSET OF EFFECTIVE EDUCATORS

A number of key components comprise the mindset of educators who work effectively with at-risk students. We begin with a basic feature of this mindset, which if absent compromises all other features. It directs attention to the significance of the teacher-student relationship in promoting hope and optimism in students who often feel defeated and pessimistic about their situation improving.

### Believing that Educators Have a Lifelong Impact on Students and Their Resilience

Many students with learning and behavioral difficulties are burdened with feelings of doubt and anxiety about their future and do not envision success in the future. It is important for educators to believe that what they say and do each day in their classrooms can have a lifelong influence on their students (Brooks, 1991, 2002; Brooks & Goldstein, 2001). In our consultations to schools, we have often heard, "We know that we can have an impact on students, but this student comes from a dysfunctional family (or this student has been abused; or this student has significant behavioral problems). What can I possibly do?" We certainly appreciate this kind of question, but in response we emphasize, "For some students the only moments of sanity, security, or acceptance they will experience is in your classroom. Don't let the opportunity go by."

When educators take advantage of this opportunity, lives are changed. There are many adults who as children experienced years of frustration, failure, and humiliation and are now leading satisfying, successful lives. This prompts the question, "Why are some students with learning and behavioral problems successful as adults while others are not?" Answering this question is perhaps one of the most important tasks of teachers and other caregivers. If we can understand those factors that contribute to children bouncing back, to becoming more hopeful and resilient, then we are better equipped to design and implement interventions that will provide children a fighting chance in life.

Fortunately, during the past two decades there has been a burgeoning literature focusing on the concept of resilience (Brooks, 1994; Brooks & Goldstein, 2001, 2003, 2004; Goldstein & Brooks, 2005; Katz 1994, 1997; Mather & Ofiesh, 2005; Rutter, 1985, 1987; Thomsen, 2002; Werner, 1993; Werner & Smith, 1992). Researchers and clinicians have identified three interrelated domains that influence the emergence of resilience, namely, the inner characteristics of the child, the family, and the larger social environment (Hechtman, 1991). The inner resources of the child that contribute to resilience include an "easy" temperament from birth, solid problem-solving skills, good social skills, and effective coping strategies. Very importantly, resilient youngsters possess a high level of self-esteem, a realistic sense of personal control, a feeling of competence, and a belief that mistakes are experiences from which to learn rather than feel defeated. Brooks and Goldstein (2001) describe these attributes as part of a "resilient mindset."

Concerning the family, it is not surprising to find that resilient children are more likely to grow up in homes characterized by warmth, affection, emotional support, and clear-cut and reasonable guidelines, limits, and consequences. Supportive adults outside the immediate family have also proven to be a major source of resilience. When resilient adults were asked what they believed was one of the most important factors in their childhood or adolescence that assisted them to be resilient, invariably they responded "an adult who believed in me." Schools have been spotlighted as environments that can provide children with experiences that enhance their self-esteem and resilience. For example, Segal (1988) noted:

> From studies conducted around the world, researchers have distilled a number of factors that enable such children of misfortune to beat the heavy odds against them. One factor turns out to

be the presence in their lives of a charismatic adult—a person with whom they can identify and from whom they gather strength. And in a surprising number of cases, that person turns out to be a teacher. (p. 2)

Part of the problem is that many educators do not realize they are or have been charismatic adults in the lives of students. In our workshops for educators, we often pose two questions, the first geared for those who have been teaching at least five years or more, the second for all educators. The questions are:

> How many of you have unexpectedly received an expression of thank you via an e-mail, letter, or phone call from a former student in which the latter acknowledges the important role you played in his or her life?
>
> How many of you have written such a thank you to an educator who served as a charismatic adult in your life, but you never really conveyed your appreciation to that person?

In many of our workshops, less than 25% of those in attendance raise their hands in response to both of these questions. The implication is that even without receiving direct feedback from current or former students, the mindset of effective educators carries the following belief: Today may be the day that I say or do something that will change a student's life in a positive way and help that student to be more hopeful and resilient.

This point is eloquently captured by Tracy Kidder in his book *Among Schoolchildren* (1989):

> Teachers usually have no way of knowing that they have made a difference in a child's life, even when they have made a dramatic one. But for children who are used to thinking of themselves as stupid or not worth talking to or deserving rape and beatings, a good teacher can provide an astonishing revelation. A good teacher can give a child at least a chance to feel, "She thinks I'm worth something. Maybe I am." Good teachers put snags in the river of children passing by, and over the years, they redirect hundreds of lives. Many people find it easy to imagine unseen webs of malevolent conspiracy in the world, and they are not always wrong. But there is also an innocence that conspires to hold humanity together, and it is made up of people who can never fully know the good that they have done. (pp. 312–313)

## The Case of Nicholas

One student who communicated to his teacher the impact she had on him was 13-year-old Nicholas Walker. At the end of the school year he wrote a poem about Ms. Alex Scott, one of his eighth-grade teachers. His mother, Tammy Young, is also an educator. She told us about the impact Ms. Scott had on Nicholas, an articulate, likeable, young adolescent who struggles with learning and attention problems. Nicholas titled the poem "The Black Sea" and he wrote a moving dedication—"Dedicated to Ms. Alex Scott, the teacher who saved me."

> Before I met you
> I lay trapped beneath the black sea,
> Where the ordinary was mandatory.
> You pulled me up—unconscious,
> And waited for me to awaken.
> It took me some time,
> But I did pull through.

You taught me so much,
Now I must move on.
Your job, however, is not complete,
For others lie stranded
Beneath the Black Sea.
Waiting for you,
To reach them—like me.

Educators are in an excellent position to serve as charismatic adults for their students. They can provide angry, resistant, vulnerable, or alienated youth with experiences that enhance their self-dignity and competence, lessen their sadness and bitterness, and strengthen their resilience. In this regard, a report issued by the U.S. Department of Education (Dwyer, Osher, & Warger, 1998) about "safe schools" is well worth considering:

> Research shows that a positive relationship with an adult who is available to provide support when needed is one of the most critical factors in preventing student violence. Students often look to adults in the school community for guidance, support, and direction. Some children need help overcoming feelings of isolation and support in developing connections to others. Effective schools make sure that opportunities exist for adults to spend quality, personal time with children (pp. 3–4).

At several of our workshops, participants have stated, "I want to be a charismatic adult. What do I do?" While such a comment is often uttered with some levity, it challenges us to ask, "In addition to believing that students with learning and behavior problems can overcome adversity and be resilient, what are the other features of the mindset of effective educators that allow us to become charismatic adults in the lives of students?" In the next section, we examine some of the features of the mindset of effective educators.

### Addressing the Social-Emotional Needs of a Student Is Not an Extra Curriculum Activity

At one of our workshops, we were highlighting the significant influence that educators have on the social-emotional life of students. A high school science teacher challenged the emphasis we placed on social-emotional factors, contending, "I am a science teacher. I know my science and I know how to convey science facts to my students. Why should I have to spend time thinking about the student's emotional or social life? I don't have time to do so and it will distract me from teaching science."

We are certain that there are many teachers and school administrators who would take issue with the views expressed by this science teacher, who believe as we do that focusing on a student's social and emotional life in the classroom may be as integral as teaching specific academic skills and content (Brooks, 1999; Cohen, 1999). However, we are also aware that others would concur with this teacher's opinion, especially in today's climate of high stakes testing. It is unfortunate that a dichotomy has emerged prompting some educators to perceive that nurturing a student's emotional and social health takes valuable time away from the task of teaching academic skills and preparing students for high stakes testing.

Based on our experiences as well as the observations we have heard from many educators, strengthening a student's sense of self-esteem is not an "extra" curriculum; if anything, a student's perception of belonging, security, and self-confidence in a classroom provides the scaffolding that supports the foundation for enhanced learning, motivation, self-discipline, responsibility, and the ability to deal more effectively with obstacles and mistakes (Brooks, 1991).

This focus on social-emotional factors is of special importance when working with children and adolescents with learning disabilities. These youngsters, given their history of learning difficulty and failure, are especially vulnerable to feelings of frustration, low self-worth, and helplessness (Brooks, 1999b, 2001a; Canino, 1981; Deci, Hodges, Pierson, & Tomassone, 1992; Licht, 1983). These feelings were vividly captured in interviews and therapy we conducted with students with learning disabilities. The following are a representative sample of their comments when describing their learning disabilities:

> "I was born to quit and God made me that way."
> "It (the learning disability) makes me feel terrible. It makes me realize that there is a barrier that stops me from having a happy and successful future."
> "I always get confused. I don't think I'll ever learn. I must have half a brain."
> "I have no friends. Everyone teases me. I wish I was never born."
> "Sometimes I feel unrespected, unconfident, lower than other people. I also feel I could never do half the stuff I want to do and that makes me feel frustrated."

## The Cases of Caitlin and Matt

Caitlin was seven years old when we first met her in therapy. She had reading and attention problems, and was referred by her parents and teacher because of her lack of confidence, her frustration and disappointment about not learning to read as quickly as her peers, and her reported headaches. In therapy we invited Caitlin to write a story about her difficulties. We informed her, as we do with other children, that we often read stories written by our clients at our workshops so that parents, teachers, and doctors can gain a better understanding of how children feel and can be more helpful to them.

Caitlin was motivated to write such a story with our assistance. She decided to use as a main character a dog named Hyper who had difficulty learning and concentrating, an obvious representation of herself. The theme of low self-esteem and a feeling of hopelessness were apparent at the beginning of the story when she wrote:

> Hyper told herself that she would get over this problem some day, but she wondered if she really would. She was worried that when she grew up and her own puppies asked her something, she would not know the answer and they would wonder why their mother was not very smart. Thinking about this made Hyper feel very upset. She wasn't sure what to do about it.

We met Matt when he was a young adolescent. He was diagnosed with both learning disabilities and ADHD, was depressed, and entertained little hope for the future. His description of school reminds us of the way in which many youngsters with special needs experience school and should prompt us to become even more committed to creating school environments that truly provide accommodations for and accept students with learning and attention problems. Matt wrote:

> School has been and still is something I dread profusely. Going to school has been like climbing up a tremendous, rocky mountain with steep cliffs and jagged, slippery rocks. This mountain is very grey and always covered in dark, murky, cold clouds. I step forth to take on this task of climbing this huge mountain. Each step is a battle against strong, howling, icy winds. The winds contain frigid rain that slams against my body, trying to push me down. I keep battling my way up. Sometimes I am knocked down and sometimes I have to stop to regain my strength. My body

is numb. My hands shake like leaves in the wind as I claw myself up the mountainside. Not being able to open my eyes, I blindly claw myself up the steep cliff. I stop because I am in such great pain. I look up and see that my struggle has hardly begun. Sometimes I just do not want to go on any further.

In college, Matt, feeling more self-confident, expanded on his story of "The Mountain" and noted that the mountain could become "your grave or your greatest triumph."

Caitlin's words poignantly captured not only her low self-esteem, but also a fear expressed by many children and adolescents with learning disabilities, namely, that their condition in life will not improve. In essence, they have lost one of the most important gifts there is, the gift of hope. As you reflect upon the words of Caitlin and Matt as well as other youngsters with learning and behavioral struggles, place yourself in their shoes as they sit in a classroom. If we do not address their social-emotional concerns, their negative feelings about learning, and their sense of helplessness and hopelessness, they will not benefit from our instruction. We are not advocating that teachers become therapists, but that they recognize that the psychological readiness and emotional state of a student to learn is an integral part of the educational process.

## Believing that All Students Wish to Learn and to Succeed and If They Seem Unmotivated or Disengaged, They May Believe They Lack the Ability to Achieve in School

We often hear teachers refer to students as lazy or unmotivated. When these accusatory labels are used and a negative mindset emerges, educators are more likely to respond to these students with a lack of understanding and annoyance. The mindset of an effective educator constantly echoes, "I believe that all students come to school desiring to learn. It they are disinterested and feel defeated, we must figure out how best to reach and teach them."

Subscribing to this view has a profound impact on the ways in which we respond to students, especially those who are struggling. When students lose faith in their ability to learn and when feelings of hopelessness pervade their psyche, they are vulnerable to engaging in counterproductive or self-defeating ways of coping. They may quit at tasks, clown around, pick on other students, or expend little time and effort in academic requirements. When a student feels that failure is a foregone conclusion, it is difficult to muster the energy to consider alternative ways of mastering learning demands.

Teachers who observe such counterproductive behaviors may easily reach the conclusion that the student is unmotivated, or lazy, or not caring about school. As negative assumptions and mindsets dominate, teachers are less likely to consider more productive strategies for reaching the student. Instead, thoughts turn to punitive actions (e.g., what punishments would finally get through to the student). However, if educators subscribe to the belief that each student wishes to succeed, negative assumptions are less likely to prevail.

### Case of Sarah

A shift in perspective was obvious in a consultation we did about Sarah, a problematic high school student. One of her teachers began by asking, "Don't you think it's okay for a 16 1/2-year-old to drop out of school?" The agenda was clear. These teachers, who typically displayed a caring and encouraging attitude, were very frustrated and angry with Sarah to the extent of wishing her to leave school. The teachers elaborated that Sarah was a student who "sabotaged" all of their efforts. "Even if Sarah agrees to do something, she doesn't follow through. It's obvious that she dislikes school and she's disruptive and disrespectful. She couldn't care less about how she does in school."

As we shall see, Sarah cared a great deal about wanting to achieve in school, but entertained little hope for doing so. It was only when her teachers truly accepted that each student desperately wants to succeed that a positive mindset emerged, which permitted them to consider new solutions. A turning point occurred when we empathized with the teachers about their frustration but then asked, "Can anyone tell us how you think Sarah feels each day when she enters the school building?" After several moments of silence, one teacher responded, "How Sarah feels? I never really thought about that before."

Another teacher followed, "I never really thought about that before either, but as I'm doing so now, only one word comes to mind, defeated. I think everyday when Sarah comes in to the school building she feels defeated." As this teacher shared her observation, the shift in mindset that permeated the room was palpable, highlighted by one teacher asking us, "You've written a lot about helping kids be more confident and resilient in the school setting. So what can we do to help a student who feels defeated begin to feel less defeated?"

A lively, creative discussion ensued, filled with ideas that had not been considered previously, including having Sarah, who relished being helpful, assist in the office. The teachers also shifted their focus from what punitive action to take to a desire to "get to know" Sarah, not via a tense, confrontational meeting but rather by having lunch with her. This new approach prompted Sarah to be more responsible and a positive cycle was set in motion. The catalyst for this new cycle was when her teachers shifted their mindset, no longer viewing Sarah's behaviors as oppositional, but rather as a reflection of the despair and defeatism she experienced. They adopted the assumption that students wish to succeed, but at times obstacles appear on the road to success—obstacles that teachers working in concert with students could remove.

### If Our Strategies Are Not Effective, We Must Ask, "What Is It that I Can Do Differently?" Rather Than Continuing to Wait For the Student to Change First.

A basic underpinning of resilience is the belief of "personal control," namely, that we are the "authors of our own lives" and it makes little sense to continue to do the same thing repeatedly if our actions are not leading to positive results (Brooks & Goldstein, 2004). While many educators and others say they subscribe to this assumption, their actions frequently belie their assertion. For example, it is not unusual to hear the following statements offered by educators at consultations we have conducted:

> "This student is unmotivated to change. She just won't take responsibility for her behavior."
>
> Or, "We've been using this strategy with this student for five months. He's still not responding. He's resistant and oppositional."

We believe in perseverance, but if a staff has been employing the same approach for five months without any positive outcome, one can ask, "Who are the resistant ones here?"

As one perceptive teacher emphasized, "Asking what is it that I can do differently should not be interpreted as blaming ourselves but rather as a source of empowerment." She continued, "Isn't it better to focus on what we can do differently rather than continue to wait for someone else to change first? We may have to wait forever and continue to be frustrated and unhappy."

This same teacher summarized her belief with the statement, "If the horse is dead, get off." We have found many dead horses strewn on the grounds of a school.

## Empathy Is One of the Most Vital Skills of an Effective Educator

If teachers are to become charismatic adults, they must be empathic, placing themselves inside the shoes of their students and perceiving the world through a student's eyes. Goleman (1995) highlighted empathy as a major component of emotional intelligence.

Being empathic invites educators to ask, "Whenever I say or do things with students, am I saying or doing these things in a way that my students will be most responsive to my message? Would I want anyone to say or do to me what I am saying or doing with my students?" For example, a teacher may desire to motivate a student with learning disabilities by exhorting the student to "just try harder." While the teacher may be well-intentioned, such a remark is frequently experienced in a negative, accusatory way. When students feel accused, they are less likely to be cooperative. Consequently, the teacher's comments are not likely to lead to the desired results. However, if this teacher had been empathic, he or she would have wondered, "If I were struggling in my role as a teacher, would I want another teacher or my principal to say to me, 'If you just tried harder you wouldn't have this problem?'" We believe that the teacher would answer "no" to this question.

Instead, as noted earlier, a teacher serving as a charismatic adult would be guided by the belief that all students want to learn and to succeed. If students are not succeeding, such a teacher would ask, "What is it I can do differently so that this student can learn more effectively?" Guided by this mindset, the teacher might replace the accusatory words "try harder" with, "I think one of the reasons you are having trouble learning is that I am not using the best strategies to teach you or perhaps you are not using the best strategies to learn. We have to figure out what are the best ways for me to teach and you to learn." This statement is free of accusation and judgment, inviting students with learning problems to join with us rather than resent and avoid us.

To highlight the significance of empathy, we have asked educators at our workshops to think of a teacher they liked and one that they did not like when they were students. We next ask them to think of words they would use to describe each of these teachers. We observe, "Just as you have words to describe your teachers, your students have words to describe you?" We then pose the following questions:

"What words would you hoped your students used to describe you?"
"What have you done in the past month or two so they are likely to use these words?"
"What words would they actually use to describe you?"
"How close would the words you hope they use parallel the words they would actually use?"
"If the descriptions are not close, what do you plan to do so that the words they would actually use become similar to the words you hope they would use?"

Another exercise that educators have found useful in reinforcing empathy is to recruit their own memories of school when they were students. We have asked teachers and school administrators:

"Of all the memories you have as a student, what is one of your favorite ones, something that a teacher or school administrator said or did that boosted your motivation and self-dignity?"
"Of all the memories you have as a student, what is one of your worst ones, something a teacher or school administrator said or did that eroded your motivation and self-dignity?"
"As you reflect upon both your positive and negative memories of school, what did you learn

from both and do you use these memories to guide what you are doing with your students today?"

Recalling one's own positive and negative memories of school, especially as a group exercise with one's colleagues, often proves to be very emotional, prompting educators to ask:

"What memories are my students taking from their interactions with me?"
"Are they the memories I would like them to take?"
"If not, what must I do to change so that the memories they take will be in concert with the memories I hope they take?"

Teachers who appreciate the importance of empathy as a critical teaching skill regularly ask these questions of themselves. We have been fortunate to meet teachers who have assumed a proactive stance by requesting anonymous feedback from students; they have had the courage to ask students to draw and describe them, to list what they like about the class and what they would like to see changed. Such an exercise communicates the message to students, "I respect your opinion. I value your input. You are a vital participant in the learning process." Empathic educators connect more effectively and constructively with students so that learning is enhanced.

## We Must Define and Create "Motivating Environments"

Educators who touch the hearts and minds of students consider what they must do to create what we have called "motivating environments," that is, environments in which students are eager to participate and cooperate. While motivating environments are of benefit to all children, they hold special value for youngsters with learning and behavioral problems who have experienced little, if any, success in school. If anything, the main motivation of many of these students is to avoid the learning task, a task that they perceive as leading to further frustration and failure. Given the strength-based model to which we subscribe, we have been drawn to two frameworks that offer a blueprint for designing such an environment.

## Attribution Theory

One promising framework originally proposed by psychologist Bernard Weiner (Weiner, 1974) and applied by many clinicians and researchers to students with special needs is called "attribution theory" (Brooks, 1991; Canino, 1981; Licht, 1983). Children encounter numerous challenges as they grow, some of which result in success, others in failure. What attribution theory highlights is that youngsters assume different reasons for why they succeed or fail and that these reasons, which vary from one child to the next, are strongly tied to their self-esteem and subsequent motivation. In terms of success experiences, research indicates that children with high self-esteem believe that their successes are determined in large part by their own efforts, resources, and abilities. These youngsters assume realistic credit for their accomplishments and feel a genuine sense of control over their lives. They are typically children who experience success early in their life within a responsive and encouraging environment. They are likely to be very motivated to face new challenges (Brooks & Goldstein, 2001).

In contrast, youth who have encountered many frustrations and disappointments and whose self-esteem has suffered erosion are more likely to assume that their achievements are predicated on luck, or chance, or fate, on variables outside of their control, thus weakening their confidence of being able to succeed in the future. For instance, we have worked with many children with learning problems who quickly dismiss a high grade with such comments as, "I was lucky" or "The teacher made the test easy." These children minimize the role that they have played in achieving any success; unfortunately, the cumulative effect of perceived failure outweighs any success experiences.

Self-esteem and motivation are also strongly implicated in how children comprehend their mistakes and failure. As an example, two children in the same third-grade class have failed a spelling test. One child thinks, "I can do better than this. Maybe I have to study more or ask the teacher for extra help." The second child explains the low grade by saying, "The teacher stinks. He never told us these words would be on the test. It's his fault I failed." Or, to take another example, a child who felt he was incapable of learning, constantly hit other students. As he gained insight into his difficulties, he told us in therapy, "I'd rather hit another kid and be sent to the principal's office than have to be in the classroom where I felt like a dummy."

The child who is willing to seek additional help and/or work more diligently, basically believes that mistakes are experiences from which to learn rather than feel defeated. Such children typically attribute making mistakes to factors that are within their power to modify, such as a lack of effort (especially if the task is realistically achievable) or ineffective strategies (e.g., poor study habits). In marked contrast, students who resort to blaming or hitting others typically adhere to the painful view that "I am a failure, I cannot change. I cannot do well." Rather than believing that mistakes are the foundation for future learning, children with low self-esteem frequently experience each new mistake as another rock being placed around their necks, weighing them down more and more. To such youngsters mistakes result from conditions that cannot be easily modified, such as lack of ability or low intelligence; given this belief, their motivation suffers and often their anger increases.

A vicious cycle is set in motion when children believe they cannot learn from mistakes. Feeling hopeless and wishing to avoid further perceived humiliation, they are apt to quit, offer excuses, cast blame on others, or resort to other ineffective ways of coping, such as assuming the role of class clown or class bully. As these youngsters reach teenage years, our attempts to teach and encourage them may be met with angry retorts such as "Leave me alone!" "I don't care!" "It's my life and I'll do what I want with it" and/or acting out behaviors. It has been our experience that these children care much more than they acknowledge, but feeling hopeless and believing they are unable to change their situation, they do not even want to entertain the notion that things may improve—for them, any hope is false hope that eventuates in further disappointment. While the adults in their lives may believe that such youngsters are quitters or lack perseverance or are bullies, what we often fail to comprehend is that these behaviors are rooted in a sense of hopelessness and a desperate attempt to avoid further humiliation (Brooks, 2004). Working with these at-risk youth involves helping to change their negative attributions and mindsets (Brooks, 2002; Brooks & Goldstein, 2001).

Attribution theory offers significant guideposts for designing classroom climates that will reinforce the self-confidence and motivation of angry and defiant students. The following questions stem from this theory:

1. How do we create a school environment that maximizes the probability that students will not only succeed but that they will experience their achievements as predicated in large measure on their own abilities and efforts? Or, stated somewhat differently, how do we assist youngsters to assume an increasing sense of ownership and responsibility for what occurs in their lives?

2. How do we create a school environment that reinforces the belief that mistakes are frequently the foundation for learning, that mistakes are not only *accepted*, but *expected*?

How do we create an environment that lessens fears of being humiliated or embarrassed, fears that often trigger sadness and anger?

## Deci's Approach to Self-Esteem and Motivation

A second framework that we have found helpful is based on the work of psychologist Edward Deci who has studied self-esteem and motivation through the lens of youngsters' needs (Deci & Chandler, 1986; Deci & Flaste, 1995; Deci, Hodges, Pierson, & Tomassone, 1992). A great deal of Deci's research has involved children with learning problems. His model has many similarities to Glasser's (1997) "choice theory" (formerly called "control theory") and the work of Brendtro, Brokenleg, and Van Bockern (1990). It suggests that youngsters will be more motivated to engage and persevere at school tasks when the adults in their lives have created a school environment that satisfies basic needs. Deci highlights the following three needs that provide direction for fostering self-esteem and motivation:

1. To belong and feel connected. Youngsters are more likely to thrive when they are in environments in which they feel they belong and are comfortable, in which they feel appreciated. Many adolescents join gangs to satisfy this need for connectedness and identity. When youngsters feel alienated or detached they are more likely to act out and fail at school (Strahan, 1989). Related to this feeling of belonging, is the importance of helping each child to feel welcome in the school environment. When we asked students of all ages what a teacher could do each day to help them to feel welcome in school, the two most frequent responses we received were: (a) being greeted warmly by a teacher who uses your name, and (b) having a teacher smile at you. Obviously, small gestures can go a long way toward assisting at-risk children to feel welcome at school and in other environments. If students do not feel welcome, they are more prone to becoming angry.

2. To feel autonomous and have a sense of self-determination. At the core of most theories of self-esteem and motivation, including attribution theory, is the concept of ownership and self-determination (Brooks, 1991). Motivation is increased when people genuinely believe that their voice is being heard and respected and they feel they have some control over what is occurring in their lives (Dicintio & Gee, 1999). If students feel they are constantly being told what to do and that their lives are being dictated by adults, they are less likely to be enthused about engaging in learning tasks that they feel are being imposed upon them. If anything, their main motivation may be to avoid or oppose the desires of others. A power struggle or angry outbursts are likely to ensue. An emphasis on reinforcing self-determination requires that educators use classroom experiences to teach youngsters how to solve problems and make wise choices and decisions. In addition, we must provide these children with ongoing opportunities to develop and refine these skills.

3. To feel competent. We all hope to be successful, to possess skills in our lives that help us feel competent and accomplished, skills that generate satisfaction and pride. Unfortunately, many children do not feel competent. As we have noted, feelings of incompetence, which are often associated with anger and sadness, prompt children to retreat from challenges and to engage in self-defeating behaviors, including aggression, that serve to intensify an already difficult problem.

All students require positive feedback and encouragement from educators. However, a focus on encouragement should never be confused with giving false praise or inflated grades since children are quite perceptive in knowing when they are receiving undeserved positive evaluations.

Positive feedback must be rooted in actual accomplishment and success. This requires teachers to provide opportunities for children to succeed in areas judged important by themselves and others. Their accomplishments should be displayed for others to see (what good is listing a child's strengths on an educational plan, for example, if no one witnesses these strengths?).

In addition, a focus on competencies and positive feedback is not mutually exclusive with offering feedback to correct a child's performance or behavior. However, corrective feedback must be undertaken in a nonaccusatory, nonjudgmental manner that does not humiliate the child. Instead, corrective feedback is most effective when presented to the student as a problem to be solved.

To assist at-risk students to feel competent, educators must identify and reinforce what we have termed each student's "islands of competence" (Brooks, 1991; Brooks & Goldstein, 2001). These islands are areas that are (or have the potential to be) sources of pride and accomplishment. Researchers and clinicians have emphasized the importance of identifying and reinforcing islands of competence in promoting self-esteem, motivation, and resilience. For instance, Rutter (1985), in describing resilient individuals, observed, "Experience of success in one arena of life led to enhanced self-esteem and a feeling of self-efficacy, enabling them to cope more successfully with subsequent life challenges and adaptation" (p. 604). Katz (1994) proposed, "Being able to showcase our talents, and to have them valued by important people in our lives, helps us to define our identities around that which we do best" (p. 10).

## The Case of Billy

The case of a young boy who was referred to us offers a vivid illustration of the importance of identifying a child's islands of competence. Billy was an angry and depressed ten-year-old boy with learning and behavior problems who dealt with his anxieties about school by bullying peers or hiding behind the bushes of the school instead of entering the building. In our first session, we discussed with Billy why he hid behind the bushes. He responded quickly and directly, "I like the bushes better than I like school." Rather than engage in a debate about the merits of bushes versus schools, we decided to discover what he saw as his islands of competence. He responded that he enjoyed taking care of his pet dog. With his permission, we mentioned Billy's expertise in taking care of animals to the school principal, suggesting that the school might benefit from the presence of a "pet monitor."

The following day the principal scheduled a meeting with Billy. He told Billy that there were pets in many of the classrooms and each class took care of its own pet. However, he added, "I want to make certain that all of the pets are well taken care of and I would like you to become the first pet monitor the school has ever had." He even handed Billy a pet monitor "union card" that he had created to emphasize the position's importance.

Billy asked about a pet monitor's responsibilities. The principal responded that initially Billy would be expected to come to school 10 minutes early each day to take care of a rabbit the school had recently purchased and would soon be responsible for checking on the welfare of the other pets as well.

Billy accepted the offer and handled his duties in a very responsible manner, in marked contrast to his history with academic requirements. Within a short time, he began to take care of other pets. Billy's teacher communicated how impressed she was with his knowledge of pets and helped him to write a manual about animal care. Billy had always been reluctant to write, but under these circumstances his hesitancy disappeared since he felt more confident and recognized that he had information to communicate. His manual was bound and placed in the school library. In addition, by the end of the school year, Billy "lectured" in every classroom in the building about taking care of pets.

Billy's aggressive outbursts and his avoidance of the school building decreased significantly once he assumed the position of pet monitor and had opportunities to display his islands of competence. Very importantly, Billy's teacher and principal had been willing to take a risk and change the way in which they had been approaching his avoidant behavior. Rather than seeing Billy as a "resistant," annoying child who had to change his behavior, they had the courage to ask what they could do differently so that he would not feel like a failure in school.

## Understanding and Implementing Strategies to Foster Motivation, Hope, and Resilience and Incorporating an "Orientation Period"

A number of classroom strategies, predicated on resilience research, attribution theory, and Deci's framework, build upon the strengths or islands of competence of students to reinforce their level of confidence, motivation, hope, and resilience. These strategies are especially important for students with learning and behavior difficulties. The following are a selected group of these interventions together with some recommendations for the implementation of an "orientation" period at the beginning of the school year.

### Intervention and Recommendation #1

*Developing Realistic Expectations and Goals and Making Accommodations in a Student's Educational Program whenIndicated.*    We are frequently asked at our workshops, "What are realistic expectations and goals for students in a particular grade?" Without avoiding the question, we typically answer, "We don't know. First, tell us about the student and then we can decide what are realistic expectations and goals." While there is a great deal of overlap among students, our response is to highlight their differences as well and the importance of respecting and honoring the unique learning abilities and capabilities of each student.

Although a wealth of research proves that children have different temperaments from birth (Chess & Thomas, 1987; Keogh, 2003), possess different learning styles (Levine, 1994, 2002; Rief & Heimburge, 1996), and that multiple intelligences are distributed differently among children (Gardner, 1983), we believe that all too often we give lip service to accepting children for whom they are; instead we respond to students as if they were a homogeneous group. When we fail to make appropriate accommodations based on the unique attributes of each student, children are more likely to fail and become sad and angry and either withdraw or display aggressive outbursts. This scenario is often seen in the school environment, especially with students with learning and attention problems.

Even with our increasing knowledge of individual differences among students, it is not unusual to hear a teacher say that it would not be "fair" to offer accommodations for one child because how would the other children feel. We can understand the teacher's point of view, but we also believe that if children are different, the least fair thing we can do is to treat them all the same. If we do not teach students in the ways that they are able to learn best, then we will continue to have many youngsters who feel mistreated, ill-at-ease, alienated, and angry in our schools. However, the issue of fairness must be addressed lest other students begin to resent those students who are receiving accommodations.

One suggestion we advocate is for schools to use the first couple of days of the new school year as an "orientation" period (Brooks, 1999). During this period, teachers would not take out any books, but instead would use the time to set the foundation for a classroom climate in which all students would have the opportunity to thrive. Key questions and concerns would be considered and possible obstacles to learning would be confronted before they became obstacles.

As an illustration, to minimize the possibility of children feeling a teacher is unfair because some children might be doing more reading or homework than others, on the first day of school, the teacher can discuss with the class how each one of them is different, how some students can read more quickly than others, that some can solve math problems more efficiently, and that some can run a mile in less time than others. The teacher can say that in light of these differences, there will be different expectations of the amount and kind of work that is done by each student.

Next, the teacher can say, "Since I will treat each of you somewhat differently because you are different, one of my concerns is if you begin to feel I am not being fair it will interfere with your learning. Thus, if at any time during the year you feel I am not being fair, I want you to tell me so that we can discuss it."

Feedback we have received indicates that when a teacher brings up the issue of "fairness" before it has become an issue, it remains a non-issue and permits teachers to accommodate to each student's needs without negative feelings emerging. It lessens frustration and the anger and sadness that are typically by-products of frustration. We also suggest that teachers communicate the same message about fairness to parents, perhaps through a short, written statement of class philosophy that is sent home. This will help teachers and parents to be on the same page.

The kinds of accommodations we typically recommend do not require major modifications in a student's program, nor do they demand that a teacher develop extremely different educational plans for each student in the classroom. We believe that effective accommodations need not be complicated. What is required is that all parties—students, teachers, therapists, parents—appreciate a child's strengths and weaknesses, share an understanding of appropriate expectations and goals, and define what each has to do to maximize the probability of success in meeting these goals. We must help at-risk students to understand their strengths and vulnerabilities and the accommodations that will help them to succeed. Realistic expectations lessen frustration and disappointment. A few examples of typical accommodations follow.

Some youngsters experience attending school as the equivalent of climbing Mt. Everest each day. Then, they are required to do homework after school, which one student claimed was "like climbing Mt. Everest twice each day." If students have learning problems, they often must spend two or three times as long to do homework than their peers. By bedtime they are frustrated and exhausted, as are their parents. Commonsense would dictate that a time limit be established for homework, regardless of how much work is actually finished. For example, if most students can complete a homework assignment in an hour, then the limit should be approximately an hour for all students even those with special needs. Some might contend that this approach will result in some students not completing as many of the problems as other students in the class and thus, not learning as much of the material; however, to ask these children to spend several more hours per evening on homework will typically prove counterproductive and may intensify sadness and defiance.

Students with learning or attention problems usually encounter more difficulty taking timed tests than their peers. As one child with learning difficulties once asked us with tears in his eyes, "Why did they ever invent timed tests?" We have witnessed the test scores of students increase noticeably when taking untimed tests and yet, they only required another 10 minutes. With the pressure of a timed test removed, the students were more relaxed.

Similarly, some students will display far more of what they know when answering questions orally, than when having to write these same answers. We should test students under the best possible conditions for them to display their knowledge. These kinds of accommodations should not be viewed as spoiling these youngsters, but rather as treating them with fairness and dignity. In doing so, we lessen the probability of acting out behaviors.

We have worked with many youth who engage in ongoing battles with parents about homework. The nightly routine is filled with frustration and anger, and family harmony is almost nonexistent. The reasons that students do not do homework are varied. Among them are difficulties copying homework assignments from the blackboard. Providing the child with a monthly "syllabus" of assignments (it is interesting to note, that professors in colleges typically distribute a syllabus for the entire semester during the first class—we're not certain why we cannot do the same in our elementary, middle schools, and high schools) can be helpful as well as assigning a "buddy" to ensure that the child has an accurate picture of what homework is required.

A number of books are lost being transported between home and school. We have found that providing two sets of books to a student, one for home, the other for school, so that no textbooks have to go back and forth, has served as a helpful intervention for many students. It is one less pressure that students have to worry about, giving them more time to focus on learning the material in the books and less time to be angry or depressed. In addition, the necessary books are always available, rather than being left in a locker at school the night before an exam.

### Intervention and Recommendation #2

*Developing Responsibility by Providing Opportunities to Contribute to Others.* When children develop a sense of accomplishment and pride, they are less likely to feel sad or angry and less likely to engage in defiant, uncooperative behaviors. It is therefore essential to provide youth with opportunities for assuming responsibilities, especially those that help them to feel that they are making a contribution to their home, school, or community environments. The experience of making a positive difference in the lives of others reinforces self-respect and a sense of hope. It serves as a powerful antidote to feelings of defeat, anger, and despair (Brooks, 1991). Self-esteem and motivation are enhanced when youngsters believe they are making a positive difference to others. As Werner (1993) has noted from the findings of her longitudinal study of resilience:

> Self-esteem and self-efficacy also grew when youngsters took on a responsible position commensurate with their ability, whether it was part-time paid work, managing the household when a parent was incapacitated, or, most often, caring for younger siblings. At some point in their young lives, usually in middle childhood and adolescence, the youngsters who grew into resilient adults were required to carry out some socially desirable task to prevent others in their family, neighborhood, or community from experiencing distress or discomfort. (p. 511)

The child who was asked to become the "pet monitor" of the school is an example of a youngster making a contribution. Other examples include an educator that we know who enlisted adolescents with learning difficulties to create piggy banks to sell and sponsor a bake sale and raffle, with the proceeds going to a needy family. The educator noted that the students' self-esteem and cooperation improved as did the many academic skills that were involved in the charitable project. Another example involved an elementary school we visited in which fifth graders were "buddies" with kindergarten and first-grade students. They would spend time each week with their buddies in a variety of possible activities including reading to them, helping them with their work, or playing a sport with them. All of the students benefited from this approach and we were impressed by the atmosphere of cooperation that permeated the building. A third example involved a school social worker who established a committee composed of five elementary school students who were often absent from school. The committee focused on the question of what prompted students to be absent and the five students engaged in "research" to answer the question. Not only did they prepare a report of their findings, but they also recommended keeping track of the attendance of first graders and intervening early for all first graders who were absent a great deal. Since becoming members of this committee the attendance and behavior of the five students improved significantly. They now had a reason to come to school. Their input was valued.

In addition, youngsters can take care of plants in school, or paint murals on the wall, or hang up favorite drawings. Requesting students to decorate the walls of a school is a strong antidote to vandalism. Co-operative learning as well as tutoring younger children is also a powerful way of increasing a sense of belonging and competence in the school setting (Brooks, 1991). We are reminded of the impressive results of the Valued Youth Partnership Program reported by the Carnegie Council on Adolescent Development (Hornbeck, 1989). This highly successful program, which involved at-risk older students assisting younger students, was developed to address the large percentage of youth dropping out of school before they reached high school. The Carnegie report described:

> A rise in tutors' self-esteem is the most noticeable effect of the program. . . . As a result, only 2 percent of all tutors have dropped out of school. This is remarkable, given that all of these students had been held back twice or more and were reading at least two grade levels below their current grade placement. Disciplinary problems have become less severe, grades have improved, and attendance of tutors has soared. (p. 47)

## Intervention and Recommendation #3

*Providing Opportunities for Making Choices and Decisions and Solving Problems: Reinforcing a Sense of Ownership.*    Theories of self-esteem and motivation as well as research about hope and resilience emphasize the importance of reinforcing the belief that one has some control over one's life (Brooks & Goldstein, 2004). A sense of powerlessness is often one trigger for anger and a failure to meet the requirements of school. To develop a sense of control, ownership, and autonomy, children require opportunities to learn the skills necessary to make sound choices and decisions and to solve problems. They also need opportunities, in keeping with their developmental level and interests, to apply and develop these skills, especially in those situations that have an impact on their lives (Adelman & Taylor, 1983; Deci & Chandler, 1986; Deci & Flaste, 1995; Deci, Hodges, Pierson, & Tomassone, 1992; Dicintio & Gee, 1999; Glasser, 1997; Kohn, 1993; Shure, 1994; Shure & Aberson, 2005).

If children and adolescents feel that they are always being told what to do, if they feel they have little control over their lives, they are less likely to be cooperative. Teachers and other professionals have many opportunities to reinforce problem-solving and decision-making skills, which is an especially important goal when teaching students with learning and behavior problems; some examples follow.

We spoke with a group of teachers who always offered their students a choice in what homework problems to do. For example, if there were eight math problems on a page, the students were told that they had to do six of the eight and it was their choice which six to do. The teachers told us that they actually received more homework on a regular basis when permitting their students some choice since it reinforced a sense of ownership for doing the homework. Similarly, a resource room teacher found that students were more likely to write when he gave them several pens each with a different color ink and asked them which color they would most like to use on that day. When students are provided these kinds of options, they are less likely to view school as an unbending, rigid environment.

Teachers should incorporate time in a class schedule to elicit the input of students about solving particular problems. Assisting students to articulate what the problem is, to think of possible solutions to the problems, and to consider the likely consequences of each solution, increases the probability of children not only learning to solve problems, but also following through on the solutions (especially since they have helped to formulate the solutions). For instance, when the first author was principal of a school in the locked door unit of a psychiatric hospital, he established a Student Council; the opportunity and structure for the student patients to discuss their concerns and criticisms noticeably lessened hostility while increasing a more responsible attitude.

From an early age, we must involve students in providing input about their own education. An article in *Teacher Magazine* (Jacobson, 1999) titled, "Three's Company" about parent-teacher conferences supports this belief:

> When Michelle Baker first learned that her son Colin would take part in a parent-teacher conference, she was skeptical. "I thought, This is going to be a fiasco," she recalls. Instead, the meeting turned out to be a big success: Colin showed unusual insight into his academic strengths and weaknesses. "He had the opportunity to hear his teacher talk about him with him sitting there," Baker says. "He was able to communicate and understand better what he was being judged on." (p. 23)

It is interesting to note that Colin was only in the first grade.

## Intervention and Recommendation #4

*Establishing Self-discipline by Learning to Discipline with Respect.*   As might be expected, many of the questions asked at our workshops, especially about students with behavior problems, revolve around the issue of discipline. In turn, we frequently ask the audience to reflect upon the purpose of discipline. Not surprisingly, the first response we typically receive focuses on the importance of establishing rules and guidelines in order to ensure that our home and school environments are safe and that both children and caregivers feel secure. We are in total agreement with this purpose of discipline, especially since we have seen what can occur in an environment in which rules, limits, and consequences are vague and inconsistently followed.

However, we must not lose sight of a second very important purpose of discipline, namely, to promote self-discipline and self-control in children and adolescents. It is difficult to conceive of children developing high self-esteem, motivation, and resilience if they do not possess a comfortable sense of self-discipline, that is, a realistic ability to reflect upon their behavior and its impact on others, and then to change the behavior if necessary (Brooks & Goldstein, 2001). In essence, self-discipline implies ownership for one's own discipline.

Before examining more closely strategies that nurture self-discipline without a loss of self-esteem, we believe that one point about discipline deserves special mention. As much as possible, parents, teachers, and other professionals should anticipate those situations that may prove very difficult for particular youngsters, situations that are likely to result in disruptive behaviors. We should consider ways to help children either avoid these situations, until we know that they are better able to manage them, or to provide them with alternative behaviors. One illustration of a preventative approach was the child who was appointed the "pet monitor." Other examples teacher have implemented include: (a) having an active child take messages to the office every half hour to provide needed physical activity, and (b) asking a disruptive child who was constantly being sent to the assistant principal's office for disciplinary purposes, to become the "assistant to the assistant principal." This position required the child to work in the assistant principal's office for a short time at the beginning of each day. The disruptive behavior ceased, especially as the child formed a more positive relationship with the assistant principal and the latter's secretary. In addition, the child's self-esteem and cooperation increased.

Even if we create school environments that lessen the probability of students misbehaving, we still know that children will, at times, act in ways that invite disapproval from other peers and adults. Many angry and resistant students require more limits and guidelines than their peers, but they are the first to experience limits as significant impositions on their life, arguing that the teachers are not being "fair." We must remember that discipline stems from the word disciple and should be understood as part of a teaching process. In helping children to develop self-discipline, it is essential not to humiliate or intimidate them (Charney, 1991; Curwin & Mendler, 1988; Mendler, 1992). Humiliation and intimidation are more likely to result in increased anger and uncooperativeness, the very feelings and behaviors we wish to change.

If we want students to assume responsibility for their actions and to perceive rules as being fair, they must understand the purpose of the rules and participate within reason in the process of creating these rules and the consequences that follow should the rules be broken (Brooks, 1991; Gathercoal, 1997; Marshall & Weisner, 2004; Nelsen, Lott, & Glenn, 1997). Adults often walk a tightrope when discipline is involved, maintaining a delicate balance between rigidity and flexibility, striving to blend warmth, nurturance, acceptance, and humor with realistic expectations, clear-cut guidelines, and logical and natural consequences; several examples follow.

An assistant principal of a middle school asked students to write a brief essay while serving detention. They were given a choice of over 30 topics including what they would do if they ran the school, what they could do in the future to avoid detention, or what dreams they had for their future. As we reviewed some of the themes the students had written about, we were impressed with their ability to reflect upon their lives and their behaviors and to consider alternative ways of behaving in the future. In addition, the exercise led to a decrease in defiant behaviors.

During the "orientation" period in the first couple of days of school, teachers may ask students what rules they considered necessary in the classroom or school, the best ways to remember these rules (so that adults did not have to remind or "nag" them), and the most effective consequences when rules are broken. Students should also be informed about nonnegotiable rules that are related to safety and security issues. Although some teachers have voiced reservations about allowing students to have an input in the creation of rules and consequences (they predicted that students would take advantage of the opportunity and eliminate all rules), we have found that the students often create rules and consequences similar to those of the teacher. If anything, many teachers have reported that they must help students with behavior problems to develop less rigid and harsh rules and consequences.

The key point is that students are more likely to remember and adhere to rules that they have helped to create since they feel a greater sense of ownership for these rules (McGinnis, Frederick, & Edwards, 1995; Rademacher, Callahan, & Pederson-Seelye, 1998). In addition, if students have a difficult time following their own rules, teachers can use their difficulty as an opportunity to discuss more effective ways of remembering these rules.

One other important point about discipline is that perhaps the most powerful forms of discipline involve positive feedback and encouragement. We will include a discussion of this when we consider ways to help students feel appreciated (point #6).

## Intervention and Recommendation #5

*Helping Children to Deal More Effectively with Mistakes and Failure.*   All children worry about making mistakes and feeling foolish. Students with learning and behavior problems are typically more self-conscious and/or worried about making mistakes than their peers. As attribution theory highlights, these children often believe that mistakes cannot be modified and are an ongoing source of embarrassment and humiliation. Many children spend more time and energy attempting to avoid a task they believe will result in failure than in seeking solutions. This avoidance is often manifested in seemingly oppositional behaviors. Since self-esteem and resilience are linked to a child's response to mistakes and failure, we must convey the message to students that mistakes are part of the learning process. We can do so in a number of ways.

Parents, teachers, and other professionals serve as models. We frequently ask youngsters to describe how their parents or teachers handle mistakes or frustrations. We have heard a wide array of responses including, "They scream," "They yell," "They don't talk with each other," "They walk around with a frown on their face, " "They blame us." Obviously, these parents and teachers are not modeling an effective way of dealing with frustration.

Similarly, teachers must reflect upon how they respond to a child's mistakes. This implies that we must have realistic expectations for children and not overreact to their mistakes or shortcomings. All of us from time to time become frustrated with the behavior of youngsters, but we must avoid disparaging remarks such as: "You have to pay closer attention" or "Were you listening to what I had to say?" The goal is to communicate that mistakes will occur and we should learn from them. We can also invite a child to problem solve by asking what might help to minimize the mistake from occurring in the future.

Since the fear of failure has such a strong influence in classrooms, it should be addressed directly even before any student makes a mistake. This can be accomplished during the "orientation" period. One illustration is for a teacher to ask at the beginning of the new school year, "Who in this class feels that he or she is going to make a mistake or not understand something in class this year?" Before any of the students can respond, the teacher raises his or her own hand and then asks why they think this question was posed. The students' responses can serve as a catalyst to discuss how fears of making mistakes interfere with offering opinions, answering questions, and learning. The teacher can then engage the class in problem solving by asking what he or she can do as their teacher and what they can do as a class to minimize the fear of failing and looking foolish.

To acknowledge openly the fear of failure renders it less potent and less destructive. Early in the school year youngsters can be taught that not understanding material is to be expected and that the teacher's job is to help them to learn. Mistakes can be "celebrated" as part of the educational process. This intervention for dealing with mistakes is important for all students, but even more so for those youngsters who feel insecure, vulnerable, and angry.

Adults who focus on children's strengths and capabilities rather than on what they cannot do lessen children's fear of failure. For instance, the seemingly simple practice of teachers marking tests by adding points for correct answers rather than subtracting points for incorrect answers places the spotlight on the positive. At one school, teachers used green rather than red ink, feeling that the use of red ink for indicating errors on papers had a negative impact on children. The students we interviewed were strong supporters of this practice.

### Intervention and Recommendation #6

*Letting Students Know that They Are Welcome and Appreciated.*    In our workshops we often ask the audience, "In the past week or two, what have you done to help another person to feel appreciated?" We pose this question since we have found that although most of us are thrilled to receive a note or phone call of appreciation, many well-intentioned people do not make use of opportunities to show appreciation. We are reminded of an article about discipline that we once read that contended that many adults have a "praise deficit." We must make certain that we find ways to welcome and appreciate all students and not just those who are cooperative and well-liked.

Self-esteem, motivation, hope, and resilience are nurtured when we convey appreciation and encouragement to students, when we become the "charismatic adults" in their lives. Words and actions that communicate encouragement are always welcome and energizing. They are vital for at-risk students, many of whom are burdened with anger and self-doubt, and may not at first accept the positive feedback. However, we must persevere and never forget that even a seemingly small gesture of appreciation can generate a long lasting positive effect; examples follow.

We met a high school teacher who each year had more than 150 students in his different classes. At the beginning of the school year, he told his students that he planned to call each of them at least twice at home in the evening during the school year to find out how they were doing. He told us that the practice took only about seven to eight minutes an evening, but had very positive effects, including students being more respectful and more disciplined in class, and doing their homework more regularly. This particular teacher was gifted in knowing how to help his students to feel welcome and appreciated. Similarly, research indicates that when students have at least one adult in school who they feel cares about them and is an advocate for them, they are less likely to be violent or drop out and more likely to attend (Brooks, 1991, 2002).

Schools can hold recognition assemblies not just to acknowledge the achievements of students with high grades, but also to spotlight the islands of competence of students whose grades do not qualify for the honor role, but who have made other contributions to the school environment.

## We Must Learn to Take Care of Ourselves, Striving to Become Stress Hardy Rather than Stressed Out

At the conclusion of one of our workshops, a teacher said, "I love your ideas, but I'm too stressed out to use them." While the remark had a humorous tone, it also captured an important consideration. At first glance, the remark seems paradoxical since numerous educators have informed us that the strength-based approach and strategies we advocate, especially for working with challenging students, do not take time away from teaching, but rather help create a classroom environment that is more conducive to learning and less stressful. Yet, we can appreciate their frustration that change requires additional time, a commodity that is not readily available. Some are hesitant to leave their "comfort zone" even when this zone is filled with stress and pressure. They would rather continue with a known situation that is less than satisfying than engage in the task of entering a new, unexplored territory that holds promise but also uncertainty.

If educators are to become charismatic adults who apply many of the ideas described in this chapter, they must venture from their "comfort zone" and utilize techniques for dealing with the stress and pressure that are inherent in their work. Each teacher can discover his or her own ways for managing stress. For instance, some can rely on exercise, others on relaxation or meditation techniques, all of which can be very beneficial. In addition to these approaches, research conducted by Kobasa and her colleagues (Holt, Fine, & Tollefson, 1987; Kobasa, Maddi, & Kahn, 1982; Martinez, 1989) under the label of "stress hardiness" examines the characteristics or mindset of individuals who experience less stress than their colleagues while working in the same environment.

This mindset involves "3 C's" (the first letter of each of the words of the mindset begins with the letter "C"). The three components are interrelated and when we describe them at our workshops we encourage educators to reflect upon how they might apply this information to lessen stress and burnout.

The first "C" represents "commitment." Stress hardy individuals do not lose sight of why they are doing what they are doing. They maintain a genuine passion or purpose for their work. While we may all have "down" days, it is sad to observe educators who basically say to themselves each morning in a resigned way, "I've got to go to school. I've got to see those kids." Once a feeling of "I've got to" or "being forced to" pervades one's mindset, a sense of commitment and purpose is sacrificed, replaced by feelings of stress and burnout. As an antidote to burnout, a staff meeting might be dedicated to sharing why one became a teacher, a school administrator, a counselor, a nurse, or a school psychologist. Such an exercise helps staff to recall and invigorate their dreams and goals.

The second "C" is for "challenge." Educators who deal more effectively with stress have developed a mindset that views difficult situations as opportunities for learning and growth rather than as stress to avoid. For example, a principal of a school faced a challenging situation. Her school was located in a neighborhood that had changed in a few short years from a middle-class population with much parent involvement to a neighborhood with a lower socioeconomic make-up and less parent involvement. Several key factors contributed to the decrease in parent involvement, including less flexibility for many parents to leave work in order to attend a school meeting or conference, as well as many parents feeling unwelcome and anxious in school, based upon their own histories as children in the school environment.

Instead of bemoaning this state of affairs and becoming increasingly upset and stressed, this particular principal and her staff realized that the education of their students would be greatly enhanced if parents became active participants in the educational process; consequently, they viewed the lack of involvement as a challenge to meet rather than as a stress to avoid. Among other strategies, they scheduled several staff meetings in the late afternoon and moved the site of the meetings from the school building to a popular community house a few blocks away. These changes encouraged a number of the parents to attend the meetings since the new time was more accommodating to their schedules and the new location helped them to feel more comfortable since it was held on their "turf." The relationship between parents and teachers was greatly enhanced and the children were the beneficiaries.

The third "C" is "control" or what we call "personal control" and is closely related to the "dead horse" phenomenon we described earlier in this chapter. Control, as used in stress hardiness theory, implies that individuals who successfully manage stress and pressure focus their time and energy on factors over which they have influence rather than attempting to change things that are beyond their sphere of control. Although many individuals believe they engage in activities over which they have influence or control, in fact, many do not. We worked with a group of teachers who were feeling burned out. We reviewed the basic tenets of stress hardiness theory and asked if they focused their energies on factors within their domain of control. They replied in the affirmative.

We then asked them to list what would help make their jobs less stressful. Their answers included, "If the students came from less dysfunctional families, if they came to school better prepared to learn, if they had more discipline at home." After a few moments one of the teachers smiled and said, "We first said that we focus on what we have control over, but everything that we are mentioning to help us feel less stressed are things over which we have little control."

After the teacher said this, the group engaged in a lively discussion focusing on what educators might do to create classroom climates that nurtured learning even if the students came from home environments that were less than supportive of education. One teacher astutely noted, "We are expecting our students to come to school excited about learning and, when they do not, we get frustrated and annoyed. Instead, what I'm hearing is that we must ask, 'What can we do differently to help motivate students who are not motivated and what can we do to help students who feel hopeless about learning to feel more hopeful.'" As the discussion continued, the teachers recognized that by focusing on what they could do differently to improve the learning environment was empowering and lessened stressful feelings. The mood of pessimism and burnout that had pervaded the room began to change. Effective teachers appreciate that they must make certain they take care of their own physical and emotional needs if they are to successfully meet the needs of their students.

## A CLOSING REFLECTION

In this chapter we have shared the evidence defining the characteristics of the mindset of effective educators as well as the behaviors that accompany this mindset. These educators touch the hearts and minds of students and assist even at-risk students to be more comfortable, secure, cooperative, motivated, hopeful, and resilient in the school setting. As we have emphasized, the actions of teachers have a lifelong impact on students. This impact is captured in the often-cited observation of psychologist and educator Haim Ginott:

> I've come to the frightening conclusion that I am the decisive element in the classroom. It's my personal approach that creates the climate. It's my daily mood that makes the weather. As a teacher, I possess a tremendous power to make a person's life miserable or joyous. I can be a tool of torture or an instrument of inspiration. I can humiliate or humor, hurt or heal. In all situations, it is my response that decides whether a crisis will be escalated or de-escalated or a person humanized or de-humanized.

Ginott's words are well worth considering as we seek to enrich the lives of students in our care.

## NOTE

1. Since the case illustrations in this chapter are taken from both of our clinical and consultation practices, we are using the plural (e.g., we and us) for each example, not only to simplify the writing style, but also to acknowledge the contributions of material from both of our practices.

## REFERENCES

Adelman, H., & Taylor, L. (1983). Enhancing motivation for overcoming learning and behavior problems. *Journal of Learning Disabilities, 16,* 384–392.

Beardslee, W. R. (1989). The role of self-understanding in resilient individuals: The development of a perspective. *American Journal of Orthopsychiatry, 59,* 266–278.

Brendtro, L., Brokenleg, M., & Van Bockern, S. (1990). *Reclaiming youth at risk: Our hope for the future.* Bloomington, IN: National Educational Service.

Brooks, R. B. (1991). *The self-esteem teacher.* Loveland, OH: Treehaus Communications.

Brooks, R. B. (1994). Children at risk: Fostering resilience and hope. *American Journal of Orthopsychiatry, 64,* 545–553.

Brooks, R. B. (1999). Creating a positive school climate: Strategies for fostering self-esteem, motivation, and resilience. In J. Cohen (Ed.), *Educating minds and hearts: Social emotional learning and the passage into adolescence* (pp. 61–73). New York: Columbia Teachers College Press.

Brooks, R. B. (2001a). Fostering motivation, hope, and resilience in children with learning disorders. *Annals of Dyslexia, 51,* 9–20.

Brooks, R. B. (2001b). To touch a student's heart and mind: The mindset o the effective educator. *Proceedings of the 1999 Plain Talk conference sponsored by the Center for Development and Learning, New Orleans* (pp. 167–177). Cambridge, MA: Educators Publishing Service.

Brooks, R. B. (2002). Creating nurturing classroom environments: Fostering hope and resilience as an antidote to violence. In S. Brock, P. Lazarus, & S. Jimerson (Eds.), *Best practices in school crisis prevention and intervention* (pp. 67–93). Bethesda, MD: NASP Publications.

Brooks, R. B., & Goldstein, S. (2001). *Raising resilient children.* New York: McGraw-Hill.

Brooks, R. B., & Goldstein, S. (2003). *Nurturing resilience in our children: Answers to the most important parenting questions.* New York: McGraw-Hill.

Brooks, R. B. (2004). To touch the hearts and minds of students with learning disabilities: The power of mindsets and expectations. *Learning Disabilities: A Contemporary Journal, 2,* 9–18.

Brooks, R. B., & Goldstein, S. (2004). *The power of resilience: Achieving balance, confidence, and personal strength in your life.* New York: McGraw-Hill.

Canino,, F. J. (1981). Learned-helplessness theory: Implications for research in learning disabilities. *Journal of Special Education, 15,* 471–484.

Charney, R. S. (1991). *Teaching children to care: Management in the responsive classroom.* Greenfield, MA: Northeast Foundation for Children.

Chess, S., & Thomas, A. (1987). *Know your child.* New York: Basic Books.

Cohen, J. (2006). Social, emotional and academic education: Creating a climate for learning, participation in democracy and well being. *Harvard Educational Review, 76,* 201–237.

Cohen, J. (Ed.) (1999). *Educating minds and hearts: Social emotional learning and the passage into adolescence.* New York: Columbia Teachers College Press.

Curwin, R. L., & Mendler, A. N. (1988). *Discipline with dignity.* Reston, VA: Association for Supervision and Curriculum Development.

Deci, E. L., & Chandler, C. (1986). The importance of motivation for the future of the LD field. *Journal of Learning Disabilities, 19,* 587–594.

Deci, E. L., & Flaste, R. (1995). *Why we do what we do: Understanding self-motivation.* New York: Penguin Books.

Deci, E. L., Hodges, R., Pierson, L., & Tomassone, J. (1992). Autonomy and competence as motivational factors in students with learning disabilities and emotional handicaps. *Journal of Learning Disabilities, 25,* 457–471.

Dicintio, M. J., & Gee, S. (1999). Control is the key: Unlocking the motivation of at-risk students. *Psychology in the Schools, 36,* 231–237.

Dwyer, K., Osher, D., & Warger, C. (1998). *Early warning, timely response: A guide to safe schools.* Washington, D.C.: U.S. Department of Education.

Gardner, H. (1983). *Frames of mind.* New York: Basic Books.

Gathercoal, F. (1997). *Judicious discipline.* San Francisco, CA: Caddo Gap Press.

Glasser, W. (1997). A new look at school failure and school success. *Phi Delta Kappan, 78,* 596–202.

Goldstein, S., & Brooks. R. B. (Eds.) (2005). *Handbook of resilience in children.* New York: Springer.

Goldstein, S., & Brooks, R. B. (2007). *Understanding and managing children's classroom behavior: Creating resilient, sustainable classrooms.* New York: Wiley.

Goleman, D. (1995). *Emotional intelligence.* New York: Bantam.

Hechtman, L. (1991). Resilience and vulnerability in long-term outcome of attention deficit hyperactivity disorder. *Canadian Journal of Psychiatry, 36,* 415–421.

Holt, P., Fine, M., & Tollefson, N. (1987). Mediating success: Survival of the hardy. *Psychology in the Schools, 24,* 51–58.

Hornbeck, D. W. (1989). *Turning points: Preparing American youth for the 21st century.* New York: Carnegie Council on Adolescent Development.

Jacobson, L. (1999). Three's company: Kids prove they have a place at the parent-teacher conference. *Teacher Magazine, 11,* 23.

Katz, M. (1994, May). From challenged childhood to achieving adulthood: Studies in resilience. *Chadder,* pp. 8–11.

Katz, M. (1997). *On playing a poor hand well.* New York: Norton.

Keogh, B. K. (2003). *Temperament in the classroom: Understanding individual differences.* Baltimore, MD: Brookes Publishing.

Kidder, T. (1989). *Among schoolchildren.* Boston: Houghton Mifflin.

Kobasa, S., Maddi, S., & Kahn, S. (1982). Hardiness and health: A perspective inquiry. *Journal of Personality and Social Psychology, 42,* 168–177.

Kohn, A. (1993). Choices for children: Why and how to let students decide: *Phi Delta Kappan, 75,* 8–20.

Levine, M. D. (1994). *Educational care: A system for understanding and helping children with learning problems at home and at school.* Cambridge, MA: Educators Publishing Company.

Levine, M. D. (2002). *A mind at a time.* Cambridge, MA: Educators Publishing Company.

Licht, B. G. (1983). Cognitive-motivational factors that contribute to the achievement of learning-disabled children. *Journal of Learning Disabilities, 16,* 483–490.

Martinez, J. (1989). Cooling off before burning out. *Academic Therapy, 24,* 271–284.

Mather, N., & Ofiesh, N. (2005). Resilience and the child with learning disabilities. In S. Goldstein & R. Brooks (Eds.), *Handbook of resilience in children* (pp. 239–255). New York: Springer.

Marshall, M. & Weisner, K. (2004). Using a discipline system to promote learning, *Phi Delta Kappan, 85,* 498–507.

McGinnis, J. C., Frederick, B. P., & Edwards, R. (1995). Enhancing classroom management through proactive rules and procedures. *Psychology in the Schools, 32,* 220–224.

Mendler, A. N. (1992). *What do I do when . . . ? How to achieve discipline with dignity in the classroom.* Bloomington, IN: National Educational Service.

Nelsen, J., Lott, L., & Glenn, H. S. (1997). *Positive discipline in the classroom.* Rocklin, CA: Prima Publishing.

Rademacher, J. A., Callahan, K., & Pederson-Seelye, V. (1998). How do your classroom rules measure up? Guidelines for developing an effective rule management routine. *Intervention in school and clinic, 33,* 284–289.

Rief, S., & Heimburge, J. (1996). *How to reach and teach all students in the inclusive classroom.* West Nyack, NY: The Center for Applied Research in Education.

Rutter, M. (1985). Resilience in the face of adversity: Protective factors and resistance to psychiatric disorder. *British Journal of Psychiatry, 147,* 598–611.

Rutter, M. (1987). Psychosocial resilience and protective mechanisms. *American Journal of Orthopsychiatry, 57,* 316–331.

Segal, J. (1988). Teachers have enormous power in affecting a child's self-esteem. *The Brown University Child Behavior and Development Newsletter, 4,* 1–3.

Shure, M. B. (1994). *Raising a thinking child.* New York: Holt.

Shure, M. B., & Aberson, B. (2005). Enhancing the process of resilience through effective thinking. In S. Goldstein & R. Brooks (Eds.), *Handbook of resilience in children* (pp. 373–394). New York: Springer.

Strahan, D. (1989). Disconnected and disruptive students. *Middle School Journal, 21,* 1–5.

Thomsen, K. (2002). *Building resilient students.* Thousand Oaks, CA: Corwin Press.

Weiner, B. (1974). *Achievement motivation and attribution theory.* Morristown, NJ: General Learning Press.

Werner, E. E. (1993). Risk, resilience, and recovery: Perspectives from the Kauai Longitudinal Study. *Development and Psychopathology, 5,* 503–515.

Werner, E. E., & Smith, R. S. (1992). *Overcoming the odds: High risk children from birth to adulthood.* Ithaca, NY: Cornell University Press.

# Index

Comprehension
  defined, 201–202
  reading difficulties
    older readers, 200–207
      applying comprehension strategies, 203–207, *205*
      improving connections between content and prior knowledge, 202–203
      monitoring understanding, 204–206
      multiple-strategy interventions, 206–207
      National Reading Panel Report, 201–202, *202*
      questioning, 203–204, *205*
      reading comprehension defined, 201–202
      relating content to prior knowledge, 202
      summarization, 204–206, *205*
    younger readers, 179
Computation, mathematics instruction, 239–242, 243–246
Computer-assisted instruction, attention-deficit/hyperactivity disorder, *46, 50*
Conduct disorder
  characterized, 62
  oppositional defiant disorder
    comorbidity of, 62
    distinction between, 62
Consequent-based interventions, 39–42, *40*
Contingency contract, attention-deficit/hyperactivity disorder, *40,* 41–42
Contribution, 400–401
*Coping Cat* program, 87–88
Coping with Depression course, 110, 123
Coping with Stress course, 110
Council for Exceptional Children, standards, 21
Counseling, gifted students, 351–352
Counseling psychology, standards, 21

**D**
Decision making, 401–402
Decoding
  language impairments, 168–170
    phonics, 168–169
    sight word recognition, 169–170
    structural analysis, 168–169
  reading difficulties, younger readers, 168–170
Delinquent acts, 62–63
Depression, 103–126
  ACTION Program, 124
    parent training, 125–126
    teacher consultation, 125
  assessment, 108–109
  cognitive-behavioral therapy, 109–111, 115–123

comorbidity, 107–108
conceptualized, 103
course, 107
definitions, 104–105
diagnostic categories, 105
ethnicity, 106–107
evidence-based interventions
  evaluation, 112–113
  implementation, 112–113
  overview, 113, *116–122*
  prevention, 109–111
gender, 106
Interpersonal Psychotherapy for Depressed Adolescents, 123–124
lack of diagnosis, 103–104
lack of treatment, 104
magnitude of problem, 103
medication, 113–114
minority students, 106–107
overview, 104–109
prevalence, 105
prognosis, 107
psychotherapeutic interventions, 114–115
school factors, 109
symptoms, 104–105
Direct instruction, mathematics instruction, 237
Direct observation, fears and related anxieties, 86
Disruptive behavior, 59–74, *see also* Specific type
  characteristics, 60–64
  collaborative development and implementation of interventions, 70
  definitions, 60–64
  effect on student, 60
  evidence-based interventions
    individualized interventions, *68,* 70–72
    research-based interventions, 65–72, *68*
    responsiveness to intervention, 65
    small group interventions, *68,* 68–69
    system-wide interventions, 65–68, *68*
  extinction, 67–68
  function-based intervention, 70–72
    functional assessment, 71
    Function Matrix, 71, *71*
    intervention plans, 71–72
    teach and reinforce replacement behavior, 72, *73*
  instruction in dealing effectively with, 66–67
  performance feedback, 67–68
  prevention, 66
  psychiatric diagnoses, 61–64
  school administrators, 59–60
  self-management, 69

CPSIA information can be obtained at www.ICGtesting.com
Printed in the USA
LVOW10s0823270814

401119LV00007B/131/P